# Why Do You Need This New Edition?

If you're wondering why you should buy the seventh edition of *Between Worlds,* here are eight good reasons!

1. **New material on writing in-class essays** offers a si[...] strategy for managing timed assignments and a cha[...] words in writing prompts to help you focus and stay [...]

2. **New learning objectives** in all the rhetoric chapters (Part II) help you anticipate and master the key material in each chapter.

3. **New readings in Chapter 5, *Between Points of View,*** offer provocative paired essays on current topics including iPods, multitasking, and going green.

4. **New content—and a new checklist—on avoiding plagiarism** offers expanded guidance and resources for integrating material from other sources into your paper.

5. **New treatment of film** adds film content to each of the five chapters in Part I, including intriguing essays on *The King's Speech, Crash, An Inconvenient Truth,* and contemporary romantic comedy, and offers you exciting guidance for "reading" film actively.

6. **Illustrated source "maps"** for MLA citations, including a Web site and a database, help you find essential information as you cite sources.

7. **New readings on more varied topics** revitalize each of the existing chapters to reflect the conflicting realms—the "between worlds"—in which most of us live. New readings show divergent views about technology and its impact (including cellphone use, how our brain works on computers, and whether Twitter is a boon or a bane, as well as offering a sociological study of romantic comedies, and readings on the nature of family relationships, gender and culture identification, and how we spend our time).

8. **Updated content in Chapter 12, on research,** not only includes the most current versions of both the MLA and the APA style guides but also offers expanded guidance for using, evaluating—and abusing—online materials as well as for documenting electronic sources.

PEARSON

# Between Worlds

## A Reader, Rhetoric, and Handbook

### *Seventh Edition*

**Susan Bachmann**

*El Camino College*

**Melinda Barth**

*El Camino College*

**PEARSON**

Boston   Columbus   Indianapolis   New York   San Francisco   Upper Saddle River
Amsterdam   Cape Town   Dubai   London   Madrid   Milan   Munich   Paris   Montreal   Toronto
Delhi   Mexico City   São Paulo   Sydney   Hong Kong   Seoul   Singapore   Taipei   Tokyo

Again, and again, to the men in our lives:
Ron, Dylan, and Evan Barth
and
Walter, Ryan, and Adam Gajewski

**Senior Sponsoring Editor:** Katharine Glynn
**Assistant Editor:** Rebecca Gilpin
**Senior Marketing Manager:** Sandra McGuire
**Senior Supplements Editor:** Donna Campion
**Production Manager:** S. S. Kulig
**Project Coordination, Text Design, and Electronic Page Makeup:** PreMediaGlobal

**Cover Design Manager:** Wendy Ann Fredericks
**Cover Designer:** Nancy Sacks
**Cover Art:** Dale Chihuly, *Niijima Floats*, 1993, photo by Terry Rishel.
**Senior Manufacturing Buyer:** Roy Pickering
**Printer/Binder:** R. R. Donnelley
**Cover Printer:** R. R. Donnelley

Credits and acknowledgments borrowed from other sources and reproduced, with permission, in this textbook appear on the appropriate page within text [or on pages 587–589].

**Library of Congress Cataloging-in-Publication Data**

Between worlds: a reader, rhetoric, and handbook / Susan Bachmann, Melinda Barth. – 7th ed.
   p. cm.
   ISBN 978-0-205-05923-2 – ISBN 978-0-495-90288-1 – ISBN 978-0-495-90370-3
   1. College readers.   2. English language—Rhetoric—Handbooks, manuals, etc.   3. English language—Grammar—Handbooks, manuals, etc.   4. Report writing— Handbooks, manuals, etc.
   I. Bachmann, Susan.   II. Barth,  Melinda.
   PE1417.B43 2011
   808'.0427—dc23
                                                                                      2011033026

10 9 8 7 6 5 4 3 2 1—DOC—14 13 12 11

**PEARSON**

ISBN 13: 978-0-205-25126-1
ISBN 10:     0-205-25126-9

# Contents

## Chapter 12   Writing the Research Paper

# Chapter 15　Understanding Punctuation

Editing Symbols chart appears opposite page 598.

# Preface

The seventh edition of *Between Worlds* remains a Reader, Rhetoric, and Handbook—a three-in-one textbook, thereby saving students money and providing instructors all the essentials under one cover. "The Reader" features topics that students care about, ranging from Twitter and tattoos to relationships and stereotyping—all designed to prompt lively discussions and spirited writing. Following the readings, a concise "Rhetoric" guides students through every aspect of the writing process with modeled writing assignments, including two student research papers. "The Handbook" is particularly student-friendly, providing succinct explanations to correct those common errors typically noted on students' essays. Although each part of this textbook can be used independently, both instructors and students value our instructive connections between readings and writing assignments.

Since the publication of the first edition, we have received overwhelming support for combining three texts within one cover, for our selection of lively readings, and for a voice that students find appealing. Instructors appreciate the meaningful discussion questions and writing topics for each reading—huge time savers for faculty and helpful prompts for students. We have connected each of the readings not only by theme but also by authors' techniques and intentions. Further, those same readings are analyzed in "The Rhetoric" to demonstrate writing strategies that students can emulate. The seventh edition retains our successes and includes some exciting changes and additions:

***A Frequently Requested Addition: How to Write an In-Class Essay*** In response to popular demand, we have included a section on writing in-class essays—a must in nearly all comp classes. We focus on the "3-D effect"—details, development, and depth—so that students take advantage of the full time period allotted for writing. We also provide a six-step strategy for managing timed writing assignments and a definition chart of key words used in writing prompts to help students get started and stay on task. Further, we have modeled a sample sentence outline for instructors to use for preparing out-of-class essays.

***All New Provocative Paired Readings: Between Points of View*** In this chapter, we have replaced most essays with current controversies. We pair writers with contrasting views on subjects that students will want to discuss, debate, and write about—whether Internet use makes us smarter or dumber, whether Twitter is innovative or inane, whether we can impede the negative effects of climate change, and whether all cellphone use while driving should be illegal. Other authors offer compelling arguments to counter popular trends involving iPod use, multitasking, and going green.

***New Student Learning Objectives for Each Chapter of the Rhetoric*** In responding to our reviewers—and our colleagues who have used this book for over two decades—we have created a bulleted list of learning objectives for each chapter. These SLOs are designed to help students anticipate the achievements they will attain as they master the material in each chapter.

***Developed Materials and a New Checklist to Prevent Plagiarism*** Because it is so easy for students to access materials through the Internet and incorporate others' ideas and words, either inadvertently or deliberately, we have expanded and developed our sections on avoiding plagiarism. We have created a new Checklist for Preventing Plagiarism for students to use throughout their drafts and before they submit their final paper.

***New Graphic Illustrations of MLA Forms*** When students search for materials online, they are often overwhelmed by confusing screens with more information than they can handle. To help students find the essentials buried in the clutter, we have provided visuals to illustrate the elements of an MLA citation for a Web site and for a database. The graphics show students where to find the required information on the screen and where to insert it in their Works Cited page.

***New Use of Films in Each Chapter of the Reader*** Because film is a dynamic text for classroom instruction and for writing topics, we have added film-related essays to each of our five chapters of readings. In "Between Perceptions," we feature both a review of the critically acclaimed film *The King's Speech* and a personal account of handling a speech impediment. We show how film can be read on multiple levels by providing a range of writing topics—character analyses, biographical accounts, personal narratives, studies of disabilities, and interpretations of history, as well as film analyses. In "Between Genders" we have added a lively argument about current and classical romantic comedies, sure to stir student responses in debates and essays. In "Between Generations," a new essay profiles an intriguing celebrity with significant student appeal. In "Between Cultures," we provide two contrasting views of *Crash,* a film popular with both students and professors. In "Between Points of View," we complement essays on climate change with reviews and research on Al Gore's film *An Inconvenient Truth.* How to analyze a film is described in "The Rhetoric."

***Expanded Rhetoric to Include Film Analysis*** Instructions for reading a film as text and guidelines for "active viewing" of films are included in the "Analysis" chapter of "The Rhetoric." We feature an essay of a professional film critic and discuss the writer's strategies and choices as he analyzes the film *Crash.* Common film terms and concepts are explained so that students are comfortable reading and writing film reviews and analyses.

***New Essays Featuring the Latest Technology***   Recognizing the prevalence of technology in our academic and personal lives, we have increased the number of essays about electronic devices and media: "iHuh?," "What the Cellphone Industry Won't Tell You," "Does the Internet Make You Smarter?," "Does the Internet Make You Dumber?," "Your Brain on Computers," "I Don't Give a Tweet What You're Doing," and "Twitter? It's What You Make It."

***New Readings and More Varied Topics***   New selections revitalize each of the existing chapters to reflect the conflicting realms—the "between worlds"—in which most of us live. Like us, the individuals in these readings are caught *between* balancing the burdens of work and school, *between* satisfying family obligations and meeting personal needs, and *between* defining self while relating with others. New readings show divergent views about cellphone use, how our brain works on computers, whether Twitter is a boon or a bane, and whether the environment can be altered by the individual. Other topics include a sociological study of romantic comedies, the nature of family relationships, gender and culture identification, and how we spend our time. Recognizing the value of wit in creating memorable writing (and keeping readers awake!), we have added more humorous selections as well as cartoons that complement our essays. In response to instructors' recommendations, we have also added many more provocative argument essays.

***New Voices and Favorite Voices***   In addition to the esteemed writers *new* to this edition—Sean Smith, David Pogue, Nicholas Carr, and Clay Shirky—we have retained famous favorites J. K. Rowling, Ellen Goodman, John Leonard, Jeff Z. Klein, Joyce Carol Oates, Dan Neil, Michael Pollan, Judith Ortiz Cofer, Meghan Daum, Martin Luther King Jr., Anne Lamott, Brent Staples, Neil Steinberg, Carol Tavris, Luis Valdez, and Jane E. Brody and popular reviewers Roger Ebert, David Denby, and A. O. Scott.

***More Essays Featuring Humor and Irony***   Recognizing that humor helps create memorable writing and that students—and we—like to laugh, we have included more wit in this edition in the form of both essays and cartoons. New work includes "A Fine Romance," "I Don't Give a Tweet What You're Doing," "Twitter? It's What You Make It," "Time Lost and Found," and "Greed in the Name of Green." Your students will be pleased that we have retained some funny favorites: "Who's Cheap?," "O.K., So I'm Fat," "Coke," "Mr. Z," *Los Vendidos*, "You Call That Irony?," and "Short Assignments."

***New Reading Questions and Writing Assignments***   The "Thinking About the Text" questions have been revised to focus as much on audience and purpose as on content—to encourage students to examine the writer's strategies and to experiment with their own. The "Writing from the Text" sections provide students with varied writing prompts for each reading. In "Connecting with Other Texts," both the new and retained readings are linked by theme, technique, and purpose.

***Diverse Forms, Styles, and Techniques*** Our varied genres include lively essays; film reviews, analyses, and interviews; editorials and commentaries; paired arguments with contrasting positions; stirring narratives; and short stories, poems, biographies, memoirs, and a play. In addition, we include photos and cartoons that visually complement the writings and films.

***New Materials on Research*** Chapter 12 includes the 2009 MLA documentation forms as well as updated and expanded APA guidelines and documentation forms that reflect the 2010 APA *Publication Manual*. Because so much of the research process is now done online, we continue to offer a section on using, evaluating, and abusing electronic sources—"The Good, the Bad, and the Ugly"—as well as on documenting electronic sources.

***Succinct Handbook*** Part III, a handbook designed to empower students but not overwhelm them, focuses on the most common errors—the "terrible ten"—that persist in student writing. To help students interpret their instructors' comments, a list of marginal symbols is included on the inside back cover.

***New Instructor's Manual*** An updated *Instructor's Manual* features answers to "Thinking About the Text" questions, including extraordinarily detailed analyses of select films, subthemes found in each chapter, cross-referencing of readings between chapters, and sample course syllabi.

***Online Resource*** MyCompLab is an eminently flexible application that empowers student writers and teachers by integrating a composing space and assessment tools with multimedia tutorials, services (such as online tutoring), and exercises for writing, grammar, and research. Students can use MyCompLab on their own, benefiting from self-paced diagnostics and a personal study plan that recommends the instruction and practice each student needs to improve his or her writing skills. Teachers can recommend MyCompLab to students for self-study, set up courses to track student progress, or leverage the power of administrative features of the site to be more effective and save time. The assignment builder and commenting tools, developed specifically for use in writing courses, bring instructors closer to their student writers, make managing assignments and evaluating papers more efficient, and put powerful assessment within reach. Students receive feedback within the context of their own writing, which encourages critical thinking and revision and helps them develop skills based on their individual needs. Learn more at www.mycomplab.com.

# Applause

This textbook could never have been written without the help of many people who have been particularly supportive and generous with their time as we worked on this book. Superb librarians and computer specialists assisted us in countless ways. We continue to be grateful to Ed Martinez, Claudia Striepe, and Moon Ichinaga from the El Camino College library, and librarian Eileen Wakiji and computer specialist Walter Gajewski, both from California State University at Long Beach. All of these knowledgeable individuals gave their time and technological expertise to help us teach students and improve this book. Over the years, colleagues at El Camino College have readily and generously shared readings, strategies, and writing ideas that inspired many aspects of this book. We are indebted to these colleagues: Amanda Ackerman, Marilyn Anderson, Mimi Ansite, Nancy Armstrong, Sara Blake, Debra Breckheimer, Allison Carr, Matt Cheung, Dana Crotwell, Nancy Currey, Stefanie Elwood, Paul Freeborn, Elise Geraghty, Julia Hackner, Yvette Hawley, Greta Hendricks, Zahid Hossain, Dalia Juarez, Mandy Kronbeck, Debra Mochidome, Kareema Nasouf, Leah Pate, Kim Runkle, Cynthia Silverman, Eric Takamine, Cindy Tino-Sandoval, Evelyn Uyemura, Kathy Vertullo, Steve Waterworth, and Rachel Williams.

We are also grateful to our Humanities Division Associative Dean Barbara Jaffe and to our administrative staff member Charlotte Koyanagi for their support of our book. We are especially pleased to include the work of our fine students: Marianela Enriquez, Rebekah Hall-Naganuma, Marin Kheng, Leselle Norville, Shannon Paaske, Robert Sakatani, and Chris Thomas, all of whom exemplify the extraordinary commitment of so many college writers. They, and all of our students, have helped us select readings and develop instructional materials for each new edition. They merit hearty applause.

A number of fine academic reviewers brought insights from their teaching to improve this book:

Irene Anders, Indiana University-Purdue University Fort Wayne

Lisa Angius, Long Island University, C.W. Post Campus

Evelyn Beck, Harrisburg Area Community College

Edna Boris, LaGuardia Community College

Dana Crotwell, El Camino College

Gregory Hagan, Madisonville Community College

Amy Hundley, Merced College

Michael F. Johanyak, The University of Akron

We are grateful to our sponsoring editor at Pearson Longman, Ginny Blanford, whose enthusiasm and support encouraged us through several editions of the book. We wish her well as she heads off to retirement—the land of choice and leisure. We look forward to reading her writings and cheering her publications. We are thankful to our dedicated assistant editor Rebecca Gilpin, for her speedy responses and dependable problem-solving, and to our fine production manager for her expert proofreading and timely help while we were between editors. We welcome Katharine Glynn, our new sponsoring editor, as we conclude this edition of the book and begin to contemplate changes for the next. Our Pre-Press editor Marie Desrosiers has diligently corrected errors, supervised last-minute changes, and determined the layout of each page of our text. Special thanks must go to Ken Clark at Chihuly Studios for his persistent searches through the archives for yet another astonishingly beautiful photo for our cover. We hope that instructors who adopt our book are as pleased as we are with our return to the images of worlds, Dale Chihuly's striking spheres. We are indebted to our permissions editor Lisa Yakmalian for her tireless efforts contacting authors to let us include their work. We also value Teresa Ward's flexibility with the schedule and her conscientious work on the *Instructor's Manual*.

Finally, we want to try to thank our families who have, for two decades, lived *Between Worlds* with us. As the book has grown and changed its shape, our families, too, have metamorphosed, and one now has expanded to include two women, Tia and Delaiah, both English teachers. The children we once banished so we could write—Dylan, Evan, Ryan, and Adam—are now adults who use the book in their writing and teaching. We have come to count on their valuable suggestions. In addition to providing creative insights, Walter and Ron continue to support our book by resolving the technical emergencies and by handling the domestic spheres we have abandoned in order to write. Our family members and friends often send us relevant articles and recommend significant films. As we revise and expand each edition, they often inquire when our work on the book will be done. We honestly and consistently reply, "Never!" However, one of us, Melinda Barth, has replied "Now!" to the question of retirement. After more than thirty years of teaching at El Camino College, she looks forward to devoting even more time to finding good material for *Between Worlds*, traveling to interesting parts of the world, and living a little bit less on the edge of the world. We both thank our families and friends for their support, and we applaud their willingness to live "between worlds" with us.

Susan Bachmann

Melinda Barth

# Part I
# The Reader

The readings in this book have been chosen to reflect the interests of college students like you, who are juggling school and work as well as social lives and family expectations. The selections in Part I have been arranged into five chapters:

Ch. 1.  *Between Generations:* Many of the authors in this chapter are caught between generations and, like you, may be trying to understand themselves in relation to parents and grandparents.

Ch. 2.  *Between Genders:* Just as you may be examining the roles that define your gender, many authors in this chapter argue for a reexamination of the roles that limit the lives of people of both sexes.

Ch. 3.  *Between Cultures:* Whether you are a newcomer to the United States, a second- or third-generation American, or a native whose roots go back for generations, you may find that the writers in this chapter describe experiences you have had, living between cultures.

Ch. 4.  *Between Perceptions:* Your self-perception is inevitably colored by the images that others have of you. Yet your desire to be perceived as an individual, rather than a stereotype, is shared by many college students and the authors who write about being between perceptions.

Ch. 5.  *Between Points of View:* Examining the contrasting ideas of the authors included in this chapter will help you to assess your own convictions, something that you may be doing more seriously since you started college.

We chose these readings to stimulate your thinking and to enable you to write meaningful essays—the goal of any composition course.

Each chapter contains readings, all arranged to illustrate parallels or contrasts with each other. Three sets of exercises follow each reading. The first, called "Thinking About the Text," consists of questions designed as a review prior to class and for small-group discussions during class. These questions are followed by "Writing from the Text," which includes writing assignments drawn from the readings and from your own experience. Your instructor may assign these topics, or you may use them for practice writing in a journal. You will find help for writing these assignments in Part II, the rhetoric portion of this book. The last set of exercises, "Connecting with Other Texts," asks you to compare two or more readings in this book. Some assignments encourage you to find additional material in the library or view a film—useful if your instructor assigns a paper that requires research. You will find information on how to write research papers of various lengths in Part II.

# Getting the Most from Your Reading

How often have you spent time reading something only to discover that you have no idea what you've just read? Worse still, have you ever found yourself supposedly reading but, instead, daydreaming about your last date, a great play-off game, or a conversation with friends? The hours that you waste in unproductive reading can be saved. Here's how.

## Active Reading

Active reading is a strategy that helps you to remain focused on the text and retain what you have read. Useful in all of your courses, active reading enables you to perceive the author's thesis and key points, supporting details, and meaningful lines, as well as to discover your own thoughts about the material.

Active reading involves reading with a pen in your hand. Although highlighters are popular with many students, it is impossible to use them to write summary notes in the margin, and it is too difficult to switch between highlighter and pen. If you are using your own book, you can make marks directly on your copy as you are reading. If you are using a library book, you will need to photocopy the pages you intend to read actively. With either method, you should do the following as you read:

- *Underline* the thesis (if it is explicitly stated), key points, and supporting details.
- *Mark* meaningful or quotable language.
- *Place checkmarks and asterisks* next to important lines.

- *Jot* brief summary or commentary notes in the margins. Infer the thesis and write it in the margin if it is not explicitly stated.
- *Circle* or *put a box around* unfamiliar words and references to look up later.
- *Ask* questions as you read.
- *Seek* answers to those questions.
- *Question* the writer's assumptions and assertions as well as your own.

Reading actively allows you to enter into a conversation with your authors—to examine and challenge their ideas. Active reading also helps you find important lines more easily so that you don't have to reread the entire work each time that you refer to it during class discussions or in your essays. Having the key points underlined means you can quickly review them for a quiz. If your instructor asks you to keep a journal of your responses to readings, you can use the meaningful lines you have marked or the marginal notes to begin your journal entry. Don't underline or highlight *everything*, however, or you will defeat your purpose of finding just the important points.

Let's now look at an active reading of Ellen Goodman's "Thanksgiving." What comments or questions can you add?

 **Thanksgiving**

*Ellen Goodman*

A journalist who has worked for *Newsweek*, CBS, NBC, and a number of metropolitan newspapers, Ellen Goodman (b. 1941) wrote a widely syndicated column from her home paper, the *Boston Globe*, from 1967 until her retirement in 2010. Goodman won the Pulitzer Prize in 1980 for distinguished commentary. She is author of *Paper Trails: Common Sense in Uncommon Times* (2004), coauthor with Patricia O'Brien of *I Know Just What You Mean: The Power of Friendship in Women's Lives* (2000), and the author of *Value Judgments*, a collection of newspaper columns (1993). Goodman asserts that it is "important to look at the underlying values by which this country exists." The essay included here, on the importance of family, was first published in the *Boston Globe* in 1980.

*nice image!*

1     Soon they will be together again, all the <u>people who travel between their own lives and each other's</u>. The package tour of the season will lure them this week to the family table. By Thursday, feast day, family day, Thanksgiving day, Americans who value individualism like no other people will collect around a million tables in a <u>ritual of belonging</u>.

*Thanksgiving: "a ritual of belonging"*

2    They will assemble their families the way they assemble dinner: each one bearing a <u>personality as different as cranberry sauce and pumpkin pie.</u> For one dinner they will cook for each other, fuss for each other, feed each other and argue with each other. They will nod at their <u>common heritage, the craziness and caring of other generations.</u> They will measure their <u>common legacy ... the children.</u>

*"craziness and caring"*

*thesis*

3    All these complex cells, these men and women, old and young, with different dreams and disappointments will give homage again to the group they are <u>a part of</u> and <u>apart from:</u> their family. <u>Families and individuals.</u> The <u>"we" and the "I."</u> As good Americans we <u>all travel between these two ideals.</u> We take value trips from the great American notion of individualism to the great American vision of family. We wear out our tires driving back and forth, using speed to shorten the distance between these two principles.

*"We" & "I"*

*2 ideals: families & individuals*

4    There has always been some pavement between a person and a family. From the first moment we recognize that we are separate we begin to wrestle with aloneness and togetherness. Here and now these conflicts are especially acute. We are, after all, <u>raised in families . . . to be individuals.</u> This double message follows us through life. We are taught about the freedom of the "I" and the safety of the "we." The loneliness of the "I" and the intrusiveness of the "we." The selfishness of the "I" and the burdens of the "we."

*ironic →*

*"we" and "I" again*

5    We are taught what André Malraux said: "<u>Without a family, man, alone in the world, trembles with the cold.</u>" And taught what he said another day: "The denial of the supreme importance of the mind's development accounts for many revolts against the family." In theory, the <u>world rewards</u> "the supreme importance" of the individual, <u>the ego.</u> We think alone, inside our heads. We write music and literature with an enlarged sense of self. We are graded and paid, hired and fired, on our own merit. The ⏍rank⏌ individualism is both exciting and cruel. Here is where the fittest survive.

*ideal quote for journal*

*World rewards the "ego"— meaning?*

*meaning?*

6    The family, on the other hand, at its best, works very differently. <u>We don't have to achieve to be accepted by our families.</u> We just have to be. Our membership is not based on credentials but on birth. As Malraux put it, "A friend loves you for your intelligence, a mistress for your charm, but your family's love is unreasoning: You were born into it and of its flesh and blood."

*True?*

7 The <u>family</u> is formed <u>not</u> for the <u>survival of the fittest</u> but for the <u>weakest</u>. It is not an economic unit but an emotional one. This is not the place where people ruthlessly compete with each other but where they work for each other. Its business is taking care, and <u>when it works</u>, it is <u>not callous but kind</u>.

*[margin: family → where the <u>weakest</u> survive]*

8 There are fewer heroes, fewer stars in family life. While the world may glorify the self, the family asks us, at one time or another, to submerge it. While the <u>world may abandon</u> us, the family promises, at one time or another, to protect us. So we commute daily, weekly, yearly <u>between one world and another.</u> Between a life as a family member that can be nurturing or smothering. Between life as an individual that can free us or flatten us. We [vacillate] between two separate sets of demands and possibilities.

*[margin: * "world may abandon us" family should "protect us" meaning?]*

*[margin: "between worlds" theme]*

9 The people who will gather around this table Thursday <u>live in both of these worlds, a part of</u> and <u>apart from</u> each other. With any luck the territory they travel from one to another can be a fertile one, rich with care and space. It can be a place where the "I" and the "we" interact. On this day at least, they will bring to each other something both special and <u>something to be shared: these separate selves.</u>

*[margin: <u>thesis</u> restated (words varied)]*

## Discussion of Active Reading

As we read Ellen Goodman's essay, we were on the lookout for key phrases, important concepts, unfamiliar words, and the thesis or focus of the essay. We immediately underlined her description of "people who travel between their own lives and each other's" and noted "nice image!" in the margin. As soon as we found memorable phrases such as the definition of Thanksgiving as "a ritual of belonging" or the simile comparing personalities of family members "as different as cranberry sauce and pumpkin pie," we underlined these as well and made relevant notations in the margin. We also underlined Goodman's description of people's "common heritage, the craziness and caring of other generations" and "their common legacy . . . the children," noting "craziness and caring" in the margin.

We boxed in two words—"rank" and "vacillate"—that we thought students might not be familiar with, and we wrote "meaning?" in the margin as a reminder to look them up in the dictionary. When we spotted what we thought was Goodman's thesis, we identified it in the margin: "All these complex cells, these men and women, old and young, with different dreams and disappointments will give homage again to the group they are a part of and apart from: their family." We continued to underline key phrases or meaningful lines and noted a brief response to each in the margin.

We also noted how Goodman begins her conclusion by repeating her thesis but in different words: "The people who will gather around this table Thursday live in both of these worlds, a part of and apart from each other." You will find another example of active reading on page 186 and advice for active viewing of a film on pages 428–435.

## Active Reading as Prewriting

Because active reading is a natural warm-up for writing, we encourage you, as we do our students, to keep a journal of meaningful lines from readings. It helps to copy each quotation at the top of a journal page as a prompt for your response. You can respond with your personal feelings about the ideas in the quoted line. These ideas might remind you of an experience from your childhood or comments made by a family member or friend.

Sometimes you may react vehemently to the author's tone or idea in the quoted line and write responses you wouldn't feel comfortable giving in class discussion. The journal responses to these quoted lines can become a part of future writing assignments or can just help you sort out your own ideas in an uncensored place.

 ### PRACTICE ACTIVE READING

1. Select any reading in the first chapter, "Between Generations," or use the first reading assigned by your instructor to practice active reading. Follow the steps described above to interact with the text.

2. Actively read Robert L. Heilbroner's essay "Don't Let Stereotypes Warp Your Judgments" (p. 424), underlining meaningful lines and making summary notes in the margin. Look for his thesis and infer it if it is not explicitly stated.

3. Select a line from "Thanksgiving" that you find meaningful and copy it at the top of a page. Then write an uncensored response that expresses your feelings or your analysis of that quotation. If you keep your journal on a computer, you will be amazed by how much you have to express.

# Chapter 1

# Between Generations

In the essay that we used to demonstrate active reading (p. 3), author Ellen Goodman quotes André Malraux's belief that "without a family" the individual "alone in the world, trembles with the cold." The family often nurtures its members and tolerates differences and failings that friends and lovers cannot accept. If you have, or have had, a strained bond with a grandparent, you will value Danzy Senna's ultimate acceptance of her strong-willed grandmother. If you and your parents are at odds over your decisions to change your body image, you will find Andres Martin's views on tattoos instructive.

The differences between generations can be both illuminating and poignant, as you will see in Caroline Hwang's and Waheeda Samady's essays and Janice Mirikitani's poem. But as you may realize from your own experiences and observations, people also suffer anxieties even within the family unit. John Leonard illustrates in his essay that family members sometimes are forced to turn from one another, while Debra Dickerson dramatizes how a family tragedy can draw its members together for physical and emotional support. Sean Smith's interview with Johnny Depp shows that having children often helps parents to make more sense of their own lives and feelings. The writers in this chapter show the family as a source of both nurturing and anxiety.

Your awareness of gaps between generations, as well as a deeper sense of family connection, may inspire your own writing. The works in this chapter attest to the will of the human spirit to mitigate family tension, to smile at some of the chaos, and to survive and thrive from one generation to the next.

# The Good Daughter

### Caroline Hwang

Having earned a BA in English from the University of Pennsylvania and an MFA from New York University, Caroline Hwang (b. 1969) has worked as an editor at *American Health, Mademoiselle, Glamour,* and *Redbook.* Hwang's novel *In Full Bloom* was published in 2003. Constantly juggling her varied projects as both a writer and an editor, Hwang observes, "I've often heard it said that the difference between being an editor and writer is that the editor has power and the writer gets the glory. I don't know that the difference is so clear-cut, but I can say that being on both sides has helped my writing and editing." The following essay was first published in *Newsweek* in 1998.

1    The moment I walked into the dry-cleaning store, I knew the woman behind the counter was from Korea, like my parents. To show her that we shared a heritage, and possibly get a fellow countryman's discount, I tilted my head forward, in shy imitation of a traditional bow.

2    "Name?" she asked, not noticing my attempted obeisance.

3    "Hwang," I answered.

4    "Hwang? Are you Chinese?"

5    Her question caught me off-guard. I was used to hearing such queries from non-Asians who think Asians all look alike, but never from one of my own people. Of course, the only Koreans I knew were my parents and their friends, people who've never asked me where I came from, since they knew better than I.

6    I ransacked my mind for the Korean words that would tell her who I was. It's always struck me as funny (in a mirthless sort of way) that I can more readily say "I am Korean" in Spanish, German and even Latin than I can in the language of my ancestry. In the end, I told her in English.

7    The dry-cleaning woman squinted as though trying to see past the glare of my strangeness, repeating my surname under her breath. "Oh, *Fxuang,*" she said, doubling over with laughter. "You don't know how to speak your name."

8    I flinched. Perhaps I was particularly sensitive at the time, having just dropped out of graduate school. I had torn up my map for the future, the one that said not only where I was going but who I was. My sense of identity was already disintegrating.

9    When I got home, I called my parents to ask why they had never bothered to correct me. "Big deal," my mother said, sounding more flippant than I knew she intended. (Like many people who learn English in a classroom, she uses idioms that don't always fit the occasion.) "So what if you can't pronounce your name? You are American," she said.

10    Though I didn't challenge her explanation, it left me unsatisfied. The fact is, my cultural identity is hardly that clear-cut.

11    My parents immigrated to this country 30 years ago, two years before I was born. They told me often, while I was growing up, that, if I wanted to, I could be president someday, that here my grasp would be as long as my reach.

12    To ensure that I reaped all the advantages of this country, my parents saw to it that I became fully assimilated. So, like any American of my generation, I whiled away my youth strolling malls and talking on the phone, rhapsodizing over Andrew McCarthy's blue eyes or analyzing the meaning of a certain upperclassman's offer of a ride to the Homecoming football game.

13    To my parents, I am all American, and the sacrifices they made in leaving Korea—including my mispronounced name—pale in comparison to the opportunities those sacrifices gave me. They do not see that I straddle two cultures, nor that I feel displaced in the only country I know. I identify with Americans, but Americans do not identify with me. I've never known what it's like to belong to a community—neither one at large, nor of an extended family. I know more about Europe than the continent my ancestors unmistakably come from. I sometimes wonder, as I did that day in the dry cleaner's, if I would be a happier person had my parents stayed in Korea.

14    I first began to consider this thought around the time I decided to go to graduate school. It has been a compromise: my parents wanted me to go to law school; I wanted to skip the starched-collar track and be a writer—the hungrier the better. But after 20-some years of following their wishes and meeting all of their expectations, I couldn't bring myself to disobey or disappoint. A writing career is riskier than law, I remember thinking. If I'm a failure and my life is a washout, then what does that make my parents' lives?

15    I know that many of my friends had to choose between pleasing their parents and being true to themselves. But for the children of immigrants, the choice seems more complicated, a happy outcome impossible. By making the biggest move of their lives for me, my parents indentured me to the largest debt imaginable—I owe them the fulfillment of their hopes for me.

16    It tore me up inside to suppress my dream, but I went to school for a PhD in English literature, thinking I had found the perfect compromise. I would be able to write at least about books while pursuing a graduate degree. Predictably, it didn't work out. How could I labor for five years in a program I had no passion for? When I finally left school, my parents disappointed, but since it wasn't what they wanted me to do, they devastated. I, on the other hand, felt I was staring at the bottom abyss. I had seen the flaw in my life of halfwayness, in my plot compromises.

17      I hadn't thought about my love life, but I had a vague plan to make concessions there, too. Though they raised me as an American, my parents expect me to marry someone Korean and give them grandchildren who look like them. This didn't seem like such a huge request when I was 14, but now I don't know what I'm going to do. I've never been in love with someone I dated, or dated someone I loved. (Since I can't bring myself even to entertain the thought of marrying the non-Korean men I'm attracted to, I've been dating only those I know I can stay clearheaded about.) And as I near that age when the question of marriage stalks every relationship, I can't help but wonder if my parents' expectations are responsible for the lack of passion in my life.

18      My parents didn't want their daughter to be Korean, but they don't want her fully American, either. Children of immigrants are living paradoxes. We are the first generation and the last. We are in this country for its opportunities, yet filial duty binds us. When my parents boarded the plane, they knew they were embarking on a rough trip. I don't think they imagined the rocks in the path of their daughter who can't even pronounce her own name.

## Thinking about the Text

1. What might be Hwang's strategy for opening her essay with a brief narration of her encounter with the Korean dry-cleaning woman? What multiple issues does she introduce with this personal anecdote?

2. Explain how the dry cleaner's comment "You don't know how to speak your name" functions not simply as an observation but as a symbol throughout the essay.

3. What details does Hwang use to support the claim that "I straddle two cultures" and "I feel displaced in the only country I know"? (9).

4. Using your own words along with phrases from the essay, identify Hwang's *aim* or purpose in this essay as well as her key *claim* or thesis.

## Writing from the Text

1. Including details from this essay and your own experiences and observations, write an evaluative response essay agreeing or disagreeing with Hwang's claim that "children of immigrants are living paradoxes" (10). Use examples from the essay to define "living paradoxes" and to support your key claim.

2. Incorporate specific details from Hwang's essay to write an analysis of the causes and effects of her parents' expectations.

## CONNECTING WITH OTHER TEXTS

1. Focusing on "The Good Daughter" and "Breaking Tradition" (p. 20), write an essay analyzing the pressures and demands on children of immigrants.

2. Create a thesis about effective or ineffective parenting and write an essay incorporating support from any three of the following: "The Good Daughter," "Breaking Tradition" (p. 20), "Where Are You Going, Where Have You Been?" (p. 70), "Living in Two Worlds" (p. 99), and "Peaches" (p. 49). Include direct quotations and analyze them fully.

# A Cabdriver's Daughter

## Waheeda Samady

Born in Kabul, Afghanistan, in 1981, Waheeda Samady and her family escaped the country during the Afghan-Soviet war. They lived in a refugee community in Islamabad, Pakistan, for several years before coming to San Diego, California, where Samady has continued to live. In 2003, Samady completed her undergraduate degrees in molecular and cell biology and in international studies at the University of California, Berkeley. She obtained her MD from the University of California, San Diego in 2010. Currently the chief resident in pediatrics at UCSD's Rady Children's Hospital, Samady enjoys teaching medical students and residents as well as conducting research in preparation for her academic fellowship in hospital medicine. She is an active executive committee member for the San Diego branch of the Council on American Islamic Relations (CAIR). A version of the essay below appeared in the anthology *Snapshots: This Afghan American Life*. The essay reprinted here appeared in the *Los Angeles Times* on October 3, 2010.

1   In the morning, before my father and I go our separate ways to work, we chat amiably. "Good luck on your day." "Hope business is good." And our one response to everything: "Inshallah." God willing.

2   I get into my mini-SUV and head off to the hospital, groaning about the lack of sleep, the lack of time, but also knowing that I am driving off to what has always been my dream.

3   My father gets into his blue taxi, picks up his radio and tells the dispatcher he's ready. Then he waits. He waits for someone wanting to go somewhere. He waits to go home to my mother, the woman he calls "the boss." Maybe today will be a good day. He will call her up and tell her he is taking her out tonight. He can do that now that we're all grown up; now that he doesn't have to save every dime for the "what-ifs" and the "just-in-cases."

4   There is very little complaining in his car. His day starts off with a silent prayer, then a pledge: Hudaya ba omaide hudit. God, as you wish. Then he

hums or sings. Some songs are about love and some about loss. They are all about life. He sings. He smiles the whole time.

5   My father is the type of person who is content to listen, but I love it when he speaks. There is wisdom there, although he does not intend there to be.

6   "What's new?" he'll ask over a Saturday morning breakfast.

7   "Not much," I reply. "My life revolves around these books, Dad; there is little to say unless you want to hear about the urinary tract."

8   "You know when Gandhi's minister of foreign affairs died, his only true possessions were books. It is the sign of a life worth living," he replies and begins to butter his toast.

9   Sometimes, the years of education and learning shine through the injuries and lost dreams. I get a glimpse of the man who once existed, and the one who never will. Who would he have been, I wonder, if the bombs hadn't come down in 1978? What if I could take away the time he spent in a coma, the years of treatment and surgery, the broken bones and disabilities. What if there were no refugee ghettos, no poverty, no fear, no depression written in his life history? Who could he have been? The thought saddens me, but intrigues me as well. Is it possible that he is who he is because the life he has lived has been filled with such tragedy? Perhaps these stories were the making of my hero.

10   Sometimes he'll tell me about his college days, about an Afghanistan I have never known and very few people would believe ever existed.

11   "In the College of Engineering, there was this lecture hall, with seats for 1,000 students," his says as eyes begin to get bigger. "At the end of the lecture, the seats would move. The whole auditorium would shift as you spun along the diameter. The engineering of the building itself was very interesting." He continues to describe the construction details, then sighs. "I wonder if it's still around?"

12   There is a pause. For 25 years I have tried to fill that silence, but I have never quite figured out what to say. I guess silence goes best there. He is the next one to speak. "You see, even your old-age father was once part of something important."

13   When he says things like that, I want to scream. I don't want to believe that the years can beat away at you like that. I don't want to know that if enough time passes, you begin to question what was real or who you are. I am unconcerned with what the world thinks of him, but it is devastating to know that he at times thinks less of himself.

14   We are the same, but we are separated. People don't see him in me. I wish they would. I walk in with a doctor's white coat or a suit or my Berkeley sweatshirt and jeans. High heels or sneakers, it doesn't matter, people always seem impressed with me. "Pediatrician, eh?" they say. "Well, good for you."

15     I wonder what people see when they look at him. They don't see what I see in his smile. Perhaps they see a brown man with a thick accent; perhaps they think, another immigrant cabdriver. Or perhaps it is much worse: Maybe he is a profile-matched terrorist, aligned with some axis of evil.

16     Sometimes the worst things are not what people say to your face or what they say at all; it is the things that are assumed. I am in line at the grocery store, studying at a cafe, on a plane flying somewhere.

17     "Her English is excellent; she must have grown up here," I hear a lady whisper. "But why on earth does she wear that thing on her head?"

18     "Oh, that's not her fault," someone replies. "Her father probably forces her to wear that."

19     I am still searching for a quick, biting response to comments like that. The trouble is that things I'd like to say aren't quick. So I say nothing. I want to take their hands and pull them home with me. Come, meet my father. Don't look at the wrinkles; don't look at the scars; don't mind the hearing aid, or the thick accent. Don't look at the world's effect on him; look at his effect on the world. Come into my childhood and hear the lullabies, the warm hand on your shoulder on the worst of days, the silly jokes on mundane afternoons. Come meet the woman he has loved and respected his whole life; witness the confidence he has nurtured in his three daughters. Stay the night; hear his footsteps come in at midnight after a long day's work. That sound in the middle of the night is his head bowing in prayer although he is exhausted. Granted, the wealth is gone and the legacy unknown, but look at what the bombs did not destroy. Now tell me, am I really oppressed? The question makes me want to laugh. Now tell me, is he really the oppressor? The question makes me want to cry.

20     At times, I want to throw it all away: the education, the opportunities, the potential. I want to slip into the passenger seat of his cab and say: This is who I am. If he is going to be labeled, then give me those labels, too. If you are going to look down on him, then you might as well peer down on me as well. Close this gap. Erase this line. There is no differentiation here. Of all the things I am, of all the things I could ever be, I will never be prouder than to say that I am of him.

21     I am this cabdriver's daughter.

## THINKING ABOUT THE TEXT

1. What is the author's intention of starting her essay with the scene of her and her father's morning brief conversation followed by their separate departures by car? What is created for the reader in Samady's description of the scene?

2. When the author acknowledges that her life of studying does not give her much opportunity for interesting stories to relate to her father, how does he convert her admission into an affirming reply?

3. What does the author reveal of her father's background? What part of his history saddens her? How might his life have been positively shaped by the tragedies of his past?

4. The author reveals that she does not care how the world regards her father, but she is distressed when she perceives that at times he "thinks less of himself." What feelings does Samady reveal? When she acknowledges that "we are the same, but we are separated" (12), what does she mean?

5. How does the ethnicity of the author and her father contribute to the author's sorrow in realizing how they are perceived? What is the "gap" between them that others see but which the author wants to close? List the many ways the author must live "between worlds."

6. Although the author has many academic and professional triumphs in her life, of what is she most proud?

## WRITING FROM THE TEXT

1. Write an analysis of the author's father that supports a thesis based on character inference and includes details from the essay. Your discussion of the supporting details will reflect both your understanding of the character and your judgment of him. (See Character Analysis, pp. 445–468.)

2. Write an essay that shows your perception of what makes a good family. Reflect on the relationship you see between Waheeda Samady and her father as you consider points to include in your analysis. Your thesis will be supported with details from the essay and inferences you can make based on what the author provides in her work.

3. Write a comparison-contrast essay to show how the author's life reflects joy, pride, and sorrows that conflict with her contentment. Your thesis should reflect your position on these conflicting emotions as you illustrate with material from the essay.

## CONNECTING WITH OTHER TEXTS

1. Read "An Identity Reduced to a Burka" (p. 113) to learn how the points made by Semeen Issa and Laila Al-Marayati are also reflected in Samady's essay. Write an analysis examining what these authors believe Muslim women most value, and support your thesis with examples from both texts.

2. Read "Terra Firma—A Journey from Migrant Farm Labor to Neurosurgery" (p. 102) and write an essay showing how Alfred Quinones-Hinojosa

and Waheeda Samady exemplify the values and high achievements of many immigrants and children of immigrants in the United States. Use the examples of people you personally know, in addition to the experiences of these authors, to develop your essay.

#  The Color of Love
## *Danzy Senna*

The daughter of an African Mexican father, author Carl Senna, and Irish American writer Fanny Howe, Danzy Senna (b. 1970) earned a BA from Stanford University and an MFA from the University of California, Irvine. She won several awards for her best-selling novel *Caucasia* (1988), and in 2002 was honored with the Whiting Award, presented each year to ten outstanding writers who demonstrate ability and promise. She published the psychological thriller *Symptomatic* (2004) and a memoir *Where Did You Sleep Last Night?: A Personal History* (2009). The following essay originally appeared in *O: The Oprah Magazine* in 2000.

1    We had this much in common: We were both women, and we were both writers. But we were as different as two people can be and still exist in the same family. She was ancient—as white and dusty as chalk—and spent her days seated in a velvet armchair, passing judgments on the world below. She still believed in noble bloodlines; my blood had been mixed at conception. I believed there was no such thing as nobility or class or lineage, only systems designed to keep some people up in the big house and others outside, in the cold.

2    She was my grandmother. She was Irish but from that country's Protestant elite, which meant she seemed more British than anything. She was an actress, a writer of plays and novels, and still unmarried in her thirties when she came to America to visit. One night while in Boston, she went to a dinner party, where she was seated next to a young lawyer with blood as blue as the ocean. Her pearl earring fell in his oyster soup—or so the story goes—and they fell in love. My grandmother married that lawyer and left her native Ireland for New England.

3    How she came to have black grandchildren is a story of opposites. It was 1968 in Boston when her daughter—my mother—a small, blonde Wasp poet, married my father, a tall and handsome black intellectual, in an act that was as rebellious as it was hopeful. The products of that unlikely union—my older sister, my younger brother, and I—grew up in urban chaos, in a home filled with artists and political activists. The old lady across the river in Cambridge seemed to me an endangered species. Her walls were covered with portraits

of my ancestors, the pale and dead men who had conquered Africa and built Boston long before my time. When I visited, their eyes followed me from room to room with what I imagined to be an expression of scorn. Among the portraits sat my grandmother, a bird who had flown in to remind us all that there had indeed been a time when lineage and caste meant something. To me, young and dark and full of energy, she was the missing link between the living and the dead.

4    But her blood flowed through me, whether I liked it or not. I grew up to be a writer, just like her. And as I struggled to tell my own stories—about race and class and post–civil rights America—I wondered who my grandmother had been before, in Dublin, when she was friend and confidante to literary giants such as William Butler Yeats and Samuel Beckett. Once, while snooping in her bedroom, I discovered her novels, the ones that had been published in Ireland when she was my age. I stared at her photograph on the jacket and wondered about the young woman who wore a mischievous smile. Had she ever worried about becoming so powerful that no man would want her? Did she now feel that she had sacrificed her career and wild Irishwoman dreams to become a wife and mother and proper Bostonian?

5    I longed to know her—to love her. But the differences between us were real and alive, and they threatened to squelch our fragile connection. She was an alcoholic. In the evening, after a few glasses of gin, she could turn vicious. Though she held antiquated racist views, my grandmother would still have preferred to see my mother married and was saddened when my parents split in the seventies. She believed that a woman without a man was pitiable. The first question she always asked me when she saw me: "Do you have a man?" The second question: "What is he?" That was her way of finding out his race and background. She looked visibly pleased if he was a Wasp, neutral if he was Jewish, and disappointed if he was black.

6    My mother ignored her hurtful comments but felt them just the same. She spent her visits to my grandmother's house slamming dishes in the kitchen, hissing her anger just out of hearing range, then raving, on the drive home, about what awful thing her mother had said this time. Like my mother, I knew the rule: I was not to disrespect elders. She was old and gray and would soon be gone. But I had inherited my grandmother's short temper. When I got angry, even as a child, I felt as if blood were rushing around in my head, red waves battering the shore. Words spilled from my mouth—cutting, vicious words that I regretted.

7    One autumn day in Cambridge, at my grandmother's place, I lost my temper. I was home from college for the holidays, staying in her guest room. I woke from a nap to the sound of her enraged voice shouting at what I could only imagine was the television.

8    "Idiot! You damn fool!" she bellowed. "You stupid, stupid woman!" It has to be *Jeopardy!*, I thought. She must be yelling at those tiny contestants on the screen. She knows the answers to those questions better than they do. But when the shouting went on for a beat too long, I went to the top of the stairs and looked down into the living room. She was speaking to a real person: her cleaning lady, a Greek woman named Mary, who was on her hands and knees, nervously gathering the shards of a broken vase. My grandmother stood over her, hands on hips, cursing.

9    "You fool," my grandmother repeated. "How in bloody hell could you have done something so stupid?"

10   "Grandma." I didn't shout her name but said it loudly enough that she, though hard of hearing, glanced up.

11   "Oh, darling!" she piped, suddenly cheerful. "Would you like a cup of tea? You must be dreadfully tired."

12   Mary was on her feet again. She smiled nervously at me, then rushed into the kitchen with the pieces of the broken vase.

13   I told myself to be a good girl, to be polite. But something snapped. I marched down the stairs, and even she noticed something on my face that made her sit in her velvet chair.

14   "Don't you ever talk to her that way," I shouted. "Where do you think you are? Slavery was abolished long ago."

15   I stood over her, tall and long-limbed, daring her to speak. My grandmother shook her head. "It's about race, isn't it?"

16   "Race?" I said, baffled. "Mary's white. This is about respect—treating other human beings with respect."

17   She wasn't hearing me. All she saw was color. "The tragedy about you," she said soberly, "is that you are mixed." I felt those waves in my head: "Your tragedy is that you're old and ignorant," I spat. "You don't know the first thing about me."

18   She cried into her hands. She seemed diminished, a little old woman. She looked up only to say, "You are a cruel girl."

19   I left her apartment trembling yet feeling exhilarated by what I had done. But my elation soon turned to shame. I had taken on an old lady. And for what? Her intolerance was, at her age, deeply entrenched. My rebuttals couldn't change her.

20   Yet that fight marked the beginning of our relationship. I've since decided that when you cease to express anger toward those who have hurt you, you are essentially giving up on them. They are dead to you. But when you express anger, it is a sign that they still matter, that they are worth the fight.

21   After that argument, my grandmother and I began a conversation. She seemed to see me clearly for the first time, or perhaps she, a "cruel girl"

herself, had simply met her match. And I no longer felt she was a relic. She was a living, breathing human being who deserved to be spoken to as an equal.

22     I began visiting her more. I would drive to Cambridge and sit with her, eating mixed nuts and sipping ginger ale, regaling her with tales of my latest love drama or writing project. In her presence, I was proudly black and young and political, and she was who she was: subtly racist, terribly elitist, and awfully funny. She still said things that angered me: She bemoaned my mother's marriage to my father, she said that I should marry not for love but for money, and she told me that I needn't identify myself as black, since I didn't look it. I snapped back at her. But she, with senility creeping in, didn't seem to hear me; each time I came, she said the same things.

23     Last summer I went into hiding to work on my second novel at a writer's retreat in New Hampshire. The place was a kind of paradise for creative souls, a hideaway where every writer had his or her own cabin in the woods with no phone or television—no distractions to speak of. But I was miserable. I could not write. Even the flies outside my window seemed to whisper, "Go out and play. Forget the novel. Leave it till tomorrow."

24     I woke one morning at four, the light outside my window still blue. I felt panic and sadness, though I didn't know why. I got up, dressed, and went outside for a walk through the forest. But the panic persisted, and I began to cry. I assumed that my writer's block had seized me suddenly.

25     That night I ate dinner in the main house and received a call on the pay phone from my mother. She told me my grandmother had fallen and broken her leg. But that wasn't all; she had subsequently suffered a heart attack. Her other organs were failing. I had to hurry if I wanted to say good-bye.

26     I drove to Boston that night, not believing that we could be losing her. She would make it. I was certain. Sure, she was ninety-two, frail, unable to walk steadily. But she was lucid, and her tongue was as sharp as ever. Somehow I had imagined her as indestructible, made immortal by power and cruelty and wit.

27     The woman I found in the hospital bed was barely recognizable. My grandmother had always been fussy about her appearance. She never showed her face without makeup. Even in the day, when it was just she and the cleaning lady, she dressed as if she were ready for a cocktail party. At night she usually had cocktail parties; doddering old men hovered around her, sipping Scotch and bantering about theater and politics.

28     My grandmother's face had swollen to twice its normal size, and tubes came out of her nose. She had struggled so hard to pull them out that the nurses had tied her wrists to the bed rails. Her hair was gray and thin. Her body was withered and bruised, barely covered by the green hospital gown.

29     Her hazel eyes were all that was still recognizable, but the expression in them was different from any I had ever seen on her—terror. She was terrified to die. She tried to rise when she saw me, and her eyes pleaded with me to help her, to save her, to get her out of this mess. I stood over her, and I felt only one thing: overwhelming love. Not a trace of anger. That dark gray rage I'd felt toward her was gone as I stroked her forehead and told her she would be okay, even knowing she would not.

30     For two days, my mother, her sisters, and I stood beside my grandmother, singing Irish ballads and reading passages to her from the works of her favorite novelist, James Joyce. For the first time, she could not talk. At one point, she gestured wildly for pen and paper. I brought her the pen and the paper and held them up for her, but she was too weak for even that. What came out was only a faint, incomprehensible line.

31     In death we are each reduced to our essence: the spirit we are when we are born. The trappings we hold on to our whole lives—our race, our money, our sex, our age, our politics—become irrelevant. My grandmother became a child in that hospital bed, a spirit about to embark on an unknown journey, terrified and alone, no matter how many of us were crowded around her. In the final hours, even her skin seemed to lose its wrinkles and take on a waxy glow. Then, finally, the machines around us went silent as she left us behind to squabble in the purgatory of the flesh.

## THINKING ABOUT THE TEXT

1. Compare and contrast Senna and her grandmother. Which differences most threaten their "fragile connection"?

2. Describe what provokes "the fight" between Senna and her grandmother and how both verbally attack each other.

3. Why is it important to Senna to "express anger"? In what ways does their fight ironically help their relationship?

4. How do both Senna's writer's block and her grandmother's deathbed scene bring a sense of resolution to this essay? What ultimately matters most to Senna and what are the "trappings" that seem irrelevant?

## WRITING FROM THE TEXT

1. Focusing on your view of Senna's relationship with her grandmother, write an essay comparing and contrasting these two female writers. Include specific details to support your analysis and assessment of them. (See Comparison-Contrast, pp. 407–413.)

2. Based on details from this essay, write a character analysis of Senna's grandmother, and include specific characteristics and illustrations for support.

3. Write an essay about a conflict you have had with a relative or with someone who discriminated against you. Dramatize what led up to the conflict, how both of you interacted, and how the tension was resolved or intensified.

4. Considering Senna's realistic details of her grandmother dying, write an essay describing your own encounter with someone who was ill or dying. Focus on those details that support your thesis about how that person changed or how your view of him or her was altered by this experience.

### CONNECTING WITH OTHER TEXTS

1. After reading "Race Is A Four-Letter Word" by Teja Arboleda (p. 108), write an essay showing how Senna's experience with her grandmother illustrates Arboleda's sense of the "barriers, pedestals, doors, and traps that form the boundaries that confine human beings to dominant and minority groups" (111). Include details from both essays to support your thesis.

2. In "Living in Two Worlds" (p. 99), Marcus Mabry discusses the guilt, helplessness, and embarrassment he often feels at leaving his family behind. Write an essay comparing and contrasting Senna's and Mabry's attitudes and experiences as they move between their new environments and the worlds of their families.

3. Read Heilbroner's "Don't Let Stereotypes Warp Your Judgments" (p. 424). Then write an essay showing specific examples of what Senna's grandmother could learn from Heilbroner's essay and how her judgment has been "warped" by stereotypes and prejudgments.

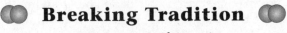

## ⊙⊙ Breaking Tradition ⊙⊙
### *Janice Mirikitani*

A third-generation Japanese American, Janice Mirikitani (b. 1942) was interned at a relocation camp during World War II. Since then, she has emerged as both poet and proponent for social change. Serving as president of the Glide Foundation, she directs thirty-five programs that assist the homeless and poor in San Francisco. Mirikitani is also a founding member of Third World Communications, editing the works of other Japanese American writers. Her collections of poetry include *Awake in the River* (1978), *We the*

*Dangerous* (1995), and *Love Works* (2003). Her poems typically illustrate her opposition to oppression and her support for those seeking their own American identity rather than following traditional customs, as in this poem from *Shedding Silence* (1987).

*For* my daughter

My daughter denies she is like me,
Her secretive eyes avoid mine.
She reveals the hatreds of womanhood
5 already veiled behind music and smoke and telephones.
I want to tell her about the empty room of myself.
This room we lock ourselves in
where whispers live like fungus,
giggles about small breasts and cellulite,
10 where we confine ourselves to jealousies,
bedridden by menstruation.
This waiting room where we feel our hands
are useless, dead speechless clamps
that need hospitals and forceps and kitchens
15 and plugs and ironing boards to make them useful.
I deny I am like my mother. I remember why:
She kept her room neat with silence,
defiance smothered in requirements to be otonashii,
passion and loudness wrapped in an obi,
20 her steps confined to ceremony,
the weight of her sacrifice she carried like
a foetus. Guilt passed on in our bones.
I want to break tradition—unlock this room
where women dress in the dark.
25 Discover the lies my mother told me.
The lies that we are small and powerless,
that our possibilities must be compressed
to the size of pearls, displayed only as
passive chokers, charms around our neck.
30 Break Tradition.
I want to tell my daughter of this room of myself
filled with tears of violins,
the light in my hands,
35 poems about madness,
the music of yellow guitars—
sounds shaken from barbed wire and

goodbyes and miracles of survival.
This room of open window where daring ones escape.
40  My daughter denies she is like me
her secretive eyes are walls of smoke
and music and telephones,
her pouting ruby lips, her skirts
swaying to salsa, teena marie and the stones,
45  her thighs displayed in carnivals of color.
I do not know the contents of her room.
She mirrors my aging.
She is breaking tradition.

## THINKING ABOUT THE TEXT

1. The narrator repeats "room" numerous times throughout this poem in relation to herself, her mother, and her daughter. What are some reasons that she uses "room" and what might this word symbolize?

2. Early in the poem, how does the narrator describe "the empty room of myself"?

3. Analyze the images that the narrator uses to describe her mother's "room." What is the impact of these details on the narrator?

4. Later, after the narrator recognizes her own attempts to break tradition and to deny she is like her mother, she describes the room that she would now like to reveal to her daughter. Analyze specific images from this "room of myself." How does this new "room of myself" contrast with that earlier "empty room of myself"?

5. How does the narrator characterize her daughter? Examine specific images.

6. How do the last two lines of the poem signal a shift in the narrator's tone from the opening two lines? What might account for this change in attitude?

7. Analyze the author's extensive use of repetition, not only of "room" but also of the title and of both daughters' denial that they are like their mothers. Are these repetitions purposeful and effective? Support your views with details from the poem.

8. Speculate why the narrator includes the dedication "for my daughter" at the beginning of the poem? Did that phrase affect your reading of this work?

## WRITING FROM THE TEXT

1. Considering your responses to exercises 1 and 7 above, analyze Mirikitani's use of repetition throughout the poem. Write an essay showing how

the repetition of certain key words and phrases not only helps unify the poem but also develops the poem's themes.

2. In an analytic essay, evaluate whether the issues addressed in this poem are ones of universal concern or if any seem more limited to one particular generation, gender, or culture. Use specific quotations to support your views.

3. Write an essay comparing and contrasting your own "room"—especially your views and values—with the "room" that best characterizes your mother or father. Describe the details in both "rooms" and explain any attempts made to "break tradition."

### CONNECTING WITH OTHER TEXTS

1. Focusing on the narrator's mother in "Breaking Tradition" as well as the parents in "The Good Daughter" (p. 8), write an essay analyzing the parents' strategies, efforts, and results as they attempt to pass on certain traditions and expectations to their children.

2. Unlike the narrator's mother in "Breaking Tradition," some parents and grandparents may or may not understand the need for children to reject certain paths in order to find their own. Focusing on the narrator in "Breaking Tradition" as well as the parents in "The Fringe Benefits of Failure, and the Importance of Imagination" (p. 154) or the grandmother in "The Color of Love" (p. 15), discuss why these individuals seem able to support and understand the need for change.

#  Who Shot Johnny?
### *Debra J. Dickerson*

After serving for twelve years as an intelligence officer in the United States Air Force, Debra J. Dickerson (b. 1959) earned a BA in politics and government, an MA in international relations, and a JD from Harvard Law School. While at Harvard, she began writing a column for the Harvard Law Record and decided to pursue a full-time writing career instead of practicing law. Dickerson's work has appeared in the *Washington Post*, the *New York Times Magazine, Good Housekeeping, VIBE, Mother Jones, Slate*, the *Village Voice, Salon*, and many other publications. Dickerson has also published two books, *An American Story*, a memoir (2001) and *The End of Blackness: Returning the Souls of Black Folk to Their Rightful Owners* (2004). Dickerson edited *The Best African American Essays: 2009*. Initially published in the *New Republic* in 1996, the following essay was selected by Ian Frazier for *The Best American Essays 1997* and is credited by Dickerson for "jump-starting" her writing career.

1  Given my level of political awareness, it was inevitable that I would come to view the everyday events of my life through the prism of politics

and the national discourse. I read the *Washington Post*, the *New Republic*, the *New Yorker*, *Harper's*, the *Atlantic Monthly*, the *Nation*, *National Review*, *Black Enterprise*, and *Essence* and wrote a weekly column for the Harvard Law School *Record* during my three years just ended there. I do this because I know that those of us who are not well-fed white guys in suits must not yield the debate to them, however well-intentioned or well-informed they may be. Accordingly, I am unrepentant and vocal about having gained admittance to Harvard through affirmative action; I am a feminist, stoic about my marriage chances as a well-educated, thirty-six-year-old black woman who won't pretend to need help taking care of herself. My strength flags, though, in the face of the latest role assigned to my family in the national drama. On July 27, 1995, my sixteen-year-old nephew was shot and paralyzed.

2      Talking with friends in front of his house, Johnny saw a car he thought he recognized. He waved boisterously—his trademark—throwing both arms in the air in a full-bodied, hip-hop Y. When he got no response, he and his friends sauntered down the walk to join a group loitering in front of an apartment building. The car followed. The driver got out, brandished a revolver, and fired into the air. Everyone scattered. Then he took aim and shot my running nephew in the back.

3      Johnny never lost consciousness. He lay in the road, trying to understand what had happened to him, why he couldn't get up. Emotionlessly, he told the story again and again on demand, remaining apologetically firm against all demands to divulge the missing details that would make sense of the shooting but obviously cast him in a bad light. Being black, male, and shot, he must apparently be involved with gangs or drugs. Probably both. Witnesses corroborate his version of events.

4      Nearly six months have passed since that phone call in the night and my nightmarish headlong drive from Boston to Charlotte. After twenty hours behind the wheel, I arrived haggard enough to reduce my mother to fresh tears and to find my nephew reassuring well-wishers with an eerie sang-froid.

5      I take the day shift in his hospital room; his mother and grandmother, a clerk and cafeteria worker, respectively, alternate nights there on a cot. They don their uniforms the next day, gaunt after hours spent listening to Johnny moan in his sleep. How often must his subconscious replay those events and curse its host for saying hello without permission, for being carefree and young while a would-be murderer hefted the weight of his uselessness and failure like Jacob Marley's chains? How often must he watch himself lying stubbornly immobile on the pavement of his nightmares while the sound of running feet syncopate his attacker's taunts?

6      I spend these days beating him at gin rummy and Scrabble, holding a basin while he coughs up phlegm and crying in the corridor while he

catheterizes himself. There are children here much worse off than he. I should be grateful. The doctors can't, or won't, say whether he'll walk again.

7    I am at once repulsed and fascinated by the bullet, which remains lodged in his spine (having done all the damage it can do, the doctors say). The wound is undramatic—small, neat, and perfectly centered—an impossibly pink pit surrounded by an otherwise undisturbed expanse of mahogany. Johnny has asked me several times to describe it but politely declines to look in the mirror I hold for him.

8    Here on the pediatric rehab ward, Johnny speaks little, never cries, never complains, works diligently to become independent. He does whatever he is told; if two hours remain until the next pain pill, he waits quietly. Eyes bloodshot, hands gripping the bed rails. During the week of his intravenous feeding, when he was tormented by the primal need to masticate, he never asked for food. He just listened while we counted down the days for him and planned his favorite meals. Now required to dress himself unassisted, he does so without demur, rolling himself back and forth valiantly on the bed and shivering afterward, exhausted. He "ma'am"s and "sir"s everyone politely. Before his "accident," a simple request to take out the trash could provoke a firestorm of teenage attitude. We, the women who have raised him, have changed as well; we've finally come to appreciate those boxer-baring, oversized pants we used to hate—it would be much more difficult to fit properly sized pants over his diaper.

9    He spends a lot of time tethered to rap music still loud enough to break my concentration as I read my many magazines. I hear him try to sound-lessly mouth the obligatory "mothafuckers" overlaying the funereal dirge of the music tracks. I do not normally tolerate disrespectful music in my or my mother's presence, but if it distracts him now . . .

10    "Johnny," I ask later, "do you still like gangster rap?" During the long pause I hear him think loudly, I'm paralyzed Auntie, not stupid. "I mostly just listen to hip-hop," he says evasively into his *Sports Illustrated*.

11    Miserable though it is, time passes quickly here. We always seem to be jerking awake in our chairs just in time for the next pill, his every-other-night bowel program, the doctor's rounds. Harvard feels a galaxy away—the world revolves around Family Members Living with Spinal Cord Injury class, Johnny's urine output, and strategizing with my sister to find affordable, accessible housing. There is always another long-distance uncle in need of an update, another church member wanting to pray with us, or Johnny's little brother in need of some attention.

12    We Dickerson women are so constant a presence the ward nurses and cleaning staff call us by name and join us for cafeteria meals and cigarette breaks. At Johnny's birthday pizza party, they crack jokes and make fun of

each other's husbands (there are no men here). I pass slices around and try not to think, Seventeen with a bullet.

13    Oddly, we feel little curiosity or specific anger toward the man who shot him. We have to remind ourselves to check in with the police. Even so, it feels pro forma, like sending in those $2 rebate forms that come with new pantyhose: you know your request will fall into a deep, dark hole somewhere, but still, it's your duty to try. We push for an arrest because we owe it to Johnny and to ourselves as citizens. We don't think about it otherwise—our low expectations are too ingrained. A Harvard aunt notwithstanding, for people like Johnny, Marvin Gaye was right that only three things are sure: taxes, death, and trouble. At least it wasn't the second.

14    We rarely wonder about or discuss the brother who shot him because we already know everything about him. When the call came, my first thought was the same one I'd had when I'd heard about Rosa Parks's beating: a brother did it. A non-job-having, middle-of-the-day malt-liquor-drinking, crotch-clutching, loud-talking brother with many neglected children born of many forgotten women. He lives in his mother's basement with furniture rented at an astronomical interest rate, the exact amount of which he does not know. He has a car phone, an $80 monthly cable bill, and every possible phone feature but no savings. He steals Social Security numbers from unsuspecting relatives and assumes their identities to acquire large TV sets for which he will never pay. On the slim chance that he is brought to justice, he will have a colorful criminal history and no coherent explanation to offer for his act. His family will raucously defend him and cry cover-up. Some liberal lawyer just like me will help him plea-bargain his way to yet another short stay in a prison pesthouse that will serve only to add another layer to the brother's sociopathology and formless, mindless nihilism. We know him. We've known and feared him all our lives.

15    As a teenager, he called, "Hey, baby, gimme somma that boodie!" at us from car windows. Indignant at our lack of response, he followed up with, "Fuck you, then, 'ho!" He called me a "white-boy-lovin' nigger bitch oreo" for being in the gifted program and loving it. At twenty-seven, he got my seventeen-year-old sister pregnant with Johnny and lost interest without ever informing her that he was married. He snatched my widowed mother's purse as she waited in predawn darkness for the bus to work and then broke into our house while she soldered on an assembly line. He chased all the small entrepreneurs from our neighborhood with his violent thievery and put bars on our windows. He kept us from sitting on our own front porch after dark and laid the foundation for our periodic bouts of self-hating anger and racial embarrassment. He made our neighborhood a ghetto. He is the poster fool behind the maddening community knowledge that there are still some black mothers who raise their daughters but merely love their sons. He and his cancerous carbon copies

eclipse the vast majority of us who are not sociopaths and render us invisible. He is the Siamese twin who has died but cannot be separated from his living, vibrant sibling; which of us must attract more notice? We despise and disown this anomalous loser, but for many he *is* black America. We know him, we know that he is outside the fold, and we know that he will only get worse. What we didn't know is that, because of him, my little sister would one day be the latest hysterical black mother wailing over a fallen child on TV.

16   Alone, lying in the road bleeding and paralyzed but hideously conscious, Johnny had lain helpless as he watched his would-be murderer come to stand over him and offer this prophecy: "Betch'ou won't be doin' nomo' wavin', mothafucker."

17   Fuck you, asshole. He's fine from the waist up. You just can't do anything right, can you?

## THINKING ABOUT THE TEXT

1.  How does the introductory paragraph both establish the author's persona and provide the compelling focus for her essay?

2.  What are the shocking details that we initially are told about how Johnny was shot?

3.  Why does the author not reveal, until the very end, what the shooter said to Johnny who was bleeding in the street? What is the effect of concluding with those words and with the author's response?

4.  How is Johnny portrayed, both before he is shot and afterwards, while he is suffering in the hospital? Which details give the reader the most vivid picture of how his life has changed?

5.  Without knowing the actual identity of Johnny's shooter, why does the author refer to him ironically as "a brother" and claim, "We already know everything about him"? What are the many details that she offers to characterize Johnny's shooter?

6.  Is the author guilty of stereotyping Johnny's shooter in this essay—or do her life experiences and the fact that Johnny's shooting was cold-blooded and unprovoked justify Dickerson's assumptions about this "brother"?

## WRITING FROM THE TEXT

1.  If you or a family member has ever been the victim of a crime, write an essay dramatizing that experience as Dickerson has done. You may choose to compare and contrast your experience with Johnny's or to use Dickerson's essay as an example of how to focus on a strong thesis and to select vivid details for support.

2. Focusing on Johnny and including details from Dickerson's narration, write an essay about the emotional and physical difficulties—for both victim and family members—of surviving a crime.

3. Write an evaluative response of Dickerson's essay as you take a stance on her thesis, tone, and main points. (See Evaluative Response, pp. 391–397.)

### CONNECTING WITH OTHER TEXTS

1. After reading Brent Staples's essay "Black Men and Public Space" (p. 164), write an essay comparing and contrasting his thesis, focus, and style with Dickerson's. Although Staples's and Dickerson's personas and attitudes may seem quite different, be careful to show how their concerns, fears, and choices overlap, too.

2. Referring to Dickerson's essay and to works by Staples (p. 164) and Thayer (p. 169), write an argument convincing readers who may be tempted to use aggression or rage that their impulsive behavior could have deadly consequences for themselves and others. Include details from all three essays to illustrate your points.

3. Using details from Dickerson's essay and from the film *Crash,* write an analysis of the causes and the consequences (for both perpetrator and victim) of street crimes and attacks.

#  On Teenagers and Tattoos
## *Andres Martin*

Professor of child psychiatry, psychiatry director of medical studies at the Yale Child Study Center, and medical director of children's psychiatric inpatient service at the Yale-New Haven Children's Hospital, Andres Martin (b. 1966) is also editor-in-chief of the *Journal of the American Academy of Child and Adolescent Psychiatry.* He is widely published in professional journals of pediatric and adolescent psychology. The essay below was published in the *Journal of Child and Adolescent Psychiatry* (1997) and reprinted in *Reclaiming Children and Youth* (2000). You will notice that the in-text citations, in paragraphs 2 and 12, and the end "References" follow APA documentation form.

> The skeleton dimensions I shall now proceed to set down are copied verbatim from my right arm, where I had them tattooed: as in my wild wanderings at that period, there was no other secure way of preserving such valuable statistics.
>
> —MELVILLE, *Moby Dick*

1        Tattoos and piercing have become a part of our everyday landscape. They are ubiquitous, having entered the circles of glamour and the mainstream of fashion, and they have even become an increasingly common feature of our urban youth. Legislation in most states restricts professional tattooing to adults older than 18 years of age, so "high end" tattooing is rare in children and adolescents, but such tattoos are occasionally seen in older teenagers. Piercings, by comparison, as well as self-made or "jailhouse" type tattoos, are not at all rare among adolescents or even among school-age children. Like hairdo, makeup, or baggy jeans, tattoos and piercings can be subject to fad influence or peer pressure in an effort toward group affiliation. As with any other fashion statement, they can be construed as bodily aids in the inner struggle toward identity consolidation, serving as adjuncts to the defining and sculpting of the self by means of external manipulations. But unlike most other body decorations, tattoos and piercings are set apart by their irreversible and permanent nature, a quality at the core of their magnetic appeal to adolescents.

2        Adolescents and their parents are often at odds over the acquisition of bodily decorations. For the adolescent, piercing or tattoos may be seen as personal and beautifying statements, while parents may construe them as oppositional and enraging affronts to their authority. Distinguishing bodily adornment from self-mutilation may indeed prove challenging, particularly when a family is in disagreement over a teenager's motivations and a clinician is summoned as the final arbiter. At such times it may be most important to realize jointly that the skin can all too readily become but another battleground for the tensions of the age, arguments having less to do with tattoos and piercings than with core issues such as separation from the family matrix. Exploring the motivations and significance [underlying] tattoos (Grumet, 1983) and piercings can go a long way toward resolving such differences and can become a novel and additional way of getting to know teenagers. An interested and nonjudgmental appreciation of teenagers's surface presentations may become a way of making contact not only in their terms but on their turfs: quite literally on the territory of their skins.

3        The following three sections exemplify some of the complex psychological underpinnings of youth tattooing.

4        Tattoos and piercing can offer a concrete and readily available solution for many of the identity crises and conflicts normative to adolescent development. In using such decorations, and by marking out their bodily territories, adolescents can support their efforts at autonomy, privacy, and insulation. Seeking individuation, tattooed adolescents can become unambiguously demarcated from others and singled out as unique. The intense and often disturbing reactions that are mobilized in viewers can

help to effectively keep them at bay, becoming tantamount to the proverbial "Keep Out" sign hanging from a teenager's door.

5      Alternatively, feeling prey to a rapidly evolving body over which they have no say, self-made and openly visible decorations may restore adolescents' sense of normalcy and control, a way of turning a passive experience into an active identity. By indelibly marking their bodies, adolescents can strive to reclaim their bearings within an environment experienced as alien, estranged, or suffocating or to lay claim over their evolving and increasingly unrecognizable bodies. In either case, the net outcome can be a resolution to unwelcome impositions: external, familial, or societal in one case; internal and hormonal in the other. In the words of a 16-year-old girl with several facial piercings, and who could have been referring to her body just as well as to the position within her family: "If I don't fit in, it is because I say so."

6      Imagery of a religious, deathly, or skeletal nature, the likenesses of fierce animals or imagined creatures, and the simple inscription of names are some of the time-tested favorite contents for tattoos. In all instances, marks become not only memorials or recipients for dearly held persons or concepts: they strive for incorporation, with images and abstract symbols gaining substance on becoming a permanent part of the individual's skin. Thickly embedded in personally meaningful representations and object relations, tattoos can become not only the ongoing memento of a relationship, but at times even the only evidence that there ever was such a bond. They can quite literally become the relationship itself. The turbulence and impulsivity of early attachments and infatuations may become grounded, effectively bridging oblivion through the visible reality to tattoos.

7      Case Vignette: "A," a 13-year-old boy, proudly showed me his tattooed deltoid. The coarsely depicted roll of the dice marked the day and month of his birth. Rather disappointed, he then uncovered an immaculate back, going on to draw for me the great "piece" he envisioned for it. A menacing figure held a hand of cards: two aces, two eights, and a card with two sets of dates. "A's" father had belonged to Dead Man's Hand, a motorcycle gang named after the set of cards (aces and eights) that the legendary Wild Bill Hickock had held in the 1890s when shot dead over a poker table in Deadwood, South Dakota. "A" had only the vaguest memory of and sketchiest information about his father, but he knew he had died in a motorcycle accident: The fifth card marked the dates of his birth and death.

8      The case vignette also serves to illustrate how tattoos are often the culmination of a long process of imagination, fantasy, and planning that can start at an early age. Limited markings, or relatively reversible ones such as piercings, can at a later time scaffold toward the more radical commitment of a permanent tattoo.

9    The popularity of the anchor as a tattoo motif may historically have had to do less with guild identification among sailors than with an intense longing for rootedness and stability. In a similar vein, the recent increase in the popularity and acceptance of tattoos may be understood as an antidote or counterpoint to our urban and nomadic lifestyles. Within an increasingly mobile society, in which relationships are so often transient—as attested by the frequencies of divorce, abandonment, foster placement, and repeated moves, for example—tattoos can be a readily available source of grounding. Tattoos, unlike many relationships, can promise permanence and stability. A sense of constancy can be derived from unchanging marks that can be carried along no matter what the physical, temporal, or geographical vicissitudes at hand. Tattoos stay, while all else may change.

10    Case Vignette: A proud father at 17, "B" had had the smiling face of his 4-month-old baby girl tattooed on his chest. As we talked at a tattoo convention, he proudly introduced her to me, explaining how he would "always know how beautiful she is today" when years from then he saw her semblance etched on himself.

11    The quest for permanence may at other times prove misleading and offer premature closure to unresolved conflicts. At a time of normative uncertainties, adolescents may maladaptively and all too readily commit to a tattoo and its indefinite presence. A wish to hold on to a current certainty may lead the adolescent to lay down in ink what is valued and cherished one day but may not necessarily be in the future. The frequency of selfmade tattoos among hospitalized, incarcerated, or gang-affiliated youths suggests such motivations: A sense of stability may be a particularly dire need under temporary, turbulent, or volatile conditions. In addition, through their designs teenagers may assert a sense of bonding and allegiance to a group larger than themselves. Tattoos may attest to powerful experiences, such as adolescence itself, lived and even survived together. As with Moby Dick's protagonist, Ishmael, they may bear witness to the "valuable statistics" of one's "wild wandering(s)": those of adolescent exhilaration and excitement on the one hand; of growing pains, shared misfortune, or even incarceration on the other.

12    Adolescents' bodily decorations, at times radical and dramatic in their presentation, can be seen in terms of figuration rather than disfigurement, of the natural body being through them transformed into a personalized body (Brain, 1979). They can often be understood as self-constructive and adorning efforts, rather than prematurely subsumed as mutilatory and destructive acts. If we bear all of this in mind, we may not only arrive at a position to pass more reasoned clinical judgment, but become sensitized through our patients' skins to another level of their internal reality.

**References**

Brain, R. (1979). *The decorated body.* New York: Harper & Row.
Grumet, G. W. (1983). Psychodynamic implications of tattoos. *American Journal of Orthopsychiatry, 53,* 482–92.

## THINKING ABOUT THE TEXT

1. After acknowledging the prevalence and relative permanence of tattoos, Martin may surprise his readers with his argument for adults to accept teenagers' "bodily adornment." How does the wording of his thesis reflect his position? How does Martin's professional background possibly contribute to his position being accepted by his readers?

2. What three specific areas does Martin analyze to support his understanding and acceptance of tattoos? What appears to be the focus or assertion for each of Martin's three points?

3. How does Martin explain the symbols of the playing cards, anchor, and face tattooed on the subjects in his essay? What motif have you seen in tattoos that might also support Martin's analyses?

4. Martin discusses both the role of "limited markings, or relatively reversible ones" (30) as well as the tattoos that "promise permanence and stability" (31). How do you interpret these apparently contrasting types of tattoos?

5. Martin's original audience is readers of the *Journal of Child and Adolescent Psychiatry*. What does the author want his fellow psychiatrists to keep in mind as they work with patients who bear tattoos and body piercings?

6. How does the quotation from Melville's *Moby Dick* at the start of Martin's essay foreshadow the content of the essay? What is Martin's rhetorical strategy in returning to Melville's words at the end of his essay?

## WRITING FROM THE TEXT

1. Using specific details from Martin's essay for support, write an essay that explains your decision to pierce or tattoo your body.

2. In light of Martin's analysis that tattoos "are often the culmination of a long process of imagination, fantasy, and planning" (30), write an essay analyzing one of your tattoos, or a tattoo you might design for yourself, or the specific tattoo of a friend. The case story of "A" might serve as inspiration for your essay.

3. If you regret a tattoo that you have, write an analysis of that tattoo that illustrates how your thinking about it has changed. Use explanations and analysis from Martin's essay to present your evolution in understanding of your tattoo.

## CONNECTING WITH OTHER TEXTS

1. After reading "Breaking Tradition" (p. 20), write an essay using details from this poem and from Martin's essay to explain how young adults often feel compelled to depart from family traditions to assert their own individuality.

2. Read David Pogue's "Twitter? It's What You Make of It" (p. 235) and write an analytic essay that shows the possibilities of self-expression through abbreviated images (tattoos) or language (Tweets).

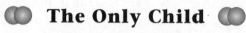

# The Only Child

## *John Leonard*

After studying at Harvard and Berkeley, where he received his BA in 1962, John Leonard (1939–2008) worked as a book reviewer, a producer of dramas and literature programs, a publicity writer, a staff writer for the *New York Times*, and a cultural critic for *Variety*, the *Nation*, and *CBS This Morning*. He is the author of *Smoke and Mirrors: Violence, Television, and Other American Cultures* (1997), *When the Kissing Had to Stop* (1999), a collection of previously published pieces, and *Lonesome Rangers: Homeless Minds, Promised Lands, Fugitive Cultures* (2002). Leonard intends his writing to ask moral questions: How do you want your children to grow up? What do you think is decent and fair? Who are your friends, and why? The work included here, from *Private Lives in the Imperial City* (1976), probes family tensions and concerns.

1     He is big. He always has been, over six feet, with that slump of the shoulders and tuck in the neck big men in the country often affect, as if to apologize for being above the democratic norm in size. (In high school and at college he played varsity basketball. In high school he was senior class president.) And he looks healthy enough, blue-eyed behind his beard, like a trapper or a mountain man, acquainted with silences. He also grins a lot.

2     Odd, then, to have noticed earlier—at the house, when he took off his shabby coat to play Ping-Pong—that the white arms were unmuscled. The coat may have been a comment. This, after all, is southern California, where every man is an artist, an advertiser of himself; where every surface is painted and every object potted; where even the statues seem to wear socks. The entire population ambles, in polyesters, toward a Taco Bell. To wear a brown shabby cloth coat in southern California is to admit something.

3     So he hasn't been getting much exercise. Nor would the children have elected him president of any class. At the house they avoided him. Or, since he was too big to be avoided entirely, they treated his presence as a kind of

odor to pass through hurriedly, to be safe on the other side. They behaved like cats. Of course, he ignored them. But I think they were up to more than just protecting themselves from his lack of curiosity. Children are expert readers of grins.

4    His grin is intermittent. The dimples twitch on and off; between them, teeth are bared; above them, the blue eyes disappear in a wince. This grin isn't connected to any humor the children know about. It may be a tic. It could also be a function of some metronome made on Mars. It registers inappropriate intervals. We aren't listening to the same music.

5    This is the man who introduced me to the mysteries of mathematical science, the man I could never beat at chess, the man who wrote haiku and played with computers. Now there is static in his head, as though the mind had drifted off its signal during sleep. He has an attention span of about thirty seconds.

6    I am to take him back to where he lives, in the car I have rented in order to pretend to be a Californian. We are headed for a rooming house in one of the beach cities along a coast of off-ramps and oil wells. It is a rooming house that thinks of itself as Spanish. The ruined-hacienda look requires a patio, a palm tree and several miles of corrugated tile. He does not expect me to come up to his room, but I insist. I have brought along a six-pack of beer.

7    The room is a slum, and it stinks. It is wall-to-wall beer cans, hundreds of them, under a film of ash. He lights cigarettes and leaves them burning on the windowsill or the edge of the dresser or the lip of the sink, while he thinks of something else—Gupta sculpture, maybe, or the Sephiroth Tree of the Kabbalah. The sink is filthy, and so is the toilet. Holes have been burnt in the sheet on the bed, where he sits. He likes to crush the beer cans after he has emptied them, then toss them aside.

8    He tells me that he is making a statement, that this room is a statement, that the landlord will understand the meaning of his statement. In a week or so, according to the pattern, they will evict him, and someone will find him another room, which he will turn into another statement, with the help of the welfare checks he receives on account of his disability, which is the static in his head.

9    There are no books, no newspapers or magazines, no pictures on the wall. There is a television set, which he watches all day long while drinking beer and smoking cigarettes. I am sufficiently familiar with the literature on schizophrenia to realize that this room is a statement he is making about himself. I am also sufficiently familiar with his history to understand that,

along with his contempt for himself, there is an abiding arrogance. He refuses medication. They can't make him take it, any more than they can keep him in a hospital. He has harmed no one. One night, in one of these rooms, he will set himself on fire.

10    He talks. Or blurts: scraps from Oriental philosophers—Lao-tzu, I think—puns, incantations, obscenities, names from the past. There are conspiracies; I am part of one of them. He grins, winces, slumps, is suddenly tired, wants me to get out almost as much as I want to get out, seems to have lapsed in a permanent parenthesis. Anyway, I have a busy schedule.

11    Well, speed kills slowly, and he fiddled too much with the oxygen flow to his brain. He wanted ecstasy and revelation, the way we grew up wanting a bicycle, a car, a girlfriend. These belonged to us by right, as middle-class Americans. So, then, did salvation belong to us by right. I would like to thank Timothy Leary and all the other sports of the 1960s who helped make this bad trip possible. I wish R. D. Laing would explain to me, once again and slowly, how madness is a proof of grace. "The greatest magician," said Novalis, "would be the one who would cast over himself a spell so complete that he would take his own phantasmagorias as autonomous appearances."

12    One goes back to the rented car and pretending to be a Californian as, perhaps, one had been pretending to be a brother. It is odd, at my age, suddenly to have become an only child.

## Thinking about the Text

1. Discuss how each "telling detail" about Leonard's brother provides a glimpse of his early promise. Then explain how these same details now underscore his sad transformation.

2. Why does Leonard's brother feel that his lifestyle and room are "making a statement"? What type of "statement" does the author feel his brother is making?

3. In this autobiographical essay, Leonard, a New Yorker, can only "pretend to be a Californian." Find details that illustrate what California represents for him.

4. Who or what does Leonard seem to blame for his brother's experimentation with drugs? Why? What is Leonard's implied thesis?

5. Discuss all possible meanings of the title. Why does Leonard wait until the end to focus on it?

## WRITING FROM THE TEXT

1. Write an essay contrasting Leonard's recollection of his brother before taking drugs with his perception of him now.

2. If drug addiction or mental illness has plagued any members of your own family, write an essay that illustrates an important insight you have learned from this experience.

3. Find a photograph that shows you with one of your relatives—a sibling, a parent, a cousin, or grandfather. Write an analysis of your relationship with that relative based on the dynamics that you perceive in the photograph.

## CONNECTING WITH OTHER TEXTS

1. Read "Living in Two Worlds" (p. 99) and write an essay that shows how both Marcus Mabry and John Leonard live between worlds because of their families.

2. Using "The Only Child," "Thanksgiving" (p. 3), or "The Color of Love" (p. 15), write an essay describing and analyzing the positive and negative aspects of family members reuniting and discovering how they have changed.

## Johnny Depp: A Pirate's Life
### Sean Smith

As senior writer at *Newsweek*, Sean Smith has examined the art and business of the film industry. Smith "has reported and written features on some of the most pivotal and controversial films of our time, including *Brokeback Mountain, United 93, The Passion of the Christ,* and *Fahrenheit 9/11,* and has explored the cultural significance of blockbusters such as *Spider-Man, Superman Returns,* and the *Harry Potter* films." Before joining *Newsweek,* Smith was the West Coast Editor of *Premiere* magazine. Smith earned a BA in magazine journalism from the University of Oregon and an MA from the Graduate School of Journalism at Columbia University. Smith has profiled numerous high-powered figures in the film industry, including Steven Spielberg, Denzel Washington, Annette Bening, Jodie Foster, Tom Hanks, Brad Pitt, Drew Barrymore, Julia Roberts, and Angelina Jolie. The following essay was published in *Newsweek* in June 2006.

1    Fatherhood has a way of changing people, even iconoclasts. "When I became a dad for the first time, it was like a veil being lifted," Johnny Depp says, as he leans forward, rolling loose tobacco into dark brown paper and using his knee as a table. "I've always loved the process of acting, but I didn't find the occupational hazards particularly rewarding." Occupational hazards like being stalked by paparazzi, mauled by strangers, packaged to sell bubble gum and other side effects of fame. "I can't use the word 'fame' with myself, but yeah," he says. "I just. . . there was a long period of confusion and dissatisfaction, because I didn't understand any of it. There was no purpose to it." He leans back, lights the cigarette, exhales. "I was never horribly self-obsessed or wrapped up in my own weirdness, but when my daughter was born, suddenly there was clarity. I wasn't angry anymore. It was the first purely selfless moment that I had ever experienced. And it was liberating. In that moment, it's like you become something else. The real you is revealed."

2     The Real Johnny Depp. How long have we searched for him? No one in Hollywood, it's fair to say, has worked harder at *not* being a movie star than Depp has, and yet he has evolved into one of the most adored actors of his generation not in spite of that persistence but because of it. *Pirates of the Caribbean: The Curse of the Black Pearl* may have grossed $653 million worldwide, made Depp a $20 million man and earned him an Oscar nomination, but he still seems an unlikely addition to the A-list. Top-tier stars, even those who are great actors, stay on top by being true to their personas. We pay $10 to see Will Smith or Julia Roberts precisely because they don't surprise us. It's not that they're playing themselves. It's just that the force of their personalities swamps everything else. They're more than actors. They're brands. Depp, 43, is almost pathologically unpredictable. He can be bizarre, hilarious, unsettling—even annoying. But he is never the same. He's the anti-Tom Cruise. "Nothing against Tom, but Johnny may be a bigger star now," says director John Waters, who cast Depp in 1990's *Cry-Baby*. "Nobody is sick of Johnny Depp."

3     *Pirates of the Caribbean: Dead Man's Chest*, which opened in 2011, will likely be the highest-grossing movie of that summer. And judging from *Newsweek*'s first look in the editing room, it also promises to be a welcome blast of sunshine in a season when Cruise has crashed and burned, and *The Da Vinci Code* has proved to be a joyiess blockbuster. In this second leg of the *Pirates* trilogy—the third installment will be released next summer—lovebirds Wili (Orlando Bloom) and Elizabeth (Keira Knightley) are arrested on their wedding day for aiding the escape of Depp's louche Narcissus, Capt. Jack Sparrow. To win freedom for his bride and himself, Will must find Captain Jack, get him to hand over his mysterious compass, and give it to the wormy Lord Beckett, who plans to use it to rid the world of pirates forever. Jack, meanwhile, has more immediate problems. He owes his soul to undersea Capt. Davey Jones, is in danger of being destroyed by a giant sea creature called a kraken, and has landed on an island of cannibals who have made him their god. This would be great if the natives didn't make a habit of eating their gods.

4     Returning director Gore Verbinski, producer Jerry Bruckheimer and team have cranked up the action this time around. One huge set piece includes an elaborate three-way sword fight on a massive water wheel that has snapped off its frame and is rolling at top speed through the jungle. ("It's those moments when you realize how absurd your job is," Depp says. "It's great fun, but it was a bastard to shoot.") Luckily, they've also given Depp plenty of playtime, too. Even more than in the first film, Depp's exaggerated expressions and unexpected line deliveries turn "cute" moments into hilarious ones. At one point, Elizabeth tells Jack, "You're a good man." Depp replies, sloppily, under his breath, "All evidence to the contrary."

5    Sitting in a bungalow at the Chateau Marmont in Los Angeles, Depp flashes a bit of Captain Jack every time he opens his mouth. Those gold pirate teeth are bonded onto his own. With the shoot for the third *Pirates* resuming in August, Depp figured it was just easier to keep them. "They don't come off until the ride stops," he says, and smiles. "It's a horrible process. I didn't want to go through yanking them off and putting them back on. And it leaves some residue of the character behind." Time slows down when you're with Johnny Depp. He seems like a man who has never rushed to, or from, anywhere in his life. He is chronically late for interviews—sometimes four or five hours, sometimes days—but this time around just a gentlemanly 50 minutes. And once he's with you, he never seems in a hurry to leave. His voice is a soft, low mumble. His body is in almost constant motion—rolling those cigarettes, rubbing an elbow, reaching for a glass—but the rhythm is tranquil and fluid, like a cat licking its paw. He's a calm, almost hypnotic presence. "He's always been true to who he is," says director Tim Burton, who has made five films with Depp, including last year's *Charlie and the Chocolate Factory*. "He's never been ruled by money, or by what people think he should or shouldn't do. Maybe it's just in America, but it seems that if you're passionate about something, it freaks people out. You're considered bizarre or eccentric. To me, it just means you know who you are."

6    Depp arrived in Hollywood in the early '80s. Despite a physical beauty that had studio executives slobbering to make him into a Romantic Leading Man and hordes of teenage girls (and a few boys) dreaming of touching his hair *just once*, Depp escaped from the Hollywood star machine around 1990, and managed to elude capture for almost two decades. He hid out in strange, sometimes beautiful films, playing unforgettable characters—Edward Scissorhands, Ed Wood, Hunter S. Thompson, Gilbert Grape—in movies that rarely made a dent at the box office. Of the 20 films Depp starred in before 2003, only one, Burton's *Sleepy Hollow*, squeaked past the $100 million mark. Depp got a reputation for being outré and unbankable. "Oh, yeah," he says, then rolls off the list of his crimes: "'That guy can't open a film. He does all those weird art movies. He works with directors whose names we can't pronounce'." He smiles. "But there are worse things they could say."

7    When news hit years ago that Depp was going to make the first *Pirates*, the buzz around town was that he must be broke, and that after years of taking the artistic high road, he had finally sold out. Depp says he never worried about that. "Never, not once, and I don't know why, because one would think that I would have," he says. "I suppose it's because I feel like I have a voice. The idea of commercial success never bothered me necessarily. What bothered me was *striving* for that, and lying to get that. If I was going to do something, it had to be on my terms—not because I'm some hideous

control freak—but because I don't want to live a lie. You really don't want to look back on your life and go, 'I was a complete fraud'."

8　　That battle to remain authentic has been long and bloody, and it made Depp an angry young man for most of his 20s. Born in Kentucky, the youngest of four kids, and raised in Florida by parents who fought and finally divorced when he was 15, Depp's dream was to play guitar in a band. By 16 he had dropped out of school and was doing just that, his group opening for acts like Iggy Pop. "It was wonderful," he says. "I couldn't have been happier." But after the band arrived in Los Angeles, Depp found himself broke. A musician he was briefly married to at the time introduced Depp to Nicolas Cage, who suggested that he give acting a try. On little more than a whim, he did, and ended up with a supporting role in *A Nightmare on Elm Street* and a small part in *Platoon*. Still struggling financially, he signed up for *21 Jump Street*, a slick TV series about young cops going undercover in high schools. It made Depp a teen idol, and made him miserable just as fast. "Everything flips," he says. "Suddenly, you go into restaurants and people are pointing at you and whispering. You feel spooked by it because that freedom of anonymity is gone. You never get used to that. You'd leave the hotel to go to dinner and there'd be tons of cameras and flashbulbs. 'Smile, Johnny! Smile!'" He looks annoyed by it, even now. "I thought, 'Jesus, I just want to go home.' But there was no home."

9　　Depp was locked into a multiyear contract with the Fox network. "They turned me into this product, and I didn't have a say in it," he says. "You have no voice, you know? I felt like I was a captive." So he lashed out, becoming a disruptive force on the *Jump Street* set in the hope that the network would fire him. "I was the only one who confronted him on what an a—hole he was being," says costar Holly Robinson Peete. "I totally understood his position, but I was over the moon to be a part of this show, and it's hard to come to work every day with someone who is p—ing all over it. So I went into his dressing room and told him how I felt, and right after that he trashed his Winnebago." Peete doesn't have any hard feelings toward Depp, and chalks it up to youth and inexperience. "He's got a really great heart, but he was frustrated," she says. "He just hated the idea of being on a lunch box or some teenage girl's wall."

10　　Finally freed from *Jump Street*, Depp played a succession of iconic loners and dreamers for visionary, unconventional directors, such as Waters, Burton, Jim Jarmusch and Terry Gilliam. But the anger, which Depp calls his "hillbilly rage," never quite dissipated. He was famously arrested for trashing a New York City hotel room in 1994, and while Depp says the incident was blown out of proportion—"I wasn't the Wild Man of Borneo"—he still believed that his fame and success lacked a point, meaning. "I had these sort of self-destructive periods," he says. "We all go through times where we poison ourselves a bit. Looking back on it now, it was simply a waste of time, all that self-medicating and boozing."

11      Depp was rescued, in part, by Marlon Brando. The two worked together on 1995's *Don Juan DeMarco*, and hit it off at the first rehearsal. "Within minutes, Johnny was in Marlon's lap with, I think, a bottle of gin," says director Jeremy Leven. "And I think he stayed there the whole time." It's easy to imagine the bond between the two men, both actors with unconventional visions, talent to burn and a disdain for art compromised by commerce. "Marlon was a pioneer," Depp says, quietly. "So I wouldn't even put myself in the same thought bubble with him, but he understood a lot of things about me, and was incredibly generous and helpful and caring. Very rarely did we talk about movies or acting, so it wasn't that. He saw me going through stuff that he had been through—my weird hillbilly rage—so yeah, the connection was strong and deep."

12      But it wasn't until Depp met and fell in love with French actress-singer Vanessa Paradis that everything seemed to fall into place for the actor. After a series of highly public, long-term romances—Sherilyn Fenn, Jennifer Grey, Winona Ryder, Kate Moss—his relationship with Paradis seemed to anchor him. The couple's daughter, Lily-Rose, was born in 1999; their son, Jack, in 2002. Being a father released him from the pressure of finding meaning and identity exclusively in his work. "I think it softened him on one level, and then invigorated him on an artistic one," says Burton. "It's an interesting juxtaposition." Depp himself puts it more directly: "Now I know where home is."

13      It was Depp's desire to make a movie for his kids that led him to *Pirates*. In a visit to the Disney lot about five years ago, he mentioned to studio chairman Dick Cook that he'd been watching a lot of Disney movies with his daughter, loved them and was hoping to voice a character in a Pixar movie. Cook mentioned that the studio was developing a movie based on the theme-park ride *Pirates of the Caribbean*. "And he got very excited," Cook recalls. "He said, 'Like a real pirate movie? With swords?' And I said, 'Yeah—with swords.' And he said, 'I'm in'."

14      As is now well known to *Pirates* fans, studio executives were nonplused when they began to see the footage of Depp in character. Whereas Capt. Jack Sparrow was initially conceived as a young Burt Lancaster, Depp had re-imagined him as a debauched, vain, slightly fey rock star, inspired by Rolling Stones icon Keith Richards and cartoon skunk Pepe Le Pew. "The studio was, like, 'Is he gay? Is he drunk? We don't know *what* he's doing!'" says producer Bruckheimer. "It took a little while to calm everybody down." For his part, Verbinski, the director, loved it. "You know, there's a lot of conspiring that goes on between actors and directors that I think is very healthy," he says.

"You should be a little concerned as a director if you're *not* making the studio nervous."

15    Depp's off-kilter performance, of course, was the very thing that catapulted *Pirates* into a cultural phenomenon. "First of all, Johnny is a pirate in real life," says John Waters. "It's the closest part he's ever played to his real self, but the fact that he played it kind of nelly was a big risk." Pause. "If only real gay pirates were that much fun." After decades of being daring and unexpected in daring and unexpected little films, Depp was now staying true to himself in a big summer blockbuster. He didn't have to be an outsider on the outside. He could be an outsider on the inside. "You feel like you have infiltrated the enemy camp, like you got in there somehow and chiseled your name in the castle wall," he says. The huge success of the film "made perfect sense to me on the one hand, and at the same time, it made no sense at all, which I kind of enjoyed." He takes another drag, exhales. "Yeah, it just felt right. Even now, with the dolls and the cereal boxes and snacks and fruit juices, it all just feels fun to me, in a Warholian way. It's absurd. It doesn't get more absurd." Depp's not ready to let go of Captain Jack just yet. "He's a blast to play," he says. "I'll be in a deep, dark depression saying goodbye to him." He laughs. "I'll keep the costume and just prance around the house, entertain the kids." Or the rest of the world. "Maybe *Pirates* 4, 5, and 6," he says. "If they had a good script, why not? I mean, at a certain point, the madness must stop, but for the moment, I can't say that he's done."

16    These days, Depp and his family divide their time between homes in Los Angeles and France, when they're not on some movie set or other. He says the media perception of him as an expat and wanna-be Frenchman has been overstated. "But, yeah, I love it there," he says. "I've always loved it there. The phones don't ring as much. Movies are never brought up in conversation. I'll take the kids and we'll go out to the trampoline and the swing set, and we'll stop by the garden and see how our tomatoes are doing. You know, old-fart stuff. Good stuff." At last, Depp has learned to quit fighting fate/fame/whatever. "I think everything happened the way it was meant to happen, but I don't know why," he says. "I remember every bump in the road, and I still don't know how I got here. But who am I to ask why? The fact is, this is where I am. So I enjoy it, salute it and keep moving forward." He smiles, a flash of gold. "None of it makes any sense to me, but then, why should it?"

---

## THINKING ABOUT THE TEXT

1. Why does Smith's opening about fatherhood seem ideal for this character study of Johnny Depp? How did Depp change once he became a father?

2. In what ways is Depp "the anti-Tom Cruise"? Why does Smith feel that Depp "escaped from the Hollywood star machine around 1990" (39)? What are the various roles that Depp played before he did the *Pirates* series?

3. How does Depp explain his anger—what he refers to as his "weird hillbilly rage" (41)? How did this anger express itself and what caused it to dissipate?

4. How is Depp rather like a pirate himself? Why did Depp accept the role of Captain Jack Sparrow and how did he make it his own?

5. What does Smith reveal about Depp's personal life that helps readers better understand him? How and where does he prefer to spend his time when not making films?

## WRITING FROM THE TEXT

1. Using specific traits and supportable inferences that you can draw from this essay, write a character analysis of Johnny Depp. Focus on a strong thesis that features 3-4 key aspects of his personality and analyze specific statements from Depp and from others about him. (See Character Analysis, pp. 445–468.)

2. Write a character analysis of a close friend or family member who, like Johnny Depp, refuses to fit into a stereotype or mold. Dramatize a few key scenes and include telling details so that the portrait is as detailed and convincing as Sean Smith's profile of Depp.

## CONNECTING WITH OTHER TEXTS

1. After reading "Don't Let Stereotypes Warp Your Judgment" (p. 424), write an essay analyzing how Johnny Depp defies the stereotype of superstar. Include specific quotations from both essays to show how Depp's character might be misjudged if audiences rely on stereotypes about celebrities.

2. Read "The Fringe Benefits of Failure, and the Importance of Imagination" (p. 154) and write an analysis of the ways that Johnny Depp deliberately chose creative roles and risked failure rather than become a commodity and fit a certain Hollywood mold. Include quotations from both essays to support your thesis about the value of risking failure.

# Chapter 2

# Between Genders

As the selections in this chapter reveal, women and men still live with gender-related issues, but the tensions of even a decade ago seem remarkably reduced. The women's and men's movements of the past decades have helped to identify, address, and correct problems that previous generations ignored. Yet both genders still experience challenges in trying to move beyond traditional male and female roles while developing relationships and becoming allies. You and your friends may be in the process of exploring or resolving some of the same gender issues that the writers in this chapter discuss.

Some of the writers show how traditional dating patterns and problems have persisted, as in Adair Lara's essay about who pays for the date. Reginald McKnight dramatizes flawed communication between the genders, and Dana Beardsley Crotwell underscores the daily work required to maintain a relationship. Film critic David Denby laments how couples featured in today's romantic comedies are mismatched in goals and intelligence—the female typically seems a "striver" and the male a "slacker." You might question whether the new romantic comedies accurately reflect your dating experiences or the relationships between couples you know.

Ellen Goodman and Joyce Carol Oates explore, in an analytical essay and a short story, a problem affecting both genders—violence against women. Don Sabo further shows how a patriarchal system that encourages violent and self-destructive competition between men also fosters violence against women. More positively, Jeff Z. Klein applauds his girlfriend as an ally and respects her ability to defend them in a street attack.

You most likely have found that gender issues are everywhere, showing up in such diverse places as pop music lyrics, films, magazine articles, and the Internet. In this chapter our writers question stereotypes, explore alternatives, deplore injustice and violence against both men and women, and celebrate improved alliances between the genders.

*"She's texting me, but I think she's also subtexting me."*

## 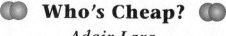 Who's Cheap?

### *Adair Lara*

Former columnist for the *San Francisco Chronicle*, Adair Lara (b. 1952) is also a teacher of writing and the author of *Welcome to Earth, Mom: Tales of a Single Mother* (1992), *Slowing Down in a Speeded-Up World* (1994), *The Best of Adair Lara* (1999), and *Hold Me Close, Let Me Go: A Mother, A Daughter, an Adolescence Survived* (2001), and *The Granny Diaries* (2008). Lara's work has appeared in *Cosmopolitan, Reader's Digest, Parenting, Glamour, Redbook, Ladies' Home Journal, American Woman, Departures, Westways, American Way, Via, Fitness, Good Housekeeping*, and many other magazines and newspapers. The essay included here originally appeared in the *San Francisco Chronicle*.

1    It was our second date, and we had driven one hundred miles up the coast in my car to go abalone-diving. When I stopped to fill the tank at the only gas station in sight, Craig scowled and said, "You shouldn't get gas here. It's a rip-off."

2    But he didn't offer to help pay. And that night, after dinner in a restaurant, he leaned over and whispered intimately, "You get the next one." Though he was sensitive and smart, and looked unnervingly good, Craig was as cheap as a two-dollar watch.

3    This is not an ethical dilemma, you're all shouting. *Lose the guy,* and fast.

4    Lose the guy? Is this fair? My friend Jill is always heading for the john when the check comes, but I don't hear anybody telling me to lose *her.* And she's far from the only cheap woman I know. A lot of us make decent money these days, yet I haven't seen women knocking over tables in fights for the lunch tab. In fact, many women with 20/20 vision seem to have trouble distinguishing the check from the salt, pepper and other tabletop items. But if a guy forgets to chip in for gas or gloats too long over the deal he got on his Nikes, he's had it.

5    Why is this double standard so enduring? One reason is that, while neither sex has a monopoly on imperfection, there *are* such things as flaws that are much more distasteful in one sex than in the other. Women seem especially unpleasant when they get drunk, swear or even insist on pursuing an argument they'll never win. And men seem beneath contempt when they're cheap.

6    These judgments are a holdover from the days when women stayed home and men earned the money. Though that old order has passed, we still associate men with paying for things. And besides, there's just something appealing about generosity. Buying something for someone is, in a sense, taking care of her. The gesture says, "I like you, I want to give you something." If it comes from a man to whom we are about to entrust our hearts, this is a comforting message. We miss it when it's not forthcoming.

7    Then why *not* dump on cheap men?

8    Some men are just skinflints and that's it. My friend Skye broke up with her boyfriend because when they went to the movies he doled out M&Ms to her one at a time. Craig, my date back at the gas station, liked to talk about how he'd bought his car—which in California, where I live, is like buying shoes—as a special present to himself.

9    This kind of cheapness is ingrained; you'll never change it. That guy who parks two miles away to avoid the parking lot fee was once a little boy who saved his birthday money without being told to. Now he's a man who studies the menu and sputters, "Ten dollars for *pasta?*" His stinginess will always

grate on you, since he is likely to dole out his feelings as parsimoniously as his dollars.

10    On the other hand, I know a wonderful man, crippled with debts from a former marriage, who had to break up with a woman because she never paid her share, and he was simply running out of money. Though she earned a lot more than he did, she couldn't expand her definition of masculinity to include "sometimes needs to go Dutch treat."

11    To men, such women seem grasping. One friend of mine, who spends a lot of money on concerts and theater and sailing but not on restaurants he considers overpriced, has evolved a strategy for women who are annoyed at the bohemian places he favors. If his date complains, he offers to donate to the charity of her choice the cost of an evening at her favorite spot. "Some women have bad values," he says, "And if the idea of spending money on a good cause, but not on her, makes her livid, I know she's one of them."

12    I had a bracing encounter with my own values when I told my friend Danny the humorous (I thought) story of a recent date who asked if I wanted a drink after a concert, then led me to the nearest water fountain.

13    Danny gave one of his wry looks. "Let's get this straight," he said, laughing. "As a woman, you are so genetically precious that you deserve attention just because you grace the planet. So, of course, he should buy you drinks. He should also drive the car, open the door, ask you to dance, coax you to bed. And then when you feel properly pampered, you can let out that little whine about how he doesn't treat you as an equal."

14    On second thought, I guess I'd rather buy my own drink.

15    So here's the deal. Before dumping a guy for ordering the sundowner dinner or the house white, better first make sure that you aren't burdening the relationship with outdated ideas of how the sexes should behave. Speaking for myself, I know that if a man looks up from the check and says, "Your share is eleven dollars," part of me remembers that, according to my mother, *my* share was to look charming in my flowered blouse.

16    Wanting the man to pay dies hard. What many of us do now is *offer* to split the check, then let our purses continue to dangle from the chair as we give him time to realize that the only proper response is to whip out his own wallet.

17    Is this a game worth playing? It's up to you, but consider that offering to help pay implies that the check is his responsibility. And this attitude can work both ways. My sister gets angry when her husband offers to help clean the house. "Like it's *my* house!" she snorts.

18    Like it's *his* check.

## THINKING ABOUT THE TEXT

1. Authors may use humor to engage an audience—even when their intention is to argue a serious point. Is Lara's main purpose in this essay mostly to entertain or to persuade her audience?

2. Does Lara have a claim? If so, what is it? Does she have support?

3. What does Lara mean when she writes that some flaws seem "much more distasteful in one sex than in the other" (46)? *Are* women more unpleasant than men when they "get drunk, swear or even insist on pursuing an argument they'll never win" (46) or are these the author's sexist generalizations? (If they are generalizations, what is her goal in using them?)

4. In what way is the point of Lara's essay embedded in Danny's response to Lara's anecdote about the after-concert drink? Why does Lara manipulate her essay so that its central wisdom appears in Danny's words? What is the author's strategy?

5. What conventional and sexist ideas are challenged in this essay?

## WRITING FROM THE TEXT

1. Lara cites a number of specific ways that people save money—avoiding commercial parking lots, eating the "sundowner" or "early bird" dinner, and drinking the house wine. Make a list of all of the ways that you save money. How many of your habits would be regarded by a date or friends as "cheap"? Develop your list into supporting examples for a thesis of your own.

2. Describe the habits of your dates and friends when it comes to ignoring a bill or saving money. The focus of your essay can be to laud or deplore your friends' habits.

3. Using Lara's essay for support, write an essay arguing that the double standard Lara describes hurts both men and women.

## CONNECTING WITH OTHER TEXTS

1. After reading "In Groups We Shrink" (p. 151), write an essay analyzing how pressure from others and within social groups can condition our behavior on a date. Incorporate the ideas of both Tavris and Lara as you focus on group conventions and individual expectations.

2. Using Lara's essay and Jeff Z. Klein's "Watching My Back" (p. 57), write an essay that illustrates how couples might redefine romantic relationships free from stereotypical role playing.

#  Peaches
## *Reginald McKnight*

The Hamilton Holmes Professor of English at the University of Georgia in Athens, Reginald McKnight (b. 1956) received a BA from Colorado College and an MA from the University of Denver in 1987. He has taught English and creative writing in Senegal as well as at the Metropolitan State University in Denver.

McKnight is the author of *Moustapha's Eclipse* (1988), *I Get on the Bus* (1990), *The Kind of Light That Shines on Texas: Stories* (1992), *White Boys* (1998), and *He Sleeps* (2001). He also is the editor of *African-American Wisdom* (1994) and *Wisdom of the African World* (1996). In addition, his work has been published in literary magazines such as *Leviathan*, *Prairie Schooner*, *Kenyon Review*, and the *Black American Literature Forum*. McKnight has said that his work generally "deals with the deracinated African Americans who came of age after the civil rights struggle. These are people who are at the front lines of the current struggle for human rights." The following story is from *Moustapha's Eclipse*.

1    J.C. crosses the sun-faded carpet looking truculent and surly. He looks at me with his woman-get-out-my-seat-face. His tail points straight up to the ceiling. He lets out with his most irate meow, stomps back and forth in front of me in that stiff-legged strut that drives me crazy. He always does this when I sit in "his" chair. "Looks like everybody's mad at me today," I say, crossing my arms and legs at the same time. Momma doesn't say a word so I know what's up with her. Daddy drops the paper to his lap, and sits up in his chair. Its old, arthritic wood creaks. "Ain't nobody mad, Baby Sister," he says, removing his glasses. "Ain't nobody disappointed, hurt, upset—' cept that little pea-brain cat of yours. Mystery to me why you even sit in that chair after he done rubbed all his hair off in it."

2    "Have you heard from Marc lately, Rita?" asks Momma, not looking up from her puzzle.

3    "Good Lord Almighty have I heard from him. Tuesday I got four letters. Four separate letters. In four separate envelopes."

4    "What's all this 'Lord Almighty' business, girl," says Daddy. "I ain't sending you to no twenty-thousand-dollar-a-year college to hear you talk like a imitation me. You gonna be a scientist. Let me hear my money's worth."

5    "Your money?" Momma says, "You mean Uncle Sam's money."

6    "I'll take his money too if it help put Baby Sis through school. I ain't proud."

7    "You ain't rich neither," Momma says, snapping a puzzle piece into place.

8    J.C. leaps up into my lap. His purring irritates me so I get up and move to the other side of the room.

9    "We got a postcard from him a couple of days before you got here, Rita," my mother says, still not looking up from the table. "Didn't say much though."

10   "Why didn't you tell me when I got home, Momma?"

11   "Moody as you was? No ma'am. I got better things to do than listen to you bawl from sunup to sundown. Anyway, we already talked about your plans before you got here. Now if I'd been bringing up his name all the time you might have thought I was trying to push you into sending him that . . . the—"

12   "How 'bout 'Dear John,' Lucille."

13   "James!"

14   "Daddy—"

15   "Well, that's the truth. I'm calling a spade a spade. Just like he did."

16   "James! Now I am not going to have you—"

17   "All right now, I'm just playing. But I don't care how much ass that boy kiss. And I don't care how long he stay in Africa to sensitize hisself. Cain't no rich white boy call my child no nigger and—"

18   "Maybe not, but she grown, James. It's her life. Her decision. You and I got nothing to say whatsoever about what Rita decide. Now you promised me you'd leave the poor girl alone. Can't you see she upset as it is?" Momma snaps another piece into the puzzle, pushes her glasses up on her nose and looks up at Daddy. Daddy picks up the newspaper, crosses his legs, clears his throat. "You right," he grunts, then clears his throat again. "Yeah, you right. But if you ask me, you an apple, he an orange." I can tell from his eyes that he is staring at but not reading the paper. The room is as silent as the moon. Dust motes swim through the lamplight around Daddy's head. He looks hurt and I'd like to tell him he needn't be, because I myself am not hurting. I am numb. I don't know what to think or feel or do. I veer toward anger, then careen toward love, then roll toward regret and guilt. But as has been the case since the fight, I end up weightless and static like one of those motes around Daddy's head.

19   Daddy tosses the paper to the floor and in the silence it sounds like firecrackers. J.C. springs up from the chair and scoots under the couch. The room again falls silent, the brief flurry of sound and action is swallowed up like stones tossed into the ocean.

20   After awhile Daddy's chair squeaks and cracks. He inhales deep and slow, then slips on his glasses. "I believe," he says, "I could use a little help outside picking some peaches for old Mrs. Li's sweet and sour sauce. She says she gonna make some extry for you to take back to school with you. Come on."

21   The fog has not yet lifted, but the air feels dryer than usual. Mr. Givens's dog yaps at us from behind the gray cedar fence. In the thirteen years my

parents and I and my two sisters have lived here, I've never seen the old dog and I don't know its name. Each evening, when chastising the dog, when telling it to shut up, when calling it in, Mr. Givens calls it, "Git-yer-dumb-ass-outta-that-garden, Shut-the-hell-up-ya-stupid-mutt, and Giddin-here-ya-damn-dog." As far as I can tell the dog seldom obeys. In the evenings Mr. Givens can often be heard bellowing, "OK, then don't eat, ya stupid!"

22 When the dog has barked long enough, my father picks up the usual peach pit, zings it in the area of Mr. Givens's garden, and finally we hear: "How many times I gotta tell ya to keep yer dumb ass outta that garden?" Silence. My father and I are alone in the backyard which is redolent with the smell of peaches, the sight of peaches. We feel peach pits beneath our feet.

23 "Grab that raggedy-looking box over next to the fence, Baby Sis," Daddy says. "Half them bushel baskets old Givens give me cain't hold air."

24 "This one?"

25 "Um hmm."

26 "Do we need a stepladder?"

27 "Well, they should be plenty of good ones on the ground. And if we shake us a branch or two we won't need a ladder." He kneels and begins sorting peaches, asks me a few questions about how school is going. I answer him in monosyllables, hoping the conversation won't drift toward anything that will upset us both. The afternoon air becomes cool all of a sudden. Goose-bumps erupt on my arms and neck. "Daddy, I'll be right back," I say, "I need a jacket."

28 In my room I stand before the closet door, looking at my reflection in the full-length mirror. I look at myself, forgetting for several moments why I have come into the room. There I stand in baggy white pants and what Marcus calls my "favorite Dinty Moore shirt." He never told me he disliked the way I dress, but when I was clad in my flannels and baggies his eyes often glanced around—toward the bookshelf, "Hey, a new one by Mishima?" or my stereo, "Let's listen to some Marvin Gaye," or the Dali prints, "When did you say that one was painted?" He, like most men, wants to see women dress in anything tight enough to keep the blood static. He always told me he wasn't particularly a breast man, or a leg man—"I'm not an anything man," he'd say. "I'm an everything man. Legs, ass, brains, conscience." But he only seemed to tell me that kind of thing when I was wearing flannels and baggies.

29 "What does he see in me?" I think as I peruse the frizzy, uncombable black hair, the burdensome breasts, the face that he insisted no guy on campus could forget, the legs he insisted are not birdlike. "And look at my legs," he'd say, indicating with both hands, "They look like a couple of Venus number twos." He told me never to change a thing about myself. "I'm the one

who needs to change," he'd say. And I'd tell him, in the beginning, he didn't need to change. That he was fine the way he was. But he would always sneer, "Simmons, you don't know the half of it." He kept saying things like that, becoming more strident, histrionic, and distant. "I'm no goddamned good," he'd say over and over. And soon enough, I began to feel as though his kisses were trying to smother something, that the walls of his apartment enfolded secret passages and chambers, that his conversation, numinous and trivial, full of New Age jargon, spoke around rather than of something. There was always something fleeting about him. Something just out the corner of my eye, something just out of reach. I imagined that an invisible incubus paced between us when we were together, thumbing its invisible nose at us, flipping us the invisible finger. I felt its presence so acutely sometimes, that I could almost see it burst forth in hyperactive, muscled flesh. Sometimes it made me fear him. Sometimes I think it made me love him more.

30    The more I loved him, the less I understood him, the farther I slipped from him. And when he started punching walls, calling me at two in the morning to apologize for no reason at all, threatening to slash his wrists every time I told him I was busy, I sensed how ripe he was for procreation.

31    "You never have time anymore, Rita. What's the matter, you mad at me?"

32    "Why should I be mad at you? I'm mad at me. I've got to really get going on my thesis."

33    "I know, I understand. I just want to see you. Why are you hiding from me all of a sudden?"

34    I'd say nothing.

35    "What's wrong, Rita? I just want to see you for one hour."

36    "Marc, I just haven't got the time."

37    He never let up. He'd set his heels and push. And push.

38    "Is it something I said to you? Is it my beliefs? When we first met, you always said I was too rarefied for you. You said I strut around 'up there' acting fey while you're 'down here' accepting life for what it is. 'Fey,' you said. Jesus Christ, Rita, I got no problem with your science. Why can't you give me what's mine?"

39    "I know, Marc. I know. I should. I do. It's got nothing to do with your beliefs. Really. I'm just preoccupied. I've got two midterms tomorrow. I've got that lousy seminar. We can talk about this tomorrow, at dinner."

40    And push.

41    "It's because you think I got no soul or some crap like that, isn't it? I just can't give you what a black guy can give you, right? That's what you think, isn't it? Well if it is, Rita, then you're wrong. It's all an illusion. It's maya. If anything, I can give you more because my world is so different from yours."

42      "Marc, there's only this world—"

43      "Look, Rita, I've been through this before. I've had relationships with Black women and Hispanic women, and Asian women. You can tell me. I think I'd understand. You probably think I don't take you seriously. You think I'm just using you."

44      He'd ask me if it was his disapproving family, his derisive friends, his age, his intellect, or that he was an undergraduate English major and I was a semester away from a master's degree in chemistry. It often left us very little to talk about at dinner. He'd ask if his beard looked silly, or if he dressed poorly, or if my family really hadn't liked him but had simply been Oscar-winning polite, or if he was too easily depressed, irascible, antisocial, untruthful, or was I sure-really-sure "it's not because I'm white?" I'd always say no.

45      I'd say no because it was easy to say no. Easier than unleashing untenable fears, easier, after awhile, than holding him close, feeling his diffuse heat. He'd push, and it was as if he'd started pushing too deeply inside himself, rummaging and scraping, uncovering things that I'm not sure were ever there. "What's wrong with me?" he'd demand. "Tell me. Just tell me something. Do you still love me? Do I offend you in some way?" I couldn't tell him. I knew I'd just have to wait, then I'd see, he'd know. I'd tried to tell him once or twice, but everything would lock up inside me when I'd try to explain. And then it finally just slid out from him, loud and ugly. The word. The beast-incubus word, the inevitable issue of the "yin-yang" relationship. His phrase, "yin-yang relationship." Had I drawn it from him, headfirst screaming, kicking into the world? Or did he plant it in me, water it with his tears, incubate it in the heat of my womblike reticence? I don't know.

46      All I could say that night was, "That, Marc. That's just what I was afraid of. Wasn't but a matter of time, was it?"

47      How would things have gone if I had just told him of my fears and talked it out with him? I never did because to do so would have implied that he had transcended nothing. I flat would have been calling him a liar, or blind. And he was neither. He had transcended something, somehow. Or what if I had just buried myself in his auburn beard, his ginseng breath, the bend and curve of his body, and listened to his nonsense about the Ghosts of Lemuria, the Light of Atlantis, the Race of Tan just for the sake of hearing his voice. His voice was so nice to listen to, a little raspy, a little flutelike. Sometimes it seemed he told his stories in song. Sweet nonsense. And when I actually heard him say the word I was so sure he would eventually say, I was shocked. Shocked both because it always shocks you when someone calls you nigger and because the word fell from his mouth so awkwardly—as if he had never heard it before, said it before, imagined saying it before.

48    So he bought a ticket to Liberia. I didn't know what to feel. He told me he wouldn't come back till he knew, till he really, really understood what blackness was. I didn't know what to say. He hugged me, kissed me longer than I could stand, said goodbye, promised he'd change, we'd get it straight, he'd return reborn, we'd marry and raise fat, tan, unrarefied babies. He got on the plane. He called me from Denver. He called me from New York. He called me from Dakar. He called me from Monrovia. I got his first letter in two weeks. By six weeks I'd received eight more. In three months over forty letters, bombarded by missives of love, the seed of self-discovery. They came daily, weekly. Tidings of hope, love, joy. Peace Profound. Images of beautiful babies, beautiful ocean, sleek, cat-black men, women in rich Day-glo rags. The taste of this. The smell of that. The size, shape, volume of his ever-expanding, ever-pregnant African love. But I just didn't. His seed fell on unsettled dust, a haze of motes never coming to rest.

49    "It won't lie still," I say aloud, suddenly remembering why I've come up to my room. I grab something warm-looking and bluish, then run back outside.

50    I stand on the stoop and watch Daddy kneeling in the grass, peach in hand. He sniffs, squeezes, removes his glasses and inspects it, then tosses it aside. His face is grave, almost sullen. I cross the yard and kneel beside him, trying to imitate the way he inspects the peaches, but I'm not really sure what he's looking for.

51    I've always loved the way my father throws himself into the task at hand. Whether it be selecting peaches for Mrs. Li's sauce, adjusting a bicycle seat, or expounding to three enraptured daughters at the dinner table just what it is that makes a grocery clerk's job so much more dangerous than a San Francisco cop's, there is no one I know with the intensity, the undivided surrender to the action, the moment.

52    While we sort through hard, woody peaches and soft, muddy peaches, peaches bruised and scarred, peaches clear-complected, he tells me the secret of Mrs. Li's sauce: "She take a whisk broom to J.C.'s chair and use all them cat hairs and cookie crumbs y'all leave in it." And he hints at the secret secret to his peach cobbler, which he says he extracted, through torture, from a Japanese POW. "If I told you, you wouldn't eat it." He tells me it once rained peaches in San Francisco when I was "just a baby, and couldn't possibly remember." And that old Moses told God that no way on earth would he sign those "commandoes or commandants, or whatever you call em, till you take peaches off the list." He tells me he never would have looked twice at Momma had she never stuffed peaches under her sweater back in '47, that peaches, at one time, contained an explosive substance instead of sugar, and the last recorded use of the exploding peach was in the Boer War. "That was

before your time," he is quick to add. He tells me about the Peach Bowl of 1968 (LSU won because they ate more peaches. "Well, why you think they call it Peach Bowl?").

53  "Paul Robeson couldn't sing note one 'less he had two, three quarts of peach wine in him," he says. And he tells me about the peachy-keen people he had ever known (me, Juanita, and Theresa May, "and sometimes that hard-head mother of yours"). He tells me how Big Daddy used to push his cart around the streets of Alabaster, Alabama, hollering, "Waaaatermelon? Strawberries and Peeeeachez! Cold, sweet Peeeeachez! Peaches and cream, peach ice cream, peacherinoes and peacherines, peach yogurt, peach pop-sicles, peach lipstick, peach pie, jam, and jelly. Cold, sweet peeeeachez!"

54  The box is full of what he assures me are the finest peaches that soil could possibly produce. I offer him a peach from the brimming box; he frowns and says, "Shooot, naw, Baby Sister, I cain't eat them things." We laugh for a long time, leaning away from each other, folding toward each other, like jazz dancers. And then I start to cry. I cry so hard I can scarcely breathe. Daddy holds me, saying nothing. He doesn't even try to shush me, just holds me till I stop. Then he reaches in the box, takes out a peach, examines it, sniffs it, throws it aside. He takes another one and does the same thing. Then another, and another, and another.

55  Finally, he turns the whole box over. Peaches tumble across the lawn. He in-spects every last one. His long fingers caress each, every one. His nose and eye, inspecting, seed-deep, each, every one. And then he finds what he is looking for. It is very large, the color of a sunrise, flows into a sunset, flows into the color of Mrs. Li's blush. He rubs it on his sleeve, holds it out to me in the palm of his hand. I wipe my nose with a finger, regard the peach for a long, long time. Till Daddy's arm trembles a bit. "Naw," I say, "I can't eat "em." He drops the fruit and it cracks on the green grass. He takes my hand, and we walk inside.

## THINKING ABOUT THE TEXT

1. What is the effect of beginning and ending the story with Rita interacting with her family? Give details that characterize Rita and her parents, and that show their sensitivity toward each other.

2. Consider McKnight's strategy to have Rita escape to her room and to use the "mirror device." From her descriptions, speech, and behaviors, what do we learn about Rita when she is in her room and reflecting on her rela-tionship with Marc?

3. To prepare for a character analysis, write a list of observations about Rita in one column and, in another column next to it, write the corresponding

inferences that you have drawn from each observation. Then write another two columns of observations and inferences about Marc. (See Character Analysis, pp. 445–453.)

4. Rita claims that Marc's conversation, "full of New Age jargon, spoke around rather than of something" (52). Look up some of the terms he uses—"incubus," "fey," "maya," "yin-yang," "Ghosts of Lemuria," "Light of Atlantis"—and explain what Marc's language and his use of this particular vocabulary reveal about him.

5. Describe the different "worlds" that Rita and Marc inhabit. What has contributed to the gulf between them and how likely is it that they will marry and resolve their differences?

6. Referring to the title and closing scene, what are some possible meanings of "peaches" that relate to this story? Consider the father's litany of references to peaches and his search for one that "is very large, the color of a sunrise, flows into a sunset, flows into the color of Mrs. Li's blush" (55). Analyze this quotation in terms of the story and explore what the peach might symbolize.

7. What is ironic about the revelation that neither Rita nor her father can eat peaches? How might this revelation relate to the story and particularly to the central conflict between Rita and Marc? How does it contribute to the resolution of the story?

## WRITING FROM THE TEXT

1. Using your lists for exercise 3 on the previous page, write a character analysis of either Rita or Marc. Focus on a strong assertion about your chosen character and include supporting details and direct quotations to illustrate your points. (See Character Analysis, pp. 445–453.)

2. Working from your responses to exercise 5 above, write an analysis of the factors contributing to the conflict between Rita and Marc. Assess which factors seem more difficult to resolve and whether a more lasting relationship between Marc and Rita seems likely. Support your assessment with specific details from the story.

3. Write an analysis of the multiple meanings of "peaches" in this story and show how this symbolism relates to the characters and central conflict.

4. If you have ever had someone call you an offensive name or if you have ever blurted out a racial or ethnic slur, write an essay explaining and dramatizing what prompted this name calling, what effect it had at the moment, how the incident ended, and what lasting effect it has had on you.

## CONNECTING WITH OTHER TEXTS

1. Read "Living in Two Worlds" (p. 99) and examine Mabry's contrasting worlds—home and university—in terms of Rita's. Write an essay comparing their "between worlds" experiences and their ways of managing an attachment to family and a commitment to their own goals.

2. In "Race is a Four-Letter Word" (p. 108), Arboleda argues that one's race should not ultimately matter, that his identity cannot be defined in terms of race. But Marc seems focused on race and on his experience dating women of diverse ethnicity and cultures. Write an essay contrasting these two positions as you show how Marc is limited in ways that Arboleda is not.

#  Watching My Back
### *Jeff Z. Klein*

Employed as staff editor of the *New York Times* since 1996, Jeff Z. Klein previously was sports editor of the *Village Voice* for five years and has been an avid ice hockey fan. He is the author of *Mario Lemieux: Ice Hockey Star* (1995) and *Messier* (2004), which "takes readers behind the headlines and statistics for a revealing look at a hockey legend." Klein is also coauthor of *The Coolest Guys on Ice* (1996), *The Death of Hockey* (1998), and two editions of *The Hockey Compendium.* The following essay was first published in the *New York Times Magazine* in 2001.

1    He charged at me, shouting something in Czech. It was the middle of the night in Prague. My girlfriend and I were there for New Year's, and as we strolled through a deserted business district, two young men came bounding out of a pedestrian underpass. Loud, menacing and drunk, one ran up and shoved me, then missed with a liquor-slow karate kick. I shoved back. We squared off, staring.

2    Here I should say that my girlfriend had just completed an advanced self-defense course. She was standing to my left. I couldn't see her, but I could hear her firmly addressing the attacker— "Back off! Go away!" —as she had been taught. I hadn't been in a punch-up since I was 10 and had no idea what to do in an actual fight. But I had seen her in class, whupping two heavily padded mock attackers. I knew what she could do.

3    As my assailant and I faced each other, another couple, a big man and a woman, walked unaware onto the scene. My assailant suddenly went after the big guy, who simply threw him to the ground. That was plenty for me. "He's got it," I said to my girlfriend. "Let's go." We backed away, but after a few steps, she stopped and said: "Wait. We should go back. They may need our help."

I wasn't keen on the idea, but back we went. We saw the big guy standing over the assailant, who was down and out. It was over. Everyone dispersed.

4     My girlfriend and I walked down into Wenceslas Square to an all-night cash machine. "I've got your back," she assured me jokingly as I went into the bank. As we waited for a cab, I admitted that I was still pretty wired. "I'm not," she said. "I was ready to fight, but I'm fine now. Of course, I wasn't the one the guy tried to start a fight with."

5     Once we were back where we were staying, I asked my girlfriend how she would have handled it if he had attacked her. "Let's say I'm the guy, and I try to kick you like this," I said.

6     She demonstrated, pantomiming a series of blocks and strikes. "But something worries me," she said as I stood there, utterly blown away. "I'm afraid I'd make a mistake." I thought she meant she was afraid she would forget what to do in the heat of action. But that wasn't it.

7     "We're trained to start fighting as soon as an attacker throws a punch and to keep going until he can't get up again," she said. "But you got out of it without fighting, even though he actually came at you. So I'm worried that I'd start fighting and really hurt the guy—or maim him, or even kill him—when it could've ended without anyone getting hurt at all."

8     Now I was really blown away. Months earlier, while she was taking the basic self-defense course for women, she told me about a man who approached her on a train. "He was kind of creepy," she said, "but I figured it was O.K. because I knew I could beat him up." At the time, I was impressed by how quickly she had absorbed the confidence that the course was supposed to impart, but I wasn't convinced. I was now. Fully.

9     I tried to fall asleep, but I couldn't. So I went to find her. There she was, supercool, soaking her feet in the tub, reading *Bridget Jones's Diary*.

10    The next night, we were out having a drink, still rehashing what happened. "I've got to tell you something," I said. "I know this might sound weird, but do you know how attractive it is that you can do this?"

11    She looked somewhat astonished, because obviously she hadn't learned how to fight to titillate me or anyone else. "I never thought of it in those terms," she said. "I just like knowing that in a situation like the one last night, I can be of help."

12    At that point, I resolved to take the men's course. It turned out, several weeks later, that half the men were in the class precisely because their wives or girlfriends had taken it, and they were dazzled by how capable the women were. Since then I've taken a couple of other courses, both in the company of my girlfriend. Some of the mystery, I must admit, is gone, but I still love the way she moves, and I love the idea that she knows exactly what to do to defend herself.

13    The day after we got back to New York, she offered to do some of my laundry. "I can't let you," I said. "It's too, I don't know, *traditional.*"

14    "Look," she said. "A few days ago, I was willing to beat some guy up for you. So, come on, I can do your laundry."

15    I happened to be facing away from her as I spoke. "Do you really think," I asked, "you would've done a better job beating up that guy than I would have?"

16    "Not a *better* job," she said. "But I would've been much less likely to get hurt doing it. Especially if he wasn't drunk and had been thinking clearly."

17    I turned and looked at her. "I think you're right," I said, and I leaned in to kiss her. It's nice to have a girlfriend who's got your back.

## THINKING ABOUT THE TEXT

1. Explain Klein's strategy in opening his essay in the middle of the action—specifically, this unexpected street assault.

2. How does the narrator's initial reaction to the attacker contrast with his girlfriend's immediate response? What are some reasons for this difference?

3. Explain what still worries the narrator's girlfriend about this incident. Why is the narrator "blown away" by her explanation?

4. Rather than being intimidated or embarrassed by his girlfriend's ability to defend them, what does the narrator initially admit about her skill? What is her response? How does her training later influence his behavior?

5. From the title of his essay to his concluding line, analyze the author's attitude toward the changing roles of males and females in a romantic relationship.

6. How does the girlfriend's attitude and behavior resist any attempt to reduce her to a stereotype? Include examples from the essay to show how multifaceted she appears.

## WRITING FROM THE TEXT

1. Using details from this essay and from your own experience, write an essay arguing that the changing roles and expectations of men and women today are or are not contributing to healthier romantic relationships. (See Evaluative Response, pp. 391–397).

2. Write an analysis showing how Klein's dramatizing techniques—choice actions, characterization, and dialogue—work to illustrate any one of the important insights drawn from this essay.

CONNECTING WITH OTHER TEXTS

1. After reading "Pigskin, Patriarchy, and Pain" (p. 60), write an essay contrasting Sabo's previous expectations for the roles of men and women with Klein's views. Include details from both essays as you develop a point-by-point comparison-contrast (see p. 409).

2. After reading "Who's Cheap?" (p. 45), write an essay contrasting Lara's depiction of women's roles with Klein's view of women.

#  Pigskin, Patriarchy, and Pain
## *Don Sabo*

A professor of social science, Don Sabo (b. 1947) has lectured and written on men's issues. He is a fitness enthusiast and a former NCAA Division I defensive football captain. Sabo is the coauthor of *Jock: Sports and Male Identity; Humanism in Sociology;* and *Sport, Men, and the Gender Order: Critical Feminist Perspectives.* Sabo is currently working on *Man Scam: Gender, Patriarchy and Patsyarchy.* The following essay first appeared in *Sex, Violence and Power in Sports* (1994).

1    I am sitting down to write as I've done thousands of times over the last decade. But today there's something very different. I'm not in pain.

2    A half year ago I underwent back surgery. My physician removed two disks from the lumbar region of my spine and fused three vertebrae using bone scrapings from my right hip. The surgery is called a "spinal fusion." For seventy-two hours I was completely immobilized. On the fifth day, I took a few faltering first steps with one of those aluminum walkers that are usually associated with the elderly in nursing homes. I progressed rapidly and left the hospital after nine days completely free of pain for the first time in years.

3    How did I, a well-intending and reasonably gentle boy from western Pennsylvania, ever get into so much pain? At a simple level, I ended up in pain because I played a sport that brutalizes men's (and now sometimes women's) bodies. *Why* I played football and bit the bullet of pain, however, is more complicated. Like a young child who learns to dance or sing for a piece of candy, I played for rewards and payoffs. Winning at sport meant winning friends and carving a place for myself within the male pecking order. Success at the "game" would make me less like myself and more like the older boys and my hero, Dick Butkus. Pictures of his hulking and snarling form filled my head and hung over my bed, beckoning me forward like a mythic Siren. If I could be like Butkus, I told myself, people would adore me as much as I adored him.

I might even adore myself. As an adolescent I hoped sport would get me attention from the girls. Later, I became more practical-minded and I worried more about my future. What kind of work would I do for a living? Football became my ticket to a college scholarship which, in western Pennsylvania during the early 'sixties, meant a career instead of getting stuck in the steelmills.

4    My bout with pain and spinal "pathology" began with a decision I made in 1955 when I was 8 years old. I "went out" for football. At the time, I felt uncomfortable inside my body—too fat, too short, too weak. Freckles and glasses, too! I wanted to change my image, and I felt that changing my body was one place to begin. My parents bought me a set of weights, and one of the older boys in the neighborhood was solicited to demonstrate their use. I can still remember the ease with which he lifted the barbell, the veins popping through his bulging biceps in the summer sun, and the sated look of strength and accomplishment on his face. This was to be the image of my future.

5    That fall I made a dinner-table announcement that I was going out for football. What followed was a rather inauspicious beginning. First, the initiation rites. Pricking the flesh with thorns until blood was drawn and having hot peppers rubbed in my eyes. Getting punched in the gut again and again. Being forced to wear a jockstrap around my nose and not knowing what was funny. Then came what was to be an endless series of proving myself: calisthenics until my arms ached; hitting hard and fast and knocking the other guy down; getting hit in the groin and not crying. I learned that pain and injury are "part of the game."

6    I "played" through grade school, co-captained my high school team, and went on to become an inside linebacker and defensive captain at the NCAA Division I level. I learned to be an animal. Coaches took notice of animals. Animals made first team. Being an animal meant being fanatically aggressive and ruthlessly competitive. If I saw an arm in front of me, I trampled it. Whenever blood was spilled, I nodded approval. Broken bones (not mine of course) were secretly seen as little victories within the bigger struggle. The coaches taught me to "punish the other man," but little did I suspect that I was devastating my own body at the same time. There were broken noses, ribs, fingers, toes and teeth, torn muscles and ligaments, bruises, bad knees, and busted lips, and the gradual pulverizing of my spinal column that, by the time my jock career was long over at age 30, had resulted in seven years of near-constant pain. It was a long road to the surgeon's office.

7    Now surgically freed from its grip, my understanding of pain has changed. Pain had gnawed away at my insides. Pain turned my awareness inward. I blamed myself for my predicament; I thought that I was solely responsible for every twinge and sleepless night. But this view was an illusion. My pain, each individual's pain, is really an expression of a linkage

to an outer world of people, events, and forces. The origins of our pain are rooted *outside,* not inside, our skins.

8      Sport is just one of the many areas in our culture where pain is more important than pleasure. Boys are taught that to endure pain is courageous, to survive pain is manly. The principle that pain is "good" and pleasure is "bad" is crudely evident in the "no pain, no gain" philosophy of so many coaches and athletes. The "pain principle" weaves its way into the lives and psyches of male athletes in two fundamental ways. It stifles men's awareness of their bodies and limits our emotional expression. We learn to ignore personal hurts and injuries because they interfere with the "efficiency" and "goals" of the "team." We become adept at taking the feelings that boil up inside us—feelings of insecurity and stress from striving so hard for success—and channeling them in a bundle of rage which is directed at opponents and enemies. This posture toward oneself and the world is not limited to "jocks." It is evident in the lives of many nonathletic men who, as tough guys, deny their authentic physical or emotional needs and develop health problems as a result.

9      Today, I no longer perceive myself as an *individual* ripped off by athletic injury. Rather, I see myself as just *one more man among many men* who got swallowed up by a social system predicated on male domination. Patriarchy has two structural aspects. First, it is a hierarchical system in which men dominate women in crude and debased, slick and subtle ways. Feminists have made great progress exposing and analyzing this dimension of the edifice of sexism. But it is also a system of *intermale dominance,* in which a minority of men dominates the masses of men. This intermale dominance hierarchy exploits the majority of those it beckons to climb its heights. Patriarchy's mythos of heroism and its morality of power-worship implant visions of ecstasy and masculine excellence in the minds of the boys who ultimately will defend its inequities and ridicule its victims. It is inside this institutional framework that I have begun to explore the essence and scope of "the pain principle."

10      Patriarchy is a form of social hierarchy. Hierarchy breeds inequity and inequity breeds pain. To remain stable, the hierarchy must either justify the pain or explain it away. In a patriarchy, women and the masses of men are fed the cultural message that pain is inevitable and that pain enhances one's character and moral worth. This principle is expressed in Judeo-Christian beliefs. The Judeo-Christian god inflicts or permits pain, yet "the Father" is still revered and loved. Likewise, a chief disciplinarian in the patriarchal family, the father has the right to inflict pain. The "pain principle" also echoes throughout traditional Western sexual morality; it is better to experience the pain of *not* having sexual pleasure than it is to have sexual pleasure.

11      Most men learned to heed these cultural messages and take their "cues for survival" from the patriarchy. The Willie Lomans of the economy pander to

the profit and the American Dream. Soldiers, young and old, salute their neo-Hun generals. Right-wing Christians genuflect before the idols of righteousness, affluence, and conformity. And male athletes adopt the visions and values that coaches are offering: to take orders, to take pain, to "take out" opponents, to take the game seriously, to take women, and to take their place on the team. And if they can't "take it," then the rewards of athletic camaraderie, prestige, scholarship, pro contracts, and community recognitions are not forthcoming.

12     Becoming a football player fosters conformity to male-chauvinistic values and self-abusing lifestyles. It contributes to the legitimacy of a social structure based on patriarchal power. Male competition for prestige and status in sport and elsewhere leads to identification with the relatively few males who control resources and are able to bestow rewards and inflict punishment. Male supremacists are not born, they are made, and traditional athletic socialization is a fundamental contribution to this complex social-psychological and political process. Through sport, many males, indeed, learn to "take it"—that is, to internalize patriarchal values which, in turn, become part of their gender identity and conception of women and society.

13     My high school coach once evoked the pain principle during a pre-game peptalk. For what seemed like an eternity, he paced frenetically and silently before us with fists clenched and head bowed. He suddenly stopped and faced us with a smile. It was as though he had approached a podium to begin a long-awaited lecture. "Boys," he began, "people who say that football is a 'contact sport' are dead wrong. Dancing is a contact sport. Football is a game of pain and violence! Now get the hell out of here and kick some ass." We practically ran through the wall of the locker room, surging in unison to fight the coach's war. I see now that the coach was right but for all the wrong reasons. I should have taken him at his word and never played the game!

## THINKING ABOUT THE TEXT

1. Why did the author decide, as a child, to play football? What were the specific rewards he gained by engaging in the sport? Can you relate Sabo's decision to one you have made in your own life?

2. What were the initiation rites that preceded his involvement with the football team? What do you imagine is the purpose of these rites?

3. Sabo relates that he became "an animal" inflicting pain on others and also incurring his own body injuries and pain. Why do boys (and increasingly girls) accept the pain of the game?

4. Sabo concludes that men suffer more than physical injury playing football. They suffer because they stifle their awareness of their bodies

and they limit their emotional expression by directing their feelings, instead, to the team and its goals. School counselors often recommend that children play team sports to learn cooperation and willingness to apply themselves to a group goal. How might Sabo respond to this advice?

5. Today, Sabo sees himself as "one more man among many men who got swallowed up by a social system predicated on male domination" (62). What is the hierarchical system the author perceives and how does playing football support this system?

6. What is Sabo's strategy in examining the verb "to take"? In how many ways does he use the verb? What is the strategy of his title?

7. What does the author conclude are the serious social and psychological results of participation in football?

## WRITING FROM THE TEXT

1. Sabo writes that "male supremacists are not born, they are made, and traditional athletic socialization is a fundamental contribution to this complex social-psychological and political process" (63). Show your agreement or disagreement with this assertion in an essay that uses specific examples from your involvement with or observations of team sports.

2. Write an essay that reveals how your ability "to take it" in some athletic activity helped you achieve a goal in your life outside of athletics.

3. Describe a time when you engaged in a socially approved activity because you wanted the rewards of friendship or public adoration. Review the strategies on how to write a narrative (pp. 383–390) after you have done some freewriting on the topic.

4. Write an essay that analyzes activities other than football that foster "conformity to male-chauvinistic values and self-abusing lifestyles." You might try using humor or irony in your essay.

## CONNECTING WITH OTHER TEXTS

1. Read "King Curtis's Echo" (p. 169) and write an analysis of how the messages that males learn playing football may interfere with Thayer's notion of self-restraint.

2. Write an essay contrasting Sabo's early view of masculinity with the male image Jeff Z. Klein represents in "Watching My Back" (p. 57).

#  The Work

## *Dana Beardsley Crotwell*

Poet and professor Dana Beardsley Crotwell (b. 1968) earned a BA in English, an MA in world literature, and an MFA in creative writing at Chapman University in California. Her writing has been featured in *Calliope* and *Earth's Daughters*. A full-time professor at El Camino College, Crotwell teaches literature, composition, critical thinking, and poetry courses. She "loves teaching Modern Literature of Latin America and Creative Writing: Poetry" and offers this encouragement to student writers: "It is so freeing to study and write. We often stifle ourselves when writing and forget that it is play; we just need to play sometimes." The following poem is from *Proposing on the Brooklyn Bridge: Poems About Marriage* published in 2003.

Sometimes marriage is like a dirty refrigerator
you think about making a change
but it would be so much work
taking everything out and examining it
really checking every corner
and crevice, the underside of what's there
not everything can be solved
with 409 and a sponge

you could defrost
but that would be really messy
and taking that bottom grill off
and seeing what's inside
could be dangerous and frightening
it could hurt you
so you think – how much easier it would be just to
trash it and get a new one
thinking you'll never let the new one get this dirty
you'll devote more time and energy
you'll watch what you put into it
and you'll know what's under the grill
before you get started –

But – looking at this icebox
studying its contents that
were distributed by two people
you realize that five years ago

this was new and clean and white
just like your wedding dress
only this box is used many times daily –
not hung covered and protected in a closet –
it is open and slammed shut
sometimes sticky, touched all over
dumped on, dirty and left unattended
except for surface touch ups –
and you decide,
put on the rubber gloves
take everything out and cover the floor with towels
and you defrost.

## THINKING ABOUT THE TEXT

1. Why does Crotwell open her poem with such a jarring simile–"sometimes marriage is like a dirty refrigerator"?

2. Focusing on specific images in the first stanza, determine how cleaning the refrigerator applies to what is needed throughout marriage.

3. Explain the multiple meanings of "defrost" in this poem. Use details from the poem to show why defrosting is often so "messy" and "frightening" in a relationship.

4. When a relationship is troubled, why might it be tempting to "trash it and get a new one"? Analyze images that show why people think that they will prevent the new partnership from getting "this dirty"?

5. After "looking at this icebox/studying its contents that/were distributed by two people," what are some multiple realizations that partners might discover that prompt them to "defrost"?

6. Why is the second-person perspective—you—so effective in this poem?

## WRITING FROM THE TEXT

1. Write an analysis of this poem that explains its key images, word choices, and meanings. Be careful to develop your essay fully and to employ the sandwich strategy to incorporate all quotations. (See 319–333.) Focus on a strong thesis that you can support throughout your essay. (See Poetry Analysis, pp. 436–444.)

2. Focusing on the main simile, "sometimes marriage is like a dirty refrigerator," write a narrative about a marriage familiar to you that needed this cleaning and "defrosting." Dramatize how it became so "dirty" and what

was done to get it clean again. Illustrate scenes from before and after the "cleaning." (See Narration, pp. 382–396.)

3. Taking the poet's advice to be creative and "play," write your own poem, beginning with your own simile to complete her first line: "Sometimes a marriage is like . . ." Find an image that is unexpected and fresh, as Crotwell did. You might choose to be humorous, ironic, playful, or somber throughout your poem, but follow her example and extend the image through various word choices and related images. You might also choose a different word for "marriage," if you prefer to write your poem about friendship, childhood, dating, or having a job, for example. Aim for concrete, vivid language.

## CONNECTING WITH OTHER TEXTS

1. Read "Through the Cracks" (p. 386) and use the images in Crotwell's poem to analyze the "work" that needed to be done in "Through the Cracks." Illustrate what was "under the grill" when the narrator explored more deeply, why the family had shut the door on certain issues, and why the family needed more than "surface touch ups" (66). What did it take to "defrost" in this family and how successful was the work?

2. After reading "Time Lost and Found" (p. 239), write an essay analyzing how both Lamott and Crotwell, in very different works and genres, emphasize that lasting relationships require time, energy, and effort that sometimes may get neglected. Include specific details from both works to illustrate the similar values and attitudes that both writers promote.

#  When a Woman Says No
### *Ellen Goodman*

A widely syndicated columnist whose home paper was the *Boston Globe*, Ellen Goodman (b. 1941) has won a Pulitzer Prize for her outstanding journalism. Goodman believes that she writes about issues more important than politics, like the "underlying values by which this country exists . . . the vast social changes in the way men and women lead their lives and deal with each other." The essay included here, first published in the *Boston Globe* in 1984, is indicative of Goodman's concerns.

Another essay by Goodman and additional biographical information appears on page 3.

1      There are a few times when, if you watch closely, you can actually see a change of public mind. This is one of those times.

2      For as long as I can remember, a conviction for rape depended as much on the character of the woman involved as on the action of the man. Most often

the job of the defense lawyer was to prove that the woman had provoked or consented to the act, to prove that it was sex, not assault.

3    In the normal course of events the smallest blemish, misjudgment, misstep by the woman became proof that she had invited the man's attentions. Did she wear a tight sweater? Was she a "loose" woman? Was she in the wrong part of town at the wrong hour? A woman could waive her right to say no in an astonishing number of ways.

4    But in the past few weeks, in Massachusetts, three cases of multiple rape have come into court and three sets of convictions have come out of juries. These verdicts point to a sea change in attitudes. A simple definition seems to have seeped into the public consciousness. If she says no, it's rape.

5    The most famous of these cases is the New Bedford barroom rape. There, in two separate trials, juries cut through complicated testimony to decide the central issue within hours. Had the woman been drinking? Had she lied about that in testimony? Had she kissed one of the men? In the end none of these points were relevant. What mattered to the juries that found four of these six men guilty was that they had forced her. If she said no, it was rape.

6    The second of these cases involved a young woman soldier from Ft. Devens who accepted a ride with members of a rock band, the Grand Slamm. She was raped in the bus and left in a field hours later. Had she flirted with the band members? Had she told a friend that she intended to seduce one of the men? Had she boarded the bus willingly? The judge sentencing three of the men to jail said, "No longer will society accept the fact that a woman, even if she may initially act in a seductive or compromising manner, has waived her right to say no at any further time." If she said no, it was rape.

7    The third of these cases was in some ways the most notable. An Abington woman was driven from a bar to a parking lot where she was raped by four men, scratched with a knife, had her hair singed with a cigarette lighter and was left half-naked in the snow. The trial testimony showed that she previously had sex with three of the men, and with two of them in a group setting. Still, the jury was able to agree with the district attorney: "Sexual consent between a woman and a man on one occasion does not mean the man has access to her whenever it strikes his fancy." If she said no, it was rape.

8    Not every community, courtroom or jury today accepts this simple standard of justice. But ten years ago, five years ago, even three years ago these women might not have even dared press charges.

9    It was the change of climate that enabled, even encouraged, the women to come forward. It was the change of attitude that framed the arguments in the courtroom. It was the change of consciousness that infiltrated the jury chambers.

10     The question now is whether that change of consciousness has become part of our own day-to-day lives. In some ways rape is the brutal, repugnant extension of an ancient ritual of pursuit and capture. It isn't just rapists who refuse to take no for an answer. It isn't just rapists who believe that a woman says one thing and means another.

11     In the confusion of adolescence, in the chase of young adulthood, the sexes were often set up to persist and to resist. Many young men were taught that "no" means "try again." Many young women were allowed to excuse their sexuality only when they were "swept away," overwhelmed.

12     The confused messages, the yes-no-maybes, the overpowered heroines and overwhelming heroes, are still common to supermarket gothic novels and *Hustler* magazine. It isn't just X-rated movies that star a resistant woman who falls in love with her sexual aggressor. It isn't just pornographic cable-TV that features the woman who really "wanted it." In as spritely a sitcom as *Cheers,* Sam blithely locked a coyly ambivalent Diane into his apartment.

13     I know how many steps it is from that hint of sexual pressure to the brutality of rape. I know how far it is from lessons of sexual power plays to the violence of rape. But it's time that the verdict of those juries was fully transmitted to the culture from which violence emerges. If she says no, it means no.

## THINKING ABOUT THE TEXT

1. In this essay, Goodman gives a brief history of social response to rape. In the past, how did lawyers defend alleged rapists? What seems to be the present attitude toward a charge of rape?

2. Goodman recounts three different rape trials. What is the logic of her arrangement of the three examples to support her thesis?

3. Beyond the assertion in the title of Goodman's essay, what is the important point she makes?

## WRITING FROM THE TEXT

1. Describe a time when the "confused messages, the yes-no-maybes" resulted in an incomplete or erroneous understanding of a point you were trying to make.

2. Write a response to Goodman's allegation that "many young men were taught that 'no' means 'try again'" (69). Argue that she is correct or incorrect. Use specific examples to support your view.

CONNECTING WITH OTHER TEXTS

1. Use "Who's Cheap?" (p. 45) and "When a Woman Says No" to write an analytical essay about the "confused messages" that women may give men in a dating situation.

2. Read recent periodical accounts of rape trials. Is Goodman accurate in her essay that there has been a "sea change" in public consciousness about rape?

 # Where Are You Going,  Where Have You Been?

### Joyce Carol Oates

A novelist, poet, playwright, editor, and critic, Joyce Carol Oates (b. 1938) also teaches creative writing at Princeton. Since her first collection of short stories appeared when she was 25, Oates has been averaging almost two books a year. Although she writes in a variety of genres and literary styles, Oates may be best known for her ability to write suspenseful tales and to create a sense of terror in an apparently ordinary situation, as the story included here illustrates. Oates has responded to critics' comments about the terror that permeates her work: "Uplifting endings and resolutely cheery world views are appropriate to television commercials but insulting elsewhere. It is not only wicked to pretend otherwise, it is futile." Some of Oates's book titles—*The Crosswicks Horror, Will You Always Love Me?* and *Zombie*—suggest the kinds of terror and anxieties embedded in her work. Recent books include *Middle Age: A Romance* (2001), *Beasts* (2002), *I'll Take You There* (2002), *Rape: A Love Story*, and *The Tattooed Girl* (2003), *The Falls: A Novel* (2004), *Missing Mom* (2005), *My Sister, My Love* (2008), and *A Fair Maiden* (2010). The story included here, from *The Wheel of Love*, has been widely anthologized since its first publication in 1965.

For Bob Dylan

1    Her name was Connie. She was fifteen and she had a quick nervous giggling habit of craning her neck to glance into mirrors or checking other people's faces to make sure her own was all right. Her mother, who noticed everything and knew everything and who hadn't much reason any longer to look at her own face, always scolded Connie about it. "Stop gawking at yourself, who are you? You think you're so pretty?" she would say. Connie would raise her eyebrows at these familiar complaints and look right through her

mother, into a shadowy vision of herself as she was right at that moment: she knew she was pretty and that was everything. Her mother had been pretty once too, if you could believe those old snapshots in the album, but now her looks were gone and that was why she was always after Connie.

2    "Why don't you keep your room clean like your sister? How've you got your hair fixed—what the hell stinks? Hair spray? You don't see your sister using that junk."

3    Her sister June was twenty-four and still lived at home. She was a secretary in the high school Connie attended, and if that wasn't bad enough—with her in the same building—she was so plain and chunky and steady that Connie had to hear her praised all the time by her mother and her mother's sisters. June did this, June did that, she saved money and helped clean the house and cooked and Connie couldn't do a thing, her mind was all filled with trashy daydreams. Their father was away at work most of the time and when he came home he wanted supper and he read the newspaper at supper and after supper he went to bed. He didn't bother talking much to them, but around his bent head Connie's mother kept picking at her until Connie wished her mother were dead and she herself were dead and it were all over. "She makes me want to throw up sometimes," she complained to her friends. She had a high, breathless, amused voice which made everything she said sound a little forced, whether it was sincere or not.

4    There was one good thing: June went places with girlfriends of hers, girls who were just as plain and steady as she, and so when Connie wanted to do that her mother had no objections. The father of Connie's best girlfriend drove the girls the three miles to town and left them off at a shopping plaza, so that they could walk through the stores or go to a movie, and when he came to pick them up again at eleven he never bothered to ask what they had done.

5    They must have been familiar sights, walking around that shopping plaza in their shorts and flat ballerina slippers that always scuffed the sidewalk, with charm bracelets jingling on their thin wrists: they would lean together to whisper and laugh secretly if someone passed by who amused or interested them. Connie had long dark blond hair that drew anyone's eye to it, and she wore part of it pulled up on her head and puffed out and the rest of it she let fall down her back. She wore a pullover jersey blouse that looked one way when she was at home and another way when she was away from home. Everything about her had two sides to it, one for home and one for anywhere that was not home: her walk that could be childlike and bobbing, or languid enough to make anyone think she was hearing music in her head, her mouth which was pale and smirking most of the time, but bright and pink on these evenings out, her laugh which was cynical and drawling

at home— "Ha, ha, very funny" —but high-pitched and nervous anywhere else, like the jingling of the charms on her bracelet.

6    Sometimes they did go shopping or to a movie, but sometimes they went across the highway, ducking fast across the busy road, to a drive-in restaurant where older kids hung out. The restaurant was shaped like a big bottle, though squatter than a real bottle, and on its cap was a revolving figure of a grinning boy who held a hamburger aloft. One night in mid-summer they ran across, breathless with daring, and right away someone leaned out a car window and invited them over, but it was just a boy from high school they didn't like. It made them feel good to be able to ignore him. They went up through the maze of parked and cruising cars to the bright-lit, fly-infested restaurant, their faces pleased and expectant as if they were entering a sacred building that loomed out of the night to give them what haven and what blessing they yearned for. They sat at the counter and crossed their legs at the ankles, their thin shoulders rigid with excitement, and listened to the music that made everything so good: the music was always in the background like music at a church service, it was something to depend upon.

7    A boy named Eddie came in to talk with them. He sat backward on his stool, turning himself jerkily around in semicircles and then stopping and turning again, and after a while he asked Connie if she would like something to eat. She said she did and so she tapped her friend's arm on her way out— her friend pulled her face up into a brave droll look—and Connie said she would meet her at eleven, across the way. "I just hate to leave her like that," Connie said earnestly, but the boy said that she wouldn't be alone for long. So they went out to his car and on the way Connie couldn't help but let her eyes wander over the windshields and faces all around her, her face gleaming with a joy that had nothing to do with Eddie or even this place; it might have been the music. She drew her shoulders up and sucked in her breath with the pure pleasure of being alive, and just at that moment she happened to glance at a face just a few feet from hers. It was a boy with shaggy black hair, in a convertible jalopy painted gold. He stared at her and then his lips widened into a grin. Connie slit her eyes at him and turned away, but she couldn't help glancing back and there he was still watching her. He wagged a finger and laughed and said, "Gonna get you, baby," and Connie turned away again without Eddie noticing anything.

8    She spent three hours with him, at the restaurant where they ate hamburgers and drank Cokes in wax cups that were always sweating, and then down an alley a mile or so away, and when he left her off at five to eleven only the movie house was still open at the plaza. Her girlfriend was there, talking with a boy. When Connie came up the two girls smiled at each other and Connie said, "How was the movie?" and the girl said, "*You* should know." They rode

off with the girl's father, sleepy and pleased, and Connie couldn't help but look at the darkened shopping plaza with its big empty parking lot and its signs that were faded and ghostly now, and over at the drive-in restaurant where cars were still circling tirelessly. She couldn't hear the music at this distance.

9     Next morning June asked her how the movie was and Connie said, "So-so."

10     She and that girl and occasionally another girl went out several times a week that way, and the rest of the time Connie spent around the house—it was summer vacation—getting in her mother's way and thinking, dreaming, about the boys she met. But all the boys fell back and dissolved into a single face that was not even a face, but an idea, a feeling, mixed up with the urgent insistent pounding of the music and the humid night air of July. Connie's mother kept dragging her back to the daylight by finding things for her to do or saying, suddenly, "What's this about the Pettinger girl?"

11     And Connie would say nervously, "Oh, her. That dope." She always drew thick clear lines between herself and such girls, and her mother was simple and kindly enough to believe her. Her mother was so simple, Connie thought, that it was maybe cruel to fool her so much. Her mother went scuffling around the house in old bedroom slippers and complained over the telephone to one sister about the other, then the other called up and the two of them complained about the third one. If June's name was mentioned her mother's tone was approving, and if Connie's name was mentioned it was disapproving. This did not really mean she disliked Connie and actually Connie thought that her mother preferred her to June because she was prettier, but the two of them kept up a pretense of exasperation, a sense that they were tugging and struggling over something of little value to either of them. Sometimes, over coffee, they were almost friends, but something would come up—some vexation that was like a fly buzzing suddenly around their heads—and their faces went hard with contempt.

12     One Sunday Connie got up at eleven—none of them bothered with church—and washed her hair so that it could dry all day long, in the sun. Her parents and sister were going to a barbecue at an aunt's house and Connie said no, she wasn't interested, rolling her eyes to let her mother know just what she thought of it. "Stay home alone then," her mother said sharply. Connie sat out back in a lawn chair and watched them drive away, her father quiet and bald, hunched around so that he could back the car out, her mother with a look that was still angry and not at all softened through the windshield, and in the back seat poor old June all dressed up as if she didn't know what a barbecue was, with all the running yelling kids and the flies. Connie sat with her eyes closed in the sun, dreaming and dazed with the warmth about her as if this were a kind of love, the caresses of love, and her mind slipped over onto

thoughts of the boy she had been with the night before and how nice he had been, how sweet it always was, not the way someone like June would suppose but sweet, gentle, the way it was in movies and promised in songs; and when she opened her eyes she hardly knew where she was, the back yard ran off into weeds and a fence line of trees and behind it the sky was perfectly blue and still. The asbestos "ranch house" that was now three years old startled her—it looked small. She shook her head as if to get awake.

13    It was too hot. She went inside the house and turned on the radio to drown out the quiet. She sat on the edge of her bed, barefoot, and listened for an hour and a half to a program called *XYZ Sunday Jamboree,* record after record of hard, fast, shrieking songs she sang along with, interspersed by exclamations from "Bobby King": "An' look here you girls at Napoleon's—Son and Charley want you to pay real close attention to this song coming up!"

14    And Connie paid close attention herself, bathed in a glow of slow-pulsed joy that seemed to rise mysteriously out of the music itself and lay languidly about the airless little room, breathed in and breathed out with each gentle rise and fall of her chest.

15    After a while she heard a car coming up the drive. She sat up at once, startled, because it couldn't be her father so soon. The gravel kept crunching all the way in from the road—the driveway was long—and Connie ran to the window. It was a car she didn't know. It was an open jalopy, painted a bright gold that caught the sunlight opaquely. Her heart began to pound and her fingers snatched at her hair, checking it, and she whispered "Christ, Christ," wondering how bad she looked. The car came to a stop at the side door and the horn sounded four short taps as if this were a signal Connie knew.

16    She went into the kitchen and approached the door slowly, then hung out the screen door, her bare toes curling down off the step. There were two boys in the car and now she recognized the driver: he had shaggy, shabby black hair that looked crazy as a wig and he was grinning at her.

17    "I ain't late, am I?" he said.

18    "Who the hell do you think you are?" Connie said.

19    "Toldja I'd be out, didn't I?"

20    "I don't even know who you are."

21    She spoke sullenly, careful to show no interest or pleasure, and he spoke in a fast bright monotone. Connie looked past him to the other boy, taking her time. He had fair brown hair, with a lock that fell onto his forehead. His sideburns gave him a fierce, embarrassed look, but so far he hadn't even bothered to glance at her. Both boys wore sunglasses. The driver's glasses were metallic and mirrored everything in miniature.

22    "You wanta come for a ride?" he said.

23    Connie smirked and let her hair fall loose over one shoulder.

24    "Don'tcha like my car? New paint job," he said. "Hey."

25    "What?"

26    "You're cute."

27    She pretended to fidget, chasing flies away from the door.

28    "Don'tcha believe me, or what?" he said.

29    "Look, I don't even know who you are," Connie said in disgust.

30    "Hey, Ellie's got a radio, see. Mine's broke down." He lifted his friend's arm and showed her the little transistor the boy was holding, and now Connie began to hear the music. It was the same program that was playing inside the house.

31    "Bobby King?" she said.

32    "I listen to him all the time. I think he's great."

33    "He's kind of great," Connie said reluctantly.

34    "Listen, that guy's *great*. He knows where the action is."

35    Connie blushed a little, because the glasses made it impossible for her to see just what this boy was looking at. She couldn't decide if she liked him or if he was just a jerk, and so she dawdled in the doorway and wouldn't come down or go back inside. She said, "What's all that stuff painted on your car?"

36    "Can'tcha read it?" He opened the door very carefully, as if he was afraid it might fall off. He slid out just as carefully, planting his feet firmly on the ground, the tiny metallic world in his glasses slowing down like gelatine hardening and in the midst of it Connie's bright green blouse. "This here is my name, to begin with," he said. ARNOLD FRIEND was written in tarlike black letters on the side, with a drawing of a round grinning face that reminded Connie of a pumpkin, except it wore sunglasses. "I wanta introduce myself, I'm Arnold Friend and that's my real name and I'm gonna be your friend, honey, and inside the car's Ellie Oscar, he's kinda shy." Ellie brought his transistor radio up to his shoulder and balanced it there. "Now these numbers are a secret code, honey," Arnold Friend explained. He read off the numbers, 33, 19, 17 and raised his eyebrows at her to see what she thought of that, but she didn't think much of it. The left rear fender had been smashed and around it was written, on the gleaming gold background: DONE BY CRAZY WOMAN DRIVER. Connie had to laugh at that. Arnold Friend was pleased at her laughter and looked up at her. "Around the other side's a lot more—you wanta come and see them?"

37    "No."

38    "Why not?"

39    "Why should I?"

40    "Don'tcha wanta see what's on the car? Don'tcha wanta go for a ride?"

41    "I don't know."

42    "Why not?"

43    "I got things to do."

44    "Like what?"

45    "Things."

46    He laughed as if she had said something funny. He slapped his thighs. He was standing in a strange way, leaning back against the car as if he were balancing himself. He wasn't tall, only an inch or so taller than she would be if she came down to him. Connie liked the way he was dressed, which was the way all of them dressed: tight faded jeans stuffed into black, scuffed boots, a belt that pulled his waist in and showed how lean he was, and a white pullover shirt that was a little soiled and showed the hard small muscles of his arms and shoulders. He looked as if he probably did hard work, lifting and carrying things. Even his neck looked muscular. And his face was a familiar face, somehow: the jaw and chin and cheeks slightly darkened, because he hadn't shaved for a day or two, and the nose long and hawklike, sniffing as if she were a treat he was going to gobble up and it was all a joke.

47    "Connie, you ain't telling the truth. This is your day set aside for a ride with me and you know it," he said, still laughing. The way he straightened and recovered from his fit of laughing showed that it had been all fake.

48    "How do you know what my name is?" she said suspiciously.

49    "It's Connie."

50    "Maybe and maybe not."

51    "I know my Connie," he said, wagging his finger. Now she remembered him even better, back at the restaurant, and her cheeks warmed at the thought of how she sucked in her breath just at the moment she passed him—how she must have looked at him. And he had remembered her. "Ellie and I come out here especially for you," he said. "Ellie can sit in back. How about it?"

52    "Where?"

53    "Where what?"

54    "Where're we going?"

55    He looked at her. He took off the sunglasses and she saw how pale the skin around his eyes was, like holes that were not in shadow but instead in light. His eyes were like chips of broken glass that catch the light in an amiable way. He smiled. It was as if the idea of going for a ride somewhere, to some place, was a new idea to him.

56    "Just for a ride, Connie sweetheart."

57    "I never said my name was Connie," she said.

58    "But I know what it is. I know your name and all about you, lots of things," Arnold Friend said. He had not moved yet but stood still leaning back against the side of his jalopy. "I took a special interest in you, such a pretty girl, and found out all about you like I know your parents and sister are gone somewheres and I know where and how long they're going to be

gone, and I know who you were with last night, and your best girlfriend's name is Betty. Right?"

59    He spoke in a simple lilting voice, exactly as if he were reciting the words to a song. His smile assured her that everything was fine. In the car Ellie turned up the volume on his radio and did not bother to look around at them.

60    "Ellie can sit in the back seat," Arnold Friend said. He indicated his friend with a casual jerk of his chin, as if Ellie did not count and she should not bother with him.

61    "How'd you find out all that stuff?" Connie said.

62    "Listen: Betty Schultz and Tony Fitch and Jimmy Pettinger and Nancy Pettinger," he said, in a chant. "Raymond Stanley and Bob Hutter—"

63    "Do you know all those kids?"

64    "I know everybody."

65    "Look, you're kidding. You're not from around here."

66    "Sure."

67    "But—how come we never saw you before?"

68    "Sure you saw me before," he said. He looked down at his boots, as if he were a little offended. "You just don't remember."

69    "I guess I'd remember you," Connie said.

70    "Yeah?" he looked up at this, beaming. He was pleased. He began to mark time with the music from Ellie's radio, tapping his fists lightly together. Connie looked away from his smile to the car, which was painted so bright it almost hurt her eyes to look at it. She looked at that name. ARNOLD FRIEND. And up at the front fender was an expression that was familiar—MAN THE FLY-ING SAUCERS. It was an expression kids had used the year before, but didn't use this year. She looked at it for a while as if the words meant something to her that she did not yet know.

71    "What're you thinking about? Huh?" Arnold Friend demanded. "Not worried about your hair blowing around in the car, are you?"

72    "No."

73    "Think I maybe can't drive good?"

74    "How do I know?"

75    "You're a hard girl to handle. How come?" he said. "Don't you know I'm your friend? Didn't you see me put my sign in the air when you walked by?"

76    "What sign?"

77    "My sign." And he drew an X in the air, leaning out toward her. They were maybe ten feet apart. After his hand fell back to his side the X was still in the air, almost visible. Connie let the screen door close and stood perfectly still inside it, listening to the music from her radio and the boy's blend together. She stared at Arnold Friend. He stood there so stiffly relaxed, pretending to be relaxed, with one hand idly on the door handle as if he were keeping

himself up that way and had no intention of ever moving again. She recognized most things about him, the tight jeans that showed his thighs and buttocks and the greasy leather boots and the tight shirt, and even that slippery friendly smile of his, that sleepy dreamy smile that all the boys used to get across ideas they didn't want to put into words. She recognized all this and also the singsong way he talked, slightly mocking, kidding, but serious and a little melancholy, and she recognized the way he tapped one fist against the other in homage of the perpetual music behind him. But all these things did not come together.

78    She said suddenly, "Hey, how old are you?"

79    His smile faded. She could see then that he wasn't a kid, he was much older—thirty, maybe more. At this knowledge her heart began to pound faster.

80    "That's a crazy thing to ask. Can'tcha see I'm your own age?"

81    "Like hell you are."

82    "Or maybe a coupla years older, I'm eighteen."

83    "Eighteen?" she said doubtfully.

84    He grinned to reassure her and lines appeared at the corners of his mouth. His teeth were big and white. He grinned so broadly his eyes became slits and she saw how thick the lashes were, thick and black as if painted with a black tarlike material. Then he seemed to become embarrassed, abruptly, and looked over his shoulder at Ellie. "*Him,* he's crazy," he said. "Ain't he a riot, he's a nut, a real character." Ellie was still listening to the music. His sunglasses told nothing about what he was thinking. He wore a bright orange shirt unbuttoned halfway to show his chest, which was a pale, bluish chest and not muscular like Arnold Friend's. His shirt collar was turned up all around and the very tips of the collar pointed out past his chin as if they were protecting him. He was pressing the transistor radio up against his ear and sat there in a kind of daze, right in the sun.

85    "He's kinda strange," Connie said.

86    "Hey, she says you're kinda strange! Kinda strange!" Arnold Friend cried. He pounded on the car to get Ellie's attention. Ellie turned for the first time and Connie saw with shock that he wasn't a kid either—he had a fair, hairless face, cheeks reddened slightly as if the veins grew too close to the surface of his skin, the face of a forty-year-old baby. Connie felt a wave of dizziness rise in her at this sight and she stared at him as if waiting for something to change the shock of the moment, make it all right again. Ellie's lips kept shaping words, mumbling along with the words blasting in his ear.

87    "Maybe you two better go away," Connie said faintly.

88    "What? How come?" Arnold Friend cried. "We come out here to take you for a ride. It's Sunday." He had the voice of the man on the radio now. It was

the same voice, Connie thought. "Don'tcha know it's Sunday all day and honey, no matter who you were with last night today you're with Arnold Friend and don't you forget it!—Maybe you better step out here," he said, and this last was in a different voice. It was a little flatter, as if the heat was finally getting to him.

89     "No. I got things to do."

90     "Hey."

91     "You two better leave."

92     "We ain't leaving until you come with us."

93     "Like hell I am—"

94     "Connie, don't fool around with me. I mean, I mean, don't fool *around*," he said, shaking his head. He laughed incredulously. He placed his sunglasses on top of his head, carefully, as if he were indeed wearing a wig, and brought the stems down behind his ears. Connie stared at him, another wave of dizziness and fear rising in her so that for a moment he wasn't even in focus but was just a blur, standing there against his gold car, and she had the idea that he had driven up the driveway all right but had come from nowhere before that and belonged nowhere and that everything about him and even about the music that was so familiar to her was only half real.

95     "If my father comes and sees you—"

96     "He ain't coming. He's at a barbecue."

97     "How do you know that?"

98     "Aunt Tillie's. Right now they're—uh—they're drinking. Sitting around," he said vaguely, squinting as if he were staring all the way to town and over to Aunt Tillie's back yard. Then the vision seemed to get clear and he nodded energetically. "Yeah. Sitting around. There's your sister in a blue dress, huh? And high heels, the poor sad bitch—nothing like you, sweetheart! And your mother's helping some fat woman with the corn, they're cleaning the corn—husking the corn—"

99     "What fat woman?" Connie cried.

100     "How do I know what fat woman, I don't know every goddam fat woman in the world!" Arnold laughed.

101     "Oh, that's Mrs. Hornby . . . Who invited her?" Connie said. She felt a little light-headed. Her breath was coming quickly.

102     "She's too fat. I don't like them fat. I like them the way you are, honey," he said, smiling sleepily at her. They stared at each other for a while, through the screen door. He said softly, "Now what you're going to do is this: you're going to come out that door. You're going to sit up front with me and Ellie's going to sit in the back, the hell with Ellie, right? This isn't Ellie's date. You're my date. I'm your lover, honey."

103     "What? You're crazy—"

104  "Yes, I'm your lover. You don't know what that is, but you will," he said. "I know that too. I know all about you. But look: it's real nice and you couldn't ask for nobody better than me, or more polite. I always keep my word. I'll tell you how it is. I'm always nice at first, the first time. I'll hold you so tight you won't think you have to try to get away or pretend anything because you'll know you can't. And I'll come inside you where it's all secret and you'll give in to me and you'll love me—"

105  "Shut up! You're crazy!" Connie said. She backed away from the door. She put her hands against her ears as if she'd heard something terrible, something not meant for her. "People don't talk like that, you're crazy," she muttered. Her heart was almost too big now for her chest and its pumping made sweat break out all over her. She looked out to see Arnold Friend pause and then take a step toward the porch lurching. He almost fell. But, like a clever drunken man, he managed to catch his balance. He wobbled in his high boots and grabbed hold of one of the porch posts.

106  "Honey?" he said. "You still listening?"

107  "Get the hell out of here!"

108  "Be nice, honey. Listen."

109  "I'm going to call the police—"

110  He wobbled again and out of the side of his mouth came a fast spat curse, an aside not meant for her to hear. But even this "Christ!" sounded forced. Then he began to smile again. She watched this smile come, awkward as if he were smiling from inside a mask. His whole face was a mask, she thought wildly, tanned down onto his throat but then running out as if he had plastered makeup on his face but had forgotten about his throat.

111  "Honey—? Listen, here's how it is. I always tell the truth and I promise you this: I ain't coming in that house after you."

112  "You better not! I'm going to call the police if you—if you don't—"

113  "Honey," he said, talking right through her voice, "honey, I'm not coming in there but you are coming out here. You know why?"

114  She was panting. The kitchen looked like a place she had never seen before, some room she had run inside but which wasn't good enough, wasn't going to help her. The kitchen window had never had a curtain, after three years, and there were dishes in the sink for her to do—probably—and if you ran your hand across the table you'd probably feel something sticky there.

115  "You listening, honey? Hey?"

116  "—going to call the police—"

117  "Soon as you touch the phone I don't need to keep my promise and can come inside. You won't want that."

118  She rushed forward and tried to lock the door. Her fingers were shaking. "But why lock it," Arnold Friend said gently, talking right into her face.

"It's just a screen door. It's just nothing." One of his boots was at a strange angle, as if his foot wasn't in it. It pointed out to the left, bent at the ankle. "I mean, anybody can break through a screen door and glass and wood and iron or anything else if he needs to, anybody at all and specially Arnold Friend. If the place got lit up with a fire honey you'd come runnin' out into my arms, right into my arms an' safe at home—like you knew I was your lover and'd stopped fooling around. I don't mind a nice shy girl but I don't like no fooling around." Part of those words were spoken with a slight rhythmic lilt, and Connie somehow recognized them—the echo of a song from last year, about a girl rushing into her boyfriend's arms and coming home again—

119  Connie stood barefoot on the linoleum floor, staring at him. "What do you want?" she whispered.

120  "I want you," he said.

121  "What?"

122  "Seen you that night and thought, that's the one, yes sir. I never needed to look anymore."

123  "But my father's coming back. He's coming to get me. I had to wash my hair first—" She spoke in a dry, rapid voice, hardly raising it for him to hear.

124  "No, your Daddy is not coming and yes, you had to wash your hair and you washed it for me. It's nice and shining and all for me. I thank you, sweetheart," he said, with a mock bow, but again he almost lost his balance. He had to bend and adjust his boots. Evidently his feet did not go all the way down; the boots must have been stuffed with something so that he would seem taller. Connie stared out at him and behind him Ellie in the car, who seemed to be looking off toward Connie's right into nothing. This Ellie said, pulling the words out of the air one after another as if he were just discovering them, "You want me to pull out the phone?"

125  "Shut your mouth and keep it shut," Arnold Friend said, his face red from bending over or maybe from embarrassment because Connie had seen his boots. "This ain't none of your business."

126  "What—what are you doing? What do you want?" Connie said. "If I call the police they'll get you, they'll arrest you—"

127  "Promise was not to come in unless you touch that phone, and I'll keep that promise," he said. He resumed his erect position and tried to force his shoulders back. He sounded like a hero in a movie, declaring something important. He spoke too loudly and it was as if he were speaking to someone behind Connie. "I ain't made plans for coming in that house where I don't belong but just for you to come out to me, the way you should. Don't you know who I am?"

128  "You're crazy," she whispered. She backed away from the door but did not want to go into another part of the house, as if this would give him permission to come through the door. "What do you . . . You're crazy, you . . ."

129     "Huh? What're you saying, honey?"

130     Her eyes darted everywhere in the kitchen. She could not remember what it was, this room.

131     "This is how it is, honey; you come out and we'll drive away, have a nice ride. But if you don't come out we're gonna wait till your people come home and then they're all going to get it."

132     "You want that telephone pulled out?" Ellie said. He held the radio away from his ear and grimaced, as if without the radio the air was too much for him.

133     "I toldja shut up, Ellie," Arnold Friend said, "you're deaf, get a hearing aid, right? Fix yourself up. This little girl's no trouble and's gonna be nice to me, so Ellie keep to yourself, this ain't your date—right? Don't hem in on me. Don't hog. Don't crush. Don't bird dog. Don't trail me," he said in a rapid meaningless voice, as if he were running through all the expressions he'd learned but was no longer sure which one of them was in style, then rushing on to new ones, making them up with his eyes closed, "Don't crawl under my fence, don't squeeze in my chipmunk hole, don't sniff my glue, suck my popsicle, keep your own greasy fingers on yourself!" He shaded his eyes and peered in at Connie, who was backed against the kitchen table. "Don't mind him honey he's just a creep. He's a dope. Right? I'm the boy for you and like I said you come out here nice like a lady and give me your hand, and nobody else gets hurt, I mean, your nice old bald-headed daddy and your mummy and your sister in her high heels. Because listen: why bring them in this?"

134     "Leave me alone," Connie whispered.

135     "Hey, you know that old woman down the road, the one with the chickens and stuff—you know her?"

136     "She's dead!"

137     "Dead? What? You know her?" Arnold Friend said.

138     "She's dead—"

139     "Don't you like her?"

140     "She's dead—she's—she isn't there anymore—"

141     "But don't you like her, I mean, you got something against her? Some grudge or something?" Then his voice dipped as if he were conscious of a rudeness. He touched the sunglasses perched on top of his head as if to make sure they were still there. "Now you be a good girl."

142     "What are you going to do?"

143     "Just two things, or maybe three," Arnold Friend said. "But I promise it won't last long and you'll like me the way you get to like people you're close to. You will. It's all over for you here, so come on out. You don't want your people in any trouble, do you?"

144     She turned and bumped against a chair or something, hurting her leg, but she ran into the back room and picked up the telephone. Something

roared in her ear, a tiny roaring, and she was so sick with fear that she could do nothing but listen to it—the telephone was clammy and very heavy and her fingers groped down to the dial but were too weak to touch it. She began to scream into the phone, into the roaring. She cried out, she cried for her mother, she felt her breath start jerking back and forth in her lungs as if it were something Arnold Friend were stabbing her with again and again with no tenderness. A noisy sorrowful wailing rose all about her and she was locked inside it the way she was locked inside this house.

145     After a while she could hear again. She was sitting on the floor with her wet back against the wall.

146     Arnold Friend was saying from the door, "That's a good girl. Put the phone back."

147     She kicked the phone away from her.

148     "No, honey. Pick it up. Put it back right."

149     She picked it up and put it back. The dial tone stopped.

150     "That's a good girl. Now you come outside."

151     She was hollow with what had been fear, but what was now just an emptiness. All that screaming had blasted it out of her. She sat, one leg cramped under her, and deep inside her brain was something like a pinpoint of light that kept going and would not let her relax. She thought, I'm not going to see my mother again. She thought, I'm not going to sleep in my bed again. Her bright green blouse was all wet.

152     Arnold Friend said, in a gentle-loud voice that was like a stage voice, "The place where you came from ain't there any more, and where you had in mind to go is canceled out. This place you are now—inside your daddy's house—is nothing but a cardboard box I can knock down any time. You know that and always did know it. You hear me?"

153     She thought, I have got to think. I have to know what to do.

154     "We'll go out in a nice field, out in the country here where it smells so nice and it's sunny," Arnold Friend said. "I'll have my arms tight around you so you won't need to try to get away and I'll show you what love is like, what it does. The hell with this house! It looks solid all right," he said. He ran a fingernail down the screen and the noise did not make Connie shiver, as it would have the day before. "Now put your hand on your heart, honey. Feel that? That feels solid too, but we know better, be nice to me, be sweet like you can because what else is there for a girl like you but to be sweet and pretty and give in?— and get away before her people come back?"

155     She felt her pounding heart. Her hand seemed to enclose it. She thought for the first time in her life that it was nothing that was hers, that belonged to her, but just a pounding, living thing inside this body that wasn't really hers either.

156    "You don't want them to get hurt," Arnold Friend went on. "Now get up, honey. Get up all by yourself."

157    She stood.

158    "Now turn this way. That's right. Come over here to me—Ellie, put that away, didn't I tell you? You dope. You miserable creepy dope," Arnold Friend said. His words were not angry but only part of an incantation. The incantation was kindly. "Now come out through the kitchen to me honey, and let's see a smile, try it, you're a brave sweet little girl and now they're eating corn and hot dogs cooked to bursting over an outdoor fire, and they don't know one thing about you and never did and honey you're better than them because not a one of them would have done this for you."

159    Connie felt the linoleum under her feet; it was cool. She brushed her hair back out of her eyes. Arnold Friend let go of the post tentatively and opened his arms for her, his elbows pointing in toward each other and his wrists limp, to show that this was an embarrassed embrace and a little mocking, he didn't want to make her self-conscious.

160    She put out her hand against the screen. She watched herself push the door slowly open as if she were safe back somewhere in the other doorway, watching this body and this head of long hair moving out into the sunlight where Arnold Friend waited.

161    "My sweet little blue-eyed girl," he said, in a half-sung sigh that had nothing to do with her brown eyes but was taken up just the same by the vast sunlit reaches of the land behind him and on all sides of him, so much land that Connie had never seen before and did not recognize except to know that she was going to it.

## THINKING ABOUT THE TEXT

1.  Identify Connie's character traits and illustrate each. How is she a rather typical 15-year-old, and how is she unique?

2.  List the various ways that Arnold Friend initially appeals to Connie.

3.  Identify the numerous intimidation tactics that Friend uses to manipulate Connie.

4.  Study Ellie's role in this story. How does Oates use him to illuminate Arnold Friend's character, temperament, and motives?

5.  Although the ending is ambiguous, Oates has revealed that this story was based on details from actual rapes and murders committed by Charles Schmid and his accomplice John Saunders in Tucson, Arizona, during the 1960s. How do various details in the story and, particularly, in the ending suggest that a crime was committed?

6. Without reducing this story to simple morals, discuss the insights (about subjects such as adolescence, parenting, role playing, manipulation, and intimidation) that we can draw from this story.

### WRITING FROM THE TEXT

1. Write a character analysis (pp. 445–453) of Arnold Friend, demonstrating how he knows and preys upon the insecurities and fantasies of a 15-year-old girl. Include details from the story to support your thesis.

2. In an essay, argue that Connie does or does not *choose* to go with Arnold Friend at the end. Could she have resisted more than she did? Cite specific evidence from the story to support your thesis.

3. Considering Connie's character and lifestyle, is Oates suggesting that Connie is to be blamed for what happened to her, or does the blame fall on Arnold Friend for taking advantage of a vulnerable 15-year-old? Write an essay to support your argument.

### CONNECTING WITH OTHER TEXTS

1. Read "When a Woman Says No" (p. 67) and write an essay applying Ellen Goodman's comments to Connie's experience.

2. Find and read the article in *Life* magazine (March 4, 1966) about the Charles Schmid case. Then write an essay comparing the actual details of his rapes and murders with this story.

3. Joyce Chopra's 1985 feature film *Smooth Talk,* based on Oates's story, is available on video, and Oates is reported to have been pleased with this adaptation. Note the differences between the video and the story versions, and write an essay analyzing the changes made in the film.

#  A Fine Romance
## *David Denby*

Book author and long-time film critic for the *New Yorker*, David Denby (b.1943) graduated from Columbia University in 1965 and also earned an MA in journalism in 1966. Denby returned to Columbia three decades after his graduation to write his account of the Western canon; *Great Books* was published in 1996. His 2004 book *American Sucker* chronicles his misadventures in investment and as a divorced man. His book *Snark: It's Mean, It's Personal, and It's Ruining Our Conversation* (2009) argues that the Internet has accelerated our snarkiness, our urge to write something nasty. In an interview with Lori

Kozlowski, Denby said: "The Internet reproduces things so quickly—that a post gets traffic and goes everywhere—accelerates things. People are trying to be funny and to be quoted or be memorable. Something that is sensible isn't necessarily catchy and isn't going to spread like wildfire. Whereas something that is nasty is and does." In the essay below, which appeared in the *New Yorker* July 23, 2007, Denby transcends film review to contribute to film history with his perception of a particular film genre, romantic comedies.

1      His beard is haphazard and unintentional, and he dresses in sweats, or in shorts and a T-shirt, or with his shirt hanging out like the tongue of a Labrador retriever. He's about thirty, though he may be younger, and he spends a lot of time with friends who are like him, only more so—sweet-natured young men of foul mouth, odd hair, and wanker-mag reading habits. When he's with them, punched beer cans and bongs of various sizes lie around like spent shells; alone, and walrus-heavy on his couch, he watches football, basketball, or baseball on television, or spends time memorializing his youth— archiving old movies, games, and jokes. Like his ancestors in the sixties, he's anti-corporate, but he's not bohemian (his culture is pop). He's more like a sullen back-of-the-classroom guy, who breaks into brilliant tirades only when he feels like it. He may run a used-record store, or conduct sightseeing tours with a non-stop line of patter, or feed animals who then high-five him with their flippers, or teach in a school where he can be friends with all the kids, or design an Internet site that no one needs. Whatever he does, he hardly breaks a sweat, and sometimes he does nothing at all.

2      He may not have a girlfriend, but he certainly likes girls—he's even, in some cases, a hetero blade, scoring with tourists or love-hungry single mothers. But if he does have a girlfriend she works hard. Usually, she's the same age as he is but seems older, as if the disparity between boys and girls in ninth grade had been recapitulated fifteen years later. She dresses in Donna Karan or Ralph Lauren or the like; she's a corporate executive, or a lawyer, or works in TV, public relations, or an art gallery. She's good-tempered, honest, great-looking, and serious. She wants to "get to the next stage of life"—settle down, marry, maybe have children. Apart from getting on with it, however, she doesn't have an idea in her head, and she's not the one who makes the jokes.

3      When she breaks up with him, he talks his situation over with his hopeless pals, who give him bits of misogynist advice. Suddenly, it's the end of youth for him. It's a crisis for her, too, and they can get back together only if both undertake some drastic alteration: he must act responsibly (get a job, take care of a kid), and she has to do something crazy (run across a baseball field during a game, tell a joke). He has to shape up, and she has to loosen up.

4    There they are, the young man and young woman of the dominant romantic-comedy trend of the past several years—the slovenly hipster and the female straight arrow. The movies form a genre of sorts: the slacker-striver romance. Stephen Frears's *High Fidelity* (2000), which transferred Nick Hornby's novel from London to Chicago, may not have been the first, but it set the tone and established the self-dramatizing underachiever as hero. Hornby's guy-centered material also inspired *About a Boy* and *Fever Pitch*. Others in this group include *Old School, Big Daddy, 50 First Dates, Shallow Hal, School of Rock, Failure to Launch, You, Me and Dupree, Wedding Crashers, The Break-Up,* and—this summer's hit—*Knocked Up*. In these movies, the men are played by Vince Vaughn, Owen Wilson, Adam Sandler, John Cusack, Jimmy Fallon, Matthew McConaughey, Jack Black, Hugh Grant, and Seth Rogen; the women by Drew Barrymore, Jennifer Aniston, Kate Hudson, Sarah Jessica Parker, and Katherine Heigl. For almost a decade, Hollywood has pulled jokes and romance out of the struggle between male infantilism and female ambition.

5    *Knocked Up*, written and directed by Judd Apatow, is the culminating version of this story, and it feels like one of the key movies of the era—a raw, discordant equivalent of *The Graduate* forty years ago. I've seen it with audiences in their twenties and thirties, and the excitement in the theatres is palpable—the audience is with the movie all the way, and, afterward, many of the young men (though not always the young women) say that it's not only funny but true. They feel that way, I think, because the picture is unruly and surprising; it's filled with the messes and rages of life in 2007. The woman, Alison (Katherine Heigl), an ambitious TV interviewer in Los Angeles, gets pregnant after a sozzled one-night stand with Ben (Seth Rogen), a nowhere guy she meets at a disco. Cells divide, sickness arrives in the morning—the movie's time scheme is plotted against a series of pulsing sonograms. Yet these two, to put it mildly, find themselves in an awkward situation. They don't much like each other; they don't seem to match up. Heigl has golden skin, blond hair, a great laugh. She's so attractive a person that, at the beginning of the movie, you wince every time Rogen touches her. Chubby, with curling hair and an orotund voice, he has the round face and sottish grin of a Jewish Bacchus, though grape appeals to him less than weed. At first, he makes one crass remark after another; he seems like a professional comic who will do anything to get a laugh. It's not at all clear that these two should stay together.

6    Authentic as Ben and Alison seem to younger audiences, they are, like all the slacker-striver couples, strangers to anyone with a long memory of romantic comedy. Buster Keaton certainly played idle young swells in some of his silent movies, but, first humiliated and then challenged, he would exert himself to heroic effort to win the girl. In the end, he proved himself

a lover. In the nineteen-thirties, the young, lean James Stewart projected a vulnerability that was immensely appealing. So did Jack Lemmon, in his frenetic way, in the fifties. In succeeding decades, Elliott Gould, George Segal, Alan Alda, and other actors played soulful types. Yet all these men *wanted* something. It's hard to think of earlier heroes who were absolutely free of the desire to make an impression on the world and still got the girl. And the women in the old romantic comedies were daffy or tough or high-spirited or even spiritual in some way, but they were never blank. What's going on in this new genre? *Knocked Up*, a raucously funny and explicit movie, has some dark corners, some fear and anxiety festering under the jokes. Apatow takes the slacker-striver romance to a place no one thought it would go. He also makes it clear, if we hadn't noticed before, how drastically the entire genre breaks with the classic patterns of romantic comedy. Those ancient tropes fulfill certain expectations and, at their best, provide incomparable pleasure. But *Knocked Up* is heading off into a brave and uncertain new direction.

7      Shakespeare knew the Roman farces—by Plautus, Terence, and others—in which a scrambling boy chases after a girl and lands her. He varied the pattern. His comedies were rarely a simple chase, and the best American romantic comedies have drawn on the forms that he devised—not so much, perhaps, in the coarse-grained *Taming of the Shrew* but in *Much Ado About Nothing*, with its pair of battling lovers, Beatrice and Benedick. Why is the contact between those two so barbed? Because they are meant for each other, and are too proud and frightened to admit it. We can see the attraction, even if they can't. They have a closely meshed rhythm of speech, a quickness to rise and retort, that no one else shares. Benedick, announcing the end of the warfare, puts the issue squarely: "Shall quips and sentences and these paper bullets of the brain awe a man from the career of his humor? No, the world must be peopled."

8      Romantic comedy is entertainment in the service of the biological imperative. *The world must be peopled.* Even if the lovers are past child-rearing age or, as in recent years, don't want children, the biological imperative survives, as any evolutionary psychologist will tell you, in the flourishes of courtship behavior. Romantic comedy civilizes desire, transforms lust into play and ritual—the celebration of union in marriage. The lovers are fated by temperament and physical attraction to join together, or stay together, and the audience longs for that ending with an urgency that is as much moral as sentimental. For its amusement, however, the audience doesn't want the resolution to come too quickly. The lovers misunderstand each other; they get pixie dust thrown in their faces. Befuddled, the woman thinks she's in love with a gas-station attendant, who turns out to be a millionaire; an unsuitable

suitor becomes a proper suitor; and so on. It's always the right guy in the end. Romantic drama may revel in suffering, even in anguish and death, but romantic comedy merely nods at the destructive energies of passion. The confused lovers torment each other and, for a while, us. Then they stop.

9      The best directors of romantic comedy in the nineteen-thirties and forties—Frank Capra, Gregory La Cava, Leo McCarey, Howard Hawks, Mitchell Leisen, and Preston Sturges—knew that the story would be not only funnier but much more romantic if the fight was waged between equals. The man and woman may not enjoy parity of social standing or money, but they are equals in spirit, will, and body. As everyone agrees, this kind of romantic comedy—and particularly the variant called "screwball comedy"—lifted off in February, 1934, with Frank Capra's charming *It Happened One Night*, in which a hard-drinking reporter out of a job (Clark Gable) and an heiress who has jumped off her father's yacht (Claudette Colbert) meet on the road somewhere between Florida and New York. Tough and self-sufficient, Gable contemptuously looks after the spoiled rich girl. He's rude and overbearing, and she's miffed, but it helps their acquaintance a little that they are both supremely attractive—Gable quick-moving but large and, in his famous undressing scene, meaty, and Colbert tiny, with a slightly pointed chin, round eyes, and round breasts beneath the fitted striped jacket she buys on the road. When she develops pride, they become equals.

10     The cinema added something invaluable to the romantic comedy: the camera's ability to place lovers in an enchanted, expanding envelope of setting and atmosphere. It moves with them at will, enlarging their command of streets, fields, sitting rooms, and night clubs; rapid cutting then doubles the speed of their quarrels. Out on the road, in the middle of the Depression, Gable and Colbert join the poor, the hungry, the shysters and the hustlers; they spend a night among haystacks, get fleeced, practice their hitchhiking skills. In screwball comedy, the characters have to dive below their social roles for their true selves to come out: they get drunk and wind up in the slammer; they turn a couch in an upstairs room of a mansion into a trampoline; they run around the woods at a country estate—the American plutocrats' version of Shakespeare's magical forest in *A Midsummer Night's Dream,* where young people, first confused and then enlightened, discover whom they should marry.

11     In many of the screwball classics, including *Twentieth Century, My Man Godfrey, The Awful Truth, Easy Living, Midnight, Bringing Up Baby, Holiday, The Philadelphia Story, The Lady Eve*—all made between 1934 and 1941—the characters dress for dinner and make cocktails, and the atmosphere is gilded and swank. The enormous New York apartments, the country houses with porticoes, the white-on-white night clubs in which swells listen to a warbling singer—all this

establishes a façade of propriety and manners, a place to misbehave. Except for the Fred Astaire–Ginger Rogers dance musicals, in which evening clothes are integral to the lyric transformation of life into movement, the lovers are no more than playing at formality. The characters need to be wealthy in order to exercise their will openly and make their choices. The screwball comedies are less about possessions than about a certain style of freedom in love, a way of vaulting above the dullness and petty-mindedness of the sticks. (In these films, no matter how rich you may be, you are out of the question if you hail from Oklahoma or Albany—you are Ralph Bellamy.)

12      Many of the heroines were heiresses, who, in those days, were prized for their burbling eccentricities—Carole Lombard's howl, Irene Dunne's giggle, Katharine Hepburn's Bryn Mawr drawl. Pampered and dizzy, they favored spontaneity over security when it came to choosing a man. As for the men, they came in two varieties. Some owned a factory or a mine, or were in finance—worldly fellows who knew how to float a debenture or hand a woman into a taxi—and others were gently cartooned intellectuals. Innocents preoccupied with some intricate corner of knowledge, they gathered old bones (Gary Grant, in *Bringing Up Baby*), or new words (Gary Cooper, in *Ball of Fire*), or went up the Amazon and discovered unspeakable snakes (Henry Fonda, in *The Lady Eve*). The man is the love object here—passive, dreamy, and gentle, a kind of Sleeping Beauty in spectacles—and the woman is the relentless pursuer. Katharine Hepburn in *Baby* nearly drives Cary Grant crazy with her intrusions into his work, her way of scattering his life about like pieces of lawn furniture. She's attracted by his good looks but also by what's unaroused in him, and she will do anything to awaken him. Equality in these comedies takes a new shape. The man is serious about his work (and no one says he shouldn't be), but he's confused about women, and his confusion has neutered him. He thinks he wants a conventional marriage with a compliant wife, but what he really wants is to be overwhelmed by the female life force. In the screwball comedies, the woman doesn't ask her man to "grow up." She wants to pull him into some sort of ridiculous adventure. *She* has to grow up, and he has to get loose—the opposite of the current pattern.

13      The screwball comedies were not devoted to sex, exactly—you could hardly describe any of the characters as sensualists. The Production Code limited openness on such matters, and the filmmakers turned sex into a courtship game that was so deliriously convoluted precisely because couples could go to bed only when they were married. The screwball movies, at their peak, defined certain ideal qualities of insouciance, a fineness of romantic temper in which men and women could be aggressive but not coarse, angry but not rancorous, silly but not shamed, melancholy but not ravaged. It was the temper of American happiness.

14      Sometimes the couple in a romantic comedy are already married, or were formerly married, but husband and wife go at each other anyway, because they enjoy wrangling too much to stop. Who else is there to talk to? In a case like that, romance becomes less a dazed encounter in an enchanted garden than a duel with slingshots at close quarters—exciting but a little risky. The most volatile of these comedies was *His Girl Friday*. Howard Hawks's 1940 version of the 1928 Ben Hecht–Charles MacArthur play *The Front Page*. In the original, the star reporter Hildy Johnson is a man. In Hawks's version, Hildy (Rosalind Russell) is a woman who has fled the barbarous city desk and plans to marry a timid businessman (Ralph Bellamy). Her former husband and editor, Walter Burns (Cary Grant), will do anything to get her back to the paper. He doesn't seem drawn to her as a woman, yet he woos her in his way, with scams, lies, and one important truth—that she's the only person good enough to cover the hottest story in town. She knows him as an indifferent and absent husband, yet she's attracted, once again, by the outrageous way this man fans his tail. And, despite her misgivings, she's caught, too, by the great time they have together toiling in the yellow journalism that they both love. Vince Vaughn, in some of his recent roles, has displayed a dazzling motormouth velocity, but he has never worked with an actress who can keep up with him. Rosalind Russell keeps up with Grant. These two seize each other's words and throw them back so quickly that their dialogue seems almost syncopated. Balance between the sexes here becomes a kind of matched virtuosity more intense than sex.

15      If Russell and Grant were exactly alike in that movie, Spencer Tracy, slow-talking, even adamantine, with a thick trunk and massive head, and Katharine Hepburn, slender, angular, and unnervingly speedy and direct, were opposites that attracted with mysterious force. In the classic comedy *Adam's Rib* (1949), their sixth movie together (they made nine), they were an established onscreen married couple, rising, drinking coffee, and getting dressed for work. How can you have romantic comedy in a setting of such domestic complacency? *Adam's Rib*, which was written by a married couple, Garson Kanin and Ruth Gordon, and directed by George Cukor, takes these two through combat so fierce that it can be ended only with a new and very desperate courtship. They become opposing lawyers in a murder case. He prosecutes, and she defends, a woman (Judy Holliday) who put a couple of slugs in her husband when she caught him in the arms of his mistress. As the two lawyers compete in court, and Tracy gets upstaged by Hepburn, the traditional sparring at the center of romantic comedy intensifies, turns a little ugly, and then comes to an abrupt stop with a loud slap—Tracy smacking Hepburn's bottom in a proprietary way during a late-night rubdown session. The slap is nothing, yet it's everything. The husband has violated the

prime rule of mating behavior by asserting a right over his wife physically. The drive for equality in movies can lead to bruising competitions, and in *Adam's Rib* the partnership of equals nearly dissolves. Suddenly anguished, the movie uneasily rights itself as husband and wife make concessions and find their way back to marriage again.

16    Achieving balance between a man and a woman in a romantic comedy can be elusive. Marilyn Monroe, her tactile flesh spilling everywhere, was either lusted after or mocked, but only Tony Curtis, appearing in Cary Grant drag in *Some Like It Hot*, knew how to talk to her. Rock Hudson and Doris Day, in their films together, were exclusively preoccupied with, respectively, assaulting and defending Day's virtue, and they both seemed a little demented. Tom Hanks matched up nicely with Daryl Hannah and with Meg Ryan, as did Richard Gere and Hugh Grant with Julia Roberts, whose eyes and smile and restless, long-waisted body charged up several romantic comedies in the nineties.

17    In recent decades, however, Woody Allen and Diane Keaton have come closest to restoring the miraculous ease of the older movies. Short and narrow-jawed, with black-framed specs that give him the aspect of a quizzical Eastern European police inspector, Allen turned his worried but demanding gaze on Keaton, the tall, willowy Californian. In their early films together, they seemed the most eccentric and singular of all movie couples; it was the presence of New York City, in *Annie Hall* (1977) and *Manhattan* (1979), that sealed their immortality as a team. Allen, narrating, presented himself as the embodied spirit of the place, sharp and appreciative, but also didactic, overexplicit, cranky, and frightened of lobsters off the leash and everything else in the natural world. The idea was that beauty and brains would match up, although, early in *Annie Hall*, the balance isn't quite there—Keaton has to rise to his level. Initially, she's nervously apologetic—all floppy hats, tail-out shirts, and tremulous opinions—and she agrees to be tutored by Allen, who gives her books to read and takes her repeatedly to *The Sorrow and the Pity*. For a while, they click as teacher and student. If Tracy and Hepburn were like a rock and a current mysteriously joined together, these two neurotics were like agitated hummingbirds meeting in midair.

18    Working with the cinematographer Gordon Willis, Woody Allen created the atmosphere of a marriage plot in conversations set in his beloved leafy East Side streets—his version of Shakespeare's magical forest. But *Annie Hall*, surprisingly, shifts away from marriage. The quintessential New Yorker turns out to be a driven pain in the neck, so insistent and adolescent in his demands that no woman can put up with him for long. And the specific New York elements that Allen added to romantic comedy—the cult of psychoanalysis and the endless opinions about writers, musicians, and artists—also threaten the stability of the couple. Psychoanalysis yields "relationships" and "living

together," not marriage, as the central ritual, and living together, especially in the time of the Pill and the easy real-estate market of the seventies, is always provisional. Opinions about art—the way the soul defines itself in time—are provisional, too. In *Annie Hall*, Keaton outgrows Allen's curriculum for her and moves on, and in *Manhattan*, perhaps the best American comedy about selfishness ever made, she returns to the married man she was having an affair with. Allen loses her both times; the biological imperative goes no-where. *Annie Hall* and *Manhattan* now seem like fragile and melancholy love lyrics; they took romantic comedy to a level of rueful sophistication never seen before or since.

19     The louts in the slacker-striver comedies should probably lose the girl, too, but most of them don't. Yet what, exactly, are they getting, and why should the women want *them*? That is not a question that romantic comedy has posed before.

20     The slacker has certain charms. He doesn't want to compete in business, he refuses to cultivate macho attitudes, and, for some women, he may be attractive. He's still a boy—he's gentler than other men. Having a child with such a guy, however, is another matter, and plenty of women have com-plained about the way *Knocked Up* handles the issue of pregnancy. Alison has a good job, some growing public fame, and she hardly knows the unap-pealing father—there's even some muttering about "bad genes." Why have a baby with him? Well, a filmmaker's answer would have to be that if there's an abortion, or if Alison has the child on her own, there's no movie—or, at least, nothing like this movie. And this movie, just as it is, has considerable interest and complication as fiction.

21     What's striking about *Knocked Up* is the way the romance is placed within the relations between the sexes. The picture is a drastic revision of classic romantic-comedy patterns. Ben doesn't chase Alison, and she doesn't chase him. The movie is not about the civilizing of desire, and it offers a marriage plot that couldn't be more wary of marriage. *Knocked Up*, like Apatow's earlier *40-Year-Old Virgin*, is devoted to the dissolution of a male pack, the ending of the juvenile male bond. Ben and his friends sit around in their San Fernando Valley tract house whamming each other on the head with rubber bats and watching naked actresses in movies. The way Ben lives with his friends is tremendous fun; it's also as close to paralysis as you can get and continue breathing. Apatow, of course, has it both ways. He squeezes the pink-eyed doofuses for every laugh he can get out of them, but at the same time he sug-gests that the very thing he's celebrating is sick, crazy, and dysfunctional. The situation has to end. Boys have to grow up or life ceases.

22     Ben and Alison's one-night stand forces the issue. Willy-nilly, the world gets peopled. Yet the slowly developing love between Ben and the pregnant

Alison comes off as halfhearted and unconvincing—it's the weakest element in the movie. There are some terrifically noisy arguments, a scene of Rogen's making love to the enormous Heigl ("I'm not making love to you like a dog. It's doggy *style*. It's a *style*"), but we never really see the moment in which they warm up and begin to like each other. That part of the movie is unpersuasive, I would guess, because it's not terribly important to Apatow. What's important is the male bond—the way it flourishes, in all its unhealthiness, and then its wrenching end. Alison lives with her sister, Debbie (Leslie Mann), and brother-in-law, Pete (Paul Rudd), and Ben begins to hang out with Alison at the house of the married couple, who are classically mismatched in temperament. Pete is restless, disappointed, and remorselessly funny, and Ben links up with him. Whooping with joy, they go off to Las Vegas, but they don't gamble or get laid. Instead, they hang out and eat "shrooms." They merely want to be together: it's as if Romeo and Mercutio had left the women and all that mess in Verona behind and gone off to practice their swordsmanship. When Ben and Pete get high, crash, and then return, chastened, to the women, the male bond is severed at last, the baby can be born, and life continues. In generic terms, *Knocked Up* puts the cart before the horse—the accidental baby, rather than desire, pulls the young man, who has to leave his male friends behind, into civilization.

23     As fascinating and as funny as *Knocked Up* is, it represents what can only be called the disenchantment of romantic comedy, the end point of a progression from Fifth Avenue to the Valley, from tuxedos to tube socks, from a popped champagne cork to a baby crowning. There's nothing in it that is comparable to the style of the classics—no magic in its settings, no reverberant sense of place, no shared or competitive work for the couple to do. Ben does come through in the end, yet, if his promise and Alison's beauty make them equal as a pair, one still wants more out of Alison than the filmmakers are willing to provide. She has a fine fit of hormonal rage, but, like the other heroines in the slacker-striver romances, she isn't given an idea or a snappy remark or even a sharp perception. All the movies in this genre have been written and directed by men, and it's as if the filmmakers were saying, "Yes, young men are children now, and women bring home the bacon, but men bring home the soul."

24     The perilous new direction of the slacker-striver genre reduces the role of women to vehicles. Their only real function is to make the men grow up. That's why they're all so earnest and bland—so *nice,* so *good.* Leslie Mann (who's married to Apatow) has some great bitchy lines as the angry Debbie, but she's not a lover; she represents disillusion. As Anthony Lane pointed out in these pages, Apatow's subject is not so much sex as age, and age in his movies is a malediction. If you're young, you have to grow up. If you grow

up, you turn into Debbie—you fear that the years are overtaking you fast. Either way, you're in trouble.

25    Apatow has a genius for candor that goes way beyond dirty talk—that's why *Knocked Up* is a cultural event. But I wonder if Apatow, like his fumy youths, shouldn't move on. It seems strange to complain of repetition when a director does something particularly well, and Apatow does the infantilism of the male bond better than anyone, but I'd be quite happy if I never saw another bong-gurgling slacker or male pack again. The society that produced the Katharine Hepburn and Carole Lombard movies has vanished; manners, in the sense of elegance, have disappeared. But manners as spiritual style are more important than ever, and Apatow has demonstrated that he knows this as well as anyone. So how can he not know that the key to making a great romantic comedy is to create heroines equal in wit to men? They don't have to dress for dinner, but they should challenge the men intellectually and spiritually, rather than simply offering their bodies as a way of dragging the clods out of their adolescent stupor. "Paper bullets of the brain," as Benedick called the taunting exchanges with Beatrice, slay the audience every time if they are aimed at the right place.

## THINKING ABOUT THE TEXT

1. What is the author's strategy in starting his essay with character analyses of the typical male and female leads of current romantic-comedies? How does Denby identify this new genre of romantic comedy? What is his perception of its primary plot? What specific titles does he give to illustrate the genre?

2. By the fifth paragraph of the essay, the reader learns that Denby is reviewing *Knocked Up*, a summer hit of 2007. However, the film review is only part of Denby's intention in this essay. What is his larger purpose beyond a single film analysis?

3. Denby examines the history of romantic comedies in order to contrast the elements of the classical romantic comedies and screwball romantic classics with the new genre he calls the "slacker-striver romances." What are the distinguishing characteristics of the hero, the heroine, and the couples in classical or screwball romantic comedies? Make a list of specific details that Denby uses to illustrate his points.

4. What is Denby's intention in looking at Shakespeare's *Much Ado About Nothing*? How does Denby characterize Beatrice and Benedick as individuals and their relationship within the comedy? In what ways are their personalities and their courtship a paradigm for many classical romantic comedies?

5. In what way did the romantic comedies in the 1930s and 1940s feature a couple who were equals? In what ways might they be unequals? Why does Denby note the various ways inequality is a tendency in some of the films of that time period? Why does he chronicle the comedies where characters dress for dinner and play in "gilded and swank" settings?

6. What is Denby's intention in analyzing the "most eccentric and singular of all movie couples," the roles played by Woody Allen and Diane Keaton (92)? In what ways does Denby's analysis of the two films by Allen and Keaton work as transitions to his analysis of the slacker-striver comedy *Knocked Up*?

7. Denby concludes that *Knocked Up* is "fascinating and funny" but it "represents what can only be called the disenchantment of romantic comedy, the end point of a progression from Fifth Avenue to the Valley, from tuxedos to tube socks, from a popped champagne cork to a baby crowning" (94). In what other specific ways does Denby indict the film? Is he correct in seeing the slacker-striver genre as a "perilous new direction" in film? What is his strategy in returning to Benedick's line in *Much Ado About Nothing*?

8. The title of Denby's essay comes from a 1930s song "A Fine Romance," lyrics by Dorothy Field and music by Jerome Kern. It was one of many popular songs in the film *Swing Time* and was sung in the film by Fred Astaire and Ginger Rogers. Others who have sung the song include Frank Sinatra, Marilyn Monroe, Ella Fitzgerald, and Billie Holiday. The lyrics have the singer attempting to romance a "strong, aged-in-the-wood woman" who ignores the singer who laments, among other complaints, that she treats his gifts of orchids as if they were cactus plants, and she won't "nestle" or even "wrestle." Access the lyrics online to see how many ways the allusion to the song is an effective title for Denby's essay.

## WRITING FROM THE TEXT

1. Write your own analysis of *Knocked Up*. If you think the film is a good one, show why in your analysis of the film's characters, plot, and theme. You might refer to some of Denby's specifically harsh judgments in order to contrast with your own views of the film.

2. Write an essay that lauds or deplores David Denby's analysis of current romantic comedies. In your essay, you may illustrate how accurately Denby portrays the leads and plots of the latest comedies or how much he fails to appreciate in these films. You will need to support your thesis with discussions of specific films in order to persuade your reader of your position.

3. David Denby scathingly attacks the "slacker" as a "slovenly hipster," who is "not bohemian" and whose "culture is pop," a "sullen back-of–the-classroom guy" who seems more interested in male bonding and recreational drugs than achieving a goal in life or developing a lasting relationship with a woman. Write a character analysis of a person you know who reflects or contrasts with the film image Denby describes. In your thesis, project the areas you intend to support in your analysis. Your conclusion would ideally provide your reader some insight you have about this person and the culture in which he lives. (See Character Analysis, pp. 445–453.)

## Connecting with Other Texts

1. Write an essay that illustrates how current romantic comedies feature characters and issues that show our culture as it really is, in contrast to the worlds reflected in those films Denby cites. Your thesis should project those elements you intend to analyze, and your specific support should be from films that you know well enough to analyze persuasively.

2. Consider key points made by Denby to write an analysis of a film that you believe shows couples who are admirably equal in their intelligence and life goals. Write your essay from a thesis that projects which areas of the leads' personality traits you intend to analyze in your paper. Your overview of the film's plot will be brief, a mere introduction to your thesis that projects your view of the characters and their relationship.

3. View one of the classic comedies described or noted by David Denby and write a comparison or contrast study of that film and *Knocked Up*. Review how to write a comparison contrast analysis, pp. 407–413, to help you structure your paper. You will want to project in your introduction the elements of the film you intend to compare or contrast, and your thesis might forecast the position you intend to support in your analysis.

# Chapter 3

# Between Cultures

Every year, more than a million people from different countries come to live in the United States. Your classrooms no doubt reflect this diversity—and your life after class probably does, too. You may find yourself enjoying sushi, falafel, or tacos, digesting cultural diversity as easily as you munch a Big Mac. Or you may find yourself perplexed by cultural pluralism, unsure of its merits. The readings in this chapter illustrate the joys and stresses of living with cultural differences. As you will discover, assimilation and rejection are issues not only for immigrants, but also for longtime residents of the United States who experience the psychological, political, and economic realities of living between cultures.

This chapter begins with an essay by someone like yourself, a college student, who describes the contrasts between his home and college environments. Marcus Mabry, an African American from New Jersey, writes of the discomfort he experiences traveling "between the two worlds" of poverty at home and affluence at Stanford. This discomfort may be felt by Muslim women living in the United States, as both Semeen Issa and Laila Al-Marayati attest in their study of bias against the burka. Even if you have not lived in a foreign country, you sometimes may feel like you are living in a foreign environment. For example, you may have grown up in the tranquil suburbs but now attend a busy city university surrounded by street vendors and honking horns. Thus you can find yourself between cultures even in your own country.

Cultural characteristics may be important because they suggest who we are, but they can also lead to misunderstanding and stereotyping as Judith Ortiz Cofer dramatically illustrates in her essay. Such tensions between cultures are dramatized in the film *Crash* which is reviewed in this chapter by both Roger Ebert and A. O. Scott. Teja Arboleda cautions against sorting people according to race or ethnicity, and certainly it would be a mistake to stereotype the illegal, migrant farmworker Alfredo Quiñones-Hinojosa, who was able to achieve the extraordinary in education and his life's work. M. Carl Holman's poem satirizes people's efforts to deny race and culture in order to create an artificial persona, and Luis Valdez's short play satirizes the use and abuse of Latinos.

Most people would agree that the United States has been enriched by multiculturalism. American art, music, literature, food, sports, dance, clothing—and so much more—all reflect the contributions of a diverse society. This chapter celebrates those contributions without ignoring the controversies.

#  Living in Two Worlds
## *Marcus Mabry*

After completing his BA in English and French literature at Stanford, Marcus Mabry (b. 1967) also earned a BA in international relations and an MA in English, all within the four years of his scholarship agreement. He has served as a correspondent for *Newsweek* at the State Department and in Paris and Johannesburg. In addition to freelance writing for *Emerge* and *Black Collegiate*, Mabry also conceived, wrote, produced, and narrated a documentary on African American families for French television. His 1995 memoir, *White Bucks and Black-Eyed Peas: Coming of Age Black in White America*, examines Mabry's decision to live in the white world where he decides he is "more comfortable" because "it demanded less role-playing" of him. In "No Father, and No Answers," an essay appearing in *Newsweek* in 1992, Mabry addresses the concerns he has had in trying both to understand and to establish a relationship with the father he only recently met (who twenty years earlier left Mabry's unwed mother to raise her son without emotional or economic support). Mabry is currently the international business editor of the *New York Times* and the author of *Twice as Good: Condoleezza Rice and Her Path to Power* (2008). The selection included here also appeared in *Newsweek on Campus*.

1    A round, green cardboard sign hangs from a string proclaiming, "We built a proud new feeling," the slogan of a local supermarket. It is a souvenir from one of my brother's last jobs. In addition to being a bagger, he's worked at a fast-food restaurant, a gas station, a garage and a textile factory. Now, in the icy clutches of the Northeastern winter, he is unemployed. He will soon be a father. He is 19 years old.

2    In mid-December I was at Stanford, among the palm trees and weighty chores of academe. And all I wanted to do was get out. I joined the rest of

the undergrads in a chorus of excitement, singing the praises of Christmas break. No classes, no midterms, no finals . . . and no freshmen! (I'm a resident assistant.) Awesome! I was looking forward to escaping. I never gave a thought to what I was escaping to.

3      Once I got home to New Jersey, reality returned. My dreaded freshmen had been replaced by unemployed relatives; badgering professors had been replaced by hard-working single mothers, and cold classrooms by dilapidated bedrooms and kitchens. The room in which the "proud new feeling" sign hung contained the belongings of myself, my mom and my brother. But for these two weeks it was mine. They slept downstairs on couches.

4      Most students who travel between the universes of poverty and affluence during breaks experience similar conditions, as well as the guilt, the helplessness and, sometimes, the embarrassment associated with them. Our friends are willing to listen, but most of them are unable to imagine the pain of the impoverished lives that we see every six months. Each time I return home I feel further away from the realities of poverty in America and more ashamed that they are allowed to persist. What frightens me most is not that the American socioeconomic system permits poverty to continue, but that by participating in that system I share some of the blame.

5      Last year I lived in an on-campus apartment, with a (relatively) modern bathroom, kitchen and two bedrooms. Using summer earnings, I added some expensive prints, a potted palm and some other plants, making the place look like the more-than-humble abode of a New York City Yuppie. I gave dinner parties, even a *soirée française.*

6      For my roommate, a doctor's son, this kind of life was nothing extraordinary. But my mom was struggling to provide a life for herself and my brother. In addition to working 24-hour-a-day cases as a practical nurse, she was trying to ensure that my brother would graduate from high school and have a decent life. She knew that she had to compete for his attention with drugs and other potentially dangerous things that can look attractive to a young man when he sees no better future.

7      Living in my grandmother's house this Christmas break restored all the forgotten, and the never acknowledged, guilt. I had gone to boarding school on a full scholarship since the ninth grade, so being away from poverty was not new. But my own growing affluence has increased my distance. My friends say that I should not feel guilty: what could I do substantially for my family at this age, they ask. Even though I know that education is the right thing to do, I can't help but feel, sometimes, that I have it too good. There is no reason that I deserve security and warmth, while my brother has to cope with potential unemployment and prejudice. I, too, encounter prejudice,

but it is softened by my status as a student in an affluent and intellectual community.

8    More than my sense of guilt, my sense of helplessness increases each time I return home. As my success leads me further away for longer periods of time, poverty becomes harder to conceptualize and feels that much more oppressive when I visit with it. The first night of break, I lay in our bedroom, on a couch that let out into a bed that took up the whole room, except for a space heater. It was a little hard to sleep because the springs from the couch stuck through at inconvenient spots. But it would have been impossible to sleep anyway because of the groans coming from my grandmother's room next door. Only in her early sixties, she suffers from many chronic diseases and couldn't help but moan, then pray aloud, then moan, then pray aloud.

9    This wrenching of my heart was interrupted by the 3 A.M. entry of a relative who had been allowed to stay at the house despite rowdy behavior and threats toward the family in the past. As he came into the house, he slammed the door, and his heavy steps shook the second floor as he stomped into my grandmother's room to take his place, at the foot of her bed. There he slept, without blankets on a bare mattress. This was the first night. Later in the vacation, a Christmas turkey and a Christmas ham were stolen from my aunt's refrigerator on Christmas Eve. We think the thief was a relative. My mom and I decided not to exchange gifts that year because it just didn't seem festive.

10    A few days after New Year's I returned to California. The Northeast was soon hit by a blizzard. They were there, and I was here. That was the way it had to be, for now. I haven't forgotten; the ache of knowing their suffering is always there. It has to be kept deep down, or I can't find the logic in studying and partying while people, my people, are being killed by poverty. Ironically, success drives me away from those I most want to help by getting an education.

11    Somewhere in the midst of all that misery, my family has built, within me, "a proud feeling." As I travel between the two worlds it becomes harder to remember just how proud I should be—not just because of where I have come from and where I am going, but because of where they are. The fact that they survive in the world in which they live is something to be very proud of, indeed. It inspires within me a sense of tenacity and accomplishment that I hope every college graduate will someday possess.

## THINKING ABOUT THE TEXT

1. Describe Mabry's university world and his role in it. Then contrast the university world with details from his family's home.

2. Mabry describes living "between the universes of poverty and affluence" (100). Detail the emotional toll this takes.

3. What happens during Christmas break to restore his sense of guilt?

4. How is the supermarket sign, hanging in the bedroom, both ironic and deeply symbolic of Mabry's life between worlds?

## WRITING FROM THE TEXT

1. Using details from the story, compare and contrast Mabry's "worlds." What is ironic about the impact of success on his life?

2. For Mabry, attending college has secured him a spot in a new world vastly different from his past. Focus on your own between-worlds experience—college and home life, school and work worlds, high school and college relationships. Help the reader see each world as vividly as Mabry does; include your emotional responses, too.

3. Write about a time when you tried to escape one world and exchange it for another. How successful were you? What was your emotional toll?

## CONNECTING WITH OTHER TEXTS

1. Analyze the between-worlds experiences of Judith Ortiz Cofer in "The Myth of the Latin Woman" (p. 118) and of Mabry. How do they compare? What conclusions can you draw about the "cultural tug of war"?

2. Compare and contrast the home and college environments of Rita Simmons in "Peaches" (p. 49) with those of Mabry. Use specific details from each essay to support your points.

3. Write an essay contrasting the high achievements of Marcus Mabry, Alfredo Quiñones-Hinojosa (below), and Brent Staples (p. 164) with their family's and peers' low expectations for them.

 ## Terra Firma—A Journey from Migrant Farm Labor to Neurosurgery

### *Alfredo Quiñones-Hinojosa*

An illegal immigrant when he crossed into the United States in the mid-1980s, Alfredo Quiñones-Hinojosa (b. 1966) is an assistant professor of neurosurgery and oncology, director of the brain-tumor stem-cell laboratory at Johns Hopkins School of Medicine, and director of the brain-tumor program at the Johns Hopkins Bayview campus.

In an interview which you can hear at www.nejm.org, Quiñones-Hinojosa discusses his concerns about how immigrants today face discrimination and often feel unwelcome in emergency rooms, where they may come too late for appropriate medical treatment. Quiñones-Hinojosa's inspiring personal narrative below appeared in the *New England Journal of Medicine* on August 9, 2007.

1    "You will spend the rest of your life working in the fields," my cousin told me when I arrived in the United States in the mid-1980s. This fate indeed appeared likely: a 19-year-old illegal migrant farm worker, I had no English language skills and no dependable means of support. I had grown up in a small Mexican farming community, where I began working at my father's gas station at the age of 5. Our family was poor, and we were subject to the diseases of poverty: my earliest memory is of my infant sister's death from diarrhea when I was 3 years old. But my parents worked long hours and had always made enough money to feed us, until an economic crisis hit our country in the 1970s. Then they could no longer support the family, and although I trained to be a teacher, I could not put enough food on the table either.

2    Desperate for a livable income, I packed my few belongings and, with $65 in my pocket, crossed the U.S. border illegally. The first time I hopped the fence into California, I was caught and sent back to Mexico, but I tried again and succeeded. I am not condoning illegal immigration; honestly, at the time, the law was far from the front of my mind. I was merely responding to the dream of a better life, the hope of escaping poverty so that one day I could return home triumphant. Reality, however, posed a stark contrast to the dream. I spent long days in the fields picking fruits and vegetables, sleeping under leaky camper shells, eating anything I could get, with hands bloodied from pulling weeds—the very same hands that today perform brain surgery.

3    My days as a farm worker taught me a great deal about economics, politics, and society. I learned that being illegal and poor in a foreign country could be more painful than any poverty I had previously experienced. I learned that our society sometimes treats us differently depending on the places we have been and the education we have obtained. When my cousin told me I would never escape that life of poverty, I became determined to prove him wrong. I took night jobs as a janitor and subsequently as a welder that allowed me to attend a community college where I could learn English.

4    In 1989, while I was working for a railroad company as a welder and high-pressure valve specialist, I had an accident that caused me to reevaluate my life once again. I fell into a tank car that was used to carry

liquefied petroleum gas. My father was working at the same company. Hearing a coworker's cry for help, he tried to get into the tank; fortunately, someone stopped him. It was my brother-in-law, Ramon, who climbed in and saved my life. He was taken out of the tank unconscious but regained consciousness quickly. By the time I was rescued, my heart rate had slowed almost to zero, but I was resuscitated in time. When I awoke, I saw a person dressed all in white and was flooded with a sense of security, confidence, and protection, knowing that a doctor was taking care of me. Although it was clear to me that our poverty and inability to speak English usually translated into suboptimal health care for my community, the moment I saw this physician at my bedside, I felt I had reached terra firma, that I had a guardian.

5   After community college, I was accepted at the University of California, Berkeley, where a combination of excellent mentorship, scholarships, and my own passion for math and science led me to research in the neurosciences. One of my mentors there convinced me, despite my skepticism, that I could go anywhere I wanted for medical school. Thanks to such support and encouragement, I eventually went to Harvard Medical School. As I pursued my own education, I became increasingly aware of the need and responsibility we have to educate our country's poor.

6   It is no secret that minority communities have the highest dropout rates and the lowest educational achievement levels in the country. The pathway to higher education and professional training programs is not "primed" for minority students. In 1994, when I started medical school, members of minority groups made up about 18% of the U.S. population but accounted for only 3.7% of the faculty in U.S. medical schools. I was very fortunate to find outstanding minority role models, but though their quality was high, their numbers were low.

7   Given my background, perhaps it is not surprising that I did not discover the field of neurosurgery until I was a medical student. I vividly remember when, in my third year of medical school, I first witnessed neurosurgeons peeling back the dura and exposing a real, live, throbbing human brain. I recall feeling absolute awe and humility—and an immediate and deep recognition of the intimacy between a patient and a doctor.

8   That year, one of my professors strongly encouraged me to go into primary care, arguing that it was the best way for me to serve my Hispanic immigrant community. Although I had initially intended to return to Mexico triumphant, I had since fallen in love with this country, and I soon found myself immersed in and committed to the betterment of U.S. society. With my sights set on neurosurgery after medical school, I followed my heart and

instincts and have tried to contribute to my community and the larger society in my own way. I see a career in academic medicine as an opportunity not only to improve our understanding and treatment of human diseases but also to provide leadership within medicine and support to future scientists, medical students, and physician scientists from minority and nonminority groups alike.

9      My grandmother was the medicine woman in the small town in rural Mexico where I grew up. As I have gotten older, I have come to recognize the crucial role she played not only in instilling in me the value of healing but also in determining the fate and future of others. She was my first role model, and throughout my life I have depended on the help of my mentors in pursuing my dreams. Like many other illegal immigrants, I arrived in the United States able only to contemplate those dreams—I was not at that point on solid ground. From the fields of the San Joaquin Valley in California to the field of neurosurgery, it has been quite a journey. Today, as a neurosurgeon and researcher, I am taking part in the larger journey of medicine, both caring for patients and conducting clinical and translational research on brain cancer that I hope will lead to innovative ways of fighting devastating disease. And as a citizen of the United States, I am also participating in the great journey of this country. For immigrants like me, this voyage still means the pursuit of a better life—and the opportunity to give back to society.

## THINKING ABOUT THE TEXT

1. What specific details of Quiñones-Hinojosa's account are most characteristic of an illegal immigrant's life?

2. What features of his life contributed to his eventually becoming a medical doctor and professor of neurosurgery and oncology?

3. This narration of an amazing personal history does not have an explicit thesis. What position is implicit in Quiñones-Hinojosa's inspiring account?

4. What does the title "Terra Firma" mean? In what ways does the term have significance in the author's life story?

## WRITING FROM THE TEXT

1. Write an essay to encourage someone to come to the United States. Use details of Quiñones-Hinojosa's life story to inspire your reader.

2. Using specific examples from Quiñones-Hinojosa's narration, write an essay arguing for increased mentoring for immigrant college students.

3. Write a response to Alfredo Quiñones-Hinojosa to tell him your feelings and ideas after reading of his triumphant, inspiring success. You might want to hear an interview with Dr. Quiñones-Hinojosa at www.nejm.org.

### CONNECTING WITH OTHER TEXTS

1. After reading Judith Ortiz Cofers "The Myth of the Latin Woman" (p. 118), write an essay to illustrate the forces that thwart immigrant assimilation. Use details from both Cofer's and Quiñones-Hinojosa's works in your analysis.

2. In "Race Is a Four-Letter Word" (p. 108), Teja Arboleda offers himself "as a case study in transcending the complex maze of barriers, pedestals, doors, and traps that form the boundaries that confine human beings to dominant and minority groups" (111). Write an analysis of Quiñones-Hinojosa's life story that supports Arboleda's self-impression.

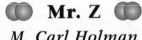

# Mr. Z

## *M. Carl Holman*

A poet, professor, and civil rights activist, M. Carl Holman (1919–1988) taught at Clark College in Atlanta, Georgia, from 1949 to 1962. He also worked as an editor on the *Atlanta Inquirer* and was on the U.S. Commission for Civil Rights. He served as president of the National Urban Coalition from 1971 until his death in 1988. Throughout his life, he won numerous awards for public service and for his poetry. The following poem, written in 1967, demonstrates his ability to meld his two passions—poetry and civil rights.

Taught early that his mother's skin was the sign of error,
He dressed and spoke the perfect part of honor;
Won scholarships, attended the best schools.
Disclaimed kinship with jazz and spirituals;
5   Chose prudent, raceless views for each situation.
Or when he could not cleanly skirt dissension
Faced up to the dilemma, firmly seized
Whatever ground was Anglo-Saxonized.

In diet, too, his practice was exemplary;
10  Of pork in its profane forms he was wary;
Expert in vintage wines, sauces and salads.
His palate shrank from cornbread, yams and collards.

He was as careful whom he chose to kiss;
His bride had somewhere lost her Jewishness.
15  But kept her blue eyes; an Episcopalian
Prelate proclaimed them matched chameleon.
Choosing the right addresses, here, abroad,
They shunned those places where they might be barred;
Even less anxious to be asked to dine
20  Where hosts catered to kosher accent or exotic skin.

And so he climbed, unclogged by ethnic weights,
An airborne plant, flourishing without roots.
Not one false note was struck—until he died;
His subtly grieving widow could have flayed
25  The obit writers, ringing crude changes on a clumsy phrase:
"One of the most distinguished members of his race."

## THINKING ABOUT THE TEXT

1. The opening line reveals that Mr. Z was "taught early that his mother's skin was the sign of error" (1), as if it were a mistake, something to correct or avoid. Why does the poet emphasize that this was "taught?" How can \ readers be sure what "his mother's skin" symbolizes? What does he shun?

2. List all the details that support the poet's claim that Mr. Z "dressed and spoke the perfect part of honor" (2). What does "perfect part" imply? What other words are used to show that every decision is calculated?

3. How does Mr. Z's bride seem ideal for him? What is she denying and avoiding? Why are they described as "matched chameleon"? What is telling about the contrast in the emotion that she exhibits over his death and the emotion that she feels for the "obit writers" who change his obituary?

4. Explain the significance of these lines: "And so he climbed, unclogged by ethnic weights, / An airborne plant, flourishing without roots" (21–22).

5. How is this poem a satire and what is the poet satirizing?

6. Irony is key to this poem. The poem reads like a list of praises, but what is the attitude of the poet toward Mr. Z? How can the reader be sure? Explain the irony in the last line.

7. What are possible meanings related to the name, "Mr. Z"? How is this name ironic?

### Writing from the Text

1. Write an analysis of the use of irony in "Mr. Z." Include specific images for support and analyze them fully. (See Poetry Analysis, pp. 436–444.)

2. Focusing on "Mr. Z," write an essay about any experiences that you or someone close to you has had denying his or her heritage. Were the successes worth the sacrifices? Can you infer Holman's view?

### Connecting with Other Texts

1. Read "The Myth of the Latin Woman" (p. 118) and contrast the author's self-concept and values with those of Mr. Z. In your essay try to account for these differences.

2. Read "Black Men and Public Space" (p. 164) and compare Brent Staples's "solution" to being misperceived by others with the choices that Mr. Z makes. Compare and contrast their motives and their acceptance of their identity.

##  Race Is a Four-Letter Word
### *Teja Arboleda*

An assistant professor at The New England Institute of Art in Brookline, Massachusetts, where he teaches media production as well as race and ethnic relations courses, Teja Arboleda founded Entertaining Diversity, Inc. in 1992 with the intention of teaching through entertainment about race, cultural diversity, and human potential. He has earned degrees in filmmaking and sociology, and an M.Ed. in education and media. Having worked as a television producer, director, writer, and entertainer, Arboleda directed a series on cultural diversity on PBS in 2001. Arboleda has appeared before the Senate Committee on Racial Classifications where he testified for changes in federal racial and ethnic categories. His father is African American/Native American and Filipino Chinese, and his mother is German Danish, a personal history that informs Arboleda's work, including the essay below from his book *In the Shadow of Race* (1998).

1    I've been called *nigger* and a neighbor set the dogs on us in Queens, New York.

2   I've been called *spic* and was frisked in a plush neighborhood of Los Angeles.

3   I've been called *Jap* and was blamed for America's weaknesses.

4   I've been called *Nazi* and the neighborhood G.I. Joes had me every time.

5   I've been called *Turk* and was sneered at in Germany.

6   I've been called *Stupid Yankee* and was threatened in Japan.

7   I've been called *Afghanistani* and was spit on by a Boston cab driver.

8   I've been called *Iraqi* and Desert Storm was America's pride.

9   I've been called *mulatto, criollo, mestizo, simarron, Hapahaoli, masala, exotic, alternative, mixed-up, messed-up, half-breed,* and *in between.* I've been mistaken for Moroccan, Algerian, Egyptian, Lebanese, Iranian, Turkish, Brazilian, Argentinean, Puerto Rican, Cuban, Mexican, Indonesian, Nepalese, Greek, Italian, Pakistani, Indian, Black, White, Hispanic, Asian, and being a Brooklynite. I've been mistaken for Michael Jackson and Billy Crystal on the same day.

10   I've been ordered to get glasses of water for neighboring restaurant patrons. I've been told to be careful mopping the floors at the television station where I was directing a show. Even with my U.S. passport, I've been escorted to the "aliens only" line at Kennedy International Airport. I've been told I'm not dark enough. I've been told I'm not White enough. I've been told I talk American real good. I've been told, "Take your hummus and your pita bread and go back to Mexico!" I've been ordered to "Go back to where you belong, we don't like *your* kind here!"

11   I spent too much time and energy as a budding adult abbreviating my identity and rehearsing its explanation. I would practice quietly by myself, reciting what my father always told me: "Filipino-German." He never smiled when he said this.

12   My father's dark skin told many stories that his stern face and anger-filled tension couldn't translate. My mother's light skin could never spell empathy—even suntanning only made her turn bright red. My brother Miguel and I became curiosity factors when we appeared in public with her. During the past 34 years, my skin has lightened, somewhat, but then in the summers (even in New England where summers happen suddenly, and disappear just as quickly), I can darken several degrees in a matter of hours. This phenomenon seems a peculiar paradigm to which people's perceptions of my culture or race alter with the waning and waxing of my skin tone. I can almost design others—perceptions by counting my minutes in the sun. My years in Japan, the United States, Germany, and the numerous countries, cities, and towns through which I've traveled, have proven that my flesh is irrelevant to the language I speak, to the way I walk and talk, or the way I jog or mow my lawn or to the fact that I often use chopsticks to eat.

It is irrelevant to *who* or *what* I married, my political viewpoints, my career, my hopes, desires and fears.

13  I don't remember being taught by my parents never to *question* skin color, yet when I compare the back of my hand to these pages, I cannot help myself—I must know. Like a sickness coursing through my veins with the very blood that makes me who I am, I ask: What color am I? And, what color was I yesterday? Tomorrow? There is also that pesky, familiar feeling I get when, in the corner of my eye, I catch passing strangers with judgments written on their brows. Maybe paranoia, maybe vanity, but the experiences and memories of too often being "different" or "undefinable" have left me with a weary sense of instant verdict on my part. And sometimes I study their thousands of faces, hoping somehow to connect. I know that they ask themselves the same questions, as they are plagued by the same epidemic, asking and reasking themselves, ourselves, "Who and what are we?"

14  Overadapting to new environments has become second nature to me, as my father and my mother eagerly fed me culture. As a child I felt like I was being dragged to different corners of the planet with my parents, filling their need for exploration and contact, and teaching us the value and beauty of difference. Between packing suitcases and wandering through unfamiliar territory, all I had ever wanted was to be "the same."

15  The United States is going through growing pains. The immigrants coming to the United States and becoming citizens are no longer primarily of European origin. But let's not fool ourselves into thinking that America is only now becoming multicultural.

16  In 1992, *Time* magazine produced a special issue entitled, "The New Face of America" with the subtitle, "How immigrants are shaping the world's first multicultural society." The cover featured a picture of a woman's face. Next to the face was a paragraph that suggested her image was the result of a computerized average of faces of people of several different races.

17  The operative words on the cover are "races," "culture," and "first." Race and culture are very different words. Race in America is predominantly determined by skin color. Culture is determined by our experiences and our interactions within a society, large or small.

18  Then there is this idea of being "first." Are we to say that this continent was never populated by a mix of people? Are we to say that the Locata and Iroquois were of exactly the same culture? What about the different Europeans who settled here later on? Of course, African slaves were not all from the same tribe, and they certainly were not of the same culture as the slave traders.

19    In the middle of the magazine, there was a compilation, more like a chart of photographs of people from all over the world. The editor and computer artist scanned all the pictures into a computer. Then, by having the computer average the faces together, they produced a variety of facial combinations. Remember, however, they said on the cover, "People from different *races* . . . to form the world's first *multicultural* society." But in the body of the article and its accompanying pictures, many people were not identified by their *race*, but rather by their *nationalities*—such as Italian and Chinese—in other words *citizenship*, a very different word.

20    Through it all, *Time* was trying to educate us, but at the same time, we're miseducated. The world—not just this country—has always been and always will be a multicultural environment. So what is it about the words *multicultural* or *diversity* that is confusing or overwhelming?

21    In the next 20 years, the average American will no longer be technically White. This will have to be reflected in the media, in the workplace, and in the schools, not out of charitable interest, but out of necessity. More people are designating themselves as multiracial or multicultural. People continue to marry across religious, cultural, and ethnic barriers. A definition for "mainstream society" is harder to find.

22    My mother's father, Opa, died a year after Oma passed away. The day after the funeral in Germany, my mother's relatives told her, for the first time, that her father was not really her father (i.e., biologically). All the people who knew the true identity of her father have long since passed away. So, if my mother's biological father was, let's say, Italian or Russian, does that make her German Italian or German Russian? She says no. German, only German, because that's how she was raised.

23    My brother, Miguel, married a Brazilian. (*Pause.*) Do you have an image in your head of what she looks like? I did when he first told me about her over the phone. Well, she is Brazilian by culture and citizenship, but her parents are Japanese nationals who moved to Brazil in their early 20s to escape poverty in Japan after World War II. So she *looks stereotypically* Japanese. But she speaks Portuguese and doesn't interact socially like most Japanese do.

24    I offer myself as a case study in transcending the complex maze of barriers, pedestals, doors, and traps that form the boundaries that confine human beings to dominant and minority groups.

25    I am tired. I am exhausted. I am always looking for new and improved definitions for my identity. My very-mixed heritage, culture, and international experiences seem like a blur sometimes, and I long for a resting place.

A place where I can breathe like I did in my mother's womb: without having to open my mouth.

## THINKING ABOUT THE TEXT

1. What is Teja Arboleda's racial ethnic identity? What seems to be his cultural identity and what are the distinctions he makes between the terms?

2. Why does Arboleda open with conflicting and negative impressions of how he has been perceived? What tone of voice do you hear in the rest of Arboleda's essay? What does he mean when he describes himself as "exhausted"?

3. Arboleda describes, in great detail, a 1992 *Time* magazine issue on "The New Face of America." How does the author use the images and text from *Time* to support his points?

4. How is Arboleda's account of his brother's marriage to a Brazilian relevant to his essay? Why the "(pause)"?

5. Why does Arboleda devote two paragraphs to describing his and his parents' skin color? What conclusion does he ultimately come to through his analysis of skin tone?

6. Arboleda does not have an explicit thesis, a strong assertion that serves as a controlling idea for his essay. Try to write what you think might serve as Teja Arboleda's thesis.

## WRITING FROM THE TEXT

1. Arboleda writes: "My flesh is irrelevant to the language I speak, to the way I walk and talk, or the way I jog or mow my lawn or the fact that I often use chopsticks to eat" (109). Write an essay analyzing your behavior or that of some of your multicultural friends to illustrate that you or they can not easily be categorized by a racial designation.

2. Write a narrative describing a time when you were misperceived as being of a race, ethnicity, or culture that you don't feel was accurate. What conclusions can you draw from this experience?

## CONNECTING WITH OTHER TEXTS

1. After reading "The Myth of the Latin Woman" (p. 118), write an essay comparing Arboleda's experiences with those of Judith Ortiz Cofer. Use examples from both essays and try to draw some conclusions about race and culture based on the author's narrations.

2. Using examples from the film *Crash* and the ideas expressed in "Don't Let Stereotypes Warp Your Judgments" (p. 424), write an essay arguing that "race" is a delimiting and often derogatory word based more on stereotypes than accurate observations.

 **An Identity Reduced to a Burka**

*Semeen Issa* and *Laila Al-Marayati*

Born in Tanzania in 1962, Semeen Issa is a teacher and also the president of the Muslim Women's League. She came to the United States in 1970 and graduated with both undergraduate and graduate degrees in education from the University of Southern California. Issa believes that "it is important in this country of great diversity that we take advantage of what others have to offer and that we stop judging people by how they look."

A practicing gynecologist as well as a writer, Laila Al-Marayati (b. 1962) is the author of articles on women's rights, women's sexuality, and female circumcision. She was born in the United States to a Palestinian father and a mother of French, German, and Native American heritage. The following article originally appeared in the *Los Angeles Times* on January 20, 2002, and was written because of the authors' growing frustration with the media's reductive perception of Muslim women.

1    A few years ago, someone from the Feminist Majority Foundation called the Muslim Women's League to ask if she could "borrow a burka" for a photo shoot the organization was doing to draw attention to the plight of women in Afghanistan under the Taliban. When we told her that we didn't have one, and that none of our Afghan friends did either, she expressed surprise, as if she'd assumed that all Muslim women keep *burkas* in their closets in case a militant Islamist comes to dinner. She didn't seem to understand that her assumption was the equivalent of assuming that every Latino has a Mexican sombrero in their closet.

2    We don't mean to make light of the suffering of our sisters in Afghanistan, but the *burka* was—and is—not their major focus of concern. Their priorities are more basic, like feeding their children, becoming literate and living free from violence. Nevertheless, recent articles in the Western media suggest the *burka* means everything to Muslim women, because they routinely express bewilderment at the fact that all Afghan women didn't cast off their *burkas* when the Taliban was defeated. The Western press' obsession with the dress of Muslim women is not surprising, however, since the press tends to view Muslims, in general, simplistically.

3    Headlines in the mainstream media have reduced Muslim female identity to an article of clothing—"the veil." One is hard-pressed to find an article, book or film about women in Islam that doesn't have "veil" in the title: "Behind the Veil," "Beyond the Veil," "At the Drop of a Veil" and more. The use of the term borders on the absurd: Perhaps next will come "What Color is Your Veil?" or "Rebel Without a Veil" or "Whose Veil Is It, Anyway?"

4    The word "veil" does not even have a universal meaning. In some cultures, it refers to a face-covering known as a *niqab*; in others, to a simple head scarf, known as *hijab*. Other manifestations of "the veil" include all-encompassing outer garments like the ankle-length *abaya* from the Persian Gulf states, the *chador* in Iran or the *burka* in Afghanistan.

5    Like the differences in our clothing from one region to another, Muslim women are diverse. Stereotypical assumptions about Muslim women are as inaccurate as the assumption that all American women are personified by the bikini-clad cast of "Baywatch." Anyone who has spent time interacting

with Muslims knows that, despite numerous obstacles, Muslim women are active, assertive and engaged in society. In Qatar, women make up the majority of graduate-school students. The Iranian parliament has more women members than the U.S. Senate. Throughout the world, many Muslim women are educated and professionally trained; they participate in public debates, are often catalysts for reform and champions for their own rights. At the same time, there is no denying that in many Muslim countries, dress has been used as a tool to wield power over women.

6    What doesn't penetrate Western consciousness, however, is that forced uncovering is also a tool of oppression. During the reign of Shah Mohammad Reza Pahlavi in Iran, wearing the veil was prohibited. As an expression of their opposition to his repressive regime, women who supported the 1979 Islamic Revolution marched in the street clothed in *chadors*. Many of them did not expect to have this "dress code" institutionalized by those who led the revolution and then took power in the new government.

7    In Turkey, the secular regime considers the head scarf a symbol of extremist elements that want to overthrow the government. Accordingly, women who wear any type of head-covering are banned from public office, government jobs and academia, including graduate school. Turkish women who believe the head-covering is a religious obligation are unfairly forced to give up public life or opportunities for higher education and career advancement.

8    Dress should not bar Muslim women from exercising their Islam-guaranteed rights, like the right to be educated, to earn a living, and to move about safely in society. Unfortunately, some governments impose a strict dress code along with other restrictions, like limiting education for women, to appear "authentically Islamic." Such laws, in fact, are inconsistent with Islam. Nevertheless, these associations lead to the general perception that "behind the veil" lurk other, more insidious examples of the repression of women, and that wearing the veil somehow causes the social ills that plague Muslim women around the world.

9    Many Muslim men and women alike are subjugated by despotic, dictatorial regimes. Their lot in life is worsened by extreme poverty and illiteracy, two conditions that are not caused by Islam but are sometimes exploited in the name of religion. Helping Muslim women overcome their misery is a major task. The reconstruction of Muslim Afghanistan will be a test case for the Afghan people and for the international community dedicated to making Afghan society work for everyone. To some, Islam is the root cause of the problems faced by women in Afghanistan. But what is truly at fault is a misguided, narrow interpretation of Islam designed to serve a rigid patriarchal system.

10    Traditional Muslim populations will be more receptive to change that is based on Islamic principles of justice, as expressed in the Koran, than they will be to change that abandons religion altogether or confines it to private life. Muslim scholars and leaders who emphasize Islamic principles that support women's rights to education, health care, marriage and divorce, equal pay for equal work and participation in public life could fill the vacuum now occupied by those who impose a vision of Islam that infringes on the rights of women.

11    Given the opportunity, Muslim women, like women everywhere, will become educated, pursue careers, strive to do what is best for their families and contribute positively according to their abilities. How they dress is irrelevant. It should be obvious that the critical element Muslim women need is freedom, especially the freedom to make choices that enable them to be independent agents of positive change. Choosing to dress modestly, including wearing a head scarf, should be as respected as choosing not to cover. Accusations that modestly dressed Muslim women are caving in to male-dominated understandings of Islam neglect the reality that most Muslim women who cover by choice do so out of subservience to God, not to any human being.

12    The worth of a woman—any woman—should not be determined by the length of her skirt, but by the dedication, knowledge and skills she brings to the task at hand.

## THINKING ABOUT THE TEXT

1. What is the authors' strategy in opening their essay with a narrative? How does the anecdote embody the authors' point of view?

2. What do you infer is the authors' thesis? Despite the seriousness of their claim, the authors' tone is humorous throughout. What is their strategy in employing humor? What is their aim?

3. What did you learn about the "veil" in different Muslim countries? How do the differences in styles and purposes for covering relate to the authors' point about Muslim women?

4. The authors insist that enforced dress codes are not the major problem facing most Islamic women, and their religion is not the delimiting factor in their lives. What are the problems facing these women? How do the authors' points help non-Muslim readers perceive the situation of Muslim women?

## Writing from the Text

1. Remember a time when a clothing code was imposed on you—for school, work, or for a social event within your peer group or family. Describe how you felt about the requirement, and whether you rebelled or conformed. Are identities reduced or enhanced by clothing regulations?

2. The authors observe that we tend to see Muslim women "simplistically" or stereotypically, in part because of our fixation on the *burka*. Write an essay that examines other nationalities and cultures that have been stereotyped by dress and analyze the consequences of such stereotyping.

3. Imagine yourself a traditional Muslim woman from an Afghan village who is transported to a city in the United States. You start to observe Western dress styles for women and now, in an essay, must show your approval or disapproval of American women's choices.

4. After this essay appeared in the *Los Angeles Times*, one letter to the editor pointed out that how women dress is not irrelevant, and that women who wear *burkas* would not become surgeons, for example, because veiling of any kind would not be possible in an operating room. Make a list of other activities or professions that you imagine could not reasonably be done by someone wearing a head covering. Write an essay that comes to some conclusion about whether the way women dress is relevant.

## Connecting with Other Texts

1. The authors write that "in many Muslim countries, dress has been used as a tool to wield power over women," and they note that "forced uncovering is also a tool of oppression" (115). Write an essay that analyzes how clothing codes have wielded power over women and men in many cultures. You might consider styles of clothing in affluent nations, as well as compulsory garments or uniforms throughout the world.

2. Write an essay comparing the experience of Waheeda Samady (p. 11) with the observations of Issa and Al-Marayati. Focus your essay on the reasons for and consequences of women wearing a veil.

3. Interview two Muslim women you know or can meet on your campus, one who wears a head covering of some kind and one who does not. In your prepared questions for the interview, you might consider asking why each has chosen "to veil or not to veil" and what experiences each has had as a result of her decision, including how she is perceived in the Muslim and non-Muslim cultures. In your comparative essay, come to some conclusion about the nature of "the veil."

# The Myth of the Latin Woman

### Judith Ortiz Cofer

Born in Puerto Rico in 1952, poet, essayist, and novelist Judith Ortiz Cofer has written extensively on being reared with her parents' traditional island culture while growing up in New Jersey. In an interview, Cofer described the contradictions in her cultural identity: "I write in English, yet I write obsessively about my Puerto Rican experience. . . . I am a composite of two worlds." A professor of English at the University of Georgia, Cofer has published essays, poems, and fiction. Her work includes *Woman in Front of the Sun: On Becoming a Writer* (2000), *The Meaning of Consuelo* (2003), *Call Me Maria* (2004), and *A Love Story Beginning in Spanish: Poems* (2005). The piece included here is from *The Latin Deli*, published in 1993.

1    On a bus trip to London from Oxford University where I was earning some graduate credits one summer, a young man, obviously fresh from a pub, spotted me and as if struck by inspiration went down on his knees in the aisle. With both hands over his heart, he broke into an Irish tenor's rendition of "Maria" from *West Side Story*. My politely amused fellow passengers gave his lovely voice the round of gentle applause it deserved. Though I was not quite as amused, I managed my version of an English smile: no show of teeth, no extreme contortions of the facial muscles—I was at this time of my life practicing reserve and cool. Oh, that British control, how I coveted it. But "Maria" had followed me to London, reminding me of a prime fact of my life: you can leave the island, master the English language, and travel as far as you can, but if you are a Latina, especially one like me who so obviously belongs to Rita Moreno's gene pool, the island travels with you.

2    This is sometimes a very good thing—it may win you that extra minute of someone's attention. But with some people, the same things can make *you* an island—not a tropical paradise but an Alcatraz, a place nobody wants to visit. As a Puerto Rican girl living in the United States and wanting like most children to "belong," I resented the stereotype that my Hispanic appearance called forth from many people I met.

3    Growing up in a large urban center in New Jersey during the 1960s, I suffered from what I think of as "cultural schizophrenia." Our life was designed by my parents as a microcosm of their *casas* on the island. We spoke in Spanish, ate Puerto Rican food bought at the *bodega,* and practiced strict Catholicism at a church that allotted us a one-hour slot each week for mass, performed in Spanish by a Chinese priest trained as a missionary for Latin America.

4    As a girl I was kept under strict surveillance by my parents, since my virtue and modesty were, by their cultural equation, the same as their honor.

As a teenager I was lectured constantly on how to behave as a proper *senorita.* But it was a conflicting message I received, since the Puerto Rican mothers also encouraged their daughters to look and act like women and to dress in clothes our Anglo friends and their mothers found too "mature" and flashy. The difference was, and is, cultural; yet I often felt humiliated when I appeared at an American friend's party wearing a dress more suitable to a semiformal than to a playroom birthday celebration. At Puerto Rican festivities, neither the music nor the colors we wore could be too loud.

5      I remember Career Day in our high school, when teachers told us to come dressed as if for a job interview. It quickly became obvious that to the Puerto Rican girls "dressing up" meant wearing their mother's ornate jewelry and clothing, more appropriate (by mainstream standards) for the company Christmas party than as daily office attire. That morning I had agonized in front of my closet, trying to figure out what a "career girl" would wear. I knew how to dress for school (at the Catholic school I attended, we all wore uniforms), I knew how to dress for Sunday mass, and I knew what dresses to wear for parties at my relatives' homes. Though I do not recall the precise details of my Career Day outfit, it must have been a composite of these choices. But I remember a comment my friend (an Italian American) made in later years that coalesced my impressions of the day. She said that at the business school she was attending, the Puerto Rican girls always stood out for wearing "everything at once." She meant, of course, too much jewelry, too many accessories. On that day at school we were simply made the negative models by the nuns, who were themselves not credible fashion experts to any of us. But it was painfully obvious to me that to the others, in their tailored skirts and silk blouses, we must have seemed "hopeless" and "vulgar." Though I now know that most adolescents feel out of step much of the time, I also know that for the Puerto Rican girls of my generation that sense was intensified. The way our teachers and classmates looked at us that day in school was just a taste of the cultural clash that awaited us in the real world, where prospective employers and men on the street would often misinterpret our tight skirts and jingling bracelets as a "come-on."

6      [Mixed cultural signals have perpetuated certain stereotypes—for example, that of the Hispanic woman as the "hot tamale"] or sexual firebrand. It is a one-dimensional view that the media have found easy to promote. In their special vocabulary, advertisers have designated "sizzling" and "smoldering" as the adjectives of choice for describing not only the foods but also the women of Latin America. From conversations in my house I recall hearing about the harassment that Puerto Rican women endured in factories where the "bossmen" talked to them as if sexual innuendo was all they understood,

and worse, often gave them the choice of submitting to their advances or being fired.

7     It is custom, however, not chromosomes, that leads us to choose scarlet over pale pink. As young girls, it was our mothers who influenced our decisions about clothes and colors—mothers who had grown up on a tropical island where the natural environment was a riot of primary colors, where showing your skin was one way to keep cool as well as to look sexy. Most important of all, on the island, women perhaps felt freer to dress and move more provocatively since, in most cases, they were protected by the traditions, mores, and laws of a Spanish/Catholic system of morality and machismo whose main rule was: *You may look at my sister, but if you touch her I will kill you.* The extended family and church structure could provide a young woman with a circle of safety in her small pueblo on the island; if a man "wronged" a girl, everyone would close in to save her family honor.

8     My mother has told me about dressing in her best party clothes on Saturday nights and going to the town's plaza to promenade with her girlfriends in front of the boys they liked. The males were thus given an opportunity to admire the women and to express their admiration in the form of *piropos:* erotically charged street poems they composed on the spot. (I have myself been subjected to a few *piropos* while visiting the island, and they can be outrageous, although custom dictates that they must never cross into obscenity.) This ritual, as I understand it, also entails a show of studied indifference on the woman's part; if she is "decent," she must not acknowledge the man's impassioned words. So I do understand how things can be lost in translation. When a Puerto Rican girl, dressed in her idea of what is attractive, meets a man from the mainstream culture who has been trained to react to certain types of clothing as a sexual signal, a clash is likely to take place. I remember the boy who took me to my first formal dance leaning over to plant a sloppy, over-eager kiss painfully on my mouth; when I didn't respond with sufficient passion, he remarked resentfully: "I thought you Latin girls were supposed to mature early," as if I were expected to *ripen* like a fruit or vegetable, not just grow into womanhood like other girls.

9     It is surprising to my professional friends that even today some people, including those who should know better, still put others "in their place." It happened to me most recently during a stay at a classy metropolitan hotel favored by young professional couples for weddings. Late one evening after the theater, as I walked toward my room with a colleague (a woman with whom I was coordinating an arts program), a middle-aged man in a tuxedo, with a young girl in satin and lace on his arm, stepped directly into our path. With his champagne glass extended toward me, he exclaimed "Evita!"

10    Our way blocked, my companion and I listened as the man half-recited, half-bellowed "Don't Cry for Me, Argentina." When he finished, the young girl said: "How about a round of applause for my daddy?" We complied, hoping this would bring the silly spectacle to a close. I was becoming aware that our little group was attracting the attention of the other guests. "Daddy" must have perceived this too, and he once more barred the way as we tried to walk past him. He began to shout-sing a ditty to the tune of "La Bamba"—except the lyrics were about a girl named Maria whose exploits rhymed with her name and gonorrhea. The girl kept saying "Oh, Daddy" and looking at me with pleading eyes. She wanted me to laugh along with the others. My companion and I stood silently waiting for the man to end his offensive song. When he finished, I looked not at him but at his daughter. I advised her calmly never to ask her father what he had done in the army. Then I walked between them and to my room. My friend complimented me on my cool handling of the situation, but I confessed that I had really wanted to push the jerk into the swimming pool. [This same man—probably a corporate executive, well-educated, even worldly by most standards—would not have been likely to regale an Anglo woman with a dirty song in public.] He might have checked his impulse by assuming that she could be somebody's wife or mother, or at least *somebody* who might take offense. [But, to him, I was just an Evita or a Maria: merely a character in his cartoon-populated universe.

11    Another facet of the myth of the Latin woman in the United States is the menial, the domestic—Maria the housemaid or countergirl. It's true that work as domestics, as waitresses, and in factories is all that's available to women with little English and few skills. But the myth of the Hispanic menial—the funny maid, mispronouncing words and cooking up a spicy storm in a shiny California kitchen—has been perpetuated by the media in the same way that "Mammy" from *Gone with the Wind* became America's idea of the black woman for generations. Since I do not wear my diplomas around my neck for all to see, I have on occasion been sent to that "kitchen" where some think I obviously belong.

12    One incident has stayed with me, though I recognize it as a minor offense. My first public poetry reading took place in Miami, at a restaurant where a luncheon was being held before the event. I was nervous and excited as I walked in with notebook in hand. An older woman motioned me to her table, and thinking (foolish me) that she wanted me to autograph a copy of my newly published slender volume of verse, I went over. She ordered a cup of coffee from me, assuming that I was a waitress. (Easy enough to mistake my poems for menus, I suppose.) I know it wasn't an intentional act of cruelty. Yet of all the good things that happened later, I remember that scene most clearly, because it reminded me of what I had to overcome before anyone

would take me seriously. In retrospect I understand that my anger gave my reading fire. In fact, I have almost always taken any doubt in my abilities as a challenge, the result most often being the satisfaction of winning a convert, of seeing the cold, appraising eyes warm to my words, the body language change, the smile that indicates I have opened some avenue for communication. So that day as I read, I looked directly at that woman. Her lowered eyes told me she was embarrassed at her faux pas, and when I willed her to look up at me, she graciously allowed me to punish her with my full attention. We shook hands at the end of the reading and I never saw her again. She has probably forgotten the entire incident, but maybe not.

13    Yet I am one of the lucky ones. There are thousands of Latinas without the privilege of an education or the entrees into society that I have. For them life is a constant struggle against the misconceptions perpetuated by the myth of the Latina. My goal is to try to replace the old stereotypes with a much more interesting set of realities. Every time I give a reading, I hope the stories I tell, the dreams and fears I examine in my work, can achieve some universal truth that will get my audience past the particulars of my skin color, my accent, or my clothes.

14    I once wrote a poem in which I called all Latinas "God's brown daughters." This poem is really a prayer of sorts, offered upward, but also, through the human-to-human channel of art, outward. It is a prayer for communication and for respect. In it, Latin women pray "in Spanish to an Anglo God/with a Jewish heritage," and they are "fervently hoping/that if not omnipotent,/at least He be bilingual."

## THINKING ABOUT THE TEXT

1.  What is the author's strategy in opening her essay with the anecdote about the bus passenger singing to her? What does the author mean when she claims that "you can leave the island" and travel to distant places, "but if you are Latina . . . the island travels with you" (118)? Do you think her awareness reflects the experience of members of other ethnicities as well?

2.  Cofer describes the "cultural schizophrenia" of growing up in New Jersey but living in a home that reflected her family's Puerto Rican heritage. In which specific areas did this between-worlds schizophrenia appear?

3.  The author is aware that most adolescents feel "out of step much of the time" (119), but how did the codes of her Puerto Rican family intensify the separation she felt from the Anglo culture she lived in?

4.  The author writes that "mixed cultural signals have perpetuated certain stereotypes" (119) about the Hispanic woman. What are those stereotypes

and how can they be perceived as dangerous as well as irritating? Why are the dress styles and behavior patterns of mothers who grew up on a tropical island not easily transported to a northern, urban society?

5. In addition to being identified with the Maria of *West Side Story* and Evita Peron, the author has also been assumed to be Maria the domestic. In her essay's conclusion, in what specific ways does Cofer use the anecdote about being presumed the waitress?

## Writing from the Text

1. Write about a time when you or a friend were stereotyped because of how you looked, perhaps by your "gene pool" that travels with you. Were you amused, irritated, frightened? In your narrative, show how you were treated and how you felt. (See Narration, pp. 382–390.)

2. Describe particular customs that you have observed in your family or the families of friends that seem to keep you or your friends "out of step" in the United States. Is a compromise in style possible or desirable, or is "cultural schizophrenia" inevitable? Perhaps that awareness will be a part of your conclusion.

3. Describe the myths that are attached to particular ethnicities, in a way similar to Cofer's observations of how Latinas are stereotyped as "sexual firebrands" or "domestics." In your analysis, speculate on the origins of the myths connected to certain groups, and in your conclusion speculate on the consequences of such stereotyping.

## Connecting with Other Texts

1. Both Judith Ortiz Cofer and Brent Staples (p. 164) deal with the problems of being perceived as other than one actually is. Write an essay that illustrates how frustrating and potentially dangerous it is to be stereotyped based on appearance. Use the specific experiences of the authors, as well as your own observations, to support your points.

2. Use films such as *Mississippi Massala, East Is East,* and *My Big Fat Greek Wedding,* as well as others that you know, to write about the "cultural schizophrenia" described by Judith Ortiz Cofer. Include specific statements from Cofer as well as detailed descriptions and analyses of scenes from the films.

3. In an essay, argue that immigrant parents work against their children's assimilation and personal happiness by adhering to values and customs that don't transport to a different country. Use "The Good Daughter" (p. 8) and "The Myth of the Latin Woman" to support your point.

# Los Vendidos[1]

### *Luis Valdez*

Director, actor, and playwright, Luis Valdez (b. 1940) is acclaimed in the worlds of stage and film. The son of migrant farmworkers, Valdez earned his BA in English from San Jose State University and worked as a lecturer at the University of California, Berkeley and Santa Cruz. In 1965, he founded El Teatro Campesino to support the grape boycott and farmworkers' strike. His major plays include *Zoot Suit* (1978), which was made into a film in 1982, and *I Don't Have to Show You No Stinking Badges* (1986). In 1987 he directed *La Bamba*, a film about Chicano pop musician Ritchie Valens, and in 1994 he wrote and directed the television screenplay *The Cisco Kid. Mummified Deer and Other Plays* was published in 2005. In his theatrical works Valdez created the *acto*—a drama written in both English and Spanish intended to educate and entertain farmworkers as well as urban audiences. *Los Vendidos*, first produced in 1967, is an example of this form.

CHARACTERS

HONEST SANCHO
SECRETARY
FARMWORKER
JOHNNY
REVOLUCIONARIO
MEXICAN AMERICAN

*[Scene: Honest Sancho's Used Mexican Lot and Mexican Curio Shop. Three models are on display in Honest Sancho's shop: to the right, there is a Revolucionario, complete with sombrero, carrilleras,[2] and carabina 30-30. At center, on the floor, there is the Farmworker, under a broad straw sombrero. At stage left is the Pachuco,[3] filero[4] in hand.]*

*[Honest Sancho is moving among his models, dusting them off and preparing for another day of business.]*

SANCHO: Bueno, bueno, mis monos, vamos a ver a quien vendemos ahora, ¿no? [*To audience.*] ¡Quihubo![5] I'm Honest Sancho and this is my shop. Antes fui contratista pero ahora logré tener mi negocito.[6] All I need now is a customer. [*A bell rings offstage.*] Ay, a customer!

SECRETARY: [*entering*] Good morning, I'm Miss Jimenez from—

---

[1] The Sellouts
[2] Cartridge belts.
[3] Chicano youths of the 1940s and 1950s who belonged to street gangs.
[4] Knife (pachuco slang)
[5] Okay, okay, my darlings, let's see which one of you we're going to sell now—right? What's up?
[6] I used to be a labor contractor, but now I have my own little business.

SANCHO: ¡Ah, una chicana! Welcome, welcome Señorita Jiménez.

SECRETARY: [*Anglo pronunciation*] JIM-enez.

SANCHO: ¿Qué?

SECRETARY: My name is Miss JIM-enez. Don't you speak English? What's wrong with you?

SANCHO: Oh, nothing, Señorita *Jim*-enez. I'm here to help you.

SECRETARY: That's better. As I was starting to say, I'm a secretary from the state office building, and we're looking for a Mexican type for the administration.

SANCHO: Well, you come to the right place, lady. This is Honest Sancho's Used Mexican Lot, and we got all types here. Any particular type you want?

SECRETARY: Yes, we were looking for somebody suave—

SANCHO: Suave.

SECRETARY: Debonair.

SANCHO: De buen aire.

SECRETARY: Dark.

SANCHO: Prieto.

SECRETARY: But of course not too dark.

SANCHO: No muy prieto.

SECRETARY: Perhaps, beige.

SANCHO: Beige, just the tone. Así como cafecito con leche, ¿no?[7]

SECRETARY: One more thing. He must be hardworking.

SANCHO: That could only be one model. Step right over here to the center of the shop lady. (*They cross to the Farmworker.*) This is our standard farmworker model. Take special notice of his four-ply Goodyear huaraches, made from the rain tire. This wide-brimmed sombrero is an extra added feature—keeps off the sun, rain, and dust.

SECRETARY: Yes, it does look durable.

SANCHO: And our farmworker model is friendly. Muy amable.[8] Watch. (*Snaps his fingers.*)

FARMWORKER: (*lifts up head*) Buenos días, señorita. (*His head drops.*)

SECRETARY: My, he's friendly.

SANCHO: Didn't I tell you? Loves his patrones![9] But his most attractive feature is that he's hardworking. Let me show you. (*Snaps fingers. Farmworker stands.*)

---

[7] Somewhat like the color of coffee with milk—right?
[8] Very friendly.
[9] Bosses

FARMWORKER: ¡El jale!¹⁰ (*He begins to work.*)

SANCHO: As you can see, he is cutting grapes.

SECRETARY: Oh, I wouldn't know.

SANCHO: He also picks cotton. (Snap. Farmworker begins to pick cotton.)

SECRETARY: Versatile, isn't he?

SANCHO: He also picks melons. (*Snap. Farmworker picks melons.*) That's his slow speed for late in the season. Here's his fast speed. (*Snap. Farmworker picks faster.*)

SECRETARY: Chihuahua . . . I mean, goodness, he sure is a hard worker.

SANCHO: *(pulls the Farmworker to his feet)* And that isn't the half of it. Do you see these little holes on his arms that appear to be pores? During those hot sluggish days in the field when the vines or the branches get so entangled it's almost impossible to move, these holes emit a certain grease that allows our model to slip and slide right through the crop with no trouble at all.

SECRETARY: Wonderful. But is he economical?

SANCHO: Economical? Señorita, you are looking at the Volkswagen of Mexicans. Pennies a day is all it takes. One plate of beans and tortillas will keep him going all day. That, and chile. Plenty of chile. Chile jalapeños, chile verde, chile colorado. But, of course, if you do give him chile (*Snap. Farmworker turns left face. Snap. Farmworker bends over.*), then you have to change his oil filter once a week.

SECRETARY: What about storage?

SANCHO: No problem. You know the farm labor camps our Honorable Governor Reagan has built out by Parlier or Raisin City? They were designed with our model in mind. Five, six, seven, even ten in one of those shacks will give you no trouble at all. You can also put him in old barns, old cars, riverbanks. You can even leave him out in the field overnight with no worry!

SECRETARY: Remarkable.

SANCHO: And here's an added feature: every year at the end of the season, this model moves on and doesn't return until next spring.

SECRETARY: How about that. But tell me, does he speak English?

SANCHO: Another outstanding feature is that last year this model was programmed to go out on *strike!* (*Snap.*)

FARMWORKER: ¡HUELGA! ¡HUELGA! Hermanos, sálganse de esos files.¹¹ (*Snap. He stops.*)

SECRETARY: No! Oh no, we can't strike in the state capital.

---

¹⁰Work! (pachuco slang)
¹¹STRIKE! STRIKE! Get out of those fields, brothers.

SANCHO: Well, he also scabs. *(Snap.)*

FARMWORKER: Me vendo barato, ¿y qué?[12] *(Snap.)*

SECRETARY: That's much better but you didn't answer my question. Does he speak English?

SANCHO: Bueno . . . no, pero[13] he has other—

SECRETARY: No.

SANCHO: Other features.

SECRETARY: *No!* He just won't do!

SANCHO: Okay, okay pues.[14] We have other models.

SECRETARY: I hope so. What we need is something a little more sophisticated.

SANCHO: Sophisti—¿qué?

SECRETARY: An urban model.

SANCHO: Ah, from the city! Step right back. Over here in this corner of the shop is exactly what you're looking for. Introducing our new Johnny Pachuco model! This is our fastback model. Streamlined. Built for speed, low-riding, city life. Take a look at some of these features. Mag shoes, dual exhausts, jet black paint-job, dark-tint windshield, a little poof on top. Let me just turn him on. *(Snap. Johnny walks to stage center with a pachuco bounce.)*

SECRETARY: What was that?

SANCHO: That, señorita, was the Chicano shuffle.

SECRETARY: Okay, what does he do?

SANCHO: Anything and everything necessary for city life. For instance, survival: he knife-fights. *(Snap. Johnny pulls out switchblade and swings at Secretary.)*

[Secretary screams.]

SANCHO: He dances. *(Snap.)*

[Johnny sings and dances. Sancho snaps his fingers.]

SANCHO: And here's a feature no city model can be without. He gets arrested, but not without resisting, of course. *(Snap.)*

JOHNNY: I didn't do it! I didn't do it! (Johnny turns and stands up against an imaginary wall, legs spread out, arms behind his back.)

SECRETARY: Oh no, we can't have arrests! We must maintain law and order.

SANCHO: But he's bilingual!

SECRETARY: Bilingual?

SANCHO: Simón que yes.[15] He speaks English! Johnny, give us some English. *(Snap.)*

---

[12] I sell myself cheap'so what?

[13] Well . . . no, but

[14] then

[15] Yes indeedy. (pachuco slang)

JOHNNY: *(comes downstage)* Down with whites! Brown power!

SECRETARY: *(gasps)* Oh! He can't say that!

SANCHO: Well, he learned it in your school.

SECRETARY: I don't care where he learned it.

SANCHO: But he's economical!

SECRETARY: Economical?

SANCHO: Nickels and dimes. You can keep Johnny running on hamburgers, Taco Bell tacos, Lucky Lager beer, Thunderbird wine, yesca—

SECRETARY: ¿Yesca?

SANCHO: Mota.

SECRETARY: ¿Mota?

SANCHO: Leños . . . Marijuana. (Snap. Johnny inhales on an imaginary joint.)

SECRETARY: That's against the law!

JOHNNY: (big smile, holding his breath) Yeah.

SANCHO: He also snorts coke. (Snap. Johnny snorts coke. Big smile.)

JOHNNY: That's too much, ése.[16]

SECRETARY: No, Mr. Sancho, I don't think this—

SANCHO: Wait a minute, he has other qualities I know you'll love. For example, an inferiority complex. (*Snap.*)

JOHNNY: *(to Sancho)* You think you're better than me, huh, ése? *(Swings switchblade.)*

SANCHO: He can also be beaten and he bruises; cut him and he bleeds; kick him and he—*(He beats, bruises, and kicks Johnny.)* Would you like to try it?

SECRETARY: Oh, I couldn't.

SANCHO: Be my guest. He's a great scapegoat.

SECRETARY: No really.

SANCHO: Please.

SECRETARY: Well, all right. Just once. *(She kicks Johnny.)* Oh, he's so soft.

SANCHO: Wasn't that good? Try again.

SECRETARY: *(kicks Johnny)* Oh, he's so wonderful! *(She kicks him again.)*

SANCHO: Okay, that's enough, lady. You ruin the merchandise. Yes, our Johnny Pachuco model can give you many hours of pleasure. Why, one police department just bought twenty of these to train their rookie cops on. And talk about maintenance. Señorita, you are looking at an entirely self-supporting machine. You're never going to find our Johnny Pachuco model on the relief rolls. No, sir, this model knows how to liberate.

SECRETARY: Liberate?

SANCHO: He steals. (Snap. Johnny rushes the secretary and steals her purse.)

---

[16] Man (pachuco slang)

JOHNNY: ¡Dame esa bolsa, vieja![17] (He grabs the purse and runs. Snap by Sancho. He stops.)

*[Secretary runs after Johnny and grabs purse away from him, kicking him as she goes.]*

SECRETARY: No, no, no! We can't have any more thieves in our state administration. Put him back.

SANCHO: Okay, we still got other models. Come on, Johnny, we'll sell you to some old lady. *(Sancho takes Johnny back to his place.)*

SECRETARY: Mr. Sancho, I don't think you quite understand what we need. What we need is something that will attract the women voters. Something more traditional, more romantic.

SANCHO: Ah, a lover. *(He smiles meaningfully.)* Step right over here, señorita. Introducing our standard Revolucionario and/or Early California Bandit type. As you can see, he is well built, sturdy, durable. This is the International Harvestor of Mexicans.

SECRETARY: What does he do?

SANCHO: You name it, he does it. He rides horses, stays in the mountains, crosses deserts, plains, rivers, leads revolutions, follows revolutions, kills, can be killed, serves as a martyr, hero, movie star—did I say movie star? Did you ever see *Viva Zapata? Viva Villa, Villa Rides, Pancho Villa Returns, Pancho Villa Goes Back, Pancho Villa Meets Abbott and Costello* . . .

SECRETARY: I've never seen any of those.

SANCHO: Well, he was in all of them. Listen to this. *(Snap.)*

REVOLUCIONARIO: *(scream)* ¡VIVA VILLAAAAA!

SECRETARY: That's awfully loud.

SANCHO: He has a volume control. *(He adjusts volume. Snap.)*

REVOLUCIONARIO: *(mousy voice)* Viva Villa.

SECRETARY: That's better.

SANCHO: And even if you didn't see him in the movies, perhaps you saw him on TV. He makes commercials. *(Snap.)*

REVOLUCIONARIO: Is there a Frito Bandito in your house?

SECRETARY: Oh yes, I've seen that one!

SANCHO: Another feature about this one is that he is economical. He runs on raw horsemeat and tequila!

SECRETARY: Isn't that rather savage?

SANCHO: Al contrario,[18] it makes him a lover. *(Snap.)*

---

[17] Gimme that purse, lady!
[18] On the contrary

REVOLUCIONARIO: (to Secretary) ¡Ay, mamasota, cochota, ven pa'cá![19] (He grabs Secretary and folds her back, Latin-lover style.)

SANCHO: (Snap. Revolucionario goes back upright.) Now wasn't that nice?

SECRETARY: Well, it was rather nice.

SANCHO: And finally, there is one outstanding feature about this model I *know* the ladies are going to love: he's a *genuine* antique! He was made in Mexico in 1910!

SECRETARY: Made in Mexico?

SANCHO: That's right. Once in Tijuana, twice in Guadalajara, three times in Cuernavaca.

SECRETARY: Mr. Sancho, I thought he was an American product.

SANCHO: No, but—

SECRETARY: No, I'm sorry. We can't buy anything but American made products. He just won't do.

SANCHO: But, he's an antique!

SECRETARY: I don't care. You still don't understand what we need. It's true we need Mexican models such as these, but it's more important that he be *American.*

SANCHO: American?

SECRETARY: That's right, and judging from what you've shown me, I don't think you have what we want. Well, my lunch hour's almost over, I better—

SANCHO: Wait a minute! Mexican but American?

SECRETARY: That's correct.

SANCHO: Mexican but . . . *(A sudden flash) American*! Yeah, I think we've got exactly what you want. He just came in today! Give me a minute. *(He exits. Talks from backstage.)* Here he is in the shop. Let me just get some papers off. There. Introducing our new Mexican American! Ta-ra-ra-ra-ra-RA-RAAA!

*[Sancho brings out the Mexican American model, a clean-shaven middle-class type in a business suit, with glasses.]*

SECRETARY: *(impressed)* Where have you been hiding this one?

SANCHO: He just came in this morning. Ain't he a beauty? Feast your eyes on him! Sturdy U.S. steel frame, streamlined, modern. As a matter of fact, he is built exactly like our Anglo models except that he comes in a variety of darker shades: Naugahyde, leather, or leatherette.

SECRETARY: Naugahyde.

SANCHO: Well, we'll just write that down. Yes, señorita, this model represents the apex of American engineering! He is bilingual, college-educated, ambitious! Say the word *acculturate* and he accelerates. He is intelligent,

---

[19] Oh mama, you cute thing, come over here!

well-mannered, clean—did I say clean? *(Snap. Mexican American raises his arm.)* Smell.

SECRETARY: *(smells)* Old Sobaco,[20] my favorite.

SANCHO: *(Snap. Mexican American turns toward Sancho.)* Eric? *(To Secretary)* We call him Eric García. *(To Eric)* I want you to meet Miss *Jim*-enez, Eric.

MEXICAN AMERICAN: Miss *Jim*-enez, I am delighted to make your acquaintance. *(He kisses her hand.)*

SECRETARY: Oh, my, how charming!

SANCHO: Did you feel the suction? He has seven especially engineered suction cups right behind his lips. He's a charmer, all right!

SECRETARY: How about boards—does he function on boards?

SANCHO: You name them, he is on them. Parole boards, draft boards, school boards, taco quality control boards, surfboards, two-by-fours.

SECRETARY: Does he function in politics?

SANCHO: Señorita, you are looking at a political *machine.* Have you ever heard of the OEO, EEOC, COD, War on Poverty? That's our model! Not only that, he makes political speeches.

SECRETARY: May I hear one?

SANCHO: With pleasure. *(Snap.)* Eric, give us a speech?

MEXICAN AMERICAN: Mr. Congressman, Mr. Chairman, members of the board, honored guests, ladies and gentlemen. *(Sancho and Secretary applaud.)* Please, please. I come before you as a Mexican American to tell you about the problems of the Mexican. The problems of the Mexican stem from one thing and one thing alone: he's stupid. He's uneducated. He needs to stay in school. He needs to be ambitious, forward-looking, harder-working. He needs to think American, American, American, AMERICAN, AMERICAN, AMERICAN. GOD BLESS AMERICA! GOD BLESS AMERICA! GOD BLESS AMERICA!! *(He goes out of control.)*

*[Sancho snaps frantically and the Mexican American finally slumps forward, bending at the waist.]*

SECRETARY: Oh my, he's patriotic too!

SANCHO: Sí, señorita, he loves his country. Let me just make a little adjustment here. *(Stands Mexican American up.)*

SECRETARY: What about upkeep? Is he economical?

SANCHO: Well, no, I won't lie to you. The Mexican American costs a little bit more, but you get what you pay for. He's worth every extra cent. You can keep him running on dry Martinis and steaks.

SECRETARY: Apple pie?

---

[20] Old Armpit

SANCHO:  Only Mom's. Of course, he's also programmed to eat Mexican food at ceremonial functions, but I must warn you: an overdose of beans will plug up his exhaust.

SECRETARY:  Fine! There's just one more question: *How much do you want for him?*

SANCHO:  Well, I tell you what I'm gonna do. Today and today only, because you've been so sweet, I'm gonna let you steal this model from me! I'm gonna let you drive him off the lot for the simple price of—let's see, taxes and license included—fifteen thousand dollars.

SECRETARY:  Fifteen thousand *dollars?* For a *Mexican?*

SANCHO:  Mexican? What are you talking, lady? This is a Mexican *American!* We had to melt down two pachucos, a farmworker, and three gabachos[21] to make this model! You want quality, but you gotta pay for it! This is no cheap runabout. He's got class!

SECRETARY:  Okay, I'll take him.

SANCHO:  You will?

SECRETARY:  Here's your money.

SANCHO:  You mind if I count it?

SECRETARY:  Go right ahead.

SANCHO:  Well, you'll get your pink slip in the mail. Oh, do you want me to wrap him up for you? We have a box in the back.

SECRETARY:  No, thank you. The Governor is having a luncheon this afternoon, and we need a brown face in the crowd. How do I drive him?

SANCHO:  Just snap your fingers. He'll do anything you want.

*[Secretary snaps. Mexican American steps forward.]*

MEXICAN AMERICAN:  ¡RAZA QUERIDA, VAMOS LEVANTANDO ARMAS PARA LIBERARNOS DE ESTOS DESGRACIADOS GABACHOS QUE NOS EXPLOTAN! VAMOS—[22]

SECRETARY:  What did he say?

SANCHO:  Something about lifting arms, killing white people, and so on.

SECRETARY:  But he's not supposed to say that!

SANCHO:  Look, lady, don't blame me for bugs from the factory. He's your Mexican American, you bought him, now drive him off the lot!

SECRETARY:  But he's broken!

SANCHO:  Try snapping another finger.

*[Secretary snaps. Mexican American comes to life again.]*

---

[21] Anglos

[22] Beloved Chicano people, let us take up arms to liberate ourselves from these despicable Anglos that exploit us! Let us—

MEXICAN AMERICAN: ¡ESTA GRAN HUMANIDAD HA DICHO BASTA! ¡Y SE HA
    PUESTO EN MARCHA! ¡BASTA! ¡BASTA! ¡VIVA LA RAZA! ¡VIVA LA
    CAUSA! ¡VIVA LA HUELGA! ¡VIVAN LOS BROWN BERETS! ¡VIVAN LOS
    ESTUDIANTES![23] CHICANO POWER!

> *[The Mexican American turns toward the Secretary, who gasps and backs up.
> He keeps turning toward the Pachuco, Farmworker, and Revolucionario, snap-
> ping his fingers and turning each of them on, one by one.]*

PACHUCO: *(Snap. To Secretary)* I'm going to get you, baby! Viva la Raza!

FARMWORKER: *(Snap. To Secretary)* ¡Viva la huelga! ¡Viva la huelga! ¡VIVA LA
    HUELGA!

REVOLUCIONARIO: *(Snap. To Secretary)* ¡Viva la revolucion! ¡VIVA LA REVOLUCION!

> *[The three models join together and advance toward the Secretary, who backs up
> and runs out of the shop screaming. Sancho is at the other end of the shop hold-
> ing his money in his hand. All freeze. After a few seconds of silence, the Pachuco
> moves and stretches, shaking his arms and loosening up. The Farmworker and
> Revolucionario do the same. Sancho stays where he is, frozen to his spot.]*

JOHNNY: Man, that was a long one, ése. *(Others agree with him.)*

FARMWORKER: How did we do?

JOHNNY: Perty good, look all that lana,[24] man! (He goes over to Sancho and
    removes the money from his hand. Sancho stays where he is.)

REVOLUCIONARIO: En la madre, look at all the money.

JOHNNY: We keep this up, we're going to be rich.

FARMWORKER: They think we're machines.

REVOLUCIONARIO: Burros.

JOHNNY: Puppets.

MEXICAN AMERICAN: The only thing I don't like is, how come I always got to play
    the Mexican American?

JOHNNY: That's what you get for finishing high school.

FARMWORKER: How about our wages, ése?

JOHNNY: Here it comes right now. Three thousand dollars for you, three thousand
    for you, three thousand for you, and three thousand for me. The rest we
    put back into the business.

MEXICAN AMERICAN: Too much, man. Hey, where you vatos[25] going tonight?

---

[23] This great mass of humanity has said, Enough! And it begins to march! Enough! Enough! Long live
the Chicano people! Long live La Causa! Long live the strike! Long live the Brown Berets! Long live
the students!

[24] Money (colloquial).

[25] Guys; dudes (pachuco slang)

FARMWORKER: I'm going over to Concha's. There's a party.

JOHNNY: Wait a minute, vatos. What about our salesman? I think he needs an oil job.

REVOLUCIONARIO: Leave him to me.

[*The Pachuco, Farmworker, and Mexican American exit, talking loudly about their plans for the night. The Revolucionario goes over to Sancho, removes his derby hat and cigar, lifts him up and throws him over his shoulder. Sancho hangs loose, lifeless.*]

REVOLUCIONARIO: *(to audience)* He's the best model we got! ¡Ajua! *(Exit.)*

## THINKING ABOUT THE TEXT

1. What is Valdez's strategy of setting this play in "Honest Sancho's Used Mexican Lot and Mexican Curio Shop"? How does this setting establish the tone and theme of this play?

2. How does Valdez depict the secretary and how does she see herself? Use specific quotations to support your interpretations.

3. Identify the stereotypes that Valdez uses and analyze his purpose in doing so.

4. What is ironic about "Honest Sancho" and how do you explain the twist at the end? What is Valdez suggesting in this ending?

5. What is the significance of the title, "The Sellouts"? According to Valdez, who are the sellouts and why?

6. Why does Valdez use both English and Spanish in this play? How do you feel about this mixing of languages? If you don't understand Spanish, would you have been able to follow the play without translations in the footnotes? Why?

7. Examine this play as a satire: a literary work that uses humor, ridicule, and exaggeration to expose or criticize certain values, beliefs, myths, practices, or institutions. What are the targets of Valdez's satire and what is he criticizing about each?

## WRITING FROM THE TEXT

1. Focusing on the mixture of English and Spanish in *Los Vendidos*, write an essay arguing that the mixing of languages adds to or detracts from an understanding of the play. Include specific quotations from the play to illustrate your claims.

2. In an essay on stereotypes, analyze how Valdez's use of Mexican stereotypes underscores the themes of this play.

3. If you have experienced stereotyping or exploitation because of your culture, write an evaluative response essay relating your experiences to specific conflicts or attitudes in this play.

4. Using materials gathered for exercise 7, write an analytic essay examining the targets of Valdez's satire. Explain what he is exposing and criticizing throughout this play.

### CONNECTING WITH OTHER TEXTS

1. Read "Don't Let Stereotypes Warp Your Judgments" (p. 424) and write an essay using examples from Valdez's play to support and illustrate Heilbroner's points and cautions.

2. Read "The Myth of the Latin Woman" (p. 118), and write an essay showing how Cofer's experiences reflect those Luis Valdez satirizes. You may include your own observations to create an amusing essay.

3. Write an essay contrasting the attitudes, values, and experiences of the fictional characters in Luis Valdez's play with the actual experiences of Alfredo Quiñones-Hinojosa (p. 108).

##  Film Analyses of *Crash*

Two contrasting views of the film *Crash* appear below and a third essay is used as a model of a film analysis (see p. 435). These reviews can help you respond to the "Writing" and "Connecting" assignments on pp. 141–142. Shot as a series of vignettes, *Crash* features characters whose lives collide—in car accidents, emotional outbursts, and racially charged confrontations. Sandra Bullock plays Jean, the DA's wife, and Brendan Fraser plays her husband Rick. Don Cheadle is Graham, the detective, and his partner and girlfriend, Ria, is played by Jennifer Esposito. Matt Dillon is Officer Ryan and Ryan Phillippe plays the rookie cop; Terrence Howard plays Cameron, a television director, and Thandie Newton plays his wife Christine. The two car thieves are Anthony played by Ludacris and Graham's brother played by Larenz Tate. This film was written by Paul Haggis and Robert Moresco and directed by Haggis. *Crash* runs 100 minutes.

##  Crash

### *Roger Ebert, film critic,* Chicago Sun-Times

1    *Crash* tells interlocking stories of whites, blacks, Latinos, Koreans, Iranians, cops and criminals, the rich and the poor, the powerful and powerless, all defined in one way or another by racism. All are victims of it, and all are

guilty [of] it. Sometimes, yes, they rise above it, although it is never that simple. Their negative impulses may be instinctive, their positive impulses may be dangerous, and who knows what the other person is thinking?

2    The result is a movie of intense fascination; we understand quickly enough who the characters are and what their lives are like, but we have no idea how they will behave, because so much depends on accident. Most movies enact rituals; we know the form and watch for variations. *Crash* is a movie with free will, and anything can happen. Because we care about the characters, the movie is uncanny in its ability to rope us in and get us involved.

3    *Crash* was directed by Paul Haggis, whose screenplay for *Million Dollar Baby* led to Academy Awards. It connects stories based on coincidence, serendipity, and luck, as the lives of the characters crash against one another other like pinballs. The movie presumes that most people feel prejudice and resentment against members of other groups, and observes the consequences of those feelings.

4    One thing that happens, again and again, is that peoples' [sic] assumptions prevent them from seeing the actual person standing before them. An Iranian (Shaun Toub) is thought to be an Arab, although Iranians are Persian. Both the Iranian and the white wife of the district attorney (Sandra Bullock) believe a Mexican American locksmith (Michael Pena) is a gang member and a crook, but he is a family man.

5    A black cop (Don Cheadle) is having an affair with his Latina partner (Jennifer Esposito), but never gets it straight which country she's from. A cop (Matt Dillon) thinks a light-skinned black woman (Thandie Newton) is white. When a white producer tells a black TV director (Terrence Dashon Howard) that a black character "doesn't sound black enough," it never occurs to him that the director doesn't "sound black," either. For that matter, neither do two young black men (Larenz Tate and Ludacris), who dress and act like college students, but have a surprise for us.

6    You see how it goes. Along the way, these people say exactly what they are thinking, without the filters of political correctness. The district attorney's wife is so frightened by a street encounter that she has the locks changed, then assumes the locksmith will be back with his "homies" to attack them. The white cop can't get medical care for his dying father, and accuses a black woman at his HMO with taking advantage of preferential racial treatment. The Iranian can't understand what the locksmith is trying to tell him, freaks out, and buys a gun to protect himself. The gun dealer and the Iranian get into a shouting match.

7    I make this sound almost like episodic TV, but Haggis writes with such directness and such a good ear for everyday speech that the characters seem

real and plausible after only a few words. His cast is uniformly strong; the actors sidestep cliches and make their characters particular.

8     For me, the strongest performance is by Matt Dillon, as the racist cop in anguish over his father. He makes an unnecessary traffic stop when he thinks he sees the black TV director and his light-skinned wife doing something they really shouldn't be doing at the same time they're driving. True enough, but he wouldn't have stopped a black couple or a white couple. He humiliates the woman with an invasive body search, while her husband is forced to stand by powerless, because the cops have the guns—Dillon, and also a liberal young cop (Ryan Phillippe), who hates what he's seeing but has to back up his partner.

9     That traffic stop shows Dillon's cop as vile and hateful. But later we see him trying to care for his sick father, and we understand why he explodes at the HMO worker (whose race is only an excuse for his anger). He victimizes others by exercising his power, and is impotent when it comes to helping his father. Then the plot turns ironically on itself, and both of the cops find themselves, in very different ways, saving the lives of the very same TV director and his wife. Is this just manipulative storytelling? It didn't feel that way to me, because it serves a deeper purpose than mere irony: Haggis is telling parables, in which the characters learn the lessons they have earned by their behavior.

10     Other cross-cutting Los Angeles stories come to mind, especially Lawrence Kasden's more optimistic *Grand Canyon* and Robert Altman's more humanistic *Short Cuts*. But *Crash* finds a way of its own. It shows the way we all leap to conclusions based on race—yes, all of us, of all races, and however fair-minded we may try to be—and we pay a price for that. If there is hope in the story, it comes because as the characters crash into one another, they learn things, mostly about themselves. Almost all of them are still alive at the end, and are better people because of what has happened to them. Not happier, not calmer, not even wiser, but better. Then there are those few who kill or get killed; racism has tragedy built in.

11     Not many films have the possibility of making their audiences better people. I don't expect *Crash* to work any miracles, but I believe anyone seeing it is likely to be moved to have a little more sympathy for people not like themselves. The movie contains hurt, coldness and cruelty, but is it without hope? Not at all. Stand back and consider. All of these people, superficially so different, share the city and learn that they share similar fears and hopes. Until several hundred years ago, most people everywhere on earth never saw anybody who didn't look like them. They were not racist because, as far as they knew, there was only one race. You may have to look hard to see it, but *Crash* is a film about progress.

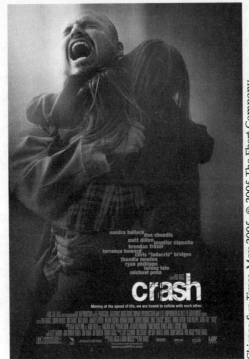

## Bigotry as the Outer Side of Inner Angst

### *A. O. Scott, film critic,* The New York Times

1    What kind of movie is *Crash*? It belongs to a genre that has been flourishing in recent years—at least in the esteem of critics—but that still lacks a name. A provisional list of examples might include *Monster's Ball*, *House of Sand and Fog* and *21 Grams*. In each of these films, as in *Crash*, Americans from radically different backgrounds are brought together by a grim serendipity that forces them, or at least the audience, to acknowledge their essential connectedness.

2    The look of these movies and the rough authenticity of their locations create an atmosphere of naturalism that is meant to give force to their rigorously pessimistic view of American life. The performances, often by some of the finest screen actors working today, have the dense texture and sober discipline that we associate with realism. But to classify these movies as realistic would be misleading, as the stories they tell are, in nearly every

respect, preposterous, and they tend to be governed less by the spirit of observation than by superstition.

3    This is not necessarily bad, and some of these movies are very good indeed. But in approaching *Crash,* we should be more than usually cautious about mistaking its inhabitants—residents of Los Angeles of various hues, temperaments and occupations—for actual human beings. This may not be easy, for they are played by people of such graven, complex individuality as Matt Dillon, Don Cheadle and Terrence Howard, as well as by less established but equally gifted actors like Michael Pena and Chris Bridges (better known to the world by his rap name, Ludacris).

4    Their characters—and the dozen or so others whose lives intersect in the course of an exceedingly eventful day and a half—may have names, addresses, families and jobs, but they are, at bottom, ciphers in an allegorical scheme dreamed up by Paul Haggis, the screenwriter (most recently of Clint Eastwood's *Million Dollar Baby*), here making his directorial debut.

5    As he demonstrated to galvanizing effect in the *Million Dollar Baby* script, Mr. Haggis is not unduly concerned with subtlety. At a time when ambitious movies are dominated by knowing cleverness and showy sensation, he makes a case for blunt, earnest emotion, and shows an admirable willingness to risk sentimentality and cliché in the pursuit of genuine feeling. Many of the scenes in *Crash* unfold with great dramatic power, even when they lack a credible narrative or psychological motive.

6    Mr. Haggis's evident sincerity and intelligence are reflected in the conviction of the cast, and may also leave an impression on the audience. So much feeling, so much skill, so much seriousness, such an urgent moral agenda— all of this must surely answer our collective hunger for a good movie, or even a great one, about race and class in a modern American city.

7    Not even close. *Crash* writes its themes in capital letters—Race, Class, Life, Fate—and then makes them the subjects of a series of speeches and the pivot points for a succession of clumsy reversals. The first speech, which doubles as introductory voice-over narration, is by Mr. Cheadle's character, a detective named Graham, addressing his partner (and lover), Ria (Jennifer Esposito), after their car has been in a minor accident. He takes the event as a metaphor for the disjunctive, isolated character of life in Los Angeles, while she insists that it is merely a literal, physical occurrence that requires a practical response.

8    It does not take long to figure out whose side Mr. Haggis is on. Metaphor hangs in the California air like smog (or like the snow that is incongruously falling on the Hollywood Hills). The other major element in the atmosphere is intolerance. Ria, who is Hispanic, climbs out of the car and confronts the other driver, an Asian-American woman, and before long their argument

has descended into racial name-calling. This sets the pattern for just about every other conversation in the movie.

9      In the next scene, which takes place earlier on the previous day, a hot-tempered Iranian shopkeeper is insulted by the owner of a gun store, who calls him "Osama." And so it goes, slur by slur, until we come full circle, to the original accident, after which a few lingering questions are resolved.

10     In the meantime, quite a lot happens. Guns are pulled, cars are stolen, children are endangered, cars flip over, and many angry, hurtful words are exchanged, all of it threaded together by Mr. Haggis's quick, emphatic direction and Mark Isham's maundering electronic score.

11     Mr. Haggis is eager to show the complexities of his many characters, which means that each one will show exactly two sides. A racist white police officer will turn out to be physically courageous and devoted to his ailing father; his sensitive white partner will engage in some deadly racial profiling; a young black man who sees racial profiling everywhere will turn out to be a carjacker; a wealthy, mild-mannered black man will pull out a gun and start screaming. No one is innocent. There's good and bad in everyone. (The exception is Mr. Pena's character, a Mexican-American locksmith who is an island of quiet decency in a sea of howling prejudice and hypocrisy).

12     That these bromides count as insights may say more about the state of the American civic conversation than about Mr. Haggis's limitations as a storyteller, and there is no doubt that he is trying to dig into the unhappiness and antagonism that often simmer below the placid surface of everyday life. "I'm angry all the time, and I don't know why," says Jean (Sandra Bullock), the wife of the city's district attorney (Brendan Fraser), the day after their S.U.V. has been stolen at gunpoint.

13     Her condition is all but universal in Mr. Haggis's city, but its avenues of expression are overwrought and implausible. The idea that bigotry is the public face of private unhappiness—the notion that we lash out at people we don't know as a form of displaced revenge against the more familiar sources of our misery—is an interesting one, but the failure of *Crash* is that it states its ideas, again and again, without realizing them in coherent dramatic form.

14     It is at once tangled and threadbare; at times you have trouble keeping track of all the characters, but they run into one another with such frequency that, by the end, you start to think that the population of Los Angeles County must number in the mid-two figures—all of it strangers who hate one another on sight.

15     So what kind of a movie is *Crash*? A frustrating movie: full of heart and devoid of life; crudely manipulative when it tries hardest to be subtle; and profoundly complacent in spite of its intention to unsettle and disturb.

---

## Works Cited

*Crash.* Dir. Paul Haggis. Perf. Sandra Bullock, Don Cheadle, Matt Dillon, Jennifer Esposito, Brendan Fraser, Terrence Howard, Chris (Ludacris) Bridges, Thandie Newton, and Michael Peña. Lions Gate, 2004. Film.

Denby, David. "Angry People." Rev. of *Crash.* Dir. Paul Haggis. *The New Yorker.* 2 May 2005: 110–111. Print.

Ebert, Roger. "*Crash.*" Rev. of *Crash.* Dir. Paul Haggis. *rogerebert.com. Chicago Sun-Times,* 5 May 2005. Web. 19 July 2005.

Scott, A. O. "Bigotry as the Outer Side of Inner Angst." Rev. of *Crash.* Dir. Paul Haggis. *newyorktimes.com, The New York Times,* 6 May 2005. Web. 29 June 2004.

## THINKING ABOUT THE FILM

1. Our first impression of every character changes as the film progresses. Describe how you see each of these characters initially and then at the end of the film:

   - Anthony, the car thief
   - Peter, Graham's brother and Anthony's accomplice
   - Officer Ryan
   - Jean, the district attorney's wife
   - Cameron, the television director
   - Graham, the detective
   - Tommy, the rookie cop

2. In addition to the audience's altered impressions of the characters, how do the characters' impressions of each other change as the film progresses?

3. Identify the social conditions that put pressure on well-intentioned individuals like Graham (the detective), Tommy (the rookie cop), and Cameron (the TV director).

4. What insights about stereotyping does the film ultimately offer the viewer?

## WRITING FROM THE FILM

1. Write a paper contrasting your initial impressions of several main characters with your perceptions of them by the end of the film. Use specific details to illustrate your points.

2. In the opening of the film, the detective, Graham, claims that people in the city miss a sense of touch so much that "we crash into each other just so we can feel something." Write an essay evaluating this statement as a reflection of the film and include specific scenes to support your views.

3. Write an essay that analyzes how racism and cultural stereotypes function as an insidious force in this film.

4. After Cameron, the television director, hides Anthony from the police, Cameron tells the young car thief, "You embarrass me; you embarrass yourself." Write an essay showing how this line might be delivered by a family member to Jean, to Graham's mother, and to the Iranian father.

## CONNECTING WITH OTHER TEXTS

1. Read David Denby's review of *Crash* in the film analysis section of Chapter 11, pp. 426–435. Denby views *Crash* as a strong film, "hyper-articulate and often breathtakingly intelligent and always brazenly alive" (430). In contrast, A. O. Scott claims that *Crash* is "a frustrating movie: full of heart and devoid of life; crudely manipulative when it tries hardest to be subtle; and profoundly complacent in spite of its intention to un-settle and disturb" (140). Write an essay comparing and contrasting these two views, and supporting or refuting either critic.

2. In his review, Roger Ebert observes that the characters "learn things, mostly about themselves. Almost all of them are still alive at the end, and are better people because of what has happened to them" (137). Focusing on any three characters, write an analysis of what they have learned and in what specific ways they are better people.

3. Read "Black Men and Public Space" (p. 164) and especially Staples's de-scription of his boyhood friends who were "seduced by the perception of themselves as tough guys" (167). In an essay illustrate how *Crash* drama-tizes the "bravado" that Staples describes and condemns.

# Chapter 4

# Between Perceptions

How we perceive ourselves is intrinsically related to our racial and ethnic roots, as well as to our gender. Our sense of self, however, goes beyond any definition of male or female, race or culture. Self-perception is often conditioned by the roles we assume—as students, workers, family members—but our self-image and how others see us may be distinct from the roles we play. You regard yourself as a college student, but when you are at home you might be the "baby" in the family, or the one diapering the baby. You know that by working extra hours you can earn much-needed overtime pay, but your perception of yourself as an "A" student prompts you to cut back on hours instead. A woman who is physically disabled may not define herself as "handicapped," and a man who qualifies for financial assistance may not see himself as "disadvantaged." Perceiving oneself beyond labels or stereotypes is an essential process, as the readings in this chapter indicate.

However, others' images of you do influence your self-perception. If you feel that you are constantly trying to exist among worlds that perceive you differently, you will relate to the tensions described in the essays by Matthew Soyster and Jennifer Coleman as they resist others' limited perceptions of them. Dan Slater's essay reveals how the extent of his stuttering is conditioned by people's responses to him and his impediment. Their essays express the frustrations of productive individuals whose self-acceptance is threatened by the delimiting views of others. The critically-acclaimed film *The King's Speech*, reviewed by Philip French, dramatizes the personal struggle of the Duke of York to manage his speech impediment as he becomes King of England.

Martin Luther King Jr. and Carol Tavris argue that we must take a stand as individuals to correct social injustice.

Self-perception can be altered in a moment of intense reflection, as we see in the epiphanies narrated by John Vaughn and Max Thayer. Focusing on her own life epiphanies, J. K. Rowling, the creator of the *Harry Potter* series, encourages readers to perceive the benefit of "failure" and the "crucial importance of imagination" in our lives. Our perceptions of others and their life choices can alter from one generation to the next, as Stephen Perry shows in his poem.

Sometimes negative self-perceptions may prompt people to make unwise choices that threaten their health. Pamela Erens chronicles the problems of many women who have eating disorders and who struggle toward self-understanding and acceptance rather than perpetuating destructive behavior. Neil Steinberg humorously accepts the fact that he's fat even as he regrets the attitudes of some thin people around him. In contrast, Jane E. Brody wants to change people's complacent perception of obesity and improve everyone's eating habits. Dan Neil wants to alter his readers' judgmental perceptions of homosexuality, arguing that sexual orientation is as innate in homosexuals as it is in heterosexuals.

To be perceived as an individual rather than as a racial or ethnic stereotype may be a challenge for you or some of your friends. Fighting stereotypes can be life-threatening, as Brent Staples reveals in his essay. Balancing how others see us with who we think we are is the condition of being between perceptions—and the basis of the writings in this chapter.

## Living Under Circe's Spell
### *Matthew Soyster*

A freelance writer, editor, and college instructor, Matthew Soyster (b. 1954) earned a BA in French and Italian literature from Stanford and an MA in English and Norwegian literature from the University of California, Berkeley. His work has appeared in *Newsweek*, *Stanford Magazine*, the *San Francisco Examiner*, and numerous other publications. Soyster has been associate editor of *Change Magazine* and a repeated guest on KPFA-FM radio, discussing images of the disabled—"Monster/Victim/Hero"—in Western film literature and popular culture. In 1989 he organized a $10,000 benefit concert for the Multiple Sclerosis Society, and in 1991 he wrote and performed "Shape Shifter," a monologue for the premiere of the Contemporary Dance Company at a Berkeley theater. The following article appeared in *Newsweek* in 1993.

1    "Life is brief, time's a thief." This ribbon of pop lyricism keens from an apartment-house radio into the hot afternoon air. Across the street I am

sprawled in the gutter behind my minivan, bits of glass and scrap metal chewing at my knees and elbows, a cut on my hand beginning to well crimson.

2    There has been no assailant, no wound except to my psyche. I'm just a clumsy cripple whose legs buckled before he reached his wheelchair. A moment ago I yanked it from my tailgate, as I've done a thousand times. But when it spun off at a crazy angle I missed the seat and slumped to the ground.

3    Now the spasms start, shooting outward from the small of my back, forcing me prone, grinding my cheek into the asphalt. What will I look like to the first casual passerby before he catches sight of the telltale chair? A wine-soaked rummy? A hit-and-run victim? Maybe an amateur mechanic checking the rear suspension, wrong side up.

4    I'm too young and vital looking to be this helpless. I shrink from the inevitable clucking and concern. Then again, this isn't the best neighborhood. The first person to come along may simply kick me and take my wallet. No wonder I'm ambivalent about rescue, needing but not wanting to be discovered. With detachment I savor the hush of this deserted street, the symphony of birdsong in the treetops.

5    I am trying to remember T. S. Eliot's line about waiting without hope, because hope would be hope for the wrong thing. Instead, that idiot TV commercial for the medical alarm-pager keeps ringing through my brain: "Help me. I've fallen and I can't get up."

6    It was only a matter of time. I've known for months that my hair's-breadth maneuvering would eventually fail me. For years, in fact. When I first learned that I had multiple sclerosis I was a marathon runner and white-water-rafting guide, a cyclist and skier, the quintessential California golden boy. Cardiovascular fitness had long since become our state religion. I lived for and through my legs.

7    But that's only the ad-slick surface of the California dream, the sunshine without the shadow. The town I live in is also the mecca of the disabled, the home of the Independent Living Movement, the place where broken people come to patch together their dignity and their dreams.

8    Yin and yang. In Berkeley, there are wheelchair users on every corner. Propped in sagging hospital-issue chairs. Space-age sports chairs. Motor-driven dreadnoughts. When I could still walk, I crossed the street to avoid them. What an odd tribe they seemed, with their spindly, agitated limbs, always hurtling down the avenue on some manic errand.

9    How could I imagine my own swift decline? A few months or years passed. Soon I was relying on a cane, then crutches, and finally—after many thigh-bruising falls and a numbness so intense it turned my legs to driftwood—a wheelchair. My response to these limitations was compensation and denial.

I thought I could become a disabled Olympian: wheelchair racing, tennis, rugby. I thought I could go on as before.

10    Wrong again. To paraphrase Tolstoy, all able-bodied people are alike, but each disabled person is crippled in his own way. MS not only played havoc with my upper-body strength and agility; it clouded my mind and sapped my energy. I could totter a few steps supported at both wrists, but my days in the winter surf, high peaks and desert canyons were over.

11    So what is it like to spend your life forked at the waist, face-level with children? The syndrome has been amply described. People see through me now, or over me. They don't see me at all. Or they fix me with that plangent, aching stare: sympathy.

12    They offer too much assistance, scurrying to open doors, scrambling out of my way with unnecessary apologies, or they leave me no space at all, barking their shins on my foot pedals. My spirit rallies in the face of such humiliations; they have their comic aspect. What disturbs me most is not how others see me, but how I've lost my vision of myself.

13    Growing crippled is a bitch. First your body undergoes a strange enchantment: Circe's spell. Then your identity gives way. You become someone or something other, but for a long time you're not sure what that other is.

14    Along the way, I've had to give up activities and passions that define me, my safe position in society, my very sense of manhood. In our species, the pecking order is distinctly vertical. True for women. Doubly true for men. A man stands tall, stands firm, stands up for things. These are more than metaphors. The very act of sitting implies demotion. Anyone who's witnessed boardroom politics knows this much. Have a seat, barks the boss. It's not an invitation, it's an order.

15    All of this brings me back to the gutter, where I lie listening to birdsong, recognizing but not apologizing for the obstinacy that landed me here. For months my friends and family have watched my legs grow weaker. They've prodded me relentlessly to refit my van with a wheelchair lift in order to avoid just this disaster. But I've refused.

16    Twice a day at least, I've dragged my reluctant legs from beneath the steering column, hauled myself erect beside the driver's seat, inched my way down the roof rail to the rear stowage. And removed the chair by hand, standing.

17    Why have I clung to this ritual, knowing it's dangerous and futile? It's the only task I rise for anymore, in a sitting life. For a moment in the driver's doorway, I'm in control, unreliant on technology or assistance, upright. Or so I've told myself. But that moment is so fragile, the control so illusory.

18    When the time comes to change, I've said, I'll know.

19    Now I know.

20    I feel the lesson, sharp as the rap of a Zen master's stick. Lying in the hot gutter, I take a deep breath and my whole body relaxes. Tuning in to Rod Stewart's tinny wisdom from the window. Listening for a passing car or pedestrian.

21    Waiting.

## THINKING ABOUT THE TEXT

1. This essay opens with the writer "sprawled in the gutter" and ends with him still "waiting" for a passing car or pedestrian to help. Analyze the effect of creating such a scene to prompt his discussion and of using the present tense (even though this event happened in the past).

2. Describe, in detail, the writer's life and his attitude about the disabled before he himself became "a clumsy cripple."

3. Soyster explains, "What disturbs me most is not how others see me, but how I've lost my vision of myself" (146). What does he mean by this, and how does his threatened self-image relate to his refusal to refit his van with a wheelchair lift?

4. Throughout this essay Soyster includes a number of *allusions*—indirect references to sources outside the work: pop lyrics, singer Rod Stewart, poet T. S. Eliot, novelist Leo Tolstoy, the myth of Circe, the Zen religion, and yin and yang. Look up these allusions in a dictionary, reader's encyclopedia, or online and explain how each contributes to your understanding of the writer and his perspective.

## WRITING FROM THE TEXT

1. Using the information you gathered for exercise 4, write an essay explaining how the allusions in this essay are essential to helping us see the writer as a unique and intriguing individual and not just "a clumsy cripple."

2. Write about an event in your life that caused you to lose a vision of yourself. Dramatize your life before this crisis or event and contrast it with your current life.

## CONNECTING WITH OTHER TEXTS

1. Matthew Soyster and Shannon Paaske (p. 342) both examine the attitudes that many harbor toward the disabled. Using details from these works, write an essay supporting your own thesis about how and why people feel uneasy around the disabled—and what can be done about it.

2. Matthew Soyster, Brent Staples (p. 164), and Jennifer Coleman (p. 175), and Don Slater (p. 195), describe how others have incorrectly stereotyped

and humiliated them. Using details from any of these narratives and from "Don't Let Stereotypes Warp Your Judgments" (p. 424), write an analysis of the causes and effects of such stereotyping on the stereotyped person and on the one doing the stereotyping.

# The Difference Between Pity and Empathy
## *John A. Vaughn*

Serving as both physician and senior editor for Health Care Multi-Media Communications at the Ohio State University Student Health Services, John A. Vaughn (b. 1971) has been able to combine his talents as a doctor and a writer. In addition to practicing medicine, Vaughn has written numerous reviews of medical books as well as guest columns and articles for publications such as the *Los Angeles Times*, the *San Francisco Chronicle*, and the *Cleveland Plain Dealer*. Vaughn offers this advice for student writers: "Read as much and as widely as possible. Revise, revise, revise. Always remember that no matter how fantastic the situation, it is the personal element of a story that connects to your reader." The following essay first appeared in the *Los Angeles Times*, March 28, 2005, and clearly shows that Vaughn follows his own advice.

1    He was the first patient I cared for in medical school. At first glance, he looked pretty good. He sat on the covers of his hospital bed in a button-down shirt that was tucked neatly into creased khakis. His shoes gleamed from polish.

2    But I quickly saw that the fastidious clothes were a disguise. His skin looked like old china: yellowed and glassy with a damp patina. His dyed blond hair was matted down in a wide part and his precisely trimmed mustache was covered by a fine mist of sweat.

3    He had AIDS, Pneumocystis pneumonia clogged his lungs, cytomegalovirus retinitis clouded his eyes and Kaposi's sarcoma ulcerated his esophagus. He was dying an agonizing death. And he was only 30. I stumbled through my painfully thorough evaluation, pulling reflex hammers, flashlights and tuning forks out of my lab coat like a bad magician.

4    I did a rectal exam to check for internal bleeding and gamely tried to explain the mechanics of the exam—only to be met with a statement that he was gay, followed by a humorless joke about his sexual practices.

5    Despite my inexperience, I knew that men often deflect their embarrassment at this exam with locker room humor. But his comment still caught me off guard. I awkwardly laughed at the joke and pulled gloves onto my shaking hands.

6    Apparently this wasn't the response he was looking for, because as he dropped his pants he continued, this time with a comment about romance.

7    He wasn't simply deflecting his embarrassment; he was throwing it back at me with as much resentment as he could muster. My first instinct was to retaliate. To say "Hey, pal, don't blame me. You got yourself in this mess. I'm just trying to help." Instead, I finished the exam in silence and left the room as quickly as possible. We were both so furious and afraid; he at being eaten away by this horrible disease, and me at feeling like an inadequate idiot because I had no idea how to help him.

8    I went to visit him the next day, determined that things would go better. His room revealed no signs of a life beyond its walls: not a single get-well card tacked to the bulletin board, not one little fold-up tent card on the bedside table notifying him of a missed call from a friend. I had never seen someone so alone. I asked him what he did for a living. He told me that he worked in computer networking and was hoping to finish his design for a new audiovisual coupling technique before he died.

9    He said it was his last chance to make a mark on the world. This seemed to sadden him more than his physical suffering; it wasn't that his life was ending, but that he would have so little to show for it.

10    I asked him about his family. Unlike many gay AIDS victims, his parents were tolerant of his lifestyle and even offered to care for him during his illness. I offered to call them but he adamantly refused. He said it would be too hard on his mom.

11    The familiarity with which he said this caught my breath. The outside world flooded into the room, and I suddenly saw this man not as a patient, but as someone's son. I finally got a taste of the anguish he was trying to make me feel the day before. His condition worsened precipitously the next night and I finally convinced him to let me call his parents. They said they would leave as soon as they could but they lived in New Jersey, nine hours away.

12    He died during rounds the following morning. As his pupils dilated and his breathing became a rhythmic, mechanical gasp, his nurse reached out and held his hand. I grabbed his other wrist as if to check for a pulse, hoping the gesture appeared sufficiently clinical to my attending physician.

13    An hour later, his parents called from a rest stop in Pennsylvania about four hours away. I thought his mother would be more upset, but I got the feeling, that she expected things to end this way. He had underestimated her; she had been strong enough to respect his need to spare her suffering, even though she knew it meant that she might never see him again. He had underestimated himself too. He never saw the doctor that he helped me

become, but every patient I have cared for since has benefited from the lesson he taught me.

14    I had leaned into our conversations with all the sympathetic voice inflections and reassuring touches I could muster from my doctor-patient relationship class. But I had looked at him with pity, not empathy, and he saw right through me. It wasn't until he made me see him as a person that I was able to effectively treat him as my patient. The mark he made on the world extended further than he'd imagined.

## THINKING ABOUT THE TEXT

1. How does Vaughn's detailed description of his patient both prepare readers for his patient's illness and yet shock readers as they discover that the patient is only 30 and yet "dying an agonizing death"? What are his AIDS-related ailments?

2. Why are both doctor and patient "furious and afraid"? What seems to sadden the patient more than his physical suffering and imminent death?

3. What prompts the new doctor to see his patient differently? Explain the doctor's before-and-after perceptions of his patient.

4. What lasting legacy has the patient left this world? Explain Vaughn's distinction between pity and empathy.

## WRITING FROM THE TEXT

1. Using illustrations from Vaughn's work, write an essay contrasting "pity" and "empathy" in order to support the author's argument that the latter is essential for the best patient care. You may include illustrations of doctors whom you've known to support Vaughn's claims.

2. Write an essay describing a situation when you initially felt pity for another or were pitied by someone—and then later when that emotion changed to empathy. Let the reader see what prompted the change and how it affected the way you reacted.

## CONNECTING WITH OTHER TEXTS

1. Using Vaughn's essay, Quiñones-Hinojosa's "Terra Firma" (p. 102), and Soyster's "Living Under Circe's Spell" (p. 144), write an essay demonstrating the importance of empathy, rather than pity, in the treatment of those with an illness.

2. Including details from Vaughn's essay, "The Color of Love" (p. 15), and "The Only Child" (p. 33), write an essay analyzing the barriers to empathizing with others, as well as ways to overcome these barriers.

#  In Groups We Shrink
### *Carol Tavris*

After studying sociology and comparative literature at Brandeis, Carol Tavris (b. 1944) earned her PhD in social psychology at the University of Michigan. Tavris has worked as a freelance writer, taught in UCLA's psychology department, written for *Vogue*, *Harper's*, and *G.Q.*, and served as an editor for *Psychology Today*. She has published extensively in the field of psychology, with emphasis on emotions, anger, sexuality, and gender issues. She has taught at the New School for Social Research in New York City since 1983. Her works include *The Mismeasure of Woman* (1992), *Psychobabble & Biobunk: Using Psychology to Think Critically About Issues in the News: Opinions, Essays and Book Reviews* (2001), *Mistakes Were Made (But Not by Me): Why We Justify Foolish Beliefs, Bad Decisions, and Hurtful Acts* (2007). The essay printed here appeared in the *Los Angeles Times* in 1991.

1    The ghost of Kitty Genovese would sympathize with Rodney King. Genovese, you may remember, is the symbol of bystander apathy in America. Screaming for help, she was stabbed repeatedly and killed in front of her New York apartment, and not one of the 38 neighbors who heard her, including those who came to their windows to watch, even called for help.

2    One of the things we find appalling in the videotape of King's assault is the image of at least 11 police officers watching four of their colleagues administer the savage beating and doing nothing to intervene. Whatever is the matter with them, we wonder.

3    Something happens to individuals when they collect in a group. They think and act differently than they would on their own. Most people, if they observe some disaster or danger on their own—a woman being stabbed, a pedestrian slammed by a hit-and-run driver—will at least call for help; many will even risk their own safety to intervene. But if they are in a group observing the same danger, they hold back. The reason is not necessarily that they are lazy, cowardly or have 50 other personality deficiencies; it has more to do with the nature of groups than the nature of individuals.

4    In one experiment in behavioral psychology, students were seated in a room, either alone or in groups of three, as a staged emergency occurred: Smoke began pouring through the vents. Students who were on their own usually hesitated a minute, got up, checked the vents and then went out to

report what certainly seemed like fire. But the students who were sitting in groups of three did not move. They sat there for six minutes, with smoke so thick they could barely see, rubbing their eyes and coughing.

5    In another experiment, psychologists staged a situation in which people overheard a loud crash, a scream and a woman in pain, moaning that her ankle was broken. Seventy percent of those who were alone when the "accident" occurred went to her aid, compared with only 40 percent of those who heard her in the presence of another person.

6    For victims, obviously, there is no safety in numbers. Why? One reason is that if other people aren't doing anything, the individual assumes that nothing needs to be done. In the smoke-filled room study, the students in groups said they thought that the smoke was caused by "steam pipes," "truth gas" or "leaks in the air conditioning"; not one said what the students on their own did: "I thought it was fire." In the lady-in-distress study, some of those who failed to offer help said, "I didn't want to embarrass her."

7    Often, observers think nothing needs to be done because someone else has already taken care of it, and the more observers there are, the less likely any one person is to call for help. In Albuquerque, New Mexico, 30 people watched for an hour and a half as a building burned to the ground before they realized that no one had called the fire department. Psychologists call this process "diffusion of responsibility" or "social loafing": The more people in a group, the lazier each individual in it becomes.

8    But there was no mistaking what those officers were doing to Rodney King. There was no way for those observers to discount the severity of the beating King was getting. What kept them silent?

9    One explanation, of course, is that they approved. They may have identified with the abusers, vicariously participating in a beating they rationalized as justified. The widespread racism in the Los Angeles Police Department and the unprovoked abuse of black people is now undeniable. A friend who runs a trucking company told me recently that one of her drivers, a 50-year-old black man, is routinely pulled over by Los Angeles cops for the flimsiest of reasons "and made to lie down on the street like a dog." None of her white drivers has been treated this way.

10    Or the observers may have hated what was happening and been caught in the oldest of human dilemmas: Do the moral thing and be disliked, humiliated, embarrassed and rejected. Our nation, for all its celebration of the Lone Ranger and the independent pioneer, does not really value the individual— at least not when the person is behaving individually and standing up to the group. (We like dissenters, but only when they are dissenting in Russia or China.) Again and again, countless studies have shown that people will go along rather than risk the embarrassment of being disobedient, rude or disloyal.

11    And so the banality of evil is once again confirmed. Most people do not behave badly because they are inherently bad. They behave badly because they aren't paying attention, or they leave it to Harry, or they don't want to rock the boat, or they don't want to embarrass themselves or others if they're wrong.

12    Every time the news reports another story of a group that has behaved mindlessly, violently and stupidly, including the inevitable members who are just "going along," many people shake their heads in shock and anger at the failings of "human nature." But the findings of behavioral research can direct us instead to appreciate the conditions under which individuals in groups will behave morally or not. Once we know the conditions, we can begin to prescribe antidotes. By understanding the impulse to diffuse responsibility, perhaps as individuals we will be more likely to act. By understanding the social pressures that reward groupthink, loyalty and obedience, we can foster those that reward whistle-blowing and moral courage. And, as a society, we can reinforce the belief that they also sin who only stand and watch.

## THINKING ABOUT THE TEXT

1. What is Tavris's thesis? How does she support her position?

2. How does the psychologist's term for the behavior Tavris describes explain what actually happens?

3. How does Tavris imagine this condition will right itself?

## WRITING FROM THE TEXT

1. Write about an incident that you observed or were a part of that confirms Carol Tavris's point.

2. Write about an incident that you observed or were a part of that shows an exception to Tavris's point.

## CONNECTING WITH OTHER TEXTS

1. Read "Discrimination at Large" (p. 175) and argue that people's ridicule of fat people is often part of a group dynamic. Use Tavris's reasoning to show how people in groups sanction such ridicule. As part of your essay, consider Coleman's suggestion that the group can work as a whole to exert pressure on those who discriminate against the fat.

2. Research the Rodney King incident of 1991 to find interviews and court testimony from the police officers involved as participants or observers of the beating. Do their own words and feelings confirm or refute Tavris's thesis?

# The Fringe Benefits of Failure, and the Importance of Imagination

### *J. K. Rowling*

The author of the world-famous *Harry Potter* fantasies that have sold nearly 400 million copies, Joanne "Jo" Rowling (b. 1965), who writes under the name J. K. Rowling, is a graduate of Exeter University and a teacher. She is almost as famous for her rise to millionaire status from being an unemployed single parent on welfare as she is for her popular books. Rowling's fortune, estimated at $1.1 billion, is philanthropically used to support such charities as Comic Relief, One Parent Families, and the Multiple Sclerosis Society of Great Britain. Noting her social, moral, and political commitments, in 2007 *Time* magazine named her a runner-up for its Person of the Year Award. Rowling's humanity and wisdom are evident in the text of her June 2008 Harvard University Commencement Address, reprinted here.

1    President Faust, members of the Harvard Corporation and the Board of Overseers, members of the faculty, proud parents, and, above all, graduates.

2    The first thing I would like to say is 'thank you.' Not only has Harvard given me an extraordinary honour, but the weeks of fear and nausea I've experienced at the thought of giving this commencement address have made me lose weight. A win-win situation! Now all I have to do is take deep breaths, squint at the red banners and fool myself into believing I am at the world's best-educated Harry Potter convention.

3    Delivering a commencement address is a great responsibility; or so I thought until I cast my mind back to my own graduation. The commencement speaker that day was the distinguished British philosopher Baroness Mary Warnock. Reflecting on her speech has helped me enormously in writing this one, because it turns out that I can't remember a single word she said. This liberating discovery enables me to proceed without any fear that I might inadvertently influence you to abandon promising careers in business, law or politics for the giddy delights of becoming a gay wizard.

4    You see? If all you remember in years to come is the 'gay wizard' joke, I've still come out ahead of Baroness Mary Warnock. Achievable goals: the first step towards personal improvement.

5    Actually, I have wracked my mind and heart for what I ought to say to you today. I have asked myself what I wish I had known at my own graduation, and what important lessons I have learned in the 21 years that has expired between that day and this.

6    I have come up with two answers. On this wonderful day when we are gathered together to celebrate your academic success, I have decided to talk

to you about the benefits of failure. And as you stand on the threshold of what is sometimes called 'real life,' I want to extol the crucial importance of imagination.

7    These might seem quixotic or paradoxical choices, but please bear with me.

8    Looking back at the 21-year-old that I was at graduation, is a slightly uncomfortable experience for the 42-year-old that she has become. Half my lifetime ago, I was striking an uneasy balance between the ambition I had for myself, and what those closest to me expected of me.

9    I was convinced that the only thing I wanted to do, ever, was to write novels. However, my parents, both of whom came from improverished backgrounds and neither of whom had been to college, took the view that my overactive imagination was an amusing personal quirk that could never pay a mortgage, or secure a pension.

10    They had hoped that I would take a vocational degree; I wanted to study English Literature. A compromise was reached that in retrospect satisfied nobody, and I went up to study Modern Languages. Hardly had my parents' car rounded the corner at the end of the road than I ditched German and scuttled off down the Classics corridor.

11    I cannot remember telling my parents that I was studying Classics; they might well have found out for the first time on graduation day. Of all subjects on this planet, I think they would have been hard put to name one less useful than Greek mythology when it came to securing the keys to an executive bathroom.

12    I would like to make it clear, in parenthesis, that I do not blame my parents for their point of view. There is an expiry date on blaming your parents for steering you in the wrong direction; the moment you are old enough to take the wheel, responsibility lies with you. What is more, I cannot criticise my parents for hoping that I would never experience poverty. They had been poor themselves, and I have since been poor, and I quite agree with them that it is not an ennobling experience. Poverty entails fear, and stress, and sometimes depression; it means a thousand petty humiliations and hardships. Climbing out of poverty by your own efforts, that is indeed something on which to pride yourself, but poverty itself is romanticised only by fools.

13    What I feared most for myself at your age was not poverty, but failure.

14    At your age, in spite of a distinct lack of motivation at university, where I had spent far too long in the coffee bar writing stories, and far too little time at lectures, I had a knack for passing examinations, and that, for years, had been the measure of success in my life and that of my peers.

15    I am not dull enough to suppose that because you are young, gifted and well-educated, you have never known hardship or heartbreak.

Talent and intelligence never yet inoculated anyone against the caprice of the Fates, and I do not for a moment suppose that everyone here has enjoyed an existence of unruffled privilege and contentment.

16      However, the fact that you are graduating from Harvard suggests that you are not very well-acquainted with failure. You might be driven by a fear of failure quite as much as a desire for success. Indeed, your conception of failure might not be too far from the average person's idea of success, so high have you already flown academically.

17      Ultimately, we all have to decide for ourselves what constitutes failure, but the world is quite eager to give you a set of criteria if you let it. So I think it fair to say that by any conventional measure, a mere seven years after my graduation day, I had failed on an epic scale. An exceptionally short-lived marriage had imploded, and I was jobless, a lone parent, and as poor as it is possible to be in modern Britain, without being homeless. The fears my parents had had for me, and that I had had for myself, had both come to pass, and by every usual standard, I was the biggest failure I knew.

18      Now, I am not going to stand here and tell you that failure is fun. That period of my life was a dark one, and I had no idea that there was going to be what the press has since represented as a kind of fairy tale resolution. I had no idea how far the tunnel extended, and for a long time, any light at the end of it was a hope rather than a reality.

19      So why do I talk about the benefits of failure? Simply because failure meant a stripping away of the inessential. I stopped pretending to myself that I was anything other than what I was, and began to direct all my energy into finishing the only work that mattered to me. Had I really succeeded at anything else, I might never have found the determination to succeed in the one arena I believed I truly belonged. I was set free, because my greatest fear had already been realised, and I was still alive, and I still had a daughter whom I adored, and I had an old typewriter and a big idea. And so rock bottom became the solid foundation on which I rebuilt my life.

20      You might never fail on the scale I did, but some failure in life is inevitable. It is impossible to live without failing at something, unless you live so cautiously that you might as well not have lived at all—in which case, you fail by default.

21      Failure gave me an inner security that I had never attained by passing examinations. Failure taught me things about myself that I could have learned no other way. I discovered that I had a strong will, and more discipline than I had suspected; I also found out that I had friends whose value was truly above rubies.

22      The knowledge that you have emerged wiser and stronger from setbacks means that you are, ever after, secure in your ability to survive. You will never

truly know yourself, or the strength of your relationships, until both have been tested by adversity. Such knowledge is a true gift, for all that it is painfully won, and it has been worth more to me than any qualification I ever earned.

23    Given a time machine or a Time Turner, I would tell my 21-year-old self that personal happiness lies in knowing that life is not a check-list of acquisition or achievement. Your qualifications, your CV, are not your life, though you will meet many people of my age and older who confuse the two. Life is difficult, and complicated, and beyond anyone's total control, and the humility to know that will enable you to survive its vicissitudes.

24    You might think that I chose my second theme, the importance of imagination, because of the part it played in rebuilding my life, but that is not wholly so. Though I will defend the value of bedtime stories to my last gasp, I have learned to value imagination in a much broader sense. Imagination is not only the uniquely human capacity to envision that which is not, and therefore the fount of all invention and innovation. In its arguably most transformative and revelatory capacity, it is the power that enables us to empathise with humans whose experiences we have never shared.

25    One of the greatest formative experiences of my life preceded Harry Potter, though it informed much of what I subsequently wrote in those books. This revelation came in the form of one of my earliest day jobs. Though I was sloping off to write stories during my lunch hours, I paid the rent in my early 20s by working in the research department at Amnesty International's headquarters in London.

26    There in my little office I read hastily scribbled letters smuggled out of totalitarian regimes by men and women who were risking imprisonment to inform the outside world of what was happening to them. I saw photographs of those who had disappeared without trace, sent to Amnesty by their desperate families and friends. I read the testimony of torture victims and saw pictures of their injuries. I opened handwritten, eye-witness accounts of summary trials and executions, of kidnappings and rapes.

27    Many of my co-workers were ex-political prisoners, people who had been displaced from their homes, or fled into exile, because they had the temerity to think independently of their government. Visitors to our office included those who had come to give information, or to try and find out what had happened to those they had been forced to leave behind.

28    I shall never forget the African torture victim, a young man no older than I was at the time, who had become mentally ill after all he had endured in his homeland. He trembled uncontrollably as he spoke into a video camera about the brutality inflicted upon him. He was a foot taller than I was, and seemed as fragile as a child. I was given the job of escorting him to the Underground Station afterwards, and this man whose life had been

shattered by cruelty took my hand with exquisite courtesy, and wished me future happiness.

29   And as long as I live I shall remember walking along an empty corridor and suddenly hearing, from behind a closed door, a scream of pain and horror such as I have never heard since. The door opened, and the researcher poked out her head and told me to run and make a hot drink for the young man sitting with her. She had just given him the news that in retaliation for his own outspokenness against his country's regime, his mother had been seized and executed.

30   Every day of my working week in my early 20s I was reminded how incredibly fortunate I was, to live in a country with a democratically elected government, where legal representation and a public trial were the rights of everyone.

31   Every day, I saw more evidence about the evils humankind will inflict on their fellow humans, to gain or maintain power. I began to have nightmares, literal nightmares, about some of the things I saw, heard and read.

32   And yet I also learned more about human goodness at Amnesty International than I had ever known before.

33   Amnesty mobilises thousands of people who have never been tortured or imprisoned for their beliefs to act on behalf of those who have. The power of human empathy, leading to collective action, saves lives, and frees prisoners. Ordinary people, whose personal well-being and security are assured, join together in huge numbers to save people they do not know, and will never meet. My small participation in that process was one of the most humbling and inspiring experiences of my life.

34   Unlike any other creature on this planet, humans can learn and understand, without having experienced. They can think themselves into other people's minds, imagine themselves into other people's places.

35   Of course, this is a power, like my brand of fictional magic, that is morally neutral. One might use such an ability to manipulate, or control, just as much as to understand or sympathise.

36   And many prefer not to exercise their imaginations at all. They choose to remain comfortably within the bounds of their own experience, never troubling to wonder how it would feel to have been born other than they are. They can refuse to hear screams or to peer inside cages; they can close their minds and hearts to any suffering that does not touch them personally; they can refuse to know.

37   I might be tempted to envy people who can live that way, except that I do not think they have any fewer nightmares than I do. Choosing to live in narrow spaces can lead to a form of mental agoraphobia, and that brings its

own terrors. I think the wilfully unimaginative see more monsters. They are often more afraid.

38    What is more, those who choose not to empathise may enable real monsters. For without ever committing an act of outright evil ourselves, we collude with it, through our own apathy.

39    One of the many things I learned at the end of that Classics corridor down which I ventured at the age of 18, in search of something I could not then define, was this, written by the Greek author Plutarch: What we achieve inwardly will change outer reality.

40    That is an astonishing statement and yet proven a thousand times every day of our lives. It expresses, in part, our inescapable connection with the outside world, the fact that we touch other people's lives simply by existing.

41    But how much more are you, Harvard graduates of 2008, likely to touch other people's lives? Your intelligence, your capacity for hard work, the education you have earned and received, give you unique status, and unique responsibilities. Even your nationality sets you apart. The great majority of you belong to the world's only remaining superpower. The way you vote, the way you live, the way you protest, the pressure you bring to bear on your government, has an impact way beyond your borders. That is your privilege, and your burden.

42    If you choose to use your status and influence to raise your voice on behalf of those who have no voice; if you choose to identify not only with the powerful, but with the powerless; if you retain the ability to imagine yourself into the lives of those who do not have your advantages, then it will not only be your proud families who celebrate your existence, but thousands and millions of people whose reality you have helped transform for the better. We do not need magic to change the world, we carry all the power we need inside ourselves already: we have the power to imagine better.

43    I am nearly finished. I have one last hope for you, which is something that I already had at 21. The friends with whom I sat on graduation day have been my friends for life. They are my children's godparents, the people to whom I've been able to turn in times of trouble, friends who have been kind enough not to sue me when I've used their names for Death Eaters. At our graduation we were bound by enormous affection, by our shared experience of a time that could never come again, and, of course, by the knowledge that we held certain photographic evidence that would be exceptionally valuable if any of us ran for Prime Minister.

44    So today, I can wish you nothing better than similar friendships. And tomorrow, I hope that even if you remember not a single word of mine, you remember those of Seneca, another of those old Romans I met when I fled down the Classics corridor, in retreat from career ladders, in search of ancient wisdom: As is a

tale, so is life: not how long it is, but how good it is, is what matters. I wish you all very good lives. Thank you very much. Copyright 2008 / JK Rowling.

JK Rowling, "The Fringe Benefits of Failure, and the Importance of Motivation," Commencement Address at Harvard University, June 2008. Copyright © 2008 by JK Rowling. Reprinted by permission of Harvard University.

## Thinking about the Text

1. What specific techniques does Rowling use to engage her audience? What qualities of her original audience—graduates of Harvard University—does she seem aware of and play to in her speech?

2. What two important lessons does Rowling wish she had known at her own university graduation that she wishes to impart to her audience?

3. How did her parents' impoverished backgrounds affect Rowling's personal and academic goals? Why does she not blame her parents for what might be seen as their negative impact on her decisions?

4. Acknowledging that Harvard graduates may not be as experienced in knowing failure as the average person, Rowling describes her own "epic scale" failure and its subsequent benefits. How does she describe the values of being at "rock bottom"? In what way does she believe some failure is essential?

5. What does Rowling believe personal happiness is *not*, and how is that belief a valuable insight for a university graduate?

6. What are the values of imagination, according to Rowling?

7. What awareness did Rowling gain from her work with Amnesty International? Which specific narratives from her job resonate with you? How does her work experience contribute to the person she is and the writing she does?

8. How does Rowling perceive people who lack the imagination or will to imagine the suffering of others?

9. How does Rowling connect her wisdom about the benefits of failure and the value of imagination to create a directive for the college graduates she addresses?

10. How does Rowling's concluding reference to a quotation from Seneca reinforce her views on the benefits of both failure and imagination?

## Writing from the Text

1. Using Rowling's acknowledged "epic scale" failures as inspiration for your own revelations, describe a period of failure in your life. Then recount in your essay what you did to create a solid foundation from

the "rock bottom" where you temporarily resided. Incorporate some of Rowling's language as you write your own account.

2. Define "failure" by analyzing the specific life choices and values of people you know. Perceive a way to categorize the examples of failure in order to organize your presentation.

3. Write an analysis of others' expectations for you that conflict with or support your personal notion of success and achieving a good life.

## CONNECTING WITH OTHER TEXTS

1. After reading "The Good Daughter" (p. 8), write an analysis that shows both comparison and contrast between Hwang's and Rowling's history and choices. What conclusions can you draw as you contrast the reasoning and decisions of these authors?

2. Read "The Difference Between Pity and Empathy" (p. 148) to compare Vaughn's understanding of empathy with what Rowling perceives as the value of imagination. Using both works, write an essay that illustrates how imagination is vital to achieving a life of goodness.

3. Do an Internet investigation of Amnesty International in order to write a descriptive analysis of the organization for someone who does not know its philosophy, procedures, and ability to help others.

 # If the Genes Fit

### *Dan Neil*

Journalist and writer of feature articles for publications, Dan Neil (b. 1960) was a *Los Angeles Times* regular columnist and is now automotive columnist for the *Wall Street Journal*. In 2004, Neil won a Pulitzer Prize for his original approach to car reviews, an example of which can be seen in his description of driving a Ferrari: "I have one weekend and a $185,000 Italian sports car so sexy it appears to have been forged from metal bra clasps and garter belt snaps, so fast it can blow the foam off lattes outside of any Starbucks it passes." The essay below, published in the *Los Angeles Times* in June 2005, reflects Neil's characteristic style even as it argues a critical point.

1      I didn't decide to be straight, never came to a sexually orienting fork in the road to choose the road more traveled. I was never indoctrinated by anyone advancing a heterosexual agenda. Talk about coals to Newcastle.

2    And it's the same for every gay person I've ever talked to. From the earliest stirrings of sexual proclivity, they were somehow aware that they belonged in the same-sex sandbox. This was the case with Brad, one of my best friends. But perhaps, I ventured, something environmental, something learned, accounted for his sexual orientation? "Yeah, right," he said, "I read a book on it when I was 3 years old."

3    Just in time for Gay Pride Month—and in time to be rushed to the battlefields of the culture wars—comes *When I Knew,* edited by fashion photographer Robert Trachtenberg, a collection of stories from gays and lesbians, famous and not so famous, describing their Eureka! moments. Of course, writes contributor Brian Leitch, you know, then you know-know, then you really, *really* know. 'Nuf said.

4    This is a funny, sad, wonderful little book, full of mordant vignettes of self-discovery and disclosure. When comic Michele Balan told her grandmother that she was a lesbian, her grandmother replied: "No you're not, you're Romanian. On your father's side!" For political fundraiser Barry Karas, it happened when he was 8 years old. After watching the boy skip around, playing hopscotch, a family friend leaned over to Karas' father and said, "Ben, I think you got a problem."

5    These childhood annunciations occur in strange ways. Makeup artist Jeff Judd remembers edging under the TV to look up the loincloth of Ron Ely, who played Tarzan. Composer Marc Shaiman had a crush on Dick Gautier, who played Hymie the robot on *Get Smart.* As a child, *Will & Grace* producer Jon Kinnally became obsessed with the man's naked back on a box of Doan's pills.

6    What is striking is that they had such revelations to begin with. It never dawned on me that I was straight. I just was. For gays and lesbians, it seems, there is always a moment when they realize that what they want isn't officially sanctioned. A cognitive moment that marks a cleaving away from the larger heterosexual world, the opening of an otherness, like jets peeling off in the missing-man formation.

7    Also conveniently timed, a June 3 article in the biology journal Cell that describes a gene-modifying experiment in which scientists switched fruit flies' sexual orientation from straight to gay. In the words of the study's authors: "The splicing of a single neuronal gene thus specifies essentially all aspects of a complex innate behavior." At least for *Drosophila melanogaster,* sexual orientation is genetic.

8    A month ago, researchers in Sweden released the results of a brain-scanning study suggesting the existence of human pheromones—scent chemicals that govern sexual behavior in many species—and demonstrating

that gay males react to male sweat pheromones the same way heterosexual women do. There was no mention of socks.

9    Sexuality is bewildering and complex and fantastically varied—on this, I think, all sides agree—and yet there is a growing body of evidence suggesting that sexual orientation has a biological foundation, and that homosexuality is not "unnatural" in the sense of not occurring in nature. Biologist Bruce Bagemihl's book *Biological Exuberance* (1999) documents hundreds of examples of homosexual behavior in the animal kingdom.

10    The common shorthand for all this is the "gay gene," a term popularized by geneticist Dean Hamer and journalist Peter Copeland's book *The Science of Desire* (1994).

11    The notion of a gay gene, or anything like it, is anathema to organizations such as the rabidly anti-gay Focus on the Family. If homosexuality is a natural variation in the human genome, homosexuals are not guilty of anything except being human. If it is established that homosexuality is genetically, or at least biologically, rooted—regardless of how such feelings are behaviorally shaded—then the campaign to marginalize and criminalize gays is revealed as the bigoted pogrom that it is.

12    How bad do Christian fundamentalists want to refute this idea? Watergate con and prison minister Charles Colson, in a piece last month responding to a *New York Times* op-ed article by Harvard cognitive scientist Steven Pinker, argues that "of course" homosexuality is "evolutionarily maladaptive," according to the tenets of natural selection. It took homophobia to rehabilitate Darwin in the eyes of fundamentalists.

13    In the long run, this is a fight homophobes cannot hope to win, simply because the fear they traffic in—somehow America's children will be seduced into the homosexual lifestyle—is so at odds with common experience. Most people know, at the core of their self-conception, that they were born straight or gay, and no amount of indoctrinating, no agenda from either side, could change that.

## THINKING ABOUT THE TEXT

1. Describe Dan Neil's purpose in writing and his position in this essay. How does he support his views?

2. The author acknowledges a contrast between his lack of a defining moment in perceiving himself as a heterosexual and the experiences of homosexuals who can and do relate a "cognitive moment that marks a cleaving away from the larger heterosexual world" (162). Why do you think homosexuals have this moment of "you know, then you know-know, then you really *really* know" (162)?

3. Dan Neil uses material from *When I Knew,* an edited collection of narrations from gays and lesbians relating their moments of sexual self-discovery. The author also relates findings from the biology journal *Cell,* the results of a study on scent chemicals and their relationship to sexual behavior, and he cites two books on biology and genetics. What is the author's intention in referring to so many sources in this short essay?

4. What is the author's strategy in twice referring to himself as a male who never questioned his sexual orientation, one who never decided to be straight?

5. Describe how the wordplay in Dan Neil's title establishes his writer's voice and implied thesis.

## WRITING FROM THE TEXT

1. Write an account of your own awareness of sexual orientation to illustrate Dan Neil's point that "most people know, at the core of their self-conception, that they were born straight or gay" (163). You might write an analysis of early crushes or middle-school romantic feelings to show how you developed an awareness of yourself as a sexual person.

2. Using the points made in Dan Neil's piece, write an essay that argues for improved high school counseling and school clubs based on homosexual orientation.

## CONNECTING WITH OTHER TEXTS

1. After reading "Don't Let Stereotypes Warp Your Judgments" (p. 424), write an essay that shows your awareness of how stereotyping can influence young people's views and lack of acceptance of homosexuals. Propose a solution to the problem.

2. Read Marcus Mabry's essay "Living in Two Worlds" (p. 99) and then write an essay showing how Mabry's and Neil's essays illustrate the guilt, helplessness, and embarrassment experienced by individuals traveling between majority and minority worlds, whether racial or sexual.

 # Black Men and Public Space
### *Brent Staples*

After earning his PhD in psychology from the University of Chicago, Brent Staples (b. 1951) worked at the *Chicago Sun-Times* and wrote for other periodicals. He became an assistant metropolitan editor of the *New York Times* in 1985, and he is presently on that paper's editorial board. In his book *Parallel Time: Growing Up in Black and White* (1994), Staples writes about his poor childhood and his present position at the *New York Times*. Staples "despises" the expression "the black experience," and insists that "black people's lives in this country are too varied to be reduced to a single term." He says that he is writing about "universal themes—family and leaving home and developing your own identity.... Being black enriches my experience; it doesn't define me." Staples has co-authored *An American Love Story* (1999). The essay included here was first published in the September 1986 issue of *Ms.* magazine as one article in a section on men's perspectives.

1    My first victim was a woman—white, well dressed, probably in her early twenties. I came upon her late one evening on a deserted street in Hyde Park, a relatively affluent neighborhood in an otherwise mean, impoverished section of Chicago. As I swung onto the avenue behind her, there seemed to be a discreet, uninflammatory distance between us. Not so. She cast back a worried glance. To her, the youngish black man—a broad six feet two inches with a beard and billowing hair, both hands shoved into the pockets of a bulky military jacket—seemed menacingly close. After a few more quick glimpses, she picked up her pace and was soon running in earnest. Within seconds she disappeared into a cross street.

2    That was more than a decade ago. I was twenty-two years old, a graduate student newly arrived at the University of Chicago. It was in the echo of that terrified woman's footfalls that I first began to know the unwieldy inheritance I'd come into—the ability to alter public space in ugly ways. It was clear that she thought herself the quarry of a mugger, a rapist, or worse. Suffering a bout of insomnia, however, I was stalking sleep, not defenseless wayfarers. As a softy who is scarcely able to take a knife to a raw chicken—let alone hold it to a person's throat—I was surprised, embarrassed, and dismayed all at once. Her flight made me feel like an accomplice in tyranny. It also made it clear that I was indistinguishable from the muggers who occasionally seeped into the area from the surrounding ghetto. That first encounter, and those that followed, signified that a vast, unnerving gulf lay between nighttime pedestrians—particularly women—and me. And I soon gathered that being perceived as dangerous is a hazard in itself. I only needed to turn a corner into a dicey situation, or crowd some frightened, armed person in a foyer somewhere, or make an errant move after being pulled over by a policeman. Where fear and weapons meet—and they often do in urban America—there is always the possibility of death.

3    In that first year, my first away from my hometown, I was to become thoroughly familiar with the language of fear. At dark, shadowy intersections in Chicago, I could cross in front of a car stopped at a traffic light and elicit the *thunk, thunk, thunk, thunk* of the driver—black, white, male, or female—hammering down the door locks. On less traveled streets after dark, I grew

accustomed to but never comfortable with people who crossed to the other side of the street rather than pass me. Then there were the standard unpleasantries with police, doormen, bouncers, cab drivers, and others whose business it is to screen out troublesome individuals *before* there is any nastiness.

4      I moved to New York nearly two years ago and I have remained an avid night walker. In central Manhattan, the near-constant crowd cover minimizes tense one-on-one street encounters. Elsewhere—visiting friends in SoHo, where sidewalks are narrow and tightly spaced buildings shut out the sky—things can get very taut indeed.

5      Black men have a firm place in New York mugging literature. Norman Podhoretz in his famed (or infamous) 1963 essay, "My Negro Problem—And Ours," recalls growing up in terror of black males, they "were tougher than we were, more ruthless," he writes—and as an adult on the Upper West Side of Manhattan, he continues, he cannot constrain his nervousness when he meets black men on certain streets. Similarly, a decade later, the essayist and novelist Edward Hoagland extols a New York where once "Negro bitterness bore down mainly on other Negroes." Where some see mere panhandlers, Hoagland sees "a mugger who is clearly screwing up his nerve to do more than just *ask* for money." But Hoagland has 'the New Yorker's quick-hunch posture for broken-field maneuvering," and the bad guy swerves away.

6      I often witness that "hunch posture," from women after dark on the warrenlike streets of Brooklyn where I live. They seem to set their faces on neutral and, with their purse straps strung across their chests bandolier style, they forge ahead as though bracing themselves against being tackled. I understand, of course, that the danger they perceive is not a hallucination. Women are particularly vulnerable to street violence, and young black males are drastically overrepresented among the perpetrators of that violence. Yet these truths are no solace against the kind of alienation that comes of being ever the suspect, against being set apart, a fearsome entity with whom pedestrians avoid making eye contact.

7      It is not altogether clear to me how I reached the ripe old age of twenty-two without being conscious of the lethality nighttime pedestrians attributed to me. Perhaps it was because in Chester, Pennsylvania, the small, angry industrial town where I came of age in the 1960s, I was scarcely noticeable against a backdrop of gang warfare, street knifings, and murders. I grew up one of the good boys, had perhaps a half-dozen fist fights. In retrospect, my shyness of combat has clear sources.

8      Many things go into the making of a young thug. One of those things is the consummation of the male romance with the power to intimidate. An infant discovers that random flailings send the baby bottle flying out of the

crib and crashing to the floor. Delighted, the joyful babe repeats those motions again and again, seeking to duplicate the feat. Just so, I recall the points at which some of my boyhood friends were finally seduced by the perception of themselves as tough guys. When a mark cowered and surrendered his money without resistance, myth and reality merged—and paid off. It is, after all, only manly to embrace the power to frighten and intimidate. We, as men, are not supposed to give an inch of our lane on the highway; we are to seize the fighter's edge in work and in play and even in love; we are to be valiant in the face of hostile forces.

9    Unfortunately, poor and powerless young men seem to take all this nonsense literally. As a boy, I saw countless tough guys locked away; I have since buried several, too. They were babies, really—a teenage cousin, a brother of twenty-two, a childhood friend in his mid-twenties—all gone down in episodes of bravado played out in the streets. I came to doubt the virtues of intimidation early on. I chose, perhaps even unconsciously, to remain a shadow—timid, but a survivor.

10    The fearsomeness mistakenly attributed to me in public places often has a perilous flavor. The most frightening of these confusions occurred in the late 1970s and early 1980s when I worked as a journalist in Chicago. One day, rushing into the office of a magazine I was writing for with a deadline story in hand, I was mistaken for a burglar. The office manager called security and, with an ad hoc posse, pursued me through the labyrinthine halls, nearly to my editor's door. I had no way of proving who I was. I could only move briskly toward the company of someone who knew me.

11    Another time I was on assignment for a local paper and killing time before an interview. I entered a jewelry store on the city's affluent Near North Side. The proprietor excused herself and returned with an enormous red Doberman pinscher straining at the end of a leash. She stood, the dog extended toward me, silent to my questions, her eyes bulging nearly out of her head. I took a cursory look around, nodded, and bade her good night. Relatively speaking, however, I never fared as badly as another black male journalist. He went to nearby Waukegan, Illinois, a couple of summers ago to work on a story about a murderer who was born there. Mistaking the reporter for the killer, police hauled him from his car at gunpoint and but for his press credentials would probably have tried to book him. Such episodes are not uncommon. Black men trade tales like this all the time.

12    In "My Negro Problem—And Ours," Podhoretz writes that the hatred he feels for blacks makes itself known to him through a variety of avenues—one being his discomfort with that "special brand of paranoid touchiness" to which he says blacks are prone. No doubt he is speaking here of black men.

In time, I learned to smother the rage I felt at so often being taken for a criminal. Not to do so would surely have led to madness—via that special "paranoid touchiness" that so annoyed Podhoretz at the time he wrote the essay.

13    I began to take precautions to make myself less threatening. I move about with care, particularly late in the evening. I give a wide berth to nervous people on subway platforms during the wee hours, particularly when I have exchanged business clothes for jeans. If I happen to be entering a building behind some people who appear skittish, I may walk by, letting them clear the lobby before I return, so as not to seem to be following them. I have been calm and extremely congenial on those rare occasions when I've been pulled over by the police.

14    And on late-evening constitutionals along streets less traveled by, I employ what has proved to be an excellent tension-reducing measure: I whistle melodies from Beethoven and Vivaldi and the more popular classical composers. Even steely New Yorkers hunching toward nighttime destinations seem to relax, and occasionally they even join in the tune. Virtually everybody seems to sense that a mugger wouldn't be warbling bright, sunny selections from Vivaldi's *Four Seasons*. It is my equivalent of the cowbell that hikers wear when they know they are in bear country.

## THINKING ABOUT THE TEXT

1. What is the effect on the reader of Staples's opening paragraph? How does it function to underscore the point of his essay?

2. In what places is Staples's effect on people related to his being black? Where is his maleness or stature a threat? Which aspect of his physiology does Staples believe is more threatening?

3. How has Staples adjusted his life to make himself less intimidating?

## WRITING FROM THE TEXT

1. Write about a time when you unwittingly threatened someone. Describe the occasion using Staples's essay as a model, so that your reader can see and hear ("thunk, thunk, thunk, thunk") the scene.

2. Write an essay in which you describe the problems of being stereotyped as a member of a group that is perceived as threatening. What, if anything, have you done to counter or handle the dangerously charged or uncomfortable environment?

3. Write an essay describing the problem of being intimidated by a group or a member of a group. What have you done to avoid feeling intimidated or threatened?

## CONNECTING WITH OTHER TEXTS

1. In what way is Staples "living in two worlds"? After reading Marcus Mabry's essay (p. 99), write a comparison contrast essay that shows how both of these authors have learned to straddle two distinct realms. (See Comparison-Contrast, pp. 407–413.)

2. After reading "Don't Let Stereotypes Warp Your Judgments" (p. 424), write an analysis of how people who discriminate against Staples "impoverish" themselves. Use specific details from both essays to support your thesis.

  # King Curtis's Echo
### *Max Thayer*

After being drafted into the Army in 1966 and serving for three years, Max Thayer (b. 1946) decided to move to Los Angeles to break into the movies. With no acting training or Hollywood connections, he began studying plays and books on acting, and he performed with experimental and street theater groups. When he joined the Screen Actors Guild in 1972, he changed his name from Michael to Max, after a character in Harold Robbins's novel *The Carpetbaggers*. Thayer has performed on stage in New York and Los Angeles and has appeared in numerous action movies shot in Hollywood and around the world. Neither a stuntman or martial-artist, Thayer credits his love of sports and his childhood experiences with ice hockey, baseball, football, basketball, boxing, and swimming for helping him in his film work. In addition to numerous B-movies, Thayer has had small, background roles in *Pearl Harbor, The Man Who Wasn't There, Collateral Damage, American Gun, S.W.A.T.,* and *Terminator 3*. The following essay first appeared in the *Los Angeles Times Magazine* in 2005.

1     I don't know what made me do it, but I'm glad, in a strange way, that I did.

2     When I heard my neighbor call out "You can't park there," I knew what was going on. Someone had pulled into our single-lane driveway, which serves four apartments that sit atop a pawn shop and a Russian deli on Santa Monica Boulevard in West Hollywood. When I heard a muffled response and my neighbor's more urgent "No! Someone is coming. We need to keep that space clear," I jumped up to look out my window.

3     Despite the no parking signs, deli customers routinely park in the mouth of the driveway, blocking exit or entrance, though most of the time a simple request to move is met with sheepish compliance. But today a man in his

30s, fit and full of himself, nonchalantly waved off the appeal and sauntered around the corner just as I leaned out the window and got off a "Hey!"

4      Maybe if I'd just kept my mouth shut I wouldn't have taken it personally. After all, just two minutes before, I had been sprawled out in my bedroom, windows wide open, enjoying a balmy Sunday morning leafing through the newspaper while monitoring the two football games in progress on TV. Absolute bliss.

5      My first bad move was slipping into a pair of flip-flops and trundling down to the landing to right this slight to my dignity. I wasn't going to yell, just walk up to him in the deli and murmur something along the lines of: "You were asked politely to move; would you please?"

6      When I turned the corner at the end of the driveway, Mr. Park Where I Want was striding away from the deli and toward me. Smugly self-assured and dressed in one of those velour warm-up suits, he was bouncing along as if he'd just won the lottery.

7      He smirked when we passed each other. I turned and retraced my steps as he approached his car. I pointed to the signs posted near the entrance. "In the future, no parking, OK?"

8      Our eyes met as he smirked again. "Caaalm down."

9      Calm down? "I'm calm, just don't park here."

10     At this point I should have kept on walking back to the funny papers and football.

11     "Caaalm down," he said again in a pat-on-the-head tone.

12     You know how annoying that is?

13     I gave him my best withering look. "It's real simple, no parking, *parksi nyetski*, right?"

14     He grinned as he slid into his car. He offered up an unoriginal obscenity, followed by "low-life."

15     I felt my anger surge into a raging boil.

16     I proffered my middle finger, cocked and ready to see what Mr. Big Shot in His Big Mercedes wanted to do about it.

17     More grinning as he slowly backed out of the driveway, returning the salute.

18     That's when I lost it, spewing every unprintable phrase that welled up in my febrile brain. I questioned his courage, his sexual proclivities, his family, his—you know the drill.

19     And that's when he braked in the middle of the street, grin gone and in its place an icy stare.

20     At that movement, a car barreling around the corner blared its horn and we lost eye contact. He maneuvered out of the way and drove off.

21   I was shaking when I went back inside. Where had this venom come from? I had been ready to go to fist city with a stranger, for what? I wanted everything the way it was 10 minutes ago, but the smudge of stupidity wouldn't wash out. As I paced and ranted with the incident churning through my mind like a Class V rapids, I shoved a stool piled high with vinyl LPs, a stack of shellac we used to call records. I had culled the essentials from my collection to download to my hard drive and now they were scattered across the floor in a hap-hazard display of rash behavior.

22   I was slumped over, gazing dejectedly at the LPs, when I saw him staring up at me with an almost baleful look.

23   King Curtis.

24   The album cover for *Blues at Montreux* was at my feet. Recorded live at the jazz festival in Switzerland, it's an unrehearsed, once-in-a-lifetime session of King Curtis and Champion Jack Dupree. King was a monster sax player of his time and Champion Jack was a pure blues barrelhouse piano player. Their chance meeting produced some of the most exuberant, joyous music you'll ever hear.

25   It snapped me out of my funk and sent me back to the early '70s, when I lived in New York. The way I heard it, one night some guy relieved himself in front of a brownstone that King Curtis owned in the upper 80s on the Westside. An argument led to a stabbing that led to King's death. Some jerk was making a mess on his property and King took offense. King ended up bleeding out, dead at 37.

26   That night, not yet aware of the tragedy, I was standing on the corner of 90th and Amsterdam, a few blocks from where the stabbing had happened. I was waiting for the light to change when I heard a saxophone wailing away with loose abandon. I crossed the street, turned a corner, went down and back up, tried the other corner and crossed the street again, but the player remained elusive.

27   I read about King the next day in the *Herald Tribune*, and these many years later the memory echoed. Do I want to die over a parking space? Do I want to live in a world where my response to a personal affront is going to land me in jail, an emergency room or the morgue?

28   I laughed and it set me free—finally. I won't choose to live that way, or worse.

29   Now, long after the anger over the driveway affront has dissipated, it's something I strive to remember when some idiot swerves into my lane without signaling or an eager shopper jostles me in the grocery store. The obscene waste of King Curtis's life and my memory of his jubilant horn give me pause and, on a good day, a touch of grace. I have to thank the Russian deli customer for that.

## THINKING ABOUT THE TEXT

1. How do Thayer's title and opening line capture reader interest? What other elements in his next two narrative paragraphs keep readers intrigued?

2. How does Thayer's description of himself before the confrontation contrast with his behavior when he "lost it"? How does this tirade affect "Mr. Park Where I Want"?

3. What aspect of Thayer's character surprises him and causes him to question, "Where had this venom come from? I had been ready to go to fist city with a stranger, for what?" (171).

4. What is relevant about Thayer's flashback to an earlier incident involving "monster sax player" King Curtis? What is significant about Thayer searching for the elusive sax player—and his "echo"?

5. Why is Thayer *thankful* for this encounter with the Russian deli customer, and what has he learned from it?

## WRITING FROM THE TEXT

1. Write an essay analyzing how Thayer uses narration and its elements (dialogue, action, characterization, conflict, flashback, and symbolism) to present a strong argument against angry confrontations. Show how each story detail supports his thesis that insignificant squabbles can too easily escalate into deadly confrontations if they are not avoided.

2. Although Thayer's story is about deadly confrontations, write an essay arguing that it is as much about self-discovery as it is about dealing with other people. Use details from this story to support your claims.

3. Write a narrative about an experience that showed a surprising aspect of yourself that you hadn't expected or seen fully. Dramatize your typical behavior before that incident and then analyze what you learned about yourself and others through that encounter.

## CONNECTING WITH OTHER TEXTS

1. After reading "Watching My Back" (p. 57), write an essay comparing and contrasting Klein's treatment of confrontations with Thayer's. Consider their similar concerns as well as the differences in their theses, initial provocation, and conclusions.

2. Using Thayer's essay, Staples's "Black Men and Public Space" (p. 164), and Dickerson's "Who Shot Johnny?" (p. 23), write an essay analyzing what each author seems to be exploring and exposing about aggression and "bravado." Examine any solutions or answers that the authors offer.

#  Blue Spruce
### *Stephen Perry*

While teaching creative writing—at Long Beach City College; University of California, Irvine; and the UCLA Extension Writers' Program—Stephen Perry (b. 1950) has published more than sixty-five poems in anthologies and in journals such as the *New Yorker, Yale Review, Virginia Quarterly Review, Kenyon Review, Antioch Review,* and *Salmagundi.* Perry has also served as poetry consultant to the Disney Corporation—the only such consultant in the company's history. He is currently seeking a publisher for his collection of poems, *Homecoming.* Perry shares a "co-dependent" Web site with his author wife, Susan Perry, and invites readers to visit and interact with them at www.bunnyape.com.

Referring to "Blue Spruce," Perry reveals, "When I read this poem at poetry readings, I usually tell people that everything in the poem is true, except for the title. There were no blue spruces (that I know of) in the little town in Missouri where I set the poem. I just like the double pun on 'blue' and 'spruce.'" The poem was published in the *New Yorker* in 1991.

> My grandfather worked in a barbershop
> smelling of lotions he'd slap on your face,
> hair and talc. The black razor strop
>
> hung like the penis of an ox. He'd draw
> 5  the sharp blade in quick strokes over
> the smooth-rough hide, and then carefully
>
> over your face. The tiny hairs would gather
> on the blade, a congregation singing
> under blue spruce in winter,
>
> 10  a bandstand in the center of town
> bright with instruments, alto sax, tenor
> sax, tuba or sousaphone—the bright
>
> oompah-pahs shaving the town somehow,
> a bright cloth shaking the air
> 15  into flakes of silvering hair
>
> floating down past the houses, the horses
> pulling carriages past the town fountain,
> which had frozen into a coiffure
>
> of curly glass. My grandfather had an affair
> 20  with the girl who did their nails
> bright pink, bright red, never blue,

perhaps as the horses clip-clopped on ice
outside his shop, his kisses
smelling of lather and new skin—

25   when she grew too big and round
with his child, with his oompah love,
with his bandstand love, with his brassy love,

and the town dropped its grace notes
of gossip and whispered hiss,
30   he bundled her out of town

with the savings which should have gone
to my mom. But how could you hate him?
My mother did, my father did,

and my grandmother, who bore his neglect.
35   When she was covered in sheets
at her last death,

he flirted with the nurses, bright
as winter birds in spruces
above a bandstand—

40   I'll always remember him in snow, a deep lather
of laughter, the picture
where he took me from my mother

and raised me high, a baby, into the bell
of his sousaphone, as if I were a note
45   he'd play into light—

## THINKING ABOUT THE TEXT

1. List all the images that Perry uses to characterize the grandfather, then describe the resulting "portrait."

2. Discuss the narrator's perception of his grandfather and compare and contrast it with the views of family members and the townspeople.

3. Look up both "blue" and "spruce" in the dictionary. Which definitions relate to this poem? Discuss possible meanings of the title.

4. Cluster (see p. 283) all the references to music or anything musical in the poem. Why might the poet have chosen to connect the grandfather with

music and, specifically, with the sousaphone? How do these references add to your understanding of his character?

5. How does the winter setting contribute to the poem? What is the significance of the reference to "light" at the end and of the repetitions of the word "bright" throughout?

### WRITING FROM THE TEXT

1. Referring to the images you listed in exercise 1 of "Thinking About the Text," write a character analysis of the grandfather from his grandson's perspective.

2. Working from the clustering you did for exercise 4, write an analysis of the poet's use of music to help characterize the grandfather and the town.

3. With supporting details from this poem, write an essay analyzing Perry's depiction of life in a small town and its effect on the individual. Does he seem at all critical of the small town or of the grandfather?

### CONNECTING WITH OTHER TEXTS

1. Using details from this poem and focusing on a character from at least one other work—the schizophrenic brother in "The Only Child" (p. 33) or the narrator in "Black Men and Public Space" (p. 164), write a paper analyzing the pressures of "fitting into" a particular society and the individual's varying responses to such pressures.

2. Consider the images used to describe the grandparents in "Blue Spruce" and in "Breaking Tradition" (p. 20). With these images in mind, write a paper contrasting these two portraits.

3. Visit Perry's Web site at www. bunnyape.com and read some of his other poems. Write an essay focusing on a recurring image or theme in Perry's writing as exhibited in "Blue Spruce" and any of his other works.

##  Discrimination at Large

### *Jennifer A. Coleman*

A graduate of Boston College Law School, Jennifer A. Coleman (b. 1959) is a discrimination and civil rights lawyer in Buffalo, New York. Coleman wrote the essay printed here after seeing the film *Jurassic Park:* "The only bad person in the film is fat, and I'm tired of the stereotyping—which nobody objects to—that makes heavy people objects of ridicule and contempt." In addition to writing legal briefs, pleadings, letters, and a law review article, Coleman teaches constitutional law at Canisius College in Buffalo. The essay that follows first appeared in *Newsweek* in 1993.

1 Fat is the last preserve for unexamined bigotry. Fat people are lampooned without remorse or apology on television, by newspaper columnists, in cartoons, you name it. The overweight are viewed as suffering from moral turpitude and villainy, and since we are at fault for our condition, no tolerance is due. All fat people are "outed" by their appearance.

2 Weight-motivated assaults occur daily and are committed by people who would die before uttering anti-gay slogans or racial epithets. Yet these same people don't hesitate to scream "move your fat ass" when we cross in front of them.

3 Since the time I first ventured out to play with the neighborhood kids, I was told over and over that I was lazy and disgusting. Strangers, adults, classmates offered gratuitous comments with such frequency and urgency that I started to believe them. Much later I needed to prove it wasn't so. I began a regimen of swimming, cycling and jogging that put all but the most compulsive to shame. I ate only cottage cheese, brown rice, fake butter and steamed everything. I really believed I could infiltrate the ranks of the nonfat and thereby establish my worth.

4 I would prove that I was not just a slob, a blimp, a pig. I would finally escape the unsolicited remarks of strangers ranging from the "polite"—"You would really be pretty if you lost weight"—to the hostile ("Lose weight, you fat slob"). Of course, sometimes more subtle commentary sufficed: oinking, mooing, staring, laughing and pointing. Simulating a fog-horn was also popular.

5 My acute exercise phase had many positive points. I was mingling with my obsessively athletic peers. My pulse was as low as anyone's, my cholesterol levels in the basement, my respiration barely detectable. I could swap stats from my last physical with anyone. Except for weight. No matter how hard I tried to run, swim or cycle away from it, my weight found me. Oh sure, I lost weight (never enough) and it inevitably tracked me down and adhered to me more tenaciously than ever. I lived and breathed "Eat to win," "Feel the burn." But in the end I was fit and still fat.

6 I learned that by societal, moral, ethical, soap-operatical, vegetable, political definition, it was impossible to be both fit and fat. Along the way to that knowledge, what I got for my trouble was to be hit with objects from moving cars because I dared to ride my bike in public, and to be mocked by diners at outdoor cafés who trumpeted like a herd of elephants as I jogged by. Incredibly, it was not uncommon for one of them to shout: "Lose some weight, you pig." Go figure.

7     It was confusing for a while. How was it I was still lazy, weak, despised, a slug and a cow if I exercised every waking minute? This confusion persisted until I finally realized: it didn't matter what I did. I was and always would be the object of sport, derision, antipathy and hostility so long as I stayed in my body. I immediately signed up for a body transplant. I am still waiting for a donor.

8     Until then, I am more settled because I have learned the hard way what thin people have known for years. There simply are some things that fat people must never do. Like: riding a bike ("Hey lady, where's the seat?"), eating in a public place ("No dessert for me, I don't want to look like her"). And the most unforgivable crime: wearing a bathing suit in public ("Whale on the beach!").

9     Things are less confusing now that I know that the nonfat are superior to me, regardless of their personal habits, health, personalities, cholesterol levels or the time they log on the couch. And, as obviously superior to me as they are, it is their destiny to remark on my inferiority regardless of who I'm with, whether they know me, whether it hurts my feelings. I finally understand that the thin have a divine mandate to steal self-esteem from fat people, who have no right to it in the first place.

10    Fat people aren't really jolly. Sometimes we act that way so you will leave us alone. We pay a price for this. But at least we get to hang on to what self-respect we smuggled out of grade school and adolescence.

11    Hating fat people is not inborn; it has to be nurtured and developed. Fortunately, it's taught from the moment most of us are able to walk and speak. We learn it through Saturday-morning cartoons, prime-time TV and movies. Have you ever seen a fat person in a movie who wasn't evil, disgusting, pathetic or lampooned? Santa Claus doesn't count.

12    Kids catch on early to be sensitive to the feelings of gay, black, disabled, elderly and speech-impaired people. At the same time, they learn that fat people are fair game. That we are always available for their personal amusement.

13    The media, legal system, parents, teachers and peers respond to most types of intolerance with outrage and protest. Kids hear that employers can be sued for discriminating, that political careers can be destroyed and baseball owners can lose their teams as a consequence of racism, sexism or almost any other "ism."

14    But the fat kid is taught that she deserves to be mocked. She is not OK. Only if she loses weight will she be OK. Other kids see the response and incorporate the message. Small wonder some (usually girls) get it into their heads that they can never be thin enough.

15    I know a lot about prejudice, even though I am a white, middle-class, professional woman. The worst discrimination I have suffered because of my gender is nothing compared to what I experience daily because of my weight.

I am sick of it. The jokes and attitudes are as wrong and damaging as any racial or ethnic slur. The passive acceptance of this inexcusable behavior is sometimes worse than the initial assault. Some offensive remarks can be excused as the shortcomings of jackasses. But the tacit acceptance of their conduct by mainstream America tells the fat person that the intolerance is understandable and acceptable. Well it isn't.

## THINKING ABOUT THE TEXT

1. Jennifer Coleman's focus is evident from the first paragraph of her essay. After you have read the entire essay, what do you assume is her thesis or complete assertion?

2. What is the author's personal history, and how does knowing her background contribute to your understanding of her point?

3. *Are* the jokes and slurs about overweight people "as wrong and damaging as any racial or ethnic slur" (15)?

4. Examine Coleman's word choice in this essay. Which words and expressions specifically contribute to her making her point powerfully?

5. What are *your* feelings as you read the comments that people have made to and about Coleman?

## WRITING FROM THE TEXT

1. Write an essay arguing that discrimination against the overweight is "as wrong and damaging as any racial or ethnic slur" (178). You will want to anticipate and counter the objection that people don't have to be overweight.

2. Describe the character traits, habits, and values of an overweight person you know. Let the description in your essay show what kinds of discrimination and problems your subject has faced.

## CONNECTING WITH OTHER TEXTS

1. Body image is a particular preoccupation for many women and, according to Rachel Krell (pp. 283–286), the world associates a thin body with beauty. Write an essay that argues that Jennifer Coleman has virtues that we admire even though she is not thin.

2. Write an essay contrasting the purpose and voice of Jennifer Coleman and Neil Steinberg, in the following essay. (See Comparison-Contrast, pp. 407–413 and What's Your Aim? p. 296.)

3. Use Heilbroner's essay on stereotyping (p. 424) as a definitive starting point for a descriptive essay on the discrimination that overweight people experience. You might contrast specific stereotypical depictions of overweight people in films and on television with an overweight person you know.

#  O.K., So I'm Fat
## *Neil Steinberg*

A graduate of Northwestern University, Neil Steinberg (b. 1960) writes a column for the *Chicago Sun-Times*. He is the author of *Complete and Utter Failure* (1994), and *If at All Possible, Involve a Cow: The Book of College Pranks* (1992), *Don't Give Up the Ship: Finding My Father While Lost at Sea* (2002), *Hatless Jack* (2004), and *Drunkard* (2008), a memoir of his struggle with alcoholism. His work has also appeared in *Rolling Stone, Esquire, Sports Illustrated, Eating Well*, and the *National Lampoon*, where he was a contributing editor. The following essay is the chapter "'F' Is For Fat" from Steinberg's book *The Alphabet of Modern Annoyances* (1996). Steinberg says he enjoys "writing about things people have trouble articulating—personal things, but not too personal."

1  Some people are no doubt fat because of glandular disorders or the wrath of an angry God. I am not one of those people. I am fat because I eat a lot.

2  Since fat people are held in such low regard, I should immediately point out that I am not *that* fat. Not fat in the Chinese Buddha, spilling-out-of-the-airplane-seat sense. The neighborhood kids don't skip behind me in the street, banging tin cans together and singing derisive songs.

3  Not yet, anyway.

4  But forget the social stigma of being fat. Ignore the medical peril, the sheer discomfort of dragging all that excess weight around. There is still a final ignominy almost too dire to mention: thin people.

5  All the drawbacks of being overweight could be shucked off—the fat are good at denial—were it not for the standing rebuke and constant insult that thin people offer, sometimes intentionally, sometimes simply by their very existence.

6  "Hey, big guy"— I get that a lot, from overly familiar office mates and, especially, from wiry panhandlers, as if it were a compliment that would inspire me to dig for change. Worse are those bent on my elevation to the sainted ranks of the thin: the sly references to fad diets, the inspirational tales of heroic weight loss. "Can I get you something?" a good friend I was visiting asked. "A Diet Coke, maybe?"

7  Others assume that thinness is forever beyond my grasp. I was once at a dinner party where the hostess was a wisp of a woman with legs like beef

jerky. She prepared some intensely fattening dessert—Bananas Foster, thick slices of ripe bananas awash in butter and sugar and cinnamon and liqueur accompanied by ice cream. The concoction was set before us. I was halfway finished and already thinking about seconds when I noticed that she wasn't eating. I challenged her, nicely. "This is great. Aren't you having any?" She fluttered her eyes and demurred. Oh, no, she said, too sweet, too fattening. And she smiled. A halo didn't form over her head, but it might as well have. The smile said it all—smug superiority, gazing down from on high.

8    I wanted to take my Bananas Foster and grind her face in it. She wasn't having any because it was bad for her. Bad for her, but fine for her piggish guests to ruin themselves on. "Here's some poison I whipped up for you. Bon appetit!"

9    Thanks.

10    That moment of shame and surprise—cheeks packed hamster-full with Bananas Foster while numbly confronting the iron resolve of your moral betters—is the heart of the fat experience. The yin of the primal pleasure of satiation, lips closing happily down on the tip of a thick triangle of stuffed Chicago pizza, balanced against the yang of stunned realization, as the mental fog parts for a moment and you catch sight of yourself in the mirror and see what's really there.

11    Small wonder we get mad at those who keep themselves in check. Envy-stoked anger is natural when dessert suddenly turns into a little lesson about restraint, a lesson I have endured for years but somehow never absorbed or profited by.

12    Surprisingly, I have less trouble with thin people who don't need to think about their weight. Those who are thin despite having eating habits that, if I practiced them, would quickly turn me into one of those elephantine men who periodically turn up on the news, dressed in sheets, removed from their homes through a hole in the wall, quickly weighed on a freight scale for the record, then placed under the personal care of Dick Gregory.

13    My wife's friend Larry, for instance, dresses in those tapered Italian suits and doesn't have enough fat on his body to make a butter pat. He actually keeps big bowls of candy scattered around his house. Not just for show. He'll casually dig his hand up to the wrist into one of the bowls, pull out a fistful of M & Ms and, tilting his head back, funnel them into his mouth.

14    Trim as a pencil. Yet, paradoxically, I find it easy to be around Larry. I'm comfortable, happy, never put off. Maybe it's because those who are effortlessly thin seem to suggest that thinness is a fluke of capricious fate, and thus out of our control. Maybe it's because Larry doesn't exhibit any of the self-control that I, in my greedy-puppy-fat-person way, would egoistically interpret as a reproach.

15    Or maybe it's just because he has all that candy scattered around his house.

## THINKING ABOUT THE TEXT

1. Reread the first paragraph and identify the specific ways that Steinberg establishes his stance toward the subject matter, his personal voice, and his purpose in writing the essay.

2. In spite of the humor in this essay, the author *is* making a point. What is it? What is the "final ignominy" that fat people must tolerate?

3. What are people's diverse responses to Steinberg's weight?

4. If Steinberg's tone and purpose were not to amuse, his thesis might be quite different. Create an angry or more intense thesis statement for this essay that Steinberg's specific examples would support.


## WRITING FROM THE TEXT

1. In a letter context—perhaps you'll even mail this to a friend—describe four thin and possibly self-righteous people you know. Try to achieve the quality of one of Neil Steinberg's well-crafted images—for example, his description of the hostess "with legs like beef jerky" (179–180).

2. If you are heavy or overweight, make a list of responses you have heard from friends and strangers about your size. Then write an essay that focuses on the intentional or unintentional comments you have endured. Adopt a voice similar to Steinberg's or one of indignation—as you prefer.

3. If you are weight conscious or very thin, write an essay that addresses the indifference, gluttony, medical problems, or laziness that you perceive in overweight people. Consider your audience and purpose as you draft your essay.


## CONNECTING WITH OTHER TEXTS

1. Compare and contrast the purpose and voice of Jennifer Coleman in "Discrimination at Large" (p. 175) and of Steinberg in this piece. Evaluate the two essays in your conclusion. See What's Your Aim? (pp. 296–297) for ideas.

2. Matthew Soyster (p. 144), Jennifer Coleman (p. 175), and Steinberg write about their perceptions of their bodies. Write an analysis of your understanding of their attitudes from a thesis that links these three writers and essays. Use details from the three texts to support your analysis.

3. Write a character analysis of Steinberg that draws supporting material from the text. You may stretch your imagination to infer character traits, but ground your analysis as much as possible in what the author reveals about himself in his essay and biographical material.

4. Read one of Steinberg's books cited in his biographical information (p. 179). Write an analysis of the kinds of humor apparent in his work.

## 🔵🔵 "Diabesity," A Crisis in an 🔵🔵 Expanding Country

### *Jane E. Brody*

Author of a widely syndicated newspaper column, "Personal Health," Jane E. Brody (b. 1941) has worked as a journalist for the *New York Times* since 1965. Initially majoring in biochemistry, Brody also enjoyed working as editor of her college literary magazine, so she decided to combine her two passions and become a science writer. Brody's best-selling books include *Jane Brody's The New York Times Guide to Personal Health* (1982), *Jane Brody's Good Food Book: Living the High Carbohydrate Way* (1985), *Jane Brody's Nutrition Book* (1987), and *Jane Brody's Guide to the Great Beyond* (2009). Brody emphasizes that good nutrition doesn't need to be unpleasant: "I wrote *Jane Brody's Good Food Book* for the average American who likes to *eat* and likes to *live.* . . . I don't like to feel deprived any more than the next person." The following essay appeared in the *New York Times* on March 29, 2005.

1      I can't understand why we still don't have a national initiative to control what is fast emerging as the most serious and costly health problem in America: excess weight. Are our schools, our parents, our national leaders blind to what is happening—a health crisis that looms even larger than our former and current smoking habits?

2      Just look at the numbers, so graphically described in an eye-opening new book, *Diabesity: The Obesity-Diabetes Epidemic That Threatens America—and What We Must Do to Stop It* (Bantam), by Dr. Francine R. Kaufman, a pediatric endocrinologist, the director of the diabetes clinic at Children's Hospital

Los Angeles and a past president of the American Diabetes Association. In just over a decade, she noted, the prevalence of diabetes nearly doubled in the American adult population: to 8.7 percent in 2002, from 4.9 percent in 1990. Furthermore, an estimated one-third of Americans with Type 2 diabetes don't even know they have it because the disease is hard to spot until it causes a medical crisis.

3    An estimated 18.2 million Americans now have diabetes, 90 percent of them the environmentally influenced type that used to be called adult-onset diabetes. But adults are no longer the only victims—a trend that prompted an official change in name in 1997 to Type 2 diabetes. More and more children are developing this health-robbing disease or its precursor, prediabetes. Counting children and adults together, some 41 million Americans have a higher-than-normal blood sugar level that typically precedes the development of full-blown diabetes.

4    And what is the reason for this runaway epidemic? Being overweight or obese, especially with the accumulation of large amounts of body fat around the abdomen. In Dr. Kaufman's first 15 years as a pediatric endocrinologist, 1978 to 1993, she wrote, "I never saw a young patient with Type 2 diabetes. But then everything changed." Teenagers now come into her clinic weighing 200, 300, even nearly 400 pounds with blood sugar levels that are off the charts. But, she adds, we cannot simply blame this problem on gluttony and laziness and "assume that the sole solution is individual change."

5    The major causes, Dr. Kaufman says, are "an economic structure that makes it cheaper to eat fries than fruit" and a food industry and mass media that lure children to eat the wrong foods and too much of them. "We have defined progress in terms of the quantity rather than the quality of our food," she wrote. Her views are supported by a 15-year study published in January in *The Lancet*. A team headed by Dr. Mark A. Pereira of the University of Minnesota analyzed the eating habits of 3,031 young adults and found that weight gain and the development of prediabetes were directly related to unhealthful fast food.

6    Taking other factors into consideration, consuming fast food two or more times a week resulted, on average, in an extra weight gain of 10 pounds and doubled the risk of prediabetes over the 15-year period. Other important factors in the diabesity epidemic, Dr. Kaufman explained, are the failure of schools to set good examples by providing only healthful fare, a loss of required physical activity in schools and the inability of many children these days to walk or bike safely to school or to play outside later.

7    Genes play a role as well. Some people are more prone to developing Type 2 diabetes than others. The risk is 1.6 times as great for blacks as for

whites of similar age. It is 1.5 times as great for Hispanic-Americans, and 2 times as great for Mexican-Americans and Native Americans. Unless we change our eating and exercise habits and pay greater attention to this disease, more than one-third of whites, two-fifths of blacks and half of Hispanic people in this country will develop diabetes.

8      It is also obvious from the disastrous patient histories recounted in Dr. Kaufman's book that the nation's medical structure is a factor as well. Many people do not have readily accessible medical care, and still many others have no coverage for preventive medicine. As a result, millions fall between the cracks until they are felled by heart attacks or strokes.

9      There is a tendency in some older people to think of diabetes as "just a little sugar," a common family problem. They fail to take it seriously and make the connection between it and the costly, crippling and often fatal diseases that can ensue. Diabetes, with its consequences of heart attack, stroke, kidney failure, amputations and blindness, among others, already ranks No. 1 in direct health care costs, consuming $1 of every $7 spent on health care. Nor is this epidemic confined to American borders. Internationally, "we are witnessing an epidemic that is the scourge of the 21st century," Dr. Kaufman wrote.

10     Unlike some other killer diseases, Type 2 diabetes issues an easily detected wake-up call: the accumulation of excess weight, especially around the abdomen. When the average fasting level of blood sugar (glucose) rises above 100 milligrams per deciliter, diabetes is looming. Abdominal fat is highly active. The chemical output of its cells increases blood levels of hormones like estrogen, providing the link between obesity and breast cancer, and decreases androgens, which can cause a decline in libido. As the cells in abdominal fat expand, they also release chemicals that increase fat accumulation, ensuring their own existence.

11     The result is an increasing cellular resistance to the effects of the hormone insulin, which enables cells to burn blood sugar for energy. As blood sugar rises with increasing insulin resistance, the pancreas puts out more and more insulin (promoting further fat storage) until this gland is exhausted. Then when your fasting blood sugar level reaches 126 milligrams, you have diabetes.

12     Two recent clinical trials showed that Type 2 diabetes could be prevented by changes in diet and exercise. The Diabetes Prevention Program Research Group involving 3,234 overweight adults showed that "intensive lifestyle intervention" was more effective than a drug that increases insulin sensitivity in preventing diabetes over three years. The intervention, lasting 24 weeks, trains people to choose low-calorie, low-fat diets; increase activity; and change their habits. Likewise, the randomized, controlled Finnish Diabetes Prevention Study of 522 obese patients showed that introducing a moderate

exercise program of at least 150 minutes a week and weight loss of at least 5 percent reduced the incidence of diabetes by 58 percent.

13    Many changes are needed to combat this epidemic, starting with schools and parents. Perhaps the quickest changes can be made in the workplace, where people can be encouraged to use stairs instead of elevators; vending machines can be removed or dispense only healthful snacks; and cafeterias can offer attractive healthful fare. Lunchrooms equipped with refrigerators and microwaves will allow workers to bring healthful meals to work. Dr. Kaufman tells of a challenge to get fit and lose weight by Caesars Entertainment in which 4,600 workers who completed the program lost a total of 45,000 pounds in 90 days. Others could follow this example.

---

## THINKING ABOUT THE TEXT

1. Cite the specific data that Brody includes from Kaufman's book on "diabesity" to support her claim that "excess weight" is "the most serious and costly health problem in America" (182).

2. What are the major causes and related factors that explain the current "diabesity" epidemic?

3. What is "Type 2 diabetes" and how can it be prevented?

4. List some of the changes in diet and guidelines for exercise that Brody recommends to combat and prevent this epidemic.

## WRITING FROM THE TEXT

1. Using data and details from Brody's essay, write an essay directed to your school district's board of education assessing your high school's nutrition and physical education policies and recommending changes.

2. Write an analysis essay that examines Brody's thesis, tone, main points, and support. Whom is she identifying as her audience and how effective are her strategies and appeal?

3. Focusing on Brody's information, write an essay fully defining "Type 2 diabetes," including both the causes and effects as well as those individuals most prone to developing this disease. (See Definition, pp. 397–401.)

## CONNECTING WITH OTHER TEXTS

1. Read "Why Stop Smoking?" (p. 291) and write a comparison-contrast of Harrison's and Brody's approaches and strategies for getting people to understand the dangers of their addictions and to make significant changes

in their lives. (See Comparison-Contrast, pp. 407–413.) Explain whether either author seems to appeal more to you and your peers—and why.

2. Read "O.K., So I'm Fat" (p. 179) and write an essay including details from Brody's article that address Steinberg's complacency.

3. After reading "Bodily Harm" (below) and "Dieting Daze: No In-Between" (p. 334), write an essay contrasting the causes and effects of the major eating disorders, anorexia and bulimia, with those of "diabesity," as described in Brody's essay.

#  Bodily Harm
### *Pamela Erens*

A 1985 graduate of Yale, Pamela Erens (b. 1963) has published work in the *New York Times, Glamour, O: The Oprah Magazine,* and *Mother Jones.* Her reviews, poetry, literary essays, and book reviews have appeared in many magazines and newspapers. She has also published a novel, *The Understory* (2007). The essay included here was first published in *Ms.* in 1985, when Erens interned there the summer after her graduation.

1    "Before I'd even heard of bulimia," said Gloria, "I happened to read an article in *People* magazine on Cherry Boone—how she'd used laxatives and vomiting to control her weight. I thought: Wow, what a great idea! I was sure that I would never lose control of my habit."

2    Recent media attention to the binge-purge and self-starvation disorders known as bulimia and anorexia—often detailing gruesome particulars of women's eating behavior—may have exacerbated this serious problem on college campuses. But why would a woman who reads an article on eating disorders want to copy what she reads? Ruth Striegel-Moore, PhD, director of Yale University's Eating Disorders Clinic, suggests that eating disorders may be a way to be like other "special" women and at the same time strive to outdo them. "The pursuit of thinness is a way for women to compete with each other, a way that avoids being threatening to men," says Striegel-Moore. Eating disorders as a perverse sort of rivalry? In Carol's freshman year at SUNY-Binghamton, a roommate showed her how to make herself throw up. "Barf buddies" are notorious on many college campuses, especially in sororities and among sports teams. Eating disorders as negative bonding? Even self-help groups on campus can degenerate into the kinds of competitiveness and negative reinforcement that are among the roots of eating disorders in the first place.

3    This is not another article on how women do it. It is an article on how and why some women stopped. The decision to get help is not always an easy one. The shame and secrecy surrounding most eating disorders and the fear or being labeled "sick" may keep a woman from admitting even to herself that her behavior is hurting her. "We're not weirdos," says Nancy Gengler, a recovered bulimic and number two U.S. squash champion, who asked that I use her real name because "so much of this illness has to do with secrecy and embarrassment." In the first stages of therapy, says Nancy, much of getting better was a result of building up the strength to (literally) "sweat out" the desire to binge and to endure the discomfort of having overeaten rather than throwing up. "I learned to accept such 'failures' and moreover, that they would not make me fat. . . ."

4    Secret shame or college fad, eating disorders among college women are growing at an alarming rate: in a recent study at Wellesley College, more than half the women on campus felt they needed help to correct destructive eating patterns. These included bingeing, chronic dieting, and "aerobic nervosa," the excessive use of exercise to maintain one's body ideal—in most women, invariably five to ten pounds less than whatever she currently weighs.

5    Why now? Wasn't the Women's Movement supposed to free women to be any body size, to explore the full range of creative and emotional possibilities? Instead, women in epidemic numbers are developing symptoms that make them feel hopeless about the future, depleting the energy they have for schoolwork and other activities, and if serious enough, send them right back home or into the infantalizing condition of hospitalization. What has gone wrong?

6    For Brenda, college meant the freedom to question her mother's values about sex. But when she abandoned her mother's guidelines, "I went to the other extreme. I couldn't set limits about sex, food, or anything else." The pressure on college women to appear successful and in control, to know what they want among the myriad new choices they are offered, is severe. So much so that many choose internal havoc over external imperfection. Naomi, a bulimic student at Ohio State University, said she would rather be alcoholic like her father than overweight like her mother because "fat is something you can see."

7    One reason college women hesitate to enter therapy, says Stephen Zimmer, director of the Center for the Study of Anorexia and Bulimia in New York City, is that the eating disorder has become a coping mechanism. It allows the person to function when she feels rotten inside. "In the first session," says Zimmer, "I tell my patients: "I'm not going to try to take your eating behavior away from you. Until you find something that works better, you get to keep it." Their relief is immense."

8    Brenda at first did not even tell the counselor whom she was seeing that she was bulimic. She started therapy because of a series of affairs with abusive men. As Brenda developed the sense that she had a right to say no to harmful relationships and to make demands on others, her inability to say no to food also disappeared.

9    However, if a woman is vomiting three times a day, she may be unable to concentrate on long-term therapy. Behavioral therapy, which directly addresses the learned habit of bingeing and purging, is a more immediate alternative. For eight years, Marlene Boskind White, PhD, and her husband, William White Jr., PhD, ran weekend workshops for bulimic women at Cornell University, usually as an adjunct to other forms of therapy. The sessions included nutritional counseling, developing techniques of dealing with binge "triggers," feminist consciousness-raising, and examining the hidden "pay-offs" that keep a woman from changing her eating behavior. Boskind-White and White report that a follow-up of 300 women they had treated one to three years earlier showed that 70 percent had entirely stopped purging and drastically reduced their bingeing.

10    Group therapy (an increasingly popular resource on college campuses) may be the first time a woman realizes she is not alone with her problem. Rebecca Axelrod, who was bulimic throughout college, and now counsels bulimics herself, found that joining the Cornell workshop and meeting other bulimic women defused many of her fears about herself: "I saw ten other women who were not mentally ill, not unable to function," Axelrod says. She remembers the moment when she understood the meaning of her bingeing and purging. "Saturday afternoon, Marlene took the women off alone, and we discussed the 'superwoman syndrome'—that attempt to be the perfect friend, lover, hostess, student . . . and perfect-looking. And bingeing, I saw, was my form of *defiance*. But if you're living life as the perfect woman, you won't cuss, you won't get drunk or laid or drive too fast. No, in the privacy of your own room you'll eat yourself out of house and home. But how dare you be defiant? And so you punish yourself by throwing it up."

11    But "groups can fall into a cycle I call 'bigger and badder,'" says Axelrod. "It starts when one person comes in and says, 'I feel terrible, I binged yesterday.' Somebody else says: 'Oh, that's okay, so did I.' Then a third person says: 'That's nothing, did you know I. . . .' Pretty soon everyone is lending support to the binge instead of to the woman who needs ways of coping with it."

12    However, Axelrod feels that there is much potential for women to help one another. She encourages bulimics to ask for help from their friends, saying that while she herself was initially frightened that being open about her bulimia would alienate her friends, most were very supportive.

"The important thing," says Axelrod, "is to be specific about what you need. Don't say: 'Be there for me.' Tell a friend exactly what she can do: for instance, not to urge you to go out for pizza if you tell her you're feeling vulnerable. And rely on three friends, not one."

13    One of the most important strategies in treating eating disorders, says Dr. Lee Combrinck-Graham of the newly opened Renfrew Center for anorectics and bulimics in Philadelphia, is breaking old patterns. Renfrew is a residential center that houses patients for between three weeks and two months, a period that can give women with eating disorders a respite from repetitive and destructive habits that are reinforced by the college environment. But Renfrew is not a "retreat"; its residents work hard. They participate in therapy workshops, take seminars in assertiveness-training and women's issues, and even participate in "new attitude" cooking classes. Dr. Combrinck-Graham stresses that therapy itself has often become a "pattern" for women who come to Renfrew. Many of Renfrew's patients, says Dr. Combrinck-Graham, can say exactly what's "wrong" with them and why, yet are still unable to control their eating habits. Renfrew combines a philosophy that recovery is the patient's responsibility—she sets her own goals and contracts for as much supervision as she needs—with innovative art and movement therapy that may bypass some of the rationalizations that block the progress of "talking" therapies.

14    Women who live close to home and whose parents are not separated may want to try family therapy. Family therapy considers the family itself, not the daughter with an eating disorder, to be the "patient." Often, the daughter has taken on the role of diverting attention from unacknowledged conflicts within the family. Family therapists behave somewhat like manic stage managers, interrupting and quizzing various members of a family, orchestrating confrontations in an attempt to expose and demolish old, rigid patterns of relating. Ideally, family therapy benefits all the members of the family. Carol, the student at SUNY-Binghamton, said that family therapy revealed how unhappy her mother was as a homemaker in a traditional Italian family.

15    Situations like Carol's are at the heart of today's epidemic of eating disorders, argues Kim Chernin in her book *The Hungry Self: Women, Eating, and Identity*. Chernin claims that today's college woman is the heir of a particular cultural moment that turns her hunger for identity into an uncontrollable urge for bodily nourishment. Young women of an earlier generation were educated to have children and remain in the home, yet our culture devalued the work they did there. Later, the Women's Movement opened up vast new emotional and career possibilities, and many daughters, on the verge of achieving their mother's suppressed dreams, are struck by panic and guilt.

16    Carol agreed: "I would try to push my mother to take classes, but my father was always against it. I was a good student, but how could I keep on

getting smarter than my mother? When I was young, we'd been like one person. I wanted to be a homemaker because she was one. But when I got older, I said to myself: 'This woman has no life. She never leaves the house except to get groceries. And she's miserable.' I wanted to stop growing up, and then she would always be able to lead me and guide me." According to Chernin, an eating disorder may be a way to postpone or put an end to one's development, one's need to choose, the possibility of surpassing one's mother. In a world hostile to the values of closeness and nurturance women learn from and associate with the mother-daughter relationship, an eating disorder can disguise a desire to return to the "nourishment" of that early bond.

17    And why do the daughter's problems focus around food? As Chernin reminds us, originally with her milk, the mother *is* food. Femininity itself has historically been associated with food gathering and preparation. Food—eating it, throwing it up—can become a powerful means of expressing aspects of the mother's life or of traditionally defined femininity that the daughter is trying to ingest or reject. And relationships with other women later in life can replicate this early pattern: food mediates hostility and love.

18    Whatever forms of therapy prove most helpful for women with eating disorders, it is clear that therapy is only half the battle. The Stone Center for Developmental Services and Studies at Wellesley College recognizes the need for early prevention and is preparing a film for adolescents that will feature women and health professionals speaking about the uses and abuses of food in our culture. Janet Surrey, PhD, a research associate at the center, stresses the need to educate girls in the 10- to 15-year-old age bracket—66 percent of whom already diet—about the psychological, physical, and reproductive danger of dieting and excessive thinness. Nutritional counseling is another imperative. But to Kim Chernin, our first priority is outreach centers and school programs that will provide developmental counseling and feminist consciousness-raising for this crucial pre-high school group. If women could learn early on to confront their conflicts over their right to development, the use of power, and their place in a still male-dominated world, there might no longer be a need for the "silent language" of eating disorders.

## THINKING ABOUT THE TEXT

1. According to Erens, how has popular press coverage of eating disorders exacerbated the problem?

2. What is Erens's purpose in quoting Rebecca Axelrod and others? What do these people and their comments contribute?

3. How can group therapy sessions, frequently joined by people with eating disorders, actually complicate the treatment?

4. What is Kim Chernin's perception of one cause of eating disorders?

5. How effective is Erens's conclusion, a proposal to curtail the number of young women with eating disorders?

### WRITING FROM THE TEXT

1. Do you think that women compete with each other by pursuing thinness? Do you think women bond in an effort to achieve thinness? Write an essay in which you describe and analyze the eating patterns of women you know.

2. Argue that the cause of eating disorders is not based in the mother-daughter relationship but in the superthin images in advertising. Cite and describe specific examples of advertising to support your view.

### CONNECTING WITH OTHER TEXTS

1. Pamela Erens, Jennifer Coleman (p. 175), and Rachel Krell (p. 293) describe the kinds of harm that can be done to women who try to conform to a standardized concept of beauty. In an analysis essay, examine the problem by connecting the ideas expressed by three of these writers.

2. This article, published in 1985, gives a good review of eating problems, but new information may provide increased or different insights. Use Erens's essay as a model but use more current material to analyze the problem of eating disorders.

# Three Ways of Meeting Oppression
## *Martin Luther King Jr.*

A graduate of Morehouse College, Crozer Theological Seminary, Boston University, and Chicago Theological Seminary, Martin Luther King Jr. (1929–1968) received numerous awards for his literary work and leadership as well as the Nobel Peace Prize in 1964. An ordained Baptist minister, King became well known as a national and international spokesperson for civil rights after his organization of the successful Montgomery, Alabama, bus boycott. In spite of threatening phone calls, being arrested, and having his home bombed, King continued to work with nonviolent resistance and to argue eloquently for racial equality. He was assassinated on April 3, 1968. The following selection is excerpted from *Stride Toward Freedom*, published in 1958.

1      Oppressed people deal with their oppression in three characteristic ways. One way is acquiescence: the oppressed resign themselves to their doom.

They tacitly adjust themselves to oppression, and thereby become conditioned to it. In every movement toward freedom some of the oppressed prefer to remain oppressed. Almost 2,800 years ago Moses set out to lead the children of Israel from the slavery of Egypt to the freedom of the promised land. He soon discovered that slaves do not always welcome their deliverers. They become accustomed to being slaves. They would rather bear those ills they have, as Shakespeare pointed out, than flee to others that they know not of. They prefer the "fleshpots of Egypt" to the ordeals of emancipation.

2    There is such a thing as the freedom of exhaustion. Some people are so worn down by the yoke of oppression that they give up. A few years ago in the slum areas of Atlanta, a Negro guitarist used to sing almost daily: "Ben down so long that down don't bother me." This is the type of negative freedom and resignation that often engulfs the life of the oppressed.

3    But this is not the way out. To accept passively an unjust system is to cooperate with that system; thereby the oppressed become as evil as the oppressor. Noncooperation with evil is as much a moral obligation as is cooperation with good. The oppressed must never allow the conscience of the oppressor to slumber. Religion reminds every man that he is his brother's keeper. To accept injustice or segregation passively is to say to the oppressor that his actions are morally right. It is a way of allowing his conscience to fall asleep. At this moment the oppressed fails to be his brother's keeper. So acquiescence—while often the easier way—is not the moral way. It is the way of the coward. The Negro cannot win the respect of his oppressor by acquiescing; he merely increases the oppressor's arrogance and contempt. Acquiescence is interpreted as proof of the Negro's inferiority. The Negro cannot win the respect of the white people of the South or the peoples of the world if he is willing to sell the future of his children for his personal and immediate comfort and safety.

4    A second way that oppressed people sometimes deal with oppression is to resort to physical violence and corroding hatred. Violence often brings about momentary results. Nations have frequently won their independence in battle. But in spite of temporary victories, violence never brings permanent peace. It solves no social problem; it merely creates new and more complicated ones.

5    Violence as a way of achieving racial justice is both impractical and immoral. It is impractical because it is a descending spiral ending in destruction for all. The old law of an eye for an eye leaves everybody blind. It is immoral because it seeks to humiliate the opponent rather than win his understanding; it seeks to annihilate rather than to convert. Violence is immoral because it thrives on hatred rather than love. It destroys a community and makes

brotherhood impossible. It leaves society in monologue rather than dialogue. Violence ends by defeating itself. It creates bitterness in the survivors and brutality in the destroyers. A voice echoes through time saying to every potential Peter, "Put up your sword." History is cluttered with the wreckage of nations that failed to follow this command.

6    If the American Negro and other victims of oppression succumb to the temptation of using violence in the struggle for freedom, future generations will be the recipients of a desolate night of bitterness, and our chief legacy to them will be an endless reign of meaningless chaos. Violence is not the way.

7    The third way open to oppressed people in their quest for freedom is the way of nonviolent resistance. Like the synthesis in Hegelian philosophy, the principle of nonviolent resistance seeks to reconcile the truths of two opposites—acquiescence and violence—while avoiding the extremes and immoralities of both. The nonviolent resister agrees with the person who acquiesces that one should not be physically aggressive toward his opponent but he balances the equation by agreeing with the person of violence that evil must be resisted. He avoids the nonresistance of the former and the violent resistance of the latter. With nonviolent resistance, no individual or group need submit to any wrong, nor need anyone resort to violence in order to right a wrong.

8    It seems to me that this is the method that must guide the actions of the Negro in the present crisis in race relations. Through nonviolent resistance the Negro will be able to rise to the noble height of opposing the unjust system while loving the perpetrators of the system. The Negro must work passionately and unrelentingly for full stature as a citizen, but he must not use inferior methods to gain it. He must never come to terms with falsehood, malice, hate, or destruction.

9    Nonviolent resistance makes it possible for the Negro to remain in the South and struggle for his rights. The Negro's problem will not be solved by running away. He cannot listen to the glib suggestion of those who would urge him to migrate en masse to other sections of the country. By grasping his great opportunity in the South he can make a lasting contribution to the moral strength of the nation and set a sublime example of courage for generations yet unborn.

10    By nonviolent resistance, the Negro can also enlist all men of good will in his struggle for equality. The problem is not a purely racial one, with Negroes set against whites. In the end, it is not a struggle between people at all, but a tension between justice and injustice. Nonviolent resistance is not aimed against oppressors but against oppression. Under its banner consciences, not racial groups, are enlisted.

11     If the Negro is to achieve the goal of integration, he must organize himself into a militant and nonviolent mass movement. All three elements are indispensable. The movement for equality and justice can only be a success if it has both a mass and militant character; the barriers to be overcome require both. Nonviolence is an imperative in order to bring about ultimate community.

## THINKING ABOUT THE TEXT

1. What are the three ways that "oppressed people deal with oppression" (191)? Is the first method that King defines actually a way to "deal" with oppression?

2. What does King decide about each of the ways he defines and describes? What are the advantages of the method he prefers? Why does he prefer this method?

3. Cite the ways that King establishes that his argument is not only about "the Negro" struggling for rights.

4. King concludes that for "the Negro" to achieve civil rights and integration, "he must organize himself into a militant and nonviolent mass movement" (194). Because King has ruled out violence as a means of meeting oppression, the word "militant" may seem inappropriate. What does the word actually mean?

5. This excerpt from King's writing functions as an essay but lacks an articulated thesis. What do you infer to be the central assertion of this selection?

6. Study King's exemplary rhetorical devices to be able to answer these questions:

   • How does King organize this section of his writing?
   • What are King's transitional devices?
   • What are the lines that remind the reader that King was a minister who spoke meaningfully and memorably from the pulpit?
   • How does King use the pronoun "it" as an effective connecting device within paragraph 5? (See pp. 341–342 for a discussion of this device.)

## WRITING FROM THE TEXT

1. King concludes this section of his writing with the awareness that "nonviolence is an imperative in order to bring about ultimate community" (194). Write an essay that describes an "ultimate community" that King would consider acceptable.

2. Write an essay that shows your own experience or observations of specific moments of acquiescence, violence, or nonviolent resistance in response to oppression. Provide details about what worked and what did not work. Does your experience confirm or refute King's position?

### CONNECTING WITH OTHER TEXTS

1. Read "Who Shot Johnny?" (p. 23) and "King Curtis's Echo" (p. 169) and write an essay showing how both essays support King's recommendations for handling oppression. In what ways are the philosophies of the three writers complementary?

2. After reading Brent Staples's "Black Men and Public Space" (p. 164), analyze how Staples's responses and methods are consistent with King's ideas.

#  Stuttering Can Be Shameful
## *Dan Slater*

With degrees in international relations (Colgate University) and law (Brooklyn Law School), Dan Slater (b. 1977) has prospered in varied careers that include the practice of law and journalism. As he describes his experience, "two weeks after being sworn in to the New York bar, I left law for a job writing about Wall Street at *The Deal* Magazine." He was the lead writer of the *WSJ (Wall Street Journal) Law Blog* from 2008-2009. As a freelance writer, Slater has had work published in the *New York Times*, the *Washington Post*, *New York* magazine, *GQ, Men's Health*, and *American Lawyer*. In 2010, Slater launched a new Internet site called LongForum, "A New Read on Old Media." Slater's essay "Stuttering Can Be Shameful" appeared first in the *Washington Post* in December, 2010, and has been reprinted in other periodicals because of the popularity of the film *The King's Speech*, to which it refers.

1    What I remember most about my stutter is not the stupefying vocal paralysis, the pursed eyes or the daily ordeal of gagging on my own speech, sounds ricocheting off the back of my teeth like pennies trying to escape a piggy bank. Those were merely the mechanics of stuttering, the realities to which one who stutters adjusts his expectations of life. Rather, what was most pervasive about my stutter is the strange role it played in determining how I felt about others, about you.

2    My stutter became a barometer of how much confidence I felt in your presence. Did I perceive you as friendly, patient, kind? Or as brash and aggressive? How genuine was your smile? Did you admire my talents, or were you wary

of my more unseemly traits? In this way I divided the world into two types of people: those around whom I stuttered and those around whom I might not.

3    The onset of my stutter occurred under typical circumstances: I was 4; I had a father who carried a stutter into adulthood; and, at the time, my parents were engaged in a bitter, protracted, Reagan-era divorce that seemed destined for mutually assured destruction.

4    My mother chronicled my speech problems in her diaries from the period. Sept. 26, 1981: "Daniel has been biting his fingernails for the past several weeks; along with stuttering up." July 8, 1982: "After phone call [with his father] Danny stuttering quite a bit, blocking on words."

5    In fact, my father and I had different stutters. His was what speech therapists consider the more traditional kind, in which the first syllable of a word gets repeated. "Bus" might sound like "aba-aba-abus." Mine was a blockage, a less extreme version of what King George VI, portrayed by Colin Firth, must deal with in the new movie *The King's Speech*.

6    My vocal cords would strangle certain sounds. Hard consonants—k's, d's, hard c's and hard g's—gave me hell. A year of speech therapy in childhood helped me develop a set of tools for defeating the impediment, or at least concealing it well enough to fool most of the people most of the time. Like many other stutterers, I evolved a verbal dexterity. Embarking on a sentence was like taking a handoff and running through the line of scrimmage: I'd look five or 10 words upfield, and if I saw a mean word, such as "camping," I'd stiff-arm it and cut back hard in search of a less-resistant path, opting perhaps for something more literal: "I want to sleep in the woods this weekend."

7    But the strategies of substitution and circumlocution were never foolproof. The stuttering rat always lurks. When I was 14 years old, I wanted to ask a girl to the high school dance. Unfortunately, her name was Kim. I sweated it out for a few days, waiting for gumption to arrive. When I finally called Kim's house, her mother answered.

8    "Yeah hi, I was wondering if ahhh . . . if ahhh . . . if . . ."

9    I needed to bust through that K. But all I could do was pant, breathless, as the K clung to the roof of my mouth like a cat in a tree.

10    I breathed deeply and said at once: "YeahhiIwaswonderingifKimwasthere."

11    "Kim?" her mother said with a laugh. "Are you sure?"

12    Another deep breath: "OhyeahI'msureKim."

13    When Kim took the phone, she told me her mom thought it was funny that I'd forgotten whom I'd called. I laughed along with them, of course, because it was preferable to forget the name of a girl you liked than to be thought an idiot.

14    More than 3 million Americans stutter, about 1 percent of the population. Stuttering afflicts four times as many males as females. Five percent of preschool children stutter as a normal developmental trend and outgrow it without therapy. While no single cause has been identified, stuttering is thought to result from a combination of genetics (about 60 percent of those who stutter have a family member who stutters), neurophysiology and family dynamics, such as a legacy of high achievement.

15    Stuttering, like other enigmatic ailments, has a checkered past. Beginning more than 2,000 years ago, one ridiculous theory followed another. Aristotle, who may have stuttered, believed the stutterer's tongue was too thick and therefore "too sluggish to keep pace with the imagination." Galen, the Greek doctor, claimed the stutterer's tongue was too wet; the Roman physician Celsus suggested gargling and massages to strengthen a weak tongue. Such quackery reached its logical climax in the 19th century, when Johann Friedrich Dieffenbach, the Prussian plastic surgeon, decided that people stuttered because their tongues were too unwieldy. In several cases he cut the organ down to size.

16    It wasn't until the early 20th century that serious steps were taken to understand and treat stuttering. Therapists tended to focus on the adolescent context in which stuttering evolves. Albert Murphy, a speech pathologist at Boston University, promoted a psychogenic theory, suggesting that the roots of stuttering "lie in disturbed interpersonal relationships and the stutterer's fractured self-image."

17    This theory is at the heart of *The King's Speech*. Screenwriter David Seidler, a stutterer, focused on the trust-building process through which an Australian speech therapist coaxes out of King George his earliest memories. In the breakthrough scene, the king recounts his childhood torments inflicted by his older brother, Edward, the sting of ridicule and his mistreatment at the hands of the royal nanny.

18    The psychogenic theory can be a seductive one—My parents screwed me up!—but it has largely fallen out of fashion, replaced with techniques such as breathing exercises and delayed auditory feedback, which uses hearing-aid-like devices that play the stutterer's speech back to him.

19    For someone who stutters, every speech hang-up carves a little more confidence out of him, leaving behind an ever-deepening sinkhole of shame and self-hatred. A child who stutters might excel at science, be a good reader, throw a perfect spiral pass or demonstrate loyal friendship. But in his mind he only stutters, and that is all that matters. Every stuttering incident intensifies that feedback loop of failure inside his head—"Everyone thinks I'm an idiot"—making the next speech attempt even more difficult.

20    Yet, small victories—even one fluent sentence—can be equally emboldening, because the stutterer is a powerful believer. "I'll keep trying to speak,"

he thinks, "because tomorrow I might just be able to." The trick, for me, was switching that internal soundtrack from: "Oh no, here we go again" to: "Breathe, relax and let it ride."

21  When I was 8, my mother took me to a speech therapist. He was a big-hearted, supremely patient man with whom I spent many afternoons discussing my favorite things: football, movies and my baseball card collection. He taught me the "airflow" technique developed by Martin Schwartz, a professor at New York University Medical Center.

22  Schwartz believed that stuttering is caused when the vocal cords clamp shut. To release them, the stutterer is instructed to sigh, inaudibly, just before speaking. Like a roller coaster, my speech therapist would tell me, the words get a free ride on the airflow.

23  After a year of therapy, I wasn't completely fluent, but I left with new confidence and a toolkit for dealing with my stutter. One of those tools entailed practicing fluency through imitation, whether quoting songs or spouting movie lines with my brother.

24  This was all about changing the feedback loop of failure: Psychologically, I could slide into a different character, no longer expecting to loathe the sound of my own voice. Physiologically, imitation provided new feedbacks to my breathing and voice mechanisms: a different pitch, a different articulation and a different rate of speaking to which I could peg my own speech.

25  However, just as the word-switching technique was never foolproof, neither was imitation. When I was 16, the stuttering rat emerged again. In a class about the legal system, I was assigned to be the prosecutor in a mock murder trial. I would have to write and deliver an opening statement. *A Few Good Men*, a movie about a military trial, had recently been released on video. I loved the way Kevin Bacon strutted before the jury, so self-assured and confident of his case against the defendants. So I practiced in his speaking style. I even wrote the last sentence of his monologue into my own statement.

26  The next morning, when I stepped to the podium, I tried to relax and breathe. But a straitjacket of stress shut me down; the muscles in my throat and chest choked off the air. Thanks to pure stubbornness, I persisted, blocking on every fifth word of a 500-word speech. By the time I reached the Kevin Bacon line—"These are the facts of the case and they are undisputed"—I couldn't move sentences with a dolly.

27  A couple of days later, the teacher stopped me in the hallway and said, "Dan, I had no idea. It was so courageous of you to try." She was a sweet woman, but it was the last thing I wanted to hear. The recognition of one's stutter can be as humiliating as the stutter itself. I'd been found out.

28  During college I ditched out on a couple of class presentations and made it through a couple of others. In law school I spoke fluently before groups on

several occasions but declined an offer to be in the mock trial club. During six years in journalism, including a stint at the *Wall Street Journal*, I've found radio interviews to be much easier than videotaped segments.

29    I'm 33 now. I believe I'm mostly cured of my stutter. Yet, when I recently visited a speech therapist in New York and spoke with him, he disagreed. He said that nothing I had said during our meeting indicated disfluency. But when I confessed that I switch words several times per day and think quite often about my stutter, he said: "A lot of energy goes into hiding it, to hoping no one finds out. You're thinking about it a lot. We would not call this a mark of success." Think about it a lot? But of course.

30    For all the empathy that can make a good speech therapist effective, perhaps there's one thing a non-stutterer can never understand: If we go to therapy, we think about it. If we don't go to therapy, we think about it. It's always there. Either it defines us or we find ways of accommodating it, working toward a state of peaceful coexistence, pushing on with the Kims and the Katies.

## THINKING ABOUT THE TEXT

1. Why does the author use the word "barometer" to describe how his stuttering helped him measure social relationships? What is the author's strategy in using the direct address—"about you"—to his readers?

2. What are the "typical circumstances" that accompanied the onset of his stuttering? What tools did Slater use to "defeat" his impediment? What does he mean by the "verbal dexterity" that he, and other stutterers, develop? How is this dexterity exemplified in his dramatization of his telephone conversation with Kim's mother?

3. What are the most interesting statistical details and historical treatments for stuttering provided by Slater?

4. If you have seen the film *The King's Speech,* do you agree that the screenwriter David Seidler intended to focus on the "disturbed interpersonal relationships and the stutterer's fractured self-image" as an explanation for Bertie's speech impediment?

5. What is the sad reality for those who are afflicted with a speech impediment but might "excel at science, be a good reader, throw a perfect spiral pass or demonstrate loyal friendship" (197)?

6. What techniques did Slater learn from the speech therapist who treated him when he was a child? In what ways did the techniques work for him? When did they fail? How does his present therapist regard his condition? How does the writer perceive his own condition and that of other stutterers?

## WRITING FROM THE TEXT

1. If you have a speech impediment or some other affliction that creates social discomfort, write an essay that shows the physical and emotional problems that exist for you. Consider using some of the strategies employed by Slater to create interest, understanding, and empathy in his reader: a briefly recounted family history, dramatizations of humiliating moments, a brief history of treatments of speech impediments, personal therapies experienced, pointed revelation of feelings about the condition, and vivid descriptions—"sounds ricocheting off the back of my teeth like pennies trying to escape a piggy bank" (195).

2. With the goal of creating both factual understanding of an affliction that you have and showing how you have come to deal with it, write a narrative that dramatizes a significant incident in your life. (See Narration, pp. 382–396.)

## CONNECTING WITH OTHER TEXTS

1. View the film *The King's Speech* and write an analytical essay that compares the family backgrounds, therapies, and personal humiliations endured by Dan Slater and King George VI. If you take notes while you screen the film, you will have specific comparisons to incorporate into your essay. (Review How to Screen a Film, pp. 429–430.)

2. Review Dan Slater's essay with the intention of determining which aspects of his speech impediment interest you most: the possible psychological causes, the techniques for dealing with the impediment, or the present therapies for stutterers. With the goal of writing a research paper, pursue other sources for more information in order to create a developed, focused, documented paper. (See Shannon Paaske's research paper "From Access to Acceptance" pp. 486–498.)

## Film Analysis of *The King's Speech*

### *Philip French, film critic,* The Guardian

A review of the film *The King's Speech* appears below. The film is based on the personal story of King George VI, who from childhood struggled with a speech impediment that threatened to ruin his reign. The film dramatizes the relationship between the king and his supportive wife as well as the bond between the king and his speech therapist. Colin Firth plays King George VI, called Bertie by family and friends, and Geoffrey Rush plays the Australian speech therapist Lionel Logue. Helena Bonham Carter plays Bertie's wife, Guy Pearce plays his brother who abdicates his position as King Edward VIII to marry his lover, American divorcee Wallis Simpson, played by Eve Best. Timothy Spall plays Prime Minister Winston Churchill, Michael Gambon plays Bertie's father, King George V, and Claire Bloom plays Bertie's mother. This film was written by David Seidler and directed by Tom Hooper. *The King's Speech* runs 118 minutes.

1    W.H. Auden wrote his poem "September 1, 1939" while sitting in a New York bar: "Uncertain and afraid/ As the clever hopes expire/ Of a low dishonest decade." *The King's Speech* takes a rather different view of Britain and the 1930s, though it's not entirely inconsistent with Auden's judgment and isn't in any sense what is sneeringly called heritage cinema. It is the work of a highly talented group of artists who might be regarded as British realists— Tom Hooper directed the soccer epic *The Damned United;* Eve Stewart was production designer on Mike Leigh's *Topsy-Turvy* and *Vera Drake;* Jenny Beavan was responsible for the costumes worn in *Gosford Park* and *The Remains of the Day;* the cinematographer Danny Cohen lit Shane Meadows's *This is England* and *Dead Man's Shoes;* Tariq Anwar's editing credits range from *The Madness of King George* to *American Beauty;* and the screenplay is by the British writer David Seidler, who co-wrote Coppola's *Tucker: The Man and His Dream.*

2    The film is the private story of a famous public man, King George VI (known in his family circle as Bertie), the woman who loved him and became his queen, and the innovative Australian speech therapist Lionel Logue, who helped him control and come to terms with the stammer that had tortured him since childhood.

3    The social and political background, acutely observed and carefully woven into the film's fabric, is the Depression at home, the rise of fascism abroad, and the arrival of the mass media as a major force in our lives. Central to the dramatic action are four crucial incidents: the death in 1936 of George V, the first monarch to address his subjects via the radio; the accession to the throne of his eldest son as Edward VIII and his almost immediate abdication in order to marry American double divorcee Wallis Simpson; the crowning of his successor, George VI; and finally, in 1939, the outbreak of a war for which the king and queen became figureheads of immeasurable national significance alongside their prime minister, Winston Churchill.

4    Although the film involves a man overcoming a serious disability, it is neither triumphalist nor sentimental. Its themes are courage (where it comes from, how it is used), responsibility, and the necessity to place duty above personal pleasure or contentment—the subjects, in fact, of such enduringly popular movies as *Casablanca* and *High Noon*. In this sense, *The King's Speech* is an altogether more significant and ambitious work than Stephen Frears's admirable *The Queen* of 2006 and far transcends any political arguments about royalty and republicanism.

5    The film begins with a brief prologue in which both Bertie as Duke of York (Colin Firth) and his contemporary audience endure agonies of

embarrassment as he attempts to deliver a speech at Wembley Stadium during the 1924 Empire exhibition. The rest takes place between 1934 when his wife (Helena Bonham Carter) arranges for him to see Logue the unorthodox therapist (Geoffrey Rush), and shortly after the beginning of the war when he makes a crucial live broadcast to the world from Buckingham Palace, with Logue almost conducting the speech from the other side of the microphone.

6    Helena Bonham Carter is a warm, charming, puckish presence as Elizabeth, very much aware of her royal status when first approaching Logue using a pseudonym, Michael Gambon is entirely convincing as George V, a peremptory man irritated by the increasing demands of democracy; having been neglected by his own father, he's incapable of expressing love for his sons. Guy Pearce is equally good as the selfish, wilful future King Edward, the movie's one truly despicable character, whose mocking of his brother's stammer places him beyond the pale. Derek Jacobi does a neat turn as Cosmo Lang, the Archbishop of Canterbury, pillar of the establishment, at once dictatorial and obsequious.

7    The movie, however, ultimately turns upon the skilfully written and impeccably played scenes between Firth's Bertie, initially almost choking on his stammer but trained to insist on court protocol, and Rush's Logue, the informal, blunt-speaking Australian, whose manners are as relaxed as his consulting room in Harley Street is modest. The interplay between them resembles a version of *Pygmalion* or *My Fair Lady* in which Eliza is a princess and Henry Higgins a lower-middle-class teacher from Sydney, and they're just as funny, moving and class-conscious as in Shaw's play. There are also, one might think, benign echoes of Prince Hal and Falstaff from *Henry IV*.

8    Across a great social gulf they become friends, the king gaining in confidence and humanity, deeply affected by the first commoner he's befriended. But to the end there remains the need to preserve a certain distance.

9    The film is not without its odd faults, the truly annoying one being the representation of Winston Churchill (Timothy Spall) as a supporter of George during the abdication. In fact, his intrigues in Edward VIII's cause nearly ruined his career. In his biography of Churchill, Roy Jenkins remarks that "had Churchill succeeded in keeping Edward VIII on the throne he might well have found it necessary in 1940 to depose and/or lock up his sovereign as the dangerously potential head of a Vichy-style state."

10    But overall the film is a major achievement, with Firth presenting us with a great profile in courage, a portrait of that recurrent figure, the stammerer as hero. He finds as many different aspects of stammering as the number of ways of photographing sand explored by Freddie Young in *Lawrence of Arabia* or John Seale in *The English Patient*. And as they did, he deserves an Oscar.

## Works Cited

*The King's Speech*. Dir. Tom Hooper. Perf. Colin Firth, Geoffrey Rush, Guy Pearce, Helena Bonham Carter, Michael Gambon, Timothy Spall, and Claire Bloom. The Weinstein Co., 2010. Film.

French, Philip. "The King's Speech." Rev. of *The King's Speech*. Dir. Tom Hooper. guardian.co.uk. *The Guardian*. 9 Jan. 2011. Web. 11. Jan. 2011.

## THINKING ABOUT THE FILM

1. What surprising facts about British royalty during this time period did you learn from this historical docudrama?

2. In what ways does this film transcend its historical and political realities? What is the film's specific focus? In what ways is the focus of the film surprising? What might have been more sensational aspects of the time period around which to create a film?

3. What specific details do we learn about King George VI (Bertie)—his childhood, his marriage and present family life and his career before he became King? How does the film create audience awareness of his character? What can we infer about Bertie's character based on what he reveals about his past and what we see of him in public and private scenes in the film? Make a list of specific details in order to respond to these questions.

4. What do we learn about the character of Lionel Logue, the speech therapist who works with Bertie? Make a list of specific details about Logue's life to support inferences about him.

5. As Logue and Bertie work together on the future King's speech impediment, what aspects of their working relationship become personal? What social realities keep them distant? How does the film dramatize the frictions and bonds between the men?

6. What do you perceive to be the most important themes of the film? Making a list of the many insights that you can draw from this film will help you resist "the moral of the story" sort of aphorisms.

## WRITING FROM THE FILM

1. Write a character analysis of Bertie, King George VI, based on inferences you can support with specific details and analysis of key scenes in the film. (Review How to Screen a Film, pp. 429–430, and Character Analysis, pp. 445–468.)

2. Using key scenes from the film and your analysis of his relationship with his family members and Bertie, write a character analysis of Lionel Logue, the speech therapist.

3. Write a comparison and contrast study of Bertie and Logue based on what they reveal about themselves and what you see of their behavior in scenes in the film. Conclude your study with some awareness you derive about the nature of relationships conditioned by social realities or differences in social class.

4. Americans often describe the British as "reserved" or "contained." Consider what the audience sees of British behavior in this film and write an analytical paper that supports and/or refutes stereotypical views of the British. A review of Alex Garcia's comparison/contrast essay (pp. 409–411) might help you with organization and inspire you to use humor in your essay.

## Connecting with Other Texts

1. In his review of *The King's Speech*, Philip French describes the film as a portrait of quiet heroism. Write an analysis of Bertie that supports French's perception of the man.

2. In her largely negative review of the film, Manohla Dargis writes that the film is "too ingratiating to resonate deeply" and that the relationship between David, who abdicates, and the scandalous American divorcee he loves, is far more interesting than the focus of the film that was made. Read Ms. Dargis's review ("*The King's English*, Albeit With Twisted Tongue," nytimes.com, published November 25, 2010) and write an essay that agrees with or refutes her perception of the film.

3. After reading Dan Slater's personal history "Stuttering Can Be Shameful" (p. 195) and other material that has been written in response to *The King's Speech*, write an essay about the problems of people who stutter and the methods used to correct speech impediments.

# Chapter 5

# Between Points of View

In this chapter we present contrasting viewpoints on timely issues and values that influence the choices we make as individuals and as citizens. The opening decades of the twenty-first century have witnessed the explosion of technology beyond what could ever have been imagined even at the close of the last century. This explosion has prompted divergent points of view on how technology should be used and whether our planet's life and our own safety will suffer the consequences of this explosion. The writers in this chapter debate those conflicting points of view.

Cellphones, for example, have provided convenient, mobile communication, but Myron Levin, Janet P. Froetscher, Marcel Just, and Tim Keller provide convincing research that driving while using cellphones, even handsfree phones, is endangering lives. Another innovation of the century, the iPod provides hours of listening pleasure. However, as Patricia Wen illustrates, if iPods are played frequently at high volume, they can impair hearing even in the young. More a time drain than a danger, Twitter is described as a potentially enriching medium by writer David Pogue, while author Meghan Daum finds Twitter "inane" and "insane." Some readers, indeed, may feel nostalgic for the past when electronic technology was not so ever-present, but poet Philip Dacey reminds readers that past eras had their own limitations, even without the anxieties of the digital world.

Certainly, digital media are ubiquitous, but whether Internet use makes us smarter, as Clay Shirky believes, or dumber, as Nicholas Carr asserts, is a hotly-debated issue. Christopher Chabris and Daniel Simons, who examine some effects of Internet use, believe that our brains can handle the bombardment of electronic stimuli. However, they acknowledge that this onslaught of online information—superficial as it can be—may give us a false sense that we know more than we really do.

A superficial response to life is Anne Lamott's fear, and her essay argues for a deeper commitment to friends, personal growth, and nature. The need to make a personal commitment to the environment—to bother to change our habits—is addressed quite differently in tone and substance by Michael Pollan and Monica Hesse. Exposing the threats of climate change, Al Gore's film *An Inconvenient Truth* is reviewed by film critics Kevin Crust and A.O. Scott and researched by Katharine Mieszkowski. All of these divergent points of view promise to enlighten, amuse, and possibly enrage you—and thereby motivate some good argumentative and analytic responses in your writings.

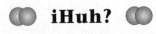

# iHuh?

## *Patricia Wen*

Award-winning journalist Patricia Wen (b. 1958) writes full-time for the *Boston Globe*, covering issues involving children, family, and social services. She previously worked on the education and health-science staff and also served for three years on the Globe's Spotlight Team, the newspaper's investigative reporting unit. In 2004, Wen was a finalist for the Pulitzer Prize in feature writing for her series about a troubled mother's decision to release her children for adoption. That series also won her a 2004 Casey Medal for Meritorious Journalism for distinguished coverage of children and family issues. Wen earned a BA in East Asian Studies from Harvard College. The following essay was published in the *Boston Globe* on May 18, 2009.

1    Seventeen-year-old Nicholas Silva has one way to escape the tensions of teenage life: He picks up his beloved iPod. The Cambridge Rindge & Latin School junior places the earbuds snugly into his ear canals and sets the volume bar as high as possible. For him, there is no such thing as a mute button standing between him and the full-pitched vocals of his favorite rappers, Kanye West and Rick Ross.

2    "When it's louder, you're in the zone," he said sitting with friends at the food court in the CambridgeSide Galleria last weekend.

3    But audiologists say that teenagers such as Silva may be heading into a new, dreaded zone: Irreparable hearing damage.

4    Since iPods were launched eight years ago, some 200 million of these MP3 players have been sold worldwide, giving young and old the convenience of storing thousands of songs on a feather-weight portable device with enduring

battery life. The advance in technology means extended listening time; for teens, that listening is often done at an especially high decibel level, research shows. And that poses some tangible risks.

5    Researchers say the sensory cells in our inner ear—which transmit sounds to our brains—can only take so much auditory bombardment before they begin to wilt, irreparably, and die. The damage teens suffer now may not show up until they're in their 40s and asking friends in crowded restaurants, "Could you repeat that?" Or it may appear sooner. Some young adults in their 20s—who listened at high levels hour after hour, day after day—are being diagnosed with hearing at the level of a typical 50-year-old, according to Dr. Brian Fligor, a former amateur rock guitarist who is now director of diagnostic audiology at Children's Hospital Boston.

6    Teens often fail to realize just how much they crank up the volume to compensate for the clanging of the subway or the chatter in the cafe, research shows. Boys tend to turn up the iPod volume louder than girls, and peer pressure can influence volume levels, according to a recent study at Children's Hospital Boston. "I tell them you can listen loud—but you have to listen smart," said Fligor, author of the study. The obvious question for iPod fanatics is: How much is too much?

7    The science of hearing loss is murky, and like a lot of areas of public health, a person's vulnerability is a combination of genetic predisposition and hard-to-measure environmental hazards. All people suffer some age-related loss that shows up anywhere from their 40s to 60s, but how much loud-noise exposure you can sustain depends on whether you are born with tough or tender ears. Some ears fully recover from an ear-ringing blaring rock concert; others are permanently weakened by it.

8    Because more men show up complaining about hearing loss, some doctors concluded that more men have susceptible ears; however some researchers believe that men's ears over the decades are just more exposed to aggravating sounds, such as loud machinery in factories or gunfire in the military.

9    When it comes to setting safe guidelines for iPod users, today's audiologists rely largely on a 1970s federal government study of more than 1,000 workers in various industries. They concluded that 8 percent of workers who were exposed to 85 decibels for more than eight hours a day, for 40 years, suffered serious, noise-related hearing impairment. It may seem arbitrary to transfer that 85-decibel level to iPod use, but many audiologists have found it a useful guide.

10   Fligor, who has authored several studies about iPod use among teens and young adults, has some general guidelines for the typical user: Based on available data, he recommends iPod users of any age listen to no more than

90 minutes a day if the volume is set at 80 percent of its capacity—roughly a 90-decibel level. If the volume bar were set at 60 percent, which reflects about 75 decibels, Fligor said, one could probably listen "all day" without risking serious damage; if it were set at 90 percent of maximum capacity, or nearly 100 decibels, a person could listen safely only for about 20 minutes a day.

11    Giving iPod advice is more art than science, and not all doctors are willing to set such specific listening guidelines. Dr. Sharon Kujawa, director of audiology at Massachusetts Eye and Ear Infirmary in Boston, said she cannot yet give specific recommendations for iPod users—not until more research is done. She said "people are all different" and it is not possible now to establish safe guidelines, other than "err on the side of caution."

12    Today's iPods can be set to automatically limit maximum volume, which Fligor measures as about 105 decibels. Dr. Roland Eavey, the former director of pediatric otolaryngology at Mass. Eye and Ear and now chief of otolaryngology at Vanderbilt University Medical Center in Nashville, said today's youth are far too oblivious to the dangers of premature hearing loss. He found that only 8 percent of adolescents ranked hearing loss as a major health problem, while more than 40 percent saw sexually transmitted diseases, substance abuse, depression, and smoking as serious issues, according to a 2005 report that examined attitudes of nearly 10,000 teenagers and young adults who responded to a Web-based survey posted on MTV.com.

13    That same survey found that 61 percent of them experienced ringing in their ears or some hearing impairment after a concert, and 43 percent after being at a club. Only 14 percent had used protective earplugs. Eavey emphasized that noise-related damage can be alleviated, in part, by giving one's ear a rest between exposures.

14    Teenagers who think their ears are immune from damage need only know about the hearing levels of the Who's guitarist, Peter Townshend, or rock guitarist Jeff Beck. These performers, now in their mid-60s, suffer from permanent noise-related hearing damage and they speak publicly about the need for more ear protections for musicians. Fligor, who confesses that he too often loves to "listen loud," tries not to be a purist. He said teenagers should remember that the occasional shriek-filled, booming rock concert is probably fine. Taking in a favorite hip-hop song at the iPod's full volume also isn't going to ruin their ears on a given day "as long as you don't listen to more than one song."

## THINKING ABOUT THE TEXT

1. Analyze the effectiveness of Wen's opening paragraph. Why is Nicholas Silva an ideal subject for her focus? What are the most important details about him?

2. Although Wen is appealing to young readers, how does her information about iPods provide *all* readers with the background needed to understand her essay?

3. How does Wen explain the danger of hearing loss? How is this explanation ideal, especially for young adult readers?

4. What is the obvious question that iPod fanatics want to have answered? How does she answer this question?

5. What are the general guidelines for iPod use that Dr. Brian Fligor, author of several iPod studies, recommends?

6. What are the indications that "today's youth are far too oblivious to the dangers of premature hearing loss" (208)? What warnings have rock guitarists Peter Townshend and Jeff Beck tried to provide?

## WRITING FROM THE TEXT

1. Using details from this reading, write an evaluative response essay, taking a stand on Patricia Wen's thesis and key points. Analyze her attempts to reach a teenage audience with these concerns about hearing loss. You may include examples from your own experience to support or refute her findings about teenagers' awareness and precautions taken to reduce hearing loss. (See Evaluative Response, pp. 391–397.)

2. If reading this essay has caused you to reconsider your own listening habits and the need for volume control and time limits, write an essay analyzing your previous habits concerning iPod listening, music at clubs and concerts, or your own playing of live instruments at practices or performances. Include specific details from the essay that have caused you to change your behavior, and explain and illustrate those changes as specifically as you can. (See Cause and Effect, pp. 402–407.)

## CONNECTING WITH OTHER TEXTS

1. After reading "Education, Backed by Law" (p. 213), write an essay arguing that a "high visibility mobilization strategy"—without any legal ramifications—is needed to make teenagers more aware of the danger of hearing loss. Use direct quotations from both Floetscher's and Wen's essays to support your stance that better education and aggressive campaigns are needed to prevent young people from taking risks that they may not fully understand.

2. Read "What the Cellphone Industry Won't Tell You" (p. 210), and use it to inspire your own essay about "What the iPod Industry Won't Tell You."

Include details from both Wen's and Levin's essays to support your claims about the difficulties of getting honest information and of changing habits to prevent risky behaviour that others seem to condone.

# What the Cellphone Industry Won't Tell You
## *Myron Levin*

Committed to safety and health concerns, Myron Levin (b. 1949) wrote for the *Los Angeles Times* for nearly 24 years. In 2008, he left the *Times* and became the founder and editor of *FairWarning* (www.fairwarning.org), a nonprofit, online investigative publication that focuses on safety and health issues facing consumers and workers as well as government and corporate conduct. Levin's stories appear on the Web site and also in online and print editions of other publications. Levin earned his BA from Indiana University. His writing tip to students is "practice, practice, practice, and read as much good writing as you can." The following article was first published under a different title in the *Los Angeles Times* on March 28, 2011 and then appeared with this title in *CSMonitor.com* on February 2, 2009.

1    In mid-January of 2009, the National Safety Council called for a nationwide ban on the use of cellphones while driving, citing overwhelming evidence of the risk of injuries and death from driver distraction. California has banned texting behind the wheel and, along with several other states, prohibits the use of hand-held phones while allowing drivers to talk with hands-free devices. But research has shown talking is risky even when both hands are free, because the mind is somewhere else.

2    About 4 in 5 cellphone owners make calls while driving, and nearly 1 in 5 sends text messages, according to a survey by Nationwide Mutual Insurance Co. The habit is so deeply ingrained that the likelihood of all-out bans seems practically nil.

3    Individuals still can make the sensible decision to hang up and drive, but they won't get any encouragement from the wireless industry. "A sensible, a responsible and a brief phone call, we think, can be made, and sometimes needs to be made, in order for life's everyday challenges to be met," said a senior official of the main industry trade group, known as CTIA—The Wireless Association. No business is comfortable telling its customers what to do—particularly when the advice weighs against its bottom line. It's not surprising then that wireless providers have taken the familiar road of denying scientific research and plain common sense.

4    Studies have shown that cellphone conversations can blind drivers to visual cues, slowing reaction time and situational awareness. Researchers at the University of Utah tested drivers and found that they performed no better, and by some measures worse, while talking on a cellphone than they did when they had a blood alcohol level of 0.08 percent and were legally drunk.

5    Such information is not available on the CTIA Web site. It features the "why pick on us?" defense that drivers engage in all manner of distracting behaviors, from eating to applying makeup—as if one bad habit justifies a worse one. It says "statistics indicate wireless use does not equate to dangerous driving," offering as proof that during a recent period, accidents dropped while the number of drivers and cellphone users was increasing. Because many factors influence crash rates—such as drunken-driving enforcement and safer highway designs—it's a specious claim that proves nothing.

6    In fact, reliable statistics on cellphone-related casualties don't exist. That's because police agencies keep records differently and because motorists who crash while on the phone rarely admit it. The number of fatalities appears to be large, however. In 2003, researchers at the Harvard Center for Risk Analysis published an estimate of 2,600 deaths a year in cellphone-related crashes. About the same time, experts at the National Highway Traffic Safety Administration produced a more conservative estimate of 955 U.S. deaths in 2002—a toll they said was sure to grow with rising on-road cellphone use.

7    Fearing the wrath of the wireless industry and its allies in Congress, federal officials suppressed the NHTSA estimate, which was first reported by the *Los Angeles Times* in March 2008. Whatever the actual number, there have been more than enough deaths and bereaved families, and drivers who suddenly became criminals through a seemingly routine act.

8    Of course, consumers don't have to rely on industry propaganda. They have access to other information and should be wise enough to trust independent authorities over self-interested business concerns. But faced with changing bad habits, we're prone to rationalization and selective hearing.

9    That's why what the cellphone industry says does matter. The appeal of chatting behind the wheel was a big factor in its phenomenal growth. Today, however, most everyone has a cellphone, and companies increasingly depend on unlimited calling plans rather than minutes sold to bored commuters. Now that we're all in their pockets, it's hard to see what they would lose by urging us, unequivocally, to hang up and drive. Their message should be that if the call is that important, it's worth pulling over.

## THINKING ABOUT THE TEXT

1. In his introduction, Levin mentions the National Safety Council's call for a nationwide ban on the use of cellphones while driving but notes that California has only banned texting and hand-held phones. What is his strategy in opening his essay with this discrepancy?

2. According to Levin, what critical research findings about cellphone use while driving have CTIA, the Wireless Association, kept from customers? What "industry propaganda" (211) is on CTIA's Web site instead?

3. What reports did the Harvard Center for Risk Analysis publish in 2003 and the National Highway Traffic Safety Administration publish that year? Why did federal officials suppress the NHTSA estimate?

4. Why does Levin believe that consumers can't be expected to seek correct information and to break bad habits on their own?

5. Why does Levin argue that "what the cellphone industry says does matter"? What does he want their message to be?

## WRITING FROM THE TEXT

1. Using information from Levin's essay and from your own observations of cellphone use while driving, write an argument to support or refute the need for legal bans against even handfree cellphone devices.

2. If you have ever been in an accident involving cellphone use, write a narrative dramatizing the activity before, during, and after the accident. Analyze your opinions and attitudes about cellphones before the accident and how these may have changed. (See Narration, pp. 382–396.)

## CONNECTING WITH OTHER TEXTS

1. Using information from this essay and from "Education, Backed by Law" (p. 213) and "How the Brain Reacts" (p. 215), write an essay arguing that the ban against handheld cellphones should be extended to include all cellphone use. Anticipate and counter objections that may be made by the cellphone industry and by motorists accustomed to cellphone chatting. (See p. 362, Strategies for Writing an Argument Essay.)

2. After reading "iHuh?" (p. 206), use details from this essay and from Levin's to write an essay persuading readers that certain technological "advances" may have hidden dangers that need to be reduced and controlled by a serious change in habits.

By permission of Mike Luckovich and Creators Syndicate, Inc.

## ◖◗ Education, Backed by Law ◖◗

### *Janet P. Froetscher*

Determined to "make a difference" in people's lives, Janet P. Froetscher (b. 1960) is currently serving as president and chief executive officer of the National Safety Council. This organization is dedicated to saving lives "by preventing injuries and deaths at work, in homes and communities, and on the roads, through leadership, research, education and advocacy." Previously, Froetscher was president and CEO of the United Way of Metropolitan Chicago. Froetscher is a member of the board of the Chicago Chamber of Commerce and a Henry Crown Fellow of the Aspen Institute. She has a BA from the University of Virginia and a Masters of Management with high distinction from Northwestern University's Kellogg Graduate School of Management. The following essay was published as part of a "Room for Debate" blog in the *NewYorkTimes.com* on July 18, 2009.

1      More than 50 research studies have reported the risks of cellphone use while driving. Talking on a cellphone while driving makes a person four

times more likely to be in a crash. This is a much higher risk than most other distracting activities, including eating, drinking, reading billboards, listening to the radio, or talking to other passengers. It's the cellphone conversation that diverts people's attention from the road.

2  The National Safety Council has called for a total ban on cellphone use while driving because more than 100 million people are engaged in this high-risk activity every day. We do not support laws that would permit the use of hands-free devices, because there is no scientific evidence that those devices are any safer for drivers.

3  Hands-free-only laws send the wrong message and may actually encourage more unsafe behavior.

4  In fact, hands-free-only laws tend to send the wrong message—that drivers can safely talk on phones without getting into crashes. And such laws may actually do harm, if drivers, lulled into a false perception of safety, start using hands-free phones to make more calls and talk longer.

5  Some argue that the cellphone laws are not enforceable. But many law enforcement officers involved in the setting of our policy don't agree. There are various approaches available, and there are some good models to follow. For example, a "high visibility mobilization" strategy—letting drivers know laws will be enforced—has been developed to enforce drunk driving, speeding, seat belts, child safety seats and graduated licensing for teens. With this approach, several times each year, people are informed that law enforcement is paying special attention to a particular law.

6  These programs are designed to increase compliance with a law, not to write more tickets. The science is clear: high visibility mobilizations can cause people to change their high-risk behavior and comply with the law. The same model could be used to increase compliance with cellphone laws.

7  Laws, of course, are not the only way to address this problem. Educating people about the risks and the science is also important. Verizon Wireless, one of the major carriers, does this well on its Web site: "For your well being and the well being of those around you, you should consider turning your phone off and allowing calls to go to Voice Mail while you are driving." That message needs to go mainstream.

## THINKING ABOUT THE TEXT

1. What is Froetscher's thesis and how does her introduction effectively prepare readers for it?

2. Why has the National Safety Council called for a total ban on cellphone use while driving? What are the problems with hands-free-only laws?

3. Explain the "high visibility mobilization" strategy, why it was developed, and which laws it has helped reinforce.

4. How is Verizon Wireless helping to educate drivers? According to Froetscher, what is their message that needs to "go mainstream"?

## WRITING FROM THE TEXT

1. Write an evaluative response essay, analyzing Froetscher's thesis and key points. Include specific quotations for support. You should also include your own experiences with "high visibility mobilization strategies" used to discourage drunk driving and speeding and to promote child safety seats, seat belt fastening, and graduated licensing for teens. Evaluate how effective these campaigns have been and whether this approach could also be used to discourage cellphone use while driving. (See Evaluative Response, pp. 391–397.)

2. Develop an argument that cellphone use while driving—even hands-free—is or is not as distracting as eating, drinking, reading billboards, listening to the radio, or talking to other passengers. Include specific quotations from Froetscher's essay as well as illustrations from your own experiences for support.

## CONNECTING WITH OTHER TEXTS

1. After reading Froetscher's essay as well as "What the Cellphone Industry Won't Tell You" (p. 210) and "How the Brain Reacts" (p. 215), write an essay comparing and contrasting the strengths and weaknesses of these three works. Include direct quotations from each reading for support.

2. Using specific details from the three cellphone essays (pp. 210–216), write your own argument convincing readers that cellphone use while driving should be completely banned. You should anticipate your readers' objections and counter them as you build your case and support your claims. (See Strategies for Writing an Argument, pp. 262–365.)

##  How the Brain Reacts
### *Marcel Just* and *Tim Keller*

Professor of psychology at Carnegie Mellon University, Marcel Just (b.1947) has worked extensively in psycho linguistics and autism. He has been a recipient of the National Institute of Mental Health Development Award, their Research Scientist Award, and their Senior Scientist Award. Co-director of the Brain Imaging Research Center, Just employs brain imaging (fMRI) to identify patterns of brain activation, as the report below illustrates.

Tim Keller (b. 1965) has a BA in psychology and English from Missouri Valley College (1987), an MA in experimental psychology (1992), and PhD in experimental psychology (1994) from the University of Missouri-Columbia. Keller has been a post-doctoral fellow at the National Institute of Mental Health. He is presently a senior research associate at Carnegie Mellon University with specialization in brain imaging (fMRI).

Just and Keller's collaboration analyzing the question "Should Cellphone Use be Illegal?" was part of a *Room for Debate Blog* which appeared in the *NewYorkTimes.com* on July 18, 2009.

1    Behavioral studies have shown that talking on a cellphone diverts the driver's attention and disrupts driving performance. We investigated that question by looking at brain activity that occurs during driving. In our study, using functional magnetic resonance imaging (fMRI), we examined the effect of listening to someone speak on the brain activity associated with simulated driving.

2    Participants steered a vehicle along a curving virtual road, either undisturbed or while listening to spoken sentences that they judged as true or false. The parietal lobe activation associated with spatial processing in driving decreased by 37 percent when participants concurrently listened to the sentences. We found that listening comprehension tasks drew mental resources away from driving and produced a deterioration in driving performance, even though the drivers weren't holding or dialing a phone.

3    These brain activation findings show the biological basis for the deterioration in driving performance (in terms of errors and staying in a lane) that occurs when one is also processing language. They suggest that under mentally demanding circumstances, it may be dangerous to combine processing of spoken language with a task like driving a car in demanding circumstances.

4    Our listening experiment did not require the participants to speak, so it was probably less disruptive to driving than an actual two-way conversation might be. It's likely that our study actually underestimates the reduction in driving performance.

5    If listening to sentences degrades driving performance, then probably a number of other common driver activities—including tuning or listening to a radio, eating and drinking, monitoring children or pets, or even conversing with a passenger—would also cause reduced driving performance.

6    It would be incorrect, however, to conclude that using a cellphone while driving is no worse than engaging in one of these other activities. First, it's not

known how much these other distractions affect driving (though that would be an interesting study). Second, talking on a cellphone is a particular social interaction, with demands different from a conversation with a passenger. Not responding in a cellphone conversation, for instance, can be interpreted as rude behavior. By contrast, a passenger in a car is more likely to be aware of the competing demands for a driver's attention. Indeed there is recent experimental evidence suggesting that passengers and drivers suppress conversation in response to driving demands. Third, with spoken language, a listener cannot willfully stop the processing of a spoken utterance. These considerations suggest that talking on cellphones while driving can be a risky choice, not just for common sense reasons, but because of the way our brains work.

## THINKING ABOUT THE TEXT

1. What is the discovery of the scientists who measured participants' ability to handle a vehicle in simulated driving situations while they were listening to someone speak? What do the authors mean by "deterioration in driving performance"?

2. Based on the results of driving errors that occur during listening exercises, what do the authors conclude about driving while concurrently processing language? What do the scientists surmise about using either hand-held or hand-free cellphones while driving?

3. Explain the distinctions the authors make between cellphone conversations and conversations with a passenger in the car. What do they concede about tuning or listening to a radio, or monitoring children of pets? Does their concession mitigate the power of their findings about processing language and driving?

4. What do the brain imaging photographs reveal? How do these images support the evidence revealed by the simulated driving tests?

5. Cite at least three specific insights the reader of this short report derives from reading it.

## WRITING FROM THE TEXT

1. Write a narrative about a time when you were in a car and the driver (you or someone else) was using a cellphone and manifested the "deterioration in driving performance" that the authors cite. How did you feel about the situation? Write your description of the event so vividly that your reader can understand your feelings and conclude your essay with any insights you derived from the experience.

2. Write an evaluative response essay that shows your understanding of the authors' findings and then develop your essay to reveal if your observations and experiences agree or disagree with their conclusions. (See Evaluative Response, pp. 391–397.)

## CONNECTING WITH OTHER TEXTS

1. Read "Education, Backed by Law" (p. 213), and write an essay that argues that given the scientific evidence of authors Just and Keller, Janet P. Froetscher is correct in her argument that favors laws and education to eliminate all cellphone use while driving. Integrate the specific details of the three writers to support your thesis.

2. In Myron Levin's essay "What the Cellphone Industry Won't Tell You" (p. 210), he concludes that the business of selling mobile phones interferes with the industry's responsibility to inform customers of the hazards of using a cellphone while driving. After reading Levin's essay, "How the Brain Reacts" above, as well as "Education, Backed by Law" (p. 213), write a persuasive essay arguing for mandatory information for cellphone purchasers, strict enforcement of the cellphone ban while driving, or for some position that you can support in your essay.

# ⬤⬤ Does the Internet Make ⬤⬤ You Smarter?
## *Clay Shirky*

A teacher at New York University's Interactive Telecommunications Program, Clay Shirky (b. 1964) is also a consultant and writer. His columns have appeared in such publications as the *New York Times*, the *Wall Street Journal*, the *Harvard Business Review*, and *Wired*. A graduate of Yale University with a BA in fine arts, Shirky founded, in 1990, the Hard Place Theatre, where he created and directed several works inspired by government documents and public records, such as transcripts of conversations recorded during a plane crash. Shirky is the author of numerous books about new media, including *The Internet by E-Mail* (1994), *Voices from the Net* (1996), *Here Comes Everybody* (2008), and *Cognitive Surplus: Creativity and Generosity in a Connected Age* (2010). Shirky's belief that "amid silly videos and spam are the roots of a new reading and writing culture" is argued in the essay below. It appeared in the online *Wall Street Journal* on June 4, 2010.

1    Digital media have made creating and disseminating text, sound, and images cheap, easy and global. The bulk of publicly available media is now

created by people who understand little of the professional standards and practices for media.

2    Instead, these amateurs produce endless streams of mediocrity, eroding cultural norms about quality and acceptability, and leading to increasingly alarmed predictions of incipient chaos and intellectual collapse.

3    But of course, that's what always happens. Every increase in freedom to create or consume media, from paperback books to YouTube, alarms people accustomed to the restrictions of the old system, convincing them that the new media will make young people stupid. This fear dates back to at least the invention of movable type.

4    As Gutenberg's press spread through Europe, the Bible was translated into local languages, enabling direct encounters with the text; this was accompanied by a flood of contemporary literature, most of it mediocre. Vulgar versions of the Bible and distracting secular writings fueled religious unrest and civic confusion, leading to claims that the printing press, if not controlled, would lead to chaos and the dismemberment of European intellectual life.

5    These claims were, of course, correct. Print fueled the Protestant Reformation, which did indeed destroy the Church's pan-European hold on intellectual life. What the 16th-century foes of print didn't imagine—couldn't imagine—was what followed: We built new norms around newly abundant and contemporary literature. Novels, newspapers, scientific journals, the separation of fiction and non-fiction—all of these innovations were created during the collapse of the scribal system, and all had the effect of increasing, rather than decreasing, the intellectual range and output of society.

6    To take a famous example, the essential insight of the scientific revolution was peer review, the idea that science was a collaborative effort that included the feedback and participation of others. Peer review was a cultural institution that took the printing press for granted as a means of distributing research quickly and widely, but added the kind of cultural constraints that made it valuable.

7    We are living through a similar explosion of publishing capability today, where digital media link over a billion people into the same network. This linking together in turn lets us tap our cognitive surplus, the trillion hours a year of free time the educated population of the planet has to spend doing things they care about. In the 20th century, the bulk of that time was spent watching television, but our cognitive surplus is so enormous that diverting even a tiny fraction of time from consumption to participation can create enormous positive effects.

8    Wikipedia took the idea of peer review and applied it to volunteers on a global scale, becoming the most important English reference work in less than 10 years. Yet the cumulative time devoted to creating Wikipedia, something

like 100 million hours of human thought, is expended by Americans every weekend, just watching ads. It only takes a fractional shift in the direction of participation to create remarkable new educational resources.

9      Similarly, open source software, created without managerial control of the workers or ownership of the product, has been critical to the spread of the Web. Searches for everything from supernovae to prime numbers now happen as giant, distributed efforts. Ushahidi, the Kenyan crisis mapping tool invented in 2008, now aggregates citizen reports about crises the world over. PatientsLikeMe, a Web site designed to accelerate medical research by getting patients to publicly share their health information, has assembled a larger group of sufferers of Lou Gehrig's disease than any pharmaceutical agency in history, by appealing to the shared sense of seeking medical progress.

10      Of course, not everything people care about is a high-minded project. Whenever media become more abundant, average quality falls quickly, while new institutional models for quality arise slowly. Today we have *The World's Funniest Home Videos* running 24/7 on YouTube, while the potentially world-changing uses of cognitive surplus are still early and special cases.

11      That always happens too. In the history of print, we got erotic novels 100 years before we got scientific journals, and complaints about distraction have been rampant; no less a beneficiary of the printing press than Martin Luther complained, "The multitude of books is a great evil. There is no measure of limit to this fever for writing." Edgar Allan Poe, writing during another surge in publishing, concluded, "The enormous multiplication of books in every branch of knowledge is one of the greatest evils of this age; since it presents one of the most serious obstacles to the acquisition of correct information."

12      The response to distraction, then as now, was social structure. Reading is an unnatural act; we are no more evolved to read books than we are to use computers. Literate societies become literate by investing extraordinary resources, every year, training children to read. Now it's our turn to figure out what response we need to shape our use of digital tools.

13      The case for digitally-driven stupidity assumes we'll fail to integrate digital freedoms into society as well as we integrated literacy. This assumption in turn rests on three beliefs: that the recent past was a glorious and irreplaceable high-water mark of intellectual attainment; that the present is only characterized by the silly stuff and not by the noble experiments; and that this generation of young people will fail to invent cultural norms that do for the Internet's abundance what the intellectuals of the 19th century did for print culture. There are likewise three reasons to think that the Internet will fuel the intellectual achievements of 21st-century society.

14     First, the rosy past of the pessimists was not, on closer examination, so rosy. The decade the pessimists want to return us to is the 1980s, the last period before society had any significant digital freedoms. Despite frequent genuflection to European novels, we actually spent a lot more time watching *Different Strokes* than reading Proust, prior to the Internet's spread. The Net, in fact, restores reading and writing as central activities in our culture.

15     The present is, as noted, characterized by lots of throwaway cultural artifacts, but the nice thing about throwaway material is that it gets thrown away. This issue isn't whether there's lots of dumb stuff online—there is, just as there is lots of dumb stuff in bookstores. The issue is whether there are any ideas so good today that they will survive into the future. Several early uses of our cognitive surplus, like open source software, look like they will pass that test.

16     The past was not as golden, nor is the present as tawdry, as the pessimists suggest, but the only thing really worth arguing about is the future. It is our misfortune, as a historical generation, to live through the largest expansion in expressive capability in human history, a misfortune because abundance breaks more things than scarcity. We are now witnessing the rapid stress of older institutions accompanied by the slow and fitful development of cultural alternatives. Just as required education was a response to print, using the Internet well will require new cultural institutions as well, not just new technologies.

17     It is tempting to want PatientsLikeMe without the dumb videos, just as we might want scientific journals without the erotic novels, but that's not how media works. Increased freedom to create means increased freedom to create throwaway material, as well as freedom to indulge in the experimentation that eventually makes the good new stuff possible. There is no easy way to get through a media revolution of this magnitude; the task before us now is to experiment with new ways of using a medium that is social, ubiquitous and cheap, a medium that changes the landscape by distributing freedom of the press and freedom of assembly as widely as freedom of speech.

## Thinking about the Text

1.  Clay Shirky begins his essay with a number of alarming assertions about how Internet use makes a negative impact on the culture, that "mediocrity" is the norm for material produced by "amateurs," and "intellectual collapse" will be the result of widespread Internet use—positions he does not support. What is his strategy in starting his essay with these views that contrast with his actual perception of the value of digital media?

2. What does Shirky mean when he writes "But of course, that's what always happens" (219)? What is it that "always happens"?

3. Explain what Gutenberg's press and the resulting publication of the Bible in many languages have in common with digital media. What are the effects of each invention? How does the invention of the press and the resulting scientific revolution compare with our present use of the Internet for work in science? What does Shirky mean by "cognitive surplus"?

4. Cite two "open source software" creations that involve "amateurs" and "volunteers." How does Shirky respond to the complaint that the quality of work in electronic media is not always high, nor are the projects "high-minded"? What is the author's intention in quoting both Martin Luther's and Edgar Allan Poe's views of books?

5. What assumed complaints about "digitally-driven stupidity" does the author give? What gives Shirky the perspective and confidence that ultimately we will use the Internet to "fuel the intellectual achievements of the 21st-century"?

## Writing from the Text

1. Write an evaluative response essay that shows that you agree or disagree with Clay Shirky's optimism about digital media increasing "the intellectual range and output of society," as the printing press did for world cultural centuries ago. You will need to represent Shirky's thesis and supporting points even as you bring in your own specific examples that support or refute his position. (See Evaluative Response, pp. 391–397.)

2. In an essay, analyze the digital media that show the mediocrity of amateurs and the lack of "high-mindedness" in some digital projects. Your goal will be to present specific examples and analyze them to show that "digitally-driven stupidity" abounds.

3. Write an analysis of projects on the Internet with the intention of showing that digital media permit users the opportunity to make "reading and writing . . . central activities in our culture," to engage in cooperative research, or to use the Internet in any other specific, positive ways. You will need specific examples and analysis of them to convince your reader of your position.

## Connecting with Other Texts

1. After reading "Does the Internet Make You Dumber?" (p. 216), write an analytical essay that compares and/or contrasts the points made by Clay Shirky and Nicholas Carr. Your thesis should make clear which writer you

believe makes the more convincing points about the Internet's role in our culture.

2. Using the material presented by authors Chabris and Simons in "Your Brain on Computers" (p. 227), as well as Shirky's essay above, write an essay that illustrates the ways using the Internet might actually make us "smarter." Include your own Internet use to support your position.

# Does the Internet Make You Dumber?

### *Nicholas Carr*

Writing about the social, economic, and business implications of technology, Nicholas Carr (b. 1959) continues to stir heated debates and to criticize the current dependence on technology. Carr authors a technology column for *BusinessWeek Online* and has written many articles and interviews for *Harvard Business Review*, where he has also served in several top editorial positions. Carr has been a speaker at MIT, Harvard, Wharton, the Kennedy School of Government, and NASA as well as at numerous industry, corporate, and professional events throughout the world. His books include the *Wall Street Journal* bestseller *The Big Switch: Rewiring the World, from Edison to Google* (2008), *Does IT Matter?* (2004), and his most recent book *The Shallows: What the Internet Is Doing to Our Brains* (2010). Carr holds a BA from Dartmouth and an MA from Harvard. In his blog "Rough Type," Carr published an essay in 2005 entitled "The Amorality of Web 2.0" that criticized the quality of volunteer Web 2.0 information projects such as Wikipedia. According to Wikipedia.com, this criticism caused Wikipedia co-founders to admit "horrific embarrassment" and to seek recommendations for improving Wikipedia's quality. The following article appeared in the *Wall Street Journal* on June 5, 2010.

1    The Roman philosopher Seneca may have put it best 2,000 years ago: "To be everywhere is to be nowhere." Today, the Internet grants us easy access to unprecedented amounts of information. But a growing body of scientific evidence suggests that the Net, with its constant distractions and interruptions, is also turning us into scattered and superficial thinkers.

2    The picture emerging from the research is deeply troubling, at least to anyone who values the depth, rather than just the velocity, of human thought. People who read text studded with links, the studies show, comprehend less than those who read traditional linear text. People who watch busy multimedia presentations remember less than those who take in information in a more sedate and focused manner. People who are continually distracted by emails, alerts and other messages understand less than those who are able

to concentrate. And people who juggle many tasks are less creative and less productive than those who do one thing at a time.

3   The common thread in these disabilities is the division of attention. The richness of our thoughts, our memories and even our personalities hinges on our ability to focus the mind and sustain concentration. Only when we pay deep attention to a new piece of information are we able to associate it "meaningfully and systematically with knowledge already well established in memory," writes the Nobel Prize-winning neuroscientist Eric Kandel. Such associations are essential to mastering complex concepts.

4   When we're constantly distracted and interrupted, as we tend to be online, our brains are unable to forge the strong and expansive neural connections that give depth and distinctiveness to our thinking. We become mere signal-processing units, quickly shepherding disjointed bits of information into and then out of short-term memory.

5   In an article published in Science last year, Patricia Greenfield, a leading developmental psychologist, reviewed dozens of studies on how different media technologies influence our cognitive abilities. Some of the studies indicated that certain computer tasks, like playing video games, can enhance "visual literacy skills," increasing the speed at which people can shift their focus among icons and other images on screens. Other studies, however, found that such rapid shifts in focus, even if performed adeptly, result in less rigorous and "more automatic" thinking.

6   In one experiment conducted at Cornell University, for example, half a class of students was allowed to use Internet-connected laptops during a lecture, while the other had to keep their computers shut. Those who browsed the Web performed much worse on a subsequent test of how well they retained the lecture's content. While it's hardly surprising that Web surfing would distract students, it should be a note of caution to schools that are wiring their classrooms in hopes of improving learning.

7   Ms. Greenfield concluded that "every medium develops some cognitive skills at the expense of others." Our growing use of screen-based media, she said, has strengthened visual-spatial intelligence, which can improve the ability to do jobs that involve keeping track of lots of simultaneous signals, like air traffic control. But that has been accompanied by "new weaknesses in higher-order cognitive processes," including "abstract vocabulary, mind-fulness, reflection, inductive problem solving, critical thinking, and imagina-tion." We're becoming, in a word, shallower.

8   In another experiment, recently conducted at Stanford University's Communication Between Humans and Interactive Media Lab, a team of researchers gave various cognitive tests to 49 people who do a lot of media multitasking and 52 people who multitask much less frequently. The heavy

multitaskers performed poorly on all the tests. They were more easily distracted, had less control over their attention, and were much less able to distinguish important information from trivia.

9    The researchers were surprised by the results. They had expected that the intensive multitaskers would have gained some unique mental advantages from all their on-screen juggling. But that wasn't the case. In fact, the heavy multitaskers weren't even good at multitasking. They were considerably less adept at switching between tasks than the more infrequent multitaskers. "Everything distracts them," observed Clifford Nass, the professor who heads the Stanford lab.

10    It would be one thing if the ill effects went away as soon as we turned off our computers and cellphones. But they don't. The cellular structure of the human brain, scientists have discovered, adapts readily to the tools we use, including those for finding, storing and sharing information. By changing our habits of mind, each new technology strengthens certain neural pathways and weakens others. The cellular alterations continue to shape the way we think even when we're not using the technology.

11    The pioneering neuroscientist Michael Merzenich believes our brains are being "massively remodeled" by our ever-intensifying use of the Web and related media. In the 1970s and 1980s, Mr. Merzenich, now a professor emeritus at the University of California in San Francisco, conducted a famous series of experiments on primate brains that revealed how extensively and quickly neural circuits change in response to experience. When, for example, Mr. Merzenich rearranged the nerves in a monkey's hand, the nerve cells in the animal's sensory cortex quickly reorganized themselves to create a new "mental map" of the hand. In a conversation late last year, he said that he was profoundly worried about the cognitive consequences of the constant distractions and interruptions the Internet bombards us with.

12    The long-term effect on the quality of our intellectual lives, he said, could be "deadly."

13    What we seem to be sacrificing in all our surfing and searching is our capacity to engage in the quieter, attentive modes of thought that underpin contemplation, reflection and introspection. The Web never encourages us to slow down. It keeps us in a state of perpetual mental locomotion.

14    It is revealing, and distressing, to compare the cognitive effects of the Internet with those of an earlier information technology, the printed book. Whereas the Internet scatters our attention, the book focuses it. Unlike the screen, the page promotes contemplativeness.

15    Reading a long sequence of pages helps us develop a rare kind of mental discipline. The innate bias of the human brain, after all, is to be distracted. Our predisposition is to be aware of as much of what's going on around us

as possible. Our fast-paced, reflexive shifts in focus were once crucial to our survival. They reduced the odds that a predator would take us by surprise or that we'd overlook a nearby source of food.

16    To read a book is to practice an unnatural process of thought. It requires us to place ourselves at what T. S. Eliot, in his poem "Four Quartets," called "the still point of the turning world." We have to forge or strengthen the neural links needed to counter our instinctive distractedness, thereby gaining greater control over our attention and our mind.

17    It is this control, this mental discipline, that we are at risk of losing as we spend ever more time scanning and skimming online. If the slow progression of words across printed pages damped our craving to be inundated by mental stimulation, the Internet indulges it. It returns us to our native state of distractedness, while presenting us with far more distractions than our ancestors ever had to contend with.

---

## Thinking about the Text

1. Analyze Carr's multiple reasons for opening his essay—about the current effect of the Internet on thinking skills—with a 2000-year-old quotation from the Roman philosopher Seneca: "To be everywhere is to be nowhere" (223). How does Carr apply this paradox to Internet use and to the type of thinking that he believes the Internet encourages?

2. According to Carr, what are the "deeply troubling" research findings about increased Internet use? Explain the "common thread in these disabilities" (224) and include the information from Nobel-Prize-winning neuroscientist Eric Kandel.

3. Describe the findings of the experiment conducted at Cornell University that permitted "half a class of students to use Internet-connected laptops during a lecture," while the other half was denied access to their computers. Discuss the conclusions drawn by developmental psychologist Greenfield about these results and about "shallower" thinking.

4. Describe the results of the experiment on multitasking conducted at Stanford University. Why were researchers surprised by these results? How does Carr use this information to advance his argument?

5. What does pioneering neuroscientist Merzenich believe is happening to our brains because of our ever-intensifying use of the Web and related media?

6. What does Carr believe is the "innate bias of the human brain"? (225). According to Carr, what are we sacrificing in all of our surfing and searching on the Internet?

7. What are the various contrasts between the skills developed via the Internet and those promoted by print media? What do we risk losing by constant use of the Internet and online media?

## WRITING FROM THE TEXT

1. Carr is definitely aware that he is writing against a popular trend today and that many readers may disagree with his concerns. Consider the strategies that he uses—thorough research and direct quotations from experts, careful explanations of the numerous experiments, anticipation of objections—as he supports his thesis. Using details from Carr's essay, write an analysis of effective persuasion strategies, especially when arguing and supporting a controversial thesis. Fully analyze the examples that you include from Carr's essay. (See Writing to Persuade, pp. 352–370.)

2. Write an evaluative response of Carr's essay, using examples from the reading and from your own experience to support or refute Carr's concern that the Internet is weakening our ability to focus on in-depth material and to retain information from lengthy texts. (See Evaluative Response, pp. 391–397.)

## CONNECTING WITH OTHER TEXTS

1. Read "How the Brain Reacts" (p. 215), "Does the Internet Make You Smarter?" (p. 216), and Carr's essay. Write an essay supporting your own thesis about Internet use, based on the readings. Clarify which authors you are supporting and which you are refuting. Include direct quotations from each reading to illustrate your claims.

2. After reading "Time Lost and Found" (p. 239), write an essay arguing the importance of contemplative thought and time away from the Internet to enrich critical thinking skills and the quality of life. Use specific details from both Lamott and Carr to support your claims. (See Writing to Persuade, pp. 352–370.)

# ⬤⬤ Your Brain on Computers ⬤⬤
## *Christopher Chabris and Daniel Simons*

A graduate of Harvard University with an BA in computer science, 1988, MA in psychology in 1997, and a PhD in 1999, Christopher Chabris (b.1966) is an assistant professor of psychology at Union College. He is the author, with Daniel Simons, of the book *The Invisible Gorilla: and Other Ways Our Intuitions Deceive Us* (2010). Chabris is especially interested in individual differences in cognitive abilities. He teaches classes in cognitive psychology, neuroscience, statistics, and individual differences.

A graduate of Carlton College with a BA in 1991 and a PhD from Cornell University in 1997, Daniel Simons (b.1969) is a professor of psychology at the University of Illinois in Champaign-Urbana. He is the author, with Christopher Chabris, of the book *The Invisible Gorilla, and Other Ways Our Intuitions Deceive Us* (2010), and numerous journal articles on attention and cognition. He is the head of the Visual Cognition Laboratory at the Beckman Institute for Advanced Science and Technology and teaches courses in visual cognition, perception, attention, and memory.

1    The latest attack on the Internet and on computers in general is Nicholas Carr's book, *"The Shallows: What the Internet Is Doing to Our Brains."* Carr and other digital alarmists make a case that seems plausible, at least on the surface. They argue that the advent of the Internet and the proliferation of new communication tools trap us in a shallow culture of constant interruption as we frenetically tweet, text and e-mail. This in turn leaves us little time for deep reading, reflection and serious conversation—pensive activities traditionally thought to build knowledge and wisdom. The alarmists cite the concept of "neural plasticity" and talk of technology "rewiring" the brain to convince us that the new distractions make us not just less willing but less able, on a physiological level, to focus.

2    Whenever you hear that something is changing your brain, you ought to be worried—or at least the person telling you wants you to be worried. But does a cultural change like this necessarily entail a fundamental change to the brain? Most of the evidence these critics offer is anecdotal: They report feeling less able to concentrate and think clearly now than they did before they started frequenting the Internet. But it could be that they are less able to concentrate now than they were 10 to 15 years ago simply because they are 10 to 15 years older.

3    The appeals to neural plasticity, backed by studies showing that traumatic injuries can reorganize the brain, are largely irrelevant. The basic plan of the brain's "wiring" is determined by genetic programs and biochemical interactions that do most of their work long before a child discovers Facebook and Twitter. There is simply no experimental evidence to show that living with new technologies fundamentally changes brain organization in a way that affects one's ability to focus. Of course, the brain changes any time we form a memory or learn a new skill, but new skills build on our existing capacities without fundamentally changing them. We will no more lose our ability to pay attention than we will lose our ability to listen, see or speak.

4    The idea that the Internet might make us dumber has some intuitive appeal, because it is easy to see how the cognitive performance of people around us drops when they are distracted. Who among us is not scared to see a driver chatting on a phone and looking back at the kids while weaving through city traffic? But the notion that prolonged focus and deep reading mark the best path to wisdom and insight is just an assumption, one that may be an accidental consequence of the printing press predating the computer. To book authors like us it seems a heretical notion, but it is possible that spending 10 or more hours engrossed in a single text might not be the optimal regimen for building brainpower.

5    Before the Computer Age, chess grandmasters used to study chess books before matches. But now they use laptops to review hundreds of games in rapid succession, in effect "downloading" into their minds knowledge that is customized for their next opponent. They access the knowledge as they need it, discarding it after the match, and the result is that today's grandmasters play the game better than their predecessors did. Visual perception and attention work the same way: They grant us conscious but temporary access to the information in our world that we need at any moment, then quickly discard it as we shift attention to other places, objects or events.

6    If we consider all the Implications of this "just in time" approach to acquiring and using information, we may be forced to reevaluate the nature of knowledge, wisdom and intelligence. It may make less sense to focus on the capabilities of an individual person, and more sense to think about the individual plus the cloud of technology and information that he or she has access to at any given moment. This human-computer-Internet collective is more knowledgeable and arguably more intelligent than a single human being could be alone. By this view, as more and more information becomes available on the Internet, we become not dumber but smarter.

7    For every way the Internet gives us to waste time, there is a way to increase the scope and diversity of our knowledge and to work collectively on problems. It was not long ago that scientists worked mostly within their own laboratories, collaborating only with students and assistants. Today scientists are more likely to collaborate in larger, more diverse teams that often span the globe. With rapid access to diverse information online, ideas, data and resources can be shared faster and on a scale that was impossible at any point in history.

8    Although the case that technology increases our intelligence is at least as plausible as the gloomy idea that it is changing our brains for the worse, there are real downsides to the instant availability of torrents of information. The danger comes not from the information itself, or from how it could rewire

our brains, but from the way we think about our own knowledge and abilities. As the psychologists Leon Rozenblit and Frank Keil discovered, people tend to suffer from an illusion of knowledge: a tendency to mistake surface-level familiarity with deep understanding. As more information becomes readily available, that sense of familiarity grows and grows, and with it the illusion of knowledge. On-demand access to reams of data can also trick us into mistaking knowledge we could obtain quickly for knowledge we already have and can act upon. And if the illusion leads us to neglect the acquisition of true knowledge, we as individuals could become dumber as a result.

9    Additionally, the more different ways technology gives us to multitask, the more chances we have to succumb to an illusion of attention—the idea that we are paying attention to and processing more information than we really are. Each time we text while we are driving and do not get into an accident, we become more convinced that we can do two (or three or four . . .) things at once, when in reality almost no one can multitask successfully and we are all at greater risk when we do so. Our capacity to learn, understand and multitask hasn't changed with the onslaught of technology, but our confidence in our own knowledge and abilities have.

10    So Google is not making us stupid, PowerPoint is not destroying literature, and the Internet is not really changing our brains. But they may well be making us think we're smarter than we really are, and that is a dangerous thing.

## THINKING ABOUT THE TEXT

1. Chabris and Simons's essay intends to counter the argument of Nicholas Carr's book *The Shallows: What the Internet Is Doing to Our Brains*. How do the authors represent Carr's position? In what ways do they think that the "digital alarmists" seem to make a plausible case?

2. How is the term "neural plasticity" of the brain described? Is the concept significant to these psychologists? What do they believe are the determiners of the brain's "wiring"?

3. The authors concede that "the idea that the Internet might make us dumber" (229) has some appeal. What observations of human behavior seem to support this perception? How do these book authors surprise the readers of their essay with their view on sustained reading of a single text?

4. What specific example do the authors cite that illustrates how the computer can actually assist the brain to improve functioning? Are there other examples of "just in time" approaches to gaining information that argue for our reevaluating the way we gain information and even knowledge? What other examples of computer-assisted gains in knowledge do the authors provide?

5. Chabris and Simons are educators and writers, and they concede that at least one aspect of computer use for gaining information should be considered. What are the "downsides to the instant availability of torrents of information"? Explain their analysis of the "illusion" we might have about "knowledge" gained on the Internet.

6. The authors acknowledge that technology affords us a way to multitask, but what problem do they concede may result from our use of technology?

## WRITING FROM THE TEXT

1. Write an evaluative response essay that reflects Chabris and Simons's position about how our brain works when we use a computer to gain information. Your thesis will show whether you agree or disagree with their findings about the advantages of working the computer for "just in time" acquisition of information or, perhaps, whether you agree or disagree about how using computers gives us illusions about what we really know. (See Evaluative Response, pp. 391–397.)

2. Write an analysis of the argument form of the essay "Your Brain on Computers." Review the material on how to write an argument essay (pp. 362–365), including concession in arguments (p. 365), in order to evaluate whether the authors have written a convincing or persuasive essay. You might also want to review the material in the rhetoric on style (p. 291) to evaluate the authors' presentation.

## CONNECTING WITH OTHER TEXTS

1. Read "Time Lost and Found" (p. 239) in order to write an essay that connects Lamott's views about technology and multitasking with those of Chabris and Simons. Your thesis should project your position that the instant availability of information and social connection via technology is positive or, as Lamott believes, a distraction that keeps us from what we really want and deeply value.

2. Read "Does the Internet Make You Dumber?" (p. 223), to write an essay that shows how Carr's argument compares and/or contrasts with the views of Chabris and Simons in the essay above. Your thesis should make clear your position on how learning is enhanced or weakened by Internet use and you should integrate your support with those of the other writers.

3. With the intention of integrating the findings of the authors to show how computers assist us in gaining information and learning, read "Does the Internet Make You Smarter?" (p. 218). Show in your essay how Shirky, Chabris, and Simons believe the Internet is positively contributing to learning in the twenty-first century.

# I Don't Give a Tweet What  You're Doing

*Meghan Daum*

A graduate of Vassar with a BA in English, Meghan Daum (b. 1970) earned an MFA in writing from Columbia University. Her work has appeared in such popular magazines as the *New Yorker, Harper's G.Q., Harper's Bazaar,* and *Vogue.* Currently on staff at the *Los Angeles Times* where her editorials appear weekly, Daum also has been a columnist at *Self* and has contributed commentaries and stories to public radio programs such as *Morning Edition, This American Life,* and the *Savvy Traveler.* Her novel *The Quality of Life Report* was published in 2003 and her "chronicle of real estate addiction," *Life Would Be Perfect If I Lived in That House,* in 2010. Daum is a "fan of the essay form" because it is one that "allows room for a variety of literary approaches—personal narrative, reportage, satire, to name just a few—and the form encourages both the writer and the reader to explore intellectual and even controversial ideas in a way that is also engaging and entertaining." You may wish to read Daum's collection of essays: *My Misspent Youth* (2001). The following piece first appeared in the *Los Angeles Times* in 2010. How controversial is the subject that Daum writes about here?

1    What am I doing right now? If you must know, I'm staring at the computer screen, toggling between this column and my e-mail program, my online bank balance and photos of my dog. Oh wait, that was a few seconds ago. Now I'm hungry. Now I'm realizing I have no bread for toast. Now an hour has passed since I started this paragraph.

2    Do you find this interesting? Me neither. But the Age of Oversharing is upon us, and those of us who lack enthusiasm for minutia are in a distinct minority. The current enabler-in-chief of this movement? Twitter, that suddenly ubiquitous "microblogging" system that lets users post updates of 140 characters or less that answer the question "what are you doing now?"

3    Most people still aren't quite sure what Twitter is—with only 14 million users, it's no Facebook yet—but it's insinuated itself into the popular lexicon so vigorously that just about everyone seems to have at least heard of it and its infinitive, "to tweet" (when you use Twitter, technically you are tweeting).

4    This is due in large part to a rather sudden media embrace. Last month, both the Doonesbury comic strip and "The Daily Show" poked fun at Twitter and its users, which now include a number of members of Congress (Jon Stewart scolded them for tweeting during hearings). Last week, election protesters in the nation of Moldova were reportedly aided and galvanized by the play-by-play rally updates afforded by Twitter. And over the weekend, when Amazon.com experienced a "glitch"—Amazon's word—that caused

tens of thousands of gay-related books to be de-ranked on the site, the Twitter outcry went viral so effectively that the company is now experiencing a major public relations crisis.

5    Meanwhile, many news outlets, ever desperate to attract even a passing glance from tech-obsessed, attention-impaired youngsters, are now tweeting about breaking news (as well as less-than-breaking, not-necessarily news) with the same vigor they bring to reporting. This week, CNN's Breaking News Twitter account (then the most popular account, according to the tracking site Twitterholic) was inching toward a record-making 1 million followers ("followers" are the people who actually read your posts). This was apparently so exciting and dramatic that Ashton Kutcher, whose account was ranked third, challenged CNN to see who could be the first to reach that 1 million mark. Guess who won.

6    Incidentally, the account of Kutcher's wife, Demi Moore, is now ranked 15th. Other popular tweeters include Britney Spears at No. 2, Barack Obama at No. 6 and Whole Foods Market at No. 24. That's right, nearly 425,000 people have signed up for updates that, presumably, let them know what a $21 jar of olive oil is doing right now.

7    Look, some of my best friends are tweeting. I know this because their e-mails now have signatures listing their Twitter account names along with their cellphone numbers, Web site urls and notices that the message has been sent from a hand-held device (as if that's not obvious because they typed "sluts met 4 lunge" instead of "let's meet for lunch.")

8    But at the risk of unilaterally offending 14 million people, I need to say this: If Twitter were a person, it would be an emotionally unstable person. It would be that person we avoid at parties and whose calls we don't pick up. It would be the person whose willingness to confide in us at first seems intriguing and flattering but eventually makes us feel kind of gross because the friendship is unearned and the confidence is unjustified. The human incarnation of Twitter, in other words, is the person we all feel sorry for, the person we suspect might be a bit mentally ill, the tragic oversharer.

9    Of course, privacy as a cultural or even personal value has been going out of style for some time now; in a world without boundaries, Twitter alone cannot be blamed for making spewing into a sport. And, to be fair, its initial function was to serve as an information conduit between close friends and family, the idea being that even if the whole world didn't care that you were buying frozen peas right now, your mother (God help her) still might.

10    But as Twitter's popularity wobbles at the tipping point between faddish distraction and worldwide obsession, it's worth wondering how much of this "connecting" is simply hastening the erosion of our already compromised

interpersonal skills. Are we tweeting because we truly want to communicate with a select group of true friends, or because typing has replaced talking and indiscretion has been stripped of all negative connotations? Are most Twitter posts merely inane, or do they carry the faint whiff of the insane?

11    The jury's still out. But, along with "what am I doing right now?" maybe it's time to ask "what the hell are we doing?"

## THINKING ABOUT THE TEXT

1. What is the author's strategy in replicating a detailed account of her activities for almost an hour? What is her position on "tweeting" and how does her essay's opening paragraph underscore her view?

2. Daum helps the reader who might not know about Twitter by giving some useful definitions, descriptions, and statistical examples including prominent users of Twitter. Do any of the explanations, examples, or statistics surprise you?

3. Daum acknowledges that many of her friends are tweeting, yet she risks "unilaterally offending 14 million people" (233). What is her condemnation of Twitter, implicit in her example of a Twitter message she received, and explicit in her harsh analogy of how Twitter would be if it were a person. List the personality traits of the personified Twitter.

4. What are the characteristics of a culture that values Twitter, according to Daum? Do you agree that the medium encourages "spewing," erodes "our already compromised interpersonal skills" (233–234), replaces talking, and promotes indiscretion (234)? Do you think that either of Daum's views about Twitter posts are correct, that the posts are "merely inane" or faintly "insane"?

5. The author concludes by repeating her initial question: "What am I doing right now?" What is her strategy? How does she expand that question into a much broader one that returns to those more far-reaching points about our culture that she has already made?

## WRITING FROM THE TEXT

1. Write an essay to persuade someone who does not use Twitter that, in spite of what Meghan Daum insists, tweeting is a positive addition to communication. You might argue that posts can be clever rather than "inane," that connections between people are enhanced through Twitter use, that boundaries might be nicely stretched through revealing tweets— or take any specific virtues you find with the medium to support your thesis.

2. In a narrative that illustrates some dramatic aspect of tweeting that you have discovered, write about an incident that has shaped your appreciation or horror of Twitter posting. You will want to review the section on how to write a narrative, pp. 382–390 in the Rhetoric, for some tips on how to tell your story in an interesting way.

### CONNECTING WITH OTHER TEXTS

1. Read David Pogue's essay "Twitter? It's What You Make of It" (p. 235) before writing a counter to Daum's essay above. Use Pogue's perceptions of the values of Twitter and his argument that the medium is "what you make of it," in order to support your own position on the values of Twitter.

2. Write an essay that integrates the views of Meghan Daum, above, with those of Anne Lamott in "Time Lost and Found" (p. 239). Use the memorable language of both writers to support your thesis and to concur that connecting via Twitter actually erodes personal connection and that "manic connectivity" (240) cannot take the place of a real, two-hour meeting with a close friend.

 # Twitter? It's What You Make It
### *David Pogue*

Renowned as a witty technology writer and speaker, David Pogue (b. 1963) is the personal-technology columnist for the *New York Times*, contributing a weekly print column, an online column, an online video, and a popular daily blog, "Pogue's Posts." He also has hosted a 4-part *PBS NOVA* mini-series about science, and he writes a monthly column in *Scientific American* magazine. His book *The World According to Twitter* (2009) features the best responses to daily questions that he "tweeted" to his 500,000 Twitter followers. Pogue is also an Emmy award-winning tech correspondent for *CBS News*, and he appears on *CNBC* each week with his "trademark comic tech videos." Pogue graduated summa cum laude from Yale, with distinction in music, and he spent ten years conducting and arranging Broadway musicals in New York. One of the world's best-selling how-to authors, Pogue has written seven books in the "for Dummies" series and has launched his own series of complete, funny computer books called the *Missing Manual* series. Pogue has been profiled on both *48 Hours* and *60 Minutes*. The following column appeared in the *New York Times* on February 12, 2009.

1   Writing can be solitary work, but not when you write a tech column. Feedback pours in so quickly—by e-mail, on blogs, in online comments—that it's almost real-time performance art.

2    For the longest time, my readers kept nagging me to check out this thing called Twitter. I'd been avoiding it, because it sounded like yet another one of those trendy Internet time drains. E-mail, blogs, chat, RSS, Facebook. . . . Who has time to tune in to yet another stream of Internet chatter?

3    True, there's nothing quite like Twitter. It's a Web site where you can broadcast very short messages—140 characters, max—to anyone who's signed up to receive them. It's like a cross between a blog and a chat room. Your "followers" might include six friends from high school, or, if you're Barack Obama, 254,484 of your most tech-savvy fans. (Incidentally, he hasn't sent out a single Twitter message since taking office. Where are his priorities?)

4    Meanwhile, you sign up to receive the utterances of other people. Eventually, your screen fills with a scrolling display of their quips—jokes, recommended links, thoughts for the day, and a lot of "what I'm doing right now" stuff. Even so, I was turned off by the whole ego thing. Your profile displays how many followers you have, as if it's some kind of worthiness tally. (See also: Facebook friend counter.)

5    Then one day, I saw Twitter in action. I was serving on a grant proposal committee, and I watched as a fellow judge asked his Twitter followers if a certain project had been tried before. In 15 seconds, his followers replied with Web links to the information he needed. No e-mail message, phone call or Web site could have achieved the same effect. (It's only a matter of time before some "Who Wants to Be a Millionaire" contestant uses Twitter as one of his lifelines.)

6    So I signed up for a free account name (pogue) and stepped in. It's not easy to figure out what's going on. Most people are supportive and happy to help you out. There is, however, such a thing as Twitter snobbery. One guy took me to task for asking "dopey questions." Others criticized me for various infractions, like not following enough other people, writing too much about nontech topics or sending too many or too few messages.

7    Determined to get the hang of it, I searched Google for "Twitter for beginners." There were 927,000 search results. (Of course, you get a staggering number of results when you search for anything on Google, which is why it's such a lame trick when journalists use Google tallies to prove their points. But I digress.)

8    Most of these articles are lists of rules. One says to use Twitter to market your business; another says never to use Twitter to market your business. One recommends writing about what you're doing right now (after all, the typing box is labeled, "What are you doing?"); another says not to. One of these rule sheets even says, "Add value. Build relationships. Think LONG term." Are we talking about Twitter, or running for Congress?

9       My confusion continued until, at a conference, I met Evan Williams, chief executive and co-founder of Twitter. I told him about all the rules, all the advice, all the "you're not doing it right" gripers. I told him that the technology was exciting, but that all the naysayers and rule-makers were dampening my enthusiasm. He shook his head apologetically—clearly, he's heard all this before—and told me the truth about Twitter: that they're all wrong. Or, put another way, that they're all right.

10      Twitter, in other words, is precisely what you want it to be. It can be a business tool, a teenage time-killer, a research assistant, a news source—whatever. There are no rules, or at least none that apply equally well to everyone. In fact, Mr. Williams said that a huge chunk of Twitter lore, etiquette and even terminology has sprouted up from Twitter users without any input from the company. For example, the people came up with the term "tweets" (what everyone calls the messages). The crowd began referring to fellow Twitterers by name like this: @pogue. Soon, that notation became a standard shorthand that the Twitter software now recognizes. The masses also came up with conventions like "RT," meaning re-tweet—you're passing along what someone else said on Twitter.

11      If you asked me to write my own "Rules for Twitter" document— No. 927,001 on Google—it would look something like this:

12      DON'T KNOCK IT TILL YOU'VE TRIED IT. Of course, this advice goes for anything in life. But listen: even my own masterful prose can't capture what you'll feel when you try Twitter. So try it. If you don't get any value from it, close the window and never come back; that's fine. Despite all the press, Twitter is still largely a geek and early-adopter phenomenon at this point.

13      DON'T USE THE WEB SITE. I couldn't believe that six million Twitter users lumber off to a Web page every time they want to send or read tweets. Turns out they don't. About 70 percent use sweet little free programs that sit at the edges of their screens (or run on their cellphones, especially iPhones) all day. They have names like TweetDeck, Twitterfeed, Twhirl and Twitterific.

14      YOU DON'T HAVE TO READ ALL THE TWEETS. It's common to check out someone's Twitter profile and read, "Following: 900 people." Baloney. Nobody has the time to read all the tweets from more than about 30 people—at least, nobody with a life. Clearly, these high subscribers just read the most recent ones, or skim for good ones, or use search.twitter.com to find messages on certain subjects.

15      YOU DON'T HAVE TO ANSWER ALL THE REPLIES. If you have a lot of followers, you get a lot of replies to your tweets. Fortunately, this isn't e-mail; nobody expects you to answer everything.

16   IF YOU'RE CONFUSED ABOUT REPLYING, YOU'RE NOT ALONE. If you reply to one of my tweets, I can write back in either of two ways. I can reply as another public tweet, but of course nobody but you will have any idea what I'm talking about. ("@puppydog: Maybe in Montana!!! LOL").

17   Or I can send you a private Direct Message—but then our dialogue may end. You can't reply to my Direct Message unless I'm also following you (it's an antispam measure, according to Twitter). Get it? Me either. Twitter Inc. says it's working on fixing this and a host of other confusing elements.

18   USE IT HOWEVER YOU LIKE. I've finally harnessed Twitter's power for my own nefarious ends. I pass on jokes. I share little thoughts that don't merit a full blog or article post. I follow links and track buddies. I un-follow people who are boring or post 50 times a day.

19   And I query the multitudes. Last week, I was writing a script for a TV segment, and needed a great example of "an arty movie that a teenage baby sitter wouldn't be caught dead watching." My followers instantly shot back a huge assortment of hilarious responses. (*Gandhi*, *My Dinner with André*, *The Red Balloon*.)

20   Other people plug their blogs, or commiserate, or break news; the first report of the plane in the Hudson came from a Twitterer. It's all good.

21   DON'T WORRY ABOUT THE RULES. Including mine. Use Twitter the way you want to. Don't let anyone tell you you're doing it wrong.

22   Oh, and one more tip: when you're trying to get real work done, it's also O.K. to close Twitter. It may be powerful, useful, addictive and fascinating—but in the end, it's still an Internet time drain.

---

## THINKING ABOUT THE TEXT

1. Pogue's witty style of writing defies all stereotyped tech experts as dry, tedious, and plodding writers. Analyze how Pogue's opening four paragraphs capture reader interest and still provide telling information about Twitter.

2. Why was Pogue initially put off by Twitter? What incident persuaded him that Twitter could be useful?

3. What are some examples of "Twitter snobbery" that Pogue experienced?

4. If Twitter can be "precisely what you want it to be," what is the range of possibilities?

5. According to Twitter co-founder Evan William, what are some examples of Twitter terminology that users have developed?

6. Illustrate some examples of how Pogue's own "Rules for Twitter" entertain readers while providing useful information. Which rules did you find most worthwhile?

7. How does Pogue find Twitter useful for his professional work? What emergency was first reported from a Twitterer?

8. How does Pogue's conclusion provide ideal closure for his essay and even return us to his opening?

## WRITING FROM THE TEXT

1. If you have had experience with Twitter, write an evaluative response essay analyzing Pogue's key points, use of humor, and diction. Include direct quotations from the essay as well as illustrations from your own experiences for support. (See Evaluative Response, pp. 391–397.)

2. Considering Pogue's concern about the "trendy Internet time drains"— e-mail, Facebook, Twitter, RSS, blogs, and chat—write a narrative dramatizing your own addiction to any online information systems or social networking sites. Illustrate their appeal, strengths and frustrations, as well as any activities sacrificed while online.

## CONNECTING WITH OTHER TEXTS

1. Read "I Don't Give a Tweet What You're Doing" (p. 232) and write a comparison-contrast of Daum's view of Twitter and Pogue's view. Analyze specific quotations from both works to support your thesis. See comparison-contrast, pp. 407–413, to insure that you use a point-by-point method rather than the block method as you develop your essay.

2. Read "Time Lost and Found" (p. 239), Pogue's essay, and any other essay about the Internet (pp. 218–238), and write an essay arguing that social networks are or are not worth the time invested in them. Include direct quotations from all three essays as well as supporting illustrations from your own experiences. (See Writing to Persuade, pp. 352–370.)

 # Time Lost and Found
### Anne Lamott

Known for her lively narrative voice, self-effacing humor, and unconventional Christian views, Anne Lamott (b. 1954) is a captivating speaker and writer. Her subjects range from alcoholism and single motherhood to Jesus. Lamott's best-selling works of nonfiction include *Operating Instructions: A Journal of My Son's First Year* (1993), *Bird by Bird: Some instructions on Writing and Life* (1994), *Traveling Mercies: Some Thoughts on Faith* (1999), *Plan B: Further Thoughts on Faith* (2005), and a collection of essays entitled *Grace (Eventually): Thoughts of Faith* (2007). Among her novels are *Hard Laughter* (1980), *Rosie* (1983), *Joe Jones* (1985), *All New People* (1980), *Crooked Little Heart* (1997), and *Imperfect Birds* (2010). She has been honored with a Guggenheim Fellowship and has taught at University of California, Davis. Lamott's ability to be funny while instructive is demonstrated in "Short Assignments" on p. 274, but she can also be outspoken and reflective as in the following essay that appeared in *Sunset* in April 2010.

1    I sometimes teach classes on writing, during which I tell my students every single thing I know about the craft and habit. This takes approximately 45 minutes. I begin with my core belief—and the foundation of almost all wisdom traditions—that there is nothing you can buy, achieve, own, or rent that can fill up that hunger inside for a sense of fulfillment and wonder. But the good news is that creative expression, whether that means writing, dancing, bird-watching, or cooking, can give a person almost everything that he or she has been searching for: enlivenment, peace, meaning, and the incalculable wealth of time spent quietly in beauty.

2    Then I bring up the bad news: You have to make time to do this. This means you have to grasp that your manic forms of connectivity—cellphone, email, text, Twitter—steal most chances of lasting connection or amazement. That multitasking can argue a wasted life. That a close friendship is worth more than material success.

3    Needless to say, this is very distressing for my writing students. They start to explain that they have two kids at home, or five, a stable of horses or a hive of bees, and 40-hour workweeks. Or, on the other hand, sometimes they are climbing the walls with boredom, own nearly nothing, and are looking for work full-time, which is why they can't make time now to pursue their hearts' desires. They often add that as soon as they retire, or their last child moves out, or they move to the country, or to the city, or sell the horses, they will. They are absolutely sincere, and they are delusional.

4    I often remember the story from India of a beggar who sat outside a temple, begging for just enough every day to keep body and soul alive, until the temple elders convinced him to move across the street and sit under a tree. Years of begging and bare subsistence followed until he died. The temple elders decided to bury him beneath his cherished tree, where, after shoveling away a couple of feet of earth, they found a stash of gold coins that he had unknowingly sat on, all those hand-to-mouth years.

5    You already have the gold coins beneath you, of presence, creativity, intimacy, time for wonder, and nature, and life. Oh, yeah, you say? And where

would those rascally coins be? This is what I say: First of all, no one needs to watch the news every night, unless one is married to the anchor. Otherwise, you are mostly going to learn more than you need to know about where the local fires are, and how rainy it has been: so rainy! That is half an hour, a few days a week, I tell my students. You could commit to writing one page a night, which, over a year, is most of a book.

6    If they have to get up early for work and can't stay up late, I ask them if they are willing NOT to do one thing every day, that otherwise they were going to try and cram into their schedule. They may explain that they have to go to the gym four days a week or they get crazy, to which I reply that that's fine—no one else really cares if anyone else finally starts to write or volunteers with marine mammals. But how can they not care and let life slip away? Can't they give up the gym once a week and buy two hours' worth of fresh, delectable moments? (Here they glance at my butt.)

7    Can they commit to meeting one close friend for two hours every week, in bookstores, to compare notes? Or at an Audubon sanctuary? Or a winery? They look at me bitterly now—they don't think I understand. But I do— I know how addictive busyness and mania are. But I ask them whether, if their children grow up to become adults who spend this one precious life in a spin of multitasking, stress, and achievement, and then work out four times a week, will they be pleased that their kids also pursued this kind of whirlwind life? If not, if they want much more for their kids, lives well spent in hard work and savoring all that is lovely, why are they living this manic way?

8    I ask them, is there a eucalyptus grove at the end of their street, or a new exhibit at the art museum? An upcoming minus tide at the beach where the agates and tidepools are, or a great poet coming to the library soon? A pond where you can see so many turtles? A journal to fill? If so, what manic or compulsive hours will they give up in trade for the equivalent time to write, or meander? Time is not free—that's why it's so precious and worth fighting for.

9    Will they give me one hour of housecleaning in exchange for the poetry reading? Or wash the car just one time a month, for the turtles? No? I understand. But at 80, will they be proud that they spent their lives keeping their houses cleaner than anyone else in the family did, except for mad Aunt Beth, who had the vapors? Or that they kept their car polished to a high sheen that made the neighbors quiver with jealousy? Or worked their fingers to the bone providing a high quality of life, but maybe accidentally forgot to be deeply and truly present for their kids, and now their grandchildren?

10    I think it's going to hurt. What fills us is real, sweet, dopey, funny life. I've heard it said that every day you need half an hour of quiet time for yourself, or your Self, unless you're incredibly busy and stressed, in which case you

need an hour. I promise you, it is there. Fight tooth and nail to find time, to make it. It is our true wealth, this moment, this hour, this day.

## Thinking about the Text

1. What specific examples does Lamott give to describe creative expression? Why does she include such a diverse range of examples? What value does she place on moments of creating?

2. How does Lamott imagine the lives of her writing students? In what ways does she meet the expectations of her reader in detailing the many ways our lives are filled with responsibilities? What does she think about "multitasking" and our "manic forms of connectivity"?

3. What specifically does Lamott ask her writing students and her readers to give up in order to make time "to pursue their hearts' desires" (240)? What do you think about the examples of activities she wants her readers to give up? Why are the ones who postpone their pursuits "delusional" and detrimental to their children?

4. In addition to time found for writing or other creative expression, Lamott expands her list to include such pleasures as visiting a beach at very low tide, hearing a poet at the local library, going to a new exhibit at an art museum. What is her intention in providing this list?

5. How does the story of the Indian beggar underscore the points Lamott is making in her essay?

6. What "fills" human beings, according to Lamott? Find key words throughout her essay to answer this question.

7. Examine the author's strategies that keep her tone light and the essay encouraging rather than didactic or judgmental, even as Lamott incites her reader to make serious changes in their lives. What does the author achieve with her writing strategy?

## Writing from the Text

1. Write an evaluative response to "Time Lost and Found," an essay that represents Lamott's thesis as well as your own point of view about whether it is at all possible or desirable to achieve the life she values. (See Evaluative Response, pp. 391–397.)

2. Write an essay, perhaps a process analysis (review pp. 415–422), to show how to achieve a life that has "fulfillment and wonder." Specific details of how you make time to create or to find meaning in your life will help your reader see what you value. Your writing might emulate the humorous tone of Lamott's essay.

## CONNECTING WITH OTHER TEXTS

1. In his essay "Does the Internet Make You Dumber?" (p. 223), Nicolas Carr describes how the Internet makes us into shallow thinkers. He presents studies that conclude that we are losing "our capacity to engage in the quieter, attentive modes of thought that underpin contemplation, reflection and introspection" (225). How do Carr's findings parallel and support the ideas expressed in Lamott's work? Write an essay that presents your view on finding "the still point of the turning world" (Eliot 226), and integrates the ideas of the two authors for support of your points.

2. In "I Don't Give a Tweet What You're Doing" (p. 232), Meghan Daum observes that our Twitter use is "simply hastening the erosion of our already compromised interpersonal skills" (233). Write an essay that shows how her view supports Lamott's position that tweeting and texting take time away from being "deeply and truly present" for the people we care about (241). Or take the opposite view and show how keeping in touch via the various electronic tools creates connections, fulfilling friendships, and helps people achieve the meaningful lives they seek.

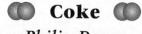

# Coke

## *Philip Dacey*

Poet Philip Dacey (b. 1939) is widely published in anthologies and poetry journals. His books include *What's Empty Weighs the Most: Twenty-four Sonnets* (1997), *The Deathbed Playboy* (1998), *The Paramour of the Moving Air* (1999), *The Adventures of Alixa Doom, and Other Love Poems* (2003), and *Mystery of Max Schmitt: Poems on the Life and Work of Thomas Eakins* (2004). Dacey has an MA in English from Stanford and an MFA in creative writing from Iowa State University. The following poem was first published in *Night Shift at the Crucifix Factory* (1991) and later in *Stand Up Poetry: The Anthology* (1994). Dacey has given numerous poetry readings and has recorded "Coke" and other poems set to music by his sons.

I was proud of the Coca-Cola stitched in red
on the pocket of my dad's shirt,
just above his heart.
Coca-Cola was America
5    and my dad drove its truck.

I loved the way the letters curved,
like handwriting, something personal,
a friendly offer of a drink
to a man in need. Bring me your poor,
10   your thirsty.

And on every road I went, faces
under the sign of Coke smiled down
out of billboards at me. We were all
brothers and sisters in the family
15    of man, our bottles to our lips,
tipping our heads back to the sun.

My dad lifted me up when he came home,
his arms strong from stacking
case after case of Coke all day. A couple of
20    cold ones always waited for us in the kitchen.

I believed our President and my dad
were partners. My dad said someday Coke
would be sold in every country in the world,
and when that happened there would be
25    no more wars. "Who can imagine," he asked,
"two people fighting while they swig their Cokes?"
I couldn't. And each night before sleep,
I thanked God for my favorite drink.

When I did, I imagined him tilting the bottle
30    up to his heavenly lips, a little Coke
dribbling down his great white beard.

And sometimes I even thought of his
son on the cross, getting vinegar
but wanting Coke. I knew that if I
35    had been there, I would have handed a Coke
up to him, who would have figured out
how to take it, even though his hands
were nailed down good, because he was God.
And I would have said when he took it,
40    "That's from America, Jesus. I hope
you like it." And then I'd have watched,
amidst the thunder and lightning
on that terrible hill, Jesus' Adam's apple
bob up and down as he drained that bottle
45    in one long divine swallow
like a sweaty player at a sandlot game
between innings, the crucial ninth
coming up next.

And then the dark, sweet flood
50  of American sleep,
sticky and full of tiny bubbles,
would pour over me.

## THINKING ABOUT THE TEXT

1. The narrator's opening words, "I was proud . . . ," characterize his attitude as a young boy. Find phrases throughout the poem that reveal the numerous sources of his pride.

2. List the various characteristics of Coca-Cola in the poem. What does Coke represent?

3. Is the poet writing this as a young boy or as a man looking back to an earlier time? How can you tell? What was his vision of the world then? Find images to support your view.

4. Characterize the poet's tone. Is he innocent and hopeful? Smiling at his past naïveté? Bitter and disillusioned? Support your interpretation.

5. A number of images are ironic or incongruous—they contradict our expectation of what seems appropriate and, in this poem, contribute to its humor. List the images that seem ironic or comical.

6. What is the poet implying about a young boy's view of the world? What does America stand for here? Why does the narrator end the poem with this image: "the dark, sweet flood / of American sleep, / sticky and full of tiny bubbles, / would pour over me"? What do these "tiny bubbles" suggest and why does he emphasize that his "American sleep" was "dark" yet "sweet"?

## WRITING FROM THE TEXT

1. Write an essay or poem focusing on a key image or symbol from your own childhood and show how your attitude toward this symbol has changed over the years.

2. Read the section on poetry analysis and write an analysis of the product Coke as a critical symbol in this poem. (See exercise 2, above for help in brainstorming this topic.)

3. Write an analysis of what the poet is suggesting about American culture and values. Is he critical or supportive of what America represents? Is this poem to be read as a satire or to be read literally? How can you tell?

4. Compare and contrast the world of the young boy with the world of the adult narrator who seems nostalgic for this earlier time.

## CONNECTING WITH OTHER TEXTS

1. Write an essay comparing and contrasting the limited vision of the individuals described in both "Mr. Z" (p. 106) and "Coke." Focus on details from both poems as you contrast the reasons for these distorted perspectives.

2. Read "Greed in the Name of Green" (below) and write a comparison-contrast essay examining Hesse's explicit use of satire with the more subtle satire present in Dacey's poem.

*"We've decided to express our concern for the environment by redecorating."*

##  Greed in the Name of Green

### *Monica Hesse*

A journalist known for her use of humor, Monica Hesse (b. 1981) is on the writing staff of the *Washington Post.* Hesse previously served as an editor at AARP, and she has written articles for numerous publications including the *San Francisco Chronicle, Houston Chronicle, People,* and *Men's Health.* Hesse earned a BA from Bryn Mawr College and an MA in nonfiction writing from Johns Hopkins University. Hesse offers this advice to student writers: "Read lots of other people, but don't try to sound like any of them. Find a writing voice that makes you laugh, or think, or feel, and then have enough confidence to believe that it will do the same for others." The following essay was published in the *Washington Post* on March 5, 2008.

1    Congregation of the Church of the Holy Organic, let us buy.

2    Let us buy Anna Sova Luxury Organics Turkish towels, 900 grams per square meter, $58 apiece. Let us buy the eco-friendly 600-thread-count bed sheets, milled in Switzerland with U.S. cotton, $570 for queen-size.

3    Let us purge our closets of those sinful synthetics, purify ourselves in the flame of the soy candle at the altar of the immaculate Earth Weave rug, and let us *buy, buy, buy* until we are whipped into a beatific froth of free-range fulfillment.

4    And let us never consider the other organic option—*not* buying—because the new green *consumer* wants to consume, to be more celadon than emerald, in the right color family but muted, without all the hand-me-down baby clothes and out-of-date carpet.

5    There was a time, and it was pre-Al Gore, when buying organic meant eggs and tomatoes, Whole Foods and farmer's markets. But in the past two years, the word has seeped out of the supermarket and into the home store, into the vacation industry, into the Wal-Mart. Almost three-quarters of the U.S. population buys organic products at least occasionally; between 2005 and 2006 the sale of organic non-food items increased 26 percent, from $744 million to $938 million, according to the Organic Trade Association.

6    Green is the new black, carbon is the new kryptonite, blah blah blah. The privileged eco-friendly American realized long ago that SUVs were Death Stars; now we see that our gas-only Lexus is one, too. Best replace it with a 2008 LS 600 *hybrid* for $104,000 (it actually gets fewer miles per gallon than some traditional makes, but, see, it is a hybrid). Accessorize the interior with an organic Sherpa car seat cover for only $119.99.

7    Consuming until you're squeaky green. It feels so good. It looks so good. It feels so good to look so good, which is why conspicuousness is key.

8    *These countertops are pressed paper.*

9    *Have I shown you my recycled platinum engagement ring?*

10    In the past two weeks, our inbox has runneth over with giddily organic products: There's the 100 percent Organic Solana Swaddle Wrap, designed to replace baby blankets we did not even know were evil. There's the Valentine's pitch, "Forget Red—The color of love this season is Green!" It is advertising a water filter. There are the all-natural wasabi-covered goji berries, $30 for a snack six-pack, representing "a rare feat for wasabi."

11    There is the rebirth of *Organic Style* magazine, now only online but still as fashionable as ever, with a shopping section devoted to organic jewelry,

organic pet bedding, organic garden decor, which apparently means more than "flowers" and "dirt."

12      When renowned environmentalist Paul Hawken is asked to comment on the new green consumer, he says, dryly, "The phrase itself is an oxymoron." Oh ho? "The good thing is people are waking up to the fact that we have a real [environmental] issue," says Hawken, who co-founded Smith & Hawken but left in 1992, before the $8,000 lawn became de rigueur. "But many of them are coming to the issue from being consumers. They buy a lot. They drive a lot."

13      They subscribe, in other words, to a destiny laid out by economist Victor Lebow, writing in 1955: "Our enormously productive economy demands that we make consumption our way of life, that we convert the buying and use of goods into rituals, that we seek our spiritual satisfaction . . . in consumption. . . . We need things consumed, burned up, replaced and discarded at an ever-accelerating rate."

14      The culture of obsolescence has become so deeply ingrained that it's practically reflexive. Holey sweaters get pitched, not mended. Laptops and cellphones get slimmer and shinier and smaller. We trade up every six months, and to make up for that, we buy and buy and hope we're buying the right *other* things, though sometimes we're not sure: When the Hartman Group, a market research firm, asked a group of devout green consumers what the USDA "organic" seal meant when placed on a product, 43 percent did not know. (The seal means that the product is at least 95 percent organic—no pesticides, no synthetic hormones, no sewage sludge, no irradiation, no cloning.)

15      This is why, when wannabe environmentalists try to change purchasing habits without also altering their consumer mind-set, something gets lost in translation.

16      Polyester = bad. Solution? Throw out the old wardrobe and replace with natural fibers!

17      Linoleum = bad. Solution? Rip up the old floor and replace with cork!

18      Out with the old, in with the green. It's done with the best of intentions, but all that replacing is problematic. That "bad" vinyl flooring? It was probably less destructive in your kitchens than in a landfill (unless, of course, it was a health hazard). Ditto for the older, but still wearable, clothes. And that's not even getting into the carbon footprint left by a nice duvet's 5,000-mile flight from Switzerland. (Oh, all right: a one-way ticket from Zurich to Washington produces about 1,500 pounds of carbon dioxide.)

19      *Really* going green, Hawken says, "means having less. It *does* mean less. Everyone is saying, 'You don't have to change your lifestyle.' Well, yes, actually, you *do*." But, but, but—buying green feels so *guilt less,* akin to the mentality that results in eating 14 of Whole Foods' two-bite cupcakes. Their first ingredient is cane sugar, but in a land of high-fructose panic, that's practically a health food, right? Have another.

20    "There's a certain thrill, that you get to go out and replace everything," says Leslie Garrett, author of *"The Virtuous Consumer,"* a green shopping guide. "New bamboo T-shirts, new hemp curtains." Garrett describes the conflicting feelings she and her husband experienced when trying to decide whether to toss an old living room sofa: "Our dog had chewed on it—there were only so many positions we could put it in" without the teeth marks showing. But it still fulfilled its basic role as a sofa: "We could still sit on it without falling through."

23    They could still make do. They could still, in this recession-wary economy, where everyone tries to cut back, subscribe to the crazy notion that conservation was about . . . conserving. Says Garrett, "The greenest products are the ones you don't buy." There are exceptions. "Certain environmental issues trump other issues," Garrett says. "Preserving fossil fuels is more critical than landfill issues." If your furnace or fridge is functioning but inefficient, you can replace it guilt-free. Ultimately, Garrett and her husband did buy a new sofa (from Ikea—Garrett appreciated the company's ban on carcinogens). But they made the purchase only after finding another home for their old couch—a college student on Craigslist was happy to take it off their hands.

24    The sofa example is what Josh Dorfman, host of the Seattle radio show "The Lazy Environmentalist," considers to be a best-case scenario for the modern consumer. "Buying stuff is intrinsically wrapped up in our identities," Dorfman says. "You can't change that behavior. It's better to say, 'You're a crazy shopaholic. You're not going to stop being a crazy shopaholic. But if you're going to buy 50 pairs of jeans, buy them from this better place.'" Then again, his show is called "The Lazy Environmentalist."

25    Chip Giller, editor of enviro-blog Grist.org, has a less fatalistic view. He loves that Wal-Mart has developed an organic line. He applauds the efforts of the green consumer. "Two years ago, who would have thought we'd be in a place where terms like locavore and carbon footprint were household terms?" he says, viewing green consumption as a "gateway" to get more people involved in environmental issues. The important thing is for people to keep walking through the gate, toward the land of reduced air travel, energy-efficient homes and much less stuff: "We're not going to buy our way out of this."

26    Congregation of the Church of the Holy Organic, let us scrub our sins away with Seventh Generation cleaning products. Let us go ahead and bite into the locally grown apple, and let us replace our incandescent light bulbs with those dreadfully expensive fluorescents.

27    But yea, though we walk through the valley of the luxury organic, let us purchase no imported Sherpa car seat covers. Let us use the old one, even though it is ugly, because our toddler will spill Pom juice on the organic one just as quickly as on the hand-me-down.

28    Amen.

## THINKING ABOUT THE TEXT

1. Analyze Hesse's tone and attitude in the opening four paragraphs as she develops a parody of a prayer. Explain her purpose and whether her tone helps or hinders it.

2. List the religious terms that she includes throughout her essay, and explain why she includes these allusions throughout.

3. Why does Hesse claim that "conspicuousness is key" to the problem of consumerism? How does this relate to the "culture of obsolescence," first coined by economist Victor Lebow in 1955?

4. What does environmentalist Paul Hawken feel about the "new green consumer"? What is both positive and negative about the green movement?

5. What does environmental author Leslie Garrett believe are the more critical environmental issues that have priority over others?

6. How does Chip Giller, editor of enviro-blog Grist.org, explain his "less fatalistic view" of the green consumer?

7. How do Hesse's concluding paragraphs return to the tone, attitude, and imagery of her introduction? In what ways is this essay an effective satire?

## WRITING FROM THE TEXT

1. Write an evaluative response essay critiquing Hesse's thesis, key points, imagery, and attitude. Explain important concepts such as the oxymoron "green consumer," "conspicuousness," and "culture of obsolescence." Include quotations to support your thesis. (See Evaluative Response, pp. 391–397.)

2. If you know a person or household that fits Hesse's description of obsessive "green consumers," write an essay exposing any flaws in their habits or behavior that seem contradictory or hypocritical. Try to parallel Hesse's satirical voice in your own work.

## CONNECTING WITH OTHER TEXTS

1. Write an essay comparing and contrasting Hesse's work with "Why Bother?" (p. 251), another essay that expresses concern about the environment. Compare and contrast the two authors' styles, attitudes, purposes, and solutions. (See Comparison-Contrast, pp. 407–413.)

2. Read "How to Get Better Gas Mileage" (p. 417) and write an essay showing how this essay supports Hesse's message even though the two essays differ in style, tone, and development. (See Comparison-Contrast, pp. 407–413.)

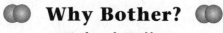

# Why Bother?

## *Michael Pollan*

Writer, educator, editor, columnist, television producer, and natural historian, Michael Pollan (b. 1955) is also a frequent lecturer on food, agriculture, gardening, and related topics. Educated at Bennington College, Mansfield College, Oxford University, and Columbia University, Pollan has been a writer in residence at the University of Wisconsin and a visiting writer in nonfiction at the University of Pittsburgh. Pollan has been published in such popular magazines as *Esquire, Vogue, Mother Jones, Travel + Leisure,* and *Smithsonian.* His full-length work includes the best sellers *The Botany of Desire: A Plant's Eye View of the World* (2001), *The Omnivore's Dilemma: A Natural History of Four Meals* (2006), and *In Defense of Food: An Eater's Manifesto* (2008). The essay reprinted below was published in the *New York Times Magazine* April 20, 2008.

1    Why bother? That really is the big question facing us as individuals hoping to do something about climate change, and it's not an easy one to answer. I don't know about you, but for me the most upsetting moment in *An Inconvenient Truth* came long after Al Gore scared the hell out of me, constructing an utterly convincing case that the very survival of life on earth as we know it is threatened by climate change. No, the really dark moment came during the closing credits, when we are asked to . . . change our light bulbs. That's when it got really depressing. The immense disproportion between the magnitude of the problem Gore had described and the puniness of what he was asking us to do about it was enough to sink your heart.

2    But the drop-in-the-bucket issue is not the only problem lurking behind the "why bother" question. Let's say I do bother, big time. I turn my life upside-down, start biking to work, plant a big garden, turn down the thermostat so low I need the Jimmy Carter signature cardigan, forsake the clothes dryer for a laundry line across the yard, trade in the station wagon for a hybrid, get off the beef, go completely local. I could theoretically do all that, but what would be the point when I know full well that halfway around the world there lives my evil twin, some carbon-footprint *doppelgänger* in Shanghai or Chongqing who has just bought his first car (Chinese car ownership is where ours was back in 1918), is eager to swallow every bite of meat I forswear and who's positively itching to replace every last pound of $CO_2$ I'm struggling no longer to emit. So what exactly would I have to show for all my trouble?

3    A sense of personal virtue, you might suggest, somewhat sheepishly. But what good is that when virtue itself is quickly becoming a term of derision? And not just on the editorial pages of the *Wall Street Journal* or on the lips of the vice president, who famously dismissed energy conservation as a "sign

of personal virtue." No, even in the pages of the *New York Times* and the *New Yorker*, it seems the epithet "virtuous," when applied to an act of personal environmental responsibility, may be used only ironically. Tell me: How did it come to pass that virtue—a quality that for most of history has generally been deemed, well, a virtue—became a mark of liberal softheadedness? How peculiar, that doing the right thing by the environment—buying the hybrid, eating like a locavore—should now set you up for the Ed Begley Jr. treatment.

4      And even if in the face of this derision I decide I am going to bother, there arises the whole vexed question of getting it right. Is eating local or walking to work really going to reduce my carbon footprint? According to one analysis, if walking to work increases your appetite and you consume more meat or milk as a result, walking might actually emit more carbon than driving. A handful of studies have recently suggested that in certain cases under certain conditions, produce from places as far away as New Zealand might account for less carbon than comparable domestic products. True, at least one of these studies was co-written by a representative of agribusiness interests in (surprise!) New Zealand, but even so, they make you wonder. If determining the carbon footprint of food is really this complicated, and I've got to consider not only "food miles" but also whether the food came by ship or truck and how lushly the grass grows in New Zealand, then maybe on second thought I'll just buy the imported chops at Costco, at least until the experts get their footprints sorted out.

5      There are so many stories we can tell ourselves to justify doing nothing, but perhaps the most insidious is that, whatever we do manage to do, it will be too little too late. Climate change is upon us, and it has arrived well ahead of schedule. Scientists' projections that seemed dire a decade ago turn out to have been unduly optimistic: the warming and the melting is occurring much faster than the models predicted. Now truly terrifying feedback loops threaten to boost the rate of change exponentially, as the shift from white ice to blue water in the Arctic absorbs more sunlight and warming soils everywhere become more biologically active, causing them to release their vast stores of carbon into the air. Have you looked into the eyes of a climate scientist recently? They look really scared.

6      So do you still want to talk about planting gardens? I do.

7      Whatever we can do as individuals to change the way we live at this suddenly very late date does seem utterly inadequate to the challenge. It's hard to argue with Michael Specter, in a recent *New Yorker* piece on carbon footprints, when he says: "Personal choices, no matter how virtuous [N.B.!], cannot do enough. It will also take laws and money." So it will. Yet it is no less accurate or hardheaded to say that laws and money cannot do enough, either; that it will also take profound changes in the way we live. Why?

Because the climate-change crisis is at its very bottom a crisis of lifestyle—of character, even. The Big Problem is nothing more or less than the sum total of countless little everyday choices, most of them made by us (consumer spending represents 70 percent of our economy), and most of the rest of them made in the name of our needs and desires and preferences.

8      For us to wait for legislation or technology to solve the problem of how we're living our lives suggests we're not really serious about changing—something our politicians cannot fail to notice. They will not move until we do. Indeed, to look to leaders and experts, to laws and money and grand schemes, to save us from our predicament represents precisely the sort of thinking—passive, delegated, dependent for solutions on specialists—that helped get us into this mess in the first place. It's hard to believe that the same sort of thinking could now get us out of it.

9      Thirty years ago, Wendell Berry, the Kentucky farmer and writer, put forward a blunt analysis of precisely this mentality. He argued that the environmental crisis of the 1970s—an era innocent of climate change; what we would give to have back *that* environmental crisis!—was at its heart a crisis of character and would have to be addressed first at that level: at home, as it were. He was impatient with people who wrote checks to environmental organizations while thoughtlessly squandering fossil fuel in their everyday lives—the 1970s equivalent of people buying carbon offsets to atone for their Tahoes and Durangos. Nothing was likely to change until we healed the "split between what we think and what we do." For Berry, the "why bother" question came down to a moral imperative: "Once our personal connection to what is wrong becomes clear, then we have to choose: we can go on as before, recognizing our dishonesty and living with it the best we can, or we can begin the effort to change the way we think and live."

10      For Berry, the deep problem standing behind all the other problems of industrial civilization is "specialization," which he regards as the "disease of the modern character." Our society assigns us a tiny number of roles: we're producers (of one thing) at work, consumers of a great many other things the rest of the time, and then once a year or so we vote as citizens. Virtually all of our needs and desires we delegate to specialists of one kind or another—our meals to agribusiness, health to the doctor, education to the teacher, entertainment to the media, care for the environment to the environmentalist, political action to the politician.

11      As Adam Smith and many others have pointed out, this division of labor has given us many of the blessings of civilization. Specialization is what allows me to sit at a computer thinking about climate change. Yet this same division of labor obscures the lines of connection—and responsibility—linking our everyday acts to their real-world consequences, making it easy

for me to overlook the coal-fired power plant that is lighting my screen, or the mountaintop in Kentucky that had to be destroyed to provide the coal to that plant, or the streams running crimson with heavy metals as a result.

12     Of course, what made this sort of specialization possible in the first place was cheap energy. Cheap fossil fuel allows us to pay distant others to process our food for us, to entertain us and to (try to) solve our problems, with the result that there is very little we know how to accomplish for ourselves. Think for a moment of all the things you suddenly need to do for yourself when the power goes out—up to and including entertaining yourself. Think, too, about how a power failure causes your neighbors—your community—to suddenly loom so much larger in your life. Cheap energy allowed us to leapfrog community by making it possible to sell our specialty over great distances as well as summon into our lives the specialties of countless distant others.

13     Here's the point: Cheap energy, which gives us climate change, fosters precisely the mentality that makes dealing with climate change in our own lives seem impossibly difficult. Specialists ourselves, we can no longer imagine anyone but an expert, or anything but a new technology or law, solving our problems. Al Gore asks us to change the light bulbs because he probably can't imagine us doing anything much more challenging, like, say, growing some portion of our own food. We can't imagine it, either, which is probably why we prefer to cross our fingers and talk about the promise of ethanol and nuclear power—new liquids and electrons to power the same old cars and houses and lives.

14     The "cheap-energy mind," as Wendell Berry called it, is the mind that asks, "Why bother?" because it is helpless to imagine—much less attempt— a different sort of life, one less divided, less reliant. Since the cheap-energy mind translates everything into money, its proxy, it prefers to put its faith in market-based solutions—carbon taxes and pollution-trading schemes. If we could just get the incentives right, it believes, the economy will properly value everything that matters and nudge our self-interest down the proper channels. The best we can hope for is a greener version of the old invisible hand. Visible hands it has no use for.

15     But while some such grand scheme may well be necessary, it's doubtful that it will be sufficient or that it will be politically sustainable before we've demonstrated to ourselves that change is possible. Merely to give, to spend, even to vote, is not to do, and there is so much that needs to be done— without further delay. In the judgment of James Hansen, the NASA climate scientist who began sounding the alarm on global warming 20 years ago, we have only 10 years left to start cutting—not just slowing—the amount of carbon we're emitting or face a "different planet." Hansen said this

more than two years ago, however; two years have gone by, and nothing of consequence has been done. So: eight years left to go and a great deal left to do.

16    This brings us back to the "why bother" question and how we might better answer it. The reasons not to bother are many and compelling, at least to the cheap-energy mind. But let me offer a few admittedly tentative reasons that we might put on the other side of the scale:

17    If you do bother, you will set an example for other people. If enough other people bother, each one influencing yet another in a chain reaction of behavioral change, markets for all manner of green products and alternative technologies will prosper and expand. (Just look at the market for hybrid cars.) Consciousness will be raised, perhaps even changed: new moral imperatives and new taboos might take root in the culture. Driving an S.U.V. or eating a 24-ounce steak or illuminating your McMansion like an airport runway at night might come to be regarded as outrages to human conscience. Not having things might become cooler than having them. And those who did change the way they live would acquire the moral standing to demand changes in behavior from others—from other people, other corporations, even other countries.

18    All of this could, theoretically, happen. What I'm describing (imagining would probably be more accurate) is a process of viral social change, and change of this kind, which is nonlinear, is never something anyone can plan or predict or count on. Who knows, maybe the virus will reach all the way to Chongqing and infect my Chinese evil twin. Or not. Maybe going green will prove a passing fad and will lose steam after a few years, just as it did in the 1980s, when Ronald Reagan took down Jimmy Carter's solar panels from the roof of the White House.

19    Going personally green is a bet, nothing more or less, though it's one we probably all should make, even if the odds of it paying off aren't great. Sometimes you have to act as if acting will make a difference, even when you can't prove that it will. That, after all, was precisely what happened in Communist Czechoslovakia and Poland, when a handful of individuals like Vaclav Havel and Adam Michnik resolved that they would simply conduct their lives "as if" they lived in a free society. That improbable bet created a tiny space of liberty that, in time, expanded to take in, and then help take down, the whole of the Eastern bloc.

20    So what would be a comparable bet that the individual might make in the case of the environmental crisis? Havel himself has suggested that people begin to "conduct themselves as if they were to live on this earth forever and be answerable for its condition one day." Fair enough, but let me propose a slightly less abstract and daunting wager. The idea is to find one thing to do in your life that doesn't involve spending or voting, that may or may not virally

rock the world but is real and particular (as well as symbolic) and that, come what may, will offer its own rewards. Maybe you decide to give up meat, an act that would reduce your carbon footprint by as much as a quarter. Or you could try this: determine to observe the Sabbath. For one day a week, abstain completely from economic activity: no shopping, no driving, no electronics.

21    But the act I want to talk about is growing some—even just a little—of your own food. Rip out your lawn, if you have one, and if you don't—if you live in a high-rise, or have a yard shrouded in shade—look into getting a plot in a community garden. Measured against the Problem We Face, planting a garden sounds pretty benign, I know, but in fact it's one of the most powerful things an individual can do—to reduce your carbon footprint, sure, but more important, to reduce your sense of dependence and dividedness: to change the cheap-energy mind.

22    A great many things happen when you plant a vegetable garden, some of them directly related to climate change, others indirect but related nevertheless. Growing food, we forget, comprises the original solar technology: calories produced by means of photosynthesis. Years ago the cheap-energy mind discovered that more food could be produced with less effort by replacing sunlight with fossil-fuel fertilizers and pesticides, with a result that the typical calorie of food energy in your diet now requires about 10 calories of fossil-fuel energy to produce. It's estimated that the way we feed ourselves (or rather, allow ourselves to be fed) accounts for about a fifth of the greenhouse gas for which each of us is responsible.

23    Yet the sun still shines down on your yard, and photosynthesis still works so abundantly that in a thoughtfully organized vegetable garden (one planted from seed, nourished by compost from the kitchen and involving not too many drives to the garden center), you can grow the proverbial free lunch—$CO_2$-free and dollar-free. This is the most-local food you can possibly eat (not to mention the freshest, tastiest and most nutritious), with a carbon footprint so faint that even the New Zealand lamb council dares not challenge it. And while we're counting carbon, consider too your compost pile, which shrinks the heap of garbage your household needs trucked away even as it feeds your vegetables and sequesters carbon in your soil. What else? Well, you will probably notice that you're getting a pretty good workout there in your garden, burning calories without having to get into the car to drive to the gym. (It is one of the absurdities of the modern division of labor that, having replaced physical labor with fossil fuel, we now have to burn even more fossil fuel to keep our unemployed bodies in shape.) Also, by engaging both body and mind, time spent in the garden is time (and energy) subtracted from electronic forms of entertainment.

24      You begin to see that growing even a little of your own food is, as Wendell Berry pointed out 30 years ago, one of those solutions that, instead of begetting a new set of problems—the way "solutions" like ethanol or nuclear power inevitably do—actually beget other solutions, and not only of the kind that save carbon. Still more valuable are the habits of mind that growing a little of your own food can yield. You quickly learn that you need not be dependent on specialists to provide for yourself—that your body is still good for something and may actually be enlisted in its own support. If the experts are right, if both oil and time are running out, these are skills and habits of mind we're all very soon going to need. We may also need the food. Could gardens provide it? Well, during World War II, victory gardens supplied as much as 40 percent of the produce Americans ate.

25      But there are sweeter reasons to plant that garden, to bother. At least in this one corner of your yard and life, you will have begun to heal the split between what you think and what you do, to commingle your identities as consumer and producer and citizen. Chances are, your garden will re-engage you with your neighbors, for you will have produce to give away and the need to borrow their tools. You will have reduced the power of the cheap-energy mind by personally overcoming its most debilitating weakness: its helplessness and the fact that it can't do much of anything that doesn't involve division or subtraction. The garden's season-long transit from seed to ripe fruit—*will you get a load of that zucchini?!*—suggests that the operations of addition and multiplication still obtain, that the abundance of nature is not exhausted. The single greatest lesson the garden teaches is that our relationship to the planet need not be zero-sum, and that as long as the sun still shines and people still can plan and plant, think and do, we can, if we bother to try, find ways to provide for ourselves without diminishing the world.

## THINKING ABOUT THE TEXT

1. According to Michael Pollan, what is the big question facing individuals concerned about climate change? What is his strategy in referring to the "dark moment" in *An Inconvenient Truth* when Al Gore asks everyone to change light bulbs? What does Pollan mean by a "drop in-the-bucket-issue"?

2. What are the international realities that Pollan recognizes we must face, even if we individually decide to be "virtuous"? What are some of the "vexing questions" we must deal with if we want to do the right thing?

3. What is Pollan's strategy in admitting that we are possibly doing "too little too late"? Shouldn't the reader be discouraged by the author's pronouncement that climate scientists are "really scared"? What is the purpose of the author's concession?

4. How does the author argue for not waiting for the government or technology to help correct the problem of climate change? Who is Wendell Berry and how does Pollan use that writer's words?

5. How does planting a garden physically work to correct the problems of climate change? What solutions are solved? What are the psychological and sociological advantages to growing your own food? How would you express Michael Pollan's thesis in this essay?

## WRITING FROM THE TEXT

1. Write an evaluative response essay showing that you understand Michael Pollan's position in "Why Bother?" and that you agree or disagree with his view. Respond to specific parts of Pollan's argument even as you also show your position on attempting to correct climate change. (See Evaluative Response, pp. 391–397.)

2. In an effort to convince a person who believes that anything we do is too little and too late to correct the problem of global warming, write a persuasive essay that argues for "bothering." Use ideas from Pollan's essay but support your own thesis with examples of how you, and the rest of the world, need to work to find personal or global solutions to the earth's environmental problems.

## CONNECTING WITH OTHER TEXTS

1. Read "Greed in the Name of Green" (p. 246) and write an essay that illustrates how in contrast to the positive views on gardening that Pollan perceives, a garden might stir consumers into a buying frenzy that works against the ecological solutions that gardening ought to perpetrate. The tone that you take in your analytical essay might use humor, as Pollan does, or irony, as Hesse demonstrates.

2. After reading Kevin Crust's review of the film *An Inconvenient Truth* (p. 260), write an essay that integrates the points Crust makes about the data Al Gore presents in the film with the views Michael Pollan presents in "Why Bother?" Your essay might take a comparison-contrast form as you bring in specific examples to support your own thesis.

*"I'm starting to get concerned about global warming."*

## Film Analyses of *An Inconvenient Truth*

This compelling 2006 documentary based on Al Gore's campaign against global warming won the 2007 Academy Award for Best Documentary, accepted by director Davis Guggenheim, and for the Best Original Song, "I Need to Wake Up," by Melissa Etheridge. With a running time of 94 minutes, the film uses graphs, animation, footage of disasters caused by climate change, and documentation of disappearing glaciers, ice shelves, plants, and animals. Al Gore and the U.N.'s Intergovernmental Panel on Climate Change won the 2007 Nobel Peace Prize. In his acceptance of the award, Gore stated, "The climate crisis is not a political issue; it is a moral and spiritual challenge to all of humanity."

# Al Gore Warms Up to a Very Hot Topic

### Kevin Crust, staff writer, The Los Angeles Times

1   Critics have labeled Al Gore and his decades-long crusade to curb global warming as "alarmist." But if you've been warning people that the sky is falling for more than 20 years and it really is falling (or at least heating up), don't you have an obligation to sound an alarm?

2   The highly persuasive documentary *An Inconvenient Truth* captures Gore delivering a multimedia presentation he has given an estimated 1,000 times since 1989. The talk is augmented with an impressive array of graphs, animation, anecdotes and statistics that convey a flurry of facts, projections and conjecture, all pointing to the ill effects the present rate of emissions has on the environment. A film with a clear point of view (and little room for others'), it is the inspiration of producers Laurie David and Lawrence Bender, who attended Gore's lecture, decided it had to be made into a film to broaden the reach of its message and recruited director Davis Guggenheim to shoot it.

3   Guggenheim intercuts the lecture with footage of Gore on the road, studiously working out his presentation on his ubiquitous laptop, and segments that effectively show the crucible moments in his life that led him to continually rededicate himself to this topic. There's the college professor who first taught him about climate change in the late 1960s, the death of Gore's sister Nancy from cancer and the 1989 accident that nearly claimed the life of his son. While the vignettes establish Gore's long-term commitment, unfortunately there's a slickness to them that plays like a campaign film that might be shown at a political convention.

4   Gore might not be anybody's idea of a pitchman, but here he's matched with the right topic, one for which he demonstrates real passion. He's charming, intelligent, professorial and one might even say . . . presidential. In fact, more than one observer has commented that if this Al Gore had been more visible during the 2000 election there may have been a different outcome.

5   Rather than alarmed, Gore comes off as poised, relaxed and confident. Guggenheim sets up Citizen Al as part rock star, part eco-Buddha. He introduces himself to a small audience saying, "I'm Al Gore, and I used to be the next president of the United States." The line gets a laugh and quickly addresses the considerable baggage that comes with being on the losing end of one of the most divisive political outcomes in U.S. history.

6   This position has its pros and cons for the film. On the plus side, Gore stands tall as an insider pushed to the fringe, a man on a mission with nothing

to lose. He's able to attack the issue without equivocation. On the minus side, it's easy for naysayers to claim that the digs he makes at conservatives are sour grapes and he's merely positioning himself to run again in 2008—though this would appear to be a longshot issue on which to do so.

7    The environment has not resonated much with voters or politicians in the past, though the increasing popularity of hybrid cars and eco-friendly products and services might indicate a shift in attitudes. That something so important could be largely ignored for so long is almost inconceivable, and among the things the film does well is an analysis as to why that is. A 2004 *Science* magazine survey of more than 900 peer-reviewed academic papers on the subject of global warming found that all supported the reality while none contested it. However, a like sampling of mainstream media found that 53% of the stories portrayed global warming as something that was in doubt in the scientific community. The mixed message has kept the automobile and oil industries in the driver's seat and the issue out of political debates.

8    Gore also does an excellent job of explaining the basic science behind climate change and the accelerated rise in temperatures since the 1970s. What could be very dry material is enlivened by Gore's geniality and desire to share the information. The potential for dreaded heaviosity is leavened at times by his dry wit and humorous moments, such as a clip from Matt Groening's animated series *Futurama*.

9    Real and projected catastrophes reveal what is at stake. Glacier erosion, the threat to wildlife and the spread of deadly viruses make for some terrifying scenarios. Hurricane Katrina and other weather-related disasters that occurred in late 2005 are included, giving the film a sense of timeliness and a powerful visual element, which Gore compares to "a nature hike through the Book of Revelations."

10    The other strong point that Gore makes is to dispute the "either/or" argument presented by big business when it comes to making the necessary changes. He uses Upton Sinclair's quote, "It is difficult to get a man to understand something when his salary depends upon his not understanding it," to not-so-subtly stress the motivation behind this line of thinking.

11    The film's title refers to politicians' apprehensiveness in addressing the problem. Attempts at strict environmental reform have long been met with gloomy projections from the right—of economic disaster in the form of lost jobs and factory closures—and Gore rebuts this by suggesting that green business can be good business.

12    Although the message of the film sounds bleak, it is actually quite rousing. Gore offers measures that can be taken on personal and community levels but also stresses that major changes require a larger response. The film's

ultimate significance is that this requires political will—which Gore labels a "renewable resource"—and that if our present representatives are not up to the challenge, we elect men and women who are.

## ◖◗ Did Al Get the Science Right? ◖◗

*Katharine Mieszkowski, senior writer,* Salon.com

1    To the tune of the Allman Brothers Band's "Ramblin Man," Al Gore's face rides a cartoon airplane across a map of the United States. As he zips from coast to coast in a Web video clip titled "Al Gore: An Inconvenient Story," a ticker at the bottom of the screen displays his rapidly rising $CO_2$ emissions next to the comparatively modest emissions of everyday folk. The climate-change Paul Revere's steed is an airplane, powered by fossil fuels. The implication: Gore's sure spewing a lot of carbon dioxide as he travels the land spreading the word about global warming.

2    Produced by the industry flacks at the Competitive Enterprise Institute, which is funded in part by Exxon-Mobil, the clip dismisses Gore as a hypocrite, leading a carbon-intensive lifestyle while scolding us plebes that we should strive to reduce our own carbon footprints. Of course, nowhere does this oil-industry-funded propaganda mention that Gore used carbon offsets to mitigate the global warming impact of his travel for *An Inconvenient Truth,* that Gore pledged to make the documentary carbon-neutral.

3    The Web clip is just one bit of the skeptic zaniness that has greeted the release of Gore's film. On Fox News, another Exxon-Mobil-funded pundit, Sterling Burnett, compared watching *An Inconvenient Truth* to learn about global warming to watching Joseph Goebbels' Nazi propaganda to learn about Nazi Germany. Over at the *New York Post,* a reviewer baldly asserted that "there is widespread disagreement about whether humans are causing global warming," a false statement that even oilman-in-chief President Bush doesn't accept anymore. Meanwhile, the College Republican National Committee encouraged skeptical students to throw global warming beach parties. Global warming? Break out the bikinis!

4    Ideological blowback or no, *An Inconvenient Truth* is drowning plenty of competition at the box office. Last weekend, playing at only 77 theaters around the country, it was the ninth most popular film, and took in more money per screen than any other film showing, with many screenings in liberal cities like San Francisco and Boston sold out. The film opens more widely this weekend.

5    Yet global warming skeptics continue to infiltrate media outlets as mainstream and reputable as PBS *The NewsHour* with Jim Lehrer, which failed

to acknowledge the industry ties of the Competitive Enterprise Institute, while giving the group a free pass to call Gore's film "alarmist." One of the most widely read critiques of the science in the film has come from longtime climate-change skeptic Robert C. Balling Jr., a professor of climatology at Arizona State University, who has received more than $400,000 from the coal and oil industries, according to the Center for Media and Democracy. On the industry-backed Web site *Tech Central Station,* Balling posted a purported fact-check of the film titled "Inconvenient Truths Indeed," which charges that the movie is "not the most accurate depiction of the state of global warming science," casting doubts on its claims about melting glaciers and intensifying hurricanes. The article has made the rounds of the right-wing blogosphere as a takedown of Gore, and the *Philadelphia Daily News* published it as an Op-Ed without any acknowledgement of Balling's well-documented ties to industry.

6    Balling's critique inspired this dismissive reaction from one climate scientist: "Some people believe the earth is flat, too." That's Eric Steig, an isotope geochemist at the University of Washington, who is one of the co-founders of the *Real Climate* Web site, where working climate scientists provide commentary and context about the news in their now-hot field. Steig e-mailed his reaction from Greenland, where he's conducting field research on the ice. He'd posted his own largely favorable review of *An Inconvenient Truth* on the *Real Climate* site before he left.

7    Judd Legum, research director at the Center for American Progress, a liberal think tank, has rebutted each of Balling's claims on the *Think Progress* Web site. For instance, some of the most dramatic images in the film show the rapid retreat of glaciers all over the world, including the melting snows of Mt. Kilimanjaro. Balling contends the snowpack retreat on Kilimanjaro is caused by declining atmospheric moisture, which has been going on for more than 100 years, not global warming. Legum counters that scientists have shown that the Kilimanjaro glacier previously survived a 300-year drought and its retreat cannot be fully accounted for by changes in atmospheric moisture, especially the shrinking that has occurred in recent decades. Besides, focusing on that one example overshadows the larger point that glaciers all over the world are disappearing.

8    Steig confirmed the facts in Legum's rebuttal. "All those points are accurate," he wrote in an e-mail. "Some of them could probably have been stronger; that is, Balling is even more wrong that Legum indicates."

9    Climate scientists who have seen Gore's film say on the whole it presents a scientifically valid view of global warming and does a good job of presenting what's likely to occur if human-induced greenhouse gas emissions continue unabated. Dr. Gavin Schmidt, a climate modeler for NASA, was pleased the

film didn't say: "You're all going to die, woo-hoo." Schmidt, who stressed that his views are his own, not NASA's, says the movie plays it relatively safe by saying, "These are the things that have happened so far. These are the things that are likely to happen should we continue on the trajectory we're on, and these are the moral consequences of it."

10     Scientists express surprise that Gore could present the science in an accurate way without putting everyone in the audience to sleep. "Such an amount of relatively hard science could have been extremely dull, and I've been to a lot of presentations on similar stuff that were very dull," says Schmidt. "Where there was solid science, he presented it solidly without going into nuts and bolts, and where there were issues that are still a matter of some debate, he was careful not to go down definitively on one side or the other."

11     Lonnie Thompson, a professor at Ohio University, whose work on re-treating glaciers from the Andes to Kilimanjaro and Tibet is featured in the film, was happy with the result. "It's so hard given the breadth of this topic to be factually correct, and make sure you don't lose your audience," he says. "As scientists, we publish our papers in *Science* and *Nature*, but very few people read those. Here's another way to get this message out. To me, it's an excellent overview for an introductory class at a university. What are the issues and what are the possible consequences of not doing anything about those changes? To me, it has tremendous value. It will reach people that scientists will never reach." John Wallace, a climate scientist at the University of Washington, agreed. "I think that he's gone to great lengths to make the science comprehensible to the layman," he says. "Given the fact that this was a film intended to bring the message to the lay public, I think it was excellent."

12     Yet some scientists who are enthusiastic about the film had their own critiques of how the science is presented. One of the biggest challenges in the film is visually portraying the likely consequences of global warming in the future. For instance, invasive species, both plants and insects, are a grow-ing scourge, which will likely be exacerbated by global warming. Yet, the film, while not saying anything technically wrong about invasive species, could leave the erroneous impression that the dandelion in your backyard was planted there by climate change, simply by omitting other contributing factors. "Anybody having to fight kudzu in their garden knows it has nothing to do with global warming. It has to do with the fact that we introduced the species from Europe," says Steig. At the same time, he says, invasive species are opportunistic, thriving in many different environments, so they're likely to thrive under climate change. "The ecological niche for certain species are

changing quite rapidly," says Schmidt. "You have situations where only a small amount of climate change can make a big difference."

13    The deadly aftermath of Hurricane Katrina is featured prominently in the film, and may lead viewers to conclude global warming is to blame for the disaster. But the truth is not that simple. As global temperatures rise, hurricane scientists predict that we'll see stronger storms as rising sea temperatures feed their fury. Yet it's hotly debated among hurricane specialists whether the intensity of tropical cyclones seen around the world over the past few years already show the impacts of global warming. Sketchy data from past decades makes nailing down that proof difficult, amplifying the debate. "There is a difference between saying "we are confident that they will increase' and "we are confident that they have increased due to this effect,'" explains Steig.

14    Also, any one event—like Hurricane Katrina—cannot be definitively linked to an overall global trend of more powerful storms, just as any specific car accident on a highway cannot be blamed on the raising of the speed limit, even if statistics show a higher speed limit makes accidents more likely to happen. Yet any one storm and its aftermath can be presented—as "An Inconvenient Truth" does—as an example of what we're likely to experience in the future because of climate change. In Gore's defense, says Steig, "Never in the movie does he say: 'This particular event is caused by global warming.'"

15    Schmidt agrees. "Gore talked about 2005 and 2004 being very strong seasons, and if you weren't paying attention, you could be left with the impression that there was a direct cause and effect, but he was very careful to not say there's a direct correlation," he says.

16    There is one example in the film that Steig says is simply a technical error. Climate scientists use ice cores from Antarctica and the Arctic to study temperature and other climatic conditions of the past. Gore says it's possible to see the influence of the Clean Air Act by observing the ice core changes in pollution concentrations over two years. In the film, the happy implication is that the ice cores show that human actions, notably political legislation, can have a quick, measurable impact, even in the ice at the ends of the earth. If we acted decisively, Gore suggests, we could do the same to stem greenhouse gases. Yet Steig, who specializes in studying ice cores by doing chemical measurements on them, says it would be impossible to isolate the years the Clean Air Act took effect. It is possible, he says, to observe the decline over the years in certain substances that have been regulated, such as lead. But he's skeptical that pinpointing the Clean Air Act in the ice can be done.

17    David Battisti, a professor of atmospheric sciences, also at the University of Washington, thinks the science in the film is well represented, yet worries

about one of the most dramatic moments in the film. "There is only one place in the film I struggled," he says. "It makes a powerful theatrical point, but it leaves open the criticism that you're stretching the truth."

18    Gore notes the relationship between $CO_2$ and temperature, as revealed in ice cores. He then shows a graph correlating the amount of $CO_2$ in the atmosphere with temperature over hundreds of thousands of years. The lines closely follow each other up and down. Literally for millenniums, the amount of $CO_2$ has hovered between 200 and 300 parts per million. But since the industrial revolution, when humans started pumping more $CO_2$ into the atmosphere with all our machines, it's risen to the current amount of 380 parts per million. Economists and climate scientists believe it will continue to rise as dramatically over the course of this century. To demonstrate the skyrocketing increase, Gore rides a mechanical lift to rise as high as the $CO_2$ is likely to go. While the temperature line does not jump up that high in the film, the audience is left to assume—with horror—that it will follow.

19    Scientists predict the jump in temperatures will be serious, but more modest than the graph implies. "The graph shows $CO_2$ going through the roof, and the thing is the temperature doesn't follow that line with the same amount of jump," says Battisti. "The good thinking person who knew nothing about the science would come away with the wrong interpretation. The world Gore paints in the future is an appropriate representation of the science. It's just that graph that is misleading."

20    "Gore is correct to link temperature and $CO_2$ in ice core records," concurs Steig. "That's very sound science. But he is incorrect to imply that you can take the one curve and use it to predict where the other curve will go in the future. It ain't so simple."

21    Steig notes that other factors, such as the earth wobbling on its axis as it revolves around the sun, have influenced temperatures in the past hundreds of thousands of years. Now, as humans continue dumping more greenhouse gases into the atmosphere—scientists predict the $CO_2$ level will rise to 1,000 parts per million by early next century—$CO_2$ will have more impact. "In the past, the oscillation between temperature and $CO_2$ were driven by the sun," says Battisti. "The $CO_2$ was a positive feedback. It wasn't the driver. The $CO_2$ is going to be the driver."

22    Yet while objecting to the way the graph is presented, Battisti agrees with the qualitative point that temperatures are rising, and will continue to do so, thanks to human-induced global warming, which is a serious problem. "Wherever you live, this is a huge change, and it dwarfs anything that we've seen in the last 150 years, or the last 1,000, or the last 10,000 years. If you want to see a change that big, you have to go back to the Ice Ages."

23    The scene that has inspired the most charges that the film is alarmist is the depiction of what would happen if the sea level rose 20 feet, with the World Trade Center Memorial site underwater, and landscapes where millions of people live, from Shanghai to San Francisco, swamped. Audiences might be left with the impression that the deluge is just around the corner, lapping at our feet.

24    Schmidt says a 20-foot rise in sea level is not unrealistic in the long run—the very long run. "The 20 feet number comes from an analog with the last time the planet was a degree warmer than it is now—120,000 years ago. Sea levels were about 20 feet higher. Where did that water come from? Half from Greenland, and half from Antarctica." How long would it take for that rise to happen again? "Maybe 1,000 years," says Schmidt. "There's some uncertainty about how quickly that could happen, but Gore was very careful not to say this is something that is going to happen tomorrow."

25    If in fact there's 800 to 1,000 parts per million of $CO_2$ in the atmosphere, Battisti says, it's going to be a very different world. Twenty feet of additional sea-level rise could occur if Greenland melts. "That's most likely if we get to 800 parts per million by the end of the century; within 500 years Greenland will be gone," he says. In fact, there was a time when there were 1,000 parts per million of $CO_2$ in the atmosphere. That was during the Eocene, about 50 million years ago, when there were crocodiles in the Arctic and palm trees in Wyoming, which was then 10 degrees farther north than it is today. "This was a time when the planet was so warm that you had amazing hot swamplike conditions," says Battisti. "You had a lot of plant life dying that was actually forming the oil and coal we're now burning."

## ◖◗  Warning of Calamities and  ◖◗ Hoping for a Change

### *A. O. Scott, film critic,* The New York Times

1    *An Inconvenient Truth,* Davis Guggenheim's new documentary about the dangers of climate change, is a film that should never have been made. It is, after all, the job of political leaders and policymakers to protect against possible future calamities, to respond to the findings of science and to persuade the public that action must be taken to protect the common interest.

2    But when this does not happen—and it is hardly a partisan statement to observe that, in the case of global warming, it hasn't—others must take up the responsibility: filmmakers, activists, scientists, even retired politicians.

That *An Inconvenient Truth* should not have to exist is a reason to be grateful that it does.

3    Appearances to the contrary, Mr. Guggenheim's movie is not really about Al Gore. It consists mainly of a multimedia presentation on climate change that Mr. Gore has given many times over the last few years, interspersed with interviews and Mr. Gore's voice-over reflections on his life in and out of politics. His presence is, in some ways, a distraction, since it guarantees that *An Inconvenient Truth* will become fodder for the cynical, ideologically facile sniping that often passes for political discourse these days. But really, the idea that worrying about the effect of carbon-dioxide emissions on the world's climate makes you some kind of liberal kook is as tired as the image of Mr. Gore as a stiff, humorless speaker, someone to make fun of rather than take seriously.

4    In any case, Mr. Gore has long since proven to be a deft self-satirist. (He recently told a moderator at a Cannes Film Festival news conference to address him as "your Adequacy.") He makes a few jokes to leaven the grim gist of *An Inconvenient Truth*, and some of them are funny, in the style of a college lecturer's attempts to keep the attention of his captive audience. Indeed, his onstage manner—pacing back and forth, fiddling with gadgets, gesturing for emphasis—is more a professor's than a politician's. If he were not the man who, in his own formulation "used to be the next president of the United States of America," he might have settled down to tenure and a Volvo (or maybe a Prius) in some leafy academic grove.

5    But as I said, the movie is not about him. He is, rather, the surprisingly engaging vehicle for some very disturbing information. His explanations of complex environmental phenomena—the jet stream has always been a particularly tough one for me to grasp—are clear, and while some of the visual aids are a little corny, most of the images are stark, illuminating and powerful.

6    I can't think of another movie in which the display of a graph elicited gasps of horror, but when the red lines showing the increasing rates of carbon-dioxide emissions and the corresponding rise in temperatures come on screen, the effect is jolting and chilling. Photographs of receding ice fields and glaciers—consequences of climate change that have already taken place—are as disturbing as speculative maps of submerged coastlines. The news of increased hurricane activity and warming oceans is all the more alarming for being delivered in Mr. Gore's matter-of-fact, scholarly tone.

7    He speaks of the need to reduce carbon-dioxide emissions as a "moral imperative," and most people who see this movie will do so out of a sense of duty, which seems to me entirely appropriate. Luckily, it happens to be a well-made documentary, edited crisply enough to keep it from feeling like 90 minutes of C-Span and shaped to give Mr. Gore's argument a real sense of

drama. As unsettling as it can be, it is also intellectually exhilarating, and, like any good piece of pedagogy, whets the appetite for further study. This is not everything you need to know about global warming: that's the point. But it is a good place to start, and to continue, a process of education that could hardly be more urgent. *An Inconvenient Truth* is a necessary film.

## Works Cited

Crust, Kevin. "Al Gore Warms Up to a Very Hot Topic." Rev. of *An Inconvenient Truth*. Dir. Davis Guggenheim. *calendarlive.com*. *Los Angeles Times*, 24 May 2006. Web. 12 Aug. 2008.

*An Inconvenient Truth*. Dir. Davis Guggenheim. Perf. Al Gore. Paramount Classics, 2006. Film.

Mieszkowski, Katharine. "Did Al Get the Science Right?" *salon.com*. Salon Media Group, Inc. 10 June 2006. Web. 28 July 2008.

Scott, A. O. "Warning of Calamities and Hoping for a Change in *An Inconvenient Truth.*" *nytimes.com*. The *New York Times*. 24 May 2006. Web. 12 Aug. 2008.

## THINKING ABOUT THE TEXT

1. Why does the film open and close with serene images of nature: lush green leaves and a gently flowing river on a sunny day, followed by Al Gore's voice-over about this peaceful place?

2. What is the intention of showing Gore delivering his slide show at town-hall-style meetings? How does Gore come across to the viewers as the camera follows him behind the scenes and on his tours?

3. What is the effect of Gore opening his presentation on a serious subject with self-irony: "I used to be the next president of the United States"? And after the audience laughs, Gore quips, "I don't find that particularly funny." Where else in this discussion of an environmental crisis do we see Gore's humor?

4. In this film, Gore narrates a moment in 1989 when his six-year-old son dropped his father's hand, ran into the street, and was severely injured. How does this personal story relate to Gore's mission?

5. Gore also tells a story of his father's tobacco farm and business and of his older sister Nancy who died of lung cancer. How is Gore's personal history relevant to this film?

6. Because so much of the film consists of scientific facts and charts, you may have been challenged to record sufficient notes. Work with classmates to answer as many of the following questions as you can:

   • Why do we have global warming?

   • What is the relationship between carbon dioxide and temperature?

- How does global warming (the increase in worldwide temperatures) contribute to an increase in the number and severity of storms, hurricanes, tornadoes, and typhoons?
- How can global warming cause both violent precipitation as well as droughts?

7. Explain the significance of each of these references from the film:

- the findings of core drills
- the thawing of the permafrost, the splitting of the Ward Hunt ice shelf, and the disappearance of the Larson ice shelf
- the Arctic ice cap disappearing
- the image of a canary in a coal mine
- the image of the frog in the cooking pot

8. Cite five ecological consequences of global warming in the animal and plant communities.

9. Explain the three factors that are causing "a collision between our civilization and the earth."

10. Gore includes several resonant quotations from important authors and creates his own memorable claims as well. Explain how each of these is illustrated in the film:

- from Mark Twain: "What gets us into trouble is not what we don't know; it's what we know that just ain't so."
- from Winston Churchill in 1936: "The era of procrastination, of half-measure, of soothing and baffling expedients, of delays is coming to its close. In its place, we are entering a period of consequences."
- from Upton Sinclair: "It is difficult to get a man to understand something when his salary depends upon his not understanding it." Cite specific ways that this statement is illustrated throughout this film.
- from Stephen Pacala and Robert Socolow in *Science* magazine: "Humanity *already* possesses the fundamental scientific, technical, and industrial know-how to solve the carbon and climate problems."
- from Al Gore: "We have everything we need save, perhaps, political will but in America, political will *is* a renewable resource."

11. How does Gore counter the myth that scientists disagree with the fact that we are causing global warming and that it is a serious problem?

12. How does Gore expose the misconception that we have to choose between the economy and the environment?

13. What historical facts about the United States does Gore cite to oppose those who claim that global warming is too big of a problem to solve?

14. When Gore took his scientific evidence of global warming to Congress, he expected that this compelling information would "cause a real sea change" in the government. He saw global warming as a moral issue that needed to be acted on and not a political issue to be derided and dismissed. What specific evidence in the film demonstrates that special interests, political corruption, and denial have prevented some necessary reforms?

15. Explain the significance of the film's title *An Inconvenient Truth*.

## WRITING FROM THE TEXT

1. Write a focused character study of Al Gore, analyzing details from the film to support the inferences established in your thesis. (See Character Analysis, pp. 445–453.)

2. Using one of the specific quotations in question 10 above, write an essay explaining its meaning and illustrating its significance in the film.

3. Using specific support from the film, write an argument convincing a skeptic that global warming is a serious problem that we are causing and that we must change our habits and behavior.

4. To reflect your understanding of specific concerns in the film, write an analysis of changes that you have made or intend to make in your life.

5. Film critic Roger Ebert has written that in his entire career of reviewing movies, he has never before claimed that viewers "owe it" to themselves to see a film, as he does for *An Inconvenient Truth*. Write an argument that supports the necessity for seeing this film.

## CONNECTING WITH OTHER TEXTS

1. Write an essay that first explains and then analyzes three or four of the negative criticisms of Al Gore's film represented in Mieszkowski's essay. Decide if these criticisms are reasonable and if they weaken the documentary for you or any viewer.

2. In his review, A. O. Scott remarks on the "jolting and chilling" effects of graphs shown in this film (268). Write an analysis of the "jolting and chilling" elements of this film, in addition to the graphs, that most affected you. Consider Gore's personal narrations and images, the animations, the photographs of glaciers taken years ago and more recently, film footage of storms, and any other material in the film that moved you.

3. After reading Kevin Crust's critique of *An Inconvenient Truth*, write an analysis that supports your perception that Crust's review of both the film and of Gore is generally positive, negative, or a combination of both. Analyze specific details from the review and film to support your claim.

4. Read Al Gore's book *An Inconvenient Truth: The Planetary Emergency of Global Warming and What We Can Do About It*. Write an essay arguing that either the book or the documentary makes a more convincing mandate for change. Include support from both works to explain your stance.

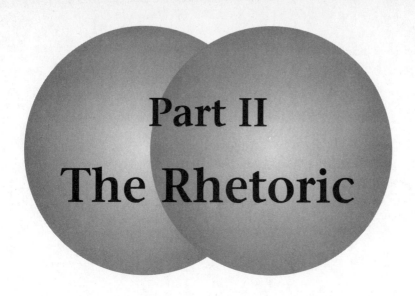

# Part II
# The Rhetoric

**P**art II—the rhetoric—is designed for you to use as an easy and constant reference, not only in class with your instructor but also at home when you are on your own. The instruction is deliberately focused and practical. We are convinced that you will only learn to write better by actually writing, and our prewriting exercises prompt you to do just that. We guide you through the entire process, from discovering a topic and writing a draft to supporting a thesis and revising the essay.

Throughout this rhetoric, you will gain skills to craft the varied types of papers that you will need to write. We provide instruction, examples, and discussions of particular methods for developing essays, and we show you how to draft these essays, too. We offer opportunities for you to practice active reading, taking notes, incorporating quotations, and interviewing—all important skills to help you write successful papers. We show how important it is to consider audience and style. In addition to the many shorter assignments, we provide instructions for all stages of a longer research paper, with guides to the most current Modern Language Association (MLA) and American Psychological Association (APA) documentation forms.

# Chapter 6

# Getting Started . . . Now!

In this chapter you will learn how to

- get started on writing assignments
- gather and sort your ideas
- find information in your readings
- consider audience as you draft

**B**efore you become anxious about your next writing assignment or bored from merely *reading* about writing, we would like to introduce you to Anne Lamott—a writer who understands anxiety and is never boring. In the following essay about starting a writing assignment, Lamott urges writers to bite off just a bit of the assignment at a time, keeping it manageable and appetizing. As you read her essay, highlight key points and vivid wordings. What do you like about her voice, tone, and attitude? What keeps you reading? What does she have to share? How persuasive is she? The following essay is from *Bird by Bird: Some Instructions on Writing and Life* (1994). You may enjoy reading Anne Lamott's brief biography and her argument essay "Time Lost and Found" (p. 239).

##  Short Assignments
### Anne Lamott

1    The first useful concept is the idea of short assignments. Often when you sit down to write, what you have in mind is an autobiographical novel about your childhood, or a play about the immigrant experience, or a history of—oh,

*say*—women. But this is like trying to scale a glacier. It's hard to get your footing, and your fingertips get all red and frozen and torn up. Then your mental illnesses arrive at the desk like your sickest, most secretive relatives. And they pull up chairs in a semicircle around the computer, and they try to be quiet but you know they are there with their weird coppery breath, leering at you behind your back.

2        What I do at this point, as the panic mounts and the jungle drums begin beating and I realize that the well has run dry and that my future is behind me and I'm going to have to get a job only I'm completely unemployable, is to stop. First I try to breathe, because I'm either sitting there panting like a lapdog or I'm unintentionally making slow asthmatic death rattles. So I just sit there for a minute, breathing slowly, quietly. I let my mind wander. After a moment I may notice that I'm trying to decide whether or not I am too old for orthodontia and whether right now would be a good time to make a few calls, and then I start to think about learning to use makeup and how maybe I could find some boyfriend who is not a total and complete fixer-upper and then my life would be totally great and I'd be happy all the time, and then I think about all the people I should have called back before I sat down to work, and how I should probably at least check in with my agent and tell him this great idea I have and see if he thinks it's a good idea, and see if *he* thinks I need orthodontia—if that is what he is actually thinking whenever we have lunch together. Then I think about someone I'm really annoyed with, or some financial problem that is driving me crazy, and decide that I must resolve this before I get down to today's work. So I become a dog with a chew toy, worrying it for a while, wrestling it to the ground, flinging it over my shoulder, chasing it, licking it, chewing it, flinging it back over my shoulder. I stop just short of actually barking. But all of this only takes somewhere between one and two minutes, so I haven't actually wasted that much time. Still, it leaves me winded. I go back to trying to breathe, slowly and calmly, and I finally notice the one-inch picture frame that I put on my desk to remind me of short assignments.

3        It reminds me that all I have to do is to write down as much as I can see through a one-inch picture frame. This is all I have to bite off for the time being. All I am going to do right now, for example, is write that one paragraph that sets the story in my hometown, in the late fifties, when the trains were still running. I am going to paint a picture of it, in words, on my word processor. Or all I am going to do is to describe the main character the very first time we meet her, when she first walks out the front door and onto the porch. I am not even going to describe the expression on her face when she first notices the blind dog sitting behind the wheel of her car—just what I can

see through the one-inch picture frame, just one paragraph describing this woman, in the town where I grew up, the first time we encounter her.

4    E. L. Doctorow once said that "writing a novel is like driving a car at night. You can see only as far as your headlights, but you can make the whole trip that way." You don't have to see where you're going, you don't have to see your destination or everything you will pass along the way. You just have to see two or three feet ahead of you. This is right up there with the best advice about writing, or life, I have ever heard.

5    So after I've completely exhausted myself thinking about the people I most resent in the world, and my more arresting financial problems, and, of course, the orthodontia, I remember to pick up the one-inch picture frame and to figure out a one-inch piece of my story to tell, one small scene, one memory, one exchange. I also remember a story that I know I've told else-where but that over and over helps me to get a grip; thirty years ago my older brother, who was ten years old at the time, was trying to get a report on birds written that he'd had three months to write, which was due the next day. We were out at our family cabin in Bolinas, and he was at the kitchen table close to tears, surrounded by binder paper and pencils and unopened books on birds, immobilized by the hugeness of the task ahead. Then my father sat down beside him, put his arm around my brother's shoulder, and said, "Bird by bird, buddy. Just take it bird by bird."

6    I tell this story again because it usually makes a dent in the tremendous sense of being overwhelmed that my students experience. Sometimes it actu-ally gives them hope, and hope, as Chesterton said, is the power of being cheerful in circumstances that we know to be desperate. Writing can be a pretty desperate endeavor, because it is about some of our deepest needs: our need to be visible, to be heard, our need to make sense of our lives, to wake up and grow and belong. It is no wonder if we sometimes tend to take our-selves perhaps a bit too seriously. So here is another story I tell often.

7    In the Bill Murray movie *Stripes*, in which he joins the army, there is a scene that takes place the first night of boot camp, where Murray's platoon is assembled in the barracks. They are supposed to be getting to know their sergeant, played by Warren Oates, and one another. So each man takes a few moments to say a few things about who he is and where he is from. Finally it is the turn of this incredibly intense, angry guy named Francis. "My name is Francis," he says. "No one calls me Francis—anyone here calls me Francis and I'll kill them. And another thing. I don't like to be touched. Anyone here ever tries to touch me, I'll kill them," at which point Warren Oates jumps in and says, "Hey—lighten up, Francis."

8    This is not a bad line to have taped to the wall of your office.

9     Say to yourself in the kindest possible way, Look, honey, all we're going to do for now is to write a description of the river at sunrise, or the young child swimming in the pool at the club, or the first time the man sees the woman he will marry. That is all we are going to do for now. We are just going to take this bird by bird. But we are going to finish this one short assignment.

## Analyzing Lamott's Purpose

Because Lamott's style is so informal and amusing, it is easy to overlook her argument. Despite her relaxed manner, her writing is focused and unified around her purpose for writing and her central points. After we read an essay, and before we write one, it helps to clarify the aim and the claim.

## What's the Aim?. . .What's the Claim?

Anne Lamott's *aim* (or purpose) seems clear—to convince writers not to become overwhelmed by the writing task or assignment. She provides suggestions, personal anecdotes, and encouragement, all chosen to propel the writer to start and to finish one short assignment.

    Anne Lamott's *claim* (or point) is that even large projects and tasks may get started sooner and be done better if we tackle them step by step or "bird by bird" rather than feeling paralyzed by the task at hand.

## Analyzing Lamott's Strategy

From the beginning, Lamott speaks in her own voice and shares her real experiences: she wonders if she could "find some boyfriend who is not a total and complete fixer-upper," she tries to decide if she is "too old for orthodontia," and she fears that she has run out of writing ideas and is "completely unemployable." These are all problems that we can identify with. Her strategy is to use a voice that sounds authentic—the voice of a friend sharing anxieties, not a professional writer offering advice from on high. Further, to engage us, she amuses us with fresh and zany images. She refers to those "mental illnesses"—an overstated image of insecurities—that arrive at your desk like "your sickest, most secretive relatives" who inhibit your writing as they "form a semicircle around the computer," condemning, criticizing, and censoring your efforts. And she depicts herself as a "dog with a chew toy" as she wrestles with the problems that keep her from getting down to work. Who hasn't had these same experiences, such as putting off an assignment or fearing the censure of a peer reader or instructor? Thus, Lamott's strategy of personal stories and self-deprecation make her credible and compelling.

    Part of her strategy also involves the use of effective language. The absence of clichés and stale language create our perception of her as a lively, spirited individual, without pretension or airs. In fact, her diction (word choice) is far from pretentious. She admits to having financial problems that are "driving me crazy" and to worrying about daily concerns that "leave me winded." Because her strategy is to make her advice accessible to the reader, she uses words that would not be appropriate in all types of assignments. Like the film character in *Stripes* who advises his fellow platoon member to "lighten up," she tries to relax her reader. "Say to yourself in the kindest possible way, Look, honey. . . ."

"Lighten up" may be just the advice you need to get started on a class assignment so that you don't start to censor yourself before you can get your ideas down on the page. In the following section, we will demonstrate prewriting techniques that may help you warm up to your writing assignments.

## Prewriting as Discovery

As soon as you are assigned a paper, begin thinking about the topic and what you already know about it. You might discover that you already have feelings about the subject or have had experiences that relate to it. These can be valuable resources for you and can help you avoid procrastinating.

## Individual Brainstorming

As soon as you let yourself think freely about the topic, your brain will both consciously and subconsciously consider anything that relates to it. You will have moments of insight or inspiration that can be exciting *and* useful. During this brainstorming stage, certain recollections can help you generate material and can trigger a chain reaction of associated ideas. Soon you will want to jot these ideas down on paper so that you don't forget them or overlook what you can learn from them.

It seems paradoxical to suggest that you will discover what you want to write by writing. But students frequently tell us—and our own writing habits confirm—that the very act of working with words, ideas, or feelings on a page or computer screen helps writers learn what they want to express about a topic.

Sometimes a spirited exchange with a friend or roommate will help you "get going" on a writing topic because you start to reconsider and refine your ideas as you discuss them, and you start to care whether your ideas have been communicated or accepted. Actually, the best thing you can do when you are assigned a writing task is immediately to jot down any responses and ideas. Consider this initial, quick writing as a conversation with yourself, because that is what it is.

To help you get moving, here are some prewriting strategies that come from the reading and writing topics in this book. Try these different methods; you may find a few that help you get beyond the blank page or screen.

# Freewriting

As the term implies, *freewriting* involves jotting down uncensored thoughts as quickly as you can. Don't concern yourself with form or correctness. Write whatever comes into your mind without rejecting ideas that may seem silly or irrelevant. In freewriting, one thought might trigger a more intriguing or significant one, so anything that comes into your head may be valuable. Here is one student's freewriting response to the topic of stereotyping:

Stereotyping? I don't think I stereotype—maybe I do. But I sure have had it done to me. When people see my tatoo they seem to think I'm in Hell's Angels or a skinhead. Talk about prejudgements! It's as if the snake coiling up my arm is going to get them, the way they look at it and pull back from me. I remember once, in a campground in Alaska, a bunch of us campers were stranded when the road washed out. As food and supplies dwindled, people started borrowing from each other. In the john one morning I asked this guy if I could borrow a razor blade and he jumped back. Not till he looked away from my arm and into my eyes did he relax. He gave me a blade, we talked, later shared some campfires together. . . . I could write about that experience, a good story. I wonder if people with tatooes have always been connected with trouble—pirates maybe, sailors, bikers and gang members today anyhow. It could be interesting to find out if the negative stereotypes about tatooes have always been there even though I just read they estimate about 20 million people have tatts now. That's some research I could get into.

Pete's response to the topic of stereotyping starts with his personal feeling that the subject doesn't really relate to him. But then he thinks about the fact that he has been stereotyped by others. As he considers how people react to his tattoo, he recalls an incident he thinks he could write as a narrative. As he thinks more about the nature of tattoos, he finds an aspect of stereotyping that concerns him and that he might like to research. If he had not written down his feelings about stereotyping, he might have settled for a more predictable response to the assignment.

Notice that Pete's freewriting starts with a question that he asks himself about the topic—a perfect way to get himself warmed up and moving. He's not worried about checking his spelling. He can consult a dictionary when he is drafting his paper to learn that *tattoos* and *prejudgments* are the correct spellings. Pete also uses language in his prewriting that might not be appropriate in his essays: "guy," "bunch," "john," "anyhow," and "get into." Most important is that Pete got started on his assignment and explored his own unique thoughts and feelings. He found a personal experience he might relate and discovered research that he would like to do.

**PRACTICE FREEWRITING**

To help you see how freewriting can lead to discovery, write for fifteen minutes, without stopping, on one of the following topics. Do not worry about form and do not censor any idea, fact, picture, or feeling that comes to you. Freewrite about the following:

1. Something that one of your parents neglected to teach you.

2. A grandparent's unexpected revelation.

3. A family gathering when you learned something.

4. Your response to "What the Cell Phone Industry Won't Tell You" (p. 210).

5. For young people, "piercing or tattoos may be seen as personal and beautifying statements" (Martin 28). With this quotation at the top of your page, respond freely.

Your freewriting may be written on a sheet of paper, composed at a computer, or jotted down in your journal.

# Journal Writing

Journal writing may be looked on as a conversation with yourself to sort out your views or ideas about a work that you've read or a movie that you've seen. A journal entry also may be a way to warm up before writing a paper or to discover your own perspective; in fact, many professional writers rely on journals to store ideas for future stories, articles, editorials, and poems.

Your professor may ask you to keep a journal while you are in a composition course. Nearly all of the "Thinking about the Text" questions and many of the "Writing from the Text" assignments in Part I make ideal topics for a journal. Using your journal to write responses to assigned readings provides many benefits:

• You will be better prepared for class discussions.

• You will retain more material from the readings.

• You will gain more writing practice.

• You will sharpen your evaluations of the readings.

For your journal entries, you can use a notebook of any size, but many students prefer to compose directly on the computer and find that they write considerably more than they would in longhand.

## Using a Journal for Pre-Reading

A journal is an ideal place to figure out how you feel about a subject *before* you have read an essay about it. If you have done some thinking about the subject, you will be more engaged and read more attentively to learn someone else's view on the subject. If an instructor assigns "Pigskin, Patriarchy, and Pain" (p. 60), your journal is a place to record your views of what high school and college football players experience on and off the field. If your instructor assigns "Twitter? It's What You Make It" (p. 235), you could use your journal to vent feelings about Twitter that you like or loathe before reading the author's argument. And if your instructor assigns "The Good Daughter" (p. 8), you may use your journal to explore your own opinions about what characterizes a "good" daughter or son.

In the Table of Contents (pp. v–xix), we provide blurbs or brief summaries as pre-reading help to stimulate your thoughts and interest even before you begin reading the essay. These blurbs can also prompt pre-reading responses in your journal. For example, the brief comment for "The Good Daughter" states: "These immigrant parents make many sacrifices for their daughter. Is she then "indentured" to her parents, forced to "straddle two cultures?"" Here is how one student might respond to this summary even before reading the essay itself:

My own parents left their family and friends behind to make a better life for themselves and their future children. When my dad arrived in the U.S., he had to take a job that he didn't like, just to pay the bills, and then had to take on another part-time job after my brother and sisters were born. It makes me feel that I need to pay them back, not only by earning money but by not dropping out of school. Almost every pay day my dad complains that he's worn out and there's never enough money. So even now while I'm in school, I'm expected to hold a job to help buy clothes for my younger brothers and sisters. The hours I have to work are hurting my grades, but I feel that I owe my parents so much for what they went through so we could grow up here.

By reading the blurb in the Table of Contents as well as the author's brief biography preceding each reading, you can stimulate your thoughts on the topic before reading each work.

## Using a Journal for Active Reading

One type of assigned active reading is a *dialectical journal*. In this kind of journal you write down specific phrases or meaningful lines from your readings and then record your thoughts about these phrases; in effect, you have a conversation with your reading material. Include specific details that you want to interpret or analyze. Record your responses to those lines and phrases; those responses may be valuable if you later decide to write a paper on the topic.

Imagine Pete, the student who did freewriting about stereotypes, responding specifically to the essay "Don't Let Stereotypes Warp Your Judgments" (p. 424). His journal response to the essay might look like this:

> "Are criminals more likely to be dark than blond?" That's a provocative question the author asks. It makes me think about all the bad guys in movies. Aren't they always dark? You never see Robert Redford playing a villain—or do you? I think some of our stereotyping comes from films, which is Heilbroner's point when he writes about "type-casts." Maybe only bad films use "types." I like what the author says about stereotypes making us "mentally lazy." I can see what he means when he says there are two people hurt in stereotyping—the person who is unjustly lumped into some category and the person who is "impoverished" by his laziness. Heilbroner says that a person can't "see the world in his own absolutely unique, inimitable and independent fashion." That makes sense about being independent. But I wonder what "inimitable" means.

Notice that Pete begins his journal entry with a question from the essay itself; he also might have started with his own question about the work. Pete jots down ideas that come to him as he responds to the reading. Note that he puts quotation marks around any words, phrases, or sentences from the text; in case he uses these later, Pete wants to remember that the ideas and language belong to the author of the essay.

In addition to moving Pete into his assigned topic, his journal writing lets him record his responses to parts of Heilbroner's essay. He is practicing finding the essence of the essay, as well as parts that he might want to quote in his own work. Further, if Pete reads "The Myth of the Latin Woman" (p. 118) and "Black Men and Public Space" (p. 164), he will have relevant material in his journal that he can connect to these other readings, either for his own interest or for writing assignments. In addition, as Pete begins reflecting on his journal entries, he may choose to develop his material in vastly different ways. On pp. 297–298, you can find some of Pete's choices.

## PRACTICE JOURNAL WRITING

Respond to any of the following quoted lines by conversing with yourself and thinking critically about these memorable quotations:

1. "First of all, no one needs to watch the news every night unless one is married to the anchor" (Lamott 241).

2. "Winning at sports meant winning friends and carving a place for myself within the male pecking order" (Sabo 60).

3. "We don't have to achieve to be accepted by our families. We just have to be" (Goodman 4).

# Clustering

*Clustering* is a more visual grouping of ideas on a page. Many students use clustering for in-class writing assignments, including essay exams, where the object is not to discover a topic but to organize information that they already have.

A student named Rachel started with the assigned question of how she was "between worlds" and used that as a center or starting point for her personal inquiry into areas where she experienced "betweenness."

She wrote the assignment as a question in the middle of the page, then she drew lines from the topics to several subtopics, which she placed in boxes. As you can see in the illustration, her subtopics are based on the chapter titles in Part I of this book. She placed "perceptions" and "genders" in the same box because, for her, these areas were closely related. Next to each subtopic, she then wrote down a brief phrase or reference to experiences and concerns that related to it. By clustering her responses, Rachel discovered topics that were important to her.

She was also able to group related issues—an immediate advantage of clustering. You may want to read the paper (p. 334) that came from this prewriting discovery work. But first look at Rachel's clustering exercise, which is reproduced below.

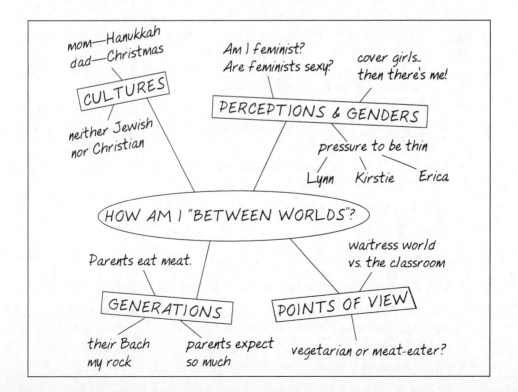

**PRACTICE CLUSTERING**

1. Center "self and family" in a box on a page. As you cluster, consider how you are "a part of" your family and how you are "apart from" your family.

2. Center "incidents that united my family" in a box on a page. Draw lines to other boxes that will include specific outings, celebrations, crises, customs, and events that have united your family. Don't forget the surprising or unlikely incidents that no one expected would draw you together.

Clustering may help you in the process of discovering topics that interest you as well as finding relationships between ideas that you have written on your page.

# Listing

*Listing* is a way of making a quick inventory of thoughts, ideas, feelings, or facts about a topic. The object is to list everything, again without censoring any notion that comes to you. In addition to clustering her "between-worlds" experiences, Rachel listed her ideas after she discovered a topic for her paper. (You can see her list on pp. 304–305.)

Another student, Marianela Enriquez, was assigned a character analysis and she chose to write her paper on Connie, the central character in the short story "Where Are You Going, Where Have You Been?" (p. 70). See her list on pp. 445–447. Notice how Marianela's list helped her find important details and then organize those details for her essay.

 **PRACTICE PRE-READING LISTING**

1. Write a list of the positive and negative consequences of using Twitter—and then read "Twitter? It's What You Make It" (p. 235) and "I Don't Give a Tweet What You're Doing" (p. 232).

2. List the advantages and disadvantages of playing football—and then read "Pigskin, Patriarchy, and Pain" (p. 60).

3. List the dangers of cellphone use while driving—and then read "How the Brain Reacts" (p. 215).

 **PRACTICE POST-READING LISTING**

4. List the reasons for getting a tattoo ("On Teenagers and Tattoos," p. 28).

5. List the advantages and disadvantages of using the Internet ("Does the Internet Make You Dumber?" p. 223, and "Does the Internet Make You Smarter?" p. 210).

6. List the behavior traits of Marcus in "Peaches" (p. 49).

# Active Reading

*Active reading* can help you focus on, retain, and perceive the organizational scheme of a work you are reading and assessing. Active reading is also an appropriate prewriting strategy when you are asked to write a specific response to something that you have read, or when you know that your own experience and knowledge provide insufficient information for a meaningful essay.

We find active reading such an imperative skill that we chose to begin the reading section of this book (pp. 2–3) with the guidelines repeated here, so you may already be familiar with this method—and we hope that you are using it! Reading with a pen in your hand—and using it to interact with the material—will save you time and frustration. As you read your own text or the photocopied pages of a library book, do the following:

- *Underline* the thesis (if it is explicitly stated), key points or topic sentence, and supporting details.
- *Mark* meaningful or quotable language.
- *Place checkmarks and asterisks* next to important lines.
- *Jot* brief summary or commentary notes in the margins. Infer the thesis and write it in the margin if it is not explicitly stated.
- *Circle* unfamiliar words and references to look up later.
- *Ask* questions as you read.
- *Seek* answers to those questions.
- *Question* the writer's assumptions and assertions as well as your own.

Reading actively will allow you to examine and challenge the ideas of an author. It will also help you find important lines more easily so that you don't have to reread the entire work each time that you refer to it during class discussions or in your essays. Don't underline or highlight *everything*, however, or you will defeat your purpose of finding just the important points.

Rachel, the student who used clustering to discover her concern about the pressure among her friends to be thin, decided to do some reading about eating disorders. The excerpt presented here from "Bodily Harm" (p. 186) illustrates her active reading.

Recent media attention to the binge-purge and self-starvation disorders known as <u>bulimia</u> and <u>anorexia</u>—often detailing gruesome particulars of women's eating behaviors—may have exacerbated this serious problem on college campuses. But why would a woman who reads an article on eating disorders want to copy what she reads? Ruth Striegel-Moore, Ph.D., director of Yale University's Eating Disorders Clinic, suggests that <u>eating disorders</u> may be a way to be like other <u>"special" women</u> and at the same time strive to outdo them. "The pursuit of thinness is a way for women to compete with each other, a way that <u>avoids being threatening to men</u>," says Striegel-Moore.

*[margin notes, left:]* check 'initions
'nness as petition— ithout eatening men.

*[margin notes, right:]* <u>Media</u> may exacerbate the problem

general term "special" = how to be unique?

Eating disorders as a perverse sort of rivalry? In Carol's freshman year at SUNY-Binghamton, a roommate showed her how to make herself throw up. "Barf buddies" are notorious on many college campuses, especially in sororities and among sports teams. Eating disorders as negative bonding? Even self-help groups on campus can degenerate into the kinds of competitiveness and negative reinforcement that are among the roots of eating disorders in the first place. *How iron* *Self-help* *groups* *as negative* *reinforceme*

*Key focus.* This is not another article on how women do it. It is an article on how and why some women stopped. The decision to get help is not always an easy one. The shame and secrecy surrounding most eating disorders and the fear of being labeled "sick" may keep a woman from admitting even to herself that her behavior is hurting her. "We're not weirdos," says Nancy Gengler, a recovered bulimic and number two U.S. squash champion, who asked that I use her real name because "so much of this illness has to do with secrecy and embarrassment." In the first stages of therapy, says Nancy, much of getting better was a result of building up the strength to (literally) "sweat out" the desire to binge and to endure the discomfort of having overeaten rather than throwing up. "I learned to accept such "failures" and moreover, that they would not make me fat." *labeled* *"sick"* *secrecy* *part of t* *problem* *Need to* *accept our* *"failures"*

Writing notes in the margins helped Rachel to stay involved as she read and to remember details from the essay.

## 🔴 PRACTICE ACTIVE READING AND CRITICAL THINKING

1. Practice the steps listed on p. 285 and actively read the next work that you have been assigned in this course. Do you feel better prepared for class discussion? Did you find the central point or thesis of the essay as a result of your active reading? Was the author's organization scheme apparent to you?

2. Actively read "The Good Daughter" (p. 8), "The Only Child" (p. 33), or "The Color of Love" (p. 15). After you have actively read one of these essays, join a small group of other students who have read the same essay. Compare your active-reading notes with those of others in your group.

# Group Brainstorming—Collaborative Learning and Critical Thinking

Writing doesn't have to be an isolated, lonely activity. In fact, much professional writing is a collaborative effort in which writers work together or consult editors. Corporations, educational institutions, and governmental organizations hold regular "brainstorming" sessions so that everyone can offer ideas, consider options, and exchange opinions. Reporters often work together on a story, business experts pool ideas to draft a proposal, and lawyers work as a team on a brief. Many of your textbooks—including this one—are the result of extensive collaboration.

Your college writing classes may offer you opportunities to work together in small groups, brainstorm for topics or supporting details, and critique and edit your classmates' writing. These small groups can stimulate new thoughts, multiple perspectives, and critical questions. Small-group discussion should prompt you to consider the ideas of others and help alleviate the fear that you have nothing to say.

In the classroom, groups of four or five work well, with each person recording the group's comments and key ideas for an assigned question. Students in the group can alternate explaining each response, so that the burden of reporting the discussion does not fall on any one group member. Your instructor, however, may ask that someone from each group serve as "group secretary," recording responses and then reading them. Either way, the goal is to generate as many different responses as possible to a given topic or question. As in all of the prewriting activities, no idea or comment should be censored.

Let's assume you have been assigned a paper about growing up with or without siblings. Each group can take a different aspect of this topic:

- The advantages of growing up with siblings
- The advantages of growing up as an only child
- The ways that only children find "substitutes" for siblings
- The reasons for sibling rivalry and competition, and the solutions to these problems
- The unexpected bonds that develop between siblings
- The reasons that sibling friendships fail

After ten to fifteen minutes of discussion, each group shares its key points with the class. After each group's report, all students should be invited to add comments or insights on that topic.

Group brainstorming is an ideal way to discuss reading assignments, and most of the "Thinking about the Text" questions in Part I are designed for collaborative work. Next you will find brainstorming exercises for both general topics and specific readings.

## PRACTICE BRAINSTORMING IN SMALL GROUPS

1. Brainstorm about the positive and negative aspects of online forums like Twitter, Facebook, MySpace, chatrooms, or YouTube.

2. Discuss the complications that there are more women than men on a college campus.

3. Discuss the various types of families currently portrayed on television. Topics:
   • Analyze the impact of the media on the family.
   • Compare sitcoms with family dramas, family reality programs, or PBS specials on the family.
   • Contrast portraits of more conventional families with those of less conventional ones.
   • Suggest programs that could help or support the family.
   • Evaluate programs for their level of violence.

4. Read "Living in Two Worlds" (p. 99) and "The Only Child" (p. 33) and discuss specific ways that family members develop different values and habits. You may add your own experiences to this discussion.

5. Read "The Good Daughter" (p. 8) and discuss how parents' expectations can affect their children's lives.

## Why Brainstorm?

Brainstorming lets you see the perspectives of others and consider their views in relation to your own—an awareness you will need when you are writing for an audience other than yourself. Collaborative work gets you away from the isolation of your own desk or computer screen and into a social context.

# Incubation

After you have tried one or more of the prewriting strategies to get started on an assignment, allow yourself an incubation period—time to think about your topic before you begin to draft the paper. Students often comment on experiencing flashes of insight about their papers while in the shower, falling asleep, or doing some physical activity.

You, too, will find that your brain will continue to "work" on your paper if you are preoccupied with it when you are away from it, and thus it is a good idea to leave time for incubation at each point in the writing process. For example, if you do some prewriting on your paper when it is first assigned, your early thoughts and ideas may develop during incubation. Later, you may also be able to refine the purpose of your essay, which in turn will help you hone your topic, improve the support of your main points, discover connections among ideas in your paper, and recall words that will sharpen your meaning.

# Considering Audience

## Identifying Your Audience

All writing is intended for readers—that is, for an audience. But who *is* the audience?

In some situations, you can easily define the audience: for example, your reader may be a friend or family member who will receive your letter. You are surely aware that your writing tone—the voice that you use that affects your word choice and emphasis—will differ if you are writing to your friend, lover, brother, elderly aunt, or mother. However, you may be less able to define the audience for other writing situations.

In general, you should not assume that your only reader is your composition instructor, for that conclusion will prompt you to write for a very small audience. Furthermore, your English teacher may be your easiest audience, because he or she is *required* to read what you have written, comment on your thinking and writing skills, and then perhaps place a grade on your work.

*Academic Audiences.* Academic readers (your instructors and classmates) expect a certain depth of response, even in a short paper. The reader expects to learn specific facts, find actual examples, discover important insights, or see particular relationships that she or he was not aware of prior to reading your paper.

An academic audience also expects you to have worked with integrity when incorporating the ideas, facts, or words of another writer. (See the discussions of plagiarism on pp. 318–323 and pp. 480–483.) An academic audience expects you to make some point and to support that point logically, with sufficient details (of description, fact, or example) to be convincing.

Academic readers expect your material to be presented in an orderly way. Finally, they expect the language of your work to be appropriate: standard English and well-chosen words without slang, jargon, or text message codes. For example, most instructors will prefer that you use "children or son and daughter" rather than "kids" and won't be pleased to see "BFF" in an essay about friendship. Academic readers will also expect that you have edited your essays to remove errors in grammar, spelling, and mechanics.

*Nonacademic Audiences.* For writing outside the classroom—for example, a letter to a newspaper, a report for your boss, or an analysis for a community project—you must engage an audience that is not required to read your writing. What are the expectations of this audience? For the most part, nonacademic audiences also expect good organization, no errors or plagiarism, and logically supported points.

In addition, you may need to convince nonacademic readers that your subject and the way you have treated it are worth their time. You may have to establish the value of your subject and the quality of your writing in the first few sentences. Developing an engaging style will help keep your reader interested.

**Voice.** Most instructors will tell you to "write in your own voice." This means that they want you to write using the vocabulary, sentence structure, and style that you use for communicating as an adult. You do not want to use pretentious words or artificial language, nor do you want to use diction that is more appropriate for rap lyrics or text-messaging a friend.

**Style, Stance, and Tone.** To engage your audience, you will want to consider style, the conscious use of language. Word choice is a key part of style; precisely chosen words, wordplay, and level of diction should be considered. (See also pp. 567–570 on word choice.) The structures of sentences—length, types, and variety—contribute to your style. You should also assume a stance and tone that is positive for all readers, even those who are disinterested in your topic. You may want to anticipate possible objections, doubts, or lack of interest by writing in a tone that does not put off any reader. Consider the style, stance, and tone of these passages from two authors expressing differing views about Twitter:

> A huge chunk of Twitter lore, etiquette and even terminology has sprouted up from Twitter users without any input from the company. For example, the people came up with the term "tweets" (what everyone calls the messages). The crowd began referring to fellow Twitterers by name like this: @pogue. Soon that notion became a standard shorthand that the Twitter software now recognizes. The masses also came up with conventions like "RT," meaning retweet—you're passing along what someone else said on Twitter. (Pogue 235)

> Look, some of my best friends are Tweeting. I know this because their e-mails now have signatures listing their Twitter account names along with their cellphone number, Websites urls and notices that the message has been sent from a hand-held device as if that's not obvious because they typed "sluts met 4 lunge" instead of "let's meet for lunch." (Daum 232)

The tone of Pogue's passage here is informative and straight-forward, with examples that reflect his stance that Twitter is creative. He illustrates that Twitter is a democratic medium because its users themselves have, in fact, shaped its terminology and conventions—inventing terms like "tweets" for messages and "RT" for information forwarded. His style is positive as he provides precise explanation of terms to enlighten readers. His style is deliberately characterized by informal diction such as "a huge chunk" and "sprouted up" and his descriptions of Twitterers as "the crowd" and "the masses."

In contrast, the tone of Daum's opening is personal and contentious as she uses her own experience to make her case. Her stance is that Twittering is often boring, "inane or insane," and a waste of time. She supports her position with an amusing and "inane" example, divulging a friend's distorted tweet—"sluts met 4 lunge"—rather than the intended "let's meet for lunch." Her style is casual and colloquial: "Look, some of my best friends are tweeting." Her relaxed diction is an appropriate reflection of the medium she is analyzing.

You need to choose the tone for your particular writing assignment. The subject matter of your work, the audience for whom you are writing, and your stance on the subject will help you determine the appropriate tone for your essay.

###  PRACTICE STYLE

1. Write two letters—one to your best friend, and one to your parents or children—describing a party that you recently attended. Your letters probably will vary in vocabulary, kinds of details, sentence structure, and tone.

2. Draft two lists describing the same television show or movie—one directed to a friend and the other for an academic essay. Use language appropriate to each audience.

## Analyzing Audience Awareness

We can profit from the study of the techniques that writers use to hold their particular audience. The following essay by William F. Harrison has been published in a number of places, including the *Los Angeles Times* on July 7, 1996. Harrison is an obstetrician and gynecologist who practices in Fayetteville, Arkansas. A smoker of twenty years, Harrison saw the effects of cigarette addiction on his own body. For ten years he tried to stop smoking and, because he limited himself to a single cigarette a day, he thought he was not harming himself. Nevertheless, he had chronic bronchitis and laryngitis. After consulting with pulmonologists and pathologists, he learned that even one cigarette a day harms the body irreparably. He knew that he needed to stop entirely, and he did. He also knew that he needed to convince his patients to stop smoking. This essay reports the results of Harrison's research. Does the writer convince his reader?

EXAMPLE: CONVINCING AN AUDIENCE

##  Why Stop Smoking?  Let's Get Clinical
### *William F. Harrison*

1    Most of us in medicine now accept that tobacco is associated with major health consequences and constitutes the No. 1 health problem in this country.

2    What smokers have not yet come to terms with is that if they continue smoking, the probability of developing one or more of the major complications

of smoking is 100 percent. It absolutely will happen. They will develop chronic bronchitis, laryngitis, pharyngitis, sinusitis, and some degree of emphysema. It is also highly probable that they will develop serious disease in the arteries of all vital organs, including the brain and heart, markedly increasing their risk of heart attack and stroke. If they continue, they increase the probability of developing cancer of the lips, gums, tongue, pharynx, larynx, trachea, bronchi and lungs, of the bladder, cervix, gallbladder and other organs. Smoking contributes to rapid aging of the skin and connective tissues—women and men who smoke usually have the skin age of a person ten to twenty years older than one who doesn't smoke, given the same degree of exposure to the sun.

3    About 415,000 people die prematurely each year in the United States as a result of smoking—the equivalent of eighteen 747s crashing every week with no survivors. Many of these victims die after long and excruciating illnesses, burdens to themselves, their families and society. The cost of this misery is incalculable, but we do know that the tobacco industry grosses about $50 billion a year from the agonies it inflicts.

4    How does all this damage come about?

5    In normal lungs, the trachea and bronchi—the large and small tubes leading to the alveoli (the tiny sacs that do the actual work of the lungs)—are lined with a film of tissue that is one cell layer thick. The surface of these cells is covered with tiny, finger-like structures called cilia. These cilia beat constantly in a waving motion, which moves small particles and toxic substances out of the lung and into the back of the throat where they are swallowed. In a smoker or someone like a coal miner, who constantly breathes in large amounts of toxic substances, many of the cilia soon disappear. If exposure continues, some ciliated cells die and are replaced by squamous cells, the same type that form the skin. Without the cleansing function of the ciliated cells, toxic materials and particles are breathed further into the lungs, staying longer in contact with all the tissue. Each group of ciliated cells killed and replaced by squamous cells decreases by a certain fraction the lungs' ability to cleanse themselves. As this occurs, the amount of damage done by each cigarette increases to a greater and greater degree. By the time one has been a pack-a-day smoker for ten years or so, extensive damage has already been done. By twenty years, much of the damage is irreversible and progresses more rapidly. After ten years of smoking, each cigarette may do as much damage to the body as three or more packs did when a smoker first started.

6    The longer one smokes, the harder it gets to quit. Smoking is one of the most addictive of human habits, perhaps as addicting as crack cocaine or

heroin. One has to quit every day, and there are no magic pills or crutches that make stopping easy. It is tough to do. Only those who keep trying ever quit. And even those who have smoked for only a short time or a few cigarettes a day will probably find it difficult to stop. But the sooner a smoker makes this self-commitment, the more probable it is that he or she will quit before having done major damage to the body.

## Analyzing the Essay

Clearly, William Harrison's purpose in writing is to convince readers who are smokers to stop smoking. His obligation as a writer is to produce plenty of research to answer the question: "Why Stop Smoking?" His intention also may be to prevent people from starting and to arm nonsmokers with specific evidence to help persuade a family member or a friend who smokes to stop.

His opening engages the reader because he is straightforward in his presentation of facts. Harrison specifically cites those diseases that all smokers definitely will get and those diseases that smokers probably will get. No organ of the body remains untouched, and Harrison might have written just that statement. But by actually citing the organs, the reader is almost overwhelmed by the catalog of specific details. In addition, to catch the interest of the person indifferent to health, Harrison appeals to the reader's vanity by stating that smokers' skin is aged ten to twenty years beyond that of nonsmokers.

When Harrison provides the number of smokers who die prematurely—415,000 per year—he also gives a disturbing equivalent for this figure: "eighteen 747s crashing every week with no survivors." The writer's purpose here is to shock us. We may be complacent about the number of smokers who die each year, but we all know the effect of a newspaper headline announcing the crash of a single plane. Imagine reading that eighteen planes crashed each week all year! Cleverly, Harrison admits he doesn't know the cost of the "excruciating illnesses"—and the misery—that precede death from smoking-related diseases. But he knows and gives the profits of the tobacco industry—"$50 billion a year."

Harrison might have generalized what happens to the lungs when people smoke, but instead he credits his readers' intelligence by providing a highly specific and scientific account of how the cilia cells that normally cleanse the lungs disappear. In fact his word choice is that the "ciliated cells die," a far more emphatic way to show that toxic material is no longer filtered out. By showing the human body as a mechanical organism, he convinces the reader that the smoker's body has no more chance to continue running well than a car would if it were deprived of oil or gasoline.

To drive home his point about the toxicity of smoking, Harrison equates the smoker with "a coal miner"; both breathe in "large amounts of toxic substances." He notes that after ten years of smoking the lungs are so vulnerable that "each cigarette may do as much damage to the body as three or more packs did when a smoker first started." He uses this startling research to convince both the smoker who planned to stop after a few years and the smoker of ten years who cuts down to an occasional cigarette, that profound harm is done to the body regardless of the smoker's intention.

Harrison's conclusion has to do with nicotine addiction, and he compares the addiction to quitting cocaine or heroin. In his frightening comparison, he provides any young person considering smoking ample reason not to start, and he gives any person who loves a smoker the impetus to seek professional help to rid the smoker of this powerful and deadly addiction.

Finally, Harrison's title is an effective play on words. He's relying on the reader to hear "Let's Get Physical," a lyric from a popular song, in "Let's Get Clinical." His essay provides vivid clinical evidence of the physical damage the smoker will do to his body, information as far from a popular tune as it can be.

### ⬤ PRACTICE AUDIENCE AWARENESS

1. Write a letter to your college president or dean of student affairs to convince the administrator that your college needs more stringently enforced "no smoking" regulations in outdoor areas.

2. Write a letter to a friend who smokes to convince that person to stop. Use the data in Harrison's essay for your letter.

## A Final Word About Audience

Good style—achieved with deliberately chosen vocabulary, sentence structure, and tone—can engage your reader immediately. Providing solid support will sustain that reader. With a realistic understanding of your audience in mind, you are ready to begin organizing and drafting your essay.

# Chapter 7

# Organizing and Drafting an Essay

In this chapter you will learn how to

- create and support a thesis
- outline your ideas
- focus and develop paragraphs
- incorporate and document sources

## From Prewriting to Purpose

The prewriting exercises presented in the previous chapter should have helped you discover focus points and different ways that you might respond to your writing assignment. You were also given some ideas about considering the audience for your writing, to help you select an appropriate stance and tone. The stance or position that you take will be influenced by your aim in writing and the assignment you have been given.

## Purpose in Writing

Clearly your purpose or aim in writing is to satisfy your instructor's assignment—and to get a good grade on your paper! Your primary purpose—assigned by your instructor or discovered on your own—may be to express, inform, analyze, or persuade. For example, if your instructor assigns an evaluative, analytic, or persuasive essay, your aim has been delineated for you. But if you have been given a more open-ended assignment—to write on a topic or respond to readings—you need to discover your aim for yourself.

## What's Your Aim?

Before you can articulate your aim, you need to make sure that your subject is manageable and not too general. During your prewriting, you have probably written about a variety of general subjects—and these may include *Between Worlds* subjects as varied as anger management, the Internet's effect on thinking skills, and stereotyping. Clearly, these subjects are too broad to write about in a college essay. Freewriting, clustering, and listing will help you hone your general subject to discover a more limited subject, one that can be handled in an essay rather than an entire book. Once you have discovered your limited subject, you will need to determine your particular purpose or aim for writing. Do you want to persuade, inform, express, or analyze? Knowing your aim, you will be able to express your point or claim.

## What's Your Claim?

Every essay requires a **thesis—an assertion or claim about a limited subject that the writer of the essay will support, prove, or describe**. Often, but not always, the view of the writer shows in the language of the thesis. Sometimes the writer constructs a thesis to forecast the plan or organization of the paper. The thesis should reflect the aim or intention of the paper and should clarify the focus of the essay for both the writer and the reader. Throughout your writing, it will help to hear your reader asking, *"What's your aim? What's your claim?"*—two questions that will ensure that you are staying focused. Remember also that your claim or thesis may change a number of times as you draft and revise your paper.

## Finding a Focus

Finding a focus often results from a prewriting exercise. After freewriting in your journal and perhaps responding to the readings, you may discover your feelings about a subject. For example, you may have been intrigued by the Table of Contents blurb for "King Curtis's Echo": "Do I want to live in a world where my response to a personal affront is going to land me in jail, an emergency room, or in the morgue?" (Thayer 171). This quotation from the essay may prompt you to write in your journal about a time when you were angered by a rude driver, an insulting customer, or an aggressive sports fan. As you prewrite on this subject, you will start to move from the general topic of anger or responses to anger to a more focused position, clarifying your aim and claim.

Or perhaps you are assigned to write about reality television programs. In your freewriting, you may discover that you have strong feelings about reality TV—that you enjoy it, find it a waste of time, or a little of both. As you express your ideas, you may start listing your positive and negative feelings. You may have been assigned to read "Don't Let Stereotypes Warp Your Judgment" (p. 424), and like the student Pete, you may have written about stereotyping—whether you have prejudged others or feel that they have preconceived ideas about you. In prewriting about stereotyping, you may discover, like Pete, that you have a number of potential paper topics embedded in the broader subject of stereotyping. Your prewriting has helped you discover a subject that you are interested in and your thoughts and feelings about that topic. Working from the general ideas in your journal, you are ready to discover your purpose in writing—your aim—and to craft a good thesis—your claim. The chart below will illustrate how writers move from a general subject to a supportable claim.

## Discovering the Claim—From General to Specific

| General Subject | Limited Subject | Aim | Claim |
|---|---|---|---|
| anger | responses to anger | to analyze the danger of impulsive responses | A moment of reflection can often prevent unnecessary violence. |
| reality TV | negative aspects | to convince readers that reality TV can endanger participants | Reality TV sacrifices participants' safety to boost ratings. |
| stereotyping | harmful effect | to persuade readers to resist stereotyping | Stereotyping can create unnecessary anxiety and deprive us of worthwhile experiences. |

## Varying the Thesis

The compact nature of this chart may suggest that the wording of each thesis is inevitable and predictable, but actually the possibilities are limitless, even for the same subject matter. Let's return again to our student Pete who did the earlier journal writing (p. 282) to discover this thesis: "Stereotyping can create unnecessary anxiety and deprive us of worthwhile experiences." His particular interest has to do with his tattoo and how he is stereotyped because of it, an awareness he gained in freewriting (p. 279). Pete realized that he had a good focus for a story he could narrate. He also discovered that he was interested in doing some reading about the history of tattoos to learn whether they were always regarded negatively.

If Pete's assignment had been to write about a personal experience involving stereotyping, he probably would have written about the incident in the Alaskan campground. Had his purpose been to define stereotyping, show its consequences, and persuade his reader that it is wrong, Pete might have recalled his dialectical journal prewriting (p. 282) on the essay "Don't Let Stereotypes Warp Your Judgments" (p. 424), and he would have developed his paper in a different way. Pete may have used any of the following for a working thesis, depending on his aim in writing the paper:

- An experience in Alaska showed me how uncomfortable stereotyping can be for the person stereotyped.
- Because tattoos have been worn by the lower classes and fringe members of various cultures throughout history, prejudice against them still exists.
- Because prominent citizens of the world have started to wear tattoos, earlier prejudice against tattoos has diminished.
- Stereotyping, or prejudgments based on "standardized pictures" in our heads, can create unnecessary anxiety and deprive us of worthwhile experiences. (This is the same thesis as shown in the chart).

Each of these assertions requires Pete to develop his paper in a slightly different way. The first thesis can be supported with his own experience. The second and third thesis statements require Pete to research material in order to support his claims. The fourth statement requires using some appropriately documented material from Heilbroner's essay on stereotyping, as well as personal experience. Like Pete, your personal interests, as well as the aim of the assignment itself, will help you decide on a suitable thesis.

##  PRACTICE RECOGNIZING A THESIS

*A thesis is a complete sentence that makes an assertion about a limited subject.* Which of the following are supportable thesis statements? Which are not? What can be done to each deficient example to make it a strong thesis?

1. Patients' use of the Internet for medical information.

2. Patients' use of the Internet for medical information should be encouraged by doctors.

3. I think that the school's cafeteria should post a nutritional analysis of every meal it offers.

4. Online romances and conventional dating are similar and different.

5. Is frequent Internet use altering the way our brain functions?

6. A moment of reflection can often prevent unnecessary violence.

7. How to get a friendship to turn romantic.

8. Planting a vegetable garden creates personal satisfaction and inspires public commitment to improve the environment.

9. In this essay, I plan to show that identifying people according to their race may limit an appreciation of their cultural identity.

10. You shouldn't eat fast food.

## Explaining the Errors

Below you will find explanations of each example as well as corrections to modify deficient attempts at a thesis. If your instructor notes that your own thesis statements are weak, you can return to this thesis-revision exercise to remind yourself of what a strong thesis statement looks and sounds like.

1. This first example may be a suitable subject or topic for an essay, but it is not a thesis. As the absence of a verb indicates, the example lacks an assertion that makes a claim about patients using the Internet for medical information. See 2 below.

2. This example does make a claim about patients using the Internet and is a reasonable thesis. It has a limited subject (patients' use of the Internet), and it has an assertion (that this use "should be encouraged by doctors").

3. This statement contains a clear assertion, but "I think" is unnecessary. The thesis should directly express this conviction: *The school's cafeteria should post a nutritional analysis of every meal it offers.*

4. While the plan to compare and contrast may be promising, this is not yet a focused thesis because it is much too general. Nearly everything, in some sense, is "similar and different." By specifying an important way that online and conventional dating are similar and/or a way that they are different, you will have a stronger thesis and may even forecast the direction of your essay:

   • Although both online romances and conventional dating involve some risk, Internet sites offer more opportunities to meet the right person and a better environment for intimate and honest communication than a bar or office can.

   • Online relationships often create and nurture a fantasy that cannot endure the real world of sustained conversations, unexpected obligations, and comfortable routines.

5. A question may be a good way to engage a reader in an introduction, but it is not an assertion, so it is not a suitable thesis. The question encourages an unfocused, disorganized response. Contrast the direction implicit in example 2 with this question, and you will see why it is not effective.

6. This example is a very explicit thesis statement. It includes a clear assertion that reflection "can often prevent" violence and it anticipates that "a moment of reflection" will be described in the essay.

7. This is not a thesis because it isn't a complete sentence and lacks a point. It is a topic or title but not a thesis. We can turn this into a thesis by writing a clear assertion:

   • Getting a friendship to turn romantic may involve unbearable embarrassment and frustration unless there is mutual determination.

   • Moving from friend to boyfriend can often sacrifice both the friendship and the romance.

8. This example is a strong thesis because it contains a clear, two-part assertion that planting a vegetable garden "creates personal satisfaction" and "inspires public commitment to improve the environment." This thesis forecasts the organization for an argument essay.

9. A thesis should not be an announcement of what the writer intends to do. Instead, as Nike insists, the writer should "just do it!" The actual assertion is strong and can stand alone: *Identifying people according to their race may limit an appreciation of their cultural identity.*

10. This may be good advice, but it is not a good thesis. Most readers would object to the preachy voice, the direct confrontation implicit in "you," and the simplistic advice. Instead, the writer could forecast reasons for avoiding fast food: *For economic, nutritional, and aesthetic reasons, we would all be better off avoiding fast food.*

## The Ideal—A Forecasting or Blueprint Thesis

Often a strong thesis not only clarifies the point of the essay but forecasts or anticipates the development of the paper. Such a thesis is ideal because it can help the writer better organize the material and can help the reader better follow the development. Several of the corrected thesis statements above provide such forecasts:

   • **Although both online romances and conventional dating involve some risk, Internet sites offer more opportunities to meet the right person and a better environment for intimate and honest communication than a bar or office can.** This thesis is especially strong because of the "although" or "even though" format that allows the writer to make a connection between the two types of dating but then promises to go beyond this link. The writer notes a specific similarity between online and offline dating (both involve risk) so the writer is promising that this will be developed and supported in the paper. But this thesis also offers two specific contrasts, arguing that online dating is preferable because it offers more opportunities to meet the right person *and* a better environment for intimacy and honesty. Both of these claims will need to be developed and supported in the essay, giving the writer plenty to develop but also giving the writer and reader a direction to follow.

- **Online relationships often create and nurture a fantasy that cannot endure the real world of sustained conversations, unexpected obligations, and comfortable routines.** This thesis requires the writer to illustrate how online relationships both create and nurture a fantasy world. Then the writer also will need to show how such fantasies may be fed by the clever, clipped communication of the computer but not be able to sustain deeper, prolonged conversations of everyday life. The writer will also need to illustrate how unexpected obligations can disrupt the fantasy as much as someone's comfortable routines can destroy the mystique of online romance.

- **Getting a friendship to turn romantic may involve unbearable embarrassment and frustration unless there is mutual determination.** Such a thesis specifies some obstacles to the goal of turning a friendship into a romance so these difficulties can be illustrated and developed. But the thesis also suggests that if both people share the attraction, a romance may be possible, again inviting the writer to support and prove this claim.

- **Moving from "friend" to "boyfriend" can often sacrifice both the friendship and the romance.** This thesis anticipates a direction that could be serious and cynical or lighthearted and ironic—or a little of both. But the assertion is clear and it promises that the writer will show how both the friendship and the romance can often be threatened by efforts to fire up the friendship.

## Changing the Thesis

A thesis statement can undergo many changes in the course of drafting and rewriting a paper. All writers have had the experience of finishing a draft only to discover that their feelings about the subject have changed. In order to reflect that new awareness in the paper, the writer will want to return to the thesis, revise it, and then reshape the points in the paper so they will adequately support the new assertion. Writers find that it is perhaps best to consider any thesis as a working thesis until they are about to edit their final draft. (See Rachel's work on developing a thesis, pp. 305–308.)

## The "Missing" Thesis

Some writers do not explicitly state their thesis, and some instructors do not demand one. Sometimes the overt assertion may spoil the sense of discovery that the writer intends for the reader. But even if a thesis is implied rather than stated, in a well-structured essay you should be able to articulate the writer's fundamental assertion.

## Positioning the Thesis

For many writers, and for many essays, placing the thesis at the end of the introduction makes sense. The thesis follows logically from the introductory materials used to engage the audience, and the plan or direction of the paper is set forth so that the reader knows not only what is coming but in what order the support will be presented. This forecasting also helps the writer of the essay to stay organized and on target.

Essays that are tightly written, with very well-organized support, may conclude with the thesis—expressed in different words—to bring a necessary sense of closure. The reader will perceive where the writer is headed, so the assertion at the end of the paper will not come as a surprise.

Many writing instructors, tired of wondering and writing "Where is all of this going?" in the margins of student papers, require that you place your thesis within the first few paragraphs of your essay. These instructors favor the clearly stated thesis that forecasts the subtopics and their order of presentation. In any case, a strong focus—whether stated in a thesis or implied—contributes to good writing, and you will want to perfect your ability to focus your work.

The more essays you read, the more you will recognize how a thesis statement sounds. Take, for example, the thesis of Don Sabo's "Pigskin, Patriarchy, and Pain" (p. 60): "Becoming a football player fosters conformity to male-chauvinistic values and self-abusing lifestyles" (63). In his essay he examines the reasons males play football and the detrimental effects of playing this sport. The author wants to show that football conditions men to perpetuate "chauvinistic values," inflict pain on others, and tolerate constant pain themselves. The author asserts his point in a statement, a thesis, that forecasts those areas that he will examine—chauvinistic values and self-abusing lifestyles—two consequences of playing football.

Although reading other writers' thesis statements will help you understand the mechanics of thesis writing, you need to practice writing your own assertions for your own papers. You also need to have readers critique the thesis statements that you have written.

### PRACTICE THESIS WRITING

1. Return to one of your prewriting exercises or freewrite for fifteen minutes on the subject of a parent's ability or inability to be open to new and possibly controversial ideas. Then reread what you have written.

Find an aspect of that material that interests you. Limit your focus and write two or three different thesis statements that you can support with the ideas in your freewriting. Use a computer to write these assertions on a sheet of paper and print out three copies prior to your next class session.

2. Work in groups of four students to comment on each other's assertions. Let each student in the group make comments about one thesis statement before you go on to look at each person's second assertion. Determine which statements are true assertions that can be supported. Then predict the type of support that is necessary (narrative of personal experience, definition, or examples from research material) for each thesis.

## Critical Thinking and the "So What?" Strategy

After you have a tentative assertion around which to direct your support, ask yourself, "So what?" A sure way to realize that your assumed assertion isn't headed anywhere meaningful is to discover yourself shrugging indifferently at your own claim. As you jot down answers to this question, you will start to see what you are actually claiming. For example, imagine what would happen if you started with this assertion:

**Thesis:** Many people in the world are victims of stereotyping.

"So what?"

Some people have preconceived ideas about others.

"So what?"

It's unfair. People see them as types, not individuals.

"So what?"

These prejudgments limit the people who are stereotyped *and* the people doing the stereotyping.

As you continue to answer the "So what?" questions, you may discover a way to state your assertion that makes your reader more eager to read your paper. Compare the following assertion with the first one. In what way is it better?

**Thesis:** Prejudgments limit the lives of the stereotyped individual *and* the person doing the stereotyping.

Notice how this statement conforms to the requirements of a thesis. It is a complete sentence, not a question or a phrase, and it articulates a definite opinion or assertion. Unlike the first attempt at a thesis, this statement establishes a definite focus on prejudgments (they "limit . . . lives"), and it suggests an order for the analysis ("the stereotyped individual" and "the person doing the stereotyping").

By asking yourself "So what?" *throughout* your writing, you will not only sharpen your thesis but also help yourself discover points and insights worth sharing with readers. If you continue to ask this question, you will prompt yourself to think more critically about each claim as you make it. You also ensure that you are writing from a worthwhile assertion and that you are explaining your points to your reader.

# Supporting a Thesis
## Drafting

No one writer drafts the same way; in fact, there are as many methods (and "non-methods") for drafting as there are writers. But there are countless strategies and approaches that help writers organize, develop, and support their ideas and assertions.

On the following pages, we trace how one student, Rachel, drafted her paper. Look back to page 283 to see Rachel's clustering exercise, where she discovered a topic related to living "between worlds." From this initial prewriting, she perceived that recurrent topics of interest were related to food: her vegetarianism, her friends, preoccupation with slimness, her awareness that her body does not fit the cover-girl mold, and even her job as a waitress.

## Developing Support

Reviewing all of these food-related topics, Rachel realized she was most interested in her friends' eating problems. She started by actively reading "Bodily Harm" (p. 186). You can read an excerpt from this prewriting exercise on pages 285–286. This active reading helped stimulate Rachel's thinking and helped her understand her friends' experiences.

## Listing

After her prewriting activities, Rachel started to list more specific ideas and experiences that related to eating disorders:

- My friend, Lynn, hospitalized for anorexia, nearly died.
- Another friend, Kirstie, was proud she could vomit automatically every time she ate.
- My friend, Erica, in a treatment program, was shocked by the number of women over 30 still plagued by eating disorders.
- Binge-and-purge syndrome needs to be explained.
- Ads depict tall models in size 3 bikinis.
- "Bodily Harm" examines psychological motives, "barf buddies," and "aerobic nervosa."
- Jane Fonda, once bulimic, hooked so many on her *Work Out* videos.

- Princess Di—bulimic and suicidal—the myth collapses.
- Kate Moss, Mary-Kate Olsen, and Kate Bosworth are skinny superstars.
- My own insecurity involves my weight.
- My cousin spent weeks in a hospital program for anorexics.
- Weight loss—the ultimate "control" mechanism?
- Women's movement trying to free women from such images.
- Young women torn between being feminist or sexy—why either/or?
- Sexy women are always pictured as thin.
- Women competing without threatening men.

## Working Thesis

From this list, Rachel linked certain topics: friends' experiences, celebrities with serious eating disorders, advertising images of women, psychological motives, the women's movement, and dieting as a control mechanism. These groupings helped her draft a working thesis so she could start planning her paper.

**Working Thesis:** Many women suffer from eating disorders.

Using this preliminary thesis as a guide, Rachel started to write.

## First Draft

In this day and age many women suffer from eating disorders. Influenced by television commercials and movies, most women have been conditioned to believe they must be thin to be beautiful. Who wouldn't want to hear friends whisper, "What a body! She really knows how to stay in shape!" or "Don't you hate someone who looks that good?" Either way, the sense of envy is clear. A thin girl has something that others don't—and this gives her power and control. She can make herself in the image of the cover girls. "The pursuit of thinness is a way for women to compete with each other, a way that avoids being threatening to men" (Erens 186).

Unfortunately, this competition keeps women from seeking or obtaining the help they might otherwise get from close friends. Many bulimics keep their secret as guarded as they can. For example, my friend Kirstie did this. She waited for years before she told friends (and later, her family) that she was bulimic. At first, only her "barf buddy" (from Erens?) knew.

Kirstie seemed to have a good life with her family and friends. But years later, she revealed to me that her greatest pride was when she discovered that she was now vomiting automatically after eating, without needing to use a finger or spoon.

Erica was another friend who needed help. In fact, her situation was so bad that she needed to go into a hospital. And my friend Lynn would have died had she not entered the hospital when she did. She had to drop out of Berkeley immediately and get prolonged therapy for herself and her family. As Erens notes, "Family therapy considers the family itself, not the daughter with the eating disorder, to be the "patient." Often the daughter has taken on the role of diverting attention from unacknowledged conflicts within the family."

One problem Lynn had was conforming to her parents' expectations. Lynn decided to major in art even though her parents wanted her to get a degree in computer science so she would have a job when she graduated. There was so much stress in that house every time Lynn enrolled in another art class. Maybe she felt that the only thing she could control in her life was how thin she could get.

The message to be thin comes from popular celebrities. Magazine covers feature the weight loss of actress and tabloid-favorite Mary-Kate Olsen who was in rehab for bulimia. In the 80s, actress Jane Fonda sold many on the value of her *Work Out* and helped spawn "aerobic nervosa" (Erens 187). Many women who admired her shape may not know that Fonda was once bulimic. And no one watching the televised spectacle of Prince Charles and Princess Diana's wedding could have predicted that years later biographers would be discussing "Di's bulimia."

Not just the supermodels like Kate Moss, or the actress Kate Bosworth, but most popular personalities seem incredibly thin today. It seems that many women—celebrities, models, and my friends—have not escaped this curse.

## Evaluating the First Draft

As Rachel was writing this draft she found herself crossing out occasional words and adding phrases, but her main concern was getting her ideas down on the page. She remembered relevant ideas from some assigned readings in *Between Worlds,* and she put some of the quoted material in her draft. She did not worry about the form of her quotes, but she was careful to copy the page numbers correctly so she wouldn't have to waste time searching for them later. Once she had written this rough draft, she reread it with a pen in hand, spotting weak areas and making quick notes to herself. Her own critique of her first draft follows.

*cliche?*               *dull*
(In this day and age) many women suffer from eating disorders. Influenced by
television commercials and movies, most women have been conditioned to believe
they must be thin to be beautiful. Who wouldn't want to hear friends whisper, "What
a body! She really knows how to stay in shape!" or "Don't you hate someone who          *maybe save...*
looks that good?" Either way, the sense of envy is clear. A thin girl has something that
others don't—and this gives her power and control. She can make herself in the image    *put thesis here?*
of cover girls. "The pursuit of thinness is a way for women to compete with each other,
a way that avoids being threatening to men" (Erens 186).

Unfortunately, this competition keeps women from seeking or obtaining the
help they might otherwise get from close friends. Many bulimics keep their secret
as guarded as they can. For example, my friend Kirstie did this. She waited for years
before she told friends (and later, her family) that she was bulimic. At first, only her
          *page?*
"barf buddy" (from Erens) knew.
                                                        *illustrate*
Kirstie seemed to have a good life with her family and friends. But years later,
*develop*    she revealed to me that her greatest pride was when she discovered that she was now  >    *too gross
                                                                                                      or OK?*
vomiting automatically after eating, without needing to use a finger or spoon.      >    *better link
                                                                                          here?*
Erica was another friend who needed help. In fact, her situation was so bad
that she needed to go into a hospital. And my friend Lynn would have died had she       *develop*
not entered the hospital when she did. She had to drop out of Berkeley immediately
and get prolonged therapy for herself and her family. As Erens notes, "Family
therapy considers the family itself, not the daughter with the eating disorder, to be
the "patient." Often the daughter has taken on the role of diverting attention from
*page?*    unacknowledged conflicts within the family." *discuss & link better
                                                           to next ¶*

One problem Lynn had was conforming to her parents' expectations. Lynn
decided to major in art even though her parents wanted her to get a degree in computer science so she would have a job when she graduated. There was so much stress
in that house every time Lynn enrolled in another art class. Maybe she felt that the
only thing she could control in her life was how thin she could get.                    *link?*

The message to be thin comes from popular celebrities like Mary-Kate Olsen.
Actress Jane Fonda has sold many on the value of her "Work Out" and has helped         *Put earlier*
spawn "aerobic nervosa" (Erens 187). Many women who admired her shape may
not know that Fonda was once bulimic. And no one watching the televised spectacle
of Prince Charles and Princess Diana's wedding could have predicted that years later
biographers would be discussing "Di's bulimia."

Not just the supermodels like Kate Moss, or actresses like Kate Bosworth, but most popular personalities seem incredibly thin today. It seems that many women—celebrities, models, and my friends—have not escaped this curse. *Ok for thesis?*

## Revising the Thesis: What's Your Aim? What's Your Claim?

Writing the draft helped Rachel realize the link between her friends' experiences and the influence of the media. Once she had a more defined aim—to criticize the media's influence on women's self-perceptions—she needed to revise her claim to reflect this criticism. Her claim is expressed in her new working thesis.

> **New Working Thesis:** Magazine ads and commercials influence how women see themselves and how they behave.

Rachel felt that her material—both her personal experiences and readings—would support her new thesis. She also realized that this thesis helped her link the influence of the media to women's actions and behavior. Rachel showed her thesis to her instructor, who suggested she apply the "So what?" response to this assertion:

Ads and commercials influence women's self-perceptions.

"So what?"

Women try to look like the skinny models.

"So what?"

It's dangerous! Women are starving themselves.

"So what?"

The media has to change—they are responsible for programming women this way.

After thinking about this conversation with herself, Rachel now had a stronger claim and she revised her working thesis again:

> **Revised Working Thesis:** The media must be forced to stop programming young women to believe that skeletal models are the ideal.

Rachel's revised thesis more accurately reflected her claim that the media must change what they are doing to women, and her reference to the "skeletal models" would permit her to discuss her friends' experiences.

# Writing an Outline
## Organizing to Highlight Key Points

Excellent ideas and interesting information can get lost or buried in a paper that is not carefully arranged and organized. If you arrange your thesis to reflect your organization scheme, you can more easily draft your essay. Notice how Rachel's thesis forecasts her essay's key points:

> The media must be forced to stop programming young women to believe skeletal models are the ideal.

Rachel's thesis suggests that she will first look at how the media is "programming" women, and then she will show how specific women become "skeletal" victims of the advertising that they see. Further, her assertion that the media "must be forced to stop" this practice invites her to propose a solution. Although Rachel devised a general scheme for organizing her paper, she knew she needed a more detailed outline.

## To Outline or Not to Outline

By helping you arrange your materials effectively, an outline can save you time and frustration. Just as most drivers need a map to direct them through unfamiliar territory, most writers need outlines in order to draft their papers.

However, you probably have had the experience of being in a car without a map, when someone could intuit the right direction and get you where you needed to be. Some writers have that intuition and therefore find detailed outlines unnecessary. But these writers still craft a strong thesis and rely on their intrinsic sense of organization to guide them as they write.

Most of us have also been in cars with drivers who were convinced they could manage without a map, but couldn't. Such indirection or "backtracking" in papers prompts instructors to note in the margins: "Order?" "Repetitious," "Organization needs work," "Relevant?" "Transition needed," or "Where is this going?" If you see these indicators on your papers, you know your sense of direction is failing you. Outline before you write! Unless your instructor requires a particular outline form, your outline may be an informal "map" of key points and ideas in whatever order seems both logical and effective.

## Ordering Ideas

You have a number of options for effective organization, and your purpose in writing will help you determine your arrangement. For example, Rachel's purpose was to convince readers that the media must stop promoting thinness as an ideal. Because this was the most important part of her argument, she saved it until the end, building support for it as she wrote. Rachel thus chose an emphatic arrangement scheme.

In an *emphatic* or *dramatic organization,* you arrange your material so that the most important, significant, worthy, or interesting material (for which you generally have the most information) is at the end of the paper. This is the principle that guides Ellen Goodman in her essay, "When a Woman Says No" (p. 67). Goodman presents summaries of three court cases involving charges of rape. She deliberately orders the three cases so that the most controversial one—involving the woman's prior sexual conduct—is last. The virtue of this type of organization is that it permits the writer to end in a dramatic way, using the most vital material or emphatic support for a concluding impression.

Some papers, however, invite a *spatial arrangement.* Often used in description, this kind of arrangement permits you to present your points in a systematic movement through space. In "The Only Child" (p. 33), John Leonard deliberately moves from external descriptions of his brother's shabby boarding house to internal descriptions of his filthy room. From these physical descriptions, he then moves further inward to an analysis of his brother's psychological condition.

In order to narrate a series of events, a *chronological ordering* may be useful. Jeff Z. Klein's essay "Watching My Back" (p. 57) chronicles a time when he and his girlfriend face drunken attackers in Prague. He describes the initial incident, their ensuing discussions of it, and finally his decision to take a self-defense class. A *chronological arrangement* is useful to tell a story, give historical detail, or contrast past and present.

## An Informal Outline

Because Rachel found it was difficult to focus her initial draft and order her supporting details, she decided to write an informal outline: a list of points, written in a logical order, that she planned to cover in her essay. She knew this outline would simply be a personal guide to help her include all relevant materials, so she didn't spend hours on the outline or concern herself with its wording.

Rachel wrote her working thesis first and then listed her key points in the order she planned to cover them. She planned to focus on the stories of three friends, and she had to decide how to order their stories. The chronology of these friendships seemed less relevant than the differences in their problems and treatment programs. She decided to begin with Kirstie, who received outpatient treatment but continued to deny her problem. She ended with Lynn, who had the most extreme eating disorder—she came close to death—and the most dramatic recovery. Lynn's experience provided the most emphatic evidence for Rachel's essay, so Rachel knew that she wanted to end her examples with Lynn's experience. Rachel also knew that she would add other points or perhaps modify this order as she wrote the paper, but at least she would have a map to head her in the right direction.

Thesis: The media must be forced to stop programming young women to believe skeletal models are the ideal.

INTRODUCTION

—Typical ad described: model in bikini

—Models as unhealthy and obsessed with being thin

—The horror: skinny models seem "right"

—Thesis

ANOREXIA AND BULIMIA AS EPIDEMICS

—Jane Fonda and her *Work Out*

—Princess Di, reputed bulimic

—Kate Moss, Mary-Kate Olsen, and Kate Bosworth perpetuate the skinny image

—Women competing with each other (use Erens)

MY FRIEND KIRSTIE, BULIMIC

—Kept this secret; only her "barf buddy" and I knew

—Obsessed with food

—Outpatient counseling didn't really work

—I didn't know how to help her

MY FRIEND ERICA, ANOREXIC

—Enrolled in in-hospital program

—Shocked by number of older women in program

—Received nutritional and emotional help

MY FRIEND LYNN, ANOREXIC, ALMOST DIED

—Dropped out of Berkeley, enrolled in hospital

—Family received treatment too (use Erens)

—These friends felt programmed by the media to be thin

—Diet industry undermines women's control

CONCLUSION

—A time for shock *and* action

—Refuse to support products that promote these images

In an informal outline like this, the ideas that you loosely group as "information blocks" may become paragraphs. In some cases, your grouping or block may end up being split into two or more paragraphs. This outline includes supporting details, but the topic sentences are not written out; therefore the outline is still rather sketchy. In Rachel's case, she didn't feel she needed more elaboration because she had already done some prewriting and initial drafting.

## A Sentence Outline

You may prefer or be required to write a more formal, full-sentence outline. Below you will find a sentence outline of Rachel's essay.

## How to Arrange a Sentence Outline

In a sentence outline, all the subtopics are complete sentences so that the reader understands not only the topics covered but the points that will be made about each topic.

The following sentence outline pertains to Rachel's final draft (pp. 334–337). Notice how the various divisions (Roman numerals, capital letters, and Arabic numbers) are organized. Whenever you divide a point (A, B, etc.) into subpoints (1, 2, etc.), you must have more than one subpoint. For example, for every "1" you must have at least a "2" for support. If you lack material for a "2," you probably need to reexamine your material and either develop more support or incorporate this solitary subpoint into your initial heading.

Also, in an outline the thesis belongs at the top; in the actual essay, however, it is usually integrated into the essay, often at the end of the introduction.

> **Thesis:** The media must be forced to stop programming young women to believe skeletal models are the ideal.

I. **Introduction: A typical ad is described and critiqued.**
   A. Ads bombard us with images of bikini-clad models.
      1. Models sip diet drinks—only thin is in.
      2. Models are always surrounded by adoring males.
      3. Models stand 5'10" and wear a size 3.
   B. Ads don't reveal the dark reality of this image.
      1. Bony ribs and hunger pangs aren't so visible.
      2. Models pop "diet pills."
      3. Models may vomit their food to stay thin.
   C. Such models don't seem skinny; they seem "right."

II. **The problem: Anorexia and bulimia plague college women.**
   A. Anorexia and bulimia remain severe problems.

1. Anorexia and bulimia are serious epidemics.
2. Media attention has not helped.
3. Women remain in bondage to their bodies.
   B. Even celebrities are victimized by eating disorders.
1. Jane Fonda, once bulimic, prompted her *Work Out* videos.
2. Princess Di was reported to be plagued by bulimia.
3. Kate Moss, Mary-Kate Olsen, and Kate Bosworth are skinny super-stars.

III. **The reasons: Thin women have advantages.**
   A. Lean shapes gain admiration and affirmation.
1. Thin girls get all the compliments.
2. They feel they have power over others.
   B. Women can compete without threatening men (Erens).

IV. **The illustrations: Female friends seem obsessed with eating.**
   A. Kirstie has a secret life with her "barf buddy."
1. She had it all: boyfriend, looks, grades.
2. Outpatient counseling didn't help.
   B. Erica met women over 30 who were still anorexic.
1. She entered an in-hospital program during her break.
2. She learned to handle emotions and food.
   C. Lynn nearly died before she got help.
1. She left Berkeley for an in-hospital program.
2. Her family joined in her therapy, too.

V. **The blame: Advertisers program women to be thin.**
   A. The ideal model today is very young and thin.
1. Fashion magazines use preteen models.
2. Weight of models continues to decline.
   B. The message of our culture is girls must starve.
1. Females feel compelled to diet constantly.
2. Skinny models were once shocking; now they are the norm.

VI. **The proposal: We must pressure the media to stop perpetrating these deadly images of women.**
   A. Send letters to producers and sponsors protesting ads.
1. One letter represents many; 10 letters mean power.
2. Models must reflect the diversity among women.
   B. Boycott products and shows that perpetrate "bodily harm."

Although a sentence outline takes more time and effort than a topic outline, the effort is seldom wasted, because many of the sentences can be transferred into the essay itself. By ensuring an ordered presentation of material, outlining often strengthens an essay and ultimately saves you time.

# Writing a Paragraph

## Focusing the Paragraph with a Topic Sentence

Once you have done some prewriting and have written a working thesis, you are ready to draft your essay. Your thesis has made an assertion you need to support, and the body of your essay consists of paragraphs that build this support. Each of those paragraphs may include a *topic sentence*—a sentence that expresses the central idea of that paragraph. The topic sentences emerge naturally from the groupings discovered in prewriting and from the subtopics of the outline.

Not all paragraphs in an essay have a topic sentence, but all paragraphs must have a focus or controlling idea. The value of a topic sentence is analogous to the value of a thesis: both keep the writer and reader on track. Again, like the thesis, the topic sentence should be deliberately placed to help the reader understand the focus of the paragraph.

Let's look at some short paragraphs that lack topic sentences.

 ### PRACTICE WRITING TOPIC SENTENCES

Practice writing your own topic sentence (the central idea) for each of the following paragraphs:

1. Lines to see an advisor extend beyond the walls of the counseling department. Because the health service requires proof of insurance, students wait in long lines to argue for exemptions. The financial aid office assigns appointment times, but invariably lines form there, too. At the bookstore, students wait twenty minutes at a register, and I need to have my out-of-state check verified in a separate line. Even before classes begin, I'm exhausted.

2. A great amount of corn is used as feed for cattle, poultry, and hogs. Corn is also distilled into ethanol—a fuel for cars and a component in bourbon. Corn is made into a sweetener used in snacks and soft drinks and a thickener for foods and industrial products. A small amount of corn is consumed at dining tables in kernel or processed form.

Although each paragraph is clearly focused, both would profit from an explicit assertion. Compare your topic sentences with your classmates' assertions before reading the following possibilities. Although topic sentences may be placed anywhere in the paragraph, the topic sentences here seem to be most effective as the first or last sentence in these paragraphs. Here are some possibilities for the first example:

- Going back to school means getting in lines.
- Lines are an inevitability at my college.
- Lines are the worst aspect of returning to school.

Here are some possibilities for the second example:

- Corn is used for extraordinarily diverse purposes.
- Humans, animals, and machines profit from products made of corn.
- Corn is a remarkably useful grain.

In addition to evaluating your classmates' topic sentences, it may be worthwhile to evaluate the relative strengths of the sentences above. Which are stronger, and why?

## Analyzing the Use of a Topic Sentence

In the following paragraph, notice how Rachel includes very good supporting details but lacks a topic sentence that expresses the central idea of the paragraph:

> During Kirstie's senior year in high school, she was dating a college guy, was enrolled in college prep classes, jogged religiously every morning and every evening, and loved to ski with her family and beat her brothers down the slope. She seemed to crave the compliments she received from her brothers and their friends because of her good looks, and she received plenty! But years later, she revealed to me that her greatest pride at that time was when she discovered that she could vomit automatically after eating, without needing to use a finger or spoon.

Rachel realized that she had not articulated the focus of her paragraph. She went back to clarify her point—that "Kirstie had it all." But Rachel also realized that her perception of her friend was an illusion. Rachel brought the two ideas together to form a topic sentence:

> Few of us ever suspected that Kirstie was in trouble because she seemed to have it all.

Rachel asserts that Kirstie "seemed to have it all" but was really "in trouble." First Rachel shows specific examples of Kirstie's seemingly happy life: "dating a college guy," being in "college prep classes," jogging "religiously," and skiing with her family. Then Rachel supports the fact that Kirstie was really a troubled young woman.

It is important that you use very specific examples to support your topic sentence. It would not have been enough for Rachel to claim that Kirstie had "everything" without showing specifically what that meant. She doesn't just mention that Kirstie had a boyfriend, but that he was a "college guy." Kirstie doesn't simply have a close family; they go skiing together, and she spends time with her brothers' friends. Rachel's support is vivid, visual, and specific. Her shocking last sentence is graphic and unforgettable because it is so detailed in its description.

## Unifying the Paragraph

Rachel's last sentence also contributes to paragraph coherence and unity. Rachel's opening sentence suggests Kirstie was in trouble, even though she did not appear to be. Subtle references to this trouble appear in the paragraph: Kirstie seems obsessed with exercise, and she craves compliments. Finally, after enumerating Kirstie's apparent successes—what she *should* be proud of— Rachel stuns the reader with the irony of Kirstie's "greatest pride," her ability to vomit automatically. Thus the concept of pride unites the paragraph. The key word in the topic sentence, "seemed," predicts the illusions that permeate and unite the paragraph. (For more on paragraph unity and coherence, see pp. 337–344.)

## Eliminating Irrelevant Details

In addition to focusing the paragraph with a topic sentence, you will need to make sure that all details in your paragraph relate to your controlling idea. This means that every sentence in your paragraph must support your topic sentence. Often when you are drafting a paragraph, you may include sentences that seem relevant at the time, but in rereading the paragraph, you discover that a certain detail doesn't contribute to that paragraph's focus. You should eliminate the sentence from that paragraph, but you may be able to use it elsewhere in your essay. Make sure that you reread your work with an eye on maintaining focus in each paragraph. Recognizing those sentences that don't fit and removing them during the revision process will strengthen the paragraph and your essay.

 ### PRACTICE HOW TO RECOGNIZE IRRELEVANT DETAILS

Read the following paragraphs and determine which sentences are irrelevant because they do not support the focus of the paragraph:

1. When it comes time to pay for a date, an awkward pause often threatens to ruin the good vibe and even the entire evening. This discomfort can be prevented if both individuals immediately pay their share, just as they

would with a friend or a co-worker, without any hesitation or reluctance. The notion that males should automatically pay or that the person who initiated the date should always pay *is* old-fashioned and outdated. It's getting ridiculous that so many restaurants and clubs charge such inflated prices, and the cost of gas keeps rising. Unless someone has made it clear that he or she is treating the other or that the date is a gift, neither should expect to be paid for or should wait around, pressuring the other into paying. It doesn't matter if the date involves a casual lunch, a costly dinner, or admission to a movie, club, or sporting event, both individuals should pay for themselves, so that neither one feels burdened or resentful.

2. In her study of how men and women communicate, Deborah Tannen claims that even in childhood, males and females socialize differently. Boys base their bonding on active play. Many boys play baseball and football in neighborhood parks. Boys struggle not to be subordinate in a group that is larger and more hierarchical than girls' groups, so physical play and a desire for dominance, rather than listening to each other, is their way of communicating. In contrast, girls base their relationships on intimate talk and exchanging secrets. Girls see conversation about their thoughts and feelings as an important way to create closeness. Girls can get really close sharing intimacies with each other, especially at pajama parties. The contrasting communication patterns of each gender continue into adulthood and cause serious problems for men and women who may marry and then discover their talking styles are in conflict.

## Analyzing the Practice Paragraphs

In the first example, the writer's controlling idea is expressed in the second sentence—that the end-of-the-date "discomfort can be prevented if both individuals immediately pay their share." The writer supports this focus by insisting that it is "old-fashioned and outdated" for males to automatically pay for everything on a date. Unless it has already been established that the date is a "treat" or a "gift," the couple should share the cost. The fourth sentence—"It's getting ridiculous that so many restaurants and clubs charge such inflated prices, and the cost of gas keeps rising"—should be removed from this paragraph. The increasing costs on dates are irrelevant to the focus of this paragraph that argues for gender equality in paying for dates. However, the fact that dates are costly could be developed in a separate paragraph even though that idea distracts the reader from the focus here.

In the second paragraph, the controlling idea is in the first sentence, "That even in childhood, males and females socialize differently." The writer notes Tannen's points that boys bond through active play and respond physically rather than sitting and listening to each other. In contrast, girls connect by talking and sharing feelings and secrets. Two sentences in this paragraph are irrelevant because they don't support the topic of communication: "Many boys play baseball and football in neighborhood parks" (third sentence) and "Girls get really close sharing intimacies with each other, especially at pajama parties" (seventh sentence). Each of these sentences may be true, but each is offering specific details that are irrelevant to the controlling idea that males and females have contrastive communication styles.

## Developing a Paragraph

When you have a topic sentence or controlling idea for a paragraph, it is essential to support it with examples and any necessary explanation. Try to anticipate questions or objections your reader may have; you can use the "So what?" response here to make sure the significance of your idea is clear. If you discover irrelevant sentences or details that don't develop your paragraph's focus, remove them. Irrelevant details work against paragraph development. Good support for your topic sentences can be drawn from your own ideas, experiences, and observations, as well as from readings and research.

# Using Sources for Support

## Giving Credit and Avoiding Plagiarism

Although in a formal research paper you may be required (or prefer) to use notecards or photocopies for recording data, for a short paper with a single source, you might choose to work directly from the margin notes you made during your active reading. No matter how you have recorded your supporting material, you must give the exact source and page number for borrowed ideas and for quoted material. In addition, you need to put quotation marks around the quoted words and around the titles of essays, short stories, or poems that you are using in your essay. The titles of longer works—books, plays, films, magazines, newspapers, Web sites, online databases—any work that can be published independently should be in italics. See p. 344 for more information about titles. By including the author's name and a page number after every idea or quotation you use, you can avoid *plagiarism*—using other writers' words or ideas without giving them credit.

## Using Others' Words

Rachel's instructor required her to use the documentation form recommended by the Modern Language Association (MLA). Therefore she gave credit by either citing the author's name before the material and then giving the source's page number in parentheses afterward or by including both the author and page citations in parentheses immediately following the quotation. For example, Rachel wrote that Jane Fonda helped spawn "aerobic nervosa"

(Erens 187). Two popularly used documentation forms (MLA and APA) are described in detail with examples in Chapter 12.

Remember, giving credit means the following:

- Using quotation marks around borrowed words or phrases
- Acknowledging the source and page number of any borrowed words or paraphrased ideas immediately afterward
- Including the complete source—author, title, and publishing information—in the list of works cited at the end of the paper.

## Incorporating Quoted Material

Quoted material should support your ideas and may be a vital component of your paper. If the original material is particularly well written or precise, or if the material is bold or controversial, it makes sense to quote the author's words so you can examine them in detail.

All quoted material needs to be introduced in some way. It is a mistake to think that quoted material can stand on its own, no matter how incisive it is.

Often, in fact, it is vital to introduce and also to comment on the quoted material. Let's look at an example from Rachel's paper:

> Lynn's family became involved in her therapy, too. Erens emphasizes the importance of the family in any treatment plan: "Often, the daughter has taken on the role of diverting attention from unacknowledged conflicts within the family" (189). In therapy, Lynn and her family gradually learned that her parents' "unacknowledged conflicts" over Lynn's choice of art as a major instead of computer science contributed to Lynn's stress. Therapy involved acknowledging these internalized conflicts as well as seeing a relationship between her eating disorder and that stress.

In this passage, Rachel uses Lynn's experience to lead into the quoted material. The quote provides an explanation of family dynamics that reflects Lynn's situation. Rather than letting the quotation stand by itself, Rachel *uses* it by discussing the connection between the quoted material and her friend's specific experience. In order to understand how Rachel has incorporated quoted material in her essay, let's look at a strategy we call "the sandwich."

## The Sandwich as a Development Technique

If you have had instructors comment that your papers need more development, or you have trouble meeting the required length for an assignment, or you find that you are merely "padding" your paper with strings of quotations, you will discover that the "sandwich" strategy is a solution to your problem.

Even if your papers seem to satisfy the page requirement but you are earning B's instead of A's on your papers, the problem may be that you have not critically thought about and *used* your supporting material.

Because effective supporting material is often quoted from sources, you need to incorporate direct quotations effectively. The "sandwich" technique helps you write better-developed and more convincing papers. Just as bread holds the contents of a sandwich together, a writer needs to use the introduction to the quotation and the discussion about it to hold the quoted material together.

It may help to visualize the "sandwich":

- **The lead-in or introduction**—the top slice of bread—appeals to the reader and helps by identifying the author or speaker and any necessary background or credentials. The introduction should provide enough of a context or an awareness of the plot for the quoted material to make sense and should anticipate and identify any pronouns used within the quotation. The lead-in may also emphasize the focus point that you intend to support with the quoted material. The introduction needs to be informative without duplicating the material in the quotation.

- **The direct quotation**—the "meat" of the sandwich—comes next.

- **The analysis or commentary**—that essential bottom slice of bread—provides those necessary lines of clarification, interpretation, analysis, or discussion after the quotation. You need to explain or define the author's terms or discuss the significance of the quotation to the work as a whole. Most importantly, your analysis demonstrates the necessity of that quoted material for the point you are making.

In the previous example (p. 319) from Rachel's paper, Rachel introduces the quotation by identifying the author's last name so that she needs to give only the page number in parentheses after the quote. In her lead-in, Rachel also anticipates Erens's focus point about "the importance of the family in any treatment plan" without repeating Erens's exact words. Her analytic comment after the quotation is a good example of how to use the author's words. When Rachel returns to Erens's observation about the family's "unacknowledged conflicts," she works with the quotation and underscores Erens's meaning.

 **PRACTICE WRITING THE SANDWICH**

The following passage appears in Brent Staples's essay "Black Men and Public Space" (p. 166):

I often witness that "hunch posture," from women after dark on the warrenlike streets of Brooklyn where I live. They seem to set their faces on neutral and, with their purse straps strung across their chests bandolier style, they forge ahead as though bracing themselves against being tackled.

Because the passage that begins "They seem to set their faces on neutral" has such memorable language to describe the women that Staples sees walking at night, students often choose to incorporate his description. In your notebook, try writing a lead-in and then your analysis of that one line.

LEAD-IN:

_____
_____
_____
_____
_____

"They seem to set their faces on neutral and, with their purse straps strung across their chests bandolier style, they forge ahead as though bracing themselves against being tackled" (166).

ANALYSIS:

_____
_____
_____
_____
_____

You might want to compare your sandwich with a classmate's. See if you both managed to avoid the following problems in your lead-in. Can you identify the reasons that these lead-ins are weak?

1. *Brent Staples says*, "They seem to set their faces on neutral and, with their purse straps strung across their chests bandolier style, they forge ahead as though bracing themselves against being tackled" (166).

2. *In paragraph 6, Brent Staples quotes*, "They seem to set their faces on neutral and, with their purse straps strung across their chests bandolier style, they forge ahead as though bracing themselves against being tackled" (166).

3. *Brent Staples feels like a criminal:* "They seem to set their faces on neutral and, with their purse straps strung across their chests bandolier style, they forge ahead as though bracing themselves against being tackled" (166).

4. *Recent statistics show that urban violence is epidemic:* "They seem to set their faces on neutral and, with their purse straps strung across their

chests bandolier style, they forge ahead as though bracing themselves against being tackled" (166).

5. *Staples's essay shows that women who walk at night* "They seem to set their faces on neutral and, with their purse straps strung across their chests bandolier style, they forge ahead as though bracing themselves against being tackled" (166).

## Explanation of the Errors

1. This lead-in effectively identifies the author, but it doesn't give a context for the quotation that follows. The reader cannot know who "they" are. (See pronoun reference, p. 538, for an explanation of this error.) Further, the writer needs to prepare the reader for what is important in the quotation so that it makes sense to the reader.

2. This lead-in also identifies the author, but there is nothing gained by starting with the paragraph number and in fact this pointless information is distracting. Furthermore, the writer does not prepare the reader for this quotation. It is also not accurate to write that "Brent Staples quotes" because Staples is not quoting anyone; he is the writer who is being quoted.

3. The writer seems to understand the discomfort that Brent Staples feels— "like a criminal"—but he has not shown how this feeling is a consequence of the women's posture. Moreover, there is no referent for "they."

4. This lead-in doesn't accurately anticipate the quotation. It may be true that "urban violence is epidemic," but this lead-in does not prepare the reader for the description of the women's posture.

5. This lead-in is effective because it identifies, before the reader is confused, that "they" are the "women who walk at night." However, the writer has a grammar error in the double subject—"women" and "they"—which prompts the reader to stumble between the lead-in and the quotation. The writer could easily correct this by starting the quotation with "seem" to avoid the double subject and moving smoothly from lead-in to quotation: *Staples's essay shows that women who walk at night* "seem to set their faces on neutral."

Here is one example of an effective sandwich—good lead-in *and* analysis— using this same quotation. If the title and author's full name have already been included in the essay, only the last name of the author is needed here:

> **Staples describes the posture of women who walk at night:** "They seem to set their faces on neutral and, with their purse straps strung across their chests bandolier style, they forge ahead as though bracing themselves against being tackled" (166).

**Staples suggests that these women need to play multiple roles. They must appear to be indifferent to their environment and not make eye contact as they "set their faces on neutral." Further, they become soldiers with bandoliers and defensive football players guarding themselves against being attacked.**

*Analyzing the Example.* Notice that the lead-in identifies the author so that only a page reference will be necessary in the parenthetical citation. Further, the referent for the pronoun "they," which begins the quotation, is clarified in the lead-in—"women who walk at night."

Students often neglect the analysis portion of the sandwich, assuming that the quotation is self-explanatory. However, the only way to convince your reader of your interpretation of the quoted material is to analyze it—to work with it.

Notice that the analysis is quite complete. The first statement—"These women need to play multiple roles"—is a general assertion drawn from the specific images of women as soldiers with their bandoliers and as football players guarding "against being tackled." Because the women are on the defensive, the student explains that they don't make eye contact and they "appear to be indifferent" as they "set their faces on neutral." The student has analyzed the word choice and imagery so that he can convince the reader of his interpretation of Staples's description.

Although Staples's language is so vivid and worth incorporating into your paper, you might also be writing an essay where you prefer to allude to Staples's experiences in a more general way, without using his specific words. You will still need to give credit, in your essay, for your use of Staples's work and ideas.

## Using Others' Ideas

As soon as you are assigned a paper topic and begin reading or Googling for information, you need to take notes and carefully record where you found ideas. It is too easy to surf the Web and gather so many ideas that you can't even remember where you found them. These ideas are *not* your own even if you put them in your own words. For example, if you are writing about how black men are often stereotyped as criminals and you refer to the vivid account of a black man in an affluent neighborhood's jewelry store barely escaping a guard dog's attack, you will need to acknowledge your debt to Brent Staples. Simply include in your essay Staples's name and the page number where he narrates the story *and* don't forget to include Staples's essay in your Works Cited. In addition to avoiding a charge of plagiarism—using someone else's words or ideas as your own—you are showing your instructor that you have prepared for your topic by reading and that you have others' support for your views. (For more discussion of plagiarism, see pp. 480–483.)

# When to Paraphrase

*Paraphrasing—putting a writer's words or ideas into your own words*—makes that information available to the reader in a condensed form. Sometimes you will want to put the essence of an entire piece that you have read into your own words; other times you will want to paraphrase just one section of the work. If the author's idea is useful but the material is wordy, filled with jargon, or contains information you do not need, you will paraphrase rather than quote the text.

# Illustrating Paraphrasing

Assume that you are writing an essay on failure—and how individuals might actually gain strength from surviving a painful failure. You might decide to include ideas from J.K. Rowling's commencement address: "The Fringe Benefits of Failure, and the Importance of Imagination" (p. 154).

### Original from "The Fringe Benefits of Failure, and the Importance of Imagination"

> The knowledge that you have emerged wiser and stronger from setbacks means that you are, ever after, secure in your ability to survive. You will never truly know yourself, or the strength of your relationships, until both have been tested by adversity. Such knowledge is a true gift, for all that it is painfully won (156–157).

### Paraphrase

> Failure is necessary because when people survive adversity, they often gain wisdom and strength from their ability to endure. Such testing brings deeper self-knowledge and a truer understanding of relationships with others (Rowling 156–157).

The important point that Rowling makes about failure is retained while her wording is condensed. Most importantly, note that her name and the page number are given in parenthesis because the ideas are Rowling's. *To fail to cite her name and a page number would be plagiarism.*

 PRACTICE PARAPHRASING

Practice paraphrasing the following paragraph—a challenging one—before you read the paraphrase that follows it.

### Original from "Why Stop Smoking? Let's Get Clinical" (p. 291)

> In normal lungs, the trachea and bronchi—the large and small tubes leading to the alveoli (the tiny sacs that do the actual work of

the lungs)—are lined with a film of tissue that is one cell layer thick. The surface of these cells is covered with tiny, finger-like structures called cilia. These cilia beat constantly in a waving motion, which moves small particles and toxic substances out of the lung and into the back of the throat where they are swallowed. In a smoker or someone like a coal miner, who constantly breathes in large amounts of toxic substances, many of the cilia soon disappear. If exposure continues, some ciliated cells die and are replaced by squamous cells, the same type that form the skin. Without the cleansing function of the ciliated cells, toxic materials and particles are breathed into the lungs, staying longer in contact with all the tissue. Each group of ciliated cells killed and replaced by squamous cells decreases by a certain fraction the lungs' ability to cleanse themselves. As this occurs, the amount of damage done by each cigarette increases to a greater and greater degree (292).

### Paraphrase

Healthy lungs contain tiny sacs that are lined with cilia, hair-like fingers that move poisons out of the lungs. In coal miners or smokers, these cilia are destroyed and are replaced by cells that can't do the cleansing so the toxics touch more tissue longer. With the cleansing cells gone, the damage continues to increase each time smoke is inhaled (Harrison 292).

This paraphrase condenses complicated scientific information while stressing Harrison's key point. Again, because the ideas are Harrison's, his name and the page source must be included in the citation. *To fail to cite his name and a page number would be plagiarism.*

## Combining Paraphrase and Quotation

Most often, the material you use to support your points will be a blend of paraphrase and direct quotation. You can capture the essence of an author's idea by paraphrasing it, but there will be well-crafted phrases and key ideas that need to be quoted to convey the flavor of the original work. When you combine paraphrase and direct quotation, you still need to be careful to give credit for both.

### Original from "Does the Internet Make You Dumber?" (p. 223)

When we're constantly distracted and interrupted, as we tend to be online, our brains are unable to forge the strong and expansive neural connections that give depth and distinctiveness to our thinking. We become mere signal-processing units, quickly shepherding disjointed bits of information into and then out of short-term memory.

### Paraphrase with Quotation

In "Does the Internet Make you Dumber?" Nicholas Carr maintains that because we are easily distracted online, our minds can't form the deeper links that help us retain information. Instead, we "become mere signal-processing units," as ideas flit in and out of our brains (224).

If you are paraphrasing an expert, you will gain credibility by introducing the title and author of the work prior to your paraphrase as illustrated here. Because the author's image of Internet users as "mere signal-processing units" is particularly strong, these words are purposefully incorporated into the paraphrase. The quotation marks need to be retained and the entire reference cited. Because Carr's name appears in the lead-in to the quotation, only the page number is needed in the parenthetical citation. (See pp. 502–503.)

 ## PRACTICE COMBINING PARAPHRASE AND QUOTATION

Practice incorporating choice quotations into your paraphrased versions of the following passages. In your lead-in, you may want to include the author's name and the source of the material. Compare your paraphrases with those written by your classmates. The page numbers given are from the essays as they appear in this textbook.

1. From "King Curtis's Echo": "Now, long after the anger over the driveway affront has dissipated, it's something I strive to remember when some idiot swerves into my lane without signaling or an eager shopper jostles me in the grocery store. The obscene waste of King Curtis's life and my memory of his jubilant horn give me pause and, on a good day, a touch of grace. I have to thank the Russian deli customer for that" (Thayer 169).

2. From "Why Stop Smoking? Let's Get Clinical": "By the time one has been a pack-a-day smoker for ten years or so, extensive damage has already been done. By twenty years, much of the damage is irreversible and progresses more rapidly. After ten years of smoking, each cigarette may do as much damage to the body as three or more packs did when a smoker first started" (Harrison 291).

As you work on refining your incorporation of paraphrased and quoted material, you also will be revising your essay. Rewriting is such a critical activity in preparing an essay that we have devoted the entire next chapter to various aspects of revision.

**Final Tips for Organizing and Drafting an Essay**

- Review your prewriting to discover your **aim** or purpose in writing.
- Formulate a tentative thesis—your **claim**—by using the "So What?" strategy.
- Make sure that your **thesis** is an assertion and not a question, phrase, or announcement.
- Consider placing your **thesis at the end of your introduction** to guide both writer and reader.
- Use the **forecasted elements** of your thesis to organize and outline your essay.
- Examine paragraphs for **sufficient focus** (topic sentences) and **support** (examples, facts, and illustrations).
- If using sources, give credit for ideas and words to **avoid plagiarism**.
- If you are including direct quotations, use the **sandwich technique** so that you have an informative lead-in before your quote and adequate analysis after it.

# Chapter 8

# Revising an Essay

In this chapter you will learn how to

- revise and edit for coherence
- write logical transitions
- vary your introductions and conclusions

## Rewriting and Rewriting

It is essential that you give yourself ample time to reconsider your rough draft in its entirety and revise it before handing it in as your final paper. Usually, this revision involves sharpening the thesis, reorganizing ideas, developing sketchy points, adding new material for support, removing irrelevant material, improving transitions between ideas, strengthening the introduction and conclusion, and editing for word choice, mechanics, and spelling.

## Thinking Critically for an Audience

Every phase of the writing process involves thinking critically—reasoning, analyzing, and assessing—so that your points are clear and understandable to your audience. The act of revision calls on these same skills.

As you begin to organize your prewriting notes into a coherent essay, ask yourself: Can a reader follow my logic? Do the examples support my main point? What, if any, examples should I cut? Your decision to remove irrelevant details reflects your awareness that irrelevant points not only weaken your support but also confuse your readers.

The need for clarity and precision continues throughout drafting and revision. As you revise, continue to question whether the depth of your analysis and support for your assertions are sufficient. You need to reconsider your focus, the logic of your organization, and the strength of your conclusion. As you edit, scrutinize your word choice, sentence structure, grammar, and mechanics so that surface flaws do not frustrate your reader.

Thinking critically requires you to recognize that your audience does not necessarily share your views. Thus the writing process forces you to challenge your own assertions and consider your readers' perspectives. Although it may appear that these stages of writing a paper involve a step-by-step process, all of these writing activities occur concurrently.

You may revise while you are drafting your paper, and possibly edit from the early drafts until the moment you hand the paper to your instructor. As noted in the previous chapter, Rachel started revising her draft as soon as she had a printout from her computer. Thinking critically about her aim in writing this essay—to persuade readers of the media's role in fostering eating disorders—Rachel made substantial changes as she revised her rough draft.

## Revising a Rough Draft

Working from her own evaluation of her rough draft (see pp. 306–308), Rachel rewrote her draft and, as required by the assignment, showed it to her instructor for comments. Rachel's paper had started out very rough, as most first drafts do, but she continued to develop her ideas and rearrange them. She felt that her second draft was stronger than the first but still could be improved. Her instructor helped her by identifying weak areas and suggesting improvements.

### EXAMPLE: DRAFT WITH INSTRUCTOR'S COMMENTS

Eating Disorders and the Media    *more striking or suggestive title*

*except for?*

Bare, (with the exception of) a bikini, the deep-tanned model poses at a

*tighten—*
*avoid*
*repeating*
*she is"*

beach. <u>She is</u> surrounded by five adoring guys. <u>She is</u> sipping a frothy soda and inviting all of us to do the same . . . if we want to get the guys . . . if we want to be *How thin? How tall?* the envy of our friends. <u>She is</u> thin but tall. Viewers don't notice the bony ribs,

(how hungry she is,) and all the "diet pills" she popped to stay that thin. A picture     *not//*
*very graphic*
doesn't reveal the vomit on her breath or the spearmint gum used to mask it. In fact,
*stronger verb?*
our magazines and T.V. commercials present us with such ads until such girls don't
seem skinny anymore—they seem right.  ✓ *clear point*

It doesn't seem to matter that, for some years now, the media has been reporting
*diction (old-fashioned?)*          *briefly distinguish*
the epidemic among college "<u>coeds</u>" of eating disorders, <u>anorexia</u> and <u>bulimia</u>. It

doesn't seem to matter that the Women's Movement has tried to free women from being so caught up on the way they look. Despite the varied opportunities now available to women, many women say they would rather lose pounds than achieve academic or career goals. In the early years of aerobics, actress Jane Fonda has sold many on the value of her *Work Out* and has helped spawn "aerobic nervosa" (Erens 186). *What is?*

Many women who admire Jane Fonda's shape may not know that Fonda was once a bulimic. And no one watching the televised spectacle of Prince Charles and Princess Diana's wedding could have predicted that years later, biographers would be discussing "Di's bulimia." ⟩ *transition? More current examples?*

*specify what is wrong with this* Who wouldn't want to hear friends whisper, "What a body! She really knows how to stay in shape!" or "Don't you hate someone who looks that good?" Either way, the sense of admiration and affirmation is clear. A thin girl has something that others don't—and this gives her power and control. She can make herself in the image of the cover girls. In "Bodily Harm," the author quotes Ruth Striegel-Moore: "The pursuit of thinness is a way for women to compete with each other, a way that avoids being threatening to men" (186) *necessary? You need Erens's name here or in you ( ) at end of this line*

Unfortunately, this competition keeps women from seeking or obtaining the help they might otherwise get from close friends. Many bulimics keep their secret as guarded as their mothers might have kept their sex life. My friend Kirstie did this. She waited for years before she told her friends (and later, her family) that she was bulimic. At first, only her "barf buddy" (Erens 186)—a cousin who had initially introduced her to this "great diet plan"—knew. Gradually, their friendship revolved exclusively around this dark secret and was eroded by their unacknowledged rivalry. *Ref?*

*awk split of subj/verb*

*develop* Few of us ever suspected Kirstie was in trouble: she seemed to have it all. But years later, she revealed to me that her greatest pride at that time was when she discovered that she was now vomiting automatically after eating, without needing to use a finger or spoon. *illustrat*

Even when Kirstie received out-patient counseling and her family thought she was "cured," she wasn't. For her it was either fasting or bingeing—there was no in-between. As her friend, I often felt trapped between either respecting her confidence or letting some adult know, so she might get the help she needed. While encouraging her to find other interests and to be open with her therapist, I felt quite helpless. I didn't want to betray her confidence and tell her parents, but I worried that my silence was betraying our friendship. ⟩ *transition?* *How could you tell?*

According to another friend, many young women continue to have obsessions with food for years afterwards. My friend Erica was shocked by the number of women ~~who where~~ over thirty in her hospital treatment program for anorexics. She admitted

*Ref?* that (this) is what made her decide she needed help while she was still in college. Unlike Kirstie, Erica decided she needed an in-hospital treatment program that cut her off from her old habits and helped her deal with her emotions and learn better nutritional habits. Erica managed to enter the program as soon as her finals were over

*good*
*transition* and therefore she didn't jeopardize her schooling.

But some don't have that choice. My friend Lynn would have died had she not entered the hospital when she did. She had to drop out of Berkeley immediately and get prolonged therapy before she could be released to her parents and begin her recovery. Her family became involved in her therapy, too. As Erens notes, "Family therapy considers the family itself, not the daughter with the eating disorder, to be the "patient." Often, the daughter has taken on the role of diverting attention from unacknowledged conflicts within the family" (189). In therapy, Lynn and her family

*shorten this*
*discussion?* gradually learned that her parents "unacknowledged conflicts" over her mother's return to work and over Lynn's choice of art instead of computer science as a major contributed to Lynn's stress. Therapy involved acknowledging these internalized conflicts as well as examining the pressure to be thin.

*effective*
*link* In addition to absorbing family conflicts, each of these friends felt that they
*between* were programmed by advertisers to accept and seek a lean look as the ideal. Fashion
*personal* magazines often use underweight preteen models who are made up and dressed
*experience* to seem older than they are. This makes women with real hips and breasts feel
*reading* overweight. In fact, the fashion world does not seem to view large bodies, strength, or maturity as attractive features for women.

It is ironic that this should happen at a time when women have more freedom to control their lives and their bodies. Unfortunately, women still spend much of their earnings on the cosmetic and diet industries. Our generation has witnessed the

*develop or*
*combine* weight of fashion models drop way down and the number of eating disorders go
*these* way up.
*short*
*paragraphs* It is time to let ourselves become shocked again. And then we need to move beyond shock and take action. Those who make the images will only change when those of us who support them stop buying products and tuning in on shows that continue to impose "bodily harm" on us. *Return to your opening image, if you can, and sharpen your thesis. Don't forget "Works Cited."*

## Revising Can Make the Difference

Every paper can benefit from careful revision and editing, but many students do not have their instructors' comments on their drafts to use as they revise. Occasionally, students can find trained tutors at the college writing center, for example, or peers who will offer feedback and suggestions. These students' comments may not be as thorough as those Rachel received, but they can help the writer see the essay from another perspective.

---

 ## A Checklist for Revising and Editing Papers

Whether you are revising your own essay or commenting on a classmate's, the following checklist should help:

- **Aim:** What is the purpose or aim of the essay? Are there any sections that seem to stray from this aim?
- **Claim:** What is the thesis? How can you make it clearer or more convincing?
- **Support:** Which points could be better illustrated and supported?
- **Organization:** Does the paper reflect the order of ideas forecast in the thesis?
- **Paragraphs:** Could any paragraph be better focused or developed? How?
- **Sentences:** Is there any sentence that is not clear or grammatical? Are the sentences varied?
- **Wording:** Circle any unnecessary or confusing words.
- **Transitions:** Locate any gaps in logic or any missing information.
- **Introduction:** How could the opening be more captivating? Does it set the right tone? Does the introduction move smoothly into the thesis?
- **Conclusion:** Is there a sense of closure or resolution? Does the conclusion return to the thesis?
- **Style:** Is the diction consistent with the purpose of the essay? Are there any words that need to be replaced?
- **Mechanics:** Correct punctuation? Grammar? Spelling?
- **Title:** Is the title fresh and enticing? Can you improve it with wordplay or by deleting unnecessary words?

Some instructors may spend time helping students work in small groups as "peer editors" who critique each other's papers. A good peer editor need not excel at grammar nor be an excellent writer. An effective editor needs to be a careful *reader*, one who is sensitive to the writer's main point and supporting details.

If you are editing a classmate's essay, you do not have to be able to correct the errors. A peer editor needs only to point out areas that seem flawed or confusing; it is then the writer's responsibility to use a handbook (like the one in this book) and correct the errors.

After studying the instructor's comments and corrections, Rachel continued modifying her draft. She rewrote certain phrases and paragraphs a number of times, shifted words and sentences, and found ways to "tighten" her prose by eliminating unnecessary words. Most of all, she tried to replace sluggish words with more precise and specific details. Notice below how her title gained more punch and how the opening is tighter and less repetitive. She also took the time to develop certain thoughts and paragraphs and to clarify her points. The following version is her final essay.

STUDENT EXAMPLE: FINAL ESSAY

Rachel Krell

Professor Ansite

English 1A

7 October 2010

Dieting Daze: No In-Between

Bare, except for a bikini, the deep-tanned model poses at a beach surrounded by five adoring and adorable guys. She is sipping a frothy diet drink and inviting us to do the same, if we want to get the guys and be the envy of our friends. She stands 5' 10" and wears a size 3. Viewers don't notice the bony ribs, the hunger pangs, and the "diet pills" she popped to stay that thin. A picture doesn't reveal the vomit on her breath or the spearmint gum used to mask it. In fact, our magazines and TV commercials bombard us with such ads until these girls don't seem skinny anymore—they seem right.

It doesn't seem to matter that, for years now, the media has been reporting the epidemic among college women of eating disorders, anorexia (self-starvation) and bulimia (binge and purge). It doesn't seem to matter that the women's movement has tried to free women from bondage to their bodies. Despite the varied opportunities now available to women, many women say they would rather lose pounds than achieve academic or career goals. In the early years of aerobics, actress Jane Fonda sold many on the value of her *Work Out* and helped spawn "aerobic nervosa"—the excessive use of exercise to maintain an ideal weight (Erens 187). Many women who admired Jane Fonda's shape may not know that Fonda was once bulimic. And no one watching the televised spectacle of Prince Charles and Princess Diana's wedding could have predicted that years later, biographers would be discussing "Di's bulimia." Current super models such as Kate Moss and popular young celebrities like actresses Mary Kate Olsen and Kate Bosworth perpetuate the concept that to be successful, one must be thin.

Such celebrities, and those females in the ads, are held up as models for all of us to mirror. A thin girl has something that others don't—and this gives her power and control. She can make her body resemble a cover girl's. In "Bodily Harm," Pamela Erens quotes Ruth Striegel-Moore, Ph.D., director of Yale University's Eating Disorders Clinic:

"The pursuit of thinness is a way for women to compete with each other, a way that avoids being threatening to men" (186). But this competition threatens and endangers the women's well-being because it keeps women from seeking the help they might otherwise get from close friends.

In fact, many bulimics—models and celebrities included—keep their secret as guarded as their mothers might have kept their sex life. My friend Kirstie waited for years before she told friends (and later, her family) that she was bulimic. At first the only one who knew about her bulimia was her cousin who had initially introduced her to "this great diet plan." This cousin became Kirstie's "barf buddy" (Erens 186). Gradually, their friendship revolved exclusively around this dark secret and was eroded by their unacknowledged rivalry.

Few of us ever suspected Kirstie was in trouble because she seemed to have it all. During her senior year in high school, she was dating a college guy, was enrolled in college prep classes, jogged religiously every morning and every evening, and loved to ski with her family and beat her brothers down the slope. She seemed to crave the compliments she received from her brothers and their friends because of her good looks—and she received plenty! But years later, she revealed to me that her greatest pride at that time was when she discovered she could vomit automatically after eating, without needing to use a finger or spoon.

Even when Kirstie received out-patient counseling and her family thought she was "cured," she would still binge and purge at will. Every conversation with Kirstie inevitably returned to the subject of food—fasting or bingeing—there was no in-between. As her close friend, I often felt helpless, trapped between either respecting her confidence and keeping her dark secret or letting an adult know and perhaps getting her more help. I didn't want to betray her confidence and tell her parents, but I worried that my silence was betraying our friendship. Even though we each went to different colleges and gradually lost touch, I find myself wondering if Kirstie ever got the help she needed.

According to another friend, even mature women continue to have obsessions with food. My friend Erica was shocked by the number of women over thirty in her hospital treatment program for anorexics. She admitted that seeing these older women is what convinced her she needed help while she was still in college. Unlike Kirstie, Erica

Krell 3

decided she needed an in-hospital treatment program that cut her off from her old habits and helped her deal with her emotions and learn better nutritional habits. Erica managed to enter the program as soon as her finals were over, and therefore she didn't jeopardize her schooling.

But some don't have that choice. My friend Lynn would have died had she not entered the hospital when she did. She had to drop out of Berkeley immediately and get prolonged therapy before she could be released to her parents and begin her recovery. Lynn's family became involved in her therapy, too. Erens emphasizes the importance of the family in any treatment plan: "Often, the daughter has taken on the role of diverting attention from unacknowledged conflicts within the family" (189). In therapy Lynn and her family gradually learned that her parents' "unacknowledged conflicts" over Lynn's choice of art as a major instead of computer science contributed to her stress. Therapy involved acknowledging these internalized conflicts as well as seeing a relationship between her eating disorder and that stress.

In addition to absorbing family conflicts, each of these friends felt that she was programmed by advertisers to accept a lean look as the ideal. Fashion magazines often use underweight, preteen models who are made up and dressed to seem older than they are. This makes women with normal hips and breasts feel overweight. In fact, the fashion world does not seem to view large bodies, strength, or maturity as attractive features for women.

It is ironic that this should happen at a time when women have more freedom to control their lives and their bodies. Unfortunately, women still spend much of their earnings on cosmetic and diet products. Our generation has witnessed the weight of fashion models decline and the number of eating disorders increase while women often feel powerless. Stripped of control, many women feel compelled to diet constantly; images of emaciated models that were once so shocking have now become commonplace.

It is time to let ourselves become shocked again—shocked by an epidemic that is destroying women's lives. And then we need to move beyond shock—and beyond the stories of Kirstie, Erica, and Lynn—and take action against the media's manipulation of the female form. Insisting that our television sponsors, magazines, and video artists stop perpetrating such deadly images of women is something we can all do. A letter from one viewer carries clout because stations often assume that each letter represents

Krell 4

many who didn't take the time to write. Ten letters from ten viewers wield even more power. It is time to protest the images of bikini-clad models parading before us and demand images that reflect the emotional and intellectual scope and diversity among women in our society. With some of our best and brightest dying among us, there is no in-between position anymore. Those who make the images will only change when those of us who support them stop buying products and stop tuning in on programs that continue to impose "bodily harm" on us.

Krell 5

Work Cited

Erens, Pamela. "Bodily Harm." *Between Worlds: A Reader, Rhetoric, and Handbook.* Ed. Susan Bachmann and Melinda Barth. 7th ed. New York: Pearson Longman, 2012. 186–190. Print.

# Rewriting for Coherence

As you may have noticed, Rachel devoted considerable attention to the way she linked information and ideas within and between her paragraphs. The goal, of course, is to ensure that all parts of the paper cohere (that is, that they hold together).

To sustain your readers' interest and ensure their comprehension of your work, you will want to examine the drafts of your essays to see if your ideas hold together. Each idea should follow logically from the one before, and all of your points must support your focus. That logical connection must be clear to the reader—not just to you, the writer of the essay, who may gloss over a link that is not obvious. All readers value clear connections between phrases, sentences, and paragraphs.

## A Paragraph That Lacks Coherence

If writing is carefully organized, the reader will not stumble over irrelevant chunks of material or hesitate at unbridged gaps. Let's examine an incoherent paragraph:

Students who commute to campus suffer indignities that dorm students can't imagine. Parking is expensive and lots are jammed. It is embarrassing to walk into class late. Often it takes over a half hour to find a spot. Commuters feel cut off from students who can return to the dorm to eat or rest. Commuters seldom have a telephone number to get missed lecture notes. Study groups readily form in dorms. Dorm students have a sense of independence and freedom. Commuters need to conform to old family rules and schedules, to say nothing of the need to baby-sit or cook for younger siblings and drive grandparents to the bank.

Although this paragraph has a clear focus and the ideas are all relevant, its coherence needs to be improved. You may sense that the information is out of order, the logic of the writer is not always obvious to the reader, sentences do not flow together, words are repeated, and emphasis is lost.

In the pages that follow, you will learn how to correct paragraphs like this and to avoid these problems in your own writing. You will also have the opportunity to correct this paragraph.

## Using Transitions

Even when material is carefully organized, well-chosen transition words and devices help you connect sentences and paragraphs and cohere your points. You are familiar with most of these words and expressions. But if you have been trying for more than five minutes to find a specific word to connect two ideas or sentences in your essay, the following list of transition terms will enable you to gain unity in your essay.

## Transition Terms

- *Time relationship:* first, second, before, then, next, meantime, meanwhile, finally, at last, eventually, later, afterward, frequently, often, occasionally, during, now, subsequently, concurrently
- *Spatial relationship:* above, below, inside, outside, across, along, in front of, behind, beyond, there, here, in the distance, alongside, near, next to, close to, adjacent, within
- *Contrast:* in contrast, on the contrary, on the other hand, still, however, yet, but, nevertheless, despite, even so, even though, whereas
- *Comparison:* similarly, in the same way
- *Examples or illustrations:* for example, for instance, to illustrate, to show, in particular, specifically, that is, in addition, moreover
- *Causes or effects:* as a result, accordingly, therefore, then, because, so, thus, consequently, hence, since
- *Conclusions or summaries:* in conclusion, finally, in summary, evidently, clearly, of course, to sum up, therefore

# Noticing Transitions

If you are writing a narrative, some part of your essay—if not the entire work—probably will be arranged chronologically. See if you can spot the *time signals* in the following excerpt from Judith Ortiz Cofer's "The Myth of the Latin Woman" and underline them.

> It is surprising to my professional friends that even today some people, including those who should know better, still put others "in their place." It happened to me most recently during a stay at a classy metropolitan hotel favored by young professional couples for weddings. Late one evening after the theater, as I walked toward my room with a colleague (a woman with whom I was coordinating an arts program), a middle-aged man in a tuxedo, with a young girl in satin and lace on his arm, stepped directly into our path. With his champagne glass extended toward me, he exclaimed "Evita!" (120).

Can you see how "even today," "still," "most recently," "late one evening," and "as I walked," are transitions used to help the reader connect the actions in the narrative?

With three or four of your classmates, read the next paragraph of this essay (121) and underline the transition words that have to do with the essay's chronological connections.

Chronological concepts may also be important for smoother transitions and improved coherence in non-narrative essays. Look at this paragraph from "Discrimination at Large" (p. 175) to see if you can identify the time concepts around which this paragraph is structured.

> Since the time I first ventured out to play with the neighborhood kids, I was told over and over that I was lazy and disgusting. Strangers, adults, classmates offered gratuitous comments with such frequency and urgency that I started to believe them. Much later I needed to prove it wasn't so. I began a regimen of swimming, cycling, and jogging that put all but the most compulsive to shame. I ate only cottage cheese, brown rice, fake butter, and steamed everything. I really believed I could infiltrate the ranks of the nonfat and thereby establish my worth.

You may rightly perceive that "since the time I first," "I began," and "much later" are the three terms that denote the passage of time within this paragraph. But you may also note that the writer uses the past tense, as if what Jennifer Coleman "really believed" at one time is different from what she believes now. The chronological ordering of the essay emphasizes this fact. Read the rest of the essay to observe how Coleman uses these time-relationship transitions—"along the way," "for a while," "still," "until," "until then," "now," and "finally"—to emphasize the history that led to her change in self-perception.

Essays that include description often require terms that connect sentences or paragraphs in a *spatial relationship*. Notice the spatial concepts that connect the descriptions in this paragraph from "The Only Child" (the complete essay starts on p. 33).

> The room is a slum, and it stinks. It is wall-to-wall beer cans, hundreds of them, under a film of ash. He lights cigarettes and leaves them burning on the windowsill or the edge of the dresser or the lip of the sink, while he thinks of something else—Gupta sculpture, maybe, or the Sephiroth Tree of the Kabbalah. The sink is filthy, and so is the toilet. Holes have been burnt in the sheet on the bed, where he sits. He likes to crush the beer cans after he has emptied them, then toss them aside.

Do you see this paragraph, as we do, as a movement from the periphery to the interior? We sense that the author moves from broad description—"wall-to-wall beer cans" around the room—to smaller, interior descriptions—"holes [that] have been burnt in the sheet on the bed, where he sits." The outside-to-inside movement of this description parallels the author's description of elements outside of his brother (in his room) to his observation of what is closer and more central to him (his thoughts, his talk, his gestures). The arrangement also complements the author's argument that his brother's life and mind were destroyed by drugs—the external environment destroying the interior.

The use of the transition words will seem contrived if you rely on them too often in any one essay, or if you use the same ones in every essay you write. You also have other, more subtle ways to gain connections between sentences and paragraphs in your essays.

## Key Word Repetition

In some cases you will want to repeat a word that emphasizes an important point that you are making. Such repetition reinforces the focus of your paragraph and essay.

In another paragraph from "The Only Child" (p. 33), the author emphasizes his disdain for his brother's living conditions by repeating his brother's explanation. Can you hear the irony or sarcasm in the author's repetition?

> He tells me that he is making a statement, that this room is a statement, that the landlord will understand the meaning of his statement. In a week or so, according to the pattern, they will evict him, and someone will find him another room, which he will turn into another statement, with the help of the welfare checks he receives on account of his disability, which is the static in his head.

Notice that the repetition of "statement" is very deliberate and strategic, rather than boring for the reader, because it emphasizes the nonreasoning to which the brother's mind has been reduced.

## Synonyms or Key Word Substitutions

You can connect the ideas or concepts within a paragraph and throughout your essay by skillfully using synonyms or key word substitutions—words that have the same or similar meanings—to emphasize your focus. Notice how Jennifer Coleman in "Discrimination at Large" (p. 175) piles word substitutions into her sentences to simulate for her reader the effect of being assaulted, as fat people are, by denigrating words:

> It was confusing for awhile. How was it I was still lazy, weak, despised, a slug, and a cow if I exercised every waking minute? This confusion persisted until I finally realized: it didn't matter what I did. I was and always would be the object of sport, derision, antipathy and hostility so long as I stayed in my body. I immediately signed up for a body transplant. I am still waiting for a donor.

How many substitutions for "lazy" did you find? How many implied substitutions for "contempt"? Coleman cites many specific terms for how she has been perceived and treated to make clear to the reader that these attacks come under many names, but the intention to denigrate is always the same.

## Pronouns

Pronouns, words substituting for nouns that clearly precede or follow them, can effectively connect parts of a paragraph. By prompting the reader to mentally supply the missing noun or see the relationship the pronouns imply, the writer also has a way to engage the reader. To emphasize the contrast between people who are fat and those who are not, Coleman uses pronoun substitutions to unite her paragraphs:

> Things are less confusing now that I know that the nonfat are superior to me regardless of their personal habits, health, personalities, cholesterol levels, or the time they log on the couch. And, as obviously superior to me as they are, it is their destiny to remark on my inferiority regardless of who I'm with, whether they know me, whether it hurts my feelings. I finally understand that the thin have a divine mandate to steal self-esteem from fat people, who have no right to it in the first place.
>
> Fat people aren't really jolly. Sometimes we act that way so you will leave us alone. We pay a price for this. But at least we get to hang on to what self-respect we smuggled out of grade school and adolescence.

In the first paragraph, *I* and *me* contrast with *they* and *their* to emphasize the separation between the author and the "nonfat" and "superior" other people. In the second paragraph the author unites herself with "fat people," repeatedly saying "we" to emphasize their unity. Coleman's entire essay coheres because she skillfully employs numerous unifying devices within and between her paragraphs. Read the essay in its entirety (pp. 175–178) to see how key word repetition, synonyms, and transitions between sentences and paragraphs create coherence within an essay.

## Transitions between Paragraphs

Key word repetition is also an important way to achieve the important goal of *connection between paragraphs*. While your reader may be able to follow your movement and sustain your ideas within a paragraph, coherence within your essay as a whole requires transition sentences and, in longer essays, entire paragraphs of transitions.

One device that works well is to offer a specific example to illustrate a general point that concludes the previous paragraph and use it toward the beginning of the new paragraph. Notice the following excerpts from Shannon Paaske's research paper, which begins on page 486. What moves the reader between paragraphs?

> According to Jan Gavlin, director of assistive technology at the National Rehabilitation Hospital in Washington, "If you can move one muscle in your body, wiggle a pinkie or twitch an eyebrow, we can design a switch to allow you to operate in your environment" (qtd. in Blackman 71).
>
> An example of one such device is the Eyegaze Response Interface Computer Aid (ERICA), developed by biomedical engineer Thomas Hutchinson at the University of Virginia. . . .

By giving a specific example of "assistive technology" introduced in theory in the previous paragraph, the author is able to connect the two paragraphs.

In another section of her research paper, Shannon uses a question to help her reader move from one paragraph to another:

> Rebecca Acuirre, 16, who has cerebral palsy, says that she recently asked a stranger what time it was and he kept walking as though he didn't hear her. "Some people are prejudiced and ignore us. That makes me angry," she says.
>
> How can these prejudices be abolished? "We need more exposure," says DeVries.

The repetition of the word "prejudice" helps these paragraphs cohere. The question engages the reader because most of us feel obliged to think about answers to questions. This rhetorical question does not merely repeat the word. Instead, it moves the reader beyond the previous aspect of prejudice to the solution Paaske will discuss in the next section.

Although all paragraphs in your essay should hold together, the device of repeating key words should not be overused or strained. You may irritate your readers if they perceive your technique as a formula. For example, let's imagine you have written a paragraph that ended with the sentence "These are rationalizations, not reasons." Avoid merely repeating the exact phrasing, like "Although these are rationalizations, not reasons," at the start of your next paragraph. Instead, you might want to begin with something like this: "Such rationalizations are understandable if one considers the. . . ." With conscious practice of the technique, you'll improve your skills.

## Avoiding Gaps

Transition terms and devices help you achieve coherence in your work, but they can't fill in for gaps in logic—sentences or paragraphs that just don't go together, or that are out of order. You can't expect your readers to move from one point to another if you have failed to put your reasoning into words. For example, in the incoherent paragraph on pages 337–338, the writer places the following two sentences together:

> Parking is expensive and lots are jammed. It is embarrassing to walk into class late.

In the writer's mind, these two thoughts are logically connected. That link is not at all apparent to readers, and a transition term like *and* or *therefore* will not bridge that gap. The writer must write something to express the connection between the two sentences so there is no gap and no need for the readers to invent their own bridge. The writer needs to explain the relationship between "jammed" and "expensive" parking lots and the embarrassment of "walking into class late." You can work on this skill in the next exercise.

 ### PRACTICE RECOGNIZING COHERENCE

In small groups, return to the incoherent paragraph on page 337 and discuss its problems. As a group, rewrite the paragraph so that all information is included, but also so that the ideas are logically linked. As you fill in the gaps in logic, practice using the transition terms and devices that ensure coherence in this paragraph. Here is one solution to improve the coherence of the paragraph.

> Students who commute to campus suffer indignities that dorm students can't imagine. Even before commuting students get to classes they have a problem. Parking on campus is expensive and hard to find because

the lots are jammed. Often it takes over half an hour to find a spot. By then class has started, and it is embarrassing to walk into class late. Commuters also feel cut off from those students who can return to the dorm to eat or rest. And while study groups readily form in dorms, commuting students seldom have even a telephone number to get missed lecture notes. Dorm students have a sense of independence and freedom from their families, but commuters need to conform to old family rules and schedules. Often the indignities of living at home include doing those tasks the students did through high school, like baby-sitting or cooking for younger siblings, or driving grandparents to the bank.

# Writing Titles

A good title sets up an expectation for readers, allowing them to anticipate the subject and tone for the essay. A captivating title is brief, suggestive, and witty. Often wordplay, imagery, alliteration—the tools of the poet—are employed to draw readers in. Notice the intriguing titles and techniques of several works in this text:

"On Teenagers and Tattoos": features alliteration; articulates the specific topic

"iHuh": alludes to iPod and to users losing their hearing

"Pigskin, Patriarchy, and Pain": uses alliteration to forecast the focus points of the essay

"Race Is a Four-Letter Word": suggests the author's anger and yet appeals with humor

"I Don't Give a Tweet What You're Doing": captures the author's feisty attitude while substituting "Tweet"—her target—for an unpublishable word

"If the Genes Fit": contains a pun on "jeans"

"Discrimination at Large": uses a pun on large people and the society as a whole ("at large")

"Greed in the Name of Green": alliterates "Greed" and "Green" and suggests the phrase "in the name of God," anticipating the author's view that "Green" has become sacred in our culture

"Does the Internet Make You Dumber?" / "Does the Internet Make You Smarter?": often an author will twist a title of a work that he is responding to

"What the Cellphone Industry Won't Tell You": creates suspense and reader interest

Notice how these titles are clever *phrases*, not wordy explanations or dry announcements. In fact, brief and appropriate humor is a plus and goes a long way to captivating readers. Moreover, you should not use another writer's exact title, even if you are analyzing that work in your essay. You may decide to play with the original title or allude to it as Robert Sakatani refers to "Breaking Tradition" in his title "Breaking the Ties that Bind" (440). Honing such a resonant title may require some thought, but if you have started the essay early enough, you will be ready for flashes of inspiration. Your title might come to you at any time: during a brainstorming session, while revising a draft, or during the incubation stage, when you are not physically working on the paper. A choice title, like an effective introduction, draws the reader to your work.

# Writing Introductions

## Introductions and Audience

Typically, a strong introduction "hooks" the reader and then expands on the hook while building to the thesis statement, which often concludes the introduction. The introduction to an essay—the aim—has two obligations: (1) to attract the reader to the subject of the essay and (2) to establish for the reader the particular purpose and focus of the writer—the claim. The focus of the writer—the claim he or she is making about a limited subject—is contained in the thesis statement. The thesis statement does not have to be at the end of the introduction, but that is often a natural place for it because both the writer and reader are then immediately aware of the key assertion that will be supported in the essay. The concept of the thesis is discussed in more detail on pages 296–302.

If you have not discovered in your prewriting activities a useful way to lead to your thesis, you may find the ideas below helpful. Some subjects will seem best introduced by one type of introduction rather than another, and it's a good idea to keep your audience in mind as you draft possible "hooks" to your topic.

## Types of Introductions

You may find that if you deliberately vary your introductions, perhaps trying each of the methods suggested here, you will not be intimidated by that blank sheet of paper or empty computer screen each time you start to write.

***Direct Quotation.*** An essay that begins with the words of another person, especially a well-known person, should help convince your reader that you are a prepared writer who has researched the views of others on the subject and found relevance in their words. For example, when we were preparing

Part I of this book, we discovered that Ellen Goodman had incorporated into her essay a particularly compelling comment by André Malraux, which we decided to use in our chapter introduction. André Malraux—a French novelist, political activist, and art critic—is not a noted authority on the sociology or psychology of family life. Nevertheless, his mildly philosophical statements about the family interested us, and we found his thoughts relevant for our introduction. Notice how we use Malraux's words throughout our introduction.

> In the essay that we used to demonstrate active reading (3), author Ellen Goodman quotes André Malraux that "without a family" the individual "alone in the world, trembles with the cold" (qtd. in Goodman 4). The family often nurtures its members and tolerates differences and failings that friends and lovers cannot accept. But as you may realize from your own experiences and observations, people also tremble with fear or anxiety even within the family unit. The writers in this chapter show the family as a source of both nurturing and anxiety.

*Description.* An introduction using description—whether it is a vivid picture of nature or of a person—can appeal to the imagination and the senses simultaneously. The power of the opening can be enhanced if the writer also postpones specific identification of the subject, place, or person until the reader is engaged. In the following paragraph from "The Only Child" (p. 33), notice that John Leonard does not reveal his subject. In fact, the reader does not know that he or she is reading about Leonard's brother until the last line of the essay.

> He is big. He always has been, over six feet, with that slump of the shoulders and tuck in the neck big men in this country often affect, as if to apologize for being above the democratic norm in size. (In high school and at college he played varsity basketball. In high school he was senior class president.) And he looks healthy enough, blue-eyed behind his beard, like a trapper or a mountain man, acquainted with silences. He also grins a lot.

*Question.* The psychology behind asking a reader a question probably lies in the fact that most of us feel obliged to at least *consider* answering a writer who has asked us something. If we don't have an immediate answer, we consider the subject and then continue with the reading—exactly what the writer wants us to do. But readers may find questions irritating if they seem silly or contrived, like "What is capital punishment?" Notice your own interest as you read the questions in the introduction to Robert Heilbroner's essay "Don't Let Stereotypes Warp Your Judgments" (p. 424).

Is a girl called Gloria apt to be better-looking than one called Bertha? Are criminals more likely to be dark than blond? Can you tell a good deal about someone's personality from hearing his voice briefly over the phone? Can a person's nationality be pretty accurately guessed from his photograph? Does the fact that someone wears glasses imply that he is intelligent?

***Anecdote or Illustration.*** Just as listeners look up attentively when a speaker begins a speech with a story, all readers are engaged by an anecdote. If the story opens dramatically, the involvement of the reader is assured. In the following example, from Brent Staples's essay "Black Men and Public Space" (p. 164), the author initially misleads the reader into thinking the writer has malicious intentions—exactly the misconception that is the subject matter of his essay.

> My first victim was a woman—white, well dressed, probably in her early twenties. I came upon her late one evening on a deserted street in Hyde Park, a relatively affluent neighborhood in an otherwise mean, impoverished section of Chicago. As I swung onto the avenue behind her, there seemed to be a discreet, uninflammatory distance between us. Not so. She cast back a worried glance. To her, the youngish black man—a broad six feet two inches with a beard and billowing hair, both hands shoved into the pockets of a bulky military jacket—seemed menacingly close. After a few more quick glimpses, she picked up her pace and was soon running in earnest. Within seconds she disappeared into a cross street.

***Definition.*** Often the definition of a term is a necessary element of an essay, and a definition may interest the reader in the subject (if the writer does not resort to that boring and cliché opener, "According to the dictionary . . ."). Sometimes the term may be unfamiliar, but often the term might be well known but the meanings may vary according to each reader. Recognizing these multiple meanings in "O.K., So I'm Fat" (p. 179), Neil Steinberg clarifies *his* definition of "fat" by using humor and by negation—explaining what "fat" does not mean.

> Some people are no doubt fat because of glandular disorders or the wrath of an angry God. I am not one of those people. I am fat because I eat a lot. Since fat people are held in such low regard, I should immediately point out that I am not that fat. Not fat in the Chinese Buddha, spilling-out-of-the-airplane-seat sense. The neighborhood kids don't skip behind me in the street, banging tin cans together and singing derisive songs. Not yet, anyway.

***Deliberate Contradiction.*** Sometimes a writer may start a paper with a view or statement that will be contradicted or contrasted with his thesis. In his essay "Does the Internet Make You Smarter?" (p. 218), Clay Shirky opens with a view that he will counter:

> Digital media have made creating and disseminating text, sound, and images cheap, easy and global. The bulk of publicly available media is now created by people who understand little of the professional standards and practices for media. Instead, these amateurs produce endless streams of mediocrity, eroding cultural norms about quality and acceptability, and leading to increasingly alarmed predictions of incipient chaos and intellectual collapse.
>
> But of course, that's what always happens. Every increase in freedom to create or consume media, from paperback books to YouTube, alarms people accustomed to the restrictions of the old system, convincing them that the new media will make young people stupid.

***Statistic or Startling Fact or Idea.*** An essay that starts with a dramatic statistic or idea engages the reader at once. Notice how the following introduction from William F. Harrison's "Why Stop Smoking? Let's Get Clinical" (p. 291) uses statistics to engage (or frighten) the reader.

> Most of us in medicine now accept that tobacco is associated with major health consequences and constitutes the No. 1 health problem in this country.
>
> What smokers have not yet come to terms with is that if they continue smoking, the probability of developing one or more of the major complications of smoking is 100 percent. It absolutely will happen. They will develop chronic bronchitis, laryngitis, pharyngitis, sinusitis, and some degree of emphysema.

***Mixture of Methods.*** Many well-crafted introductions combine the approaches described above. For example, in the introductory paragraph of "The Color of Love" (p. 15), Danzy Senna employs narration, description, comparison-contrast, illustration, allusion, definition, a startling idea, and deliberate contradiction to dramatize the differences between the writer and her grandmother.

> We had this much in common: We were both women, and we were both writers. But we were as different as two people can be and still exist in the same family. She was ancient—as white and dusty as chalk—and spent her days seated in a velvet armchair, passing judgments on the

world below. She still believed in noble bloodlines; my blood had been mixed at conception. I believed there was no such thing as nobility or class or lineage, only systems designed to keep some people up in the big house and others outside, in the cold.

# Writing Conclusions

The conclusion of an essay should give the reader a feeling of completion or satisfaction. Ideally, the conclusion will fit like the lid on a box. You might return to your introduction and thesis, select key images or phrases that you used, and reflect them in your conclusion. This return to the start of the paper assures your reader that all aspects of your assertion have been met in the essay. Furthermore, the purpose of your paper—to express, inform, analyze, or persuade—should be consistent with the tone and stance of your conclusion. If your aim has been to persuade your reader, your conclusion needs to be more forceful than if you only had intended to inform your reader. An effective conclusion echoes the tone of the introduction without merely repeating the exact words of the thesis (a type of conclusion that is contrived and dull). Although your ending may be weakened by "tacking on" a new topic or concept without sufficient explanation and development, you may want to suggest that there is some broader issue to think about, or some additional goal that might be achieved if the situation you have discussed were satisfied.

For his conclusion to the essay "Don't Let Stereotypes Warp Your Judgments" (p. 427), Robert Heilbroner returns to the images of the pictures in our mind, the ideas stirred by the questions he had asked earlier in his introduction:

> Most of the time, when we type-cast the world, we are not in fact generalizing about people at all. We are only revealing the embarrassing facts about the pictures that hang in the gallery of stereotypes in our own heads.

Another effective conclusion appears in Marcus Mabry's "Living in Two Worlds" (p. 99). Mabry refers to his opening line describing the sign that proclaims "We built a proud new feeling." Throughout his essay, he contrasts the "two universes" of his home and school environments. Now in his conclusion, he creates the phrase that will also be the title of his essay:

> Somewhere in the midst of all that misery, my family has built, within me, "a proud feeling." As I travel between the two worlds, it becomes harder to remember just how proud I should be—not just because of where I have come from and where I am going, but because of where they are. The fact that they survive in the world in which they live is

something to be very proud of, indeed. It inspires within me a sense of tenacity and accomplishment that I hope every college graduate will someday possess.

Mabry's conclusion also reflects his broader thoughts about pride, not only about his pride in where he is headed but also his pride in his family's ability to survive. He brings his reader a sense of hope and inspiration and gives his essay closure.

The student papers in this book also show effective techniques in their conclusions. Rachel, who wrote the paper on eating disorders (pp. 334–337), was advised by her instructor to strengthen the conclusion of her rough draft (pp. 329–331) by returning to the images and key words of her introduction. Rachel did this in her final paper. She was also able to echo the title of a source that she used in her essay. The following part of her conclusion mirrors her introduction:

It is time to protest the images of bikini-clad models parading before us and demand images that reflect the emotional and intellectual scope and diversity among women in our society. With some of our best and brightest dying among us, there is no in-between position anymore. Those who make the images will only change when those of us who support them stop buying products and stop tuning in on programs that continue to impose "bodily harm" on us.

Shannon Paaske also returned to her introduction to conclude her research paper on the disabled, "From Access to Acceptance: Enabling America's Largest Minority." Her thesis and conclusion are printed here, but you can read her entire essay on pages 485–501. Notice that the title of Shannon's essay also is echoed in her conclusion.

### Thesis

Although technological advances, equality-promoting legislation, and increasing media exposure have worked as a collective force to improve the lives of disabled people, ignorance and prejudice continue to plague them.

### Conclusion

The legislation and technology that were developed at the end of the twentieth century will continue to make new worlds accessible to the disabled. Ideally, these developments will permit the disabled to be viewed in terms of their capabilities rather than their disabilities. In that climate, the disabled can gain acceptance in the worlds to which they have access. With the steps being taken by government, science, and the media, individuals alone are needed to make the dream of acceptance a reality for the disabled.

**Final Tips for Revising**

Give yourself ample time to revise.

- Return to the checklist on p. 332 and reread your draft with each question in mind. Enlist the help of a peer, if you can.

- Reread your essay to see if your essay has or needs appropriate transitions.

- Reconsider your title to see if you can lighten and tighten it with humor, wordplay, and brevity.

- Revise the opening of your introduction by employing one of these hooks: a relevant quotation, vivid description, startling fact or idea, deliberate contradiction, compelling question, anecdote, definition, or a mixture of these methods.

- Develop your introduction so it flows smoothly from your opening hook to your thesis.

- Revise your conclusion to reflect a key word, image, or answer to a question posed in your introduction.

- Edit your conclusion to echo but not repeat the exact wording of your thesis.

- Consider your reader. Have you brought a sense of significant closure to your paper? Proofread carefully for grammar, punctuation, and spelling errors. Don't rely only on spellcheck.

You have been considering your reader and the aim of your paper as you have rewritten your rough drafts, verified the logic of your organization, strengthened the introduction and conclusion, and edited for surface errors. These essential revision strategies can help you convince your readers that your essays are worth their time and consideration—and may inspire them, too.

# Chapter 9

# Writing to Persuade

In this chapter you will learn how to

- persuade your audience to agree with you
- organize and develop your argument
- discover strategies for persuasion
- anticipate counter-arguments
- avoid logical fallacies

## Prevalence of Persuasion

Nearly all essays aim to persuade readers of the writer's view. Whether the writing is humorous, serious, personal, informative, or expressive, all essays have a point to make and a reader to convince. Essays that deal with issues and controversies are deliberately designed to sway readers to one view or another. In this textbook, many authors aim to persuade readers—for example, whether the Internet makes us smarter or dumber, or whether all cellphone use should be illegal while driving. Writers focusing on these topics intend to demonstrate that their views are sound, and they may even want to promote change.

But even writing that does not appear issue-driven—for example, a first-person account—often aims to convince readers. In this text one author demonstrates that even a migrant farm worker can become a neurosurgeon; another illustrates how group pressure can cause us to respond differently than we would if we were alone. These accounts may not have an explicit thesis, but they often have an implicit aim—to prompt the reader to reconsider choices or expectations, to help people realize their potential, or to be wary of social pressure.

In fact, any type of essay may have an argument embedded within. When you write a narrative, for example, your aim may be to promote a change of thinking or behavior in your reader. You may be assigned to write an evaluative response to an essay, but you will inevitably need to persuade readers that the author's conclusions do or do not reflect your own observations.

When analyzing a person's life story, you may also be persuading readers that the individual made wise or flawed decisions. In a research-based essay, you may find yourself convincing your reader, for example, that the government should increase funding for research on autism. Even when you write an analysis of a poem, you will be convincing readers that your perceptions and interpretations are correct. All of these persuasive papers, to one degree or another, involve argument.

## Persuasion as Argument

The term "argument" often conjures up images of people shouting at each other, disagreeing and disputing others' views, but a written argument does not need to be contentious and certainly not combative. In fact, an aggressive attack and tone *may* persuade the reader—to actually stop reading! A good argument depends on sound reasoning and support to persuade readers to renew their commitment to a certain perspective, to reconsider their views, or to change their course of action. Before any readers will be convinced, they will require sufficient evidence—support that the writer needs to provide and analyze.

Convincing others that your beliefs and perspectives are worth understanding, and perhaps even supporting, can be a definite challenge. Sometimes you will need to anticipate your readers' preconceptions and to counter their convictions in order to get them to modify their beliefs or change their behavior. Persuasion is a part of many writing situations, and convincing readers that a certain assertion or opinion is supportable is the heart of argument.

## The Doubting and Believing Games

Peter Elbow, respected professor and writer on composition and rhetoric, encourages writers to reconsider their understanding of the process of argument. In his paper "The Believing Game—Methodological Believing," delivered at a College Composition and Communication Conference (CCCC) in 2008, Elbow contends that it is unfortunate that skepticism and doubt have been synonymous with critical thinking. Writers and readers assume that by doubting others' ideas, "we can discover hidden contradictions, bad reasoning, or other weaknesses" (Elbow 1). Indeed, finding weaknesses in an argument is a skill often emphasized in writing classrooms because poor reasoning creates flawed and unconvincing papers. Elbow acknowledges that the "doubting game . . . develops an indispensable dimension of intelligence or rationality" (7) needed to evaluate arguments. But while Elbow recognizes the value of "the doubting game," he feels that "the believing game," a more positive approach to considering arguments, has been nearly ignored in the teaching of critical thinking. He argues that we also need to value "the believing game—the disciplined practice of trying to be as welcoming or accepting as possible to every idea we encounter" (1). This acceptance does not mean that Elbow doesn't want students to think critically and write well-reasoned, convincing papers. But Elbow asserts that "we cannot see what's good in someone else's idea (or in our own!) till we work at believing it" (2). He urges students to strive to embrace unfamiliar ideas, silence skepticism, and try to get *inside* someone else's view.

We find that Peter Elbow raises important questions about the nature of critical thinking and verifies that both doubting *and* believing are valuable tools in understanding arguments. Throughout *Between Worlds*, our readings, questions, and assignments have encouraged you to play the believing game—to value "what's good in someone else's ideas" even if the ideas seem unfashionable or alien to your own views. Elbow's point is clear: "The believing game suggests modes of writing persuasively and analytically that are nonadversarial" (9)—that is, not combative or hostile. We support Elbow's advice while we also encourage you to develop sound arguments and to avoid fallacious reasoning. And we urge you to play the believing game as energetically as you play the doubting game.

## When to Use Argument

Argument is frequently a part of all types of essay writing. Even when a particular method or mode of development is assigned, you may still be writing persuasively even if you are not writing an actual argument. For example, if you are attempting to convince a reader that one course of action is superior to another, you may be developing your essay using comparison-contrast, but you are, nevertheless, writing an argument. If you are assigned a cause-and-effect essay, you may be arguing that a particular behavior or event caused a certain consequence. When you are assigned an analysis of a poem or of a character in a story, you will be trying to convince readers of the validity of your interpretations. In all cases, your thinking and writing will be stronger if you remain open to multiple perspectives—play the believing game—even as you analyze and critique the reasoning in your own and others' work—play the doubting game.

# Brainstorming for an Argument

When you are assigned a topic and begin brainstorming for ideas and feelings, record your uncensored responses as you freewrite, list, or cluster ideas. This unrestricted prewriting—embracing the believing game—should help you discover what you know about your subject and what you will need to find out. Here are some specific questions to consider as you prepare a persuasive essay:

- What do you already know about this issue? List everything that comes to mind.

- What are your feelings about this subject and why do you feel this way? Freewriting in your journal may help here.

- Do you have any biases about this subject that block you, even tentatively, from embracing another's views—and playing the believing game?

- What questions do you have about this subject? Read for answers in your textbook and online.

- How has this reading affected your opinions or perceptions of this issue? Jot down meaningful lines and respond to these quotations in your journal.

- What is your view or position on the controversy? Why is it more convincing than the counter-argument (opposing view)?

- After considering the counter-argument, what is a possible claim or point that *you* can support? Write down this working thesis.

- Determine if your goal is to persuade your readers to agree with your position—or to both agree and to act. Will you have an implied or a clearly expressed argument?

- Would it help you to compare and contrast opposing points? Will you need to define a concept as a key part of your argument? Should you focus on the causes and effects of a certain problem? (If your brainstorming shows that any of these methods of development would be helpful, see Chapter 10, pp. 375–413.)

# Explicit and Implicit Arguments

If, in your brainstorming, you have discovered a clear aim—to overtly alter your readers' view—and if your claim is directly stated, you have an explicit argument and a thesis that you will need to support. On the other hand, if convincing your reader is secondary to your aim to express, entertain, inform, or analyze, then you are probably developing an implicit argument.

An analysis of two essays in this text may help you see this distinction between an explicit and implicit argument.

If you have not yet read these two essays, you will want to read Jennifer Coleman's "Discrimination at Large" (p. 175) and Neil Steinberg's "O.K., So I'm Fat" (p. 179). Although these writers address the same topic—what it means to be heavy in a culture that reveres thinness—their essays are quite different.

## An Explicit Argument

Coleman's argument is explicit: Her aim is to convince readers that discrimination because of weight is unjust and cannot be tolerated. This claim or thesis is explicitly stated at the end of her essay. In "O.K., So I'm Fat," Neil Steinberg's argument is implicit: His aim is to express his annoyance and his claim is that some thin people have superior attitudes that make him feel uncomfortable. His stance is softer because his argument is implicit; he is not expecting people to reform. However, Coleman *is* demanding such a change.

In "Discrimination at Large," Jennifer Coleman asserts that discrimination against heavy people, in jokes and attitudes, is as "damaging as any racial or ethnic slur" (178). In this essay, her aim is to persuade the reader that attitudes and actions against "fat people" need to be changed so that ridicule is not acceptable. She argues that people who would not tolerate jibes about someone's race, culture, disability, or sexual orientation often do mock fat people.

Coleman expresses her feelings about being harassed for simply ordering food at a restaurant or appearing on a beach, but her main purpose extends beyond expressing herself. She wants to persuade her reader that discrimination because of weight is as unfair and unacceptable as discrimination because of race and ethnicity. As in any argument, she must present evidence of how she has been harassed. She does this by reporting hostile attacks like "Move your fat ass" and unsolicited comments like "You would really be pretty if you lost weight."

Her aim, to persuade her reader, also requires her to anticipate an opponent who might argue that this harassment is not the same as racial and ethnic slurs because weight, unlike race or ethnicity, can be controlled. The average reader might contend that she should diet and exercise. Coleman anticipates this counter-argument by delineating the details of her acute exercise and dietary phase. She reveals that her pulse, cholesterol level, and respiration were excellent; she was fit but still fat. Finally, she exposes the poor reasoning of those who want her to exercise but still attack her for riding a bike ("Hey lady, where's the seat?") or denigrate her by trumpeting like elephants while she is jogging. While she exercises, she has heard people shout, "Lose some weight, you pig." She demands that her reader "go figure," emphasizing how irrational some people are, perhaps even some readers. We think that her primary goal is achieved—to persuade readers with her explicit argument that such harassment should not be tolerated or perpetuated by anyone who is sensitive and reasonable.

## An Implicit Argument

In "O.K., So I'm Fat," Neil Steinberg's argument is implicit rather than explicit. What is his aim? We see this as an expressive essay that still persuades readers because Steinberg is revealing how he feels about the "smug superiority" of some thin people (180). He probably does not aim to reform people's behavior, but readers may be persuaded to be more sensitive. He acknowledges that there is "a social stigma" in being fat as well as "medical peril" and some discomfort in "dragging all that excess weight around."

But what he wants to express is that the "ignominy" for fat people is "thin people." This is his implied argument. He cites as evidence "overly familiar office mates" and "wiry panhandlers" who address him as "big guy," and those who slyly refer to fad diets or offer him a Diet Coke, hoping to elevate him to the "sainted ranks of the thin." He cites the "wisp of a woman" hostess with "legs like beef jerky" who prepared "an intensely fattening dessert—Bananas Foster, thick slices of ripe bananas awash in butter and sugar and cinnamon and liqueur accompanied by ice cream" but who didn't have any herself.

He notes the smug superiority in her refusal as she "gazes down" on him. Steinberg also mentions that he is not bothered by thin people who don't need to watch what they eat; he is "comfortable, happy, never put off" by them.

Steinberg's purpose is to express his perceptions about the superior attitude of thin people—not to reform his readers' opinions or behavior. Steinberg makes it clear that thin people's attitude toward the obese is not, dare we say, a weighty subject. In both Coleman's and Steinberg's essays, each writer's purpose or aim is evident in the explicit or implied thesis or central claim of the essay.

## Arguments and Proposals

A distinction can be made between two types of writing that attempt to convince readers to reconsider their views and beliefs:

An *argument* employs logic to reason a point and get the reader to think.

A *proposal* employs logic to influence others and get the reader to think and act.

Although these types of writing often overlap, some assignments seem to fit more in one category than the other. If you are asked to analyze an essay and argue for or against the writer's views, your essay will involve *argumentation*. You will be expected to focus on a thesis that can provoke the reader's thoughts and to use supporting evidence that is logically presented and carefully analyzed.

If you are asked to offer a solution to a problem or to persuade others to modify or change their behavior, your essay will need to include a *proposal* in addition to argumentation. You will be expected to create a thesis that elicits a response. Therefore you will also need to suggest a reasonable plan of action or activities for your reader.

## Sound Reasoning: Balancing Logos, Pathos, and Ethos

Sound reasoning is the backbone of all convincing arguments. The ancient Greeks, whose theories of rhetoric and argument continue to influence writers today, understood that arguments have three main components: *logos, pathos*, and *ethos*. A good essay is based on the logic or *logos* of the argument. The *logos* is the reasoning, the work done with the supporting evidence—the facts, data, and statistics collected for support. However, readers often initially respond to an emotional appeal, the *pathos*, of an argument. This emotional appeal is created by stirring the readers' feelings and recognizing their needs and concerns. Finally, the ethics or *ethos* of an argument is the credibility or authority that convinces readers that the writer and his or her ideas and views are reliable and trustworthy. Ideally, the writer's ethos should ensure that the logos is sound and that the pathos is not excessive or manipulative.

Sound reasoning governs and strengthens the entire body of the essay, from the opening to the conclusion. Readers will expect all claims to be carefully explained and supported with evidence and illustrations so that the material is not distorted or misrepresented. Good critical thinkers need to be self-defense experts—on guard against attempts to manipulate their emotions or deceive them with false information or fallacious reasoning. However, good critical thinkers also need to be open to new and often unfashionable ideas, playing the believing game as they read material alien to their own way of thinking.

## Audience and Argument

It is critical to identify one's *audience* and to find an approach that would best appeal to that audience. Identification of your readers may include asking these questions:

- Are your readers aware that the problem exists?
- Will your readers find the problem sufficiently important?
- Are your readers affected by the problem?
- Do your readers have special interests or biases that will cause them to resist the information? The argument? The essay?

If the writer can determine whether the readers are likely to be sympathetic, neutral, or hostile, the approach can then be designed to reach that audience.

# Argument Introductions

Once you have identified your audience—college comp classmates, film goers, history majors—you will be able to design your introduction to appeal to those readers. If you know their interests and backgrounds, you can write your opening with this background in mind. If you realize that your readers may be hostile or indifferent to your views, you know that you need to work hard to appeal to them and convince them of your perspective. They will not overlook your flawed logic, irrelevant or insufficient examples, or sweeping generalizations and assumptions. In fact, they will be seeking reasons to dismiss your views, so you don't want to make it easy for them to reject your argument.

Even if you suspect that your audience may be sympathetic to your aim and may agree with you, it is wise to write your essay with your most adamant opponent in mind. You will want to reason clearly, support claims fully, and anticipate any objections so you can address these concerns before your reader even considers them. Acknowledging and refuting any counter-arguments (opposing views) can strengthen your stance.

Because you are attempting to convince readers of a view that may be different from their own, it often helps to begin by illustrating the problem and showing what is wrong with the current thinking or practice on this issue. If there are any myths, misconceptions, or misinformation about your subject, it may help to acknowledge them in your opening as you set out to question or disprove them.

For example, if a writer is arguing that female students in the early grades need greater encouragement to succeed in math and science classes, then it would make sense to first establish the need. The introduction and part of the body of the essay might demonstrate how females are discouraged from pursuing math and science majors and how few women today excel in these fields, even though studies indicate females are no less capable of succeeding in science and math than males are. Providing your readers with the statistical data to verify these findings will help convince both genders. However, the writer needs to be aware that females may be more interested in this topic than males or that readers in non-science fields may need to be persuaded that this subject is relevant.

# Organizing and Developing an Argument

An outline can be critical for keeping the argument focused and organized. The outline can be informal, merely an ordered list of points that the writer plans to cover. The outline may also help an instructor follow the argument and detect any flaws or gaps before the essay is actually written. In such cases, a more formal outline may be required. (For an illustration of an informal outline for an argument, see pp. 310–312 and for a formal outline, see pp. 312–314.) Outlining your material may also help you catch problems in your reasoning.

## Avoiding Logical Fallacies

Often an argument may be persuasive but still illogical. If a claim has no basis or foundation in reason, a *logical fallacy* will result, discrediting the argument and eroding the reader's trust. By recognizing these fallacies in others' arguments and avoiding them in your own writing, you can become a more effective critical thinker. Let's look at some of the most common types of logical fallacies, listed in alphabetical order:

- *Appeal to false authority:* Uses a person or celebrity who does not have expertise in that area to try and sway the reader. ("Brad Pitt wears Gap jeans so they must be well made.")

- *Appeal to fear:* Attempts to convince by implicitly threatening the audience but not offering any logical support for the fear. ("Unless you major in business, you will end up unemployed.")

- *Appeal to pity:* Occurs when an argument appeals solely to our emotions rather than our intellect or reasoning. ("If I don't receive an 'A' in your course, professor, I won't get into law school.")

- *Bandwagon appeal:* Suggests that "everyone is doing this—why don't you?" This pressures the reader to conform whether or not the view or action seems logical or right. ("All good teachers are using PowerPoint presentations.")

- *Begging the question (circular reasoning):* Does not prove anything because it simply restates the assertion. ("Instructors who teach writing are better teachers because good instructors teach writing.")

- *False analogy:* Compares two things that aren't really comparable and therefore results in a false conclusion. ("If developmental math classes can be taught effectively in a large lecture hall, developmental English classes can be, too.")

- *False cause:* Assumes a cause-effect relationship between two events just because one precedes another. It claims a causal relationship solely on the basis of a chronological relationship. ("Because Joe got a new laptop this semester, he earned an 'A' in both his English and math classes.")

- *False dilemma (either/or argument):* Sets up a false black-and-white dilemma, assuming that a particular viewpoint or course of action can have only two diametrically opposed outcomes. ("College professors either require lengthy writing assignments or they are poor teachers.")

- *Hasty generalization:* Consists of drawing a broad conclusion from a few unrepresentative generalizations ("Math teachers use Scantron tests; math teachers don't teach students to think critically.")

- *Personal or "ad hominem" ("against the man") attacks; name-calling:* Whether intentional or not, these slurs are often associated with advertisers and politicians, whose careers may depend on their power to manipulate and mislead the public. Calling someone a "leftist radical" or a "warmonger" is intended to get the audience to respond emotionally to a prejudice rather than to think rationally about an issue. Often these attacks are designed to divert attention from the issue to the opponent's personal traits or associations that may be irrelevant. ("Why should we even consider an opinion from the *New York Times*? All *Times* writers are liberals.")

- *Unqualified generalization:* Makes too broad a claim that cannot be proven but requires qualifiers such as words like "often," "seldom," "most," "may," and "could." ("All college freshmen are overwhelmed by the heavy reading assignments.")

- *Slippery slope or the domino theory (or ripple effect):* Purports that if a certain action is taken, it will necessarily cause other extreme results, whether or not the evidence supports these conclusions. ("If students use the Internet for research, they will be tempted to plagiarize and will end up failing all of their classes.")

These are only some of the many logical fallacies that can weaken an argument. Instead of relying on illogical attacks and charges, writer must seek logical support for their positions and expose fallacies in their opponent's argument.

## Preparing Your Argument

Earlier in this chapter we provided questions for use as you brainstorm for an argument (p. 355). We also have previously demonstrated freewriting, listing, and clustering, using students Rachel and Pete (pp. 279–286). These prewriting exercises can be used for all types of essays, and certainly as you prepare for an argument. In fact, Rachel's essay on eating disorders *is* an argument, using her own experiences and a reading from this text for support (pp. 334–337).

These additional suggestions for writing an argument will help to get you started after you have finished prewriting and brainstorming for a topic:

- **Identify your aim** in writing the essay and determine your stance.
- Search the library databases for articles and books or use reputable internet sites to **increase your knowledge** and understanding of the subject. The more evidence you have, the more convincing your argument will be.
- Focus on a **claim** or **working thesis** that reflects your stance on the issue.
- Consider ways to refute the counter-argument and opposing views as you build your case.
- Decide if your argument will contain a **proposal** for a solution to the problem and reflect that in your thesis.

- **Briefly outline** your ideas to correspond with your aim and claim. Consider some possible methods of developing your points: narration, comparison-contrast, cause and effect, and extended definition. See pp. 382–413 for help using these methods.
- **Consider your audience** and determine their biases or lack of information. Experiment with the most effective way to appeal to your readers.

# Strategies for Writing an Argument Essay

Once you have brainstormed to discover your specific topic and your position on it, you are ready to draft your essay. As you write to persuade your reader, certain strategies can help strengthen your essay and convince readers to consider your view. Although these points are listed in order, we do not mean to suggest that there is a correct chronology. We know from our own experience and from our students' efforts that writing is a recursive process: We return to many of these strategies again and again before we move ahead to others.

## Illustrations from the Text

Each strategy here is illustrated with an example from arguments in this text:

- **In your introduction, help the readers see that there** is **a problem, issue, or need that has prompted your argument.** If your tone is inviting and your wording is clear and accessible, readers may already be open to your views and ready to be persuaded.

In "Terra Firma: A Journey from Migrant Farm Labor to Neurosurgery" (p. 102), Alfredo Quiñones-Hinojosa knows that his subtitle may intrigue readers because it seems so implausible. His opening lines make the problem clear: "'You will spend the rest of your life working in the fields,' my cousin told me when I arrived in the United States in the mid-1980s. This fate indeed appeared likely: a 19-year-old illegal migrant farm worker, I had no English language skills and no dependable means of support. I had grown up in a small Mexican farming community, where I began working at my father's gas station at the age of 5. Our family was poor and we were subject to the diseases of poverty: my earliest memory is of my infant sister's death from diarrhea when I was 3 years old" (103). Opening with a haunting quotation and then a vivid personal narrative, Quiñones-Hinojosa depicts himself and his family as hard-working and still poor. He is careful to avoid manipulating the reader or appealing only to pity by presenting the facts and showing that he and his family didn't want or expect charity.

- **Make sure that you support your claims with plenty of evidence that you analyze fully.**

An illustration of this technique is clear in Andres Martin's essay "On Teenagers and Tattoos" (p. 28). Throughout his essay, he uses several case studies of his patients with tattoos to specifically support his thesis: that parents and psychiatrists should not harshly judge teens' tattoos but should see them as a way to better understand teenagers (28–32). Martin includes detailed descriptions and analyses of the symbolism of each patient's tattoos to convince his readers who may only see teenage tattoos as self-mutilation.

- **Anticipate your opponents' objections and refute their counter-arguments.**

In "Time Lost and Found," Anne Lamott asserts that anyone can make time for all those things we wish we could do but don't because we claim that we can't. We may long for deeper friendships and time for creative expression— "writing, dancing, bird-watching, or cooking" or any activity that can bring the joy and peace that people want in their lives. She argues that constant texting, emailing, going to the gym 4 days a week, and watching the nightly news use time that could be enjoyed in more creative ways. These busy habits also "steal most chances of lasting connection" with others (240). Lamott anticipates her readers' objections that they don't have any extra minutes to spare, and she imagines her writing students' voices: "They start to explain that they have two kids at home, or five, a stable of horses or a hive of bees, and 40-hour workweeks" (240). She acknowledges that she shares their frenetic lives even though "they don't think I understand. But I do. I know how addictive busyness and mania are" (241). However, she counters that if they want to have rich lives of connection and creativity, they have to give up or cut back on less meaningful activites. Her argument is more effective because she empathizes with her readers and anticipates their objections even as she refutes them.

- **Clarify your view as you provide reasons and analysis.**

In "Why Bother?" (p. 251), Michael Pollan analyzes the difficulty for the individual who wants to do something about climate change but begins to recognize the complexity of the issues and perhaps the futility of an individual making a change when so many others seem indifferent to the problems. He presents a situation: should he deny himself the use of a clothes dryer and string a laundry line in his yard when people elsewhere are increasing their carbon footprints with purchases and practices that exacerbate global warming? His question about "why bother?" leads to an analysis of planting a garden, an action that shows that bothering can make a significant difference. In addition to the feelings of personal virtue enjoyed by the home gardener who can grow the "proverbial free lunch," the backyard produces the most local food possible, the compost pile "shrinks the heap of garbage your household needs trucked away even as it feeds your vegetables," and the home gardener gets a good work-out without having to drive to the gym. Through his analysis of the reasons for planting a garden, Pollan convinces his reader that to bother is not only virtuous but may help improve rather than diminish the planet.

- **Offer a concession to your opponent that doesn't undermine your argument and then use it as a way to strengthen your position.**

In "Your Brain on Computers" (p. 227), Christopher Chabris and Daniel Simons argue that there is no conclusive evidence that the distracting abundance of information on the Internet interferes with our brain's ability to sustain concentration. The authors open their essay by referring to Nicholas Carr's claims that the Internet is weakening our brain's ability to focus, and the authors concede that their opponent's position "seems plausible, at least on the surface" (228). They acknowledge that all the "new communication tools trap us in a shallow culture of constant interruption as we frenetically tweet, text, and e-mail" (228). This concession shows that the writers are open to Carr's position and realize that it "seems plausible" (228). But the authors note that the evidence of the brain's inability to sustain focus is anecdotal; therefore, they qualify their concessions with "seems" and "at least on the surface." They then refute the counter argument and conclude that the Internet actually may make us smarter because it offers valuable and diverse modes of learning and sharing information, for example, to sharpen skills for a chess competition or to facilitate collaboration in science and technology.

- **Use sound reasoning and avoid logical fallacies.**

In "My Favorite School Class: Involuntary Servitude" (p. 366), Joe Goodwin writes a convincing argument even though it contains logical fallacies. One fallacy, a hasty generalization, occurs when Goodwin doesn't support his sweeping claim that values are no longer taught in the home. Goodwin adds that the values of respect, patience, and compassion must be "learned elsewhere, since we live in a world in which many families have two parents working long hours every day and many more have just a single parent" (366). Goodwin implies that single parents or families with two working parents are too busy to foster values in their children so the schools need to fulfill this obligation. However, Goodwin ignores the fact that there are plenty of families that disprove his claim. Such a fallacy may weaken Goodwin's argument, but it does not necessarily invalidate the essay if the rest of his support is convincing. You can read Joe Goodwin's complete essay and our analysis of his argument on pp. 365–369.

## Conceding and Refuting

Rather than twisting facts or attacking an opponent, it is best to anticipate objections and refute them, logically and directly, before the reader can utter "But . . .". Overlooking or ignoring potential holes in an argument can render it vulnerable to attack. Your argument will not necessarily be weakened if you recognize what may appear to be a weakness in your plan—provided you can show that it doesn't really undermine your argument.

Another effective strategy is to acknowledge counter-arguments and perhaps even admit that they have merit, but then show how your solution or viewpoint is still superior. Such a strategy suggests that you are informed, open-minded, and reasonable—qualities that make the reader more receptive to your argument.

Arguments and proposals written by students can be more than mere classroom exercises. They can be sent to newspapers, television stations, corporations, and government boards. Several of the argument assignments in the "Writing from the Text" and "Connecting with Other Texts" sections in Part I involve college-related issues and may be appropriate for the editorial or opinion page of your campus or local newspaper.

## Evaluating an Argument

As you read an argument, consider these questions to evaluate its effectiveness:

- Who is the targeted audience, and how does the writer appeal to this audience?
- What is the problem? What is the thesis?
- What are the supporting points?
- What are the strengths of the argument?
- Does the writer anticipate counter-arguments and refute them?
- What are the weaknesses? Are there any logical fallacies?
- How does the ending bring satisfying closure to the essay?

### EXAMPLE: AN ARGUMENT ESSAY

The following argument was written by Joe Goodwin, who was in high school when he published this essay in the "Campus Correspondence" section of the *Los Angeles Times* on August 9, 1992. Goodwin responds to the controversy surrounding a policy mandating community service for junior high through high school students in Maryland schools. In 1997, Maryland made it a graduation requirement that students need to complete seventy-five hours of community service. The numbers in the margin of this essay correspond to the numbers of the explanatory notes on the facing page.

My Favorite School Class: Involuntary Servitude

Like most teen-agers, I hate to be told what to do. I chafe at curfews, refuse to patronize restaurants that tell me what to wear, and complain daily about the braces my parents and dentist want me to have. Yet, I look forward to the "forced opportunity" for community service my high school requires. While criticism mounts against Maryland's action in becoming the first state to mandate students to perform 75 hours of community service over seven years, it is well to look at the experience of local school districts that have instituted similar programs.

For five years, every student at the Concord-Carlisle Regional High School in Massachusetts has been required to perform 40 hours of community service in order to graduate. Conventional wisdom would have us believe that this would be an especially burdensome task, perhaps an impossible one, for students who hold outside paying jobs. But the graduation requirement may be satisfied within the school by working as teacher's aides, library assistants, or tutors. Outside school, the requirement may be met by working at hospitals, nursing homes, senior citizens' centers, soup kitchens, or for the town's park service or recreational department.

To be sure, it would be wonderful if students volunteered such service. But the great benefit of the mandated program is the responsibility it places on the school to work with community leaders to locate the places where students can best make a solid contribution. It is unrealistic to expect students to roam from place to place in search of service opportunities. Once the arrangements for those opportunities are made, the student needs only to decide which kind of service best fits his or her personality.

Those who oppose the community-service mandate fear it will interfere with the regular school curriculum. But what more important class can a student take than one that teaches values and responsibility? Clearly it is better to be helping the elderly and homeless rather than listening to long lectures about their plight.

Some say that schools should not be in the business of fostering civic concerns among its youth. But what more important role can a school play than in shaping values—respect for the elderly, patience for those younger, compassion for those less fortunate—among its young? These and related values used to be taught in the home. Now, they must be learned elsewhere, since we live in a world in which many families have two parents working long hours every day and many more have just a single parent.

# Explanatory Notes for the Argument Essay

The numbers on these explanatory notes correspond to the numbers in the margin of the argument essay.

1. *Audience:* Goodwin's audience is students who might resist community service, or their parents who might not want the school day lengthened with extra work, or taxpayers or school boards who might be voting on whether to institute the compulsory service requirement in their communities.

2. *Appeal:* Goodwin appeals to his audience by identifying himself as a typical teenager who "hate[s] to be told what to do." He creates an image of himself as a teen who resents curfews, dress codes, and wearing braces.

3. *Thesis:* Goodwin's thesis is that in spite of his resistance to being told what to do, he sees a program of mandatory community service as a valuable "forced opportunity" for students.

4. *Problem:* Goodwin identifies the problem as those who resist mandatory community service.

5. *Objections/refutations:* Goodwin anticipates objections and refutes them:
   a. Doing community service is a burden for students who hold outside paying jobs. (Students can choose to work on campus or off.)
   b. Students should volunteer for such service. (He concedes that they should volunteer but believes that it is unrealistic to expect students to search for such opportunities on their own.)
   c. Community service will interfere with regular curriculum. (He believes that community service is as important as any class and that it teaches students to apply what they are learning in the classroom.)
   d. Schools should not be in the business of fostering civic concerns among students. (He argues that schools must help shape values, especially since many children do not get such training at home.)

      *Logical fallacy:* Goodwin's point about values is a good one, but he has a logical fallacy: *hasty generalization.* He claims that values "used to be taught in the home" and that homes with two parents working or with single parents are not teaching values. These are assumptions Goodwin can't support. He could have written "now values *may* need to be learned elsewhere" because *some* working or single parents *aren't always* available to teach values or reinforce the ones they have taught. (See pp. 360–361.)

6. *Support:* Goodwin supports his argument by insisting that it is better to be working directly with the elderly rather than reading about or hearing lectures about their "plight."

7. *Support:* Goodwin supports his argument by asserting that the school should do what many homes are not doing—teaching and reinforcing the

8   Sociologists and journalists decry the decline of American society and the disintegration of the American family. Yet, when those who find pleasure in lecturing about this decline are faced with a solution that would help strengthen society, they fall back on the past. It is this negative attitude toward change that has caused the country to reach the point of such neglect.

9   Today, the passion and commitment that marked my parents' generation—the 1960s—is gone, replaced by an ominous silence. I listen to my parents talk of their experiences with the civil-rights movement, the sit-ins, the war on poverty, and I am impatient for the time when my own generation is similarly involved in the great public events of our day. Although 40 hours of community service is not very much, it is a beginning.

My interest in community service was heightened last spring. While on a class trip to the Science Museum in Boston, a group of students in my 8th-grade class were involved in an altercation with another group of students from a largely black school in Roxbury, a neighborhood near downtown. Taunts were exchanged, a fight broke out. It was unsettling.

10   The following week, teachers from both schools arranged a daylong meeting of a representative sampling of students at each school. The discussion that resulted was an extraordinary experience. As I listened to black students describe their stereotypes of whites in the suburbs, as I heard one black girl say she cried herself to sleep the night of the fight in fear and frustration that racial relations would never improve, I realized how far America was from the ideals of equality and justice. If community service could help to bridge the gap between ideal and reality, I will feel happy indeed.

## Explanatory Notes *(continued)*

values "of respect for the elderly, patience for those younger, compassion for those less fortunate."

8. *Clarification:* Goodwin clarifies the problem: Weak values contribute to the "decline of American society" and "the disintegration of the American family" and yet many people resist a program that could strengthen values.

9. *Support:* Goodwin supports his argument by arguing that the "passion and commitment" of his parents' generation, sadly lacking in youth today, might be reinvigorated by community service.

10. *Logical fallacy:* Goodwin attempts to support his argument with a personal anecdote about a class trip to an inner-city museum. In his mind, his discovery on the trip supports the need for community service programs. However, his reasoning is not clear to the reader. Goodwin makes a leap that the reader can't comprehend. Goodwin may have meant that "community service could move students into worlds they don't routinely inhabit and could bridge communication gaps." If he had articulated the connection between the racial tension on the class trip and community service, he would have had a stronger conclusion to his argument. (See p. 360.)

Throughout his essay, Goodwin's tone is restrained and reasonable. His writing reflects a healthy balance between idealism (free choice) and realism (mandatory service). He might have been tempted to resort to name-calling or offensive attacks, but instead he relies on examples and explanations to support his case.

 ## PRACTICE WRITING ARGUMENT ESSAYS

Write an essay to convince your reader of one of the following assertions. The page numbers in parenthesis refer to readings in the text.

1. The lyrics in contemporary music reflect (or incite) societal tension.

2. Reality television is or is not compelling programming.

3. Football should (or should not) be played in high school (p. 60).

4. All cellphone use while driving should (or should not) be illegal (pp. 210–217).

5. The burka does (or does not) prejudice the world's perception of the woman who wears it (p. 113).

6. Twitter is (or is not) a worthless time drain (p. 232 and 235)

7. Buying green is (or is not) disguised consumerism (p. 246).

8. Combatting climate change is (or is not) worth the bother (p. 259).

 **Final Tips for Argument Essays**

- **Brainstorm for a topic** and freewrite or list what you already know about this subject.
- Read more about your subject. As you **gather information**, stay open to new ideas—play the believing game. By suspending judgment, you will be able to understand, and perhaps value alternative views.
- Recognize your **purpose**: argument or proposal for action.
- **Identify your readers**, consider their perspective, and prepare your appeal. Avoid insulting or attacking them.
- Word your **thesis** carefully to provoke thought or action.
- **Outline** your argument so it is focused and organized.
- **Support all claims** with convincing evidence and reasoned analysis.
- **Anticipate objections** and differing viewpoints, and show why your argument is stronger even if the counter-arguments have some merit.
- **Offer a concession** to your opponents that does not undermine your argument, and then use it as a way to strengthen your position.
- Guard against **logical fallacies**; they weaken any argument.
- Make sure that your conclusion brings satisfying **closure** to your argument. Avoid tacking on any new points.

# Chapter 10

# Methods for Developing Essays

In this chapter you will learn strategies to prepare for in-class essays and to develop out-
of-class essays using these different methods:

- summary
- narration
- evaluative response
- definition
- cause and effect
- comparison and contrast

Your instructor will ask you to write both in-class and take-home essays.
Although your methods for developing either essay assignment may be similar, your strategy will need to be different if you are writing in a timed setting.

## Writing an In-Class Essay

An in-class essay requires you to quickly retrieve information that you know, to
present it in an orderly way, and to develop your ideas with enough substance
to convince your instructor that you understand the material. Frequently,
students rush through an in-class essay, providing quick or undeveloped
answers, and then are disappointed when the essay earns only a mediocre
grade. Instead, plan to spend the entire time period allowed so that you give
yourself a chance to write full and complete responses to the prompt and to

earn the best grade possible. To write a successful in-class essay, you need to focus on the "3-D effect" for composition: Details, Development, and Depth.

## The "3-D Effect"—Details, Development, and Depth

Whenever you write an in-class essay or written responses on an exam, *details* are needed so that you support your claims with examples and illustrations, particularly from your readings and class notes. For an in-class essay, direct quotations are not expected, but the information should be as specific and detailed as possible. Your professors will be expecting you to paraphrase memorable language and original imagery from the readings. Such specifics will provide concrete support so that your paper is not filled with vague generalizations or weakly supported claims. It is not enough that the details are included; they each need to be *developed* fully. Explain each detail and example with sufficent context from the reading to demonstrate your full understanding of the material. When professors assign in-class essays or essay exams rather than multiple choice or fill-in-the-blank answers, they will expect you to explore the essay prompt fully and with considerable *depth*. You can achieve this depth by careful analysis of the full implications of your claims. Avoid quick answers or superficial treatment of complex questions and concerns.

To prepare for an in-class essay, you should review readings and notes before you come to class. If you spend time studying and anticipating possible essay prompts and test questions, you won't be nervous because you will be writing about materials that you have reviewed. Use the key words that follow to help you formulate possible questions that you might encounter in the prompt. Here is a six-step strategy to prepare for a timed writing assignment.

## A Six-Step Strategy for In-Class Writing

1. Read the prompt more than once.

2. **Determine what the prompt specifically requires you to do.** Have you been asked to *define, list, summarize, compare or contrast, explain,* or *analyze?* See the list on pages 373–374 for definitions of words that are commonly used in essay prompts.

3. **Briefly outline** the material that will satisfy the prompt. Do not spend much time on this step; the outline can be brief, with only key words or phrases to remind you of material that you need to include.

4. **Create a thesis**—placed at the end of your introduction—to focus your essay and possibly forecast the areas that you will develop.

5. **Write the essay**—an introduction, several body paragraphs, and a conclusion—to support your thesis and key points. Remember the **3-D effect: Details, Development, and Depth.**

6. **Reread your answer to correct errors in spelling and grammar.** Use a dictionary if you are permitted to bring one to the exam. Do *not* plan to rewrite; you will seldom have sufficient time. As you reread, if you recall material that would improve your essay, indicate that you have an insertion, with a small number in parentheses. Then write the added material on another sheet of paper after the corresponding number. **Use the full time period to write and proofread.**

It is most important that you understand exactly what the prompt requires you to do. For example, if the assignment asks you to *list* the chemical elements commonly called salts, you are to enumerate—present in a list or outline form—the specific chemical elements called salts. An essay is not required, would be inappropriate, and might cost you points. If the prompt asks you to *compare and contrast* two subjects, and you only show how the subjects contrast, you have missed part of the assignment—how the subjects compare. The chart that follows here will help you understand what is expected on exams. The first example in parentheses provides a typical exam topic from a college course; the second example is drawn from readings in this textbook.

## Key Words Used for Essay Prompts

| Word | Meaning and Examples |
| --- | --- |
| *analyze* | Break into elements or parts and examine: "Analyze the job of the Attorney General of the United States" or "Analyze Michael Pollan's argument that you should change your actions to improve the environment" (p. 252). |
| *compare* | Look for and bring out points of similarity, qualities that resemble each other: "Compare the intelligence required of skilled blue- and white-collar workers" or "Compare the reasons people of different ages get tattoos" (p. 28). |
| *contrast* | Stress the dissimilarities, differences: "Contrast the characteristics of an impressionist portrait with a cubist portrait" or "Contrast the advice that J.K. Rowling gives to graduates with what her parents expected of her" (p. 154). |
| *define* | Give the meaning of a word or concept: "Define the term *archetype*" or "Define a 'cheap' date according to Adair Lara" (p. 45). |
| *describe* | Give an account, word picture, or narration: "Describe the Aztec civilization at Teotihuacan," or "Describe the family tradition that Mirikitani's narrator manages to break" (p. 21). |

| Word | Meaning and Examples |
|------|---------------------|
| *discuss* | Examine, consider from different points of view: "Discuss the use of pesticides in controlling mosquitoes" or "Discuss the problems inherent in playing high school football according to Don Sabo" (p. 60). |
| *explain* | Make clear, interpret, tell the meaning of, tell how: "Explain how animals in Antarctica have been impacted by global warming" or "Explain the distinction that Vaughn makes between 'pity' and 'empathy'" (p. 148). |
| *illustrate* | Clarify with examples or analogies, exemplify: "Illustrate how current rap lyrics reflect inner-city tensions" or "Illustrate what Max Thayer learns from his reflections on King Curtis" (p. 169). |
| *justify* | Show good reason for, give evidence to support your position: "Justify changing sport team names that refer to Native Americans" or "Justify using the Internet to 'get smarter'" (p. 218). |
| *relate* | Show correlation, how things are connected: "Relate an early childhood education program to elementary school academic success" or "Relate the pressures within a group to people's responses in an emergency" (p. 151). |
| *summarize* | Give the main points or facts in condensed form, omitting details: "Summarize the myth of Oedipus" or "Summarize the plot of 'Where Are You Going, Where Have You Been?'" (p. 70). |
| *trace* | In narrative form, describe the progress, development, or history of events: "Trace the opening of the American West through the development of wagon-train trails" or "Trace the process of reducing gas expense" (p. 417). |

If you understand the meaning of words used in exams or essay prompts, you will not lose points or time by pursuing a direction that will fail to give you full credit for the information that you know.

# Writing an Out-of-Class Essay

In a take-home essay, you will have more time to reflect, research, and revise your writing than you do in an in-class, timed writing situation. More will be expected of you in an out-of-class essay because you have days to organize, draft, and rewrite your material. Unlike in-class essays, take-home essays should not contain crossed-out words or hand-written insertions but should reflect details, development, and depth as well as editing and proofreading.

# Specific Methods of Development

Whether you are writing an in-class or out-of-class essay, your instructor may ask you to write a paper using a particular method of development for presenting your support, such as a narrative or a comparison-contrast study. You may be assigned an argument essay, which is fully covered in Chapter 9, but you may find yourself using one of the following methods to structure your argument. If your instructor doesn't assign a particular type of paper, then your purpose for writing will influence the methods of development you choose. To help you better understand how these types of support differ from one another, we have identified the following models for discussion: summary, narration, evaluative response, definition, cause and effect, comparison-contrast, and, in Chapter 11, analysis. By examining these methods in isolation, we do not mean to suggest that all paper topics will fit precisely into one of these categories. Nothing could be further from our experience as students, teachers, and writers.

You may recall that Rachel's essay "Dieting Daze" (p. 334) incorporates narrative, definition, description, and comparison-contrast in a problem analysis paper that argues for a change. These multiple approaches are ideal complements, and together they helped Rachel meet her goal. Her purpose was to convince her reader that advertisers need to be more responsible for the body images they promote.

# Combining Multiple Methods

Because you may be asked to develop a paper with a single and particular strategy, we have included in this chapter models of the methods most often assigned. But because we believe that most essays are developed with combined methods, we start our discussion with Dan Neil's "If the Genes Fit" (p. 161), an essay that combines multiple development techniques.

Neil's intention is to argue that homosexuality is inborn and not a choice and that those who resist this reality are fighting a battle that they "cannot hope to win." Neil's argument relies on his use of multiple methods of development: narration, summary, comparison-contrast, definition, analysis, and cause and effect. Let's now look at how each method contributes to his argument.

## Analyzing Mixed Methods

***Narration.*** To engage his reader, Neil opens his essay with his personal history that he "did not decide to be straight, never came to a sexually-oriented fork in the road to choose the road more traveled" (161). His account of his firsthand experience is heightened by his humorous quip that he was "never indoctrinated by anyone advancing a heterosexual agenda. Talk about coals to Newcastle" (161). In this final allusion, Neil acknowledges that heterosexuals walk "the road more traveled" and that it is as unnecessary to be "indoctrinated" to this sexual orientation as it would be to bring coal to an area that mines it. His use of narration is also evident when he recounts the retort of his good friend Brad. Neil wonders if Brad's sexual orientation might be "something environmental, something learned," to which Brad replies, "Yeah, right . . . I read a book on it when I was 3 years old" (162). The use of narration and humor engages readers before the author details scientific information that might otherwise turn off the general reader.

*Summary.* Neil succinctly summarizes the "vignettes of self-discovery and disclosure" that fill the book *When I Knew,* a collection of stories from gays and lesbians who describe their epiphanies, when they realized that "they belonged in the same-sex sandbox" (162). These summarized accounts are funny ("No you're not [lesbian], you're Romanian") and poignant (the boy playing hopscotch and overhearing his father's friend say, "I think you got a problem"). To support his argument, Neil also summarizes three articles from scientific journals: one describing how gene modification alters sexual orientation in fruit flies; another illustrating that gay men respond to the scent of males just as heterosexual women do; and another documenting "hundreds of examples of homosexual behavior in the animal kingdom" (163). These succinct summaries of scientific studies substantiate Neil's claim that homosexuality is genetic, not learned behavior.

*Definition.* Neil not only uses definition to explain scientific terms but, more fundamentally, to drive home his argument. Because he is reporting on scientific information, Neil does need to define certain terms for the average reader. For example, he reports the study of brain scans that demonstrate "that gay males react to male sweat pheromones the same way heterosexual women do" (163). Then he defines the word "pheromones—scent chemicals that govern sexual behavior in many species" (162). Neil also defines "gay gene," a term that he attributes to geneticist Dean Hamer and journalist Peter Copeland, as shorthand for the evidence that sexual orientation is inborn. However, Neil's use of definition is not limited to scientific terms but is an integral part of his argument. When he defines "the campaign to marginalize and criminalize gays" as "the bigoted pogrom that it is" (163), he is clearly opposing the "rabidly anti-gay Focus on the Family" organization (163). Ultimately, the entire piece relies on definition to argue for the understanding and acceptance of homosexuality as innate and natural behavior.

*Comparison-contrast.* Although "If the Genes Fit" does not reflect characteristic comparison-contrast form (see pp. 407–409), Neil's argument is based on the initial *contrast* between heterosexuals' and homosexuals' awareness of their sexual orientation and the deeper *comparison* that all humans are genetically wired for sexual preference. Neil contends that for a heterosexual there is no moment of discovery: "It never dawned on me that I was straight. I just was" (162). Although heterosexuals don't have "Eureka! moments" but simply intuit that they are part of a statistical majority, Neil observes, "For gays and lesbians, it seems, there is always a moment when they realize that what they want isn't officially sanctioned" (162). But more significantly, the heart of Neil's argument is based on comparison—that both heterosexuals and homosexuals inherently "know, at the core of their self-conception that they were born straight or gay" (163). Because sexual orientation has a genetic foundation, Neil emphasizes the commonality, the comparison, of all humans' response to their genetic wiring.

*Analysis:* In addition to providing numerous anecdotal and scientific examples, Neil analyzes the material he incorporates. For example, when he cites the realization of sexual self-awareness that gays and lesbians have, he refers to that "cognitive moment that marks a cleaving away from the larger heterosexual world," and he describes that cleaving away as "the opening of an otherness, like jets peeling off in the missing-man formation" (162). In this striking simile, Neil captures the experience of homosexuals and helps the reader understand the separation and "otherness" that homosexuals may feel as they move away from the traditional pattern.

*Cause and Effect:* The support for Neil's thesis is dependent on cause and effect reasoning. Neil summarizes scientific studies revealing that "homosexuality is a natural variation in the human genome" and that homosexuality is genetically based. These are the causes that lead him to the effect—his conclusion that "homosexuals are not guilty of anything except being human" (163). Further, Neil contends that because homosexuality is natural, then the appropriate effect should be social acceptance, not repudiation. Therefore, "the campaign to marginalize and criminalize gays is revealed as the bigoted pogrom that it is" (163). His argument relies on cause and effect reasoning: The condemnation of homosexuality is irrational and denies scientific evidence.

# Why This Analysis?

The purpose of this analysis of "If the Genes Fit" (p. 161) is to encourage you to recognize the multiple modes and devices that professional writers use to engage and inform their readers. Employing these devices will improve your writing. By practicing the single-development assignments given in the "Writing from the Text" topics described in Part I, you will learn to employ multiple methods confidently to write an appealing and convincing paper. Let's now look at each strategy in greater detail.

# SUMMARY

Summarizing is an important skill that demonstrates your ability to understand both the content of the reading and the way the material is arranged. A summary shows your ability to read, comprehend, and write. Summaries of assigned readings in class can become particularly useful personal learning tools, serving as study guides for examinations. But you may be asked in some classes—from undergraduate through graduate studies—to submit summaries to show that you have read and understood journal articles, essays, or books. Your purpose in writing a summary is to give your audience a condensed but complete view of the original work. In a sense, you are saving your reader the time and effort of reading the original—if your summary is accurate!

## Organizing and Developing a Summary

The following steps can be used to summarize assignments in any class—from psychology, education, and philosophy to political science and English. These same steps may also be the first you take if you are asked to summarize an essay and then evaluate it, an assignment frequently given in college courses.

1. Read the work actively, marking directly on the copy (if possible) the obvious divisions or sections within the text. Underline the thesis, if one is explicitly stated, as well as any key points or examples you see as you read.

2. Reread the text. On a separate sheet of paper, write a few sentences of summary (combining paraphrased and quoted material) for each section of the work that you have marked in the margins of the original.

3. Write the author's thesis or what you infer to be the central assertion of the entire essay. You may write a general thesis or one that forecasts the points the writer will use to support the assertion.

4. Write a draft that starts with the thesis, even if the writer delayed the central assertion of the work. Continue the draft with the sentence summaries that you wrote for each of the sections of the text. Use the full name of the author of the work once, then use only his or her last name in other places in your summary. It is important to use the writer's name so that your reader is reminded who had the ideas in the original text.

5. Reread your draft to be sure of the following:

   • Your thesis reflects the author's *full* point.
   • Each section of your summary has its own assertion (or topic sentence) and sufficient support from the original.
   • Your summary parallels the original in tone and order.

- Your summary is both objective and complete. *Objective* means that none of your feelings about the text are reflected in statements or tone. *Complete* means that you have not left out any sections of the original.

6. Reread your summary to be certain that you used quotation marks around any key words or phrases that you have taken from the text. Most of the summary should be in your own words, but a particularly memorable phrase or expression will resist paraphrasing. You will want to include this memorable language in your summary within quotation marks. Be certain that the title of the work that you are summarizing is either in quotation marks (for short works) or italics (for longer works). See p. 502. Check for spelling, mechanical errors, and sentence correctness. Insert necessary transition words and phrases prior to your final writing.

7. Unlike an essay that you have written, a summary of someone else's work does not need a conclusion. End your summary with the author's final point.

## STUDENT EXAMPLE: A SUMMARY

The following is an example of one student's summary of "Three Ways of Meeting Oppression," an essay by Martin Luther King Jr. (p. 191).

Chris Thomas

Professor Blake

English 1A

3 February 2011

A Summary of "Three Ways of Meeting Oppression"

In an excerpt from his book *Stride Toward Freedom,* Dr. Martin Luther King Jr. shows that oppressed people deal with their oppression in three characteristic ways: with acquiescence, violence, or nonviolent resistance. King shows that only a mass movement committed to nonviolent resistance will bring a permanent peace and unite all people.

Although acquiescence—passive acceptance of an unjust system—is the easiest method of dealing with injustice, King insists that it is both morally wrong and the way of the coward. To acquiesce to unfair treatment is to passively condone the behavior of one's oppressors. King says, "Noncooperation with evil is as much a moral obligation as is cooperation with good. The oppressed must never allow the conscience of the oppressor to slumber" (192). King maintains that respect for Negroes and their children will never be won if they do not actively stand against the system.

However, King contends that violence is no solution because it never concerns itself with changing the belief system of oppressors. "In spite of temporary victories, violence never brings permanent peace" (192). Thus King insists that violence is impractical as well as immoral: "The old law of an eye for an eye leaves everybody blind" (192). King states that bitterness and corruption become the legacy of this destructive method that "annihilates" rather than "converts." Thus violence destroys any possibility of brotherhood.

King's principle of nonviolent resistance is his answer to how one must deal with oppression. It is confrontational without resorting to physical aggression. Nonviolent resistance avoids "the extremes and immoralities" of the other two methods while integrating the positive aspects of each. The nonviolent resister, like the person who acquiesces, agrees that violence is wrong, but like the violent resister, he believes that "evil must be resisted" (193). King insists that this is the method that oppressed people

Thomas 2

must use to oppose oppression: "Through nonviolent resistance the Negro will be able

to rise to the noble height of opposing the unjust system while loving the perpetrators

of the system" (193). Nonviolent resistance allows neither cowardice nor hatred.

King states that by using nonviolent resistance, the American Negro and other

oppressed people can "enlist all men of good will in [the] struggle for equality" (193).

He maintains that the struggle is not between people or races but is "a tension between

justice and injustice" (193). Only a mass movement of nonviolent resistance will unite

people in a community.

Thomas 3

Work Cited

King, Martin Luther, Jr. "Three Ways of Meeting Oppression." *Between Worlds: A Reader,*

*Rhetoric, and Handbook.* Ed. Susan Bachmann and Melinda Barth. 7th ed. New

York: Pearson Longman, 2012. 191–194. Print.

## Analyzing the Writer's Strategy

Chris begins his summary of the excerpt by identifying its source and the author's complete name. Notice that Chris has the title of the excerpt from King's book in quotation marks while the title of the book is in italics. (See pp. 561–562 for more information about indicating titles.) Although King does not state his thesis explicitly, Chris infers it from King's writing and then states it in the first paragraph. Chris's thesis and paragraphs reflect the three main points of King's essay, so Chris has organized his summary to parallel the original. This is a tremendous help to his readers, who immediately gain an overview of the entire work. The quoted material that he chooses from King's essay reflects what Chris finds most significant in language and specificity to support King's points. Although a different summary writer might choose other quotations to define and illustrate those points, the points and thesis would be nearly the same in each summary.

## Summary as Part of a Larger Assignment

Chris's assignment was to write a complete and objective summary of another writer's work. Other assignments might require a response or evaluation of the content in addition to the summary. A character analysis might have an introduction that summarizes the plot of the story in a few sentences. An even more abbreviated use of summary occurs when writers incorporate direct quotation into their essays and need to briefly summarize the context as they introduce the quotation. An argument essay might progress from a short summary of an experiment or survey. Even poetry analysis, which must go beyond summary to be effective, nevertheless, will employ limited summary of plot or context. The act of summarizing helps you see what you do and do not understand about a reading. Your effective summary then can convince your reader that you comprehend the original well enough to incorporate it into your own points.

---

 ### Final Tips for a Summary

- Begin with a statement of the author's complete thesis; include the author's full name.
- Focus each paragraph of your summary to reflect the sections of the original.
- Parallel the original in tone and order.
- Summarize all parts of the essay and be objective.
- Paraphrase most of the essay but incorporate memorable language in quotation marks.
- End with the author's final point; no conclusion is necessary in your summary.

---

# NARRATION

Everyone loves a good story, and most people enjoy telling one. The process of narration—telling a single story or several related ones—is often associated with myths, fairy tales, short stories, and novels, but writers of all types of essays use narrative strategies. The purpose of narration is to use firsthand experiences to engage or entertain, inform, or persuade an audience.

## When to Use Narration

Narration can be used to argue a point, define a concept, or reveal a truth. Writers in all disciplines have discovered the power of the narrative. Journalists, historians, sociologists, and essayists often "hook" their readers by opening with a personal anecdote or a human interest story to capture the reader and illustrate points. In fact, many writers use narration to persuade their audiences about a course of action.

Personal narratives can be powerful if they focus on a provocative insight and if details are carefully selected and shaped. Therefore narratives are more than mere diary entries because certain details may be omitted while others may be altered. Narratives may help the writer better understand the significance of an experience, and they help readers "see for themselves." Typically, narratives require no library research—our lives are rich with resources for this type of essay. But often writers may choose to supplement personal narration with research and outside sources to move beyond their own experience.

# Organizing and Developing a Narrative

Narratives often focus on an incident involving a conflict, whether it is between opposing people, values, or perceptions. The writer then dramatizes the incident so the reader can picture what happened and can hear what was said. Such incidents often involve some aspect of change—a contrast between "before" and "after"—even though the change may be internal (a change in awareness) rather than external or physical.

Narratives do not have to feature life-shattering incidents or have a somber tone. In fact, some superb narratives may be funny and have a humorous or ironic outcome. In "The Good Daughter," Carolyn Hwang tells about the day when she walked into the dry cleaners and the owner corrected Hwang's pronunciation of her own name. This ironic exchange prompts Hwang's self-reflective essay. Many of the best narratives involve profound changes that are not always obvious to others. In "The Color of Love" (p. 15), Danzy Senna dramatizes an intense argument with her grandmother whom she describes as "subtly racist, terribly elitist, and awfully funny" (18). Ironically, this angry encounter ultimately helps them better understand and appreciate each other.

## Brainstorming for a Subject

Writers usually need to dig deep to find those buried experiences that have changed their attitudes and views. To help generate ideas, you will find specific narrative assignments at the end of many essays, poems, and stories in the "Writing from the Text" sections in Part I. If your assignment is more general—to write about any significant moment or change in your life—it will help to consider these questions.

- What are my most vivid memories of
  - Kindergarten? First grade? Second? Third? Fourth? Fifth?
  - Middle school? High school? College?
  - Team sports?

- Learning to laugh at myself?
- Overcoming a challenge?
- Dealing with failure or illness?
- Living in another culture?
- Staying with friends or relatives?
- Getting a job or working?
- Making a costly mistake?
- When did I first
  - Try too hard to impress others?
  - Feel ashamed (or proud) of myself?
  - Stand up to my parents?
  - Realize teachers make mistakes?
  - Give in to peer pressure?
  - Pressure another to go against authority?
  - Wish I had different parents?
  - Wish someone would disappear from my life?
  - Want to change who I am?
- How did one incident show me
  - What living between two worlds really means?
  - How foolish we can be?
  - How it feels to be alone?
  - Why conformity isn't always best?
  - How stereotyping has affected me?
  - How different I am from my sister/brother/friend?
  - Why we have a certain law?
  - How it feels to live with a physical disability?
  - How little I know myself?

## Additional Prewriting

If you prefer a visual strategy, you might try clustering or mapping your ideas. One method is to write your topic—for example, "significant changes"—in a circle in the center of your page and then draw spokes outward from it. At the end of each spoke, write down a specific incident that triggered important changes in your life. Write the incident in a box and then use more spokes, radiating from the box, to specify all the changes that resulted. (For an illustration of clustering, see p. 283.)

After you have brainstormed about all possible changes, choose the incident that seems most vivid and worth narrating. Then use another sheet of paper and write about a specific change in a circle at the center and write down all the details that relate to it. After you have recorded all relevant details, you are ready to focus these thoughts and draft your paper.

# From Brainstorming to Drafting a Paper

In a narrative essay, the thesis is not always articulated in the essay itself because it can ruin the sense of surprise or discovery often associated with narratives. In fact, an explicit thesis can slow the momentum of the story or spoil the ending. Whether it is articulated or implied, however, a thesis is still essential in order to keep the writer focused and to ensure that the story has a point or insight to share.

***Beginning with a Working Thesis.*** For example, in the student essay that follows, Rebekah Hall-Nakanuma focuses on a time when her sister's illness prompted her own discoveries about family and self. When she began writing about her sister's unexpected illness, Rebekah probably did not begin with a thesis because the insight, focus, or assertion is seldom clear at first. Rebekah had only a topic, her sister's hospitalization. But after she clustered or listed some details, she probably wrote a *working* thesis—a preliminary assertion that could be changed and refined as the narrative took shape.

> **Working Thesis:** My sister's hospitalization took us all by surprise.

***Discovering the Real Thesis.*** Most writers aren't lucky enough to identify a thesis immediately. Often, particularly in a narrative, it takes considerable writing before the best thesis is discovered. Therefore writers typically continue sharpening their thesis throughout the writing process as they, too, discover the point of their story. As Rebekah narrated this experience, it developed as a genuine "between worlds" experience.

> **Discovered Thesis:** The pressure to be perfect can ultimately cause family members to bury or deny very real fears and needs.

Once the thesis becomes clear to the writer, the rough draft needs to be revised so that all the details relate to this new thesis. Notice, however, that the thesis statement does not need to be specified in the actual essay.

The following essay written by student Rebekah Hall-Naganuma describes a family's discovery that "crept in through the cracks" when least expected.

## STUDENT EXAMPLE: A NARRATIVE

Rebekah Hall-Naganuma

Professor Anderson

English 1A

20 January 2010

### Through the Cracks

It was late at night as I listened to my father's low rumble, his face buried in the phone receiver that was nearly resting on his chest. I sat on the edge of the coffee table, straining to understand the words he used. Dad was not easily disturbed. He took the unexpected in stride, so his now hushed tone scared me. I looked around, trying to clarify the moment. Craig's ears were plugged with headphones; his thoughts seemed inside the computer directly in front of him. Mom moved about the kitchen, her lips spread in the thin line that told me she was troubled. Normally voluble, her silence was foreboding.

Finally, Dad ended the conversation. I leaned forward, reaching for some kind of explanation. I watched his face, hoping for a revelation. His face was pale and closed. He didn't return my look but stood up and walked into the kitchen. I followed and stared at Mom's straightened back.

"Heather is in the hospital," Dad said, his voice raspy, as he told us about my older sister. I noticed his Adam's apple dip and heard him swallow. Mom turned around, her posture unnatural. She tilted her head in question. Dad continued, "She had a blackout and checked herself into the hospital. They're running some tests." He watched my mother's face as if to relay a secret message. She didn't get the message.

"What do you mean by 'blackout'?" she asked, with a look of confusion on her face.

"She ended up in Houston somehow and then couldn't remember how she got there." Dad began to sound matter-of-fact, as if this were secondhand local news.

We didn't say anything. I could imagine all sorts of scenarios—disease, drugs, brain tumor. I did not want to believe any of these. Mom began to bustle around the tidy kitchen, smiling and singing. Her cheerfulness, her way of pretending that everything was under control, irritated me.

But she had taught us well. We all had an uncanny ability to hide our flaws. Our unconscious goal was to be perfect. We were perfectionists stranded in the never-ending desert of dysfunctionalism. Owning up to the defects in our family would mean giving up on our ideals. It would mean sacrificing the commendation of others. People would always comment on how close we all were and how happy we always looked together. We had developed our skills well in fabricating happiness.

The next day one result was in; it turned out that Heather would be in a psychiatric ward for awhile. Her doctor didn't know for how long. "Craig . . . Rebekah . . . I don't want you talking about your sister's condition with anyone. I think this should stay in the family," Dad cautioned, after sitting us down one day. His eyes were serious, and his hands were folded in front of him, almost as if he were praying.

Mom had decided to fly to Texas, where Heather lived with her husband and children. She was going there, "to straighten things out," she said, as if it were merely a miscommunication that needed clarification. They had both told the church, where Dad pastored, that Heather needed help with her kids. I wanted to laugh aloud at them; at the same time, I wanted to pound my fists against them.

My parents had a way of being silent when matters required questions, confessions, and tears. I tried to understand it—they came from the era of church picnics, nice homes and nice cars. They dreamed of a nice family that would fit into their plans. They had us instead: Heather with her drug problems, Duane with his alcoholism, Kim with her bartending career, and me with my loud music and cigarettes. Craig was really the only one who went along with their scheme. My mother's camaraderie with him had always angered me as though he proved her point of motherhood.

The front that they kept up was like water just beginning to boil, but I knew it would someday. My dad had been the counselor and the mentor to the lost and the troubled; he had kept our image pure. We weren't allowed to listen to rock music at home, yet somehow mental illness had crept in through the cracks in our family. We could see the signs beneath the surface and behind closed doors.

Heather's problems set free a flood of dark emotion in our family. We had to admit that no matter how hard we tried, sadness and tragedy could not be avoided. It could not be covered up. Heather's honesty began to open up the doors that we had never been allowed to walk through. We gradually discovered our own humanity through the questions prompted by Heather's illness. The pictures of blood and gore that Heather drew in art therapy, the shock treatment, the crazy hairstyles that Heather flaunted at 35 years of age gave us a glimpse outside the wonderland of daisies and rainbows. And it let out the dogs that had been howling inside of me.

I hadn't been able to sleep well for weeks. I started having the most frightening nightmares. Images were in my subconscious that I never would have guessed were there: people attacking me, wars raging, fires out of control. Then the panic attacks began—the sleepless nights, the senseless roaming with friends at night. I needed someone to explain it all to me. I searched for someone to tell me what to do. Dad was never good at opening up his mind to these things. I knew what his answer would be: "It's because you're listening to that rock music" or "because you are so rebellious." And somehow, no matter how much I disliked my mother's incessant optimism, I had become like her. I could not explain my problems to anyone; I could not show my sorrows. Maybe that is part of the reason why I decided to tell Mom about my anxiety.

Her response surprised me. We were talking on the phone, and I started telling her about the nightmares and the craziness of my life. "Rebekah," she said slowly. "The time that I have been spending here with Heather has helped me to understand some things." She paused as if she were lifting a veil and not sure what she would find underneath. "I always thought that simply being a kind person would make everything okay. I thought I could be a good mother by just being thoughtful."

And she told me how, in this latest phase of her life, she had learned that people deserved more than just an occasional "please" and "thank you." People were filled with anger, sorrow, frustration, silliness, hate, exhaustion, deceit, and fear. And all of those emotions did not make a person weak, wrong, or mistaken. Those emotions made a person human. The anger turned the forgiveness into a beautiful act of love. The sorrow made the laughter more joyous. All of those years she had thought that her duty as a mother was to protect us from our dark sides, to wash away our tears with cake or promises or smiles. But instead of just letting us cry, she had made us stop.

After Heather's breakdown, we all began to talk—and cry—and to heal. It wasn't painless or automatic. But we found ways to express fears, and to listen, and to kid each other rather than to hold feelings in and stay silent. I could feel us turning onto a new road, one that would be bumpier and more cracked, but where the scenery would be fresh and often exhilarating at times.

## Analyzing the Writer's Strategy

When writers narrate a story, they try to recreate scenes—to show rather than tell—so that the reader can experience the moment as they did. Rather than simply telling us what they felt, they try to *show* us. For example, in the student model, Rebekah could have simply told us of her sister's "blackout" and subsequent hospitalization. Instead, she lets us observe and hear as her father discloses this unexpected news to her and her family:

> I watched his face, hoping for a revelation. His face was pale and closed. He didn't return my look but stood up and walked into the kitchen. I followed and stared at Mom's straightened back.

> "Heather is in the hospital," Dad said, his voice raspy, as he told us about my older sister. I noticed his Adam's apple dip and heard him swallow. Mom turned around, her posture unnatural. She tilted her head in question. Dad continued, "She had a blackout and checked herself into the hospital. They're running some tests." He watched my mother's face as if to relay a secret message. She didn't get the message.

> "What do you mean by 'blackout'?" she asked, with a look of confusion on her face.

Such a scene draws the reader in because each of us can sense the confusion and concern that the family members feel. The writer doesn't need to write, "My entire family was worried" because she has *shown* this more vividly than any claim she could make. Rebekah's use of dialogue, action, and vivid details (her father's "pale and closed" face and "raspy voice," her mother's "straightened back" and "unnatural" posture) makes us sense their anxiety.

*Selecting Telling Details.* The key to describing scenes and characters is to make sure each detail is revealing. It is not important to know the narrator's hair color or height, so such details would not be relevant or "telling." But the fact that she listens to rock music even though it wasn't allowed at home reveals that she is not willing to conform totally to the family's standards and rules. Such details help us to understand better the narrator's character as well as the dynamics within her family.

Similarly, the setting can be revealing. Although the time of day is not always important in a story, here it seems fitting that it is "late at night" when the father hears that Heather has been hospitalized and that it is during the night that the narrator roams senselessly with friends and also is awakened by panic attacks and nightmares. All of these nighttime activities underscore the inability to avoid or deny the darker reality of their lives.

 **PRACTICE WRITING ESSAYS WITH NARRATION**

Many of the topics in the "Writing from the Text" sections in Part I invite you to relate your own experience to the particular readings and to respond with a narrative. Here are some additional assignments:

1. Write an essay describing one home or school experience that taught you an unexpected lesson. Show us the incident as it happened, and describe what you learned and why it was unexpected.

2. Write an essay focusing on a time when you bullied or were bullied or embarrassed by someone else. Let us see what happened and what you discovered about yourself and others.

3. Write about an incident when you felt that your cultural or family background was incorrectly prejudged. Describe what happened so that your reader can understand the event and your response to it. Did you make any discoveries as a result of this experience?

---

 ## Final Tips for a Narrative

- Focus on a **provocative insight** so that your story reflects some real thought.

- Continue **sharpening your thesis** as your narrative develops. Remember, the thesis does not need to be explicitly stated in the essay.

- **Dramatize** a scene or two, using action and dialogue. Don't just tell the reader; show the scene.

- Include **telling details** that reveal relevant character traits. Have your characters interact with each other.

- **Rewrite sentences** and revise paragraphs to eliminate wordiness and generalizations.

- **Study other narratives** in the text, looking for techniques and strategies. Experiment!

# EVALUATIVE RESPONSE

Each day when you appraise or assess the value or quality of something—a movie, editorial, song lyric, college course—you are evaluating it. Informally, a friend may ask how you liked a particular film, and you offer your evaluation, without defining your criteria. Sometimes, however, you need to give a written evaluation. You may be asked to fill out an evaluation form on a course you are taking or on the instructor. You may be asked to write a movie or book review for a newspaper or a course. In some cases, you will need to evaluate something using specific criteria—established by you or someone else. In most cases, you will support your evaluation with examples from a text—a film, an essay, a book, or an editorial. The purpose of an evaluative response essay is to give your judgment of a work based on both your experience and a careful reading of the text.

## When to Write an Evaluative Response Essay

Throughout your college writing, you will be asked to respond to assigned readings and texts. You will be expected to summarize passages, analyze key points, incorporate direct quotations, and evaluate assertions and evidence. In English classes, such an assignment may involve your relating your own observations or experiences to the readings.

## Organizing and Developing an Evaluative Response Essay

To write an evaluative response essay, you need to present the author's thesis and key points, and then respond to them in terms of your own views, experiences, and judgments. Your essay must show that you have read the text closely, and it should include quotations from the text and a discussion of each quotation. Overall, your essay should both analyze and evaluate the text: What are the author's central points? Do you agree or disagree with them?

You may find that you agree with some of the author's points but not with others, and you will need to explain and support your stance on each. Most importantly, your thesis should articulate your main focus as well as your view of the author's key claims. For example, in the student essay that follows, Marin Kheng briefly summarizes Ellen Goodman's position in "Thanksgiving" (p. 3) but shows how she disagrees with it:

> While Goodman's essay is a suitable guide to how a family should function, it is essentially an idealistic portrayal of the family, and thus it ignores the harsher realities that are present in many American households.

Marin's essay will be a treatment of "the harsher realities" that she has observed in families she knows. She includes meaningful passages from the original text and uses her own observations to counter them. For example, Marin writes: "Goodman assures us that 'while the world may abandon us, the family promises . . . to protect us'" (5). She then uses this quotation as a departure point to describe a contrasting case of her friend Brahim, whose family deserted him. In your own essays, you will want to show how the original concurs—or doesn't concur—with your own experiences or observations. Whether you agree or disagree with the author, you will be evaluating the original and supporting your stance.

In any case, you will want to make sure that you have sufficiently understood and represented the text. It is not enough in an evaluative essay to simply give the title and author and then progress with your own story. Instead, you want to *use* the material that you have read. You might think of your response essay as a kind of conversation with the writer: You will be listening to, reflecting on, and evaluating the writer's many points and then inserting your own examples that parallel, extend, or counter the author's perspective.

## STUDENT EXAMPLE: AN EVALUATIVE RESPONSE ESSAY

To satisfy an assignment for her composition class, Marin Kheng was asked to respond to and evaluate one of the essays in *Between Worlds*. She chose Ellen Goodman's "Thanksgiving" (p. 3) because she found that her observations of friends' experiences countered the world that Goodman describes, and Marin thought that this contrast would create a compelling essay.

---

Kheng 1

Marin Kheng

Professor Barth

English 1A

11 March 2012

Thanksgiving Beyond the Cleaver Family

The boy sits alone in the darkness of the family room, his eyes wide and yearning,

hungry for the images that flash across his TV set. A family—mothers, fathers, siblings,

uncles, aunts, cousins, grandparents—all sit down at the dining table to share their

Thanksgiving dinner and a part of their lives. They are smiling, talking, laughing, at

times bickering, as cranberry sauce and slices of turkey meat are passed around from

---

person to person. The images play across the boy's face, inviting him to join in the warmth and the camaraderie before cruelly slipping away from his grasp and back into the dark black haven of the TV screen. The commercial has ended, and the boy is left alone in his family room with his 2-for-3-dollars TV dinner before him and the muffled sounds of screaming adult voices seeping through from his parents' bedroom. This is his Thanksgiving.

This is not, however, the Thanksgiving depicted in Ellen Goodman's essay, "Thanksgiving" (p. 3). According to Goodman, Thanksgiving is a time for individuals in all parts of the United States to reconvene with their families in remembrance of and appreciation for the warmth, love, and support that the family structure provides. Goodman also contends that Americans are constantly struggling between the freedom and loneliness that the world of the individual brings and the selflessness and support that the world of the family brings. They cannot deny themselves either world because both the family and the individual are intrinsically connected and dependent upon each other. While Goodman's essay is a suitable guide to how a family should function, it is essentially an idealistic portrayal of the family, and thus it ignores the harsher realities that are present in many American households. The truth is that for many Americans like the boy, the workings of the ideal family described in Goodman's essay are in sharp contrast with what actually goes on in their own families.

Goodman believes that a contradiction exists in being "raised in families . . . to be individuals" (4) because individualism must arise from a structure promoting togetherness. For my friend Nicole, there is no dilemma in being an individual within a family because there is no threat of the loss of individualism in her family. With a father who spends the little spare time he has at the neighborhood bar and a negligent mother who constantly eats to escape her marital problems, Nicole has had to be independent for most of her life, doing for herself the things most children have taken for granted. She has had to work parttime jobs to pay for basic expenses such as food and clothing, walk down to the free clinic by herself when she is ill, and spend family-oriented holidays by herself or with friends. For Nicole there will not be "a ritual of belonging" around a dining table (3). To Nicole, the idea of togetherness and unity do not align themselves with family. Instead, the only words that correspond with family are independence, maturity, and adult responsibilities forced onto a girl far from grown up.

Other families, like that of my cousin Jana's, do not force their children to raise themselves, but instead require them to earn the privilege of being accepted by the family. Contrary to Goodman's assertion that "we don't have to achieve to be accepted by our families. We just have to be" (4), Jana has to be everything that her parents desire in order to be given praise and affection, and more importantly to Jana, to stop the criticism inflicted on her by her parents. The pressure is increased when her older sister Heny, who at 21 is getting her Ph.D. in chemistry at Harvard University, comes to visit. This demand for perfection placed on Jana has led her to become an AP student with a 4.2 GPA, co-captain of the varsity swimming team and a star tennis player, president of various campus clubs, treasurer for her student council, an intern at a prestigious law firm, and a manic-depressive neurotic. In September, two weeks after the start of her senior year, she suffered a nervous breakdown and attempted suicide. When she survived, her parents stood beside her hospital bed and told her, "We are very disappointed in you. Heny would never have done something like this." While Goodman asserts that the family is "not the place where people ruthlessly compete with each other," Jana's parents clearly cultivate sibling rivalry and don't seem to understand that the family is "not for the survival of the fittest but for the weakest" (5). Although Jana's parents have given her every material comfort a teen could desire, the demands they make in return for these comforts threaten her physical, mental, and emotional well-being. But they have never given her the one thing she needs most, which ironically no amount of money could ever buy. They have never given her their acceptance.

Complete abandonment, however, is perhaps the worst thing parents can do to one of their own. Goodman assures us that "while the world may abandon us, the family promises . . . to protect us" (5). In the case of my friend Brahim, his family left one day and never came back. A straight-A student who grew up in a neighborhood infamous for its drugs and its hookers, he had been the filial son, patiently dragging his drunken brother up the stairs to their motel room, selling cheap marijuana to pay the rent when his father had spent a month's wages on a night at the Bicycle Club Casino,

Kheng 4

and assuring his teachers his black eye and the welts on his arm were caused in a fist fight with another boy when, in fact, they were caused by his own mother. Yet, despite all his efforts at holding his family together, he was abandoned in the end. At 13, he was homeless on the streets of North Hollywood with pocket change and a trash bag full of clothes. The ideal of a family that supports and protects its members and measures "their common legacy . . . the children" (4) means nothing to him because he realized at that young age the ridiculousness and cruelty of this ideal.

If Nicole, Jana, Brahim, the boy eating his TV dinner alone, or any of the countless number of Americans with dysfunctional families were to read "Thanksgiving," they would not be able to understand the ideals of family that Goodman espouses or the people she gathers around her dining table. It is not that they do not know what a family should be like, or that they do not want a family, but for them Goodman's family belongs in another world, a world that no amount of wishing and desiring could ever realize. Their eyes will linger at André Malraux's statement that "Without a family, man, alone in the world, trembles with the cold" (Goodman 4.). Some may become angry, some may snort in lonely contempt, or some may simply be perplexed, because the sad irony in their reality is that although they have families, they, too, are trembling alone in the cold.

Kheng 5

Work Cited

Goodman, Ellen. "Thanksgiving." *Between Worlds: A Reader, Rhetoric, and Handbook.* Ed. Susan Bachmann and Melinda Barth. 7th ed. New York: Pearson Longman, 2012. pp. 3–5. Print.

# Analyzing the Writer's Strategy

Marin's purpose is to show that while Goodman's essay is a suitable guide to how a family should function, it is an idealistic portrayal of the family, and thus ignores the harsher realities of many American households.

In her opening, her strategy is to use narration to dramatize an anonymous character who could be anyone her reader might know.

Marin's thesis is clear. She states that "the truth is that for many Americans like the boy, the workings of the ideal family described in Goodman's essay are in sharp contrast with what actually goes on in their own families." She builds her support by incorporating direct quotations, and she contrasts these with her own experiences. For example, Marin writes: "Goodman assures us that "while the world may abandon us, the family promises . . . to protect us." She then shows how her friend Brahim's family deserted, rather than protected, him. In Marin's conclusion, she returns to the notion that "Goodman's family belongs in another world, a world that no amount of wishing and desiring could ever bring" to the friends she describes.

Notice that Marin puts quotation marks around Goodman's essay title when she first refers to it in paragraph 2, and then in her conclusion, when she returns to Goodman's title "Thanksgiving." Remember that titles of essays, short stories, and poems are indicated by quotation marks. See p. 561 for more information on titles.

In your own evaluative essays, you will assess the original essay in light of your own views and experiences. You may find that you agree with some points that the author makes but not with all of them. Regardless of your stance, you need to examine specific quotations from the original work.

## PRACTICE WRITING AN EVALUATIVE RESPONSE ESSAY

1. Write an evaluative response to "Greed in the Name of Green" (p. 246) that takes a stand on the author's claim that consuming "green" products is motivated by greed. After fully explaining Hesse's position, use examples from your own or from your friends' experiences of "going green" to support or oppose her thesis.

2. After reading "What the Cellphone Industry Won't Tell You" (p. 210), write an evaluative response of Myron Levin's concern about the dangers of cellphone use while driving.

3. Evaluate and respond to the ideas in "The Good Daughter" (p. 8) in terms of your parents' expectations and your responses to them.

4. Respond to and evaluate any of the essays in *Between Worlds*, perhaps one that has not been discussed in class.

5. After viewing the film *Crash* and reading the reviews (pp. 430–435), write an evaluative response of one of the following essays: "Don't Let Stereotypes Warp Your Judgments" (p. 424), "Black Men and Public Space" (p. 164), "Who Shot Johnny?" (p. 23), or "Bigotry as the Outer Side of Inner Angst" (p. 138). Focus your essay on key quotations from the essay and use examples from the film *Crash* to illustrate and support your claims about the author's main points.

**Final Tips for an Evaluative Response Essay**

- **Read carefully** the essay you intend to evaluate, underlining or recording in a journal any language that you find interesting.
- Determine whether you **agree with or oppose** the author's main point and shape this view into your thesis.
- Find good material in the text, especially **choice language**, as well as examples from your own experience to support your position.
- **Reread the original essay** after you have written your evaluative response to see whether there is additional material you should pull into your paper.
- Refine your conclusion to insure that you have **restated your thesis in different words** and that your conclusion offers important insights.

# Definition

Whether your entire essay is a definition or you have incorporated a definition into your essay to clarify a term or concept for your reader, explaining what a term means is an integral part of writing. Knowing your intended audience and purpose in writing will help you determine which words you need to define.

# When to Use Definition

In a paper for a psychology class, for example, you would not need to define terms generally used in that field. But when you write for a general reader and use language unfamiliar to most people—a technical or foreign term, or a word peculiar to an academic discipline—you will need to define the term so your reader can understand it. Even if you are using a familiar word, you need to explain its meaning if you or an author you are quoting use it in a unique way.

Sometimes a brief definition is all that you need. In that case, a few words of clarification, or even a synonym, may be incorporated into your text quite easily:

*Los Vendidos,* or "The Sellouts," is the Spanish-language title of Luis Valdez's play (124).

Achondroplasia—a type of dwarfism—may affect overall bone structure and cause arms and legs to be disproportionately smaller than the rest of the body.

Eating disorders include "bingeing, chronic dieting, and 'aerobic nervosa,' the excessive use of exercise to remain one's body ideal" (Erens 186).

As these examples show, incorporating definition into your text is unobtrusive and superior to writing a separate sentence to define the term.

## Organizing and Developing a Definition Essay

When an assignment calls for an extended definition of a concept or term, the following methods may be used alone or in combination:

- *Dictionary definition:* Including a formal definition of a word from a dictionary before developing your point. Even common words may require you to take this route so that you and your reader have the same sphere of reference.

- *Expert's definition:* Presenting an expert's definition of a term to show that you have sound support for your understanding of a word.

- *Comparison-contrast:* Contrasting your definition of a word with the way it is typically used or with the actual dictionary definition of the term. If the term is unfamiliar, you might show how it is similar to another concept.

- *Description:* Defining a term by describing its characteristics: size, shape, texture, color, noise, and other telling traits.

- *Exemplification:* Giving examples and illustrations of a concept to enable your reader to understand it better. Because such examples are rather specific, they should only help supplement a definition rather than be used by themselves.

- *Negation:* Explaining what something is *not* in order to help limit the definition and eliminate misconceptions.

## The Purpose of Defining

You may be asked to write a "definition essay"—a paper that develops with the primary intention of increasing the reader's understanding of a term—in a psychology, sociology, history, philosophy, or English course. Usually, however, your goal will be something else. You may be attempting to convince your reader to consider the explained term in a positive light, or to compare it—even to prefer it—to something else. Sometimes the persuasive aspect of the essay relies on the reader's willingness to reconsider the definition of a word, as occurs in the next essay.

EXAMPLE: AN ESSAY BASED ON DEFINITION

The following essay was written by Jon Winokur, a freelance writer and author of twenty reference books and anthologies, including *Zen to Go* (1988), *True Confessions* (1992), *The Rich Are Different* (1996), and *How to Win at Golf Without Actually Playing Well* (2000). In "You Call That Irony?," published in the *Los Angeles Times* in 2007, Winokur defines irony and shows how this word is often incorrectly used.

 **You Call That Irony?**

## *Jon Winokur*

1   When it was revealed in 2003 that William J. Bennett, author of "The Book of Virtues," had a secret gambling habit, more than one commentator termed it a delicious irony, and it was indeed a pleasure to see a sanctimonious scold get his comeuppance. But it wasn't irony, just hypocrisy.

2   It was ironic when, on "The Daily Show," Jon Stewart commended Bennett for his indignation, and for "standing up to the William Bennetts of the world."

3   Here's another example of irony: the 1959 episode of "The Twilight Zone" titled "Time Enough at Last," in which Burgess Meredith plays Henry Bemis, a bookish bank teller with thick glasses and an insatiable appetite for reading. One day, knocked unconscious by a giant explosion, he awakens to find that he's the last man on Earth.

4   Wandering the desolate city, overwhelmed with loneliness, he is about to kill himself when he notices the ruins of . . . a library! Cut to: stacks of books piled high on the library's steps and Henry, giddy with joy. But as he settles down on the curb with the first book, his glasses fall off and shatter on the ground, trapping him forever in a blurry world.

5   Now that's irony.

6   Irony is one of the most misused words in the English language. Much of the confusion comes from the existence of several distinct forms of irony. Verbal irony is the act of saying one thing but meaning the opposite with the intent of being understood as meaning the opposite, as in, "Nice weather we're having" on a rainy day.

7   Cosmic irony involves quirks of fate, as when a UPS driver on his way to deliver parts to a hospital has a serious accident, is taken to the same hospital by ambulance, but the hospital can't perform necessary tests because one of its machines is down and the parts to fix it are in the driver's wrecked van.

8  Socratic irony is a strategy for refuting dogma. In the Platonic dialogues, Socrates assumes the role of the eiron, a sly dissembler who feigns naivete by asking seemingly foolish questions that gradually hang his opponents by their own admissions. A modern practitioner is Sacha Baron Cohen, whose characters Borat and Ali G expose pomposity by pretending to be stupid.

9  Irony is about the interplay of opposites, not the random proximity of events. It's ironic that Beethoven was deaf, but merely coincidental that Brad Pitt tore his Achilles tendon while playing Achilles in Troy. People miss the distinction and say "ironic" when they mean "coincidental," an abuse encouraged by Alanis Morissette's 1996 hit single, "Ironic," in which situations purporting to be ironic are merely annoying ("a traffic jam when you're already late, a no-smoking sign on your cigarette break").

10  It is ironic that "Ironic" is an unironic song about irony. Is that perfectly clear?

11  In case you're confused, here are some more examples of irony:

12  • Brewing heir Adolph Coors III was allergic to beer.

13  • County supervisors in Pima County, Ariz., held a closed meeting to discuss Arizona's open meeting law.

14  • U.S. Border Patrol uniforms are manufactured in Mexico.

15  • When the Berlin Wall came down in 1989, so many visitors were taking souvenir pieces that a protective fence was installed, so that, yes, the Berlin Wall was guarded by a wall.

16  • Zimbabwean President Robert Mugabe's 2005 state of the nation address, in which he promised to remedy his country's chronic electricity shortages, was blacked out by a power failure.

17  • A 17-year-old Amish boy was electrocuted by a downed power line that became tangled in the wheels of his horse-drawn buggy.

18  • The "Marlboro Man" died of lung cancer.

19  • A 2001 Father's Day tribute on ESPN featured "How Sweet It Is (to be Loved by You)," sung by Marvin Gaye, who was shot and killed by his father in 1984.

20  • Entries for the Florida Press Club's 2005 Excellence in Journalism Award for hurricane coverage were lost in Hurricane Katrina.

## Analyzing the Writer's Strategy

The purpose of this essay is to convince readers that there is a wide misuse of the word "irony" and that speakers and writers need to be more definitive in their word choice. Winokur uses the following methods to explain "irony":

• *Dictionary Definition:* Winokur doesn't resort to the predictable "according to Webster's dictionary . . ." to define "irony." But he does provide distinct definitions of two different types of irony: verbal irony—the act of saying one thing but intentionally meaning the opposite—and cosmic irony—the quirks of fate that afflict all human beings when the opposite of what is deserved or expected occurs. Further, he informs his reader that the word "irony" is derived from the Platonic dialogues of Socrates in which he "assumes the role of the *eiron,* a sly dissembler who feigns naivete by asking seemingly foolish questions that gradually hang his opponents by their own admissions" (400). Winokur needs to clarify the dictionary meanings of "irony" in order to support his view of its misuse.

- *Comparison-contrast:* Winokur shows what irony is and contrasts it with what irony is not: "Irony is about the interplay of opposites, not the random proximity of events" (400). The author notes that it is ironic that the composer Beethoven was deaf because he could not hear his own musical compositions, but it is merely a coincidence, or random proximity of events, that Brad Pitt tore his Achilles tendon while playing the role of Achilles.

- *Description:* In order to show what irony is, Winokur describes in great detail a *Twilight Zone* plot in which a bank teller with "an insatiable appetite for reading" is rendered unconscious by an explosion. He awakes to discover that he is alone on earth and is lonely and depressed until he discovers a pile of books at a library. Just as he is about to start reading, his glasses fall off and shatter, leaving him "forever in a blurry world" (399). Winokur's description supports his perception that this episode is ironic. The episode's title, "Time Enough At Last" is itself ironic.

- *Exemplification:* Even though this is a short essay, Winokur packs it with 14 specific illustrations of irony. Some of our favorite examples include: "Brewing heir Adolph Coors III was allergic to beer"; "County supervisors in Pima County, Ariz., held a closed meeting to discuss Arizona's open meeting law"; "The 'Marlboro Man' died of lung cancer" (400). After studying each example, the reader gets a clearer sense of this often-misused term. Although lists are typically avoided in essays, Winokur's bullets here are effective because they highlight his thorough exemplification.

- *Negation:* Because Winokur believes that the word "irony" is so often misused, he opens his essay with an example of a situation that many would claim is ironic. However, he insists that it isn't. Winokur contends that William Bennett's authorship of *The Book of Virtues*—despite Bennett's own gambling addiction—is an example of hypocrisy, not irony. Further, Winokur claims that the examples from Alanis Morissette's song "Ironic" are wrong: "a traffic jam when you're already late, a no-smoking sign on your cigarette break" are annoyances, not illustrations of irony. Ultimately, readers who have too often exclaimed, "That's ironic!" may rethink their word choice because of Winokur's use of negative illustrations.

**PRACTICE WRITING DEFINITION ESSAYS**

1. In your college papers, you will frequently use short definitions to clarify terms. In small groups, armed with dictionaries, practice writing one-sentence definitions of the following terms:

   a. satire               c. boyfriend
   b. environmentalist     d. empathy

2. Although you will use definition most often as a component of your papers, it is useful to practice writing short definition essays. In small groups, collaborate with your classmates to write a short essay that defines one of the following:

   a. green movement       d. unconditional love
   b. "between worlds"      e. disabled
   c. a cheap date

---

✔ **Final Tips for a Definition Essay**

- Is your **purpose** for defining to inform? To analyze? To persuade?
- Identify the needs of your audience; **determine which words** your readers cannot be expected to know or may misunderstand.
- Whenever possible, incorporate into your text the **necessary clarification** of a term. Avoid writing a separate sentence to define the term.
- Remember that **definitions can also be developed** by comparing and contrasting that word with other terms, by describing the characteristics of a term, by presenting examples, and by illustrating what the term is not.

---

# Cause and Effect

Throughout your life you have been made aware of the consequences of your behavior: not getting your allowance because you didn't keep your room clean; winning a class election because you ran a vigorous campaign; getting a C on an exam because you didn't review all of the material. In all of these cases, a particular behavior seems to *cause* or result in a certain *effect*. In the case of the denied allowance, for example, your parents may have identified the cause: not keeping your room clean.

Causes are not always so easy to identify, however, for there may be a number of indirect causes of an action or inaction. For example, you may have won an election because of your reputation as a leader, your popularity, your opponent's inadequacies, your vigorous campaign, or even a cause that you may not have known about or been able to control. Effects usually are more evident: homeless families, few jobs for college graduates, small businesses failing, and houses remaining on the market for years are all obvious effects of a recession. What has caused the recession typically is more difficult to discern, but good critical thinking involves speculating about possible causes and their effects.

## When to Use Cause-and-Effect Development

Cause-and-effect development can be used in diverse writing situations. For example, you would use this strategy to trace the reasons for a historical event, such as the causes and results of the American entry into World War II. You perceive cause-and-effect relationships when you analyze and write about broad social problems (like runaway teens) or more personal concerns (such as why you and your siblings are risk takers). All of these thinking and writing tasks invite you to examine the apparent effects and to question what has caused them. This questioning inevitably involves speculation about causes rather than absolute answers, but this speculation can lead to fruitful analysis and provocative papers.

## Organizing and Developing a Cause-and-Effect Essay

To get started, you may want to brainstorm and let all of your hunches emerge. In fact, a lively prewriting session is the key to a lively cause-and-effect paper. To produce a paper that goes beyond predictable or obvious discussion, take time to think about diverse causes for an effect you have observed and to contemplate the most dramatic effects of causes that you perceive.

You may find that you want to focus more on the causes or on the effects rather than trying to spend equal time on both. The wording of your thesis will be critical to forecast your emphasis and clarify your stance to your reader. For example, the following essay focuses on the effects of the writer's experience as a soldier in an unpopular war. Notice how he analyzes his feelings of shame, anger, envy, and pain—all effects of a single cause, serving in the Marines during the Vietnam War.

EXAMPLE: A CAUSE-AND-EFFECT ESSAY

Robert McKelvey's goal in "I Confess Some Envy" is to present an analysis of a social issue. McKelvey, a Bronze Star recipient for his service in Vietnam and now a child psychiatrist and professor at Baylor, analyzes the causes of the envy he felt while watching the Desert Storm troops receive public acclaim. He cites the reasons that his generation of soldiers failed to gain support and the effects of this failure on him and his peers. Veterans who have returned more recently from Afghanistan or Iraq might compare their experiences with McKelvey's. His essay first appeared in the *Los Angeles Times* on June 16, 1991, shortly after the return of American troops from the Persian Gulf.

#  I Confess Some Envy
## *Robert McKelvey*

1   Every year on the Marine Corps' birthday, the commandant sends a message to all Marine units worldwide commemorating the event. On November 10, 1969, I was stationed with the 11th Marine Regiment northwest of Da Nang in Vietnam. It was my task to read the commandant's message to the Marines of our unit.

2   One sentence, in particular, caught my attention: "Here's to our wives and loved ones supporting us at home." Ironically, that week my wife had joined tens of thousands of others marching on the nation's capital to protest U.S. involvement in Vietnam.

3   It was a divisive, unhappy time. Few people believed the war could be won or that we had any right to interfere in Vietnam's internal affairs. However, for those of us "in country," there was a more pressing issue. Our lives were on the line. Even though our family and friends meant us no harm by protesting our efforts, and probably believed they were speeding our return, their actions had a demoralizing effect.

4   Couldn't they at least wait until we were safely home before expressing their distaste for what we were doing? But by then, the military had become scapegoats for the nation's loathing of its war, a war where draft dodgers were cast as heroes and soldiers as villains.

5   Watching the Desert Storm victory parades on television, I was struck by the contrast between this grand and glorious homecoming and the sad, silent and shameful return of so many of us 20-odd years ago. Disembarking from a troop ship in Long Beach, my contingent of Marines was greeted at the pier by a general and a brass band. There were no family, friends, well-wishers, representatives of the Veterans of Foreign Wars, or children waving American flags.

6      We were bused to Camp Pendleton, quickly processed and sent our separate ways. After a two-week wait for my orders to be cut, during which time I spent most days at the San Diego Zoo, I was discharged from active duty. I packed up and flew home to begin premedical studies.

7      As the plane landed in Detroit, the on-board classical music channel happened to be playing Charles Ives's "America." The piece's ironic, teasing variations on the theme, "My Country 'Tis of Thee," seemed a fitting end to my military service.

8      My wife met me at the airport and drove me directly to Ann Arbor for a job interview. We were candidates for a job as house parents for the Religious Society of Friends (Quakers) International Co-op. Face-to-face with these sincere, fervent pacifists, I felt almost ashamed of the uniform I was still wearing with its ribbons and insignia.

9      I recalled stories of comrades who had been spat upon in airports and called "baby killers." The Friends, however, were exceptionally gentle and kind. They, at least, seemed able to see beyond the symbols of the war they hated to the individual human being beneath the paraphernalia. Much to my surprise, we got the job.

10      I took off my uniform that day, put it away and tried to resume the camouflage of student life. I seldom spoke of my service in Vietnam. It was somehow not a topic for polite conversation, and when it did come up the discussion seemed always to become angry and polarized.

11      Like many other Vietnam veterans, I began to feel as if I had done something terribly wrong in serving my country in Vietnam, and that I had better try to hush it up. I joined no veterans' organizations and, on those rare times when I encountered men who had served with me in Vietnam, I felt embarrassed and eager to get away. We never made plans to get together and reminisce. The past was buried deep within us, and that is where we wanted it to stay.

12      The feelings aroused in me by the sight of our victorious troops marching across the television screen are mixed and unsettling. There is pride, of course, at their stunning achievement. Certainly they deserve their victory parade. But there is also envy. Were we so much different from them?

13      Soldiers do not choose the wars they fight. Theirs happened to be short and sweet, ours long and bitter. Yet we were all young men and women doing what our country had asked us. Seeing my fellow Vietnam veterans marching with the Desert Storm troops, watching them try, at last, to be recognized and applauded for their now-distant sacrifices, is poignant and sad.

14      We have come out of hiding in recent years as the war's pain has receded. It has become almost fashionable to be a veteran and sport one's jungle fatigues. Still, a sense of hurt lingers and, with it, a touch of anger. Anger that the country we loved, and continue to love, could use us, abuse us, discard

and then try to forget us, as if we were the authors of her misery rather than her loyal sons and daughters. It was our curious, sad fate to be blamed for the war we had not chosen to fight, when in reality we were among its victims.

## Analyzing the Writer's Strategy

McKelvey's purpose is to express his pain and sorrow as he reviews his history as a veteran of the Vietnam War. He analyzes the causes of his personal frustrations and the effects of American response to that war in contrast to the response to the Persian Gulf War twenty years later.

McKelvey's strategy is to dramatize moments in his personal history and to lead his reader to discover the irony implicit in these events. For example, while he was reading to his unit the commandant's message applauding the support of "wives and loved ones" at home, his own wife had joined a massive demonstration in Washington protesting U.S. involvement in Vietnam. McKelvey contrasts the "grand and glorious homecoming" of the Desert Storm troops with his own "sad, silent and shameful return." He shows himself "almost ashamed" of his uniform with its ribbons and insignia when he applied to be a house parent for the Quakers. He notes that "soldiers do not choose the wars they fight," and yet the Desert Storm troops were celebrated as heroes while he and his fellow vets from Vietnam were called "baby killers" and spat upon when they returned.

Through irony, McKelvey helps his reader understand the effects of the anti-Vietnam War sentiment on one individual who articulates for many suffering but silent soldiers, also the "victims" of that war. He avoids using the terms "cause" and "effect" or the predictable "cause and effect" paragraph structure, favoring instead subtle juxtaposition of causes and their profound effects.

 ## PRACTICE WRITING ESSAYS ABOUT CAUSES AND EFFECTS

Write an essay that focuses on the causes or effects of one of the following:

1. Your having revealed an important truth about yourself to a member of your family

2. Your moving away from home

3. Your family combining cultural customs for a holiday occasion

4. Your sense of being caught living between two worlds, as described by Marcus Mabry (p. 99), Caroline Hwang (p. 8), and Judith Ortiz Cofer (p. 118)

5. Your discovery that you are unwillingly intimidating others, as Brent Staples describes (p. 164)

6. Your feeling of being manipulated by the media's depiction of ideal female body shapes as discussed by Rachel Krell (p. 334).

**Final Tips for Cause-and-Effect Development**

- **Brainstorm** to come up with every possible cause or effect for your particular topic.

- Review your list of causes and effects to **determine whether each point is reasonable** and supportable. Eliminate any that are illogical or for which you lack data. Do research if additional evidence is needed.

- Apply the **"So what?" strategy** (see p. 303). Will this cause-and-effect analysis make worthwhile reading?

- Group ideas that belong together and **order your evidence** to conclude with your most emphatic and well-developed support.

- **Develop your explanations** fully so that your reader doesn't need to guess your assumptions.

## COMPARISON AND CONTRAST

Whether you are examining your own experiences or responding to texts, you will inevitably rely on comparison and contrast thinking. To realize how two people, places, works of art, films, economic plans, laboratory procedures, or aspects of literature—or anything else—may be alike or different is to perceive important distinctions between them.

While we may start an analysis process believing that two subjects are remarkably different (how they *contrast*), after thoughtful scrutiny we may see important similarities between them. Conversely, although we may have detected clear similarities in two subjects (how they *compare*), the complete analysis may reveal surprising differences. Therefore, while comparison implies similarity and contrast implies difference, these two thinking processes work together to enhance perception.

## When to Use Comparison-Contrast Development

Subtle comparison-contrast cues are embedded in writing assignments, both in-class exams and out-of-class papers. For example, an economics instructor may ask for a study of prewar and postwar inflation; a philosophy instructor may ask for examples showing how one philosophical system departs from another; a psychology instructor may require an explanation of how two different psychologists interpret dreams; or a literature instructor may assign an analysis of how a character changes within a certain novel.

The prevalence of such assignments in all disciplines underscores the importance of comparison and contrast in many experiences and learning situations. Assignments that ask writers to explain the unfamiliar, evaluate certain choices, analyze how someone or something has changed, establish distinction, discover similarities, and propose a compromise all require some degree of comparison and contrast.

For example, a writer may initially believe that women and men have quite different complaints about their lives. Women feel that they need to be attractive; they feel limited in their choice of career and restricted by the career heights and pay they may attain; and they feel obligated to be domestic (good mothers, cooks, and housekeepers). Men feel they need to be successful at work to be attractive to women; they feel burdened to select high-status, high-paying jobs regardless of their real interests; and they must work continuously. Many feel precluded from domestic life—cut off from their children and home life.

At first, the complaints of each gender appear to be quite different. But the writer examining these complaints may perceive that they have something in common: that women *and* men suffer from "an invisible curriculum," a series of social expectations that deprive human beings of choice. A thesis for this study might look like this:

**Thesis:** Although women and men seem to have different problems, both genders feel hampered by an "invisible curriculum" that affects their self-esteem and limits their choices at work and in their families.

## Organizing and Developing a Comparison-Contrast Essay

There are two basic methods for organizing data to compare or contrast. In the *block* method, the writer would organize the material for a study of conflicts affecting gender like this:

BLOCK 1. WOMEN

1. Need to feel attractive to be successful

2. Feel limited in workplace choices, level, pay

3. Feel obligated to be mothers, domestic successes

BLOCK 2. MEN

1. Need to feel successful at work to feel attractive

2. Feel burdened to achieve high position, work continuously

3. Feel cut off from children and domestic choices

In the *point-by-point* method, the writer would organize the material like this:

POINT 1. FACTORS THAT GOVERN SELF-ESTEEM

a. Women need to feel attractive

b. Men need to feel successful at work

POINT 2. RELATIONSHIP TO WORK

a. Women feel restricted in choice, level, pay

b. Men feel burdened to achieve high position, work continuously

## Which Method to Use: Block or Point-by-Point?

Although the block method may seem easier, it tends to allow the writer to ramble vaguely about each subject without concentrating on specific points of comparison or contrast. The resulting essay may resemble two separate discussions that could be cut apart with scissors. The advantage of the point-by-point method is that it keeps the writer focused on the relationship between both works and on the similarities or differences between them. Writers are less likely to digress and wander off topic in a point-by-point arrangement and are more likely to emphasize the points that they are making. Moreover, the summary statement that appears at the end of each paragraph in point-by-point organization tends to unify the essay more emphatically than the summary statement at the end of each block.

EXAMPLE: A COMPARISON-CONTRAST ESSAY

Writers do not always announce their intention to compare and contrast in their thesis, even though comparison and contrast elements predominate in the development of their thinking and writing. The following essay, published in the *Los Angeles Times* on June 16, 1999, was written by Alex Garcia, a staff photographer who lived in Cuba for several months. Although Garcia does not articulate his contrast plan in a thesis, from the first sentence of his essay he makes clear his intention to contrast the worlds of the United States and Cuba.

##  Reality Check
### *Alex Garcia*

1     It appears Uncle Sam and El Comandante, while not quite seeing eye to eye, are exchanging curious glances. On baseball fields, in concert halls and in schoolyards, the citizens of Cuba and the United States have recently been

getting a glimpse of cultures that have been closed to one another for four decades. The United States says it hopes these exchanges will make it easier to export cultural values to Fidel Castro's Cuba. But it's worth underscoring that such exchanges go both ways.

2    I recently spent several months in Havana and the Cuban countryside as part of a language and cultural program hosted by San Francisco–based Global Exchange, one of the few organizations in the United States that legally sponsors trips to the island. As someone of Cuban origin, I stepped into such waters cautiously.

3    I have a cousin now living in the United States who risked his life swimming to the naval base at Guantánamo Bay to escape what he considers a prison. I also have a cousin who became president of his neighborhood block committee in Havana out of loyalty to what he believes is a worker's paradise. Both have made tremendous sacrifices to stay true to the values they hold dear. That I would find some of my values in conflict with those I found in Cuba came as no surprise. But I was uncomfortable with how even my most basic assumptions would be challenged.

4    For example, as one of our core values, U.S. citizens presume the inherent goodness of individualism, of being ruggedly independent, John Wayne-style. So it came as a surprise when one of my tutors said, "I would never want to think of myself as independent." "Me neither," another said coldly.

5    Come again? As a program participant, I was paired with University of Havana students who served as language tutors and cultural assistants. We had been talking about their future hopes, and I had asked what they were going to do once they were independent.

6    "Being independent means being selfish, cold, unwilling to help other people," my tutor told me. After years of struggling to be independent myself, I was at first uneasy with that idea. But I recalled the communal spirit of the many Cubans I met: the ubiquitous hitchhikers getting free rides from passing motorists; neighbors borrowing the car and the telephone as if they were family; hotel workers trading shifts and bicycles in a spirit of compañerismo, or camaraderie.

7    And there was the pedestrian who jumped into my cab to mooch a ride, defending his appropriation of my fare by saying to the driver, "Hey we're Cuban, aren't we?" I can't imagine hitchhiking in downtown Los Angeles, or even calling my neighbor "cousin," much less sharing with him a roll of toilet paper—a commodity rationed in Cuba. The U.S. model encourages people to value individual effort over shared sacrifice. But to many Cubans, it can seem a lonely path to take.

8    Expressing the values I believe the United States stands for was not simple either, in large part because Cuban television shows the flip side of them,

through news and entertainment. For instance, if I cite civil liberties, the state-run television network Cubavision will air a Hollywood movie about the Ku Klux Klan, hate crimes or out-of-control gangbangers in Los Angeles. If I advocate multi-party democracy, a Cubavision documentary will point to a two-party system in the United States tainted by special-interest money and embarrassed by a 30 percent voter turnout. If I stress the benefits of upward mobility, the government-controlled national newspaper Granma will remark that the majority of people who are born in poverty in the United States die in poverty.

9    Fair or not, the contrarian views fostered in the Cuban media take away the shine with which we like to present ourselves.

10   Wastefulness isn't exactly one of my core values, but it certainly revealed itself as a personal trait while I was in Cuba. Given the choice between buying a new backpack, or repairing an old one by hand—sewing it with used dental floss—which do you think I chose? Or using my family's old kerosene lantern during blackouts versus pulling out my fancy flashlight that, oops, used expensive and rare batteries? Or tossing plastic bottles without considering their secondary storage value? I guess seeing thousands of commercials by age 10 has pushed me to think: "Where can I go to get or buy what I need?"

11   By contrast, most Cubans first ask, "What do I already have that I could use?" Some even bragged about such resolver, or resourcefulness. My relatives, not terribly amused with my lack of resolver, were quite patient. Their frugality is probably borne of necessity rather than virtue, but my lack of it was embarrassing to me. Perhaps I've been too busy shopping for values instead of cultivating them.

12   More embarrassing was a discussion about personal hygiene and what it seems to say about one's priorities. I was blindsided when asked, "Why do you all have the habit of showering in the morning before work instead of after work? You mean to tell me you come home to be with your family or friends, and you don't shower then? You go to bed with your wife after a full day of sweat? Eeeeeyyyyewww!"

13   It was surprising for me, as an American photojournalist, to see how images in our media that seem clear-cut can have quite another meaning for a Cuban. In Havana, I met a Cuban photographer working for an international news agency who showed me a picture he'd taken that day. It was of Castro, excitedly raising his fists in the air as he stood behind a lectern. "Ha? Ha? Isn't that great?" the photographer said proudly. "This will show the exiles in Miami that Fidel is still going strong!" I looked at him, incredulous. From a certain U.S. perspective, the gray-haired leader waving his fists appeared as the stereotypical crazed pariah.

14    Becoming aware of our own preconceptions or biases, and accepting them, may well be the ultimate value of any culture exchange. Staging a sing-along, a ballgame or other cultural encounter might have great symbolic value and surface appeal. But if the two nations are to make a genuine connection and resolve the decades' old conflict, we need to look deeper and not get lost on an island of assumptions.

## Analyzing the Writer's Strategy

Garcia's stance is established in his first sentence, when he shows his footing in two worlds, the United States and Cuba. He creates the image of "Uncle Sam and El Comandante . . . not quite seeing eye to eye . . . exchanging curious glances" to establish the *differences* in the two cultures he observed during his stay in Cuba. Using these informal nicknames, he establishes a light-hearted tone that softens the negative aspects of American values as viewed through the eyes of his Cuban hosts.

Garcia notes that while the goal of the language and cultural program is that it "will make it easier to export cultural values to Fidel Castro's Cuba," ironically he returned questioning his own values. Irony abounds in his family background and in the discoveries he makes. He has family on both sides of the political spectrum: one cousin escaped Cuba, calling it "a prison," and another cousin serves as a leader in Cuba, believing it to be "a worker's paradise." Therefore, Garcia expected to find some of his values in conflict with those he found in Cuba, but he did not expect to have his "most basic assumptions" challenged. Rather than promoting American values to the Cubans, Garcia came to question them.

Garcia's sense of irony comes through in his examples of American life that don't make sense to Cubans: that American individualism is won at the expense of greater good for the group, that American civil liberties allow the existence of racist groups such as the Ku Klux Klan, that Americans enjoy the right to vote but turn out in embarrassingly low numbers, that America is praised as the land of opportunity yet most of its citizens who are born poor also die poor. As he says, "The contrarian views fostered in the Cuban media take away the shine with which we like to present ourselves."

After exposing the ironies of public and political life, Garcia moves to personal observations on his wastefulness, indifference to environmental protection, and consumerism, and he concludes that perhaps he has been "too busy shopping for values instead of cultivating them." His carefully worked out irony and well-chosen words earn him the empathy rather than the antagonism of his American readers.

To illustrate how far apart cultural perceptions can be, Garcia juxtaposes two responses to the same photo of Castro, with his fists raised. The Cuban's view is that the photo shows Fidel is "still going strong," but the American is more likely to see the gray-haired leader as "the stereotypical crazed pariah."

Garcia concludes his essay by admitting that the highest value of a cultural exchange program might be that we become "aware of our own preconceptions or biases." By acknowledging that his stay in Cuba forced him to confront his own assumptions, he creates the same opportunity for his reader. He finally hopes that both nations will "make a genuine connection" and "not get lost on an island of assumptions," a final well-crafted allusion to the isolation of cultural boundaries.

 ## PRACTICE WRITING ESSAYS THAT USE COMPARISON AND CONTRAST

Select one topic to write an essay that uses comparison or contrast.

1. A family member's response to an important decision; how you expected that person to respond

2. A perception of a family member that you held in your youth; a view of that person that you have today

3. Your understanding or interpretation of a particular movie, song, or event; a friend's view of the same thing

4. Your concept of ideal employment; a job you have held or hold now

5. The effect of the Internet on learning as described in "Does the Internet Make You Dumber?" (p. 223) and "Your Brain on Computers" (p. 227)

6. The authors' attitudes about being fat in "Discrimination at Large" (p. 175) and in "O.K., So I'm Fat" (p. 179)

---

 ### Final Tips for Comparison and Contrast Essays

- Make sure that your **thesis includes both subjects** that are being compared and contrasted, and that the wording is specific. Avoid a thesis that simply claims they are both alike and different.

- Consider using the **point-by-point** method of comparison-contrast for a more emphatic delivery of information.

- Continue **interrelating the two subjects** so that you never make a point about one without showing how it relates to the other.

- Search for **subtle links and distinctions** as well as for the obvious ones. Then analyze the reasons for those differences.

# Chapter 11

## Analysis

In this chapter you will learn how to write a

- process analysis
- problem analysis
- film analysis
- poetry analysis
- character analysis
- focused biography research paper

## ANALYSIS OF A PROCESS, PROBLEM, FILM, POEM, OR CHARACTER

All essays involve analysis. Whether the method of development is comparison-contrast, cause and effect, or any other strategy, all college writing requires analysis—a close examination of the parts in order to better understand the whole. The "parts" may include a scrutiny of a particular author's key points, supporting examples, word choice, and organizational strategy. The purpose of any analysis is not merely to take the process, problem, or poem apart, but to see the value of the individual parts and to appreciate their interaction in creating the whole.

## When to Use Analysis

Written analysis is assigned in every academic discipline. Whether you are writing a lab report on the dissection of a frog in biology, interpreting a painting in art history, examining a short story in English, reviewing curriculum in education, exploring a management problem in business, or studying a discrimination problem in law, you will be expected to write analytical papers. These papers will be specifically targeted to the subject you are studying. However, all papers involve breaking the whole into parts and examining the parts to show a reader their importance to the whole.

# Analysis of a Process

A paper that examines a process explains how to do something or how the process itself is done. Examples might include performing a swimming pool rescue, getting a classmate to ask you out, cooking in a wok, paying car insurance while earning minimum wage, or getting a roommate's friend to move out.

## Brainstorming for a Topic

If a topic has not been assigned, brainstorm for possibilities. Consider what you know how to do that others don't or what you would like to learn in order to explain that process to a reader. Don't overlook the unusual: how to get your parents to start a compost pile or how to get your roommate to shower daily. Your essay can, in fact, be quite lively if you use ingenuity and a little prewriting energy.

## Organizing and Developing a Process Analysis

If you are writing a paper that tells your reader how to do something, or one that describes how something happens, these tips will help:

1. Determine whether chronology is important. For some processes, the sequence of the steps is critical (performing a swimming pool rescue), while for others it isn't as important (getting a classmate to ask you out). If chronology is important, list the steps and reexamine your list to make sure any reader can follow the logic of your arrangement.

2. If the steps in your process resist chronological ordering, determine an arrangement that makes sense. For example, in the model below, the writer first dismisses the most efficient but least probable method to save gas before she offers gas-saving steps that everyone can achieve.

3. Write each point completely, with supporting details and analysis of each. Include all of the necessary information and remove confusing or

irrelevant details. Imagine yourself in your readers' position, trying to follow your instructions for something they have never done.

4. Write a thesis that clearly asserts your point:

   **Thesis:** Success in small-group discussions requires awareness, participation, and cooperation.

   **Thesis:** Following the proper sequence of steps will facilitate a swimming pool rescue.

5. Draft your essay by linking each step or point with appropriate transitions to move your reader smoothly through this process.

6. Rewrite and edit your essay so that the language is vivid, the directions are precise, and the analysis is complete.

### PRACTICE PROCESS ANALYSIS IN SMALL GROUPS

In small groups, write down the steps explaining how to do the following:

1. find summer employment

2. balance a diet to achieve good nutrition

3. stay awake in a dull lecture

4. convince an unwilling landlord to make a repair

Spend time reaching accord within your group to ensure that all steps follow logically and that no necessary steps are left out. Aim for clarity and precision; remove words that obscure your directions. Any one of these analyses could be drafted into a collaborative paper.

Sections throughout this book explain various processes—for example, how to conduct an interview; how to cluster, list, and read actively; how to incorporate quoted material. These sections may be useful to you as models of process analysis, and they also underscore how important process analysis is to both teaching and learning.

### EXAMPLE: A PROCESS ANALYSIS

In the following essay, "How to Get Better Gas Mileage," Katharine Mieszkowski, a senior writer at *Salon.com*, provides tips from auto experts and "obsessive hypermilers" on how to go farther on a gallon of gas. Mieszkowski's essay was first posted in 2007, and gas prices have continued to fluctuate wildly. Her advice for conserving gas remains relevant.

*"It runs on its conventional gasoline-powered engine until it senses guilt, at which point it switches over to battery power."*

##  How to Get Better Gas Mileage

### *Katharine Mieszkowski*

1    Drink less, give up sweets—the clean calender of a new year inspires many earnest vows of self-improvement. With oil flirting with $100 a barrel, and $3 gas looking like the new normal, perhaps instead of resolving to curb your gluttony in the new year, you should pledge to train your car to be a fuel sipper. "Every time you get into your car and turn on your ignition you can save money," says Bradlee Fons of Pewaukee, Wisconsin, who teaches seminars on efficient driving. "It helps the country with national security and oil dependence, and it helps the world with global warming."

2    The most efficient way to save gas, as any "one-less-car" transportation activist will attest, is to leave your car in the garage. Walk, ride your bike, take the bus or train, or carpool whenever you can. When you're in the market for a car, choose the most fuel-efficient model. That should get easier to

do in the coming years as automakers comply with the just-passed law to move America's fleet from an average fuel economy of 25 miles per gallon to 35 by 2020, a 40 percent increase. It means there should be more fuel-efficient models of all vehicle types from compact to minivan to choose from soon.

3      Yet there are also simple steps that every driver can take with an existing car, truck or SUV to save fuel simply by improving driving habits. "If you're an aggressive driver, and many, many people are, you should become a moderate driver," says Philip Reed, senior consumer advice editor for Edmunds.com. Unfortunately, most people who drive aggressively don't realize it. "Driving for most people is a completely unconscious act. Just a little bit of self-awareness about how you drive can make a huge difference," says Bradley Berman, founder of Hybridcars.com, which offers both easy and advanced tips for driving more efficiently. Adopting a mellower approach on the road not only will ameliorate your road rage but could save you the equivalent of $1 a gallon, according to the U.S. Department of Energy, by improving your fuel efficiency as much as 33 percent.

4      "We all learned how to drive when gas was cheap, and we have to relearn how to drive," says Fons. To chill out behind the wheel, first curb rapid acceleration and excessive braking. Start by avoiding so-called jack rabbit starts—aggressively accelerating from a standstill at a stop sign or a stoplight. But remember, midrange acceleration also gobbles fuel, according to Reed from Edmunds. "You're going 50, and there's an opening in traffic, and you need to accelerate to 75, and you hammer it—that requires a lot of energy." Learn to accelerate smoothly and gradually. Press down on the pedal with the light touch of a feather.

5      Adopting a lower cruising speed can also help your car go farther with less gasoline. The efficiency of most cars rapidly declines at speeds over 60. In fact, every 5 miles per hour over 60 you drive is like paying an extra 20 cents a gallon for gas, according to the Department of Energy. So the next time you're tempted to pull ahead of the guy in the Ferrari on the freeway, think of the Saudis and keep out of the fast lane.

6      Just as hammering the gas is a bad idea, so is slamming on the brakes. Instead, anticipate stoplights and stop signs so that you can back off the accelerator, whenever possible, to slow down, and then gently apply the brakes. "If your vehicle weighs 4,000 pounds, it takes a lot of energy to get that going from a dead stop," explains Fons, who drives a 2000 Honda Insight, and through his driving habits manages to wring as much as 100 mpg out of the car, which is rated at 66 mpg by the Environmental Protection Agency. In stop-and-go traffic, strive to maintain one consistent low speed instead of accelerating and braking, accelerating and braking. To do this, drive in

the slow lane, and maintain a long buffer zone in front of you, so you won't have to slam on the brakes to avoid rear-ending the next car.

7    Drivers are often unconsciously influenced by the speed of the other cars around them, which can lead to speed creep. "When a faster car passes you, you have a tendency to speed up. Soon, even though you were committed to going 70, you're going 80," says Reed. "In some cases, cars are so well insulated it's easy to go fast without realizing it." A good way to avoid that pitfall: Use the cruise control on the freeway, which will also help you avoid the temptation to constantly dart forward when you see an opening in traffic up ahead.

8    Any time you hear the engine revving high, you're gulping fuel. If you drive a stick shift, and you're cruising along in third, shift to fourth, and hear the revs of the engine drop. Your car is the most inefficient when the engine is still warming up, so taking fewer trips by combining errands into one trip will save gas. Drive to your farthest destination, and then do the errands closer to home on the way back. When choosing your route, avoid hills if possible, so you won't be wasting energy hauling thousands of pounds of steel up an incline.

9    If you've got 57 books in your trunk that you keep meaning to donate to the library, but never get around to doing, try this experiment: "Take all that stuff out, and put it in a wheelbarrow, and push it up and down the driveway once, and you'll see how much energy it takes," says Wayne Gerdes. Gerdes invented the term "hypermiler" to describe the obsessive drivers like him who strive to wring every last mile out of a gallon of gas, exceeding the EPA's estimate of how far a car can go per gallon.

10    The more weight your car has to carry the harder it works, even though the overall gas savings are small, about 1 to 2 percent per 100 excess pounds eliminated, according to the U.S. Department of Energy. Reed at Edmunds doesn't worry too much about excess weight in the trunk, since he believes this tip was crafted back in the 1970s when New Englanders would keep 150-pound bags of sand in their trunks in hopes of getting better traction in the ice and snow in winter.

11    Avoiding excessive idling is also a must. Anytime you're idling for more than 15 seconds, such as at a railroad crossing or when waiting curbside to pick up your child from school, turn off your engine, advises Fons, who co-founded the Milwaukee Hybrid Group, which gives tips on what he calls eco-driving. The bigger your engine, the more fuel you typically waste idling. But whatever car you have, when it's idling it gets—duh!—zero miles per gallon. Idling is one of those bad habits that die hard. "Cars used to be hard to start. Oil was cheap, and we didn't care about global warming," says Reed. "These days cars are fuel injected."

12     Keeping your car tuned up can also bring some gas mileage improvements. Keeping tires properly inflated and frequently changing the air filter are the two biggies. "Gasoline is only one of the fuels the car burns, "explains Reed. "The other is oxygen, so feeding it with clean oxygen is very important."

13     If you really get into saving gas, you can invest in a scan gauge, which costs about $170. It will inform you in real time what miles per gallon your car is getting. (Hybrids already come equipped with them.) Gerdes, who says he once got 127 mpg (over the course of 90 miles) in a 2004 Toyota Prius, believes drivers can realize a 15 percent savings on fuel overnight by buying and heeding a gauge.

14     It used to be said that driving with the air conditioner on was a big fuel waster. But in all but the oldest jalopies with primitive air conditioners, that turns out to be an old wives' tale. "The air conditioners that we have now are highly efficient," says Reed from Edmunds. "Yes, they do take more power from the engine, but we're talking about 1 or 2 percent." The alternative of driving with the air conditioner off and the windows open doesn't offer a significant gain in gas mileage. On the contrary, when Edmunds conducted road tests to measure whether the altered aerodynamics of driving with the windows open impacted gas mileage, they noticed a decline in fuel economy if all the windows and the sunroof were open.

15     Driving experts say there's no need to wait for years to benefit from the new fuel-efficiency law. We can see major gas savings now simply by backing off the accelerator and brakes. "Everybody and anybody can do this no matter what they own and drive," says Gerdes. With practice, you, too, can become a hypermiler, and soon be shaming your lead-foot neighbors with your superior miles per gallon.

## Analyzing the Writer's Strategy

Katharine Mieszkowski's highly useful process analysis begins with an allusion to New Year's resolutions because she is writing at the end of a calendar year. She appeals to readers who annually commit to "earnest vows of self-improvement." For this year, she suggests that instead of curbing their own gluttony, readers should train their car "to be a fuel sipper" (417). This vivid image is striking and a lively contrast to the predictable tradition of New Year's resolutions. Mieszkowski's voice is reader-friendly even while she incorporates the research of many experts who provide technical data and statistical evidence on how to improve fuel efficiency.

Mieszkowski begins with the most obvious gas-saver, "to leave your car in the garage," but then provides "simple steps that every driver can take with an existing car, truck or SUV to save fuel" (418). She realizes that most readers can't stop driving altogether or even replace their existing vehicle for a more fuel efficient one. Her tips promise to be realistic and workable.

By including advice from experts, she strengthens her argument with technological information about how "jackrabbit starts," hammering the accelerator, and "slamming on the brakes" use excessive fuel. She reports that "adopting a mellower approach on the road not only will ameliorate your road rage but could save you the equivalent of $1 a gallon . . . improving your fuel efficiency as much as 33 percent" (418). These noteworthy statistics should influence any driver.

In addition to convincing her readers with statistics, she also addresses controversies that readers may have heard debated. For example, she notes that extra weight in the trunk is significant to some experts but not to others, but that all seem to agree that an air conditioner does not guzzle fuel, as was once believed. In fact, closed windows improve the car's aerodynamics and gas mileage. By addressing experts' opposed views and by dispelling "an old wives' tale," she anticipates and answers readers' questions.

Without resorting to a bulleted list, Mieszkowski nevertheless quickly provides numerous tips for all drivers willing to change their habits: adopt a lower cruising speed ("every 5 miles per hour over 60 you drive is like paying an extra 20 cents per gallon for gas"); avoid "speed creep," unconsciously increasing your speed to match the drivers around you (use cruise control); avoid idling the car for over 15 seconds (turn off the engine instead of waiting with the engine running).

The author's conclusion affirms her universal appeal that all drivers, regardless of their vehicles, can change habits in order to save fuel: "With practice, you, too, can become a hypermiler, and soon be shaming your lead-foot neighbors with you superior miles per gallon" (420). Mieszkowski is encouraging readers to not only change habits but to change priorities and even values to respond to a pressing need.

 ## PRACTICE WRITING A PROCESS ANALYSIS ESSAY

Select and describe a process that you know well from the following list:

1. How to get a hot guy or girl to hang out with you

2. How to "withdraw" from an email, Facebook, or Internet addiction

3. How to benefit from small-group discussions

4. How to change your habits to "go green"

Write your description as precisely as you can so that a reader can learn the process. Does your interest in the topic show in your description?

**Final Tips for a Process Analysis Essay**

- Review the order of the steps you have written to determine that your reader can follow your instructions or description. Consider your tone. Would humor help you engage your reader?
- Examine the details you have given to remove any confusing instructions or irrelevant details.
- Put yourself in your reader's position to see whether you have defined necessary terms, provided relevant details, and analyzed all key points.
- Reread your work to see whether appropriate transitions link the steps or the parts of your analysis.
- Reread to strengthen your language and enliven your essay.

## ANALYSIS OF A PROBLEM

Another kind of analysis paper describes a problem; it may or may not offer a solution. The writer may trace the history of the problem, but chronology is not as vital to this type of analysis as it is in a step-by-step process analysis. It is critical that the writer establishes the problem, examines its parts, and shows how the parts are related to the problem as a whole.

### When to Use Problem Analysis

More than any other single type of writing, problem analysis appears in every academic field and profession. Our daily newspapers and monthly newsmagazines as well as the readings in this textbook all feature essays analyzing a variety of problems: drug abuse, irresponsible parenting, stereotyping, isolation of the disabled, group conformity, and racial, ethnic, and gender discrimination. In spite of the wide range of issues, writers of problem analysis share similar strategies when they examine an issue.

### Organizing and Developing a Problem Analysis Essay

Engaging your readers is critical in problem analysis. Why should your readers care about stereotypes, ethnic bias, the rights of the disabled, or any other subject that doesn't directly relate to them? It is your job to create reader interest, and you can do this in a number of ways. Sometimes startling statistics or a bold anecdote will jar complacent readers out of apathy. Sometimes posing a direct question to readers prompts them to consider their responses and become involved in the topic—at least enough to read the work. After you have engaged your readers, decide how much background information they require in order to understand the problem. For example, if you are writing an analysis of changing interest rates, you will include less background material if you are writing the paper for your business class than for your English class.

Then, as in all analysis papers, you will need to choose which parts of the problem you want to examine. You must describe the problem so that any reader can understand it. This might include a discussion of the severity of the problem, the numbers affected by it, which population is most affected, and the consequences if this problem is uncorrected. A detailed study of each aspect of the problem and how it relates to the other parts will constitute the body of your paper. If it is relevant to your analysis, you might speculate about the barriers to solving this problem (such as cost, social bias, frustration with earlier failures, indifference, or denial).

It is important that this analysis has a focus and a clear point or assertion. For example, if you are concerned about the fact that Americans are on the job more than workers in other countries, it is not enough merely to identify the number of hours that American employees work each week. Nor is it enough to show that they work more hours per week and more weeks per year than their European counterparts, or that they are not routinely given flexible work schedules so they can coordinate their family's needs with their work responsibilities. All of these important facts could support a point, but the point must be made.

You will need to clarify, in the form of a thesis or assertion, why the analysis of these facts is important: that American workers are overworked, that Americans have insufficient leisure time, that American children grow up deprived of their parents, or any other point that you deem significant as a result of your analysis. But without a point, you have no paper.

Once you have determined your assertion, you are ready to outline, draft, and revise your paper. Specific suggestions about outlining, drafting, and revising can be found in the student example of a problem analysis on eating disorders (pp. 308–315).

## EXAMPLE: A PROBLEM ANALYSIS

The following analysis was written by a Harvard-educated economist, Robert L. Heilbroner, who has written extensively on economics and business. This essay, originally published in *Reader's Digest*, contains a unique perception of a common problem.

# Don't Let Stereotypes Warp Your Judgments

*Robert L. Heilbroner*

1   Is a girl called Gloria apt to be better-looking than one called Bertha? Are criminals more likely to be dark than blond? Can you tell a good deal about someone's personality from hearing his voice briefly over the phone? Can a person's nationality be pretty accurately guessed from his photograph? Does the fact that someone wears glasses imply that he is intelligent?

2   The answer to all these questions is obviously, "No."

3   Yet, from all the evidence at hand, most of us believe these things. Ask any college boy if he'd rather take his chances with a Gloria or a Bertha, or ask a college girl if she'd rather blind-date a Richard or a Cuthbert. In fact, you don't have to ask: college students in questionnaires have revealed that names conjure up the same images in their minds as they do in yours—and for as little reason.

4   Look into the favorite suspects of persons who report "suspicious characters" and you will find a large percentage of them to be "swarthy" or "dark and foreign-looking"— despite the testimony of criminologists that criminals do not tend to be dark, foreign, or "wild-eyed." Delve into the main asset of a telephone stock swindler and you will find it to be a marvelously confidence-inspiring telephone "personality." And whereas we all think we know what an Italian or a Swede looks like, it is the sad fact that when a group of Nebraska students sought to match faces and nationalities of fifteen European countries, they were scored wrong in 93 percent of their identifications. Finally, for although horn-rimmed glasses have now become the standard television sign of an "intellectual," optometrists know that the main thing that distinguishes people with glasses is just bad eyes.

5   Stereotypes are a kind of gossip about the world, a gossip that makes us prejudge people before we ever lay eyes on them. Hence it is not surprising that stereotypes have something to do with the dark world of prejudice. Explore most prejudices (note that the word means prejudgment) and you will find a cruel stereotype at the core of each one.

6   For it is the extraordinary fact that once we have typecast the world, we tend to see people in terms of our standardized pictures. In another demonstration of the power of stereotypes to affect our vision, a number of Columbia and Barnard students were shown thirty photographs of pretty but unidentified girls, and asked to rate each in terms of "general liking," "intelligence," "beauty," and so on. Two months later, the same group were

shown the same photographs, this time with fictitious Irish, Italian, Jewish, and "American" names attached to the pictures. Right away the ratings changed. Faces which were now seen as representing a national group went down in looks and still farther down in likability, while the "American" girls suddenly looked decidedly prettier and nicer.

7 Why is it that we stereotype the world in such irrational and harmful fashion? In part, we begin to type-cast people in our childhood years. Early in life, as every parent whose child has watched a TV Western knows, we learn to spot the Good Guys from the Bad Guys. Some years ago, a social psychologist showed very clearly how powerful these stereotypes of childhood vision are. He secretly asked the most popular youngsters in an elementary school to make errors in their morning gym exercises. Afterwards, he asked the class if anyone had noticed any mistakes during gym period. Oh, yes, said the children. But it was the unpopular members of the class—the "bad guys"—they remembered as being out of step.

8 We not only grow up with standardized pictures forming inside of us, but as grown-ups we are constantly having them thrust upon us. Some of them, like the half-joking, half-serious stereotypes of mothers-in-law, or country yokels, or psychiatrists, are dinned into us by the stock jokes we hear and repeat. In fact, without such stereotypes, there would be a lot fewer jokes. Still other stereotypes are perpetuated by the advertisements we read, the movies we see, the books we read.

9 And finally, we tend to stereotype because it helps us make sense out of a highly confusing world, a world which William James once described as "one great, blooming, buzzing confusion." It is a curious fact that if we don't know what we're looking at, we are often quite literally unable to see what we're looking at. People who recover their sight after a lifetime of blindness actually cannot at first tell a triangle from a square. A visitor to a factory sees only noisy chaos where the superintendent sees a perfectly synchronized flow of work. As Walter Lippmann has said, "For the most part we do not first see, and then define; we define first, and then we see."

10 Stereotypes are one way in which we "define" the world in order to see it. They classify the infinite variety of human beings into a convenient handful of "types" toward whom we learn to act in stereotyped fashion. Life would be a wearing process if we had to start from scratch with each and every human contact. Stereotypes economize on our mental effort by covering up the blooming, buzzing confusion with big recognizable cut-outs. They save us the "trouble" of finding out what the world is like—they give it its accustomed look.

11 Thus the trouble is that stereotypes make us mentally lazy. As S. I. Hayakawa, the authority on semantics, has written: "The danger of

stereotypes lies not in their existence, but in the fact that they become for all people some of the time, and for some people all the time, substitutes for observation." Worse yet, stereotypes get in the way of our judgment, even when we do observe the world. Someone who has formed rigid preconceptions of all Latins as "excitable," or all teenagers as "wild," doesn't alter his point of view when he meets a calm and deliberate Genoese, or a serious-minded high school student. He brushes them aside as "exceptions that prove the rule." And, of course, if he meets someone true to type, he stands triumphantly vindicated. "They're all like that," he proclaims, having encountered an excited Latin, an ill-behaved adolescent.

12    Hence, quite aside from the injustice which stereotypes do to others, they impoverish ourselves. A person who lumps the world into simple categories, who type-casts all labor leaders as "racketeers," all businessmen as "reactionaries," all Harvard men as "snobs," and all Frenchmen as "sexy," is in danger of becoming a stereotype himself. He loses his capacity to be himself— which is to say, to see the world in his own absolutely unique, inimitable and independent fashion.

13    Instead, he votes for the man who fits his standardized picture of what a candidate "should" look like or sound like, buys the goods that someone in his "situation" in life "should" own, lives the life that others define for him. The mark of the stereotyped person is that he never surprises us, that we do indeed have him "typed." And no one fits this straitjacket so perfectly as someone whose opinions about other people are fixed and inflexible.

14    Impoverishing as they are, stereotypes are not easy to get rid of. The world we type-cast may be no better than a Grade B movie, but at least we know what to expect of our stock characters. When we let them act for themselves in the strangely unpredictable way that people do act, who knows but that many of our fondest convictions will be proved wrong?

15    Nor do we suddenly drop our standardized pictures for a blinding vision of the Truth. Sharp swings of ideas about people often just substitute one stereotype for another. The true process of change is a slow one that adds bits and pieces of reality to the pictures in our heads, until gradually they take on some of the blurriness of life itself. Little by little, we learn not that Jews and Negroes and Catholics and Puerto Ricans are "just like everybody else" — for that, too, is a stereotype—but that each and every one of them is unique, special, different, and individual. Often we do not even know that we have let a stereotype lapse until we hear someone saying, "all so-and-so's are like such-and-such," and we hear ourselves saying, "Well—maybe."

16    Can we speed the process along? Of course we can.

17    First, we can become aware of the standardized pictures in our heads, in other people's heads, in the world around us.

18　　Second, we can become suspicious of all judgments that we allow exceptions to "prove." There is no more chastening thought than that in the vast intellectual adventure of science, it takes but one tiny exception to topple a whole edifice of ideas.

19　　Third, we can learn to be chary of generalizations about people. As F. Scott Fitzgerald once wrote: "Begin with an individual, and before you know it you have created a type; begin with a type, and you find you have created—nothing."

20　　Most of the time, when we type-cast the world, we are not in fact generalizing about people at all. We are only revealing the embarrassing facts about the pictures that hang in the gallery of stereotypes in our own heads.

## Analyzing the Writer's Strategy

Heilbroner's immediate goal is to convince his readers that they stereotype, even though they may think that they do not. Throughout his essay, Heilbroner's tone is light and not accusatory because most people intellectually know that stereotyping is unfair—and would even deny that they do it. His strategy is to engage his readers by asking an entire paragraph of carefully chosen questions that he knows everybody answers in the same predictable way—evidence of the pervasiveness of stereotyping. Using statistical evidence from tests that have been given to college students (seemingly people of above average intelligence), Heilbroner then shows that all people "typecast the world." The author incorporates quoted statements about stereotyping from famous thinkers and philosophers to illustrate his own views.

Ultimately Heilbroner's strategy is to convince his readers that stereotyping "impoverishes" the person who does the stereotyping because it makes that person "mentally lazy." He can accomplish this only by giving many specific examples of how people substitute stereotypes for true observation. His strategy is further to convince his readers that a slow process of conscious awareness can reduce the tendency to stereotype.

 **PRACTICE WRITING A PROBLEM ANALYSIS ESSAY**

Problem analysis assignments appear after many of the readings in this text. In addition to those that reflect the theme of being "between worlds," you might write an analysis of any of these problems:

1. limited inexpensive housing available for college students

2. policies at work or school that seem poorly conceived

3. a family's inability to communicate

4. athletes' use of drugs

5. driving while using any type of cellphone

6. overdrinking and overeating in American society

---

 **Final Tips for a Problem Analysis Essay**

- Engage your readers to convince them of the importance of the problem.
- Provide sufficient background information for your intended audience.
- Make sure that your thesis expresses why your analysis of the problem is important.
- Reread and revise to ascertain that you have adequately discussed the parts of the problem that require analysis and that you have related those parts to the problem as a whole.

---

# ANALYSIS OF A FILM

## Film as Text

Film is an important part of our lives, beyond mere entertainment. The movies we see find their way into our conversations, passionate debates with friends, and even our classrooms. In fact, as soon as we leave the theater (and sometimes sooner, until viewers around us object), we rush to share our impressions, opinions, and evaluations with anyone who has seen the film.

Dialogues about films, like classroom discussions of other texts, help us to express not only our views but also our uncertainties as we attempt to get our questions answered. Further, we often seek reviews, both before the film, so we know what to anticipate, and after the film, so we can discover what we missed or how someone else might have interpreted a scene. DVD versions have become so popular because they offer those special features—running commentaries, interviews with the actors, director, and writer, and even explanations of deleted scenes. All of this information helps us better understand the moving images. And frequently, we want to express our own ideas about a film, to counter or expand on others' ideas. Writing about film, therefore, becomes an extension of this dialogue and motivates us to analyze and evaluate what we have seen and heard.

**Common Film Terms and Concepts**

- **Theme:** what the film is about, its overall concerns (loss of innocence, triumph of good over evil, shattered ideals, family endurance).
- **Plot:** what happens from beginning to end of the film, including the order or arrangement of these key events.
- **Characterization:** how the main characters are depicted and how they change; how minor characters may illuminate the main characters' struggles or values.
- **Narration:** the story line or unfolding of the story from beginning to end; some experimental films may be non-narrative and tell no story; some documentaries may focus on a real event without organizing the details into a story.
- **Point of view (POV):** films often use an objective point of view, but the camera can also create a character's more subjective perspective; in addition, the first person ("I") may also be used, often involving *voice-overs*, that is, the narrator speaking off camera in the first person.
- **Flashback:** an image, scene, or sequence that illustrates a past action or event.
- **Flashforward:** an image, scene, or sequence that illustrates a future action or event.

# Active Viewing

Just as we initially learned to read a text actively, we need to move beyond passive viewing of a film to "read" it actively. Clearly, we cannot underline key points and write notes in the margin as we do when we read printed matter, but we can learn to critically view a film and jot down key details from scenes to analyze later. Your notes on the film will become your text—to use for class discussion and for writing an essay. Learning to take effective notes can save you time and frustration. Even during the first viewing of a film, you should take careful notes. It is ideal to see a film more than once, adding to your preliminary notes as you watch.

Before you begin watching any of the films in this chapter, consider the following questions, so you can anticipate what's coming:

- What is the significance of the *title*?
- What is the *setting*—time and place—of this film?

- Why does the film *open* as it does?
- What is important about the *concluding images*?
- What is the *point of view*? Does it limit or control the viewer's vision?
- Do the main characters *change or develop* during the film? How?
- Which *four to five sequences* seem most striking to you?
- Is there any unusual *camera work*? Mixed genres?
- What were the most important *repetitions*?

If the questions focus on characterization, key scenes, or significant lines, you will be more apt to critically consider the images on the screen and not slip into passive viewing. These questions will help you focus your note taking. Once the film has ended, your notes are the only text you will have. Because watching a film takes about two hours, you will want to make each viewing count.

### EXAMPLE: A FILM ANALYSIS

The analysis that follows is on the 2005 film *Crash*. The film captures anxieties about urban life and conflicts exacerbated by racial and ethnic tension. Filmed as a series of vignettes, this intense film exposes the characters' prejudices and, at the same time, compels us to confront our own unconscious stereotyping.

In this essay, critic David Denby argues that despite the racial tensions and offensive language, *Crash* "pulls us into the multiple stories it has to tell and becomes intensely moving" (431). Notice how his analysis includes specific details of plot, setting, character development, and film techniques as he examines "the heart-swelling resolutions of the different stories" (433). This essay appeared in the *New Yorker* on May 2, 2005.

## ◐◐ Angry People ◐◐
### *David Denby, film critic, The New Yorker*

1    If there's an ill-tempered remark that has ever been uttered in the city of Los Angeles that hasn't found its way into Paul Haggis's *Crash*, I can't imagine what it is. *Crash* is about the rage and foolishness produced by intolerance, the mutual abrasions of white, black, Latino, Middle Eastern, and Asian citizens in an urban pot in which nothing melts. The characters run afoul of each other, say things better left unsaid, and get into terrible trouble. And yet the movie isn't exasperating in the way that movies about steam-heated people often are. *Crash* is hyper-articulate and often breathtakingly intelligent and always brazenly alive. I think it's easily the strongest American film since

Clint Eastwood's *Mystic River,* though it is not for the fainthearted. In the first twenty minutes or so, the racial comments are so blunt and the dialogue so incisive that you may want to shield yourself from the daggers flying across the screen by getting up and leaving. That would be a mistake. *Crash* stretches the boundaries: after the cantankerous early scenes, it pulls us into the multiple stories it has to tell and becomes intensely moving.

2      Like other recent movies set in Los Angeles (*Grand Canyon, Short Cuts, Magnolia*), the picture is structured in vignette form, a natural dramatic outgrowth of a strange automotive paradise in which people live in separate racial and class enclaves, drive to work, and stick with their own. "We're always behind this metal and glass," a melancholy police detective, Graham (Don Cheadle), says as he sits in his car with his partner and girlfriend, Ria (Jennifer Esposito). "It's the sense of touch. I think we miss that touch so much that we crash into each other just so we can feel something." This may seem a fancy conceit until one realizes that Haggis is pushing the word "crash" beyond the literal: he means any kind of rough contact between folks from different ethnic groups. But after the collision, what then? The stories, which begin on separate paths, slowly mesh; the characters are thrown together in bizarre ways, and they go past their initial distaste for each other and at least admit that they live in the same city, and are touched by the same fatality and magic.

3      Paul Haggis, who is fifty-two, was born in Canada; he crossed the border into the land of dreams and folly in his early twenties. For many years, he worked successfully in American television, and was responsible for, among other things, the short-lived but much-appreciated series *EZ Streets.* A few years ago, Haggis, working with his friend Bobby Moresco, wrote the screenplay for *Crash* on spec. Most writers who have been around as long as Haggis wouldn't write anything—not even a thank-you note—on spec, but the virtues of working this way are obvious enough: *Crash* was created freely, without the usual anxieties that shape big-budget films. The screenplay then attracted a number of people eager to take some chances, including the star, Don Cheadle, who helped raise a production budget of $6.5 million, which is roughly one-tenth the budget of the average Hollywood studio feature. Yet *Crash* doesn't look small. Haggis, in his first outing as director, has put together an extraordinary cast, and the stories are set high and low, in Brentwood and the ghetto, among cops and civilians, the young and the decrepit elderly.

4      *Crash* begins with out-of-focus lights, moving in the dark, as if a stunned post-collision consciousness were slowly coming back into focus. The time is Christmas, a very cold Christmas for Los Angeles, with dreamy flakes of snow in the air. At the side of the road the police are investigating a shooting; a young black man has been killed. Cheadle's detective examines the

crime scene and stares at something in horror. The movie then goes back to the previous afternoon and fills in the events leading up to Cheadle's unhappy moment. Two young African-Americans, Anthony (the rapper Chris "Ludacris" Bridges) and Peter (Larenz Tate), argue merrily on the street. Anthony is convinced that everything in his life, including the large windows on Los Angeles buses, is part of a white plot to humiliate blacks. His friend tries to tease him out of it. The real joke, however, is that Anthony, who rants that whites assume that all young black men are thugs, actually is a thug, and when he and Peter spy a prosperous white couple walking down the street to their Lincoln Navigator, they jump them, at gunpoint, and take off in the car.

5      The couple, it turns out, are the Los Angeles district attorney (Brendan Fraser) and his spoiled-bitch Brentwood wife (Sandra Bullock). At home after the incident, the young D.A. complains hysterically that the incident, which is sure to become public, may lose him either the black vote or the law-and-order vote, and his wife, who saw trouble coming, is mad because people might think she's a racist. Later the same evening, a prosperous black couple, Cameron (Terrence Howard) and Christine (Thandie Newton), are out on the town. A little drunk, Christine performs a companionable sex act on her husband as he drives their own Lincoln Navigator. A white cop, Officer Ryan (Matt Dillon), who's got a heavy case of L.A.P.D. malaise—he knows he's a racist but can't suppress it—pulls them over, even though it's obvious that their Navigator isn't the stolen one. As his partner (Ryan Phillippe) looks on in disgust, Ryan humiliates the couple, reaching up between Christine's thighs in a mock weapons search. Christine, shaken, taunts her husband for not standing up to the cops, a fight that sickens both of them, because it seems so old: the black manhood issue again. But also that night we see that Ryan's father is in terrible pain from a misdiagnosed prostate problem, and Ryan can't get a straight answer about his father's condition from the black supervisor at their H.M.O. What Ryan does to the black couple is not justified by his problems, but, as we later find out, a racist can also be a good son and a good cop.

6      I give so much detail about a single plot thread because the entire movie is as intricately worked as this one piece of it. Haggis's complex take on each furious encounter makes previous movie treatments of prejudice seem like easy and self-congratulatory liberalizing. Apart from a few brave scenes in Spike Lee's work, *Crash* is the first movie I know of to acknowledge not only that the intolerant are also human but, further, that something like white fear of black street crime, or black fear of white cops, isn't always irrational. In another strand, an Iranian shopkeeper named Farhad (Shaun Toub) has become a quarrelsome fool; he's sure that everyone is out to cheat him.

But this incensed man's neighbors think that he and his family are Arabs, and trash his store. In Haggis's Los Angeles, the tangle of mistrust, misunderstanding, and foul temper envelops everyone; no one is entirely innocent or entirely guilty.

7      *Crash* could have turned into an exploding nebula, the superheated pieces flying off into dramatic irrelevance (as they do in many of Lee's movies), but Haggis has imposed a tight formal organization on his narrative. He has set up parallel events and characters (two wealthy couples, two daughters who save their fathers, and so on), and also multiple echoes and variations, all of which deepen the thematic lines. Haggis sustains the temporal fiction—a long day's journey into night, then day, and then back to the film's opening moment at night—with shrewdly timed cutting among the stories and with many silent moments in which a single character, staring at the city's moving lights, falls into a brooding funk similar to Cheadle's melancholy in the first scene. The moments of rest, deepened and prolonged by Mark Isham's gentle electronic score, serve as caesuras between the high-tension scenes. There are plenty of angry people in movies and on television, but Haggis has an intimate feeling for the way rage fuels itself and redoubles—the demotic eloquence of the street, the marital quarrel, the police-station tirade. I can't think of a single flat or dramatically pointless scene, and some of the big moments play out at the edge of insanity, where contentiousness spills over into tragedy or farce.

8      The actors grab at their roles as if their careers depended on it. Thandie Newton and Terrence Howard expose the kind of torment and shame that could drive this educated, privileged couple apart. Cheadle's soft-spoken intelligence has become one of the most expressive elements in American cinema, and, as the man who sees the most, understands the most, and pays for his knowledge in suffering, he holds this movie together. But everyone steps up, including Matt Dillon, Sandra Bullock, and the angel-faced Ryan Phillippe, who pulls off a moment of near-calamity with character and force. The heart-swelling resolutions of the different stories will, I know, strike some viewers as overwrought. But hasn't Haggis earned the tears? He has laid the groundwork for emotional release by writing some of the toughest talk ever heard in American movies. Some things may be better left unsaid, but the exuberant frankness of this movie burns through embarrassment and chagrin and produces its own kind of exhilaration.

## Analyzing the Writer's Strategy

The writer of analysis will always look at the parts of the subject to be analyzed with the goal of examining how those parts contribute to an appreciation of the whole. David Denby does exactly that in his review and analysis of the film *Crash*. His essay is also an argument to convince readers that *Crash* is an extraordinary film that "produces its own exhilaration" (433).

Denby begins his analysis conceding that viewers may be driven away by the offensive language, racial tensions, and "cantankerous early scenes" of *Crash*, but he insists that leaving the film "would be a mistake" (431). Although the first twenty minutes of the movie are filled with "intolerance" and "ill-tempered" remarks and the characters "get into terrible trouble," Denby's view is that this film nevertheless "pulls us into the multiple stories it has to tell" and is ultimately "intensely moving" (431). His strategy is to acknowledge his opponents' objections to *Crash* before he presents his analysis that will show the film's value.

To convince his reader that *Crash* has value beyond that of an action thriller, Denby carefully records one character's lines early on in the film. Graham, sitting in a patrol car with his detective "partner and girlfriend," drolly remarks on a car crash they are peripherally involved in: "It's the sense of touch. I think we miss that touch so much that we crash into each other just so we can feel something" (431). Denby's goal in quoting Graham's lines is to illustrate how the director Haggis is "pushing the word 'crash' beyond the literal: he means any kind of rough contact between folks from different ethnic groups" (431). Such interpretations help convince readers that this is a film with deep thematic insights.

Another element of the film that Denby analyzes is its plot structure— its "vignette form"—and he observes that the multiple stories are "intricately worked" around several compelling plot threads. He admires how director Haggis "has imposed a tight formal organization on his narrative" (433). Denby looks at the "parallel events and characters" not only to give his reader some idea of the plot of the film but to analyze the director's intention of showing how overlapping these stories are, how the "multiple echoes and variations . . deepen the thematic lines" of the film. Ultimately, Denby will observe that "in Haggis's Los Angeles, the tangle of mistrust, misunderstanding, and foul temper envelops everyone; no one is entirely innocent or entirely guilty" (433). Denby's intention is to go beyond plot description to illustrate how the narrative form of the film contributes to its theme.

Denby also analyzes the film's techniques. He observes the camera work in the film's opening, with its "out-of-focus lights, moving in the dark," and he effectively interprets this technique "as if a stunned post-collision consciousness were slowly coming back into focus" (431). This analysis goes beyond observation; he interprets how the effects contribute to the audience's understanding of the film's themes. He further perceives how Haggis cuts "the high-tension scenes" with "many silent moments," and Denby notes that these "quiet moments are deepened and prolonged" by the "gentle electronic score" (433) of the film's soundtrack. Denby's strategy is to give his reader analysis of the film's techniques that the audience may have observed but might not have integrated into a significant understanding of how they actually work in the film.

By noting that the film's actors "grab at their roles as if their careers depended on it" (433), Denby concludes his film analysis with specific praise of their talents. Denby's accolades also extend to the director who has created a film that results in "heart-swelling resolutions of the different stories" (433) and thereby provides the audience deserved "emotional release" (433). Denby's review of *Crash* is clearly written to motivate his reader to see the film, and to appreciate its achievement.

 ### PRACTICE WRITING FILM ANALYSIS

Select one of the films reviewed in this text—*Crash* (pp. 430–433), *The King's Speech* (pp. 200–203), or *An Inconvenient Truth* (pp. 259–269)—or a film you prefer–and write an analysis that shows your understanding of the film. Review the example and analysis above before you begin writing.

---

 ## Final Tips for Writing about Film

- Review any class notes or instructions *before* you watch the film. If you are assigned to view *Crash* (pp. 430–433), *The Kings Speech* (pp. 200–203), or *An Inconvenient Truth* (pp. 259–269), review the "Thinking About the Film" questions before you begin the film.

- Use *shorthand and abbreviations* so you can jot down quick notes while keeping your eye on the film.

- If not using a bound notebook, *number your pages* as you write.

- *Leave extra lines between scenes* so you can fill in more details when the film ends.

- Try to recognize and *record key narrative facts, shots, and sequences.*

- Jot down *specific details* about the opening sequence, key scenes, and ending.

- Use *quotation marks* to designate dialogue copied exactly as spoken.

- Spend time immediately after a film *adding details* and interpreting your shorthand notes while the film is still fresh.

- See the film a second and third time, if possible, *adding to your notes* each time.

- Return to your instructor's notes or the "Thinking about the Film" questions *now* and answer them as specifically as you can.

---

# Poetry Analysis

When you are asked to write an essay about a poem, you will be expected to analyze it—that is, to study its parts and explain how they relate to the whole. This examination involves a closer scrutiny than an overview or summary. In a summary, you tell what the poem is about or what happens in the poem. In an analysis, you explain how certain elements function in the poem and why the poem is written as it is. Although summary cannot take the place of analysis, you might need to summarize as a part of analysis. But poetry analysis requires a close look at the poem's elements—key words, images, and figures of speech.

An exploration of *key words* is a productive way to analyze a poem. Even though you may feel you know what a word means, the poet may be using a less-known meaning of the word. Because most of us don't know the origin or obscure meanings of all words, a dictionary is indispensable when reading a poem. In addition to the *denotation,* or dictionary definition of a word, you may be aware of the *connotation* or emotional association that the word conveys, and the poet may be counting on your feelings about the word. Knowing the connotations, unusual definitions, or multiple meanings of a word is critical to understanding the poem.

All poems consist of *images*—words that stir the senses: sight, sound, smell, touch, and taste. Because images are such vital elements of a poem, a productive analysis of a poem often involves examining particular images or patterns of images that seem to work together. In "Blue Spruce" (p. 173), Stephen Perry weaves a pattern of musical images throughout his poem: his grandfather's sousaphone, bandstand "with instruments—alto sax, tenor sax, tuba or sousaphone," congregation singing, the "oompah-pahs" of the sousaphone, and musical "notes."

In addition, he appeals to multiple senses: our sense of sight as a baby is raised "into the bell of his sousaphone," our sense of smell with the "barbershop / smelling of lotions," our sense of touch with the "smooth-rough hide" of the black razor strop, and our sense of sound "as the horses clip-clopped on ice" (22).

Images used suggestively rather than literally are called *figures of speech,* and a study of these figures can enhance your discussion of imagery. Of the many kinds of figures of speech, the most common are metaphor, simile, and personification. A *metaphor* is an implied comparison between two unlike things. Poets aren't the only ones who use metaphors; you probably use them daily without realizing it. For example, when you say, "My boyfriend is a gem," you are comparing him to something that is valuable, dazzling, impressive! In Stephen Perry's poem, he makes a direct comparison when he pictures how "the tiny hairs would gather / on the blade, a congregation singing" (7–8). The tiny hairs become a "congregation singing."

In contrast with metaphor, a *simile* is an explicit comparison between unlike things, using the words "like" or "as." In Perry's poem, the speaker describes how his grandfather lifted him high into the bell of his sousaphone "as if I were a note / he'd play into light—" (44–45). The baby is not literally a musical note but is compared to a lively, "light" sound that the grandfather would "play." The baby is "light" in contrast to the adults who judge the grandfather's affair darkly.

Perry also uses *personification*—giving human characteristics to an inanimate object, animal, or abstraction. In this poem, the speaker describes the town fountain in winter as one that had "frozen into a coiffure / of curly glass" (18–19). In addition to the coiffeur being a metaphor (an implied comparison) for the frozen water, the fountain is given human characteristics because it has styled hair, a "coiffure."

You may hear people refer to a *symbol* or to *symbolism* when they are discussing poetry. A symbol is something concrete used to represent or suggest something more abstract. In Perry's poem, the "sousaphone"—a large commanding instrument with a deep, forceful sound—represents the grandfather who is bold and impossible to ignore.

## How to Actively Read a Poem

When you are assigned a poem to read, you need to read it through without worrying about what you don't understand. In a second or third reading, read the poem aloud, so that your ear catches connections that the poet intends. Then, just as you have been reading the essays in this book—actively—with a pen in hand, read the poem again and circle unfamiliar words, underline key words or lines, mark important ideas, and jot down comments in the margin. This is the time to use the dictionary to look up not only the words that may be new to you but words that the poet may have used differently than you would expect. You need to write down, on the page with the poem or on a separate piece of paper, the multiple meanings of each word as well as relevant origins of the word.

As you read, mark the examples of simile, metaphor, and personification, as well as images that relate to each other by similarity or contrast. Ask questions as you read: Why does the poet use a particular word, or how do two images relate? Your responses to these questions provide notes that will help you choose the focus for your analysis.

Here is an example of active reading that a student, Robert Sakatani, did to prepare for class discussion of Janice Mirikitani's poem "Breaking Tradition" (p. 20).

EXAMPLE: ACTIVE READING OF A POEM

 **Breaking Tradition**
*Janice Mirikitani*

*dedication* → For my daughter

✓ My daughter denies she is like me,
  Her secretive eyes avoid mine.                    *daughter: "secretive," "veiled"*
    She reveals the hatreds of womanhood
    already veiled behind music and smoke and telephones.
5   I want to tell her about the empty room
      of myself.
        This room we lock ourselves in          *repeats "room" = key metaphor?*
      where whispers live like fungus,
      giggles about small breasts and cellulite,
10     where we confine ourselves to jealousies,
      bedridden by menstruation.
        This waiting room where we feel our hands      ⟩ *striking metaphor*
      are useless, dead speechless clamps
      that need hospitals and forceps and kitchens
15     and plugs and ironing boards to make them useful.
✓   I deny I am like my mother, I remember why:
      She kept her room neat with silence,  —*grandmother's room: "neat with silence"*
      defiance smothered in requirements to be otonashii,
      passion and loudness wrapped in an obi,  —*meanings*
20     her steps confined to ceremony,
      the weight of her sacrifice she carried like
      a foetus. Guilt passed on in our bones.
*repeats title:*   I want to break tradition—unlock this room
      where women dress in the dark.
*grandmother's*  25   Discover the lies my mother told me.        *narrator wants to escape:*
*"lies"*           The lies that we are small and powerless,    *"unlock this room"*
      that our possibilities must be compressed
      to the size of pearls, displayed only as
      passive chokers, charms around our neck.
*repeats title:*  30   Break Tradition.
        I want to tell my daughter of this room  —*narrator's room*

of myself
filled with <u>tears of violins</u>,
*narrator*  the <u>light in my hands</u>,
*expresses*  35  poems about madness,
*all emotions*  the <u>music of</u>(yellow guitars)—— *meaning?*
*creatively*  sounds shaken from barbed wire and
goodbyes and miracles of survival.   *relocation camps?*
| This room | of open window where daring ones escape.

40  My daughter denies she is like me    *repeats opening images*
her secretive eyes are walls of smoke
*daughter is*  and music and telephones,
*hip/Westernized*  her pouting ruby lips, her skirts
swaying to salsa, teena marie and the stones,
45  her thighs displayed in carnivals of color.
<u>I do not know</u> the contents of | her room. |    *daughter's room—unknown*
She mirrors my aging.
*repeats title*  She is <u>breaking tradition</u>.    *Like mother, like daughter—each in*
*her own way*

## Active Reading Discussed

Student Robert Sakatani underlined key words and circled words he needed to look up because he didn't know the meanings or thought the word might have an unusual meaning. He also blocked off words that were repeated, and he underlined significant metaphors. He noted repeated images of "rooms"and apparently discovered a pattern: daughter, mother, and grandmother, each with her own room. His active reading not only prepared him for class discussion but also for the essay that he later wrote.

Although Robert and his classmates went through the poem line by line, questioning meanings and making observations about Mirikitani's word choices and imagery, Robert's instructor had warned the students that a written line-by-line explication could easily slip into mere summary. Therefore, the instructor required that the students write an analysis that stems from a thesis. In a thesis-driven analysis, the writer controls the organization of ideas rather than just following the lines of the poem.

The instructor also reminded students of the value of using the "sandwich" when incorporating quoted lines from the poem. (You may want to review this technique on pp. 319–323). You will notice in Robert's paper, which follows, how skillfully he introduces the line he is quoting and how deliberately he explains and analyzes the words and images in each line that he includes. Notice that poetry lines are documented by line number in parentheses and that a break between two lines of a poem is indicated by a slash with a space on each side. (See p. 561 for discussion of the slash.)

When Robert refers to the "narrator"of the poem, he means the speaker or "I" of the poem. In poetry analysis it is important not to assume that the poet and speaker in a poem are always the same person. Although Janice Mirikitani may seem to be the speaker of this poem because she is an Asian woman, Robert avoids an unprovable assumption by using the word "narrator"or "mother."

Robert used his active reading notes and ideas from class discussion to prepare the following analysis. Notice that he found the focus for his paper in the parallels and contrasts that he perceived among the three generations of "rooms."

## STUDENT EXAMPLE: POETRY ANALYSIS

Sakatani 1

Robert Sakatani

Professor Waterworth

English 1A

3 October 2010

Breaking the Ties that Bind

Adolescence is a stage in human development filled with physical and emotional changes that a child often finds difficult, frustrating, and at times, painful. It is a journey all individuals must travel as they forge their own identity. Mirroring the growing pains of their child, a mother and father experience changes in the dynamics of their role as parents. Feelings of alienation and rejection are common as the parents witness their son or daughter seeking outside role models to emulate. The mother who narrates Janice Mirikitani's poem "Breaking Tradition" (p. 20) feels this estrangement from her daughter and shares with the reader what she cannot share with her daughter. Through this process, the mother not only traces her own rebellious nature and desire to "break tradition," but she also recognizes a parallel between her daughter's life and her own past.

"Breaking Tradition" is both a poem and a letter. Mirikitani structures her poem in this manner to reveal the indirect way the mother has to express her emotions because she can't communicate this directly to her daughter. It begins with a dedication:

"For my daughter" (1). The isolation and larger typeface of this line reveals the significance of the daughter in the mother's life. This is the mother's way of telling her child that she is so important to her. In contrast, a plaintive statement of truth follows it: "My daughter denies she is like me / Her secretive eyes avoid mine" (2–3). The mother loves her daughter unconditionally, yet she feels the sting of her daughter's rejection. She is shut out of her child's world, "veiled behind music and smoke and telephones" (5). The daughter's tactics are typical of most adolescents who develop a need for privacy. Shutting the world out by slipping on headphones and listening to loud music, or talking endlessly on the telephone are smoke screens that the daughter uses to avoid communicating and revealing what is metamorphosing within her.

The narrator observes "the hatreds of womanhood" as her daughter experiences not only the physical changes of adolescence but also the changing role she will have as a woman in society. The mother empathizes with her daughter's frustration, and she yearns to have that mother/daughter relationship where she can confide in her and "tell her about the empty room / of myself" (5–6). This may be a metaphor for her soul—empty only because there is no one with whom to share her innermost thoughts about womanhood. Mirikitani uses vivid imagery to illustrate the mother's frustration with gender roles that imprison the spirit of a woman. The mother makes an acute observation that the submissive nature of women allows the cycle of male dominance to continue in their lives. The author uses the metaphor of women's hands as "useless, dead speechless clamps" (13) to illustrate how women have been reduced to objects "that need hospital and forceps and kitchens / and plugs and ironing boards to make them useful" (14–15). This further implies that many women define themselves by the gender roles established by society—those of child bearers, cooks, and housekeepers. The suppression of women by other women is just as detrimental. In the simile "whispers live like fungus" (8), Mirikitani implies that being critical of one another will "confine ourselves to jealousies" (10), allowing repressed feelings to multiply and spread.

In her attempt to understand her child, the mother begins processing her own experience as a daughter, revealing that she too denied her own mother. While her daughter resists sharing her inner thoughts with her mother, the narrator recalls her own mother's mandate to be "otanashi", a Japanese word meaning to be mild, submissive, or docile. To be a woman in her mother's time was to be "smothered" (18) and "confined to ceremony" (20). It was a culture where a woman spoke with an indirect gaze and walked behind the man softly. The narrator exposes her contempt for her mother who "kept her room neat with silence" (17) and surrendered herself to manipulation by her family and society, keeping her "passion and loudness wrapped in an obi" (19). Through her recollections, she discovers her own suppressed anger towards this legacy that has left her with an "empty room" for a soul: "want to break tradition—unlock this room / where women dress in the dark" (23–24) and "discover the lies my mother told me" (25). The mother realizes that in order to emancipate herself from her inherited guilt and shame about her body and social mandates, she needs to understand the truth about her mother.

In turn, the mother knows very little about her maturing daughter. All that the mother knows of her daughter is what she discovers through observation—that the daughter's sense of style, "pouting ruby lips, her skirts / swaying to salsa, teena marie and the stones" (43–44) celebrates her freedom to express herself openly, free from the confinements of Asian tradition. The mother wants the opportunity to bond with her daughter and let her know that she, too, has hidden desires to be self-expressive. Mirikitani uses vivid imagery of "tears of violins," "light in my hands," and "music of yellow guitars" perhaps to convey how much she values self-expression, in tears, music, and poetry—the "light" in her hands. While the daughter keeps her true feelings within the fortress of her room, the mother is ready to set herself free.

Through the mother's observations of her daughter's "secretive eyes," the mother has also discovered herself. She now understands the nature of her daughter's rebellion, for it is not unlike her own. Everything that she has wished for her daughter has been the same thing that she wished her own mother could have provided her. In the mother's confession that her daughter "mirrors my aging" (47), there is a realization that she, too, has been undergoing life-altering changes. As she sees her child in a new

perspective, she celebrates that she now can identify with her daughter in pursuit of

"breaking tradition."

### Work Cited

Mirikitani, Janice. "Breaking Tradition." *Between Worlds: A Reader, Rhetoric, and Hand-*

  *book.* Ed. Susan Bachmann and Melinda Barth. 7th ed. New York: Pearson

  Longman, 2012. 20–22. Print.

## Analyzing the Writer's Strategy

To engage the reader, Robert begins with a universal statement about adolescence, noting that both children and parents suffer during this time. Preparing the reader for the subject matter of this poem, he discusses how parents often find themselves "mirroring the growing pains of their child"and experiencing parallel feelings of alienation and rejection. Robert then gives the title and author and clarifies the context of the poem—a mother's lament about her daughter's secrecy and detachment. Now he builds to his thesis, which concludes his introduction: "Through this process, the mother not only traces her own rebellious nature and desire to "break tradition," but she also recognizes a parallel between her daughter's life and her own past." The rest of his paper needs to support this thesis, by illustrating the mother's own rebellion in the past but also her understanding of her daughter's distance.

Robert's frequent use of quotations from the poem as well as his careful analysis of each not only supports his thesis but works to convince readers that his interpretations are sound. Notice how each quotation is always preceded by a smooth lead-in and then followed by careful explanation of the images and language. These "sandwiches" provide development for Robert's ideas and support for his claims. He not only incorporates the line smoothly but also works with the language of the image.

Robert never expects the quoted line to stand on its own without him analyzing it. He also is careful to make sure that his interpretations of certain lines make sense in the context of the poem as a whole. Often there is intentional ambiguity in a poem and it is worthwhile to address it. For example, Robert speculates, using "may" and "perhaps," when he interprets that "the empty room may be a metaphor" for the mother's soul and that she refers to the "'music of yellow guitars' perhaps to convey how much she values self-expression." Another reader of the poem might infer different meanings from this metaphor. If you aren't sure about the poet's intention, you can soften your assertion with "may," "perhaps," or "probably" without resorting to "I think" or "I feel." This "I" voice is unnecessary and can be avoided in analytic writing.

In his conclusion, Robert returns to his opening ideas about both the mother's and the daughter's parallel feelings of alienation and rejection, but he does not repeat his exact words. He expresses what he has gained through his analysis of the poem—a deeper awareness of the poem's theme. He now perceives that both the mother and daughter are "undergoing life-altering changes . . . in pursuit of 'breaking tradition.'" In concluding with this insight, he returns to the title of the poem and gains a succinct final sentence.

 ## PRACTICE WRITING POETRY ANALYSIS

In small groups, select one of the following poems and write a list of images that would be interesting to analyze: "Breaking Tradition" (p. 20), "The Work" (p. 65), "Mr. Z" (106), "Blue Spruce" (p. 173), "Coke" (p. 243). Group the images that belong together, arrange the images in an order that makes sense, and write an assertion—a thesis—that would be workable for an analysis of the poem.

---

 ### Final Tips for Poetry Analysis

- Actively read the poem several times, marking key words, images, figures of speech, and your impressions.
- Note repetitions and image patterns that might help you find a focus for your analysis.
- Decide which elements provide the most productive approach to the poem and formulate a thesis based on that decision.
- Analyze the quoted words or lines you have chosen to support your thesis. Remember to use the "sandwich."
- In your introduction, engage your audience and then briefly prepare your reader for your thesis. Briefly summarize the poem so that your reader has some context for your study.
- In the conclusion, return to your opening idea and thesis without repeating yourself.

# What Is Character Analysis?

Because narratives, short stories, novels, and biographies are often read in freshman composition classes, we include here a character analysis to demonstrate the process of analyzing a subject—a fictitious character or an actual person. Whether you are examining a subject from life or print, you want to observe and record telling details—those that reveal something significant about the person. As you study a character, you will accumulate lots of facts, some that you will discard as irrelevant and others that you will decide are indicative of the person's character. From these facts you will make assumptions about your subject's personality and character. In fact, the heart of your analysis will depend on inference—that is, a hypothesis that you formulate about the character based on the facts that you have observed.

# Character Analysis: Short Story

As you actively read the narrative or short story, list specific examples of speech, behavior, and thought that reveal the character. Mix facts and your responses or inferences about them as you go along. Simply write your list; you will sort, eliminate, and reword examples later.

# Prewriting: Listing Information from a Short Story

If you are taking notes from a short story for a character analysis, you need to record telling descriptions, behaviors, and speech that will help you determine what kind of person that character is. It helps to list all revealing observations in the left column and leave room between observations so you can group similar details. As you list and group related ideas, jot down in the right column an inference about that character. An inference is a hypothesis or supposition about a character that you will later prove or refute from the data collected. Here is a list of observations and inferences about Connie in Joyce Carol Oates's short story, "Where Are You Going, Where Have You Been?" (p. 70):

| Observations about Connie | Inferences about Connie |
| --- | --- |
| "quick nervous giggling habit" | self-conscious |
| cranes neck to glance into mirrors | vain |
| ignores a boy from the high school | callous |
| leaves her friend to go off with Eddie | callous, self-absorbed |
| checks "other people's faces to make sure her own was all right" | self-conscious, insecure |

| | |
|---|---|
| "she knew she was pretty and that was everything" | self-assured, superficial |
| thought her mother preferred her to June because Connie was prettier | self-assured, superficial |
| checks her hair and worries about how bad she looks when a strange car pulls in driveway | insecure, self-conscious |
| "wished her mother were dead and she herself were dead and it were all over" | depressed |
| "everything about her had two sides to it, one for home and one for anywhere that was not home" | two-sided, sneaky? rebellious? |
| jersey | |
| her walk | |
| lipstick | |
| laughter | |
| says she is going to the movies but goes to drive-in restaurant | deceitful |
| avoids conversation with family about "movie" and "Pettinger girl" | sneaky, evasive |
| doesn't go to family barbecue—rolls her eyes at mother | indifferent, evasive, rebellious? |
| goes to Eddie's car | likes being with boys |
| "her mind slipped over into thoughts of the boy she had been with the night before" | daydreamer, romantic |
| daydreams about the boys she hangs out with, "how sweet it always was . . . the way it was in movies and promised in songs" | romanticizes about love, naive |
| "her eyes wander over the windshields and faces all around her" | always on lookout for cute guys |

| | |
|---|---|
| "smirked and let her hair fall loose over one shoulder" | flirtatious |
| couldn't decide if Arnold Friend is attractive or a jerk | naive |
| doesn't realize at first that Friend is so much older | naive |
| flattered by Friend's interest in her | naive |
| amazed by all Friend knows about her: | naive, vulnerable |
|     her name | |
|     friends' names | |
|     description of June | |
|     family at barbecue | |
|     fat woman at barbecue | |
|     neighbor with chickens | |
| appalled by Friend's graphic talk of sex | intimidated, innocent |
| cries out for mother | childlike, needy |
| can't phone police | inexperienced, terrified, paralyzed |
| realizes she will never see mother or sleep in her bed again | childlike |

## Arranging and Thesis Construction

Consider how you will arrange your character traits and the specific examples that support the traits. What do you want to emphasize in your analysis? Consider ending your character analysis with the trait that you find most significant or most indicative of character. By using your most emphatic point in the terminal spot in your paper, you will have a natural conclusion—one that gets at both the heart of your subject and the theme of the short story.

Perhaps the place to start is with the most obvious feature of the subject for analysis because it will take less effort to convince your audience of your perception if your reader shares your perception. In the case of Connie, the writer might address her preoccupation with her looks or her apparent self-assuredness. The writer might also want to look at her flawed family relationships or her boy-craziness. Depending on how you perceive Connie, you may want to order the inferences in your thesis to reflect the reasons for her behavior. Your final character inference should lead naturally to the conclusion of your paper, and you will want to keep this in mind as you order the inferences in your thesis.

***Determining a Thesis.*** You need to have a thesis for your character study, whether or not you include it in your paper. You can determine one by using the character traits that you perceived during grouping. Remember that your thesis expresses a view about a limited subject, such as Connie's character. If you have many observations on your prewriting list, you know you have good support ready.

***Possible Thesis Statements.*** Here are some possibilities for thesis statements for the character analysis of Connie. Remember, each writer's perceptions and preferences will determine the thesis and the order in which the information will be presented.

1. Although Connie appears to be a self-assured teenager, she is actually an insecure, sexually innocent, two-sided girl whose inexperience does not prepare her for the encounter with Arnold Friend.

2. Connie seeks male attention, hangs out with older kids, and affects a sexy exterior, but she is no match for someone with criminal intentions.

3. Connie's life is filled with paradoxes. She is a gregarious girl without a true friend; she lives in a traditional family but has no real bonds with family members; she craves the attention of boys but does not know how to protect herself. Ultimately, these paradoxes render her vulnerable to an attack by someone like Arnold Friend.

4. Because Connie's home life is deficient, Connie develops survival mechanisms. She daydreams, evades interaction with her family, and deceives her family and friends—behavior that could not help her withstand Arnold Friend.

5. Connie projects a brazen, rebellious exterior that masks the naive, insecure girl within.

## STUDENT EXAMPLE: CHARACTER ANALYSIS ESSAY

As you read the following character analysis by student writer Marianela Enriquez, notice that in addition to an examination of the separate qualities of Connie's character, Marianela returns to the essence of the entire work to bring closure to her study.

Marianela Enriquez

Professor Hackner

English 1A

16 April 2010

Who Were You, Connie, and Why Did You Go?

Readers of "Where Are You Going, Where Have You Been?" (p. 70) may be tempted to condemn the protagonist, Connie, as a self-absorbed and superficial 15-year-old and to reduce the story to a simple warning against risky behavior. But it would be a mistake to do so. Throughout the work, author Joyce Carol Oates takes great care to illustrate situations and describe feelings and a personality all survivors of teenage angst have experienced and can recognize. In this way, her chilling short story about a rapist and his teenage victim becomes much more than a tale of fear. It becomes a tragedy of a teenage girl struggling with adolescence on her own and dealing with all the insecurities of her age. Although Connie appears to be a self-assured teenager, she is actually an insecure, sexually innocent, two-sided, and naive girl whose inexperience cannot prepare her for the encounter with Arnold Friend.

Connie herself is pretty, with long, dark blonde hair and brown eyes, and like most girls her age, she is preoccupied with her looks. But even in realizing that this is a typical teenage trait, one can see that Connie's preoccupation is a sign of her insecurity. She has habits of always looking at herself in mirrors and "checking other people's faces to make sure her own was all right," two practices that reveal her insecurity and contradict the self-assuredness of her belief that "she was pretty and that was everything" (71).

Even when a "car she didn't know" pulls into her driveway, Connie's first concern is to check her hair and wonder "how bad she looked" (74). She feels that her physical attractiveness is at the root of everything. She reasons that the tension existing between herself and her mother is because her mother is jealous that her own looks are gone. But, in spite of that thinking, she also reasons that her mother preferred her to her sister June because Connie is the prettier of the two. Connie's beauty seems to be the only asset recognized by other people, so in her insecurity, Connie clings to people's compliments. When understood in this light, Connie can be seen not as a conceited person, but as a confused girl who attempts to work the one good quality she thinks she has.

Because Connie believes that beauty is everything, she naturally moves toward people who will appreciate her beauty—boys. Whether she is at the shopping plaza or a drive-in restaurant "where older kids hung out" (72), Connie always has her eye out for someone to fulfill her dreams of romance. While she does enter cars with boys she barely knows, there is no evidence that Connie actually has intercourse with any of them. According to Connie, her experiences are always sweet, "not the way someone like [her sister] June would suppose but sweet, gentle, the way it was in movies and promised in songs" (74). Connie doesn't have one special boyfriend about whom she dreams. In fact, "all the boys fell back and dissolved into a face that was not even a face, but an idea, a feeling"of romance. Even Arnold Friend recognizes Connie as sexually innocent when he claims he will be her "lover" but adds, "You don't know what that is, but you will" (80). Her shock at his graphic language and her insistence that "people don't talk like that" (80) confirm her innocence as well.

Perhaps the greatest key to understanding Connie's character is to understand her duality. Oates specifies that "everything about her had two sides to it, one for home and one for anywhere that was not home" (71). Connie is full of contrasts: "She wore a pullover jersey blouse that looked one way when she was at home and another when she was away from home" (71). In addition to rearranging her clothing to look older, she changes her walk "that could be childlike and bobbing" when she is at home or "languid" when she is out. "Her mouth that is pale and smirking most of the time, but bright and pink on evenings out" suggests that Connie is rebelling against her parents' make-up rules, and deliberately making herself look older when she leaves her house. Connie's laughter "was cynical and drawling at home," probably in response to family jokes, but is "high pitched and nervous anywhere else" (71). This duality includes deceit. For example, while her family thinks that she and a friend are going to the movies, they often "went across the highway, ducking fast across the busy road" (72). And when her mother bluntly asks, "What's this about the Pettinger girl?" Connie

Enriquez 3

dismisses the question, refusing to let her mother into her world. Whether consciously or unconsciously, Connie builds walls around herself and doesn't talk to anyone with any sort of depth. She can't relate to her older sister, June, who is praised by their mother, and her father ignores the family to "read the newspaper at supper" (71). The indifference of her family is damaging to Connie who is, in actuality, a lonely girl desperate for some kind of positive attention.

Her desire for attention and her teenage naiveté makes her the perfect victim for Arnold Friend. It is ironic that Connie's killer should be the only one in the story who has any kind of understanding into her character. Apparently, the man has been watching Connie for some time and knows of her love for music, of her innocent encounters with boys, and of her family situation so that he can intimidate Connie with what he knows or can guess. Friend is able to create an image of himself that Connie finds appealing. She is interested that they are listening to the same radio station, and she finds his car impressive. She "liked the way he was dressed, which was the way all of them dressed" (76) and at first she is so blinded by the familiarity of his looks that she can't tell if "she liked him or if he was just a jerk" (75). Because of her naiveté, Connie at first doesn't notice that Arnold and his friend are much older than the boys Connie knows. Because Connie craves attention, she is easily flattered by Arnold Friend even though her intuition tells her that something is wrong with these two older men.

Taking advantage of Connie's insecurity and naiveté, Friend manipulates her responses and plays upon her existing insecurities. Armed with facts about Connie's life, Friend plays upon the rivalry between June and Connie by calling her sister "fat" and a "poor, sad bitch" (79), and he plays on Connie's feelings of abandonment, created by her father's disinterest, by repeating that her father isn't coming back for her.

Arnold lets her know that locking the door will not keep him out. Connie's vulnerability is evident in the story's most disturbing scene when Connie tries to telephone the police. Arnold's abuse puts Connie in such a hysterical state that she botches her one chance to escape. Oates's description of "her breath jerking back and forth in her lungs as if it were something Arnold Friend were stabbing her with again

Enriquez 4

and again" (83) is powerful with its sexual implications, and we realize that Connie is raped emotionally before she is physically raped. He let her know that she is hopelessly trapped.

Connie becomes paralyzed by the knowledge that she is alone and vulnerable and that if she doesn't go along with Friend, her family will be murdered. She must feel guilty remembering "how she sucked in her breath just at the moment she passed him" and "how she must have looked at him" at the restaurant (76). In the end, Connie breaks and resigns herself to a sure death. No longer the teenager, Connie is a little girl who can only think, "I'm not going to see my mother again . . . I'm not going to sleep in my bed again" (83).

In creating a character so recognizable in her insecurities, duality, and naiveté, Joyce Carol Oates also creates a character we can pity. Oates creates a sense that the difference in where Connie is going and where we may have gone at the tender age of 15 may not be so much the result of differences in action but the result of differences in fate. This awareness completely destroys the security that comes with thinking that through the avoidance of certain behaviors, we can prevent negative outcomes, and this realization heightens the horror of Connie's story. We are forced to reckon with the uncontrollable nature of chance, a chance that doesn't shrink away from giving a 15-year-old innocent girl a Friend who may take her life.

Enriquez 5

Work Cited

Oates, Joyce Carol. "Where Are You Going, Where Have You Been?" *Between Worlds: A Reader, Rhetoric, and Handbook.* Ed. Susan Bachmann and Melinda Barth. 7th ed. New York: Longman, 2012. 70–84. Print.

## Analyzing the Writer's Strategy

Marienela begins her analysis by acknowledging that some readers will find Connie merely a "self-absorbed and superficial" teenager and will "reduce the story to a simple warning against risky behavior," but Marienela cautions that "it would be a mistake to do so." In fact, she defends Connie to the point of saying that Connie is not to be blamed for what happens to her, and throughout her analysis of Connie's character, Marienela illustrates the forces that contribute to Connie's personality, values, and vulnerability. Marienela supports her inferences about Connie's character with well-integrated and analyzed quoted material from the story, recognizing the importance of including and interpreting many specific illustrations to prove her claims about Connie.

 ### PRACTICE WRITING A CHARACTER ANALYSIS

In small groups, select one of the following individuals and write a list of character traits: Caroline Hwang in "A Good Daughter" (p. 8), Johnny Depp in "Johnny Depp: Unlikely Superstar" (p. 36), or Rita or Marc in "Peaches" (p. 49). Group the details that belong together, arrange the details, and write an assertion—a thesis—that would be workable for a character analysis.

# Character Analysis: Biography

Reading a good biography—the study of a person's life—can be a great pleasure. We learn something intimate, entertaining, and instructive about the subject of the book and the time period in which the person lived. Even readers who would not elect to read a history book discover that a biography vicariously connects them to a culture and time they may not know and permits them to glimpse choices that the subject of the biography made, which perhaps even influenced that epoch. Readers of biography learn about personal conviction as well as about a period of time not their own—discoveries that can be both informative and inspirational. In addition, a longer character analysis written from reading a full-length biography can be a rewarding research project.

## Gathering Information from a Book: Inference Cards

If you are taking notes for a paper based on a biographical study and are using a full-length book, keep separate index cards for each character trait that you observe while you are reading. For example, if you find that your subject was "strong-willed," even in childhood, you would head an index card with that inference. As you read the book, every time you see that trait reflected in an action of your subject or a comment made by someone about the character, simply record the page number. When you infer another trait, perhaps "maternal" or "ambitious," start new cards and continue to record page numbers. When you have completed a 400-page or longer biography, you may have twenty or thirty "inference cards," each with a different trait at the top and each with many recorded page numbers. It may seem time-consuming and even awkward to stop reading to record a page number on an existing card or to start a new card with an inferred trait, but you will not need to reread the full-length book in order to write a good paper. You will have page numbers that indicate the support you need for each inference if you keep track of traits from the beginning of your reading. You will be actively reading and inferring traits, focusing your reading from the start.

## Grouping Cards

After you have finished reading the biography and writing inference cards, group the cards that seem to belong together. For example, if you have cards with "strong-willed," "determined," and "obsessed," you would be able to combine those cards for one section of your subject analysis. The number of page references that you have noted on the cards will help you decide if the trait that you observed is supportable. In your paper, you would use only those character traits for which you have many page numbers recorded.

## A Working Thesis

Write a working thesis featuring those traits that seem to have sufficient support, based on the pages you have recorded on the index cards. You wouldn't want a thesis that features each trait that you have observed, so you'll need to be selective, even if you have grouped two or three different cards that will work together to form one section of your paper. Leselle Norville, in her analysis of Amelia Earhart (p. 457), had inference cards indicating that Earhart was "irresponsible," "indifferent," "complacent," "inept," and "careless." She ultimately selected "complacent" for her thesis, but she returned to the other words, synonyms or near-word equivalents, as she drafted her paper and included examples from each of the cards.

Decide which traits and terms most fairly and completely represent your subject. Write a thesis based on those traits, knowing that you may decide to change the thesis or rearrange it as you draft your paper.

## Arranging the Support

Decide what you want to emphasize about your subject. If the traits that you have observed are both negative and positive, determine which predominate. Arrange the traits in your thesis to project the organization of your paper. Do you want your paper to conclude with surprising information about your subject—inferences that you have discovered in reading the full study of your subject's life—or would you rather have your reader be comforted with a conclusion of familiar material about the subject of your paper? Do you want to emphasize the negative by concluding with those traits, or do you want to show that in spite of problems, your character triumphed? Further, you may see consequences that are derived from your character's strengths, weaknesses, or inconsistencies, and you may want to predict a cause-and-effect relationship in your thesis.

Leselle perceives that Amelia Earhart had contradictory character traits, and she structures her paper around these contrasting traits. For example, she sees "reserve" in Earhart but also "charisma." She sees "competence" but also "complacency." These antithetical traits alternate in the arrangement of her support. Further, Leselle deduces that Earhart's "insecurity" was the cause of these inconsistencies and she forecasts that idea in her thesis and concludes her paper with that awareness.

## From Inference Cards to Drafted Paper

After you have arranged the inference cards in an order that makes sense for your thesis, return to the note cards and look up the page numbers that support each trait. You will want to select examples of behavior, anecdotes, statements from people about your subject, and statements from your subject that most vividly show your subject's personality and character. Your goal is to render a lively portrait of your subject. Remember that you can "tell" your reader many times that your subject was "charismatic," but even one "showing" illustration or revealing anecdote will do more to create a vivid image in your reader's mind.

As you use the material from the page numbers on your cards, combine paraphrased and quoted material. Use your own words to narrate an example most of the time, but where there is vivid description by the author of your biography, or quoted material from someone about your subject, use direct quotation, too. In Leselle's paper, she uses Amelia Earhart's own voice to help her reader hear the kind of person she was. To show Earhart's restlessness, she quotes Earhart's fear that marriage would be "living the life of a domestic robot" (qtd. in Rich 42) and that her prenuptial agreement insisted she have freedom "from even an attractive cage" (qtd. in Chapman 182). By letting her subject speak in her own voice, Leselle captures the tone of a restless young woman who refuses to be confined.

Be certain as you draft that you note the page number where you derived both the paraphrased and quoted material that supports your inferred trait because you will need to include an in-text citation to inform your reader of the source of your information. Compose directly on the computer, if you can, but if you write in longhand, write on only one side of the lined paper so that if you later want to cut the draft up to rearrange sections, you will be able to do so. If you compose directly on the computer, you will be able to cut and paste to rearrange sections of your draft. Develop each section of the paper and take a break before you go on to another trait. Remember Anne Lamott's suggestion and write your focused biography one trait at a time or "bird by bird" (276). If you recognize the incremental nature of this paper, and work on single sections at a time, you won't be overwhelmed by the project.

## Transitions Within and Between Sections

When you have finished drafting each section of the paper, look for ways to create transitions between the sections of analysis. You may decide to rearrange some of your support so that the illustration or quotation that concludes one section can be used as a bridge to the next trait or section of analysis. Leselle finished one section of her analysis of Earhart's restlessness with this sentence:

> Earhart's [prenuptial] requirements of GP were bluntly but honestly stated in [a] letter and reveal that she had a true fear of settling (461).

The next section of Leselle's paper moves from restlessness or "fear of settling" to Earhart's "determination." The new section begins with this sentence:

> Perhaps the only thing to match Earhart's restlessness was her audacious drive. She had an aggressive determination and sheer willpower (461).

As you connect the parts of your paper, check to see that you are returning to the focus points of each section forecast in your thesis. In addition, use key word repetition or synonyms within each section of your paper, perhaps alternative words that were on your inference cards. For example, by showing that Earhart "neglected" to practice, "ignored" safety precautions, was "inept" in necessary skills, and was "apathetic" about equipment that she should have brought on her final flight, Leselle supports her perception that her subject was "complacent" about the realities of aviation. By using substitute words— "neglected," "ignored," "inept," and "apathetic"— to describe Earhart's "complacency," Leselle avoids monotonous repetition of the same word while still supporting her focus. See pages 338–340 for help on transitions.

## Writing the Introduction

After you have drafted each section of the paper to support a particular trait, you are ready to write an introduction. See pages 345–349 for suggestions of particular types of introductions. Leselle, for example, uses the concept of contradiction to "hook" her audience: "How fascinating that a woman slow of speech, ordinary-looking, and capable only of piloting a plane held the world spellbound for almost a decade." You may find your "hook" by reexamining any circled page numbers on your inference cards that indicate a lively anecdote or quotation that could be used to precede your thesis. Leselle was impressed by a photograph of Amelia Earhart that shows her as poised and confident, an image that Leselle perceived as "rehearsed." Further, an Earhart poem that Leselle discovered seems to capture Earhart's values. The photograph and poem, and Leselle's interpretation of them, work well to introduce Earhart's character. She decides to write two introductory paragraphs before moving to her thesis in her third paragraph. Notice as you read Leselle's paper how it is structured to support the thesis, based on inferred character traits, and that it is not a mere summary of a biography.

## STUDENT EXAMPLE: BIOGRAPHY ESSAY

Leselle Norville

Professor Breckheimer

English 1A

2 June 2010

The Earhart Appeal

How fascinating that a woman slow of speech, ordinary-looking, and capable only of piloting a plane held the world spellbound for almost a decade. She attended parades and banquets given in her honor, she mingled with royalty and celebrities, and she drew enormous crowds when she gave lectures. On March 17, 1937, just twenty-two days before her fortieth birthday, Amelia Earhart embarked with Fred Noonan, her navigator, on what promised to be her greatest adventure—an unprecedented flight around the world's equator (Rich 270). She never returned, and although the government mounted a search and rescue operation, neither the craft nor its occupants were ever recovered. Earhart became a legend and is still unquestionably the most popular aviatrix today.

It is doubtful, however, that the world ever truly saw Amelia Earhart, the person, for it is in one's most unguarded moments that true character emerges. She carried herself poised for a snapshot, and newsreels of her show that events were sometimes restaged in order to portray Earhart in the most confident light. In many of her photographs, she wore a much-rehearsed expression. However, there does exist a photograph of her dressed completely in white, from her unfastened leather flying cap to her flight suit, and, curiously enough, she is encircled by a soft, angelic glow (Lovell, plate 1). This photograph was not candid and shows her lips pressed together as she had been directed to do by her husband (Rich 58). She appeared serene and composed, but also in this photograph is an unmistakable ardor in the eyes that peer out from an otherwise restrained, calm face. That insatiable hunger is discernible in the first line of Earhart's poem, "Courage," printed in Doris L. Rich's *Amelia Earhart—A Biography*. It reads, "Courage is the price that life exacts for granting peace" (48) and is a true reflection of Earhart's belief that contentment is not acquired without risk. In that photograph, because her essence shone through, Earhart was beautiful.

Quite often, the fame achieved by beauty is fleeting; the same is true for fame by riches or by well-placed connections. The Earhart appeal knew no such limits. Earhart was captivating because of her complexity, and the result was enduring celebrity. She was an intriguing blend of reserve and charm, of restlessness and determination, and of competence and complacency; however, it is her insecurity that accounted for her varied shades of character, the sum of which made her the architect of her life as well as her unfortunate demise.

Throughout her life, Earhart was reserved. Her difficult childhood, which was spent in the care of an unreliable father and with unsupportive friends, caused her to be withdrawn because "to depend on those she loved could be disappointing, [and] to confide in others might lead to humiliation" (Rich 12). Consequently, Earhart guarded her innermost thoughts very closely. Even in high school, she alienated herself from her classmates. Mary S. Lovell, in *The Sound of Wings: The Life of Amelia Earhart*, refers to the caption beneath Earhart's yearbook photograph which reads, "the girl in brown who walks alone" (22) and which adequately captures the solitary nature of Earhart that would be a constant throughout her life. She also tended to be reserved because she valued her privacy greatly. At Ogontz, a finishing school in Pennsylvania, she wrote a letter begging her mother not to write her teachers because she would "just shrivel" at the thought of having her personal affairs being discussed with others (qtd. in Rich 15). To Earhart, even her mother's concern was no excuse for divulging private issues.

In her youth, Earhart learned that reserving one's true feelings was necessary to preserve one's confidence. These convictions never left her and eventually made public-ity a source of much distress for her. She was often overwhelmed by fans desperate to touch her and get her autograph. Soon after her first transatlantic flight, the first wave of criticism hit. She, herself, felt that her contribution to the flight, on which she was really just a passenger, was only minimal. Nevertheless, Earhart was hurt by comments made in a London newspaper that claimed her presence on the flight was no more significant than that of a sheep on board (Rich 65). Earhart "fibbed," saying that "from first to last [her] contact with the press [was] thoroughly enjoyable" (Rich 66). To say otherwise would have been to betray her injured self-image. Sally Putnam Chapman, in *Whistled Like a Bird*, has recorded the words of empathy for Earhart's situation that Dorothy Putnam entered in her diary. Seeing the erosion of Earhart's privacy, Dorothy Putnam wrote that "there [is] a penalty to being famous and one pays the price by having no privacy whatever!" (111). In light of Earhart's quiet nature, it is amazing that she was able to tactfully handle the press, giving only enough and never too much.

In an interesting twist, the unassuming Earhart seemed destined for great things. It was her reserve that made her remote, but it was her charm that allowed her to win the affection and admiration of others, and she was repeatedly called to leadership by her peers. Jean Adams and Margaret Kimball, in their book, *Heroines of the Sky*, took great pains to emphasize "the gaiety, the humor, and the real kindliness which made the charm of her face" (174). This warm side of Earhart contributed to her magnetism and led to the many leadership posts in her life. Earhart's letters have been compiled by Jean Backus, author of *Letters from Amelia—An Intimate Portrait of Amelia Earhart*, and in one of her letters written from Ogontz, Earhart told her mother that she was "secretary by popular vote" (Backus 37). She quickly elevated to class president status.

In spite of her solitary nature, Earhart was able to create a lighthearted, comfortable atmosphere with her quick wit, refreshing honesty, and gracious manner, causing others to trust and respect her. She was so charming that, according to news articles, "no private party [was] complete without her," and she was "the one essential, apparently, for a successful entertainment" (Rich 171). Her complex character made her both a mysterious loner and a socialite. Fortunately, her quietness, which was sometimes mistaken for aloofness, was offset by her charisma, making it easier to overlook her faults. Placing a distant third in the first Women's Air Derby of 1929 did not blemish her popularity or credibility (Rich 94). The Ninety-Nines, a group of aviatrixes, chose Earhart to be their president, exhibiting great confidence in her ability to represent their interests. Transcontinental Air Transport, a then newly-formed airline, also recognized that charm was an excellent persuader and employed Earhart as their spokesperson (Rich 98).

Amelia's charisma, her ability to hold people's interest and attention, required quite a bit of liveliness, and Earhart had such an abundance of it that she tended to be restless. She lacked focus and became impatient quite quickly. Her cousin, Nancy Morse, in an interview for PBS's *The American Experience*, attributes Earhart's unsettled spirit to her childhood because her family was always moving. It is her belief that "Amelia got easily bored." Earhart's educational and career goals were not concrete. Her interests were widely varied from the sciences to the arts to humanities, and she always made time for sports. She abandoned her plan to graduate from the Ogontz finishing school and decided to aid victims of World War I as a nurse's aid in Canada (Rich 18). She later returned to college to study medicine, dropping out in the end because of financial difficulties. She had as many as twenty-eight jobs including truck driver, fashion designer, social worker, and photographer. When Earhart found flying, her assertion that "[she'd] die if [she] didn't" comes as no surprise (Rich 24). She had been unfulfilled for some time and knew that she could find peace in the freedom of the air.

Earhart could not bear the thought of an uneventful life. Her aversion to settling down accounted for her late marriage. She thought that marriage was "living the life of a domestic robot" (qtd. in Rich 42). She could not bear the thought of being the typical housewife trapped in an unrelenting routine of house tending. "I don't want anything all of the time" she said, and, therefore, just before she married George Palmer Putnam, popularly known as GP, she ensured that she had some freedom "from even an attractive cage" by listing some prenuptial conditions in a letter to him (qtd. in Chapman 182). Earhart, as kindly as possible, informed GP to "let [her] go if [they found] no happiness together" (qtd. in Chapman 182). Earhart's requirements of GP were bluntly but honestly stated in the letter and revealed that she had a true fear of settling.

Perhaps the only thing to match Earhart's restlessness was her audacious drive. She had an aggressive determination and sheer willpower. In childhood, neither admonishment from her grandmother nor risk of injury could deter Earhart. For example, a seven-year-old Earhart decided that "belly-slamming," sleighing downhill in snow while prone, was fun, and she proceeded to do so despite her grandmother's view of the act as unladylike (Rich 3). Young Earhart just barely avoided collision with a horse-drawn wagon because the sleigh, moving too fast for Earhart to control it, sped right under the horse's belly. Relishing the thrill, "the grinning, triumphant speedster" (3) did not consider personal injury or warnings from her grandmother to be a deterrent. This early show of daring and determination was an indication of the resolve she would exhibit later in her life.

Her drive and her restlessness seem incongruent; however, they went hand in hand. Because she tended to be fickle, it was necessary for her to find an activity that could engage her wholly. Rich cites a London newspaper's reference to Earhart as having an "unquenchable determination to go on attempting the hitherto unachieved" (65). Aviation, because it had just begun to gain popularity, provided Earhart with limitless opportunities to set records and then surpass them. Clearly, glory was not her motivation. Earhart referred to her first unofficial altitude record in 1922 as a mere "calibration of the ceiling" because it was an accomplishment that was personally significant, and with every feat accomplished, there remained a greater one unaccomplished (qtd. in Rich 34). She pushed the ceiling higher throughout her career. In spite of the many records she set and the awards she received, however, Earhart was never satisfied. Her drive was not for the record but rather for the achieving of it.

It is not surprising, then, that health took second place to aviation in Earhart's life. Nothing consumed her more than flying. Thus, she overworked herself to finance her career. She once said, "No pay, no fly, no work, no pay," indicating her determination to fly regardless of how hard she had to work to support her passion (Rich 37). Earhart always had a hectic monthly schedule of lecturing to earn a living. She believed that illness was an acceptable cost for the privilege of flying, and as a result, she was hospitalized many times with stress-induced illnesses. Even while she was in college, Earhart never relented. A friend noted that Earhart was exhausted quite often, but "admonitions on the subject were ignored" (Rich 21). She insisted on working and playing hard and found time to study and still play tennis, field hockey, and any other sport that interested her. As long as she felt the activity challenging enough, she was interested.

Earhart's drive to succeed at whatever she attempted outweighed controversy about the motives for her 1935 flight from Honolulu to the mainland. She endured resistance from the Army, from the press, and from the sponsors of her flight (Backus 163). Regardless, she made known her intentions to "make the flight with or without" sponsorship (Backus 163). With renewed confidence in Earhart's success, her sponsors supported her.

One who is driven needs courage, and courage requires remarkable resolve. Earhart was so bent on flying that even though the fumes from the fuel that entered the cockpit sometimes made her nauseous, she preferred to be sick and fly. Earhart, in her poem "Courage," said that "each time we make a choice, we pay with courage" (Rich 49). She knew she could stand the adverse conditions in her plane so long as she could fly.

Although the determination that spawns courage is readily identified with Earhart, competence is seldom attributed to her. She was shrewd, frugal, and responsible, but she is usually portrayed as a victim of GP's fierceness. An interesting fact is that GP's "aggressive action" was excused as "his recipe for success," but Earhart's acquiescence was "less understandable" (Lovell 152). Obviously she was misunderstood. In fact, Earhart's supposed acquiescence belied her astute judgment. Adams and Kimball's *Heroines of the Sky*, even though it contains a highly romanticized account of Earhart's life titled "Amelia Earhart—She Dramatized Flying," fails to acknowledge Earhart's own role in her success. Instead, Adams and Kimball describe GP as being "the real impresario of this prima donna" (162). Earhart knew the value of a resourceful man and used him to her advantage. She valued his "brilliant mind" and "keen insight" (Lovell 117). Gore Vidal, in an interview for *The American Experience*, supported the view that Earhart's partnership with GP was an excellent tactical move because "he made life very easy for her in many ways." She was certainly not a weak person as is commonly perceived.

Furthermore, during her marriage to GP, Earhart ensured that she was responsible for her own finances by keeping them separate. In her prenuptial letter, she required that GP "not interfere with [her] work or play" (qtd. in Chapman 182). Apparently, she was wise enough to prevent problems and control issues that could arise from shared finances by establishing an unrelenting standard before the marriage. Although GP's former wife Dorothy Putnam saw Earhart as "a brainless puppet who does whatever [George] advises" (qtd. in Chapman 139), it is clear that Earhart was very much the master of her own affairs.

In fact, she had always managed her affairs wisely. In school, she was often able to tell her mother not to send money and not to worry because she had enough money to make do. Earhart "hate[d] to spend money for things [she] would never need or want," and she sometimes sewed, altered, or bought second-hand clothing (Rich 15). She chose to be resourceful, carefully avoiding the wastefulness of her parents. Earhart never wanted to inherit what she called the "family failing" (Backus 119). As a result, she "never dealt sentimentally with money" (155). Later in her life, she often asked that her mother and sister send her bills and statements before she gave out significant sums of money. She said that she needed them "just for records" (qtd. in Backus 117).

Efficient use of time was another aspect of Earhart's competence that is evidenced in her letters to her mother. While she was at Ogontz, she delighted in sharing her schedule with her mother, relishing the idea that "every minute [was] accounted for" (29). Earhart was not the kind to waste time on meaningless activities. She would read a book or spend the afternoon playing a sport rather than staying indoors with nothing to do. Later in her life, she was able to keep her appointments and business arrangements in spite of her hectic lecturing schedule, "often with two lectures booked for the same day" (Rich 148). As taxing as her career must have been, Earhart was able to lecture while designing her own clothing line, representing a major airline, and supporting her mother, sister, and a mentally retarded uncle.

As competent as Earhart was, she could also be complacent. She had many accidents throughout her career, which is understandable because airplanes lacked the technology that exists today. Nevertheless, Earhart failed to take responsibility to prevent accidents. In a television interview, Elinor Smith, who was voted the best woman pilot of 1930, pinpointed Earhart's most crucial flaw: failure to practice. Smith observed that in a time when flying was not made simple by technology, "you had to fly every single day," but Earhart "never seemed to practice" (*The American Experience*). In order to facilitate the continuation of her career in aviation, Earhart had turned much of her attention to lecturing and other pursuits, but, ironically, these activities left hardly any time for flying. Instead of slowing down the hectic pace at which she was working, Earhart allowed her skills to become dull. She was already neglecting her health, but she showed gross disregard of accidents and risks when she said she "just does not think about crackups" (qtd. in Rich 131). She seemed to be leaving herself at the mercy of fate. Referring to the Women's Derby of 1929, Smith notes that although Earhart had "the fastest and the most powered plane in that race" (*The American Experience*), Earhart still came in a distant third because she simply did not have the skills to do any better.

In addition to neglecting practice, Earhart abandoned any further instruction in the operation of her craft. Consequently, she was inept in many of the skills essential for safe, successful flying. In all her years of flying, Earhart had never learned Morse code or how to properly operate the plane's radio. Throughout the period of preparation for her ill-fated round-the-world adventure, Earhart exhibited inexcusably poor judgment. According to explorer and aerial photographer Brad Washburn, Earhart ignored "fundamentally important things" (*The American Experience*). Washburn was to have been Earhart's navigator for the trip but abandoned the project in the final stages of preparation because he doubted her judgment. He said that just minutes before her final flight, Earhart decided that taking her parachute and life raft would prove too bothersome, so she left them behind just as she had left her Morse code machine and antenna. Ultimately, Earhart's complacency—demonstrated by her failure to bring essential equipment on such a challenging flight—was greatly responsible for her tragic end.

Earhart was complex, having varied and seemingly incongruous character traits; however, the one link between her strengths and failings was her insecurity. Her fear of humiliation caused her to withdraw, while her fear of alienation sparked her charisma. She was restless, which was not only an indication of unfocused energy but revealed her indecisiveness and uncertainty. She was certainly driven but needed to reassure herself of her worth. Earhart's meticulous handling of money and time management was a shield against becoming like her parents, but her complacency revealed a lack of common sense and self-preservation. She was trapped in a vicious cycle of overwork and overplay and, perhaps, she was overwhelmed. In her poem "From an Airplane," Earhart describes darkness as unavoidable, slow, and unrelenting: "Even the watchful purple hills that hold the lake could not see so well as I the stain of evening creeping from its heart" (*The American Experience*). These lines may seem prophetic, considering Earhart's premature death.

In her final desperate communication with the world, possibly just before she fell from the sky into the lonely Pacific, Earhart stumbled over her words, her voice "shrill and breathless, her words tumbling over one another" (Rich 270). Earhart's life was undeniably remarkable, but perhaps unfulfilling. Once again, Earhart's poetry, whether intentionally or inadvertently, describes her life. An excerpt from an unfinished poem reads, "Merciless life laughs in the burning sun and only death, slow, circling down" (qtd. on *The American Experience*). And such was her end.

## Works Cited

Adams, Jean, and Margaret Kimball. "Amelia Earhart—She Dramatized Flying." *Heroines of the Sky.* Freeport, NY: Doubleday, 1942. Print.

"Amelia Earhart: The Price of Courage." Narr. Kathy Bates. *The American Experience.* PBS. 1993. Videocassette.

Norville 11

Backus, Jean L. *Letters from Amelia: An Intimate Portrait of Amelia Earhart.* Boston: Beacon
    Press, 1982. Print.

Chapman, Sally Putnam. *Whistled Like a Bird: The Untold Story of Dorothy Putnam, George
    Putnam, and Amelia Earhart.* Ed. Stephanie Mansfield. New York: Warner Books,
    1997. Print.

Lovell, Mary S. *The Sound of Wings: The Life of Amelia Earhart.* New York: St. Martin's
    Press, 1989. Print.

Rich, Doris L. *Amelia Earhart: A Biography.* Washington, DC: Smithsonian Institution
    Press, 1989. Print.

## Analyzing the Writer's Strategy

The purpose of a character analysis of a once-living person is not entirely different from a character analysis of a fictitious character. The goal is to create a vivid portrait of the subject by focusing on inferred traits that can be supported with text. The analysis must be focused around a thesis based on inferences about the person so that the paper does not become a birth-to-death summary of the subject's life, or a mere review of the book read about the subject.

## Writing the Thesis

The writer has plenty of creative opportunity to decide which character traits may best represent the subject's life. Most people are complex personalities, whose lives are filled with moments of strength and weakness, failure and triumph. Leselle was most interested in the contradictions within Amelia's character, how her life developed and may have ended because of these inconsistencies. Leselle made the decision to balance these contrasting traits so that her focused biography of Earhart fully represents the woman behind the famous pilot. Further, Leselle is insightful and sees that Earhart's insecurity accounted for the variations in her character, and she focuses her thesis to reflect that cause-and-effect perception:

> Earhart was captivating because of her complexity, and the result was
> enduring celebrity. She was an intriguing blend of reserve and charm,

of restlessness and determination, and of competence and complacency; however, it is her insecurity that accounted for her varied shades
of character, the sum of which made her the architect of her life as well
as her unfortunate demise (458).

In her opening paragraph, Leselle deliberately refers to Earhart's fatal accident rather than postponing this fact. Her strategy is to show the reader that
Earhart's premature death may have been a consequence of certain character
traits and not totally unexpected.

## Selecting Support to "Show," Not "Tell"

Leselle uses statements from other people as well as Earhart herself to support
the points in her paper and to create a vivid portrait of her subject. In order to
show that Earhart was "reserved," Leselle includes the line beneath Earhart's
high school photograph that reads: "the girl in brown who walks alone." In
that quotation, Leselle uses another's voice to show Earhart's solitary nature.
To reveal Earhart's character and values, Leselle also includes numerous
examples of Earhart's own voice; she documents these appropriately, adding
"qtd. in" within the parenthetical reference so the reader knows that the words
are from someone other than the biographer. For example, Leselle provides an
excerpt from a letter that Earhart wrote to her mother "begging her mother
not to write to her teachers because she would 'just shrivel' at the thought of
having her personal affairs being discussed with others" (459). By recording
Earhart's vivid word choice, "shrivel"—to wither, become helpless and
useless—Leselle captures Earhart's extreme fear of having her teachers talk
about her. Throughout her analysis, Leselle selects memorable descriptions
and anecdotes to show her subject, reveal Earhart's character, and promote
the reader's interest.

## Conclusions

In her conclusion, Leselle recalls her thesis, that "Earhart was complex, having varied and seemingly incongruous character traits." Leselle underscores
the cause-and-effect perception that she forecasts in her thesis by discussing
many of the incongruous traits that were the result of Earhart's insecurity.
Leselle satisfies readers need for closure, how Earhart's life ended, and she
reminds readers of the drama that she projected in her introduction—that
Earhart's plane never returned from her last flight over the Pacific. Finally,
Leselle frames her focused character study by incorporating lines from yet
another Earhart poem.

**Final Tips for Writing a Focused Biography**

- Select a good biography to read, one that has documented sources. When in doubt, get advice from your school librarian or your instructor.
- Find additional biographical sources at the library and online to complement your primary biography.
- Write a thesis based on character inference, using traits you can support.
- Arrange the traits in the thesis thoughtfully to reflect your full perception of the subject.
- Use anecdotes about the character, comments quoted from your subject, and comments made about the subject to support your thesis and to *show* your subject.
- Use a variety of transitional devices between sections of your paper in order to gain unity, coherence, and emphasis.
- Write an enticing introduction to your analysis and conclude meaningfully, perhaps with some insight about your perception of the person's life.
- Use in-text parenthetical references to document the source of ideas, facts, and quotations.
- Title your work to engage your reader.

# Chapter 12

# Writing the Research Paper

In this chapter you will learn how to write a research paper and to

- manage your time
- gather materials using databases or the Internet
- evaluate your sources
- avoid plagiarism
- benefit from a good model essay
- document your paper using MLA citations

The research paper—routinely assigned by most freshman composition in-structors and universally dreaded by freshman composition students—has a worse reputation than it deserves. Like most tasks that at first seem over-whelming, the research paper needs time and organization. The steps sug-gested here, and the model of a student paper in this section, should help you handle such an assignment.

## Planning the Research Paper

Even if you had outstanding luck in high school and welded a research paper together in a manic weekend session, your college professor certainly won't value the results of such a rushed job, and you will find your course grade threatened. Instead, admit to yourself that the research paper requires your attention through a number of steps, all of which you can handle. The research assignment is not designed to show what you don't know but to confirm what you can do.

In addition, the assignment encourages you to experience the pleasure of discovering new interests and information. If your instructor allows you to choose your topic, take advantage of this opportunity to pursue one that intrigues you, one that is worth the time and energy that you will devote to the investigation. Enjoy the discovery!

## More Tools, More Choices

Computers make the process of discovering an intriguing topic more fun than ever. All libraries now have computers that can not only direct you to books but also provide you with immediate feedback about the status of the book—whether it is in the library or when it should be returned. You can also request that the book be held for you or sent from another library. Periodical searches are equally easy and, in some cases, you can print out the full text of an article or print an abstract, a brief summary that will help you determine whether you want to find the original full text.

We encourage you to use your library's superb databases—even from your home computer—to discover alternative topics that you may not have previously considered. It won't take you long to discover that the databases provide organized searches of authored articles that you will need for college writing. Further, you are not restricted to your own library's collection but can "roam the stacks" of the best libraries worldwide.

## Time Schedule for the Research Paper

If your instructor does not assign due dates for the various stages of the paper, try dividing the time between the assigned date and the due date into four approximately equal parts. For example, if you have two months for the preparation of a paper, each stage will have two weeks. If you have one month, you can give each stage a week of your time.

### STAGE 1—DISCOVERING A TOPIC AND MATERIALS

- Determine the topic that interests you and satisfies the paper assignment. You may want to choose 2–3 alternatives, to make sure that you are interested in the material and that there are plenty of credible sources for your research. Allow a few days, but do not postpone that first decision for longer than a few days.

- Go to the library and begin your search for materials. Locate the computers with your library's catalog of books and the computers with the periodical databases of credible, previously edited and printed articles.

- Meet a reference librarian—the researcher's best friend. Ask the librarian whether your topic has additional subject headings that you should be aware of so that you can do a complete search while you are in the library.

- Gather a few choice books to explore at home. Also begin your periodical search and email yourself any full-text articles that look promising. You then can decide at home which articles will be most useful and print only those that are relevant.

## STAGE 2—TAKING NOTES

- Using pen and paper, a laptop or other electronic tool, begin a list of each of your sources, copying down *all* important information: author, title and subtitle, edition or volume number, editor or translator, city of publication and publisher, and date of publication. If you are using electronic sources, record the complete URL (Web address) and the date that you access the material, in addition to the above information. If you are only using select pages, or a chapter from an anthology, or if the book is a reference text that you can't check out, make sure that you record the exact page numbers of any paraphrased or quoted material. This precise record-keeping will eliminate hours of unnecessary frustration and return trips to the library.

- Read and take notes on the materials that you find. If you take notes in the library on works that you do not intend to photocopy, write direct quotations and paraphrase these later, when you know how much material you want to use. If you are printing from electronic sources, be selective or you will be hauling home piles of paper. Read widely; print rarely!

- As you take notes, think about how you might focus your paper.

## STAGE 3—DRAFTING AND REVISING

- Determine a working thesis and write an outline for the paper.

- Use the computer to draft your paper. The extra time you spend preparing your paper electronically will be doubly compensated in revision speed and quality. **Remember to click on** *save* **often and to save your work not only on your hard drive but also on a backup flash drive.**

- Make sure that you have put quotation marks around any borrowed phrases or lines from your sources and include the author's last name and page numbers even in your draft. Be sure also to give credit for all paraphrased material—researched ideas that you have put into your own words. (See more on plagiarism, pp. 480–483.)

- Meet with your instructor or writing center staff for feedback before you continue.

- Revise your manuscript, strengthening the thesis, improving the arrangement, using more emphatic support, improving word choice and transitions, and clarifying any writing that your reader finds ambiguous or weak.

### STAGE 4—EDITING AND PROOFREADING

- Examine your paper for coherence and unity. Read for effective transitions between paragraphs and within long paragraphs. (See pp. 337–343.) Edit carefully. Realize that spell-check and grammar-check might flag words that are correct as well as miss an incorrectly used word that appears to be spelled correctly (their/there/they're). Make sure that you have used quotation marks at the beginning and the ending of all quotations and that you have parenthetical citations for all ideas and quotations you have incorporated. (See plagiarism, pp. 480–483.)

- Print out the revised copy of your paper, the Works Cited page, and provide a heading on the first page with your name, professor's name, course number, and date in the upper left-hand corner. (See the MLA model on pp. 486–501.)

If you divide the research paper assignment into parts, you will not be overwhelmed by the task. You may also realize that you need longer to draft your paper but less time for revision because the computer has expedited this process.

# Gathering Library Material

## Getting Started

Shannon Paaske's instructor required a research paper that was more developed, and used more sources, than the shorter documented papers that had been assigned earlier in her composition course. In addition to the length and source requirements, Shannon's assignment was to respond more fully to one of the subjects included in Part I of *Between Worlds*. Shannon decided that she wanted to learn more about the world of the disabled.

Her initial response to the research paper may have been posed in the form of questions: What are the problems the disabled have in attending classes? In working? In their social lives? What technology is available for the disabled on my campus? What kind of legislation exists to help the disabled? How do the disabled feel about their conditions? Are the attitudes of Soyster characteristic of the disabled? (See p. 144.) Has he written any other articles?

With these questions in mind, Shannon went to her college library.

## Meeting the Librarian

The reference librarian can show you how to use the various computers, the periodical databases, and the Internet, and can direct you to specialized reference books and indexes that can be particularly helpful as you begin your research. There are more indexes than you can ever imagine, and a little time browsing these resources can open up new worlds of information. For example, if you have been assigned to write a biography research paper (457) and you are just beginning your search for a subject, a general index such as *Encyclopedia of World Biography* or a more selective index such as *Contemporary Black Biography* are helpful shortcuts to learning about people's lives before you head off to find a full-length biography. Reference librarians are waiting to introduce you to these resources. Also, if you are new to research or to using computers and databases to find materials, consult your reference librarian and express your concerns. Most colleges and universities have short courses or workshops to orient students to library and online research.

## Finding Information

Each library has its own computer system with particular options for searching (such as "keyword" or "browse"). Ask the librarian to recommend a method for searching for books and periodicals. If you cannot locate articles under a particular topic, ask the reference librarian for the Library of Congress Subject Headings, which will provide an alternative term. For example, if you are searching for materials on film, the correct subject heading is "motion pictures," not film or movies. Many students leave libraries empty-handed or with few sources because they have not used the correct search method or because they have not entered all the appropriate headings.

## Using Both Books and Periodicals

As you collect research materials, you should search for books as well as periodicals. Books provide greater depth and analysis, and they often include a historical overview (of legislative changes, economic patterns, fashion trends, or art or political movements). Because books take longer to publish, the material may be dated for some subjects, but historical perspective and depth are advantages in most fields. For more current information, you should also check periodicals, using the databases. These articles will provide up-to-date information: news events, current legislation, technological or medical data, or recent statistics. In addition to periodicals, books, and Internet materials, don't neglect videos, films, CD-ROMs, and interviews as potential sources of information.

## Using Electronic Sources

As you may already realize, electronic sources offer you several advantages: (1) You can locate materials that are in your local libraries and in libraries thousands of miles from your campus; (2) you can read materials on the

Internet that may not yet be available in print because they were posted as recently as the day of your search; (3) you can also tap into the knowledge of other researchers by using general search engines such as Google or Yahoo! or more specialized databases (see below); (4) you can subscribe to a *listserv,* a mailing service that will email you up-to-date articles and answer questions on specialized topics; and (5) using certain services, you can obtain maps, pictures, and graphics that will enhance your understanding of your subject.

Your library has information on just about every topic, so if you do not find what you need, realize that you may be using an incorrect heading or misspelling a term. Computers are helpful, but it often takes a human being— a librarian—to show you how to access that help.

## Beginning a Periodical Search—Head for the Databases

In addition to helping you search for books, your librarian will help you access essential databases for your particular research assignment. All of the materials in databases have been written by an author, edited for accuracy and style, previously published in respected print media, and are made available without commercial interest. On these pages, no one will try to sell you anything—other than ideas and information. Libraries subscribe to many different databases, and your librarians can tell you which services are available to you and which are appropriate for your assignment. For example, if you are writing on a current topic, databases such as *ProQuest* or *NewspaperSource* will provide articles from major national newspapers. If you need more depth and development, databases such as *Academic Search Premier* or *ERIC* (*Educational Resources Information Center*) provide articles from magazines and journals. If you need information from a particular field of study—history, fine arts, literature, science—specialized databases can help: *Issues and Controversies; CQ Researcher* (*Congressional Quarterly Researcher*); *Gale Literary Databases* (*Contemporary Authors, Dictionary of Literary Biography,* and *Contemporary Literary Criticism*); *LRC* (Literature Research Center); *Health and Wellness Center; CINAHL* (*Cumulate Index to Nursing and Allied Health Literature*); *MedlinePlus* or *Organized Wisdom.* These are just a few of the special databases that are used by students and faculty for academic research. You may be familiar with *EBSCOhost's* general database which includes popular magazines, but don't overlook the academic journals and magazines needed for most college research. For example, see *EBSCOhost's Academic Search Premier* as a better resource for your college papers.

# Beginning an Internet Search— Some Cautions

In contrast to using databases for your academic research, general searches on the Web require some cautions. The Internet is a vast information network, but you must remember that *anyone* can post material on the Web. This means that the article that you are reading about vaccinations or greenhouse gases could be a rant or spoof written by someone with no credible information or expertise. In fact, according to the Berkeley guide to *Evaluating Web Pages,* "Most pages found in general search engines for the Web are self-published or published by businesses small and large with motives to get you to buy something or believe a point of view" (8). See www.lib.berkeley.edu/TeachingLib/Guides/Internet/Evaluate.html and see also the evelation guide included below (pp. 478–479).

Further, students may be tempted to begin their research with Wikis—Web pages modified by any Internet users. One of the most popular is the online encyclopedia *Wikipedia* (www.wikipedia.org), which can provide some initial information to get you started. However, keep in mind that, unlike a published encyclopedia, *Wikipedia* can be modified by any Internet user. Therefore the information may be inaccurate and is typically not acceptable for scholarly papers. However, if your professor permits you to use open source materials in your research, you need to document those sources. This means that you need to cite, within your essay and in your Works Cited at the end, any ideas or "facts" drawn from a *Google* search.

It is also important that you move beyond easily accessible, online sources to materials with more depth and substance. Instead of limiting yourself to the same few links that your classmates are using, go to your library's home page and, using the periodical databases, search for relevant articles. Nearly all of these articles will have credible authors who are experts in their fields and editors who have checked and verified their information, and perhaps even edited for precision and clarity. If you use the library databases, your essays will reflect your effort and innovation as well as the integrity of the sources that you have used.

# Refining an Internet Search

When Shannon Paaske updated the research paper that we published in the first edition of this textbook, she knew that the databases would provide her with current and useful material. Using *Medline,* she entered the keyword "disability," and then refined her search by adding "AND" and the terms "assistive and technology," to locate articles about the current technology designed to assist the disabled. Shannon also checked the bibliographies of these articles to find additional information for her paper.

Before starting a search, define your research goal and then list on paper the terms associated with that topic. You should enter those terms in the search box of a *search engine*. As you explore each term one at a time, you may sense that your terms are too general. You can then join the key terms with common words like "and," "or," "but not," so that the selections more closely reflect your interest and the number is manageable. If your term is too general, you will have either thousands of "hits" or none—and you will most likely be overwhelmed or discouraged. Athough you won't necessarily want to restrict your search terms in your initial information-gathering phase, eventually you will refine your search to avoid being overwhelmed with sources. Because every search engine has its own system, be sure to click on the "help" icon of the particular search engine to learn the best search strategies.

## Keeping Track of Internet Sources

Quickly read the material on the screen and send to your email only those pages that you sense will be useful and will later want to print. If you want to return to an article or database, you can add a bookmark to mark it. Avoid bookmarking too many sites—a mistake similar to highlighting an entire page rather than selective passages of a textbook.

Keep accurate track of all information and addresses of sites that you use, including the access date, so that you have complete information to provide on your list of works cited. Because the reader of your paper may want to learn more about a particular aspect of your topic, your information must be accurate.

## The Abuse of Electronic Sources

It may seem a researcher's dream to discover 3,000 hits on a topic with a print button handy and a fresh supply of paper in the printer. However, our own quick searches of Internet materials have produced mixed results. We found some articles that were well written and prepared with exemplary support. We also found too many trivial, unsigned, poorly written pieces—work that no serious college student should consider using. We thus have serious reservations about students who ignore the library and its databases, and we would undoubtedly fail papers that were last-minute patch jobs of poorly reasoned Web material.

*"On the Internet, nobody knows you're a dog."*

## Evaluating Online Sources

Just as student researchers have always needed to consider the quality of their sources, you, too, will need to evaluate what you have read and printed from the Internet. Students working from books have the clear advantage of knowing that an editorial staff has evaluated the text and verified the data in it. However, no such safeguards exist on the Internet where literally *anybody* can publish *anything*. So while your job as a student researcher may be lightened in the discovery phase, your job in evaluating material from the Net is more challenging. Let's look at criteria for evaluating Web sources, entitled "The Good, the Bad, and the Ugly: or, Why It's a Good Idea to Evaluate Web Sources," distributed on the Internet by Susan E. Beck, Instruction Coordinator, New Mexico State University Library. (You can visit this site at http://lib.nmsu.edu/instruction/evalcrit.html.) Use the following questions to evaluate the authority, accuracy, objectivity, currency, and coverage of the material that you find on the Web.

## ⬤⬤ Evaluation Criteria for ⬤⬤ Web Sources: "The Good, the Bad, and the Ugly"
### *Susan E. Beck*

I. Authority
- Is there an author? Is the page signed?
- Is the author qualified? An expert?
- Who is the sponsor?
- Is the sponsor of the page reputable? How reputable?
- Is there a link to information about the author or the sponsor?
- If the page includes neither a signature nor indicates a sponsor, is there any other way to determine its origin?

   Look for a header or footer showing affiliation.

   Look at the URL. http://www.fbi.gov

   Look at the domain. .edu, .com, .ac.uk, .org, .net

Rationale

1. Anyone can publish anything on the Web.
2. It is often hard to determine a Web page's authorship.
3. Even if a page is signed, qualifications are not usually provided.
4. Sponsorship is not always indicated.

II. Accuracy
- Is the information reliable and error-free?
- Is there an editor or someone who verifies/checks the information?

Rationale

1. See number 1 above.
2. Unlike traditional print resources, Web resources rarely have editors or fact-checkers.
3. Currently, no Web standards exist to ensure accuracy.

III. Objectivity
  - Does the information show a minimum of bias?
  - Is the page designed to sway opinion?
  - Is there any advertising on the page?

Rationale

1. Frequently the goals of the sponsors/authors are not clearly stated.
2. Often the Web serves as a virtual "Hyde Park Corner," a soapbox.

IV. Currency
  - Is the page dated?
  - If so, when was the last update?
  - How current are the links? Have some expired or moved?

Rationale

1. Publication or revision dates are not always provided.
2. If a date is provided, it may have various meanings. For example,
   It may indicate when the material was first written
   It may indicate when the material was first placed on the Web
   It may indicate when the material was last revised

V. Coverage
  - What topics are covered?
  - What does this page offer that is not found elsewhere?
  - What is its intrinsic value?
  - How in-depth is the material?

Rationale

1. Web coverage often differs from print coverage.
2. Frequently, it's difficult to determine the extent of coverage of a topic from a Web page. The page may or may not include links to other Web pages or print references.
3. Sometimes Web information is "just for fun," a hoax, someone's personal expression that may be of interest to no one, or even outright silliness.

## Resisting Temptation

Even after you have evaluated your sources and verified that your authors are credible, there is another trap to avoid. Because you may have actual copies of good articles on your computer, you could easily be tempted to simply cut and paste chunks of others' work into your draft. Resist this temptation! All college papers need to reflect *your* perception, using experts to *support* your views. Most of your essay should be your own thinking and words, with supporting information from experts. This information needs to be carefully analyzed—explained and evaluated in your own words and voice—and then accurately documented.

## Plagiarism

Whether you use computer printouts, note cards, or photocopied pages from a book, you must record all of the necessary information so you can give credit and avoid **plagiarism—using someone else's ideas or language as your own**. Whether this is done accidentally or deliberately, it is a serious offense that schools may punish with expulsion. If you are desperate to complete an assigned paper, using somebody else's work, including work published on the Internet, may seem like a good idea to you. *Don't do it.* Your professors can easily search for and find the same words and ideas that you have stolen for your paper. Furthermore, many colleges subscribe to services such as TurnItIn.com with databases to help instructors verify whether their students' work is original. Failing a course and being expelled from school are not worth the risk. Realize that you are capable of doing the work that you have been assigned and that accomplishing this task with integrity will strengthen your skills and confidence as a writer.

Plagiarism most often occurs inadvertently—often because of sloppy note taking, poor record keeping, or even ignorance. One kind of ignorance is the misperception that you don't need to document general information from a quick Google search. **However, *any* information retrieved from any online source—electronic dictionaries, Wikipedia, YouTube, for example—must be accredited.** You can avoid the problem of inadvertent plagiarism by accurately recording, from your earliest notes on, the source of every idea—even in summary or paraphrased form—and of every key word or phrase of another writer that you are using. Furthermore, if you change or omit anything in the text that you are quoting, you need to use brackets (see p. 564) and ellipses (see pp. 562–563) to signify to your reader that you have made a change. It is important that you use quotation marks as soon as you begin using the author's words. Finally, you need to completely and accurately cite the source of material that you have used. Failure to adhere to these conventions may result in a charge of plagiarism, however inadvertent it may be. Examples of inadvertent plagiarism are shown below, so that you can avoid this error in your own work.

***Inadvertent Plagiarism.*** Plagiarism occurs if a quotation is not used or documented correctly. In the following excerpt, read the original, from Marcus Mabry's "Living in Two Worlds" (p. 99) and the incorrect uses of the quotation.

### Original

Most students who travel between the universes of poverty and affluence during breaks experience similar conditions, as well as the guilt, the helplessness and, sometimes, the embarrassment associated with them. Our friends are willing to listen, but most of them are unable to imagine the pain of the impoverished lives that we see every six months. Each time I return home I feel further away from the realities of poverty in America and more ashamed that they are allowed to persist. What frightens me most is not that the American socioeconomic system permits poverty to continue, but that by participating in that system I share some of the blame.

 **PRACTICE FINDING THE ERRORS**

Identify the incorrect uses of the material in each of these examples:

1. Marcus Mabry talks about the student who travels between the universes of poverty and affluence during school breaks.

2. Mabry is frightened by the fact that "the American socioeconomic system permits poverty to continue" and that "by participating in that system," he shares some of the blame (100).

3. One student who was studying at Stanford describes the guilt, helplessness, and embarrassment that he and other students feel when they move between their school lives and their home lives when they return home for vacation.

4. Mabry is concerned not that "the American socioeconomic system permits poverty to continue, but that by participating in that system he shares some of the blame" (100).

## Explanation of Errors

1. In his mistaken notion that he has "only paraphrased," this writer has failed to place quotation marks around Mabry's words ("who travel between the universes of poverty and affluence"). Additionally, the student has not documented with parenthetical information the source of the material that he has taken from Marcus Mabry. Even if the student were to use only the image of the "universes of poverty and affluence," the image is Mabry's and must be documented.

2. This writer has misrepresented Mabry. The original expresses the idea that it is *not* America's "socioeconomic system" that frightens him but his fear that "by participating in that system" he "shares some of the blame." The writer has written a combination of paraphrase and quotation that does not correctly express Mabry's point.

3. The writer here has attempted a paraphrase of Mabry's words that stays too close to the original in repeating "guilt," "helplessness," and "embarrassment," without using quotation marks and which fails, in any case, to attribute and document the source of the idea.

4. This writer has made a change in Mabry's quoted material in order to merge his or her text smoothly with Mabry's words. But the writer has failed to use brackets to inform the reader that there is a change in the quoted material. This is how the quotation should look: "'The American socioeconomic system permits poverty to continue, but that by participating in that [he shares] some of the blame.'"

If you carefully copy material from another source, double-check your paraphrases, and inspect your quoted material and compare it with the original to verify that you have been accurate in your sense as well as in the use of quotation marks, brackets, and parentheses, you will avoid the inadvertent plagiarism that threatens your integrity as a writer and flaws the writing that you produce.

# A Checklist for Preventing Plagiarism

Whether you are reading through your drafts or editing your final essay, you will find that this checklist will help you write a credible essay and avoid plagiarism:

- From the beginning of your research, did you carefully take notes and record the sources of all words and ideas gathered from your readings and Internet searches?

- As you were taking notes, did you put quotation marks around all words taken from other writers or found on Web sites? If not, track down these sources immediately, before you forget what you have used.

- If your assignment requires multiple sources—as research papers do—have you varied your sources to include diverse views so that you are not merely writing a summary of a book or article?

- Is your thesis your own idea and wording so that it reflects your own position and blueprint for development of your essay?

- Have you accurately represented the ideas, statistics, and words of the sources you have used? To avoid distortions, compare your original notes with what you have written in your essay.

- Do you have parenthetical citations for all words and summaries of ideas drawn from your sources? Have you placed all citations within your paragraphs, immediately following the information from your sources?

- For all paraphrased material, have you responsibly represented your sources and included parenthetical citations for those paraphrases?

- Did you include correct page numbers as required for *all* quotations, paraphrases, and summaries?

- If you have altered any quotations by removing words or adding a word, have you used ellipses or brackets correctly?

- Does your Works Cited page include all of the sources used in your paper?

# Developing a Working Thesis

While Shannon read from her materials and took notes, she decided to focus on these three approaches: (1) technology that equips the disabled to leave home and enter the outside world, (2) the media's recent interest in depicting the disabled, and (3) the attitudes of the nondisabled person toward the disabled. Her working thesis looked something like this:

> Technology and the media have improved life for the disabled, but they still suffer social isolation and indignities.

Shannon talked with her instructor about her working thesis and the rough outline of the three parts that she planned to write. Shannon and her instructor concluded that she did not have enough information about the social isolation of the disabled, and that her own casual observations would be insufficient for a well-developed research paper. The instructor suggested that Shannon approach the Special Resources Center on the campus to arrange interviews with disabled students who would be willing to talk about their social situations. Furthermore, both the instructor and Shannon concluded that they knew very little about legislation that gave rights to the disabled, and both realized that any reader would want to know something about this legislation.

# Gathering Additional Information: The Interview

Before she started the first draft of her paper, Shannon returned to the library to collect information on the legislation that guarantees the disabled access and ensures their rights. In the process, she discovered some old laws that were so ridiculous that they could provide a dramatic introduction for her paper.

Shannon also contacted the director of her campus Special Resources Center, who gave her names and telephone numbers of students who volunteered to talk with her. These face-to-face interviews proved to be a valuable resource in her paper. Shannon was able to describe the experiences of real individuals and to catch their actual voices in print.

## Conducting the Interview

Although you have prepared questions and ordered them, you may find that the answers cause you to skip to another question or to think up a question on the spot. Your ability to respond with follow-up questions and encouragement ("Why do you think that happened?" "How did you respond?") may determine the depth of the interview. Such follow-up questions may prompt the interviewees to move from predictable responses to those that are fresh and candid.

As you take notes, concentrate on getting down key phrases and controversial claims. Shannon recorded this from one of her interviewees: "Some people are prejudiced and ignore us. That makes me angry." Shannon put quotation marks around exact words so she could remember which words were her subject's and which she added or paraphrased. As you interview your subjects, don't hesitate to ask them to clarify points or expand on ideas so you can get the necessary information. Before you leave, remember to ask about additional sources or reference materials (reading materials, brochures, and names of other specialists). Also, check the spelling of each interviewee's name.

Because these people are giving you some valuable time for the interview, it is essential that you offer to meet where and when it is convenient for *them*. Arrive on time, don't overstay your welcome, and prepare your questions before the meeting. Remember to be exceptionally courteous and to show appreciation for their time and help.

## Writing up the Interview

Immediately after the interview, write out or type up the questions and answers while the session is still fresh in your mind. If you discover you have missed any important material or may have misunderstood a point, call back your interviewee immediately for a clarification.

When you integrate the interviewees' comments into your paper, be careful to quote exactly and to represent the context of the statement accurately. Misusing quotations or distorting their intended meaning destroys your integrity as a writer. Shannon found that her conversations with the disabled provided insights that her readings could not. The strength of her argument, however, could not rely only on interviews and personal experiences. She used nine printed sources and three electronic sources to develop her argument.

### STUDENT EXAMPLE: RESEARCH PAPER

You may be interested to know that our former student, Shannon Paaske, who wrote the research paper that we published in the first edition of *Between Worlds,* has finished her undergraduate work and is now a first-grade teacher in Los Angeles. It is probably every student's nightmare that a former teacher would track her down, but we did. Shannon agreed to update her paper using more current material, including the Internet. The numbers in the margin of the manuscript correspond to the numbers of the explanations on the facing page. These explanations will guide you through both rhetorical and mechanical considerations for your own paper.

(1) (2)

Shannon Paaske

(3)   Professor Bachmann

English 1A

3 May 2008

(4)                    From Access to Acceptance:

Enabling America's Largest Minority

In the early 1900s, a Chicago city ordinance stated that no "unsightly, deformed

(5)   or maimed person can appear on the public thoroughfares" (Davidson 62). A court case

in Wisconsin in 1919 upheld the expulsion from school of a twelve-year-old boy with

cerebral palsy because his teachers and fellow students regarded him as "depressing

(6)   and nauseating" (62). In contrast to these unjust laws of the first half of the twentieth

century, the second half drafted legislation and designed equipment to improve

life for disabled people. In 1990, the Americans with Disabilities Act was passed by

Congress. This enormous piece of legislation, among other things, requires both public

buildings and private businesses to provide architectural access for disabled persons

and it prohibits discrimination against them in the workplace. Helping to remove even

more barriers, the Assistive Technology Act was signed into law eight years later. This

act promotes the use of technological devices designed to help disabled persons lead

independent lives. A customized, computerized van allows a man paralyzed from the

chest down to operate a motor vehicle by himself. And near the end of the twentieth

century, major network television shows such as *Life Goes On*, *L.A. Law*, and *Star Trek:*

*The Next Generation* regularly featured people with all types of disabilities. Clearly,

(7)   America's institutions have come a long way in acknowledging the 43 million people

in this country with disabilities (Blackman 70). Although technological advances,

(8)   equality-promoting legislation, and increasing media exposure have worked as a

collective force to improve the lives of disabled people, ignorance and prejudice

continue to plague them.

(9)         Technological developments, almost exclusively computer-oriented, have

revolutionized the world of those who make up what is sometimes termed "America's

(10)   largest minority" (Davidson 61). Citizens who were once confined to home, forbidden

# Explanatory Notes for the Research Paper

The numbers on these explanatory notes correspond to the numbers in the margin of the research paper.

1. *Securing the paper.* When your paper is finished, staple the pages in the upper left corner. Don't use a folder or plastic binder.

2. *Form.* Type your last name and the page number, as Shannon does, in the upper right corner of each page, one-half inch from the top. All other margins will be one inch.

3. *Heading.* Begin your heading one inch from the top of the first page and flush with the left margin. Include your full name, instructor's name, the course number, and the date, double-spacing between lines. Double-space again and center the title, and then double-space between title and first line of the paper.

4. *Title.* Your title should engage your reader and establish an expectation for what the paper is about. It should please your reader's ears and eyes. If your reader stumbles while reading your title, it needs more work. Shannon's focus is unmistakable: the disabled person's wish for "access" and "acceptance." Do not underline or put quotation marks around your title.

5. *Citations.* Shannon's opening sentence includes a quotation, so she must document the source and page number in parentheses. The second time that Shannon quotes material from Davidson's article, she needs only the page number because Davidson's name has just been given.

6. *Introduction.* Shannon's introduction is a dramatic, abbreviated history of the legislation, equipment changes, and social responses to the disabled in this century. She quotes the exact language of the ordinances because the wording jolts the reader.

7. *Statistic.* Shannon notes that there are "43 million" disabled people in the United States and cites Blackman and the page where she located this figure.

8. *Thesis.* Shannon's thesis that begins with "although" forecasts her intention: to look at the technical and legislative changes, and increased media exposure, as improvements for the disabled. She will also examine the problems that plague the disabled and prevent their full "acceptance."

9. *Summarized material.* Noting past limitations, Shannon summarizes the technological developments that now "enable" the disabled.

10. *Uncommon knowledge quoted.* It is not common knowledge that the disabled are "America's largest minority," so Shannon documents the source of this statement.

11   to travel by air, and unable to attend classes or hold jobs have been liberated by recent inventions that encourage independence as well as allow for enriching life experiences. Just how extensive is the new technology? According to Jan Gavlin, director of assistive technology at the National Rehabilitation Hospital in Washington, "If you can move one muscle in your body, wiggle a pinkie or twitch an eyebrow, we can design a switch to allow you to operate in your environment" (qtd. in Blackman 71).

An example of one such device is the Eyegaze Response Interface Computer Aid (ERICA), developed by biomedical engineer Thomas Hutchinson at the University of Virginia. This eye-controlled computer empowers severely disabled yet bright people with the ability to learn and communicate. Ten years ago these people would have been misdiagnosed as mentally retarded by traditional tests that are unable to correctly measure their intelligence. Originally designed for children who previously might have been misdiagnosed, ERICA and other systems like it instead "create pathways for kids to express themselves and for teachers to engage their minds"

12   (Rab and Youcha 22).

This technology also allows severely disabled adults to pursue careers, as in the case of Brian Dickinson. "Mr. Dickinson has amyotrophic lateral sclerosis [better known

13   as Lou Gehrig's disease], which has stripped him of the power to speak, swallow, move his legs or arms, wiggle his fingers or turn his head" (Felton 1). With the help of an Eyegaze system, Dickinson continues writing his column for *The Providence Journal-Bulletin* in Rhode Island. He selects certain functions on his computer screen simply by looking at the appropriate keys.

14   Other developments include computerized "sip and puff" machines, which enable people without the use of their arms or legs to change television channels, talk on the phone, and play computer games simply by inhaling or exhaling into a plastic straw (Blackman 70). A system called DragonDictate is a computer program that prints dictation onto a monitor when the user speaks into a microphone (70). This type of program is especially useful to people who are unable to type because of poor muscle control (a characteristic of cerebral palsy) or who have various types of paralysis. The system even comes with a spell-check mode that responds to the incorrect word with an "oops."

# Explanatory Notes *(continued)*

11. *Quotation within the article.* Shannon credits a knowledgeable source, Jan Gavlin, as he is quoted in Blackman's article. Because she has wisely used Gavlin's name in her lead, Shannon needs only to cite that he is "quoted" in Blackman and give the page number. If she had not used Gavlin's name in her lead, her parenthetical reference would be: (Gavlin qtd. in Blackman 71).

12. *Two-author citation.* The parenthetical reference from an article written by two authors contains the last name of each author, connected with "and," and the page number of the article.

13. *Altering a quotation.* Shannon adds a clarification to her quoted material using brackets so that the reader knows that she has altered the quotation. A quotation should not be altered unless it is essential for clarity and then the alteration should not change the meaning of the original text.

14. *Paraphrased material.* Even though Shannon describes in her own words how the "sip and puff" machine is used, she must document the source of her information. If Shannon had felt there would be any confusion in her reader's mind about the source of her information, she would have repeated Blackman's name as she does in the next paragraph.

Modern wheelchair designs also reflect the recent advancements that permit the disabled to leave home and enter the world. Robert Cushmac, 16, who was paralyzed from the neck down in a car accident when he was 10, gets from class to class at his Virginia high school, where he is an honors student, in a wheelchair activated by a chin-controlled joystick (Blackman 71). The Hi-Rider is a "standing wheelchair" that was designed by Tom Houston who is paralyzed from the waist down. His design makes it possible for him to perform tasks previously impossible, such as reaching an object on an overhead shelf, or greeting someone face to face (Blackman 70).

As these examples show, the continuous headway being made in adaptive technology has considerably altered the way of life for many disabled people. However, it is highly unlikely that much of this progress could have been accomplished without the help of a sympathetic political climate. Federal Disability Laws passed by Congress since 1968 addressed the environmental needs of the disabled and particularly focused on independent living as a goal. This goal expressed the desire of people with disabilities to view themselves and be viewed "no longer as passive victims deserving of charitable intervention but as self-directed individuals seeking to remove environmental barriers that preclude their full participation in society" (DeJong and Lifchez 45).

Laws such as the Architectural Barriers Act of 1968 required structures built with federal funds or leased by the federal government to be made accessible, and the Urban Mass Transportation Act and Federal Aid Highway Act of 1970 and 1973 worked to make transportation a reality for the disabled (DeJong and Lifchez 42). Later laws were created to achieve the attitudinal changes implicit in the objectives of the independent living movement. One law is The Rehabilitation Act of 1973, which prohibits discrimination against disabled people in programs, services, and benefits that are federally funded. The Rehabilitation Comprehensive Services and Developmental Disability Amendments of 1978 established independent living as a priority for state vocational programs and provided federal funding for independent living centers (DeJong and Lifchez 42). The Social Security Disability Amendments of 1980 gave disabled people more incentives to work by letting them deduct independent-living

## Explanatory Notes *(continued)*

15. *Transition.* Shannon moves from her review of the technological advance-
    ments designed to enhance the lives of the disabled to a review of legis-
    lation that has given them rights. Notice that her transition establishes
    that the technological advancements would not have occurred without the
    legislative changes. This is a more critically perceptive transition, showing
    a cause-and-effect relationship, than one that suggests merely "another
    change for the disabled is in the area of legislation."

16. *Paraphrased and quoted material.* Shannon summarizes the various laws
    and acts and documents her source of information, the *Scientific Ameri-
    can* article written by the two authors noted in her parenthetical refer-
    ences throughout this portion of her text. Her review of this legislation is
    historical, and it is chronologically arranged.

expenses from their taxes (42). The Americans with Disabilities Act, signed in 1990, reinforced the legislation that was not earlier implemented.

More recently, the Assistive Technology Act of 1998 ensures funding for statewide programs to promote the use of technological devices that improve the functional capabilities of disabled persons ("The ATA"). Because of the important role that such devices play to increase the independence of individuals with disabilities, the impact of this legislation is major. The speed and extent to which this impact can be felt is heavily influenced by the advent of the Internet. Through Websites such as *AbleData*, ATA (Alliance for Technology Access), and RESNA (Rehabilitation Engineering and Assistive Technology Society of North America) users can look up specific information on assistive technology devices, get help with problems or questions, and even make personal connections in chat rooms (AbleData).

It is undeniable that new legislation, together with the flourishing of adaptive technology and Internet-based sources of support, have created greater awareness of the disabled in our communities. The increasing number of disabled characters in movies and television reflects that awareness. Deaf actress Marlee Matlin, for example, enjoyed success starring in the Academy Award-winning *Children of a Lesser God* in 1986, and later in the television series *Reasonable Doubts*. In assessing Matlin's character in *Reasonable Doubts*, Ben Mattlin (no relation), a writer with a muscular dystrophy-related disease, says he "can't say enough good things about working a highly visible disability into a major character" (Mattlin 8). Ben Mattlin also finds it significant that this character is portrayed as both intelligent and sexy. In addition, on ABC's *Life Goes On*, Christopher Burke, an actor who has Down's Syndrome, played Corky, a "competent, high-functioning integral part of his family" (Mattlin 8). Because Matlin and Burke are disabled actors who portray disabled characters—in contrast to the many able-bodied actors who play disabled roles—they have helped mark a path of new acceptance for the disabled.

In addition, retail stores that employ the disabled to model in their advertising create new public acceptance of the disabled. In 1991, retail store Kids R Us hired disabled children from hospital pediatric wards to work as professional models for their catalogues and circulars. Some of the store's executives got the idea while watching

# Explanatory Notes *(continued)*

17. *Documenting electronic sources.* Shannon used the Internet to find the most recent legislation affecting the disabled. Because there was no author, she credits the abbreviated *title* of the site in her parenthetical citation. "The ATA" is an abbreviation for "The Assistive Technology Act," found in the Works Cited section with the Web address so that the reader also can locate the information.

18. *Another electronic source.* Here again Shannon does not have an author so she uses the title of the site in her parenthetical reference.

19. *Conclusion to one section and transition to the next.* Shannon concludes her review of the legislation with a statement that the provisions of the most recent act for which she has information have not yet been fully implemented. She believes the impact will be "undeniable" when the act is fully in effect.

20. *New focus point.* Again, Shannon relates the next section of her paper to the previous sections by asserting that technology and legislation have made the disabled visible citizens in our communities. The media have reflected this visibility by increasing the number of disabled employed in film, television, and advertising.

21. *Parenthetical explanation.* Shannon makes a point of noting that the media critic, Ben Mattlin, is no relation to Marlee Matlin. She is then free to use Mattlin's name in parenthetical documentation without concern that her reader will be confused.

22. *Summary and direct quotation.* In a combination of summarized information and direct quotation, Shannon uses Ben Mattlin's article about the depictions of disabled actors in various media. She was tempted to use Mattlin's critical comments about the "distorted images" of the disabled in particular films, but she realized that this digression would change the balance and focus of her paper. From Mattlin's article, she used only what was relevant to her essay—brief references to actual programs and actors, and the appreciation of a disabled writer for positive portrayals of the disabled in film.

23 these kids play. Vice President Ernie Speranza reasoned, "They think of themselves as average kids, so we decided we should too" (Speranza qtd. in Yorks 1). Kids R Us was not the first retail store to make this move, and since 1990, Target and Nordstrom's—representing both ends of the economic spectrum—have hired disabled people of all ages as models in an effort to better represent the diversity of its clientele (Yorks 1).

Also helping to bring more exposure through the media is a television news-magazine, a series of programs created by the mother of an autistic child who wanted to create a television show devoted to disabled people. This series provides "profiles of courage and accomplishment and informs viewers of a wide range of issues and opportunities to enhance quality of life through greater self-sufficiency" (*Disabilities and Possibilities*). Winner of many awards, including an Emmy, this program has aired on PBS stations throughout North America and aims to unify abled and disabled people.

The arts community appears to be responding with greater awareness as well. In 1999, a five-day festival in Los Angeles celebrating "the arts, disability, and culture" hosted more than eight international dance companies featuring disabled performers (Haskins 108). Although efforts such as these indicate that the media have "started to

24 get a broader perspective on real life" (Olson), people with disabilities have yet to enjoy full acceptance by American society. Nancy Mairs, a woman with multiple sclerosis who balances a college teaching and lecturing career with the demands of a marriage and motherhood, finds that while her family and the people she works with have accepted her disability, she still has had to endure an end-of-the-semester evaluation by a student

25 who was perturbed by her disability (122).

While no longer blatantly discriminated against, disabled people often continue to suffer the burden of social bias. Even those remarkable individuals who are able to triumph over physical barriers have trouble surmounting social barriers. Post-polio actor Henry Holden relates his own experience with social discrimination:

26     A guy with paralyzed legs is not supposed to be able to sell insurance, but I did very well at it in New Jersey before I became an actor. A guy with paralyzed legs is not supposed to climb mountains, but I made the trek up

# Explanatory Notes *(continued)*

23. *Quotation within the article.* The vice president of a retail store is quoted within an article that Shannon read about the use of the disabled as models in advertising. She quotes him in her text and notes his name and the page of the quotation in her parenthetical reference.

24. *Quotation from an interview.* Because there are no page numbers associated with interviews, only the last name of the subject interviewed is enclosed in the parentheses. Shannon uses Steve Olson's comment about the value of images of the disabled in advertising as a transition to the final section of her paper. This section focuses on the feelings that disabled people have about nondisabled people's perceptions of them. Shannon gained these insights in interviews as well as readings.

25. *Paraphrased and summarized material.* An experience noted by an author in her essay is summarized and paraphrased by Shannon, and the source of the material is documented.

26. *Long quotations.* Because the experience of the actor Henry Holden is especially revealing, Shannon decided to include the long quotation in her paper. Because the quotation is longer than four typed lines, it cannot be incorporated within the paragraph. Instead, a longer quotation is set off from the rest of the paper with double-spacing at the top and bottom of the quotation, and it is indented ten spaces or one inch from the left margin. The quotation itself is double-spaced, and the final period precedes the parenthetical information.

the cliff at Masada in Israel at four o'clock in the morning. A guy with paralyzed legs is not supposed to ride horses, but I rode in an exhibition in Madison Square Garden. Yet I am not generally accepted by nondisabled people in social situations. The attitude in the country is that, if you have a disability, you should stay home. (Holden qtd. in Davidson 63)

27    Susan Rodde, who has cerebral palsy, confirms that in most social situations, "we, the physically challenged, have to be the icebreakers." At parties and social gatherings, the disabled person is often isolated or ignored. Having used a wheelchair since a surfing accident, Berkeley student Steve Olson confirms this experience: "Sometimes I meet people at parties who feel uncomfortable about [my disability]. I talk and tell jokes to break the ice, and soon no one realizes there's a disabled person—me—sitting in the room with them." Unfortunately, the "ice" does need to be broken because many people feel uncomfortable around disabled or disfigured people, and so far, the responsibility of making social contact lies with the disabled person.

28    But many disabled people report that fully abled people have a hard time "respecting the fact that we're the same as they are," says Diane DeVries, who was born with no legs and only partial arms. Perhaps because of ignorance or fear, our
29    disabilities "remind people of their own vulnerabilities" (DeVries). As Nancy Mairs says, "Society is no readier to accept crippledness than to accept death, war, sex, sweat, or
30    wrinkles" (119). Because they may feel vulnerable, able-bodied people tend not to form close relationships with disabled people, and some even refuse casual contact. Rebecca Acuirre, 16, who has cerebral palsy, says that she recently asked a stranger what time it was and he kept walking as though he didn't hear her. "Some people are prejudiced and ignore us. That makes me angry," she says.

31    How can these prejudices be abolished? "We need more exposure," says DeVries. Acuirre concurs, saying the media should do more to educate the public. On a personal level, Bill Davidson, in "Our Largest Minority, Americans with Handicaps," recommends the nondisabled public "help reverse centuries of discrimination" by getting to know disabled people "at work, in the marketplace, at school" and by making "contact that is real—not just casual" (63). Able-bodied people can help

# Explanatory Notes *(continued)*

27. *Brackets.* Shannon has enclosed in brackets a change that she has made in material from an interview. It is possible that her subject used a pronoun that would have been ambiguous to the reader; Shannon substituted the noun and placed the clarifying term in brackets. The reader understands that the brackets are used to clarify or change tense or other language forms to permit easy reading of the quoted material as it is integrated with the writer's text. No changes may be made and put into brackets that would alter the meaning of the material quoted. (See p. 564 for more information about brackets.)

28. *Incorporating short quotations.* Shannon incorporates into her text the specific quoted material from her reading and interviews. When the subject of an interview is named in the text, there is no need for additional documentation.

29. *Interview subject quoted.* Because Shannon does not reuse Diane DeVries's name in her text, she documents the source of the quotation by using DeVries's last name in parentheses.

30. *Documentation from a book.* Nancy Mairs's name is used in Shannon's text, so only the page number of the book is cited in parentheses.

31. *Incorporating summary and quotations.* Shannon introduces the author and title of the article in her text. This attribution within her text facilitates Shannon's documentation; she needs to note only the page number within the parentheses. Her citations document the specific quoted material as well as the paraphrased content of Davidson's article.

overcome their own preconceived notions and realize that if disabled people seem bitter, "it's not because of their disability . . . but because of society's attitude toward them." Prejudices can be stopped before they start by encouraging children "not to shun and fear" the disabled (63).

32        The legislation and technology that were developed at the end of the twentieth century will continue to make new worlds accessible to disabled people. Ideally, these developments will permit the disabled to be viewed in terms of their capabilities rather than their disabilities. In that climate, disabled people can gain acceptance in the worlds to which they have access. With the steps being taken by government, science, and the media, individuals alone are needed to make the dream of acceptance a reality for people with disabilities.

33                              Works Cited

34    *AbleData*. The National Institute on Disability and Rehabilitation Research. U.S.
          Department of Education. Web. 20 Mar. 2004.

35    Acuirre, Rebecca. Personal interview. 23 Apr. 2008.

36    "The Assistive Technology Act of 1998." *RESNA*. Web. 11 Apr. 1999.

37    Blackman, Ann. "Machines That Work Miracles." *Time* 18 Feb. 1991: 70–71. Print.

38    Davidson, Bill. "Our Largest Minority: Americans with Handicaps." *McCall's* Sept.
          1987: 61–68. Print.

39    Dejong, Gerben, and Raymond Lifchez. "Physical Disability and Public Policy."
          *Scientific American* June 1983: 40–49. Print.

40    DeVries, Diane. Telephone interview. 22 Apr. 2008.

41    *Disabilities and Possibilities Television Newsmagazine*. Web. 10 April 1999.

42    Felton, Bruce. "Technologies That Enabled the Disabled: High-tech or Low, Devices
          Enrich Work." *New York Times* 14 Sept. 1997, late ed.: Sec 3, 1+. Print.

# Explanatory Notes *(continued)*

32. *Conclusion.* In her conclusion, Shannon reviews the relationship between the points she has made in her paper. She concludes by asserting that the advancements for the disabled lie in the hands of individuals, not only institutions. She uses the language of her title to bring a more dramatic closure to her analysis.

33. *The form for the list of sources used in the text.* The Works Cited page should always begin on a new numbered page at the end of the paper. The head is centered on the line, one inch from the top of the page. The first cited work is typed two lines beneath the heading. The entire list is double-spaced. The list is alphabetically arranged by the author or speaker's last name or by the first word in the title of an unsigned article. The entry begins at the left margin. If it is longer than one complete line, its second line begins five spaces indented from the left margin. (More complete information on MLA form begins on p. 502.)

34. Entry for an electronic source.

35. Entry for a personal interview. The date of the interview is noted.

36. Entry for an electronic source.

37. Entry for a signed article in a weekly periodical.

38. Entry for a signed article in a monthly periodical.

39. Entry for a magazine article written by two authors.

40. Entry for a telephone interview. The date of the interview is noted.

41. Entry for an electronic source.

42. Entry for a signed daily newspaper article. Notice the plus sign (+) after page 1 to indicate that after the first page the article continues on nonconsecutive pages.

43    Haskins, Ann. "Dance Listings." *LA Weekly*. 28 May 1999: 108. Print.

44    Mairs, Nancy. "On Being a Cripple." *With Wings: An Anthology of Literature by and about Women with Disabilities*. Ed. Marsha Saxon and Florence Howe. New York: Feminist Press, 1987. 118–127. Print.

45    Mattlin, Ben. "Beyond *Reasonable Doubts*: The Media and People with Disabilities." *Television and Families* 13.3 (1991): 4–8. Print.

46    Olson, Steve. Telephone interview. Apr. 2008.

47    Rab, Victoria Y., and Geraldine Youcha. "Body." *Omni* June 1990: 22+. Print.

48    Rodde, Susan. Telephone interview. 20 Apr. 2008.

49    Yorks, Cindy LaFavre. "Challenging Images." *Los Angeles Times*. 22 Nov. 1991: E1–2. Print.

## Explanatory Notes *(continued)*

43. Entry for a signed column in a weekly newspaper.

44. Entry for a chapter within an anthology with two editors. Notice that the name of the author of the chapter Shannon used is listed first.

45. Entry for a signed article in a periodical with volume and number.

46. Entry for a telephone interview.

47. Entry for two authors of an article within a monthly periodical. Notice that the article started on page 22 but did not appear on continuous pages. The "1" symbol indicates that the pages were not consecutive.

48. Entry for a telephone interview.

49. Entry for a signed article in a daily newspaper. Notice the "E" prior to the page number to indicate the section of the newspaper in which the article appeared.

# Documenting the Research Paper: MLA Style

Whenever you use the words, information, or ideas of another writer—even if in your own words you summarize or paraphrase—you must credit the source. The following forms show you exactly how to provide the necessary information for documenting your sources according to the Modern Language Association (MLA) style guide. You can check the MLA Web site (www.mla. org) for additional documentation information and updating. *The MLA Handbook for Writers of Research Papers* (7th ed., 2009) is the source for this section, and it is certainly the form that your college English instructors will want you to use.

## Indicating Titles

Any titles that you refer to within your essay and in the citations at the end of your work need to be appropriately indicated. **The titles of short works—** those works typically included in anthologies or periodicals and not published independently, such as essays, short stories, poems, songs, and articles— **should be in quotation marks. The titles of longer works**—those works published independently, such as books, plays, newspapers, magazines, Web sites, online databases, television and radio broadcasts, CDs, record albums, performances, and works of art—**should be in italics**.

## Writing Parenthetical Citations

Your in-text citation should give just enough information so that your reader can find the origin of your material on the works-cited page (your bibliography) at the end of your paper. Here are sample parenthetical citations to illustrate MLA format.

*Author Not Named in the Text.* When you haven't included the author's name in your text, you must note in parentheses the author's last name and the page or pages of your source.

> "The first steps toward the mechanical measurement of time, the beginnings of the modern clock in Europe, came not from farmers or shepherds, nor from merchants or craftsmen, but from religious persons anxious to perform promptly and regularly their duties to God" (Boorstin 36).

*Author Named in the Text.* It is often advantageous to introduce your paraphrased or quoted material by noting the author's name within your text, especially if your author is an authority on the subject. If you do include the author's name in the text, your parenthetical citation will be brief and less intrusive, containing only the page number by itself.

According to Daniel Boorstin, the senior historian of the Smithsonian Institution, "the first steps toward the mechanical measurement of time, the beginnings of the modern clock in Europe, came not from farmers or shepherds, nor from merchants or craftsmen, but from religious persons anxious to perform promptly and regularly their duties to God" (36).

***Two Books by the Same Author.*** If your paper contains two different works by the same author, each parenthetical reference should give an abbreviated form of the title, with the page number, so that your reader will know which work you are citing in each section of your paper.

Ben Mattlin deplores the pity for the disabled that Jerry Lewis's yearly telethon evokes ("Open Letter" 6). Mattlin also exposes the hypocrisy in depicting the disabled as superheroes. His point is that "courage and determination are often necessary when living with a disability. But there's nothing special in that, because there's no choice. Flattering appraisals sound patronizing" ("Beyond *Reasonable Doubts*" 5).

***A Work with Two or Three Authors.*** If the work was written by two or three authors, use each of their names in your text or in the parenthetical citations.

In their study of John Irving's *The World According to Garp*, Janice Doane and Devon Hodges analyze the author's attitude toward female authority: "Even novels that contain sympathetic female characters, as Irving's novel does, may still be oppressive to women" (11).

Critics have charged that John Irving's *The World According to Garp* doesn't really support female authority: "Even novels that contain sympathetic female characters, as Irving's does, may still be oppressive to women" (Doane and Hodges 11).

***A Work with More Than Three Authors.*** If more than three authors wrote your source, you may use only the first author's last name, followed by "et al." and the page number in parentheses, or you may list all of the authors' last names in the text or with the page number in parentheses.

In *Women's Ways of Knowing: The Development of Self, Voice, and Mind*, the authors note that there are many women who "believed they were stupid and helpless. They had grown up either in actual physical danger or in such intimidating circumstances that they feared being wrong, revealing their ignorance, being laughed at" (Belenky et al. 57).

In *Women's Ways of Knowing: The Development of Self, Voice, and Mind*, the authors note that many women "believed they were stupid and helpless. They had grown up either in actual physical danger or in such intimidating circumstances that they feared being wrong, revealing their ignorance, being laughed at" (Belenky, Clinchy, Goldberger, and Tarule 57).

In *Women's Ways of Knowing: The Development of Self, Voice, and Mind*, Belenky, Clinchy, Goldberger, and Tarule note that there are many women who "believed they were stupid and helpless. They had grown up either in actual physical danger or in such intimidating circumstances that they feared being wrong, revealing their ignorance, being laughed at" (57).

***Author's Name Not Given.*** If the author is anonymous, use the complete title in your text or an abbreviated form of the title with the page number in the parentheses.

The obituary for Allan Bloom in *Newsweek* describes him as the man who "ignited a national debate on higher education" and "defended the classics of Western Culture and excoriated what he saw as the intellectual and moral relativism of the modern academy" ("Transition" 73).

***Corporate Author or Government Publication.*** Either name the corporate author in your text or include an abbreviated form in the parentheses. If the name is long, try to work it into your text to avoid an intrusive citation.

Southern California Edison, in a reminder to customers to "Conserve and Recycle," gives the shocking statistic that "every hour, Americans go through 2.5 million plastic bottles, only a small percentage of which are now recycled" (*Customer Update* 4).

***Literature: Novel, Play, Poem.*** Because works appear in various editions, it is best to give the chapter number or part in addition to the page number to help your reader find the reference you are citing.

### Novel
In the novel *Invisible Man*, Ralph Ellison uses a grotesque comparison to describe eyes: "A pair of eyes peered down through lenses as thick as the bottom of a Coca-Cola bottle, eyes protruding, luminous and veined, like an old biology specimen preserved in alcohol" (230; ch. 11).

**Play**
The parenthetical citation includes just the arabic numbers for the act, scene, and lines. These numbers are separated by periods: (4.3.89–90).

In William Shakespeare's *Othello*, Emilia sounds like a twenty-first-century feminist when she claims that "it is their husbands' faults" if their wives have affairs (4.3.89–90).

**Poem**
The parenthetical citation includes the line or lines of the poem cited: (13–14).

Poet Robert Hass, in "Misery and Splendor," describes the frustration of lovers longing to be completely united: "They are trying to become one creature, / and something will not have it" (13–14).

*Indirect Source.* When you use the words of a writer who is quoted in another author's work, begin the citation with the abbreviation "qtd. in" and both writers' last names if you have not used them in your text.

Women and men both cite increased "freedom" as a benefit of divorce. But Riessman discovered that women meant that they "gained independence and autonomy" while men meant that they felt "less confined," "less claustrophobic," and had "fewer responsibilities" (Kohler Riessman qtd. in Tanner 40–41).

*More Than One Work.* If you want to show that two works are the sources of your information, separate the references with a semicolon.

Two recent writers concerned with men's issues observe that many women have options to work full-time or part-time, stay at home, or combine staying at home with a career. On the other hand, men need to stay in the corporate world and provide for the family full-time (Allis 81; Farrell 90).

## Online Sources

### Online Source—Author Given
When you incorporate online sources, use the same form as you would for a book or periodical: Give the author's name in parentheses followed by the page number if the entry is longer than one page. If it is one page or less, give only the author's name.

"Making Media a Familiar Scapegoat" concludes with the claim: "Trench coats don't kill, guns and pipe bombs do" (Rosenberg 3–4).

If the Internet material uses paragraph numbers rather than page numbers, give the relevant number or numbers preceded by the abbreviation *par.* or *pars.*

In the study "National and Colonial Education in Shakespeare's *The Tempest,*" Prospero's character is not limited to that of a dramatist: "Throughout the play Prospero teaches all the characters, and the teacher role could be seen to fit him better than even the customary playwright" (Carey-Webb par. 11).

If the material is not on numbered pages or lacks numbered paragraphs, identify by screen number, followed by the number of the screen or screens, in parentheses.

### Online Source—Author Unknown

Often no author is given for material available on the Internet. In such cases, use the same form you would for an unsigned article in a periodical or reference book: an abbreviated form of the title (first significant word or two).

An advancement such as the Eyegaze System "enables people with severe motor disabilities to do many things with their eyes that they would otherwise do with their hands" ("Unique Products").

If no author or title is available, use the name of the Web site.

Through the Internet, the disabled can look up specific information on assistive technology devices, get help with problems or questions, and even make personal connections in chat rooms (AbleData).

## Preparing the Works Cited Page

Whenever you note in parentheses that you have used someone else's material, you will need to explain that source completely in the works-cited list (the bibliography) at the end of your research paper. The Works Cited page always begins on a new and numbered page at the end of the paper. The entries are arranged alphabetically, according to authors' last names. If there are no authors named, then the works are listed according to title. If the title begins with "A" or "The," keep the article in the title but alphabetize according to the second word.

All sources—whether book or journal article—are arranged together on one list. Do not have a list of books and then a list of periodical titles. Readers can identify **book titles** (and the titles of all longer works: movies, magazines, and newspapers) because they are **italicized**. **Titles of short works**—essays, articles, and songs—are put in **quotation marks**. At the end of each entry, specify the medium of publication, followed by a period: Print, Web, CD, Laser disc, Performance, Film, Television, etc. Even if the article originally appeared in another medium, for example, a newspaper or journal, but you retrieved it online, your citation should identify the medium of publication is the Web, followed by a period and then the date of access. Do not number the entries. Double-space between all lines, both within an entry and between entries. Each entry starts at the left margin and extends to the right margin. If additional lines are needed for an entry, indent five spaces or one-half inch. To see how the Works Cited page should look, turn to the student research paper on page 498. To see how each type of entry should look, study the models below.

Because the complete source is listed only in the works cited, it is essential that each entry conform exactly to standard form so that the reader can easily locate your source. Most of the forms that you will need are illustrated here.

### Elements of a Book Citation

1.                              2.                           3.    4.    5.

Fiedler, Leslie. *Freaks: Myths and Images of the Secret Self*. New York: Simon, 1978.

7.{ Print

6.

1. Use the author's full name—last name first—followed by a comma and then the first name and any middle name or initial or suffix like Jr. or III. Omit any titles (Dr., Ph.D., Rev.). End with a period and one space.

2. Print the book's full title including any subtitles. Italicize the title and capitalize the first and last words as well as all other important words. If there is a subtitle, separate the main title and the subtitle with a colon and one space. Place a period after the title and leave one space.

3. Type the publication information beginning with the city of publication, followed by a colon and one space.

4. Print the name of the publisher, followed by a comma. Shorten the name by removing "and Co." or "Inc." Abbreviate multiple names to include only the first name. (The "Simon" in the example refers to Simon and Schuster.) If you are citing a university press, abbreviate as "UP." See the Boardman citation below.

5. Include the date of publication and end with a period.

6. Include the medium of publication. For example, the medium of publication for a book would be *Print* while the medium for an online book would be *Web*. Other examples include *CD, Film, DVD, Performance*, etc. *Web* is the medium of publication for any content that you retrieve online, even if it originally appeared in another medium—for example, a newspaper article that you retrieved from a Web site. The medium of publication is

generally the last element in your citation. When *Web* is the medium of publication, the last element should be the date of access.

7. Any line after the first line is double-spaced and indented one-half inch or five spaces, a "hanging indent."

## Sample MLA Entries

### BOOKS

### One Author

Fiedler, Leslie. *Freaks: Myths and the Images of the Secret Self*. New York: Simon, 1978. Print.

### Two or Three Authors

Doane, Janice, and Devon Hodges. Nostalgia and Sexual Difference: The Resistance to

   Contemporary Feminism. New York: Methuen, 1987. Print.

Notice that any authors' names after the first author are written with the first name before the last name.

### More Than Three Authors or Editors

Boardman, John, et al., eds. *The Oxford History of the Classical World*. New York: Oxford UP,

   1986. Print.

                                      or

Boardman, John, Jasper Griffin, and Oswyn Murray, eds. *The Oxford History of the Classical*

   *World*. New York: Oxford UP, 1986. Print.

With more than three authors, you have the choice of shortening the entry to provide only the first author's name, followed by the Latin abbreviation "et al." (which means "and others"), or you may provide all of the names. Notice that Oxford University Press is abbreviated "Oxford UP."

### Author with an Editor or Editors

Shakespeare, William. *King Lear*. Ed. Barbara A. Mowat and Paul Werstine. New York: Wash-

   ington Square, 1993. Print.

Cite the name of the author first and then, after the title of the work, give the editor's name or names, preceded by "Ed."—an abbreviation for "edited by."

### Book with an Editor and No Author Cited

Webb, Charles H., ed. *Stand Up Poetry: The Anthology*. Long Beach: UP California State U,

   1994. Print.

If the book does not have an author, cite the editor's name, followed by "ed."

## Selection from an Anthology or Collection

Mabry, Marcus. "Living in Two Worlds." *Between Worlds: A Reader, Rhetoric, and Handbook.*
    Ed. Susan Bachmann and Melinda Barth. 7th ed. New York: Longman, 2013.
    99–101. Print.

Mairs, Nancy. "On Being a Cripple." *With Wings: An Anthology of Literature by and about*
    *Women with Disabilities.* Ed. Marsha Saxton and Florence Howe. New York: Feminist
    P at City U NY, 1987. 118–127. Print.

Olds, Sharon. "True Love." *The Wellspring.* New York: Knopf, 1996. 88. Print.

Give the author and title of the selection, using quotation marks around the
title. Then give the title of the anthology, in italics. If the anthology has an
editor, note the name or names after the "Ed." Give the page numbers for the
entire selection as shown.

## Two or More Selections from the Same Anthology

Bachmann, Susan, and Melinda Barth, eds. *Between Worlds: A Reader, Rhetoric, and Hand-*
    *book.* 7th ed. New York: Longman, 2013. Print.

Holman, M. Carl. "Mr. Z." Bachmann 106–107.

Staples, Brent. "Black Men and Public Space." Bachmann 164–168.

To avoid repetition, give the full citation for the book once, under the editor's
last name. Then list all articles under the individual authors' names, followed
by the title of their work. After each title, put the editor's name as a cross-
reference to the complete citation.

## Two or More Books by the Same Author(s)

Lamott, Anne. *All New People.* New York: Doubleday, 1991. Print.

———— *Bird by Bird: Some Instruction on Writing and Life.* New York: Doubleday, 1994. Print.

Give the author's name for the first entry only. After that, type three hyphens in place of the name, followed by a period and one space and then
the next title. The three hyphens always stand for exactly the same name
as in the preceding entry. The titles of the author's works should be listed
alphabetically.

## Corporate Author

National Council of Teachers of English. *Guidelines for Nonsexist Use of Language in NCTE*
    *Publications.* Urbana, Ill.: NCTE, 1975. Print.

Use the name of the institution or corporation as the author even if it is also
the name of the publisher. Abbreviate the institution's name if it is repeated:
NCTE.

### Author Not Named

*Webster's New World College Dictionary.* 4th ed. New York: Macmillan, 1999. Print.

If a book has no author noted on the title page, begin the entry with the title and alphabetize according to the first word other than "a," "an," or "the."

### Other Than First Edition

If you are citing an edition other than the first, place the edition number between the title and the publication information, as in the entry above.

### Republication

Melville, Herman. *Billy Budd, Sailor (An Inside Narrative).* 1924. Chicago: U Chicago P, 1962.
Print.

If you are citing a work that has been published by different publishers, place the original date of publication (but not the place or publisher's name) after the title. Then provide the complete information for the source you are using.

### Book Title within the Title

Gilbert, Stuart. *James Joyce's* Ulysses. New York: Vintage, 1955. Print.

If the title of the work that you are using contains another book title, do not italicize or place the original book title in quotation marks.

### Story or Poem Title within the Title

Cisneros, Sandra. *"Woman Hollering Creek" and Other Stories.* New York: Random House,
1991. Print.

If the title of the work that you are using contains a title that is normally enclosed in quotation marks (a short story or poem), keep the quotation marks and italicize the entire title: *Dare to Eat a Peach: A Study of "The Love Song of J. Alfred Prufrock."* Print.

### Multivolume Work

Raine, Kathleen. *Blake and Tradition.* 2 vols. Princeton: Princeton UP, 1968. Print.

If you have used two or more volumes of a multivolume work, state the total number of volumes in the work. Place this information ("2 vols.") between the title and publishing information.

Malone, Dumas. *The Sage of Monticello.* Boston: Little, Brown, 1981. Vol. 6 of *Jefferson and His Time.* 6 vols. 1943–1981. Print.

If you are using only one volume of a multivolume work, give the title of that volume after the author's name and then give the publishing information. After the publishing date, note the volume number, the title of the book, and the number of volumes in the collection. If the volumes were published over a period of years, indicate the dates.

### Translation

Marquez, Gabriel García. *Love in the Time of Cholera*. Trans. Edith Grossman. New York:

>   Penguin, 1988. Print.

When citing a work that has been translated, give the author's name first. After the title, give the translator's name, preceded by "Trans."

### Introduction, Preface, Foreword, or Afterword

Grumbach, Doris. Foreword. *Aquaboogie*. By Susan Straight. Minneapolis: Milkweed, 1990.

>   Print.

If you are citing material from an introduction, preface, foreword, or after-word written by someone other than the author of the book, give the name of the writer and designate the section she or he wrote. Notice also that "Fore-word" is without underlining or quotation marks. After the title of the work, "By" precedes the author's name.

   If the author of the introduction or preface is the same as the author of the book, give only the last name after the title:

Conrad, Joseph. Author's Note. *"Youth: A Narrative" and Two Other Stories*. By Conrad.

>   New York: Heinemann, 1917. 3–5. Print.

### Article in an Encyclopedia or Other Reference Books

Benet, William Rose. "Courtly Love." *The Reader's Encyclopedia*. 1987 ed. Print.

"Hodgkin's Disease." *The New Columbia Encyclopedia*. 4th ed. 1975. Print.

If there is an author of the edition or article, alphabetize by last name. Other-wise, alphabetize in the works-cited page by the title of the entry.

## PERIODICALS: JOURNALS, MAGAZINES, AND NEWSPAPERS

### Journal with Continuous Pagination

Cooper, Mary H. "Setting Environmental Priorities." *Congressional Quarterly Researcher*

>   9.19 (21 May 1999): 425–428. Print.

Fowler, Rowena, "Moments and Metamorphoses: Virginia Woolf's Greece." *Comparative*

>   *Literature* 51.3 (1999): 217–242. Print.

Journals sometimes paginate consecutively throughout a year. Each issue, after the first one, continues numbering from where the previous issue ended. After the title, give the volume number followed by a period and the issue number, if there is one. (See the first example, "Cooper.") Provide the publication date in parentheses, followed by a colon and the page numbers. Conclude by noting that it is a print medium.

### Journal That Paginates Each Issue Separately

Anderson, Maxwell L. "Museums of the Future: The Impact of Technology on Museum Practices." *Daedalus* 128.3 (1999): 129–162. Print.

Heilbrun, Carolyn. "Contemporary Memoirs." *The American Scholar* 68.3 (1999): 35–42. Print.

If the journal numbers each issue separately, give the volume number, a period, and the issue number (as in "68.3" above) after the title of the journal.

### Monthly or Bimonthly Periodical

Barth, Melinda. "Neil Moss." *Ceramics Monthly* Oct. 2010: 53. Print.

Notice that in a monthly or bimonthly periodical, the month of publication is abbreviated (except for May, June, and July), and no volume or issue numbers are given.

### Weekly or Biweekly Periodical

Anderson, Jan Lee. "The Power of García Marquez." *New Yorker* 27 Sept. 1999: 56–71. Print.

### Daily Newspaper, Signed Article

Yee, Amy. "Please Leave Your Stereotypes at the Door." *Christian Science Monitor* 7 July 1999: 15. Print.

### Daily Newspaper, Unsigned Article or Editorial

"Jerusalem and Disney." *Jerusalem Post* 24 Sept. 1999: A26. Print.

If the newspaper is divided into numbered or lettered sections, give the section designation before the page number, as in "A26". If the article continues on a nonconsecutive page, write only the first page number followed immediately (no space) by a 1 and a period.

Rosenbaum, David E. "Budgetary Posturing." *New York Times.* 2 Mar. 1995, late ed.: A1. Print.

If the newspaper has editions (late ed., natl. ed.) include this item after the date and before the colon.

### Titled Review

Friedman, Jane. "An Artist Who Promotes Glass Consciousness." *Washington Post.* 26 Sept. 1999: G1+. Print.

The page number "G1+" in the citation indicates that the article starts on page G1 but does not continue on consecutive pages.

### Untitled Review

Shore, Paul. Rev. of *Backlash: The Undeclared War Against American Women*, by Susan Faludi. *The Humanist* Sept.-Oct. 1992: 47–48. Print.

## OTHER SOURCES

### Interview

Cuff, Ross. Personal interview. 12 Feb. 2006.

Daigh, Sarah. Telephone interview. 18 Mar. 2006.

### Film or DVD

*In the Line of Fire*. Dir. Wolfgang Petersen. Perf. Clint Eastwood, John Malkovich, Rene Russo, and Dylan McDermott. Columbia, 1993. DVD.

If you want to refer to a particular individual involved with the film, cite that person's name first:

Malkovich, John, actor. *In the Line of Fire*. Dir. Wolfgang Petersen. Perf. Clint Eastwood, Rene Russo, and Dylan McDermott. Columbia, 1993. DVD.

### Television or Radio Program

"Inspector Morse: Cherubim and Seraphim." 2 episodes. Mystery. Perf. John Thaw and Kevin Whateley. PBS. WNET, New York. 2 Mar. 1995. Television.

As in a film citation, if you wish to refer to a particular person in the program, cite that name first, followed by the rest of the listing. The episode is put in quotation marks; the program name is in italics. A series name (if any) is neither put in quotation marks nor underlined. Except for the comma between the local station and the city, a period follows every item. Narrators, directors, adapters, or performers can be listed if relevant.

### Song Lyrics

Coldplay. "Fix You." *X & Y*. Capital, 2005. CD.

Hoobastank. "The Reason." *The Reason*. Island, 2003. CD.

If you are quoting the lyrics of a song, you need to cite the title of the particular song (in quotation marks) followed by the title of the album or CD (in italics), the recording company, the date, and the medium—CD or LP.

## ELECTRONIC SOURCES

In the spring of 2009, MLA mandated a significant change in the way that electronic sources are documented: **No Web address or URL is required unless the writer feels that readers need the URL to locate the original source.** The updated citation format, described in detail below, is designed to provide the information needed to retrieve an online source in a simpler, more consistent format. Characteristic citations are illustrated here.

# An Online Article

A typical entry for a short work found online will include the following:

1. Author (if given), director, narrator, performer, editor, compiler, or producer of the work. For works with more than one author or a corporate author, or for anonymous works, follow the guidelines for print sources. If no author is given, begin the entry with item 2, the title of the work.

2. Title of the article. Italicize the title, unless it is part of a larger work. Titles that are part of a larger work should be enclosed in quotation marks.

3. Title of the journal or Web site (in italics) if this is distinct from item 2.

4. Volume and issue, if provided. For an article from a database, provide the volume number, followed by a period, and then the issue number. For example, if the volume is 12 and the issue is 3, it will be: 12.3.

5. Name of database or, for a web site, publisher or sponsor of the web site. This information can often be found at the bottom of the Web page or on an "About Us" link. If this information is not available, use N.p. (for no publisher). For many publications, the name of the Web Site and the Publisher or Sponsor may be the same (see the illustration of the "Reuters" Web Site, p. 516).

6. Date of publication: For a database, give the year of publication in parenthesis. For an article from a Web site, give the day, month, and year. If no date is given, use n.d.

7. Medium of publication. For all online sources, the medium of publication is Web.

8. Date of access (day, month, and year) concluded with a period. If some of the information is not available, cite what is available.

9. Provide the URL if your readers will have difficulty finding the source without it.

The elements of an MLA Works Cited Entry—for an article on an **online database:**

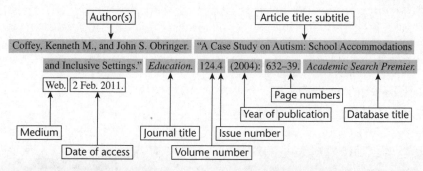

Author(s)

Article title: subtitle

Coffey, Kenneth M., and John S. Obringer. "A Case Study on Autism: School Accommodations and Inclusive Settings." *Education.* 124.4 (2004): 632–39. *Academic Search Premier.*

Web. 2 Feb. 2011.

Medium

Date of access

Journal title

Volume number

Issue number

Year of publication

Page numbers

Database title

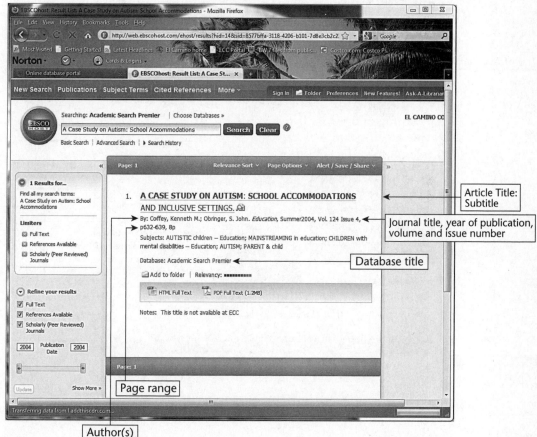

Article Title: Subtitle

Journal title, year of publication, volume and issue number

Database title

Page range

Author(s)

The elements of an MLA Works Cited Entry—for an article on a **Web site:**

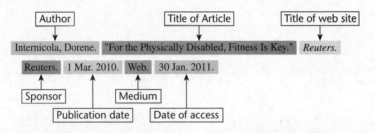

Author — Internicola, Dorene.
Title of Article — "For the Physically Disabled, Fitness Is Key."
Title of web site — *Reuters.*

Reuters. 1 Mar. 2010. Web. 30 Jan. 2011.

Sponsor — Reuters.
Publication date — 1 Mar. 2010.
Medium — Web.
Date of access — 30 Jan. 2011.

# Sample MLA Entries for Electronic Sources

## An Article from a Database

Bricker-Katz, Geraldine, Michelle Lincoln, and Patricia McCabe. "A Lifetime of Stuttering: How Emotional Reactions to Stuttering Impact Activities and Participation in Older People." *Disability and Rehabilitation.* 31.21 (2009): 1742-52. *Academic Search Premier.* Web. 27 Jan. 2011.

"Gabriel (Jose) Garcia Marquez." *Contemporary Authors.* 13 Feb. 2001: n. pag. *Gale Literary Databases.* Web. 11 Oct. 2001.

## An Article from an Online Scholarly Journal

Carey-Webb, Allen. "National and Colonial Education in Shakespeare's The Tempest." *Early Modern Literary Studies* 5.1 (1999): n. pag. Web. 5 Sept. 1999.

## An Article in an Online Magazine

Shenk, Joshua Wolf. "Lincoln's Great Depression." *The Atlantic Monthly* Oct. 2005. Web. 2 Sept. 2005.

## An Article in an Online Newspaper

Gonzalez, David. "From Margins of Society to Center of the Tragedy." The *New York Times* 2 Sept. 2005. Web. 5 Sept. 2005.

## A Review in an Online Newspaper

Ebert, Roger. Rev. of *Eternal Sunshine of the Spotless Mind*, Dir. Michael Gondry. *Chicago Sun-Times Online.* 19 Mar. 2004. 2 pp. Web. 9 May 2005.

## An Online Book Available Independently

Austen, Jane. *Pride and Prejudice.* Ed. Henry Churchyard. 1996. Web. 5 Sept. 1999.

## A Professional or Personal Site

Gajewski, Walter. "Oh, What a Web We Weave." California State U, Long Beach. Web. 25 Feb. 2003.

Perry, Stephen. Poems. Web. 5 Sept. 1999.

## An Online Government Publication

United States. CIA Publications and Handbooks. *1995 World Factbook.* Washington, D.C.: Central Intelligence Agency (1995). Web. 3 Jan. 1996.

If no author is given, as in a government publication, cite the institution or publishing agency.

### Electronic Source Not in Print

Nowviskie, Bethany. "John Keats: A Hypermedia Guide." Wake Forest U. Web. 26 Feb. 2003.

### A CD-ROM

Many journals, magazines, newspapers, and periodically published reference works are published both in print and on CD-ROM:

Nehemiah, Marcia. "Nicholas Negroponte." *Digit.* Issue #8. CD-ROM. PC Carullo. 55–60.

If you are using only a part of the work, state which part.

"Artifice." *The Oxford English Dictionary.* 2nd ed. CD-ROM. New York: Oxford UP, 1992.

# Documenting the Research Paper: APA Style

Although most English instructors require MLA form for documenting sources, instructors from other disciplines may prefer American Psychological Association (APA) form. Check with your instructors to see which of the two forms they prefer. *These two styles are very different; don't confuse them.* The following citations reflect the APA *Publication Manual* of 2010.

## Writing Parenthetical Citations

The differences between MLA and APA forms are that in APA parenthetical citations, the date of publication must be included within the essay and not just in the references at the end. The punctuation of the citations and References page is also different.

According to APA form, if the sentence preceding quoted material includes the author's name, the date of publication will immediately follow in parentheses. Then, at the end of the quotation, include the page number in parentheses.

In Ben Mattlin's recent study (1991) of the media and people with disabilities, he approves Christopher Burke's role as a "competent, high-functioning, integral part of his family" (p. 8).

Notice that the date of the study is included within the introduction to the quotation, and then the page number is abbreviated as "p." within the final parentheses.

If you do not use the author's name when you introduce the quoted material, place the author's name, the year, and the page number in parentheses at the end of the quoted material. Use commas between the items in the parentheses.

One critic approves Christopher Burke's role as a "competent, high-functioning, integral part of his family" (Mattlin, 1991, p. 8).

If you paraphrase the material rather than quoting it specifically, include the author's last name and the date of publication either in your text or in the parentheses at the end of the summarized material. Do not include the page number.

According to Ben Mattlin (1991), disabled actors are playing important roles in television dramas.

One writer who has examined the media's treatment of the disabled reports some positive changes in television (Mattlin, 1991).

To cite an Internet document in the body of a paper, provide the name of the author, followed by the date. If no author is given, begin with the name of the document. If you use a direct quotation, provide the page number or paragraph number in the parentheses, after the date: (Coffey, 2004, p. 6) or (Coffey, 2004, para. 4).

## Specific Examples of APA Form

Here are specific examples of common situations you may need to document in APA form.

*A Work with Two to Five Authors.* If your material was written by two or more authors, name all of them in the introduction to the material or in the final parentheses each time you cite the work. In the parentheses, use "&" rather than "and."

Roberts, Keane, and Clark (2008) report on a program that successfully transitioned autistice children into general education classrooms.

Researchers report that autistic children can be successfully transitioned into general education classrooms (Roberts, Keane, & Clark, 2008).

After you first cite a work by three or more authors, use only the first author's name with "et al." (which means "and others"). If you include a direct quotation or specific information, you need to provide the page number in your citation.

"The program has expanded from a single pilot class in 1992 to currently 57 classes, with the majority of students transitioning to general education classrooms. (Roberts et al., 2008, p. 1).

*Author's Name Not Given.* If the author of the material that you are using is not given, either use the complete title in your introduction to the material or use the first few words of the title in the parenthetical citation with the date.

Retired Supreme Court Justice Thurgood Marshall graduated first in his class at Howard Law School and then sued the University of Maryland Law School, which had rejected him because he was black ("Milestones," 1993).

An obituary from "Milestones" (1993) noted that Thurgood Marshall graduated first in his class at Howard Law School and then sued the University of Maryland Law School, which had rejected him because he was black.

***Corporate Author.*** If you are using a work with a corporate or group author that is particularly long, write out the full name the first time you use it, followed by an abbreviation in brackets. In later citations, use just the abbreviation.

The American Philosophical Association (APA) has prepared "Guidelines for Non-Sexist Use of Language" because philosophers are "attuned to the emotive force of words and to the ways in which language influences thought and behavior" (American Philosophical Association, 1978).

***Indirect Source.*** If you use work that is cited in another source, you need to acknowledge that you did not use the original source.

Actor Henry Holden relates his own experience with social discrimination by noting that he is "not generally accepted by nondisabled people in social situations" (cited in Davidson, 1987).

***Electronic Source.*** If you use online material, cite the author's last name and the publication date. If the article has paragraph numbers instead of page numbers, use "para." instead of "p."

"Stuttering is known to impact communication in younger adults but this has not been established in older people who stutter" (Bricker-Katz et al., 2009, p. 1742).

## Preparing the References Page

In APA form, the alphabetical listing of works used in the manuscript is titled "References." (In MLA form, this listing is titled "Works Cited.") Here are some general guidelines for the references page.

- Begin the "References" on a new page.
- Double-space within and between entries. The first line should be flush with the left margin, and all subsequent lines should be indented five spaces or one-half inch from the left margin.

- Alphabetize the list by the last name of the author or editor. If the work is anonymous, alphabetize by the first word of the title, excluding "a," "an," or "the."
- All authors' names should be listed last name first, with the parts of names separated with commas. Do not use "et al." unless there are six or more authors. Use initials for first and middle names. Use an ampersand ("&") rather than the word "and."
- In contrast to the way titles normally appear, APA style limits capitalizations of book titles and of articles to the first word of the title and subtitle as well as to all proper nouns. However, all the main words of the titles of journals or magazines are capitalized as they normally appear.
- Italicize the titles of books, journals, and any volume numbers. Do not underline or use quotation marks around the titles of articles.
- Give the full names of publishers, excluding "Inc." and "Co."
- Use the abbreviation "p." or "pp." before page numbers in books, magazines, and newspapers, but not for scholarly journals. For inclusive page numbers, include all figures (365–370, not 365–70).

## Sample APA Entries

### BOOKS

#### One Author

Fiedler, L. (1978). *Freaks: Myths and the Images of the Secret Self*. New York: Simon & Schuster.

#### Two or More Authors

Doane, J., & Hodges, D. (1987). Nostalgia and sexual difference: The resistance to contemporary feminism. New York: Methuen.

#### Editor

Allen, D. M. (Ed.). (1960). *The new American poetry*. New York: Grove Press.

#### Translator

Ibsen, H. (1965). *A doll's house and other plays* (P. Watts, Trans.). New York: Penguin Books.

#### Author Not Named

*The Oxford dictionary of quotations*. (1964). New York: Oxford University Press.

#### Later Edition

Fowler, R. H., & Aaron, J. E. (1992). *The Little, Brown handbook* (5th ed.). New York: HarperCollins.

### Multivolume Work

Raine, K. (1968). *Blake and tradition* (Vol. 2). Princeton, NJ: Princeton University Press.

    Malone, D. (1943–1981). *Jefferson and his time* (Vols. 1–6). Boston: Little, Brown.

### Work in an Anthology

Mairs, N. On being a cripple. (1987). In M. Saxton & F. Howe (Eds.), *With wings: An anthology of literature by and about women with disabilities* (pp. 118–127). New York: Feminist Press at City University of New York.

### Two or More Books by the Same Author

Olsen, T. (1979). *Silences*. New York: Dell Publishing.

Olsen, T. (1985). *Tell me a riddle*. New York: Dell Publishing.

## PERIODICALS: JOURNALS, MAGAZINES, AND NEWSPAPERS

### Journal with Continuous Pagination

Culp, M. B. (1983). Religion in the poetry of Langston Hughes. *Phylon, 48*, 240–245.

### Journal That Paginates Each Issue Separately

Hardwick, J. (1992). Widowhood and patriarchy in seventeenth-century France. *Journal of Social History, 26*(1), 133–148.

### Article in a Magazine

Mazzatenta, O. L. (1992, August). A Chinese emperor's army for eternity. *National Geographic,* pp. 114–130.

### Article in a Daily Newspaper, Signed

Soto, O. R. (1992, January 28). Putting the tag on graffiti-smearers. *Press Telegram,* sec. B, p. 3.

### Article in a Daily Newspaper, Unsigned or Editorial

    Back to Future. (1992, May 3). *Los Angeles Times,* p. M-4.

### Titled Review

    Ansa, T. M. (1992, July 5). Taboo territory [Review of *Possessing the secret of joy*]. *Los Angeles Times Book Review,* pp. 4, 8.

### Motion Picture (note: the final period is deleted).

    Petersen, W. (Director). (1993). In the line of fire [Motion picture]. United States: Columbia

### Personal Interview

Interviews that you conduct yourself are not listed in APA references. Instead, use an in-text parenthetical citation. If the subject's name is in your text, use this form: "(personal communication, February 12, 2003)." If the subject's name is not in your text, use this form: "(S. Daigh, personal communication, March 18, 2003)."

## Article from an Online Database

Bricker-Katz, G., Lincoln, M., & McCabe, P. (2009). A lifetime of stuttering: How emotional

reactions to stuttering impact activities and participation in older people. *Disability*

*& Rehabilitation. 31* (21), 1742-1752. Retrieved from Academic Search Premiere:

http://web.ebscohost.com

## Article in Print and Online

Markels, A. (1996). MCI unit finds culture shock after relocating to Colorado. *The Wall Street*

*Journal Interactive Edition.* 7 pp. Retrieved January 23, 2002, from http://www.wsj.com

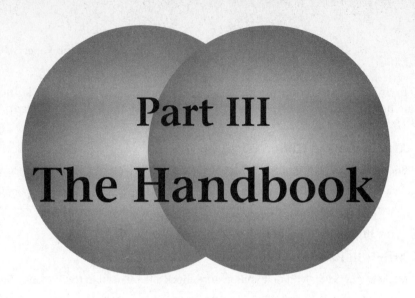

# Part III

# The Handbook

**P**art III—the handbook—is designed to help you use words and control sentences in order to write convincing, error-free papers. It will help you in drafting and revising your essays as well as in understanding the comments that your instructors write in the margins of your papers.

We do not believe that you need an extensive background in grammar in order to write clearly and well. But we are convinced that control of grammar and punctuation will give you power over both your ideas *and* your readers.

You may feel discouraged by the numerous mistakes on your papers and by the prevalence of circled words and marginal notes from your instructor. However, if you and your classmates were to examine past papers, you may discover that you do not make a great number of *different* errors so much as you repeat the same kind of error many times. For that reason, we have isolated those recurrent errors for discussion and correction. For friendly advice about grammar, visit Grammar Girl at *http://grammar.quickand dirtytips.com*.

This handbook begins with a deliberately succinct Chapter 13, entitled "Understanding How Sentences Work." We try to meet your needs in this chapter without telling you more than you ever wanted (or needed) to know about the elements of a sentence. Chapter 14 precisely identifies and describes the recurrent errors—the "terrible ten"—that typically appear in student papers. Chapter 15 discusses punctuation and helps you eliminate guesswork and punctuate accurately. Chapter 16 focuses on faulty word choice and shows you how well-chosen words can strengthen your essays. To determine quickly whether your word choice is sound, you can use the alphabetical list of Commonly Confused Words in the Glossary of Usage.

# Chapter 13

# Understanding How Sentences Work

Understanding how sentences work gives you the vocabulary you need to discuss your writing and to correct errors that have been noted in your papers. Such knowledge also increases your power and versatility as a writer. By eliminating some of the guesswork that can hamper student writers, this handbook can help give you the tools and confidence to write with conviction.

As you probably know, every sentence must contain a *subject* and a *verb*. This basic unit is called a *clause*. (For more on clauses, see pp. 530–531.) In key examples throughout this section, we have often underlined the subject once and the verb twice to help you identify them quickly.

## Subjects

A *subject* is who or what a clause is about.

> Ryan sent his agent an award-winning screenplay.

[Subjects may precede verbs.]

> There are several guitars in Adam's apartment.

[Subjects may follow verbs.]

## Noun as Subject

The subject of the clause may be a *noun* or a *pronoun*. A *noun* can be a

- *Person:* athlete, Jamie Foxx, veterinarian
- *Place:* Lake Erie, bike path, the Acropolis

- *Thing:* computer, hammock, Harley-Davidson
- *Quality/idea/activity:* wit, peace, dancing

## Pronoun as Subject

A *pronoun* takes the place of a noun and can also function as the subject of a clause. Pronouns can be

- *Personal:* I, you, he, she, it, we, they

  They reviewed their lecture notes.

- *Indefinite:* all, any, anybody, anything, each, either, everybody, everyone, neither, nobody, none, no one, nothing, one, some, somebody, someone, something

  Everybody needs to recycle.

- *Demonstrative:* that, this, such, these, those

  Those are the sale items.

- *Relative:* who, whom, whoever, whomever, whose, which, whichever, that, what

  The order that is ready is the deluxe pizza.

  [In this example, that is the subject of the dependent or relative clause. The subject of the independent clause is order.] (For more about clauses, see pp. 530–531.)

- *Interrogative:* who, whom, whoever, whomever, whose, which, that, what

  Who recommended this awful film?

## Compound Subject

Subjects may be *compound,* as in these sentences:

Julie and Joe restore old automobiles.

Books and papers collected on his desk.

Here are questions and assignments for each reading.

Ashley, Sonja, and Ryan can amuse their families for hours.

# Objects

## Direct Object

Not all nouns function as the subject of a clause. A noun that receives the action of the verb is called a *direct object.* In the sentence "Julie and Joe restore old automobiles," the noun *automobiles* answers the question, "What do Julie and Joe restore?" *Automobiles* is thus the direct object of the verb *restore.*

## Indirect Object

A noun that identifies to or for whom or what the action of the verb is performed is the *indirect object*. In the sentence "The dietician and nurses gave the patients new menus," the noun *patients* answers the question, "To whom were the menus given?"

## Object of the Preposition

A noun that follows a preposition (see list on p. 529) is called the *object of the preposition*. In the sentence "Books and papers collected on his desk," the noun *desk* is the object of the preposition *on*.

Objects may provide important information in a sentence, but they are not necessary in order to have a clause. *Verbs,* however, are essential.

# Verbs

A *verb* is what the subject does, is, has, or has done to it. The verb may be more than one word (*may be coming*). The verb also changes form to agree with the subject (*he* <u>drives</u> *; they* <u>drive</u>) and to indicate time (*he* <u>drove</u> *, he* <u>has</u> <u>driven</u>). Regular verbs form their past tense by adding *-ed*, but there are a number of irregular forms like *drive* that have special forms.

## Action Verbs

An *action verb* specifies what the subject does, has, or has done to it. The action does not have to be physical in any sense: *meditate* is an action verb. Other action verbs include *dance, think, laugh, provoke, erupt,* and *suggest:*

Every Christmas Eve, Janine and Tim <u>entertain</u> their relatives with holiday tunes.

Dr. Sanders <u>wrote</u> an insightful study of Oates's work.

## State-of-Being Verbs

A *state-of-being* or *linking verb* specifies what the subject is. State-of-being verbs include the following: *is, are, was, were, am, feel, seem, be, being, been, do, does, did, have, has, had.* These can be main verbs or helping verbs. For more on helping verbs, see the following section.

Evan <u>is</u> interested in engineering with a focus on the environment.

[<u>is</u> as main verb]

Dylan <u>is</u> <u>teaching</u> history at North High.

[<u>is</u> as a helping verb]

*Note:* Words ending in *-ing* need a helping verb in order to function as the main verb of a sentence. The *-ing* form of the verb can also function as a noun: *Playing is a form of learning for small children.* Here *playing* is the subject, and *learning* is the object of the preposition *of.* Thus, just because there is an *-ing* word in a word group, there is not necessarily a verb.

## Helping Verbs

The helping verb is always used with a main verb. Helping verbs include can, will, shall, should, could, would, may, might, and must.

> The designated driver <u>will get</u> everyone home safely.

> Some of the Friedmanns <u>could have camped</u> with the VanValkenburgh family at Yosemite.

## Adjectives and Adverbs

Many sentences contain modifying words that describe the nouns and verbs. *Adjectives* modify nouns (*corroded* pipes, *hectic* schedule) and pronouns (*the curious one*). *Adverbs* modify verbs (*cautiously* responded), adjectives (*truly generous*), adverbs (*very slowly*), and word groups (*Eventually*, he entered the room.) Adverbs answer the questions *how? when? where?* and *why?* They often end in *-ly*, but not always.

The following sentence contains both adjectives and adverbs. Can you identify each?

> According to Barbara Ehrenreich, angry young men often will vent their frustrations on vulnerable, weaker beings—typically children or women.

The adjectives *angry* and *young* modify the noun *men;* the adjectives *vulnerable* and *weaker* modify the noun *beings.* The adverbs *often* and *typically* modify the verb *will vent.*

Adjectives and adverbs can provide valuable details, but they can be overused. Being descriptive doesn't require a string of adjectives and adverbs. Often a strong verb gives a more precise picture in fewer words:

> The drunken man <u>walked</u> *unsteadily* and *unevenly* from the bar.

> The drunken man <u>staggered</u> from the bar.

The verb staggered is vivid and precise. The pile-up of adverbs in the first sentence is wordy and imprecise. Such tightening often improves writing and saves space for more necessary depth and development.

## Phrases

A *phrase* is a group of words, typically without the subject and verb of the sentence. Just as clauses do not necessarily have objects, adjectives, and adverbs, clauses also do not necessarily have any phrases. While phrases may provide additional information, they seldom contain the subject and verb in the sentence. Therefore, if you are checking to see that you have a subject and verb, in order to avoid fragments, you can eliminate phrases from your search. There are many types of phrases, but here we discuss two of the most common.

## Prepositional Phrases

A *prepositional phrase* always starts with a *preposition*—a word that shows relationships in time and space—and ends with the *object* of the preposition. The most common prepositions are listed here.

| | | | | |
|---|---|---|---|---|
| about | beside | from | outside | under |
| above | besides | in | over | underneath |
| across | between | inside | past | unlike |
| after | beyond | into | plus | until |
| against | but | like | regarding | unto |
| along | by | near | respecting | up |
| among | concerning | next | round | upon |
| around | considering | of | since | with |
| as | despite | off | than | without |
| at | down | on | through | |
| before | during | onto | till | |
| behind | except | opposite | to | |
| below | for | out | toward | |

Some prepositions are more than one word long: *along with, as well as, in addition to, next to,* and *up to* are some examples.

The object of the preposition is always a noun or pronoun:

Elaine assists the dean **of Fine Arts with registration problems.**

**On the weekends,** Becky and Joey take Kaitlyn **to the park.**

**For two weeks in January,** Anne vacations **with her daughter's family in Long Beach.**

[In the last sentence, "for two weeks," "in January," "with her daughter's family," and "in Long Beach" are all prepositional phrases. Note how much easier it is to locate the subject and verb when the prepositional phrases are eliminated from consideration.]

## Verbal Phrases

Verbal phrases resemble verbs, but they do not function as the main verb of the clause. Verbal phrases may serve as subjects, objects, adjectives, and adverbs. Two main types of verbal phrases are *infinitive phrases* and *-ing phrases*.

***Infinitive Phrases.*** If the verb is preceded by *to* (*to ski*), the verb is in the *infinitive* form. It helps to recognize infinitives because they cannot be the main verbs.

> Most <u>professors</u> <u>like</u> **to challenge** students.
>
> <u>To think</u> <u>is</u> **to question.**
>
> [Infinitives can function as subjects.]

***-ing Phrases.*** A word ending in *-ing* may look like a verb, but it needs a helping verb or a main verb elsewhere in the sentence. Notice how *working* serves a different function in each of the following sentences (only in the first sentence is it part of the main verb):

> Rise Daniels <u>is working</u> as an art instructor.
>
> <u>Working</u> as an art instructor <u>requires</u> overtime hours.
>
> [When *-ing* words function as subjects, they are called **gerunds**.]
>
> The working <u>artist</u> <u>exhibited</u> her paintings.
>
> [When *-ing* words function as adjectives, they are called **participles**.]

Words and phrases ending in *-ing* can often lead writers to believe they have a complete sentence—that is, at least one independent clause—when they may have only a fragment. For example, "In the evening after arriving home from work" is not an independent clause; it simply consists of three phrases.

One way to determine if there is an independent clause, and therefore a sentence, is to draw a line through each phrase:

> ~~In the evening~~ after arriving home ~~from work,~~ <u>Bill</u> <u>retreats</u> ~~to his studio for hours~~ ~~to play piano~~ and ~~to compose new songs.~~

Now that you can recognize the most important parts of a sentence, you can better understand how clauses work and how they can be combined.

# Clauses

A *clause* is a group of words with a subject and main verb. There are two basic types of clauses: (1) independent and (2) dependent.

## Independent Clauses

The *independent (or main) clause* has a subject and main verb and can stand alone:

> <u>Rob</u> <u>is</u> a physician's assistant in the New York area.
>
> <u>Alyssa</u> <u>loves</u> performing with Susie.
>
> The <u>band</u> <u>invited</u> Sara and Ryan backstage.

## Dependent Clauses

The *dependent (or subordinate) clause* has a subject and main verb but cannot stand alone. Dependent clauses begin with one of these subordinating conjunctions:

| | | | |
|---|---|---|---|
| after | how | unless | which, |
| although | if, even if | until | whichever |
| as, as if | in order that | what, whatever | while |
| because | since | when, whenever | who, whom, |
| before | that, so that | whether | whose |

Whenever a clause begins with one of these words (unless it is a question), it is a dependent clause. If we take an independent clause such as

> We jogged

and put one of the subordinating conjunctions in front of it, the independent clause becomes dependent (and therefore a fragment):

> After we jogged

> Because we jogged

To make a complete sentence, we need to add an independent clause (or delete the subordinating conjunction):

> After we jogged, we went for a swim.

> Because we jogged, we justified eating brownies.

Every sentence must have at least one independent clause in it.

# Sentence Variation

If you know how to control and combine clauses, you can vary your sentences for greater emphasis, more clarity, and less monotony. The four basic sentence types are illustrated here.

## Simple Sentences

Simple sentences contain one independent clause:

> Professor Hodges's students submitted fine critical analyses of the textbook.

> Despite his busy schedule, Walter edits new podcast selections each night.

## Compound Sentences

*Compound* sentences contain *two independent clauses*. There are only two ways to punctuate a compound sentence:

1. A *comma* followed by a coordinating conjunction (*and, but, for, or, nor, yet, so*):

> We arrived at the cabin, so they left.

2. A *semicolon* by itself (or it may be followed by a word like *nevertheless* or *however*):

We arrived; they left.

We arrived; therefore, they left.

Notice that the writer's decision to use a coordinating conjunction or a semicolon is not arbitrary. If the writer wishes to clarify or emphasize the relationship between the two clauses, he or she will use a coordinating conjunction (such as *so*) or a conjunctive adverb (such as *therefore*). If the writer prefers not to define the relationship between the clauses, then the semicolon by itself is more appropriate.

## Complex Sentences

*Complex* sentences contain *one independent clause and one or more dependent clauses*. The following dependent clauses are underscored with a broken underline.

When the dependent clause comes first in the sentence, a comma is necessary.

A comma isn't necessary when the dependent clause comes at the end.

## Compound-Complex Sentences

*Compound-complex* sentences contain *two or more independent clauses and one or more dependent clauses*. The dependent clause or clauses may be at the beginning, at the end, or between the independent clauses. Here one dependent clause begins the sentence, and another ends the sentence:

Although Jane was a senior citizen, she swam competitively, and we were all impressed that she won medals.

In the following sentence, the dependent clause is between the two independent clauses:

At work Tammy cares for an elderly man who requires constant help, so she enjoys returning home each night to play with Jamie, Paul, and Duane.

###  Practice Sentence Variation

Using details from the last essay that you discussed in class, write your own sentences to illustrate each sentence type: simple, compound, complex, and compound-complex. Then underline all subjects once and all verbs twice to make sure you have the necessary clauses. Manipulating these sentence types will help you vary your sentences and combine your ideas more smoothly.

# Chapter 14

# Understanding Common Errors

In the following chapters, we examine the ten errors that appear most frequently in student papers: fragments, run-on or fused sentences, pronoun reference, subject-verb agreement, shifts (in number or person, verb tense, voice, and mood), mixed sentences, misplaced (and dangling) modifiers, faulty parallelism, punctuation (Chapter 15), and faulty word choice (Chapter 16). These errors may be noted in the margins of your papers with the symbols that appear in these margins as well as on the inside back cover.

## Fragments

Although sentence fragments are used frequently in fiction and advertising copy to simulate spoken English, the sentence fragment is considered non-standard in formal writing. Fragments may confuse the reader, and they will make your writing seem choppy and your ideas disconnected.

A *fragment* is a group of words that, for some reason, *cannot stand alone*   *frag*
as a complete sentence. The reason may be any one of the following:

1.  The word group may lack a subject.

    While the students prepared their finals, they sunbathed at the same time.

    <u>Became involved</u> in discussions that distracted them from their studies.   *frag*

    [Add a subject.]

    While the students prepared their finals, they sunbathed at the same time. Soon <u>they</u> <u>became involved</u> in discussions that distracted them from their studies.

2. The word group may lack a complete verb.

*frag*    Arriving before the concert began, we enjoyed the excitement in the air. The <u>band</u> tuning up before their opening song.

[Add a helping verb.]

Arriving before the concert began, we enjoyed the excitement in the air. The <u>band</u> <u>was tuning</u> up before their opening song.

3. The word group may lack both a subject and a verb.

*frag*    I value my piano teacher. A bright and patient woman. She encourages perfection even while she tolerates my mistakes.

[Attach the phrase *a bright and patient woman* to the independent clause before or after it.]

I value my piano teacher, a bright and patient woman. She encourages perfection even while she tolerates my mistakes.

or

I value my piano teacher. A bright and patient woman, she encourages perfection even while she tolerates my mistakes.

4. The word group may contain both a subject and a verb but be simply a dependent clause.

*frag*    Native American music and dances are national treasures. Which is why our dance company performs them regularly.

[Avoid starting any sentence with *which* unless you are asking a question.]

Native American music and dances are national treasures. <u>This</u> <u>is</u> why our dance company performs them regularly.

or

Because Native American music and dances are national treasures, our dance company performs them regularly.

Another example of such a fragment is the following:

*frag*    Although rap music has been criticized for its violence and harsh language. Rap really reflects the tension in the cities rather than causes it.

Although rap music has been criticized for its violence and harsh language, rap really reflects the tension in the cities rather than causes it.

As noted earlier, writers may deliberately use a fragment for emphasis or to mimic conversation, but these uses are always controlled and planned.

Otherwise, fragments make an essay confusing or choppy. Sometimes the simplest solution is to connect the fragment to an independent clause that is either right before or after it.

# Run-on or Fused Sentences

*Run-on* or *fused sentences,* or sentences flawed with a *comma splice,* occur when a writer perceives that the thoughts in two complete sentences are related but fails to join the thoughts appropriately. Sometimes the writer makes the mistake of inserting a comma between the independent clauses, creating a comma splice. No punctuation at all between the independent clauses creates a run-on or fused sentence. Both errors occur because the writer sees a relationship between sentences and isn't sure what to do to show the relationship.

*r-o*

*fs*

The "sentence" that follows is one anyone might say, and a writer might be tempted to write:

It snowed for days the skiers were ecstatic.

*r-o*

The writer has clearly perceived a relationship between the joy of the skiers and the weather conditions. But the word group is incorrectly punctuated and is a run-on or fused sentence.

## Comma Splice

The writer may decide to "correct" the error by inserting a comma between the two independent clauses:

It snowed for days, the skiers were ecstatic.

*cs*

The comma is inadequate punctuation, however, for separating the independent clauses. That "correction" results in the sentence fault called a *comma splice,* which is noted as "*CS*" in the margin of a paper.

## Correcting Comma Splices and Run-on Sentences

The following methods illustrate alternatives for correcting comma splices and run-on sentences. Notice that the five choices are all grammatically correct, but each places different emphasis on the two clauses and may change the meaning of the sentence.

1. Separate each independent clause with a period.

   It snowed for days. The skiers were ecstatic.

2. Use a comma plus a coordinating conjunction (*and, but, for, or, nor, yet, so*) between the independent clauses.

It snowed for days, and the skiers were ecstatic.

or

It snowed for days, yet the skiers were ecstatic.

or

It snowed for days, so the skiers were ecstatic.

3. Use a semicolon between the independent clauses.

It snowed for days; the skiers were ecstatic.

4. Change one independent clause into a dependent clause.

Because it snowed for days, the skiers were ecstatic.

or

The skiers were ecstatic because it snowed for days.

Notice that when the dependent clause begins the sentence, a comma separates it from the main clause. Conversely, when the independent clause begins the sentence, there is no comma before the dependent clause that concludes the sentence. See page 531 for a list of words that begin dependent clauses.

5. Use a semicolon after the first independent clause, and then a conjunctive adverb (see below) followed by a comma:

It snowed for days; consequently, the skiers were ecstatic.

or

It snowed for days; nevertheless, the skiers were ecstatic.

## Conjunctive Adverbs

Conjunctive adverbs include *accordingly, also, anyway, besides, certainly, consequently, conversely, finally, furthermore, hence, however, incidentally, indeed, instead, likewise, meanwhile, moreover, nevertheless, next, nonetheless, otherwise, similarly, specifically, still, subsequently, then, therefore,* and *thus.*

## Style and Meaning

Grammatical correction of a run-on sentence is not the only concern of the writer. Style emphasis and meaning also should be considered when you are deciding which conjunction to use. Notice the difference in emphasis in the following examples:

It snowed for days. The skiers were ecstatic.

Because it snowed for days, the skiers were ecstatic.

In the first example, the writer asks the reader to infer the relationship between the skiers' being "ecstatic" and the fact that "it snowed for days." In the second example, the cause-and-effect relationship is defined clearly. Take the following simple sentences, also fused, and notice what happens to the meaning, emphasis, or relationship between the independent clauses when different corrections are employed:

> Renée pitched the team won.

*r-o*

1.  Renée pitched. The team won.

The writer has not defined a relationship between the facts stated in the two sentences.

2.  Renée pitched, and the team won.

A mild relationship is suggested by connecting the two events with *and*.

> Renée pitched, so the team won.

The relationship between the team's victory and the person who pitched is defined in this construction using *so*.

> Renée pitched, yet the team won.

The use of *yet*, which signals something contrary to expectation, changes the relationship between the independent clauses in this example. The word *yet* tells the reader that in spite of the fact that Renée pitched, the team won.

3.  Renée pitched; the team won.

The semicolon does not define the relationship between the two independent clauses although a subtle relationship *is* suggested by the writer's using a semicolon instead of a period. The semicolon is a compromise punctuation symbol. It is stronger than a comma, but it is not as complete a stop as a period.

4.  Whenever Renée pitched, the team won.

> The team won because Renée pitched.

> Although Renée pitched, the team won.

> The team won even though Renée pitched.

The dependent clause, whether it begins or ends the sentence, defines the exact relationship between the two clauses in the sentence. Clearly, the subordinate conjunction chosen has everything to do with the meaning of the sentence.

5.  Renée pitched; therefore, the team won.

> Renée pitched; nevertheless, the team won.

Again, the conjunctive adverb defines the precise relationship between the two clauses of the sentence. For the purpose of connecting two short independent clauses, most writers would find the combination of semicolon and conjunctive adverb and comma too cumbersome. A coordinating conjunction with a comma would probably be a better method of linking the two clauses.

# Pronoun Reference Agreement

*Pronouns* are words that *take the place of nouns*. In most cases, pronouns are an advantage to the writer because they permit reference to nouns named without the writer having to repeat the noun or finding a clear substitute (or synonym) for it. Ambiguity, vagueness, or confusion can result, however, if the *ref* writer has not used pronouns responsibly. The margin symbol *"ref"* indicates a problem with the pronoun reference.

The following chart shows the forms that personal pronouns take.

## *Singular*

| Subjective | Possessive | Objective |
|---|---|---|
| I | my, mine | me |
| you | your, yours | you |
| he | his | him |
| she | her, hers | her |
| it | its | it |

## *Plural*

| | | |
|---|---|---|
| we | our, ours | us |
| you | your, yours | you |
| they | their, theirs | them |

Indefinite pronouns include all, any, anybody, anything, each, either, everybody, everyone, everything, neither, nobody, none, no one, nothing, one, some, somebody, someone, and something.

Pronoun problems occur when the reader does not know what noun is referred to by the noun substitute, the pronoun.

1. Sometimes the pronoun used could refer to either of two nouns:

*ref*   When Karen told Pat the news, she burst into tears.

*She* can refer to either Karen or Pat. The ambiguity must be resolved for the reader:

Pat burst into tears when Karen told her the news.

or

Karen burst into tears when she told Pat the news.

2. Sometimes the subject is implied by the writer but is not stated in the sentence. The pronoun does not clearly refer to any given noun, and confusion results for the reader:

   For years, Pete carried rocks from the quarry, and it strained his back.

   *ref*

   *It* cannot refer to the plural *rocks,* and the singular noun *quarry* didn't "strain his back." The writer probably means "this work" or "the constant hauling of heavy rocks." The writer needs to make that clarification in the sentence:

   For years, Pete carried rocks from the quarry, and this work strained his back.

3. Indefinite pronouns can also pose a problem for writer and reader if the singular form of the indefinite pronoun is inconsistent with the meaning of the sentence or the gender of the pronoun is assumed by the writer to be a generic *he.* Generally, a singular pronoun should be used with an indefinite pronoun:

   <u>Each</u> boy on the football team has <u>his</u> own locker.

   <u>Anybody</u> who has <u>her</u> doubts about the safety of breast implants should read Jenny Jones's essay "Body of Evidence."

In the examples above, the gender of the possessive pronoun is clear from the context of the sentence. However, if you are not sure of the gender or number (singular or plural) of your subject, reword your sentence so that the subject pronoun is plural. For example:

Everybody running for class office should report to his counselor.

*Everybody* is a singular pronoun and requires a singular possessive pronoun: *his* or *her. Their* is plural and can't be used in this sentence. But should the writer assume the generic *his?* A reader might object that the implication of the sentence is that only males may run for class office. A similar misunderstanding would occur if the writer opted for *her* as the singular possessive pronoun. If this were a single-sentence statement, as in a school bulletin, the writer might choose *his or her* for a correct and clear mandate. But the repetitive use of *his or her* (or *his/her*) can be a burden in a lengthy manuscript.

Learn to find alternatives. A plural noun and plural possessive pronoun will take care of the problem:

All of the candidates for class office should report to their counselors.

You may also want to see the discussion of sexist language (p. 570) in Chapter 16.

# Pronoun Case

In addition to problems with pronoun referents, writers often have trouble deciding when to use the subjective case pronouns and when to use the objective case pronouns (see chart in the previous section, Pronoun Reference Agreement, p. 538).

*Subjective pronouns* are used for the subject of the sentence or clause:

<u>We</u> listen to hip-hop music.

Because Dr. Connor is so supportive, <u>he</u> brought the team home for a barbecue.

*Subjective pronouns* are also used when the pronoun follows a linking verb:

It is <u>I</u> who volunteered.

It was <u>they</u> who chose that route.

*Objective pronouns* are used for any objects:

### Direct object:

Alicia and Mary recognized <u>us</u> at the premiere of their film.

### Indirect object:

Tony's band gave <u>him</u> a standing ovation.

### Object of the preposition:

Marilyn's energetic water fitness class is ideal for <u>them</u>.

*Pronoun pairs* such as "you and I" and "you and me" tend to confuse writers, but the same principles apply. Determine whether the pronoun is serving as a subject or object and then choose the correct form (see chart, p. 538). Often it is easier to make this determination if you eliminate the first noun or name in the pair:

### Subject:

Garrick and (**I**? **me**?) went to the concert together.

Eliminate "Garrick": *I* went. So choose: Garrick and *I* went to the concert together.

### Direct Object:

Josh drove Mike and (**I**? **me**?) to the surfing competition.

Eliminate "Mike": Josh drove *me*. So choose: Josh drove Mike and *me* to the surfing competition.

### Indirect Object:

David showed Julia and (**we**? **us**?) his new stallion.

Eliminate "Julia": David showed *us*. So choose: David showed Julia and *us* his new stallion.

**Object of a Preposition:**

Tiana flew to Maui with her cousin and (**he? him?**)

Eliminate "her cousin": Tiana flew to Maui with *him*. So choose: Tiana flew to Maui with her cousin and *him*.

# Subject-Verb Agreement

The margin note *"agr"* means that there is an agreement problem; the subject   *agr* and the verb do not agree in number. Both subject and verb should be singular or both should be plural. Speakers who are comfortable with standard English usually will not have trouble selecting the correct verb form for the subject of sentences. But some sentences, especially those that have groups of words separating the subject and verb, may offer a temporary problem for any writer. Some conditions to be aware of are listed here.

1. A prepositional phrase does not influence the verb of the sentence:

   The <u>birds</u> in the nest <u>need</u> food from the mother bird.

   Our first five <u>days</u> of vacation <u>are going</u> to be in New Orleans.

   Her <u>secretary</u>, in addition to her staff, <u>prefers</u> the new computer.

   Notice that by removing the prepositional phrases from your consideration, you will use the correct verb form for the subject of the sentence.

2. Subjects connected by *and* usually have a plural verb:

   Alfredo's academic <u>load</u> and work <u>time</u> <u>keep</u> him busy.

   Some exceptions:

   a. When the compound subject (nouns connected by *and*) is regarded as a unit, the subject is regarded as singular and has a singular verb:

      <u>Peanut butter and jelly</u> <u>remains</u> Dalton's favorite lunch.

   b. If the double nouns refer to the same person or thing, the verb is singular:

      Danika's <u>home and studio</u> <u>is</u> 215 Thompson Street.

   c. When *each* or *every* precedes the multiple nouns, use a singular verb:

      <u>Each instructor</u> , <u>student</u> , and <u>staff member</u> <u>prefers</u> the new insurance plan.

   d. When nouns are connected by *or* or *nor,* the verb agrees with the noun closer to it:

      Your student ID or room <u>key</u> <u>guarantees</u> the loan of a beach chair.

      Your student ID or room <u>keys</u> <u>guarantee</u> the loan of a beach chair.

Neither the police officer nor his <u>cadets</u> <u>were attending</u> the lecture.

Either Arthur or <u>Michael</u> <u>plays</u> the solo tonight.

3. Most indefinite pronouns have a singular verb, even if the pronoun seems to convey a plural sense. Indefinite pronouns include *anybody, anyone, each, either, everybody, everyone, everything, neither, none, no one, someone,* and *something.* Notice how each indefinite pronoun is used in the following sentences:

<u>Each</u> of the band members <u>has</u> two free tickets.

<u>Everybody</u> <u>endures</u> the stress of two finals a day.

<u>Everyone</u> on the school board <u>votes</u> at each meeting.

*All, any,* or *some,* however, may be singular or plural depending on what the pronoun refers to:

<u>All</u> of the pizza <u>is gone</u>.

<u>All</u> of the books <u>are shelved</u>.

4. Collective nouns (like *band, family, committee, class, jury,* and *audience*) require a singular verb unless the meaning of the noun is plural, or individuality is to be emphasized:

The <u>jury</u> <u>presents</u> its decision today.

The <u>jury</u> <u>are</u> undecided about a verdict.

5. Even when the subject follows the verb, the verb must be in the correct form:

There <u>remains</u> too little <u>time</u> to organize the campaign.

6. Titles require singular verbs:

<u>Roots</u> <u>is</u> the book we will read next.

<u>Jacoby and Associates</u> <u>is</u> the law firm on the corner.

<u>Mysteries</u> <u>is</u> the section of the library Carlos prefers.

7. Nouns describing academic disciplines—like *economics, statistics,* or *physics*—and diseases that end in an *s*—like *mumps* and *measles*—and *news*—are treated as singular nouns:

<u>Physics</u> <u>challenges</u> Maria, but she does well in the course.

<u>Measles</u> usually <u>attacks</u> only the children who have not been inoculated.

## Shifts

*shift*    The margin note *"shift"* marks an inconsistency in the text in person, number, or verb tense.

# Shifts in Person and Number

Shifts in person and number sometimes occur because you are not certain from what point of view to write or because you move from one perspective to another without being conscious of the change. You may begin with the idea of addressing a general audience—"someone"—and then decide to address the reader as "you." Or you may begin with a singular reader in mind and switch to a plural sense of "all readers." If you start to write from one perspective and switch to another, a distracting shift occurs:

> If <u>someone</u> in the group writes a paper, <u>they</u> may present it.                    *shift*

**Corrections:**

If a <u>person</u> writes a paper, <u>he or she</u> may present it.

or, better:

If <u>people</u> write papers, <u>they</u> may present them.

<u>The vegetarian</u> learns to prepare interesting and nutritious meals with vegetables and grains, but then <u>you</u> have to assure <u>your</u> friends that <u>you're</u> getting enough protein.     *shift*

**Corrections:**

If <u>you</u> are a vegetarian, <u>you</u> learn to prepare interesting and nutritious meals with vegetables and grains, but then <u>you</u> have to assure your friends that <u>you're</u> getting enough protein.

or, better:

<u>Vegetarians</u> learn to prepare interesting and nutritious meals with vegetables and grains, but then <u>they</u> have to assure <u>their</u> friends that <u>they</u> are getting enough protein.

# Shifts in Verb Tense

Shifts in verb tense confuse a reader about when the action takes place. You have probably heard oral storytellers shift from one tense to another. Eventually you may have figured out the course of the narration, perhaps by asking the speaker to clarify the time of the action. But a shift in tense is particularly distracting in writing because you can't ask a writer for a clarification of the text. Notice how the verb tense in the following example shifts from the past to the present:

> Shortly after we <u>arrived</u> at the picnic site, it <u>started</u> to rain. So we <u>pack</u> up the bread,     *shift*
> salami, and fruit and <u>rush</u> to the cars.

**Correction for verb tense consistency:**

Shortly after we <u>arrived</u> at the picnic site, it <u>started</u> to rain. So we <u>packed</u> up the bread, salami, and fruit and <u>rushed</u> to the cars.

Use the present tense throughout to write a summary or a description of a literary work:

*shift*

> Daisy Miller first <u>meets</u> Winterbourne in Geneva, and she later <u>met</u> him in Rome where she <u>is dating</u> the charming Giovanelli. Winterbourne <u>was</u> furious that Daisy <u>doesn't</u> <u>realize</u> that Giovanelli <u>wasn't</u> a "real" gentleman.

### Correction for verb tense consistency:

> Daisy Miller first <u>meets</u> Winterbourne in Geneva, and she later <u>meets</u> him in Rome where she <u>is dating</u> the charming Giovanelli. Winterbourne <u>is</u> furious that Daisy <u>doesn't</u> <u>realize</u> that Giovanelli <u>isn't</u> a "real" gentleman.

## Shifts in Voice

Just as a shift in number or tense can be distracting, a shift from the active to the passive voice can confuse or distract your reader. Use the voice consistently.

When the subject of a sentence does the action, the sentence is in the *active voice:*

> <u>Lester</u> <u>brought</u> the tossed salad.

When the subject *receives* the action, the verb is in the *passive voice.* Notice that the passive voice is less effective than the active voice because it is less direct:

> The tossed <u>salad</u> <u>was brought</u> by Lester.

When the active and passive voice are combined, the sentence is inconsistent in voice and would be marked with a "shift" in the margin of the paper:

*shift*

> <u>Lester</u> <u>brought</u> the tossed salad, and the soft <u>drinks</u> <u>were</u> <u>brought</u> by Mike.

### Correction:

> <u>Lester</u> <u>brought</u> the tossed salad, and <u>Mike</u> <u>brought</u> the soft drinks.

In some cases, the passive voice is necessary because what might be the subject of the sentence is unknown or unimportant:

> The <u>car</u> <u>was hijacked</u> last week.

Because the hijacker is apparently unknown, the sentence is in the passive voice, with the action being done to the car, the subject of the sentence.

> NASA was granted additional funds to complete the study for the space station.

The name of the agency that granted NASA the funds for the study may be unimportant to the writer of this sentence; the important point is that NASA has the funds for the project.

Passive voice constructions may create suspicion that the writer is deliberately hiding information:

The city council was voted unlimited travel funds.

Clearly, the city resident who reads that sentence in the local paper would want to know *who* did the voting, and why the newspaper failed to name the subject of the verb *voted*. Use the active voice whenever you know and wish to identify the "doer" of a particular act.

# Shift in Mood

A shift in mood can also distract the reader. In the English language, there are three moods: **indicative** (to give information), **imperative** (to give commands or advice), and **subjunctive** (to express desires or a condition other than factual). If a writer is using one particular mood, an unexpected shift can be confusing and illogical:

### Shift from Indicative to Imperative

YouTube provides a vehicle for creative expression and entertaining viewing. Don't *shift* upload videos that your employer shouldn't see.

The first sentence provides general information (indicative mood). The second sentence shifts to a command (imperative mood). This shift can be confusing to a reader who believes that he is being given information about YouTube and then is suddenly given advice. An improvement would be the following:

### Correction:

YouTube provides a vehicle for creative expression and entertaining viewing, but certain uploads might be too revealing for a prospective employer to see.

# Mixed Sentences

The margin note *"mixed"* indicates a mixed construction involving sentence *mixed* parts that don't go together. The sentence may start with one subject and shift to another, or the verb may not fit the true subject of the sentence. The sentence also may begin with one grammatical construction and end with another. The problem, then, is a misfit in grammar or in logic, so the sentence is confusing to the reader:

Although he is active in the men's movement doesn't mean he is a misogynist. *mixed*

In this sentence the writer tries to make the dependent clause *Although he is active in the men's movement* the subject of the sentence. The writer probably intends *he* to be the subject of the sentence; rewriting the sentence to show this *and* selecting a correct verb for the subject will eliminate the confusion:

> Although he is active in the men's movement, he is not a misogynist.

## Confused Sentence Parts

Each of the mixed sentences below contains a confusion between sentence parts. In some cases, the writer has started with one subject in mind and has ended the sentence with a different or implied subject. In other cases, the grammatical form of the first part of the sentence is inconsistent with the end of the sentence. Most often the revision involves correct identification of the true subject of the sentence and then the selection of an appropriate verb.

*mixed*    Among those women suffering with eating disorders, they are not always bulimic.
           Not all women with eating disorders are bulimic.

*mixed*    By prewriting, outlining, drafting, and revising is how he wrote good papers.
           He wrote good papers by prewriting, outlining, drafting, and revising his work.

*mixed*    The subject of ecology involves controversy.
           Ecology involves controversy.

## Faulty Verb Choice

In some sentences with mixed meaning, the fault occurs because the subject is said to do or to be something that is illogical.

*mixed*    A realization between the academic senate and the dean would be the ideal policy on plagiarism.

The sentence says that "a realization" would be "the ideal policy," which is not exactly what the writer means. Correction of the faulty use of the verb *would be* will clarify the sentence.

> Ideally, a policy on plagiarism would be decided between the academic senate and the dean.

or

> Ideally, the academic senate and the dean would realize the necessity for a policy on plagiarism.

In speech, *is when* and *is where* are common constructions for defining words, but these are mixed constructions and should be corrected in writing.

*mixed*    Acquiescence is when you give in to your oppressor.
           Acquiescence means giving in to an oppressor.

*mixed*    A final exam is where you show comprehensive knowledge.
           On a final exam you show comprehensive knowledge.

# Misplaced and Dangling Modifiers

A *modifier* is a word, phrase, or clause used to describe another word in the sentence. The modifier should be as close to that word as possible or it is a *misplaced modifier*, causing confusion or unintentional humor.   *mm*

> Confused by the assignment, the professor was asked to explain the instructions   *mm*
> again to the students.

Written this way, *"confused by the assignment"* appears to describe *the professor* rather than *the students*.

The margin note *"mm"* indicates that this is a *misplaced modifier* because "confused by the assignment" should be close to the word it is modifying, *the students:*

> Confused by the assignment, the students asked the professor to explain the
> instructions again.

Other examples of misplaced modifiers show that when the modifier is oddly placed, the meaning of the sentence is absurd. Notice how easily the misplaced modifier can be moved so that the sentence makes sense:

> Robert L. Heilbroner insists that prejudging a person hurts not only the one being   *mm*
> stereotyped but also the one stereotyping in his essay.

> In his essay, Robert L. Heilbroner insists that prejudging a person hurts not only the
> one being stereotyped but also the one stereotyping.

> You will value the difficult classes you took semesters from now.   *mm*

> Semesters from now, you will value the difficult classes you took.

> Yuko's blind date was described as a six-foot-tall musician with a long ponytail   *mm*
> weighing only 160 pounds.

> Yuko's blind date was described as a 160-pound, six-foot-tall musician with a long
> ponytail.

Another kind of problem is a modifier that "dangles" because there may not be a word for the modifier to describe. In this case, the sentence needs to be rewritten:

> At the age of 12, my family hiked into the Grand Canyon.   *dm*

Here the writer probably does not mean that his or her family was 12 years old, but this sentence does not contain a word for the opening phrase to describe. Therefore, *at the age of 12* is called a *dangling modifier*—a modifier that   *dm* fails to refer logically to any word in the sentence. Dangling modifiers can be corrected by the following methods:

1. Keep the modifier as it is and add a word for the modifier to describe.

> At the age of 12, I hiked into the Grand Canyon with my family.

2. Turn the modifier into a dependent clause so that the meaning is clear.

When I was 12, my family hiked into the Grand Canyon.

Dangling and misplaced modifiers can turn even the most serious disser-
tation into a comedy of errors! Occasionally an instructor may write *"awk"*
(awkward) or *"confusing"* or *"reword"* in the margins when the problem is that
a modifier has been put in the wrong place. Becoming aware of the importance of the *placement* of each word or phrase in a sentence can help you
detect and prevent such comical and confusing meanings before you prepare
your final draft.

# Faulty Parallelism

To achieve clarity, emphasis, and harmony in writing, use *parallel construction* for parts of sentences that you repeat. The "parts" may be single words,
phrases, or clauses. Therefore, when you write any kind of list, put the items
in similar grammatical form (all *-ing* words, all infinitives, and so on). Instead
of writing "He likes hiking and to ski," you should write "He likes hiking and
skiing" or "He likes to hike and to ski."

//     If faulty parallelism is noted in the margin of your paper, you have not
kept the parts of your sentence in the same grammatical form.

## Single Words

//     The movie entertained and was enlightening.

The movie was **entertaining** and **enlightening**.

## Phrases

//     Karen enjoys telling complicated jokes, performing the latest dances, and exotic food.

Karen enjoys **telling complicated jokes, performing the latest dances,** and **eating
exotic food**.

## Dependent Clauses

//     Professor Jaffe reminded the students that papers must be submitted on time and to
prepare reading assignments before class.

Professor Jaffe reminded the students **that papers must be submitted on time** and
**that reading assignments must be prepared before class**.

# Independent Clauses

"I came, I did some learning, and I triumphed," announced the jubilant graduate.      //

"**I came, I learned,** and **I triumphed,**" announced the jubilant graduate.

You can also achieve greater clarity, emphasis, and balance by using parallel constructions with correlative conjunctions (paired terms such as *not only . . . but also; either . . . or;* and *neither . . . nor*):

We discovered that fast walking with a neighbor is good for health and also keeps us      //
friendly.

We discovered that fast walking with a neighbor is good <u>not only for health but also for friendship.</u>

Fran doesn't work as a waitress any longer, and neither does Donna.      //

<u>Neither Fran nor Donna</u> works as a waitress any longer.

# Chapter 15

# Understanding Punctuation

A "*P*" in the margin of an essay indicates some sort of error in punctuation. This chapter covers all punctuation symbols. Because the comma is the most frequently used of them, most errors occur in comma use. Commas usually function to separate elements within a sentence, but they also have standard uses in dates, in addresses, and in multiple-digit numbers. Below are models of the standard uses of the comma, with brief explanations to help you avoid comma errors.

## The Comma

1. Use a comma before a coordinating conjunction joining independent clauses. (Coordinating conjunctions are *and, but, for, or, nor, yet,* and *so.* See also pp. 535–536.)

   The school board has slashed the budget, so activity fees will increase this year.

   Many men want to take paternity leave when their babies are born, but most companies are not prepared for the requests.

   Short independent clauses may not need a comma with the conjunction, but if there is any doubt about the need or clarity, use a comma.

   He arrived so I left.

   He arrived, so I left.

2. Use a comma to separate introductory elements from the rest of the sentence:

To register for classes, bring your advisor's signature card.

If elementary schools continue to close, increased bus service will be necessary.

Exhilarated, the climber reached the summit.

By the next century, most college graduates will be in service-related careers.

3. Use a comma to separate items in a series.

The campus bookstore has been criticized for selling sexist magazines, cigarettes, and greeting cards of questionable taste.

Triathlons require quick running, swimming, and cycling.

The requirements for ownership of the condominium include a bank-approved loan, a satisfactory security rating, and a willingness to comply with the homeowners' rules and procedures.

4. Use a comma between coordinate adjectives—adjectives that modify the same word equally—if there is not a conjunction.

The shady, blooming, fragrant garden welcomed the walkers.

A shady and fragrant garden welcomed the walkers.

If the first adjective modifies the second adjective, do not use a comma.

That mansion's most interesting feature is a white oak staircase.

Professor Pierce's exams require complicated mathematical computations.

5. Use commas to set off nonrestrictive word groups. Nonrestrictive elements describe nouns or pronouns by giving extra or nonessential information. The nonrestrictive element could be removed from the sentence without sacrificing the meaning of the sentence.

Walden Pond, which is located outside of Concord, was the site of Thoreau's one-room shelter and bean field.

Amy Tan's first novel, *The Joy Luck Club*, was written in a few months.

The Rolls-Royce, its silver hood ornament gleaming in the sun, was completely out of gas.

6. Do *not* use commas with restrictive word groups. Restrictive elements limit the meaning of words or provide vital (or restricting) information.

The entrees on the left side of the menu are suitable for diners who prefer low-cholesterol diets.

The sentence gives the information that only the entrees on the left side of the menu are low in cholesterol. Presumably, the other items on the menu are not especially suited for clients who prefer low cholesterol.

Our son who lives in Texas teaches anthropology.

For a family with sons residing in different states, the restrictive clause is essential and commas should not be used.

Customers using credit cards collect free airline mileage.

Again, the lack of commas shows that the information is restrictive. Only those customers who use credit cards will collect airline mileage; customers who pay by check or cash do not.

7. Use commas to separate transitional or parenthetical expressions, conjunctive adverbs, contrasting elements, and most phrases from the main part of the sentence.

Silk, for example, can be washed by hand.

Joseph Heller, as the story goes, wanted to call his novel *Catch-18* instead of *Catch-22*.

A medium avocado contains 324 calories; therefore, it is not an ideal fruit for people watching their weight.

Darren, unlike his brother Stephen, can be reasonable.

Her medical studies completed, Nancy started a practice in Fresno.

8. Use commas to set off expressions and questions of direct address, the words *yes* or *no*, and interjections.

Sorry, Professor Hendricks, only two of those books are in the stacks.

You will complete the immigration papers, won't you?

Yes, most readers prefer the new MLA documentation form.

Oh, I can't decide if we really need an attorney.

9. Use commas for dates, addresses, and titles.

James Joyce was born on February 2, 1882, which was St. Bridget's Day and Groundhog Day, too.

The special delivery letter was sent to 10350 Dover Street, Westminster, Colorado.

Will Wood, Ph.D., begins his law practice at Duke University.

10. Use commas to set off direct quotations.

As Richard Ellmann notes, "Stephen Dedalus said the family was a net which he would fly past."

> "I too believe in Taos, without having seen it. I also believe in Indians. But they must do *half* the believing: in me as well as in the sun," wrote D. H. Lawrence to Mabel Luhan.

11. Do *not* use a comma to separate a verb from its subject or object. The following examples both show *incorrect* uses of the comma:

    Fast walking around a track, can be painless but effective exercise. *P*

    Christine explained to Larry, that practicing law has precedence over going to films. *P*

12. Do *not* use a comma between compound elements if the word groups are not independent clauses. The following examples show *incorrect* uses of the comma:

    Louise can prepare a multi-course meal, and weed her garden on the same day. *P*

    Sara understands that the conference is in June, and that she will need to grade finals while she is attending it. *P*

13. A comma should not be used to separate an adjective from the noun that follows it. The following examples are *incorrect* uses of the comma:

    It was a sunny, warm, and windless, day. *P*

    A massive, polished, ornately carved, buffet stood in the dining room. *P*

# The Apostrophe

The apostrophe is one of the more perplexing punctuation symbols for all writers. In fact, Grammar Girl, a helpful Web site that we highly recommend, devotes at least two podcasts to answering listeners' questions about how to use the apostrophe. In addition to reading the explanations below, try hearing Grammar Girl's podcasts at <http://grammar.quickanddirtytips.com/apost rophe-plural-grammar-rules.aspx>.

Most frequently, the apostrophe is used to form **contractions** and to show **possession**:

## Contractions

When two words are merged into one, the apostrophe takes the place of any missing letters:

| | |
|---|---|
| does not | doesn't |
| it is | it's |
| should have | should've |
| I would | I'd |

Contractions tend to make writing seem more conversational and informal; therefore, they are often avoided in formal writing and in research papers.

Remember that the apostrophe takes the place of the missing letter and does not ever belong in the break between the two words:

couldn't [*not* could'nt]

Other instances where apostrophes indicate a missing letter or letters are commonly found in informal writing and speech, particularly in dialogues from narratives and fiction:

| around | _'round |
| until | _'til |
| 1950s | _'50s |
| playing | playin'_ |

Again, such forms are typically reserved for writing that is intended to sound conversational.

## Possession

Possessive nouns indicate belonging or ownership and are typically placed immediately before whatever is owned. Rather than write "the trumpet of Jason" or "the office of his doctor," we eliminate the *of* and move the owner in front of the possession:

Jason's trumpet

his doctor's office

Sometimes such ownership is loosely implied:

tonight's party

Thursday's test

one day's sick leave

two weeks' vacation

In a sense, the party really does "belong" to tonight (not tomorrow) and the test "belongs" to Thursday (not Friday). Similarly, the sick leave is "of one day" and the vacation is "of two weeks." Clearly, the possessive form here makes the writing smoother and less wordy.

In some cases, the notion of ownership is open to interpretation. For example, you may wonder if you should write *farmers market* or *farmers' market*—or *homeowners association* or *homeowners' association*. It might be argued that the farmers sell at the market but don't own it (hence, *farmers market* seems right and *farmers* is used as an adjective). However, homeowners do own their association because they contribute fees and may manage it (therefore, *homeowners' association* seems reasonable). Ultimately, your sense of whether there is ownership should determine whether or not to use the apostrophe in these situations.

To indicate possession, obey the following guidelines:

1. Add 's if the possessive noun does not end in *s* (whether it is singular or plural):

   Sarah's acting

   Ben's collections

   the men's movement

   the children's enthusiasm

2. Add an apostrophe at the end of the word if the plural possessive noun ends in an *s* (including proper names):

   those actors' salaries

   five students' projects

   two months' salary

   the Knights' generosity

   the Walshes' Super Bowl party

3. If a singular proper name ends in *s*, add an ' and a second *s*.

   James's routine

   Oates's story

4. There is an exception to the above rule that an 's should follow a proper name ending in *s*. If the pronunciation would be awkward with the added 's, the writer may use only the apostrophe:

   Billy Collins' poem

   Pamela Erens' essay

***Joint Possession.*** When two or more people possess the same thing, show joint possession by using 's (or *s*') with the last noun only:

   We relaxed at Jule and Marsha's home in Colorado Springs.

   Nate and Jess's help is valuable.

***Individual Possession.*** When two or more people possess distinct things, show individual possession by using 's (or *s*') with both nouns:

   Andy's and Beth's summer projects aren't completed yet.

   Luis's and Charles's questions were both provocative.

***Compound Nouns.*** If a noun is compound, use 's (or *s*') with the last component of that noun term:

   My brother-in-law's woodworking is very professional.

   Barbara and Julie took their sisters-in-laws' advice.

***Indefinite Pronouns.*** Indefinite pronouns are those that refer to no specific person or thing: *everyone, anyone, no one,* and *something.* These pronouns also need an apostrophe to indicate possession:

> We asked everybody's opinion of the film.

> Is someone's safety in jeopardy?

***Possessive Pronouns.*** Possessive pronouns are already possessive and need no apostrophes:

| | |
|---|---|
| my, mine | its |
| you, yours | our, ours |
| her, hers | their, theirs |
| his | whose |

> *Whose* car should we drive?

> I would prefer to ride in *yours* rather than *theirs.*

***Plurals of Letters.*** Use 's to pluralize the letters of the alphabet:

> He earned three *B's* this term.

> She has two *t's* in her last name.

***Plurals of Numbers and Abbreviations.*** The apostrophe should *not* be used for plurals of numbers or abbreviations:

> They all marched in *twos.*

> By the end of the *1990s,* community recycling was widespread.

> Many students like to purchase used *CDs* at their local music stores.

> All candidates must have earned their *BAs.*

Some reminders:

1. Make sure a noun is possessive (and not merely plural) before you use an apostrophe. The noun *passengers* does not "own" anything in the following sentence; therefore, it is a simple plural.

   P  The ~~passenger's~~ *passengers* were not allowed to smoke.

2. Possessive pronouns need no apostrophes.

   P  The crowd expressed ~~it's~~ *its* pleasure.

   P  That responsibility is ~~her's~~ *hers.*

3. Many instructors prefer that their students not use contractions in formal writing and research papers.

# The Period, Question Mark, and Exclamation Point

The most obvious use of the period is to mark the end of a sentence—unless the sentence is a direct question or needs an exclamation point:

> Do you remember learning punctuation symbols in elementary school?
>
> Yes, and it all seemed so easy then!

Because the exclamation point is used for strong commands and emphatic statements, it should not be overused. Furthermore, an exclamation mark is never used with a period, a comma, or another exclamation point.

Don't use a question mark for an indirect or implied question:

> I wonder if I ever had trouble with punctuation in elementary school.

Use the period for abbreviations:

> Mr. / Mrs. / Ms.     Dr. / Rev. / Capt.     i.e. / e.g. / etc.
>
> a.m. / p.m.

Notice that no period is used with abbreviations that consist of all capital letters:

> CA    NY    TX    IL    BC    AD    US    CD-ROM

Do not use periods with acronyms (words that are made from the first letters of many words and are pronounced as words):

> NATO    UNICEF    NASA    AIDS    MADD    DARE

Usually no period is used in abbreviations of the names of organizations, schools, and some academic titles:

> NBC    UN    NBA    NYU    BS    MA    PhD    NAACP

# The Semicolon

The semicolon is most often used to connect two independent clauses:

> Students with an advisor's signature card register in their division office; students without a signature must register in the gym.

Notice that the semicolon is used in place of a period to show that the two independent ideas—clauses that could stand alone as separate sentences—are *related*. The semicolon suggests the relationship without defining it.

The semicolon is also used after an independent clause and before some transitional phrases (like *on the other hand* or *in contrast*) and after conjunctive adverbs (such as *therefore, however,* and *furthermore;* see the complete list on p. 536).

Newcomers to the United States often enjoy material advantages that they lacked in their native lands; on the other hand, they often feel spiritually deprived in their new country.

Professor Smiley will accept late papers; however, he reduces the grade for each day the paper is late.

The semicolon is used for separating items in a list if the punctuation within the list includes commas. Notice Naomi Wolf's use of the semicolon in this example from *The Beauty Myth:*

In 1984, in the United States, "male lawyers aged 25–34 earn $27,563, but female lawyers the same age, $20,573; retail salesmen earn $13,002 to retail saleswomen's $7,479; male bus drivers make $15,611 and female bus drivers $9,903; female hairdressers earn $7,603 less than male hairdressers" (49).

# The Colon

A colon is used to introduce and call attention to a statement, to introduce a list, to introduce a quotation if the quotation is at the end of a sentence, in bibliographic forms, in reporting time, for separating main titles from subtitles, and in distinguishing chapters from verses in the Bible. A colon is usually preceded by a main clause (a word group containing a subject and verb). The main clause does not need to be followed by a complete clause, but if it is a complete clause, capitalize the first word.

The candidates need to realize that women form a significant majority in this country: six million more potential votes.

The application form requires the following: a final transcript, a housing request, a medical report, and the first tuition check.

Women do not expect promotions or high salaries: "Women are often unsure of their intrinsic worth in the marketplace" (Sidel qtd. in Wolf 49).

New York: Longman

*Between Worlds: A Reader, Rhetoric, and Handbook*

The train departs at 5:30 in the morning.

In some cases, a colon should not be used. For example, do *not* place a colon between a subject and a verb, between a verb and its complements, or between a preposition and its object:

*P*        The animals in that section of the zoo include: panthers, leopards, lions, and tigers.

*P*        The courses he needs to take are: biology, chemistry, physics, and calculus.

*P*        Don't put luggage on: the bed, the desk, or the reading chair.

# The Dash

The dash (created by typing two hyphens with no spaces around or between them) is used sparingly for dramatic emphasis, to call attention to material the dash sets off. Sometimes the dash is used in places where a colon could also be used, but the dash is considered more informal. Because the dash indicates a sudden shift in thought and is used for dramatic emphasis, it should not be overused. In formal writing, a comma, colon, or period may be more appropriate punctuation symbols.

> We all believe that environmental protection is an obligation of our era—but we still use toxic cleaners in our homes.

Here the dash is used to emphasize the contrast between what "we all believe" and what we do. A comma could also be used in this sentence:

> In the past some successful and even less-successful women had the same goal—to "marry up"—so some men felt a psychological need to be successful at work.

The dash is used here to set off the definitive information, the "same goal" the writer believes women have. A comma could have been used, but the dash achieves more emphasis.

The dash may also be used in the same manner as the colon to announce a dramatic point:

> The candidates need to realize that women form a significant majority in this country—six million more potential votes.

# Quotation Marks

Quotation marks are used to enclose direct quotations, some titles, and occasionally words defined or used in a special way. Quotation marks are used in pairs.

## Direct Quotations

A *direct quotation* states in exact words what someone has said or written. It is enclosed with quotation marks.

> Brigid Brophy insists, "If modern civilisation has invented methods of education which make it possible for men to feed babies and for women to think logically, we are betraying civilisation itself if we do not set both sexes free to make a free choice."

Notice that Brophy's spelling of *civilisation* is British, and that the writer quoting her is not permitted to change her spelling without indicating the change in brackets: "civili[z]ation." See more on brackets on page 564.

An *indirect quotation* notes what has been said in a paraphrased or indirect way. No quotation marks are needed:

> Brigid Brophy believes that men and women should be free to make the choices that education and technology have made possible.

A *quotation within a quotation* requires the use of standard quotation marks around the outside quotation and single quotation marks around the interior quotation:

> According to Naomi Wolf, "Every generation since about 1830 has had to fight its version of the beauty myth. 'It is very little to me,' said the suffragist Lucy Stone in 1855, 'to have the right to vote, to own property, etcetera, if I may not keep my body, and its uses, in my absolute right.'"

Commas and periods are placed inside quotation marks:

> Brigid Brophy thinks that both genders should be "free to make a free choice."

> If we do not let men and women make choices, "we are betraying civilisation itself," believes Brigid Brophy.

Semicolons and colons are placed outside quotation marks:

> Brophy says we are all "free to make a free choice"; in fact, we let convention limit our awareness of choice.

> Brophy says we are all "free to make a free choice": about our educations, our careers, our domesticity.

Question marks go inside quotation marks if they are part of the quotation but belong outside of quotation marks if the quoted statement is being used as a question by the writer quoting the material:

> The professor asked, "Who agrees with Brigid Brophy's thesis?"

> Does Brophy think we "should be free to make a free choice"?

If you are quoting a conversation, begin a new paragraph for each speaker. Notice the punctuation of the quoted conversation in this excerpt from Rebekah Hall-Naganuma's narrative, which begins on page 386.

> "What do you mean by 'blackout?'" she asked, with a look of confusion on her face.

> "She ended up in Houston somehow and then couldn't remember how she got there."

If you are quoting poetry, integrate into your own text quoted single lines of poetry. Two or three lines of poetry may be brought into your text and enclosed in quotation marks, or they may be set off from your text, without quotation marks but indented ten spaces (one inch) from the left margin:

> The narrator in Janice Mirikitani's poem "Breaking Tradition" longs to be liberated from her mother's influence:
>
>> I want to break tradition—unlock this room
>>
>> where women dress in the dark.

Discover the lies my mother told me.

The lies that we are small and powerless. (23–26)

or

The narrator in Janice Mirikitani's poem "Breaking Tradition" longs to be liberated from her mother's influence: "I want to break tradition–unlock this room / where women dress in the dark" (23–24).

The slash ( / ) is used to indicate the end of a poetry line when poetry lines are incorporated into text. (The use of the slash is described further on pp. 565–566.) Set off poetry quotations of more than three lines and prose quotations of more than four lines.

## Titles

Titles of short stories, songs, essays, poems, articles, parts of books, and the titles of episodes on television and radio are enclosed in quotation marks:

"In Groups We Shrink"

"Imagine"

"Don't Let Stereotypes Warp Your Judgments"

"The Work"

"Tracks" in *Aquaboogie*

Do not use quotation marks around a word that you feel self-conscious about using. Instead, change the word:

The morning meeting is held to give the staff the "rundown" on the advertising goals    *p*
for the day.

The morning meeting is held to explain that day's advertising goals to the staff.

# Italics

Current MLA style requires the use of italics for titles of independently published works—books, plays, periodicals, films, Web sites, online databases, television and radio broadcasts, CDs, record albums, performances, and works of art:

*Between Worlds: A Reader, Rhetoric, and Handbook*

*A Midsummer Night's Dream*

*Time*

*Crash*

*30 Rock*

*Organized Wisdom*

*The Animal Years*

*Nighthawks*

Use italics for words and letters referred to as words, foreign words in an English text, and for emphasis.

The tidy room is not so much *neat* as it is boring.

For addresses on envelopes, use the abbreviation for the state, *AZ*, instead of Arizona.

Spanish expressions such as *adios* have become common in the United States.

He is *not* the best candidate for the job even though he is qualified.

# The Ellipsis

The ellipsis, a set of three spaced periods (. . .), informs the reader that something has been left out of a quotation. For example, a writer quoting material from Naomi Wolf's book *The Beauty Myth* might decide to leave out some material unnecessary to the text he or she is writing. Here Wolf writes about the phenomenon of eating disorders in countries other than the United States:

It is spreading to other industrialized nations: The United Kingdom now has

3.5 million anorexics or bulimics (95 percent of them female), with 6,000 new

cases yearly (183).

Here the passage is revised using an ellipsis:

It is spreading to other industrialized nations: The United Kingdom now has

3.5 million anorexics or bulimics . . . with 6,000 new cases yearly (183).

The decision to remove material and use the ellipsis must be governed by the writer's intent. But the ellipsis may not be used to remove anything that would change the meaning of the section that the writer is quoting. The fact that 95 percent of the cases of eating disorders in the United Kingdom involve women may not be relevant to the writer of the revised text, so the ellipsis is used as a convenient tool to shorten the quoted material and keep the emphasis where the writer wants it. The missing words in this case do not change the meaning of the original.

If you remove words from the quoted material at the end of the sentence, use a period before the three periods of the ellipsis. Notice this example from "How to Get Better Gas Mileage" (p. 417). Mieszkowski quotes Philip Reed, a consumer advocate, whose full statement might not be entirely relevant to someone using Mieszkowski's material. A writer eliminating a part of the work would use an ellipsis after the period in the first sentence to show that unnecessary material between the two sentences was removed:

> Drivers are often unconsciously influenced by the speed of the other cars around them, which can lead to speed creep. "When a faster car passes you, you have a tendency to speed up. Soon, even though you were committed to going 70, you're going 80," says Reed. . . . A good way to avoid that pitfall: use the cruise control on the freeway, which will also help you avoid the temptation to constantly dart forward when you see an opening in traffic up ahead. (419)

If a parenthetical reference follows an ellipsis at the end of a sentence, use three spaced periods and then place the period to conclude the sentence after the final parenthesis:

> As Lisa Appignanesi records in her biography *Simone de Beauvoir*, Beauvoir believed that "the genuinely moral person can never have an easy conscience. . ." (79).

To avoid using the ellipsis too often, integrate carefully selected parts of quoted material into your text:

> As Carol Tavris notes, people respond "in shock and anger at the failings of 'human nature.'"

By paraphrasing part of the quotation and integrating the author's text with your own, you can avoid both using lengthy quotations *and* overusing the ellipsis.

# Parentheses

Use parentheses to separate a digression or aside from the main sentence:

> Their house number (usually painted on the curb) was on the mailbox.

> Because an increasing number of women (and men) are suffering from eating disorders, we must address the problem at our next NOW conference.

Rules govern the use of punctuation within and outside of parentheses. If a sentence requires a comma in addition to parentheses, use the comma after the second or closing parenthesis:

> During the Civil War (1861–1865), African Americans were trained for active duty and fought in segregated units.

If the information within the parentheses is a complete sentence, the final punctuation is enclosed within the parentheses:

> More information on gardens that require little water appears throughout the book. (See the chapters on cactus and native plants, especially.)

Parentheses also are used in documentation to enclose the source of paraphrased or quoted information. In these cases, the terminal punctuation appears outside the parentheses:

> As Virginia Woolf says in *Orlando,* "Clothes have . . . more important offices than merely to keep us warm. They change our view of the world and the world's view of us" (187).

(For a more complete discussion of how parentheses are used in MLA documentation, see p. 502, and for their use in APA documentation, see p. 518.)

# Brackets

Use brackets to enclose words or phrases that you have added to a quotation, to show any changes that you have made in quoted material, or to record your own comments about quoted material:

> Today, more attention is being paid "to the relationship between eating disorders [anorexia and bulimia] and the compulsive eating of many women."

In the preceding example, the writer has clarified a point for the reader by defining within the quotation types of eating disorders. The brackets indicate that the words are not part of the original quotation.

> The Duke of Ferrara, in Robert Browning's poem "My Last Duchess," is disturbed that the Duchess "ranked [his] gift of a nine-hundred-years-old name / With anybody's gift."

In this example, the writer changed the original—"ranked my gift of a nine-hundred-years-old name"—to fit into a text. To show the change from *my* to *his,* the writer placed brackets around the change. The diagonal line (or slash) between "name" and "With" indicates the end of the line in the poem.

> The "Poison Pen Letters" greeting card says, "Everything has it's [sic] price . . . but I didn't know you came so cheap!"

The brackets are used to enclose *sic,* a Latin word meaning "in this manner." The *[sic]* used after *it's* in the above example indicates that the error of not using *its* is in the original, and is not an error made by the person quoting the original.

# The Slash

The slash may be used sparingly to show options, like *pass/fail* or *Dean/ Department Head.* Notice that there is no space between the words and the slash when the slash is used to show options.

The slash is also used to define the end of a line of poetry if the line is incorporated into a text. For example, notice how the writer incorporates into a poetry explication some words from Stephen Perry's poem "Blue Spruce":

> The speaker in the poem reveals that his "grandfather had an affair / with the girl who did their nails" (19–20).

The slash indicates where the line ends in the original work (which appears on p. 173). Notice that a space appears on either side of the slash when it is used to indicate the end of a line of poetry.

In bulletins, reports, and some business correspondence, the slash is used in the form *he/she,* as in this sentence:

> The person who lost a ring in the library may claim it after he/she describes it to
>
> campus police.

In formal writing, you should avoid the form *he/she* by writing *he or she,* as in this sentence:

> The student who aspires to a law degree may attain it if he or she is willing to work hard.

Both *he/she* and *he or she* can be avoided by rewriting the sentence:

> The person who lost a ring in the library may claim it by describing it to campus police.

> The student who aspires to a law degree may attain it by working hard.

## The Hyphen

The hyphen is used to divide a word or to form a compound word. To divide a word that will not fit on the typed or written line, separate the part of the word that will fit on the line with a hyphen at a syllable break, then conclude the word on the next line. The break must occur only between syllables and should not leave fewer than two letters at the end of the line or fewer than three letters at the beginning of the next line. The hyphen appears at the end of the first line, *not* at the beginning of the next line. If you are using a computer, the word processing program automatically moves the full word to the next line (unless directed to hyphenate words).

Notice how each error is corrected:

> Of all of the applicants for the job, she was the best teach-        P
>
> er for the class.

> Of all of the applicants for the job, she was the best
>
> teacher for the class.

If you choose to hyphenate, a word can be broken between syllables if the break will leave at least two letters at the end of the line and three or more letters at the beginning of the next line. Because the syllables of *teach-* and *-er* will not fit that rule, the entire word must be moved to the next line.

> After his paper was completed, the frustrated student fo-        P
>
> und another critical article.

> After his paper was completed, the frustrated student
>
> found another critical article.

[A one-syllable word cannot be broken, so *found* must be moved to the next line.]

*P*    Since the 1993 presidential inauguration, interest in the poetry of Maya Angelou has increased.

Since the 1993 presidential inauguration, interest in the
poetry of Maya Angelou has increased.

[The hyphen is used *only* at the end of the first line.]
Divide compound words only where the hyphen already exists:

He gave the family heirloom to his sis-

*P*    ter-in-law.

He gave the family heirloom to his sister-
in-law.

Histories of popular music describe the heart-throb-

*P*    bing gestures of Elvis Presley.

Histories of popular music describe the heart-
throbbing gestures of Elvis Presley.

Hyphens are also used to form compound words that modify a noun:

The grade-conscious students knew the best sequence for the courses.

The award-winning play went on to Broadway.

If the modifiers follow the noun, the hyphens are usually left out.

The students are grade conscious.

The play was award winning and went on to Broadway.

Hyphens are used in spelled-out fractions and compound whole numbers from twenty-one to ninety-nine:

Over one-half of the voters will stay home on election day.

Everyone hates that old school bus song, "Ninety-Nine Bottles of Beer on the Wall."

Hyphens are used to attach some prefixes and suffixes. Usually, prefixes are attached to a word without a hyphen: *preconceived, disinterested, unhappy.* But prefixes such as *ex-, self-,* and *all-,* prefixes that precede a capitalized word, or prefixes that are a capitalized letter usually require a hyphen; for example, *self-supporting, ex-champion, anti-European,* and *U-boat.* Sometimes, to prevent confusion, a hyphen is necessary to separate a prefix ending in a vowel and a main word that starts with a vowel, for example, *de-escalate, re-invent,* and *pre-advise.*

# Chapter 16

# Understanding Faulty Word Choice

Poor word choice weakens writing, and instructors will note these errors in the margins of your papers. (Specific examples are cited in the alphabetically arranged list of commonly confused words on pages 571–582.) The types of word choice problems are defined and illustrated here.

## Clichés

Clichés, or overused words or expressions, should be avoided. Predictable language is stale, and expressions that were once novel and even colorful inevitably lose their descriptive quality through overuse. Like a faded carpet, clichés no longer add color to the space they occupy. If you can complete the following expressions automatically, you know that you have examples of a cliché:

The bread was hard as a _____.

We searched all day, but it was like looking for a needle _____.

Good writing is clear, fresh, and vivid:

The bread was as hard as aged camel dung and about as tasty.

We searched all day, but it was like looking for a button in my mother's tool drawer.

## Slang, Jargon, and Colloquial Words

Some of our most vivid language is considered *slang* (highly informal, often coined words used in speaking) or *jargon* (the special vocabulary of people who have the same job, interest, or way of life). In fact, in conversation, if

pretentious language were substituted for some of the commonly used *colloquial* words—*intoxicated* for *drunk* or *children* for *kids*—our conversations would sound stuffy or silly. Slang is often vigorous and colorful, but it is nonstandard and therefore unacceptable in most formal writing. And the jargon that is acceptable in conversation or memos at work may be unintelligible to the general reader. If you think your "funky," "laid-back," or "awesome" word choice is going to influence negatively your reader's feelings about your integrity as a writer, elevate your language and remove the inappropriate word.

## Archaic Words, Euphemisms, and Pretentious Words

Some words that appear in literature, especially poetry, may not be appropriate for expository writing:

*wd ch*    Marcus Mabry was amongst the minority students accepted at Stanford.

Marcus Mabry was among the minority students accepted at Stanford.

The word *amongst,* used in poetry, sounds inflated in expository texts.

Writers sometimes use *euphemisms*—substitutes for words perceived as offensive—to limit emotional impact. For example, a war report might describe the results of a bombing mission as "collateral casualties" rather than "civilians killed." A *Newsweek* article states that "the collateral damage of the drug war has been immense"—a euphemism avoiding the recognition that it is human beings who are being incarcerated and homes that are being destroyed in overly aggressive police actions.

Euphemisms are often deliberately used to mask a harsher reality. At best, they are often imprecise, as in this sentence: "We lost our grandmother last week." The reader might wonder if she is still wandering in the parking lot of the local mall. To avoid this confusion and to communicate accurately, use direct and precise language: "Our grandmother died last week."

Pretentious language is used by writers who believe it will make their work appear more refined or elegant. Avoid words like *facilitate* or *utilize* when *help* and *use* are adequate. Some pretentious words have persisted and reached cliché status: *viable* and *parameters,* for example.

Writers who are insecure about their writing may be tempted to overuse a thesaurus or pad their papers with contrived and inflated diction. Readers can usually detect this as a desperate attempt to pump up flat or shallow ideas. Instead of developing their thinking and analysis, pretentious writers try to bluff it. Typically, the end result is wordy, confused, stuffy prose rather than writing that is concise, accurate, and honest. Here are some examples, from student essays, of contrived or inflated diction:

**Inflated and Wordy Diction:**

The imagery that Baldwin employs engulfs the situation to a reality status. *diction*

**Precise:**

Baldwin's imagery makes the scene realistic.

**Inflated and Wordy Diction:**

The story commences with the creation of an atmosphere that posited the couple's *diction* affluency.

**Precise:**

The setting suggests that the couple is wealthy.

# Redundancies

The legal profession has contributed some double-talk, such as *aid and abet,* to our language, and some other redundancies have persisted even though they are bulky or inane: *each and every, revert back, end result, temporary respite,* or *true fact.* You can see that *each* and *every* mean the same thing, so the words should not be used together. To revert means "to go back." And what is a fact if it isn't true? If you regard these redundancies as you would clichés—language that is predictable and imprecise—you will eliminate them from your writing.

# Sexist Language

Language that demeans women or men is *sexist*. Most writers would know not to use *chick, broad, stud,* or *hunk* in their work, but more subtle and insidious sexist language also needs to be avoided. If you exclude or offend a portion of your audience, you will lose your reader—even if the rest of your essay is strong—as in the following examples:

Every professor uses his wisdom to remain objective.

Each nurse is required to store her lunch in a locker.

A clever lawyer parks his car in the free lot.

The competent PTA president uses her gavel rarely.

Even a superficial look at job and lifestyle choices in the last decades would confirm the necessity of unbiased language in print. Nurses and lawyers are both female and male; nowhere is it prescribed that only women will be PTA presidents. Consider the following solutions illustrated below for freeing the above sentences of sexist language:

A professor uses wisdom to remain objective.

Professors use their wisdom to remain objective.

Nurses are required to store their lunches in lockers.

Each nurse is required to store his or her lunch in a locker.

Clever lawyers park their cars in the free lot.

Avoid the *his/her* construction in formal writing and the *his or her* pattern. You can eliminate both of these bulky and awkward constructions by using the article instead of a possessive pronoun, or by using a plural noun as the subject:

The competent PTA president uses the gavel rarely.

Competent PTA presidents use their gavels rarely.

Do not assume any job is gender specific. *Fireman* should be *firefighter, clergyman* should be *minister* or *member of the clergy,* and *mailman* should be *letter carrier* or *mail carrier.* Do not add *lady* to job titles; "She is a lady doctor" is as unnecessary a distinction as "He is a male artist."

You can further free your writing from sexism by eliminating the generic use of *man* in examples like the following:

Mankind is more aware of stereotypes than it was a decade ago.

Humanity is more aware of stereotypes than it was a decade ago.

People are more aware of stereotypes than they were a decade ago.

# Glossary of Usage: Commonly Confused Words

**a, an:** Use *a* before words beginning with consonant sounds, including those spelled with an initial pronounced *h* (*a* horse) and those spelled with vowels that are sounded as consonants (*a* one-hour final, *a* university). Use *an* before words beginning with vowel sounds, including those spelled with an initial *h* (*an* igloo, *an* hour).

**a/an, the:** *A* and *an* are indefinite articles and are used before nouns that are nonspecific or general (*a* game, *an* acrobat). *The* is a definite article and used before nouns that refer to something specific (*the* game, *the* acrobat).

An avid sports fan, Bill watches a televised football game every weekend.

His favorite team is the Miami Dolphins although his friend always cheers for the Buffalo Bills.

**accept, except:** *Accept* is a verb meaning "to receive." *Except* is a preposition meaning "excluding" or "but."

I accept your plan to tour all of New York City except for Central Park.

**advice, advise:** *Advice* is the noun meaning "recommendation about what to do." *Advise* is the verb meaning "to give opinion or counsel."

I advise you to follow your counselor's advice.

**affect, effect:** *Affect* is usually a verb meaning "to influence." *Effect* is a noun meaning "result." In psychology, *affect* is used as a noun meaning "a feeling or emotion." *Effect* can be used as a verb meaning "to implement, or to bring about."

The eyedrops do not affect his driving.

Candles create a romantic effect in the dining room. An examination of affect is critical in understanding personality.

Congress must effect a change in the tax laws.

**aisle, isle:** *Aisle* means a walkway between sections of seats, shelves, or counters. *Isle* means an island.

Deborah and Jeff decided it was time to amble down the <u>aisle</u> together.

The pet food <u>aisle</u> of the supermarket seems to expand each year.

Melanie and Russ were dreaming about snorkeling near some faraway <u>isle</u> in the Pacific.

**all ready, already:** *All ready* means "completely prepared." *Already* means "by now" or "before now."

We were <u>all ready</u> for the trip, but the bus had <u>already</u> left.

**all right:** *All right* is typically spelled as two words. (*Alright* appears in some dictionaries, but most readers still consider it a misspelling.)

**all together, altogether:** *All together* means "in a common location," "in unison," or "as a group." *Altogether* means "completely" or "entirely."

We are <u>altogether</u> certain that caging the rabbits <u>all together</u> is a mistake.

**allude/elude:** *Allude* means "to refer to"; *elude* means "to escape."

Mimi <u>alluded</u> to the time when Katie studied in France and managed to <u>elude</u> tedious professors.

**allusion, illusion:** An *allusion* is an "indirect reference"; an *illusion* is "a deceptive appearance" or "a fantasy that may be confused with reality."

Joyce's use of mythological <u>allusions</u> gives the <u>illusion</u> that she is a classicist.

**a lot:** *A lot* is always two words, never *alot*.

**altar, alter:** The noun *altar* means "an elevated place or structure where religious rites are performed." *Alter* is a verb that means "to change or modify."

She needed to <u>alter</u> her schedule to allow time to decorate the church <u>altar</u> with fresh daisies for the wedding.

**among, between:** Use *between* when referring to two; use *among* for three or more.

<u>Between</u> you and me, Alex is <u>among</u> the most creative students in our program.

**amount, number:** *Amount* refers to a quantity of something that cannot be counted. *Number* refers to items that can be counted.

The <u>amount</u> of flour used depends on the <u>number</u> of cookies you want to bake.

**anxious:** *Anxious* means "apprehensive" or "worried." Often it is confused with the word *eager*, which means "anticipating" or "looking forward to."

Yumiko was <u>anxious</u> about her performance review because she was <u>eager</u> to be promoted.

**a while, awhile:** *A while* is an article and a noun; *awhile* is an adverb.

> We spoke for <u>a while</u> and then parted.

> Wait <u>awhile</u> before you swim.

**basically:** This word is greatly overused and often unnecessary:

> **Avoid:** Tia and Delaiah are, <u>basically</u>, ideal daughters-in-law.

> **Better:** Tia and Delaiah are ideal daughters-in-law.

**being as, being that:** These terms should not be used for *because* or *since*.

> <u>Because</u> Quarterback Doug Flutie was so popular with fans, the games in Buffalo were always sold out.

> <u>Since</u> he signed with the Lakers, Kobe has been a top scorer for the team.

**beside, besides:** *Beside* is a preposition meaning "next to." *Besides* is a preposition meaning "except," as well as an adverb meaning "in addition to."

> Caitlin sat <u>beside</u> her camera crew so she could direct them.

> Everyone <u>besides</u> the team rides the school bus to each game.

> Leslie's instructional expertise is needed; <u>besides</u>, she knows how to have fun!

**brake, break:** *Brake* means to slow or stop a vehicle or the device used to stop a vehicle. *Break* means to smash, shatter, become separated, interrupt, or halt.

> If that driver doesn't <u>brake</u> soon, he will <u>break</u> the bikes that are in the driveway.

**can, may:** *Can* means "is able to." *May* indicates permission.

> You <u>can</u> talk on the telephone for three hours, but you <u>may</u> not in my house!

**capital, capitol:** *Capital* refers to the city and is the word to describe an uppercase letter. *Capitol* indicates the building where government meets.

> The <u>capital</u> is the destination for the class trip, but a visit to the <u>capitol</u> is impossible because the ceiling is under repair.

**censor, censure:** *Censor* functions as a verb (meaning "to suppress or remove objectionable material") and as a noun (the person who suppresses the objectionable material). *Censure* is a verb meaning "to criticize severely."

> The librarian refused to work with citizens who <u>censor</u> the classics.

> The <u>censor</u> of a few decades ago considered *The Adventures of Huckleberry Finn* subversive.

> The city council needs to <u>censure</u> neon signs in "Old Town."

**cite, site, sight:** *Cite* means "to quote by way of example, authority, or proof." *Site* is "the location of." *Sight* is a "spectacle or view."

The tourist <u>sights</u> were on the <u>site</u> of an ancient village <u>cited</u> in the guidebook.

**complement, compliment:** *Complement* means "to complete" or "something that completes or supplements another." *Compliment* is a noun or verb that means "to praise."

His sensitivity <u>complements</u> her assertiveness.

Most people see through false <u>compliments</u>.

**conscience, conscious:** *Conscience* is a noun referring to one's sense of right and wrong. *Conscious* is an adjective that means "alert to" or "aware of."

The jury member was <u>conscious</u> of his nagging <u>conscience</u>.

**could of, should of, would of:** These are incorrect forms for *could have, should have,* and *would have. Of* is a preposition, not a part of a verb.

The trainer <u>should have</u> exercised his horse today.

**desert/dessert:** *Dessert* (with the double *s*) means the sweet treat at the end of the meal. *Desert* is used for all other meanings: a barren, sandy region; a deserved reward or punishment; to abandon or forsake.

Taylor and Garrett devoured their <u>dessert</u> before they departed for the <u>desert</u>.

Karen had to <u>desert</u> the thief, but she knew he would get his just <u>deserts</u>.

**discreet/discrete:** *Discreet* means "tactful" or "diplomatic"; *discrete* means "separate" or "distinct."

Dean Lew is always <u>discreet</u> about students' comments on evaluation forms.

Kristi's and Charlotte's duties are <u>discrete</u> from each other.

**double negative:** Double negatives to emphasize negativity are nonstandard in English.

I didn't see anything [not *nothing*].

The child could hardly control [not *couldn't hardly control*] his tears.

**due to:** *Due to* is acceptable following a linking verb but is considered less acceptable at the beginning of a sentence.

Most minor injuries during earthquakes are <u>due to</u> panic.

<u>Because of</u> [not *due to*] rain, the beach party was canceled.

**due to the fact that:** Use *because* to avoid wordiness.

**each:** *Each* is singular. (See also p. 539 #3 and p. 541 #2c).

**effect:** See affect.

**e.g.:** This is a Latin abbreviation meaning "for example." It is sometimes confused with *i.e.,* which means "that is." Neither of these abbreviations should be used in the text of a manuscript, but they can be used in parenthetical expressions.

**either:** *Either* is singular. (See also pp. 538–539.)

Jim and Marti offered to tow the van; <u>either</u> is willing to drive to Coalinga.

**elicit, illicit:** *Elicit* is a verb meaning "to evoke." *Illicit* is an adjective meaning "illegal or unlawful."

The attorney was unable to <u>elicit</u> any information from her client about <u>illicit</u> drug sales in the neighborhood.

**emigrate from, immigrate to:** *Emigrate* means "to leave a country or region to settle elsewhere." *Immigrate* means "to enter another country and live there."

When Pano <u>emigrated</u> from Turkey, he missed living near the sea.

After the Revolution, many Cubans <u>immigrated</u> to the United States.

**eminent, imminent:** *Eminent* means "celebrated" or "exalted." *Imminent* means "about to happen."

The <u>eminent</u> seismologist predicted that an earthquake was <u>imminent</u>.

**especially, specially:** *Especially* means "particularly" or "more than other things." *Specially* means "for a specific reason."

Ryder <u>especially</u> values working on cabinets. He's known for <u>specially</u> ordered fine pieces of exotic woods.

**etc.:** Avoid ending a list with the abbreviation *etc.* Writers often overuse it to suggest they have more information than they do. The Latin expression is *et cetera,* which means "and others" or "and other things." The expression is best avoided in your essays because it is vague. It is also often misspelled as *ect.*

**everybody, everyone:** *Everybody* and *everyone* are singular. (See also pp. 538–539.)

**except:** See accept.

**farther, further:** *Farther* refers to distance. *Further* implies quantity or degree. *Further* is now widely accepted for both meanings.

Janae swam <u>farther</u> than everyone in her water fitness class.

Jerry is <u>further</u> along on his computer project than he expected.

**fewer, less:** *Fewer* refers to items that can be counted. *Less* refers to measurable amounts.

> Nate has <u>fewer</u> expenses and therefore needs <u>less</u> spending money because he works for the national parks.

**firstly:** *Firstly* is pretentious. Use *first*.

**fun:** *Fun* is colloquial when used as an adjective and should be avoided.

> Jess and Brian enjoyed the amusing [not *fun*] movie.

**further:** See farther.

**good, well:** *Good* is an adjective; *well* is usually an adverb.

> <u>Good</u> work is almost always <u>well</u> rewarded.

**hanged, hung:** *Hanged* refers to people. *Hung* refers to pictures and things that can be suspended.

> The criminal <u>hanged</u> himself in his prison cell.

> The Walshes <u>hung</u> Debbie's recent paintings in the living room.

**he, he/she, his/her:** The writer should no longer assume that *he* is an acceptable pronoun for all nouns. Furthermore, *he/she* or *his/her* are awkward. To avoid this construction, use the plural or a specific noun instead of the pronoun. (See also p. 570.)

> **Instead of:** When a student works in a small group, <u>he/she</u> participates more.

> **Write:** When <u>students</u> work in small groups, they participate more.

**hisself:** *Hisself* is nonstandard. Use *himself*.

**hung:** See hanged.

**i.e.:** This Latin abbreviation for *id est* should be replaced by the English *that is*.

**illusion:** See allusion.

**imminent:** See eminent.

**imply, infer:** *Imply* means "to state indirectly or to suggest." *Infer* means "to come to a conclusion based on the evidence given."

> By covering his ears, he <u>implied</u> that he no longer wanted to listen.

> We can <u>infer</u> that the Duke of Ferrara is an arrogant man because he refused to "stoop" to speak to his wife.

**irregardless:** *Irregardless* is nonstandard. Use *regardless*.

**its, it's:** *Its* is the possessive form. *It's* is the contraction for *it is* or *it has*. (See also p. 556.)

> <u>It's</u> too bad that Dick and Jean's cat has injured <u>its</u> tail.

> <u>It's</u> been a bad day for the Jacobys' cat.

**later, latter:** *Later* refers to time. *Latter* refers to the second of two things named.

> Initially many southern European immigrants came to this country, but <u>later</u> the immigration policy restricted the numbers.

> Both Diego Rivera and his wife Frida Kahlo painted, but the <u>latter</u> has gained more public recognition in the last few years.

**lay, lie:** *Lay* means "to place or put" and requires an object. (The past tense is *laid.*) *Lie* means "to rest or recline." (The past tense of *lie* is *lay,* and so the two words are sometimes confused.)

> Lay the piano music on the bench where Mrs. Main <u>laid</u> it yesterday.

> Twinkle will <u>lie</u> down exactly where she lay yesterday.

**lead, led:** The present tense of the verb is *lead* and the past tense is *led.* However, *lead* is also used as a noun, meaning a gray metal, and confusion results because it is pronounced the same as "led."

> Barbara will <u>lead</u> the tour to Istanbul, and then it will be <u>led</u> by Lexa.

> Usually plumbers replace <u>lead</u> pipes with copper.

**less:** See fewer.

**lie:** See lay.

**loose, lose:** *Loose* is an adjective meaning "unrestrained or unfastened." *Lose* is a verb meaning "to misplace" or "to be defeated."

> If his bathing suit is too <u>loose</u> , Lester will <u>lose</u> it in the next wave.

**lots, lots of:** Avoid these constructions in formal writing. Elevate the diction to *many* or *much.*

**mankind:** Avoid this term, as its sexism offends many readers. Use *humans, humanity,* or *humankind* instead.

> It was one small step for the <u>man</u> who walked on the moon, but it was a giant step for <u>humanity</u>.

**maybe, may be:** *Maybe* is an adverb meaning "perhaps." *May be* is a verb.

> <u>Maybe</u> Vince will open his own restaurant in Oregon, and Sherry <u>may be</u> ready to train their employees again.

**may of, might of:** These are nonstandard forms of *may have* and *might have.*

**media, medium:** *Media* is the plural of *medium,* when the word refers to a means of public communication.

> The <u>medium</u> most often used by political candidates is television.

> Other <u>media</u> such as public radio, newspapers, and documentary films may provide deeper political analysis.

**myself:** *Myself* is a reflexive or intensive pronoun and, like the other -*self* pronouns, should not be used in place of personal pronouns.

I drove <u>myself</u> to the hospital because no one else was home.

"I can do it <u>myself!</u>" the toddler protested.

Juan ladled the chili for his father and <u>me</u> [not *myself*].

**neither:** *Neither* is singular. (See also p. 538.)

<u>Neither</u> of us is available to babysit for the Trosts tonight.

**nohow:** *Nohow* is nonstandard for *in any way.*

**none:** *None* can be singular or plural depending on meaning.

<u>None</u> of the alternatives seem reasonable.

<u>None</u> of the football players is injured.

**nowheres:** *Nowheres* is nonstandard for *nowhere.*

**number:** See amount.

**of:** *Of* is a preposition. It should not be used in place of *have* in constructions like *should have* or *would have.*

**off of:** *Of* is not necessary with *off.* Use *off* alone or use *from.*

The marbles rolled <u>off</u> the table and continued rolling around Monahan's room.

**O.K., OK, okay:** All three forms are acceptable, but in formal writing these expressions are inappropriate.

**on account of:** A wordy way to write *because.*

**owing to the fact that:** A wordy way to write *because.*

**passed, past:** *Passed* is the past tense of the verb that means having gone by, having completed a test or course, having transferred a ball or puck to a teammate. *Past* is not a verb. Rather, it is used as a noun, adjective, adverb, or preposition and means a time gone by or having elapsed in time. If you remember to use the form "passed" when you need a verb, you will be correct.

**Verb:** Julia passed Debra in the hall and told her that Miori had <u>passed</u> the test.

**Verb:** The Maguires <u>passed</u> around reviews of the film *In the Line of Fire.*

**Verb:** During the game, Tyler <u>passed</u> the ball to David.

**Verb:** Jane and Pete <u>passed</u> their summer days at the cabin.

**Noun:** In the <u>past</u>, Julia and Debra met to discuss the student's progress.

**Adjective:** The Maguires have collected <u>past</u> reviews of *In the Line of Fire.*

**Adverb:** Tyler liked to jog <u>past</u> the pier during his morning runs.

**Preposition:** It was <u>past</u> noon when Jane and Pete arrived at their cabin.

**plus:** *Plus* is not appropriately used as a conjunction to join independent clauses. Use a standard coordinating or adverbial conjunction such as "moreover" or "in addition."

We celebrated the Fourth of July with hot dogs, corn on the cob, potato salad, and watermelon; <u>in addition</u>, [not *plus*] we enjoyed the firework display at Zaca Lake.

**precede, proceed:** The verb *precede* means "come before" (note the prefix *pre-*). The verb *proceed* means "go forward" or "move on."

Spanish 4 <u>precedes</u> Spanish 5, "Literature of Mexico."

To <u>proceed</u> without a contract would be foolish.

**prejudice, prejudiced:** *Prejudice* is a noun; *prejudiced* is an adjective. Do not leave out the *-d* from the adjective.

<u>Prejudice</u> that starts in childhood is difficult to obliterate, and he was distinctly <u>prejudiced</u> against working mothers.

**principal, principle:** *Principal* is a noun for the "chief official" or, in finance, the "capital sum." As an adjective, principal means "major" or "most important." *Principle* is a noun meaning "a law or truth, rule, or axiom."

The school's <u>principal</u> uses various <u>principles</u> for deciding the graduation speakers; the <u>principal</u> factor seems to be related to academics.

**proceed, precede:** See precede.

**quote, quotation:** In academic writing, *quote* is a verb; *quotation* is a noun. However, the word *quote* is also used colloquially as a shortened form of the noun *quotation.*

Dennis wanted to quote a line from <u>Macbeth</u>, so he selected a memorable quotation.

**raise, rise:** *Raise* is a verb meaning "to move or cause to move up," and it takes an object. *Rise* is a verb meaning "to go up," and it does not take a direct object.

The farmers who <u>raise</u> cows are concerned about the disease.

They <u>rise</u> early to attend to the livestock.

**reason is because:** In speech, this expression is common. In formal writing, it is not appropriate. A clause using *that* is the preferred form:

The <u>reason</u> the Arnolds drove their trailer was <u>that</u> [not *because*] they could transport dune buggies for the Dennis family, too.

**reason why:** The expression *reason why* is redundant. *Reason* is sufficient.

The <u>reason</u> [not *reason why*] Jorge attends law school at night is not obvious to anyone but his family.

**rise, raise:** See raise, rise.

**should of:** *Should of* is nonstandard; use *should have.*

He <u>should have</u> [not *should of*] known not to build a campfire on that windy hill.

**since:** *Since* is sometimes used to mean *because,* but it is best to use it only as a conjunction in constructions having to do with time.

Andy has been waiting <u>since</u> January for his tax forms.

<u>Since</u> [or *because*] you left, I've been dating others.

**sit, set:** *Sit* means "to rest the weight of the body" as on a chair. *Set* means "to place."

Dorothy wants you to <u>sit</u> on the black leather sofa.

Tom would rather you not <u>set</u> stoneware dishes on his cherrywood table.

**site, cite, sight:** See *cite, site, sight.*

**somebody, someone:** *Somebody* and *someone* are singular. (See also p. 538.)

**sometime, some time, sometimes:** *Sometime* is an adverb meaning "at an indefinite time." *Some time* is the adjective *some* modifying the noun *time. Sometimes* means "now and then."

<u>Sometime</u> we should get together and play tennis.

Raul devoted <u>some time</u> to perfecting his pronunciation.

<u>Sometimes</u> Ken discards every yolk from the eggs as he prepares his omelette.

**stationary/stationery:** *Stationary* is an adjective meaning "immovable, fixed in place." *Stationery* (with an "e" just as in "letter") is a noun meaning "writing material."

Despite the brisk wind, the sign remained <u>stationary</u>.

Leslie wrote the letter on <u>stationery</u> from the cruise ship.

**supposed to, used to:** Don't neglect to use the *-d* ending on these often used and often misspelled words!

He is supposed to [not *suppose to*] bring the wine for the dinner.

Ariane became <u>used to</u> [not *use to*] Dee's indifferent housekeeping.

**than, then:** *Than* is used in comparisons. *Then* is an adverb denoting time.

There are many more calories in avocados <u>than</u> in apples.

First Sylvia Plath attended the school, and <u>then</u> she taught there.

**their, there, they're:** *Their* is a possessive pronoun. *There* is an adverb denoting place. *They're* is a contraction meaning *they are.*

<u>Their</u> plans for hang gliding <u>there</u> in the park are apt to be postponed because <u>they're</u> not ready to pass the safety test.

**then, than:** See than, then.

**there is, there are:** The verb following the expletive "there" is singular or plural according to the number of the subject that follows the verb. (See also pp. 541 and 542 #5.)

There is a dictionary on the table. There are books and keys on the table.

**this here, these here, that there, them there:** Nonstandard for *this, these, that,* or *those.*

**thru:** *Thru* is a nonstandard spelling of *through* that should be avoided in all formal writing.

**thusly:** Use *thus,* which is less pretentious.

**till, until, 'til:** *Till* and *until* have the same meaning and both have standard uses. *'Til* is an informal contraction of *until.*

**to, too, two:** *To* is a preposition meaning 'toward' and is part of the infinitive form of the verb (for example, *to run*). *Too* is an adverb meaning "overly." *Two* is a number.

Two trips to the market in one day are not too many for a fine cook like Mike.

**toward, towards:** Either form is acceptable if used consistently, but *toward* is preferred.

**try and:** *Try and* is nonstandard; *try to* is preferred.

Try to [not *try and*] meet Mohammed before he locks up his bike.

**unique:** *Unique* means "distinctively characteristic." It is an absolute adjective that should not be modified by "most" or "very."

A tuxedo shirt and jacket, bow tie, and Bermuda shorts create a unique [not *most unique*] style for a hot-weather prom.

**until:** See till, until, 'til.

**usage:** The noun *use* should be used whenever possible. *Usage* refers only to convention, as in *language usage.*

The use [not *usage*] of computers has facilitated essay writing, but papers with correct usage have not increased.

**used to:** See supposed to, used to.

**weather, whether:** *Weather* refers to the atmospheric conditions. *Whether* can be used interchangeably with *if.*

Gail wasn't certain whether the stormy weather would keep John and Mark from jogging to Niagara Falls.

**well:** See good, well.

**which, in which:** Writers occasionally use *in which* in places where *which* is sufficient. Read work carefully to eliminate the unnecessary preposition.

Salma grabbed the gray cape, <u>which</u> [not *in which*] had been left on the sofa.

**which, who:** *Which* is used for things, not for people. Use *who* for people.

Martin Luther King, the American <u>who</u> defined civil disobedience for his generation, was a theologian as well as a political figure. His letter from Birmingham, <u>which</u> he wrote in jail, defines his position.

**while:** Do not use *while* to mean *although* if there is a chance of confusion for the reader. Like *since, while* should be reserved for time sense. Unless the point is to show that the actions occur at the same time, *although* is the better word.

Nick begins cooking dinner <u>while</u> Chris drives home from Richmond.

Although [not *while*] Elizabeth continues to invest their savings, Bill never resists a rug sale.

**who's, whose:** *Who's* is the contraction for *who is* or *who has. Whose* is a possessive pronoun.

<u>Who's</u> going to stay at the Sea Bird Motel in Wildwood?

<u>Who's</u> been having dinner with the Grebners every Sunday?

Mike asked Lucy <u>whose</u> design she preferred.

**would of:** *Would of* is nonstandard for the complete verb *would have.*

*Los Vendidos* <u>would have</u> [not *would of*] been a perfect theater experience for Cinco de Mayo.

**you:** The indefinite use of *you,* or even its use to mean "you the reader," can be incongruous or offensive and can be avoided:

A decade ago, the fit hiker [rather than *you*] could camp on the beach with the seals at Pt. Sal, but now even the poor trail has eroded.

It is common practice in some African tribes for prepubescent females [rather than *you*] to be scarified.

**your, you're:** *Your* is a possessive pronoun. *You're* is the contraction of *you are.*

<u>Your</u> savings will disappear if <u>you're</u> not careful.

# Common Irregular Verbs

Most verbs in English form their past tense and past participle by adding
*–ed* or *–d* to the simple form of the word: *help, helped; bake, baked*. However,
many verbs form their past tense or past participle irregularly with a changed
internal vowel (ring, rang, rung) or by adding an ending other than *–ed* or *–d*.
(bring, brought, brought). Some verbs use the same form in the present, past,
and past participle (cut, cut, cut). A dictionary can help you find the correct
form of the past tense and past participle, but you can save some time by
becoming familiar with the list below:

| base form | past tense | past participle |
|---|---|---|
| arise | arose | arisen |
| awake | awoke or awaked | awaked or awoke |
| be (is am are) | was, were | been |
| beat | beat | beaten |
| become | became | become |
| begin | began | begun |
| bend | bent | bent |
| bet | bet | bet |
| bite | bit | bitten or bit |
| blow | blew | blown |
| break | broke | broken |
| bring | brought | brought |
| build | built | built |
| burst | burst | burst |

*(continues)*

| base form | past tense | past participle |
| --- | --- | --- |
| buy | bought | bought |
| cast | cast | cast |
| catch | caught | caught |
| choose | chose | chosen |
| cling | clung | clung |
| come | came | come |
| cost | cost | cost |
| deal | dealt | dealt |
| dig | dug | dug |
| dive | dived or dove | dived |
| do | did | done |
| draw | drew | drawn |
| dream | dreamed or dreamt | dreamed or dreamt |
| drink | drank | drunk |
| drive | drove | driven |
| eat | ate | eaten |
| fall | fell | fallen |
| feed | fed | fed |
| feel | felt | felt |
| fight | fought | fought |
| find | found | found |
| flee | fled | fled |
| fly | flew | flown |
| forbid | forbade or forbad | forbidden |
| forget | forgot | forgotten or forgot |
| forgive | forgave | forgiven |
| freeze | froze | frozen |
| get | got | got or gotten |
| go | went | gone |
| grow | grew | grown |
| hang (to suspend) | hung | hung |
| hang (to execute) | hanged | hanged |
| have | had | had |
| hear | heard | heard |

| base form | past tense | past participle |
|-----------|------------|-----------------|
| hide | hid | hidden |
| hit | hit | hit |
| hurt | hurt | hurt |
| keep | kept | kept |
| know | knew | known |
| lay (to put) | laid | laid |
| lead | led | led |
| leave | left | left |
| lend | lend | lend |
| let (to allow) | let | let |
| lie (to recline) | lay | lain |
| light | lighted or lit | lighted or lit |
| lose | lost | lost |
| make | made | made |
| mean | meant | meant |
| pay | paid | paid |
| prove | proved | proved or proved |
| quit | quit | quit |
| read | read | read |
| rid | rid | rid |
| ride | rode | ridden |
| ring | rang | rung |
| rise (to get up) | rose | risen |
| run | ran | run |
| say | said | said |
| see | saw | seen |
| seek | sought | sought |
| send | sent | sent |
| set (to place) | set | set |
| shake | shook | shaken |
| shine (to glow) | shone | shone |
| shoot | shot | shot |
| show | showed | shown or showed |

*(continues)*

| base form | past tense | past participle |
|-----------|-----------|----------------|
| shrink | shrank | shrunk |
| sing | sang | sung |
| sink | sank | sung |
| sit | sat | sat |
| slay | slew | slain |
| sleep | slept | slept |
| sling | slung | slung |
| speak | spoke | spoken |
| spend | spent | spent |
| spin | spun | spun |
| spring | sprang or sprung | sprung |
| stand | stood | stood |
| steal | stole | stolen |
| sting | stung | stung |
| stink | stank or stunk | stunk |
| stride | strode | stridden |
| strike | struck | struck |
| strive | strove | striven |
| swear | swore | sworn |
| sweep | swept | swept |
| swim | swam | swum |
| swing | swung | swung |
| take care | took | taken |
| teach | taught | taught |
| tear | tore | torn |
| tell | told | told |
| think | thought | thought |
| throw | threw | threw |
| wake | woke or waked | waked or woken |
| wear | wore | worn |
| wring | wrung | wrung |
| write | wrote | written |

# Text Credits

Laila Al-Marayati and Semeen Issa, "Muslim Women: An Identity Reduced to a Burka," *Los Angeles Times*, January 20, 2002. Reprinted by permission of the author.

"Breaking Tradition", from *Shedding Silence: Poetry and Prose* by Janice Mirikitani, copyright © 1987 by Janice Mirikitani. Used by permission of Celestial Arts, an imprint of the Crown Publishing Group, a division of Random House, Inc.

Christopher Chabris and Daniel Simons, "Your brain on computers" from the *Los Angeles Times*, July 25, 2010. Reprinted by permission of the authors.

Judith Ortiz Cofer, "The Myth of the Latin Woman: I Just Met a Girl Named Maria" from *The Latin Deli: Prose and Poetry*. Copyright © by Judith Ortiz Cofer. Reprinted by permission of The University of Georgia Press.

Jennifer A. Coleman, "Discrimination at Large," *Newsweek*, August 2, 1993. Reprinted by permission of the author.

Dana Beardsley Crotwell, "The Work," originally published in *Proposing on the Brooklyn Bridge: Poems About Marriage*, Ed. Ginny Lowe Connors, Grayson Books, © 2003. Reprinted by permission of the author.

Kevin Crust, "Al Gore warms up to a very hot topic," *The Los Angeles times*, May 24, 2006. Copyright © 2006 Los Angeles Times. Reprinted by permission.

Philip Dacey, "Coke" from *Night Shift at the Crucifix Factory*. (Iowa City: University of Iowa Press, 1991). Copyright © 1991 by Philip Dacey. Reprinted by permission of the author.

Meghan Daum, "I don't give a tweet what you're doing," copyright 2009 *Los Angeles Times*. Reprinted with permission.

David Denby, "A Fine Romance", originally published in *The New Yorker*, July 23, 2007. Reprinted by permission of the author.

David Denby, "Angry People," *The New Yorker*, May 2, 2005. Reprinted by permission of the author.

Debra J. Dickerson, "Who Shot Johnny?" *The New Republic*, January 1996. Reprinted by permission of the author.

Marianela Enriquez, "Who Were You, Connie, and Why Did You Go?" Reprinted by permission of the author.

Pamela Erens, "Bodily Harm." *Ms. Magazine*, October 1985. Reprinted by permission of the author.

Philip French, Review: "The King's Speech" in the *Guardian*, January 9, 2011. Copyright Guardian News and Media Ltd 2011. Reprinted with permission.

Janet Froetscher, President of the National Safety Council, "Education, Backed by Law." Originally published in nytimes.com: Room for Debate Blog: A Running Commentary on the News, July 18, 2009.

Alex Garcia, "Reality Check," *Los Angeles Times*, June 16, 1999. Reprinted by permission of the author.

Joe Goodwin, "My Favorite School Class: Involuntary Servitude." Reprinted by permission of the author.

"In Groups We Shrink" From Loner's Heroics. Copyright © 1991 by Carol Tavris. Originally appeared in the *Los Angeles Times*. Reprinted by permission of Lescher and Lescher, Ltd. All rights reserved.

Rebecca Hall-Naganuma, "Through the Cracks." Reprinted by permission of the author.

William F. Harrison, "Why Stop Smoking? Let's Get Clinical." Reprinted by permission of the author.

Robert L. Heilbroner, "Don't Let Stereotypes Warp Your Judgments," *Think Magazine*, June 1961. Reprinted by permission of the author.

Quinones-Hinojosa, "Terra Firma—A Journey from Migrant Farm Labor to Neurosurgery" from *The New England Journal of Medicine*, Volume 357, August 9, 2007. Copyright © 2007 Massachusetts Medical Society. All rights reserved. Reprinted with permission.

Max Thayer, "King Curtis's Echo," *The Los Angeles Times Magazine*, August 21, 2005. Reprinted by permission of the author.

Chris Thomas, "A Summary of 'Three Ways of Meeting Oppression.'" Reprinted by permission of the author.

*Los Vendido* is reprinted with permission from the publisher of "Luis Valdez-Early Works" by Luis Valdez (© 1971 Arte Publico Press—University of Houston).

John A. Vaughn, "The Difference Between Pity and Empathy," *Los Angeles Times* (Doctor Files), March 28, 2005. Reprinted by permission of the author.

Jon Winokur, "You Call That Irony?" *The Los Angeles Times*, February 11, 2007. Reprinted by permission of the author.

# Photo Credits

37 AF archive / Alamy

45 Leo Cullum/ The New Yorker Collection/ www.cartoonbank.com

113 AP Images/Chris Carlson

138 Lions Gate/courtesy Everett Collection

182 Bizarro © 2005 Dan Piraro. King Features Syndicate

213 By permission of Mike Luckovich and Creators Syndicate, Inc.

246 Robert Weber/ The New Yorker Collection/ www.cartoonbank.com

259 Sam Gross/ The New Yorker Collection/ www.cartoonbank.com

417 Mick Stevens/ The New Yorker Collection/ www.cartoonbank.com

457 AF archive / Alamy

477 Cartoon by Peter Steiner/Cartoonbank.com

515 Courtesy of EBSCO

516 Courtesy of Reuters

568 Bizarro © 2006 Dan Piraro. King Features Syndicate

37 AF archive / Alamy

45 Leo Cullum/ The New Yorker Collection/ www.cartoonbank.com

113 AP Images/Chris Carlson

138 Lions Gate/courtesy Everett Collection

182 Bizarro © 2005 Dan Piraro. King Features Syndicate

213 By permission of Mike Luckovich and Creators Syndicate, Inc.

246 Robert Weber/ The New Yorker Collection/ www.cartoonbank.com

259 Sam Gross/ The New Yorker Collection/ www.cartoonbank.com

417 Mick Stevens/ The New Yorker Collection/ www.cartoonbank.com

457 AF archive / Alamy

477 Cartoon by Peter Steiner/Cartoonbank.com

515 Courtesy of EBSCO

516 Courtesy of Reuters

568 Bizarro © 2006 Dan Piraro. King Features Syndicate

# Author Index

# Subject and Title Index

Note: Boldface shows location of readings.